ELIZABETH SETON

ELIZABETH SETON

American Saint

CATHERINE O'DONNELL

Three Hills
an imprint of
CORNELL UNIVERSITY PRESS   ITHACA AND LONDON

First published 2018 by Cornell University Press

Printed in the United States of America

Library of Congress Cataloging-in-Publication Data

Names: O'Donnell, Catherine (Historian), author.
Title: Elizabeth Seton: American saint / Catherine O'Donnell.
Description: Ithaca : Three Hills, an imprint of Cornell University Press, 2018. | Includes bibliographical references and index. |
Identifiers: LCCN 2018002063 (print) | LCCN 2018003434 (ebook) | ISBN 9781501726019 (pdf) | ISBN 9781501726026 (epub/mobi) | ISBN 9781501705786 (cloth : alk. paper)
Subjects: LCSH: Seton, Elizabeth Ann, Saint, 1774–1821. | Christian saints—United States—Biography.
Classification: LCC BX4700.S4 (ebook) | LCC BX4700.S4 O36 2018 (print) | DDC 271/.9102 [B]—dc23
LC record available at https://lccn.loc.gov/2018002063

CONTENTS

Cast of Characters

THE BAYLEYS

Richard Bayley Sr. (1744–1801)—physician, author of scientific tracts, public health officer.

Catherine Charlton Bayley (d. 1777)—first wife of Richard Bayley, daughter of Rev. Richard Charlton.

Children:

> **Mary Magdalen Bayley Post** (1768–1856), m. Dr. Wright Post, a student of Richard Bayley, in 1790 and bore seven children.

> **Elizabeth Ann Bayley Seton** (1774–1821), m. William M. Seton, merchant, in 1794, and bore five children, who are to be found under **The Setons.**

Charlotte Amelia Barclay Bayley (1759–1805)—second wife of Richard Bayley, daughter of Helena Roosevelt and Andrew Barclay.

Children:

> Charlotte Bayley, called **Emma** (1779–1805), m. William Craig, relative of **Eliza Sadler.**

Richard Bayley Jr. (1781–1815), m. Catherine White in 1812.

(Andrew) **Barclay Bayley** (1783–1811), engaged to **Harriet Seton,** tried to establish himself as a physician in the West Indies.

Guy Carlton Bayley (1786–1859), m. Grace Roosevelt in 1813, worked first within the Setons' merchant enterprise, then as a physician; son **James Roosevelt Bayley** converted to Catholicism, was ordained a priest, and served as archbishop of Baltimore.

William Augustus Bayley (1788–1817), m. Jane Smith in 1811.

Helen Bayley (1790–1848), m. Samuel Craig, relative of **Eliza Sadler.**

Mary Fitch Bayley (1796–1830), m. Robert Bunch.

THE SETONS

William Seton Sr. (1746–1798), merchant.

Rebecca Curson Seton (1746–1775), first wife of William Sr., daughter of Richard Curson Sr., merchant of Baltimore, sister of **Anna Maria Curson Seton** and **Elizabeth Curson Farquhar.**

Children:

William Magee Seton (1768–1803), merchant, married **Elizabeth Bayley Seton,** their children to be found below under William Magee and Elizabeth Bayley Seton.

James Seton (1770–?), merchant, partner to **Martin Hoffman,** m. Mary Gillou Hoffman (d. 1807), sister of **Martin Hoffman;** the couple had nine children, often tended by **Cecilia Seton.**

John Curson (Jack) Seton (ca. 1771–1815), largely unsuccessful merchant, married twice, fathered children often tended by **Rebecca Mary Seton.**

Henry Seton (1774–?), largely unsuccessful merchant and naval officer.

Anna Maria Seton Vining (ca. 1775–1802), m. John Middleton Vining in 1790.

Anna Maria Curson Seton (1756–1792), second wife of William Sr., daughter of Richard Curson Sr., merchant of Baltimore, sister of **Rebecca Curson Seton** and **Elizabeth Curson Farquhar.**

Children:

> **Eliza Seton Maitland** (1779–1807), m. James Maitland, who abandoned Eliza and their children.

> **Rebecca Mary Seton** (1780–1804), "soul sister" of **Elizabeth Bayley Seton.**

> **Mary Seton Hoffman** (ca. 1785?–?), lived briefly with **Elizabeth Bayley Seton** after death of her father, m. **Martin Hoffman.**

> **Charlotte Seton Ogden** (1786–1853), lived briefly with **Elizabeth Bayley Seton** after death of her father, m. **Governeur Ogden** (1778–1851).

> **Henrietta (Harriet or Hatch) Seton** (1787–1809), lived for an extended period with Elizabeth Bayley Seton after death of her father.

> **Samuel Waddington (Sam) Seton** (1789–1869), trained as a merchant, later an educator.

> **Edward Augustus (Ned) Seton** (1790–1840s?), trained as a merchant, talented amateur artist, m. Bazilide Balome of Louisiana and established his residence there.

Elizabeth Bayley Seton (1774–1821), m. **William Magee Seton** (1768–1803) in 1794; the couple had five children, whose stories are told in this book. Readers who do not yet wish to know their fates should avoid the chart below.

Children:

> **Anna Maria (Anna, Annina) Seton** (1795–1812), took initial vows as a Sister of Charity.

William (Will) Seton II (1796–1868), merchant's clerk, naval officer, m. Emily Prime Seton; the couple's eight children include Monsignor Robert Seton and Helen Seton, who became a Sister of Mercy of New York.

Richard Bayley (Dick) Seton (1798–1823), merchant's clerk, civilian clerk on a naval ship.

Catherine Charlton (Kit, Josephine) Seton (1800–1891), entered Sisters of Mercy of New York in 1846.

Rebecca (Bec) Seton (1802–1816).

FRIENDS, CLERGY, AND SISTERS OF CHARITY

Pierre Babade (1763–1846)—Sulpician priest, professor at St. Mary's, Baltimore, confessor to Elizabeth Seton in the early days of the Emmitsburg community.

The Barrys—James (d. 1808), a Catholic merchant, and Joanna (d. 1811) had two daughters, Mary and Ann, who died in adolescence. The Barrys were confidantes of John Carroll.

Simon Bruté (1779–1839)—Sulpician priest, president of St. Mary's, Baltimore, professor at Mount St. Mary's and spiritual director of Elizabeth Seton, after Seton's death bishop of Vincennes.

The Burkes—Margaret Burke was born in Ireland and educated by Ursulines before abruptly leaving school and marrying. She emigrated to Philadelphia, where her brother **Matthew Carey** was a successful printer; widowed twice, she served as an assistant to John Dubois at the Mount. Her daughter **Maria Burke** (also known as Maria Murphy) was one of the first to join Seton's sisterhood.

Charles Carroll (1737–1832)—known as Charles Carroll of Carrollton, only Catholic signer of the Declaration of Independence, United States senator from Maryland, plantation owner, president of the American Colonization Society, and one of the largest slave owners in the country.

John Carroll (1735–1815)—Jesuit (although the order was suppressed from 1774 to 1814), a founder of Georgetown College, consecrated bishop of Baltimore in 1790 and archbishop in 1808.

The Catons—Richard Caton (1763–1845), a merchant, and wife Mary (Polly) Carroll Caton (1770–1846), daughter of Charles Carroll of Carrollton, were prominent members of Maryland society, as were their four daughters, Marianne, Elizabeth, Louisa, and Emily.

The Harpers—Robert Goodloe Harper (1765–1825), a lawyer, politician, and member of the American Colonization Society, and his wife Catherine Carroll Harper (1778–1861), daughter of Charles Carroll of Carrollton, were prominent members of Maryland society and sent children including Mary Diana, Charles Carroll, Emily, and Elizabeth to be educated at St. Joseph's Academy and Mount St. Mary's.

Jean-Louis Anne Madeleine Lefebvre (John) de Cheverus (1768–1836)—A priest who fled France to serve first in Maine, then in Boston, where he was consecrated the diocese's first bishop in 1810. After Elizabeth's death he was named bishop of Montauban and returned to France.

The Chatards—Pierre (1767–1848)—Born in Saint-Domingue (Haiti) and educated as a physician in France, he became a prominent doctor in Baltimore, married to Marie-Françoise (1777–1863), who was also from Saint-Domingue.

Samuel Sutherland Cooper (1769–1848)—A wealthy sea captain who converted to Catholicism and was eventually ordained a priest; his donation enabled Elizabeth Seton to found the Emmitsburg school and sisterhood.

Jean-Baptiste-Marie (John) David (1761–1841)—A Sulpician priest who fled France, served as professor at both Georgetown College and St. Mary's Baltimore (where he was also acting president), and became the second clerical superior of the Emmitsburg sisterhood. He served as coadjutor of the Bardstown, Kentucky, diocese and, after Seton's death, as bishop; he founded the Sisters of Charity of Nazareth, Kentucky.

Jean (John) Dubois (1764–1842)—A priest who fled France and joined the Sulpician order in the United States. The first president of Mount St. Mary's and a collaborator of Elizabeth Seton in her school and sisterhood, Dubois later served as bishop of New York.

Louis-Guillaume Valentin (William) Dubourg (1766–1833)— Born in Saint-Domingue, Dubourg was ordained a Sulpician priest in France, then fled the Revolution. He served as president of both Georgetown College and St. Mary's, Baltimore, and was the first clerical superior of the sisterhood at Emmitsburg.

Catherine Dupleix—Wife of a sea captain and friend to Elizabeth Seton

The Farquhars—**James** (ca. 1842–1831), a merchant, in 1774 married **Elizabeth Curson (Aunt) Farquhar** (ca. 1751–d. after husband, date unknown); the couple were influential within the extended Seton clan and had numerous children (as many as seventeen), one of whom, **Eliza**, or **Zide**, was close to Elizabeth Seton.

The Filicchis—**Filippo** (1763–1816) and **Antonio** (1764–1847) were merchants based in Livorno, Italy, also known as Leghorn. Filippo, who served as United States consul to Leghorn, married an American, **Mary Cowper** (1760–1821); the couple died childless. Antonio and his wife **Amabilia** (1773–1853) had several children.

Margaret George (1787–1868)—Born in Ireland, George emigrated to the United States as a child. After losing much of her family to yellow fever, she moved to Baltimore, where she was educated and married a professor at St. Mary's, Baltimore. Widowed young, she was among the first Sisters of Charity to take vows, served in a number of administrative positions and missions, and founded the American Sisters of Charity of Cincinnati.

Isabella Graham (1782–1814)—Graham became an educator and philanthropist after being widowed with small children. First in her native Scotland and then in New York City, she founded schools and charitable institutions including New York's Society for the Relief of Poor Widows with Small Children.

John Hickey (1789–1869)—The first Sulpician to be ordained after training at Mount St. Mary's, Hickey served in a variety of capacities at the Emmitsburg institutions, including as superior of the Sisters of Charity of St. Joseph's from 1829 to 1841.

John Henry Hobart (1775–1830)—Episcopalian minister and author associated with the High Church tradition who, when serving at Manhattan's Trinity Church, spurred Elizabeth Seton's interest in Christianity. Hobart eventually served as Episcopal bishop of New York and founded the General Theological Seminary in New York City.

Michael Hurley (1780–1837)—American-born Hurley was ordained an Augustinian priest in Rome in 1797. After serving in Philadelphia, he was sent to New York to assist William and Matthew O'Brien. Hurley was soon returned to Philadelphia, where he served St. Augustine's parish, participated in Catholic benevolent efforts, and served as vicarius of the Augustinian Province in the United States.

The O'Briens—William O'Brien, an Irish-born Dominican, was pastor to St. Peter's parish, Manhattan, and in his early, energetic years led it out of contention and attracted donations. **Matthew O'Brien,** likely a relative, became his assistant at the parish and gained praise for his preaching before being accused of serial misconduct.

Ambrose Maréchal (1764–1828)—A Sulpician who fled his native France and served at St. Mary's, Baltimore, and Georgetown, becoming coadjutor bishop of Baltimore. He was consecrated archbishop of Baltimore in 1817.

Cecilia (Veronica) O'Conway (1788–1865)—Daughter of a peripatetic Irish-born translator, Matthias O'Conway, Cecilia was one of the first to join the Emmitsburg community. A confidante of Elizabeth Seton, O'Conway left the Sisters of Charity and became an Ursuline in 1823.

Eliza Sadler (?–1823)—Irish-born and well-educated, Sadler was the wife and (after 1801) widow of merchant Henry Sadler, who also participated in the poor widows' society, the Orphan Asylum Society, and the House of Industry; relatives of hers married half siblings of Seton.

Julia Scott (1765–1842)—A native of Philadelphia, Julia lived in New York City and befriended Elizabeth Seton during her marriage to the politician Lewis Allaire Scott. She returned to Philadelphia after being widowed, commencing a correspondence with Seton that lasted until the latter's death. Her son, John Morin Scott, became mayor of Philadelphia.

Sarah Startin (1746–1822)—Widow of the successful merchant Charles Startin, she was Elizabeth Seton's godmother and an active participant in Trinity Church and the poor widows' society.

Jean Tisserant (dates unknown)—A French priest who had fled the Revolution and worked in the United Sates as tutor to Catholic families, he became Elizabeth Seton's spiritual director before returning to France.

Rosetta (Rose) White (1784–1841)—Left a widowed mother in her twenties, White was among the first to join the Emmitsburg sisterhood. She served as Elizabeth Seton's first assistant and began missions in Philadelphia and New York; after Seton's death, White was elected to succeed her as Mother, or superior of the sisterhood.

ELIZABETH SETON

PROLOGUE

Today

J UST SOUTH of the small town of Emmitsburg, Maryland, a low-slung marble block announces the National Shrine of Saint Elizabeth Ann Seton. On the shrine's leafy grounds rises a brick church with the dimensions of a cathedral and the demure ornamentation of a Catholic high school. Entering the building (a minor basilica, in the nomenclature of the Catholic Church) one finds a quiet, vaulted space, its walls gently sumptuous with bone-colored marble and stained glass, its air often perfumed by incense. At the Altar of Relics, within a copper casket, lie the remains of Elizabeth Bayley Seton. Seton, who died in 1821 at the age of forty-six, was canonized in 1975, becoming the United States' first native-born Catholic saint. Visitors to her shrine light candles and pray by the Altar of Relics, and a Mass is said daily.

Outside the basilica, the conventions of American tourism mingle with those of Roman Catholic commemoration. Visitors take pictures next to a statue of Mother Seton and listen to explanations of the historic significance of the shrine's buildings. Across the lawn from the basilica stands one such structure, a two-story gray building with thin white pillars and a slanting, russet-shingled roof. Known as the Stone House, the building is the carefully preserved descendant of a drafty dwelling in which Elizabeth and a small group of followers lived after their arrival in St. Joseph's Valley in 1809. Those followers now lie beneath white gravestones in a cemetery a few hundred yards from

Figure P.1. The Basilica of Elizabeth Ann Seton. Photo courtesy of the
Seton Shrine, Emmitsburg, Maryland.

the Stone House; the clustering of their death dates silently signals the
relentless losses of the settlement's early years.

The shrine's grounds bear testament to the struggles and achievements not only of Elizabeth Seton but of thousands of women who have
served in religious communities she inspired. Six congregations of sisters
trace their lineage directly to that fragile first group, and others have
joined them in the Sisters of Charity Federation, an association of communities of vowed women who draw their charism, or gifts of the spirit,
from Saints Vincent de Paul, Louise de Marillac, and Elizabeth Ann
Seton. In Elizabeth's lifetime, the American Sisters of Charity offered a
benevolent face for a Catholic Church short on priests and public trust,
and in the centuries since, members of the communities have founded
and staffed missions across the nation and the globe.[1]

Older visitors to the shrine are more likely than younger ones to have
been touched personally by the work of Sisters and Daughters of Charity.
The grounds of the shrine quietly tell that story too. Near the basilica
rises a multistoried provincial house dedicated in 1965. In its administrative offices staff were meant to oversee the women's far-flung apostolic

work; its dormitory floors were intended to house the scores of novices the community expected to welcome each year. But the number of young women choosing to enter consecrated life—to become women religious, in the nomenclature of the Church—was dropping even as the provincial house was built, and the grounds that were to brim with novices now house archives and historical exhibits. The archives ensure that Mother Seton will not be forgotten. Yet her followers are not content to have their founder's legacy reside only in history and memory. In 2011, the American Daughters of Charity consolidated their four eastern provinces into one, helped to create the professionally managed historic site and archive at Emmitsburg, and moved their provincial house to the more readily accessible city of St. Louis. Their work, and that of the other congregations, continues.

Within the shrine's peaceful grounds thus lie traces of ambition, loss, and wrenching change. The same might be said of the oft-photographed statue of Mother Seton. At the end of her life, Elizabeth had become the serenely pious figure the statue memorializes. But she had first been a miserable adolescent, a thrilled young bride, a skeptic of organized

Figure P.2. Daughters' gravestones. Photo courtesy of the Seton Shrine, Emmitsburg, Maryland.

religion, and a spiritual seeker who feared she might go catastrophically astray. It seems safe to say that no one expects to wind up with a basilica in her honor in western Maryland. But Elizabeth Seton's canonization was simply the final step—and not even, by the time it happened, the most astonishing one—in an improbable journey.

HER JOURNEY is surprisingly possible to retrace. Most Americans of Elizabeth Seton's day are visible only in glimpses: an entry in a city directory, a name in a census, perhaps a letter or two. Seton's importance to her followers has led to the preservation of an extraordinarily rich archive. Friends began to collect papers during her lifetime, and in the decades after her death, admirers gathered documents and published memoirs. The first to draw on these materials using the tools of modern historical analysis was Annabelle Melville, whose 1951 biography remains an essential guide to all who study the saint. Since Melville, other authors—often members of the Sisters of Charity federation—have explored Elizabeth's spirituality, friendships, and the continuing inspiration she offers to women religious; short treatments of her work as teacher and founder have also appeared. Judith Metz, SC, and Regina Bechtle, SC, working with Vivien Linkhauer, SC, Kathleen Flanagan, SC, and Betty Ann McNeil, DC, have completed the prodigious task of gathering and annotating Seton's papers in the three-volume *Elizabeth Bayley Seton: Collected Writings*.[2]

Despite this invaluable work, and during decades in which historians have explored the lives of women and the centrality of religion to early American life, Elizabeth Seton has rarely figured in histories of her era, and she has not been the subject of a new scholarly biography. Because Seton drew on a European monastic tradition—a tradition that required a vow of obedience, yet—she may seem a strange candidate for inclusion in histories of American women's leadership. Yet by founding a successful religious community, she created spiritual and practical possibilities for generations of American girls and women. And if it's tempting to allow Seton's sainthood to exclude her from our efforts to understand "ordinary" people within a nation and faith, that's a temptation we should resist. The archive that her sainthood has produced—decades of correspondence, journals, and reflections, as well as documentation of her family and associates—reveals not only Seton's distinctive achievements as an institution builder and thinker but also the aspects of her life that were anything but extraordinary: struggles over health and money, the dispossessions of war, the labors of motherhood, the rewards of long friendships. Mother Seton "knows what it's like," one visitor to the shrine told me, explaining that in Elizabeth's life as daughter, wife, widow, and mother, she saw elements of her own. That combination of the extraordinary and the familiar has led Catholics to turn to Seton for solace and intercession. It also makes her an illuminating subject of biography.

The woman who became Mother Seton was born on Manhattan Island in 1774, as the American colonies edged toward revolution. Her mother, Catherine Charlton Bayley, was the daughter of an Anglican rector, and her father was Richard Bayley, an ambitious physician. Elizabeth's mother died young, and her father soon remarried, bringing Elizabeth and her older sister Mary a stepmother whose unhappiness darkened their childhoods. After a tempestuous adolescence, Elizabeth fell in love with and married a fellow Manhattanite, a merchant named William Magee Seton. For a time the couple prospered, and Elizabeth bore five children. But she was left a widow at thirty-one, stripped of both her wealth and her Episcopalian faith. After a year of agonizing uncertainty, Elizabeth converted to Catholicism. Within another two years, she had moved to Maryland, founded the community that would become the Sisters of Charity of Saint Joseph, and begun to create an influential body of spiritual teachings. At the age of forty-six, she died.

In Elizabeth Seton's unofficial tagline—"first American-born Roman Catholic saint"—her nationality and her faith are each firmly fixed. In reality both were defined by cultural exchange and conflict rather than by stable borders. During her New York childhood, Elizabeth listened to Methodist hymns written in England and learned the French language that formed part of her family's Huguenot heritage. As a young woman, she read European philosophy and used goods and money produced by a plantation economy that spanned continents—a plantation economy that would come to support her work in ways she, who analyzed so much else of the world around her, declined to see. After her conversion, she weighed the appeal of forms of Catholicism practiced by Anglo-American Jesuits and immigrant French Sulpicians, and she pored over the teachings of saints from Africa and Spain.

The new American nation in which Elizabeth lived was, in short, part of a much wider world through which flowed ideas, people, goods, and gods.

During her lifetime, Revolutionary Atlantic currents eroded some forms of religious authority while augmenting others. Within both the Catholic and Protestant traditions, some believers sought to separate doctrine from custom, understanding themselves to be rendering religion fit for an enlightened era. Others questioned whether institutional religion was useful at all and whether it made sense to believe in a God who intervened in human affairs. If anyone thought, however, that the Age of Reason would bring the end of faith, he was mistaken. By Elizabeth's young womanhood, an evangelical Protestantism centered on Bible reading, individual rebirth, and Christ's redemptive power drew Americans and Britons toward newly intense and expressive forms of Christianity. In continental Europe across the same decades, the ambitions of the Bourbon monarchs, followed by the French Revolution and the rise of Napoleon, unsettled ecclesiastical hierarchies and religion's daily claims, shattering some Catholic religious traditions, reinvigorating others, and inspiring the creation of still more. On both sides of the Atlantic, relations between Protestants and Catholics, between clergy and laity, between church and state, and even between God and man, were open to question and ripe for transformation.

Elizabeth's correspondence and spiritual journals make much of this intimately visible. She was born into a family whose Anglicanism turned to Episcopalianism as a result of the cultural reconfigurations of the American Revolution. Elizabeth's own spirituality drew not only on the Catholic tradition she eventually embraced but also on the mix of philosophical inquiry, genteel Protestantism, and evangelicalism that animated the world of her youth. And although her conversion to Catholicism might appear anathema to the Second Great Awakening's Protestant inventiveness, she left her Protestant countrymen behind only in a narrow sense. In another way, Elizabeth walked in the company of contemporaries who threw over the denominations of their parents and neighbors in order to immerse themselves in intense and alien forms of Christianity.

Portraying Seton's conversion to Catholicism as simply one of many controversial choices spiritually ambitious Americans made in the early nineteenth century leaves out one important element of her era: antipopery. When the Catholic Church appears in the story of early America, it is usually as a phantom haunting the Protestant mind or a beleaguered minority evading the Protestant boot. There's good reason for that: in England and America, many Protestants believed Catholics incapable of patriotism and independent thought and sought to limit Catholics' ability to practice their faith and participate in political life. This cultural animosity is part of Elizabeth's story; through her life we witness the pain and disruption anti-Catholicism caused members of a faith now woven into the American fabric. Yet in her life we also see unmistakable evidence that anti-Catholic sentiment was less pervasive and monolithic in the early American republic than is commonly portrayed, and we witness Catholics confidently competing in the American marketplace of religion. Seton's conversion provoked heated disagreements and pained silences, but she and her critics did not simply rehash early modern sectarian controversies. Instead they confronted questions that roil the twenty-first century: If one believes there is a safest path to Heaven, shouldn't one try to convince others to follow it? What if those others do not want to be convinced? If a person believes that the purpose of life is to serve God, must she not sacrifice everything in order to pursue it? What if sacrificing her own well-being also sacrifices the well-being of others? Elizabeth Seton contemplated such questions throughout her adult life. The answers she developed sundered and remade her relationships. They also animated the religious community she founded and, through it, the American Catholic Church.

———

IN CREATING THIS PORTRAIT of Elizabeth Seton, I've had the privilege of learning something of how she lives in others' imaginations as well. She is honored not only at the Seton Shrine in Emmitsburg but at the Saint Mary's Spiritual Center and Historic Site in Baltimore and the Shrine of St. Elizabeth Ann Bayley Seton in lower Manhattan; at each place, visitors walk through buildings important in Seton's own life and hear and share stories of her meaningfulness to others'. Many who would never think to visit one of the shrines also feel her cultural presence: "Seton, she did the schools?" "Mother Seton. . . . Like the Daughters of Charity?" are questions I've come to expect and welcome when I mention my research. Her admirers are not confined to the Catholic faith; it was during a chance conversation, in the earliest stages of this project, that I learned Seton is honored on the Episcopal Church's calendar of saints as well as that of the Roman Catholic Church. I've also often listened to people explain that their interest in Seton has nothing to do with any particular faith tradition but rather with the drama and daring of her unexpected life. Elizabeth Seton was an explorer who creatively adapted each intellectual and spiritual tradition she chose to inhabit, and it seems only fitting that her life and legacy are put to uses she did not imagine.

One fact of Seton's life, however, is clear: faith lay at its center. And faith lies at the center of this book, in a way unusual, and perhaps uncomfortable, among scholarly works of history. "Faith is hard," the anthropologist Tanya Luhrmann has observed; for historians, it can also be hard to think about and describe. The realm of faith is filled with inquiry and doubt as well as belief, with dread as well as comfort, and with ruthlessness as well as benevolence. Faith is not entirely the same for all those who share a creed nor entirely different among all those who don't. Faith is not reducible to the instrumental uses that historians commonly acknowledge as real: the maintenance of social order, the creation of allegiances, the fight against modernity's dislocations. Nor, however, is faith abstracted from the societies in which it develops: faith looks away from the world but must be lived within it. It is at the scale of an individual life such as Elizabeth Seton's that the work of faith, like the workings of gender, culture, personality, and chance, comes into view. And it is from individual lives that societies, nations, and religions are made.

PART 1

A NEW YORK LIFE

1

TWO FAMILIES

A T THE TIME of Elizabeth Seton's birth, New York was a city made by empire and defined by water. Its deep harbor had drawn goods and people for generations, and the Hudson, the great river on Manhattan's western edge, was the finest road into the interior of the northeastern colonies. The city's merchants traded in patterns established by Britain's power: wealthy New Yorkers drank fortified wine shipped from Madeira, kept time on clocks imported from England, and sipped tea from cups made in China. Merchants also proved cheerfully willing to smuggle when the opportunity arose, which it often did. So fast did cargoes pile up that the men who unloaded them accidentally tipped containers into the harbor, leaving shoes and ceramics to be found by the archaeologists of later centuries.[1]

Water flowed over as well as among the islands that rose up through the waters of New York's harbors and bays. On Manhattan's western side, streams tumbled into the Hudson; on the east, farmers cut channels to drain surface water into what they called the East River, really just a splinter of the Hudson that Manhattan's landmass forced to find its own way to the bay. Convinced that the "stagnation and rottenness" of marshes caused the fevers that plagued them, New Yorkers drained swamps in lower Manhattan as a radical solution to the problem. They also pushed the city slowly out into the harbor, building wharves on land made from discarded bottles, ship parts, and animal bones.[2] Despite

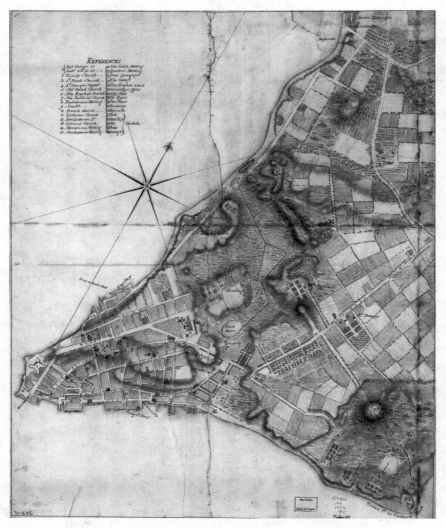

FIGURE 1.1. *A Plan of the city of New York*, 1776. Courtesy of the digital collections of the Library of Congress, Washington, DC.

the transformations wrought by its inhabitants, Manhattan Island was still as much a landscape as a city during Elizabeth's childhood, a place not only of merchants, laborers, and buildings but of hills, creeks, and trees. Most of its residents, including the Bayley and Seton families, lived within a mile of Fort George at the island's southern tip.

YOUNG MEN ON THE RISE

At Elizabeth's birth, her father, Richard Bayley, was twenty-nine years old. William Seton, the man who would become her father-in-law, was twenty-eight. Like Manhattan itself, both men were made by empire and water. Bayley was a surgeon who crossed the ocean for training in London, then returned and devoted himself to combating the fevers that thrived near the city's swamps and docks. Seton, born in England, made his money selling New Yorkers the goods they coveted from across the sea. The characters and careers of these two men shaped the circumstances of Elizabeth's life well into her young womanhood, so we will take time to know them now.

William Seton came from a Scottish clan who, like other merchant families, knit themselves into skeins of cousins and commerce: a Seton by both birth and marriage, his mother possessed the stutteringly dignified name of Elizabeth Seton Seton. Like tens of thousands of Scots during the eighteenth century, Seton sailed to the North American mainland hoping to find opportunities his home failed to provide.[3] He arrived in New York at seventeen, bearing high hopes and letters of introduction to Richard Curson, another English-born merchant who had found his way to the thriving colonial port. Curson's advertisements capture the mix of transatlantic hub and early modern village in which Seton sought his fortune. "Wines Wholesale and Retail, to be sold by Richard Curson, on Potsbakers Hill, near the new Dutch Church," reads a notice from 1757. "Also, Old Jamaica and Barbados Rum, Brandy, Geneva, and Velvet Corks. . . . Said Curson is remov'd lower down, in the House of Capt. Burchill, fronting the Street that leads to the Widow Rutgers's Brewhouse, opposite to the Sign of the Three Pidgeons."[4] In this world, personal ties were as essential to merchant life as goods and credit; amiable William Seton knew how to weave them. By 1765, still not twenty years old, he was an officer of the city's St. Andrew's Society, founded to provide charity and promote social intercourse among Scottish immigrants and their descendants.[5]

Elizabeth's father found his way to Manhattan a few years after William Seton. Richard Bayley had spent his childhood in New Rochelle, an area of tiny towns and fertile farms some twenty-five miles north of Ft. George, just across the sluice of water separating Manhattan from the mainland. New Rochelle had been settled by French Protestants fleeing the endless rounds of sectarian violence following the Reformation. The descendants of those Huguenot settlers maintained their piety, their French language, and their loathing for the religion they called popery. Bayley possessed neither the intense Protestant piety that permeated his hometown nor any other kind. Nor was he content, as his brother was, to stay and make his way amid the region's farms. Instead, he set off for Manhattan, determined to become a "scientific" physician who used observation and experimentation to understand the causes of disease.[6] Bayley was as ambitious as Seton. But Seton sought profits and never made an enemy when he could form an alliance; Bayley sought truth and relished a good fight.

Manhattan was a realm of opportunity for Seton and Bayley but a place of captivity for others: everywhere the two men looked, they were likely to see an enslaved person. In the seventeenth century, the Dutch East India Company had bought and sold slaves and used them for labor in the colony. After the English acquired the area, its labor demands exceeded its attractions for free immigrants, so those who promoted New York's settlement encouraged and forced the migration of a polyglot mix of Europeans and Africans.[7] In 1741, less than twenty-five years before Seton and Bayley arrived in the city, a series of unexplained fires led to rumors that New York's enslaved population was plotting insurrection in the company of Papists. (It was Catholics' perceived animosity toward the English, not toward the institution of slavery, that made them suspect.) White New Yorkers burned and hanged those they blamed for the rebellion, leaving rotting corpses as warnings to others. The brutal events did not slow the rise of slavery on the island. On the contrary, the institution continued to produce the capital fueling the growth of city and empire. William Seton and Richard Curson bought and sold the fruits of slaves' labor: hogsheads of tobacco from the Chesapeake, rum from Jamaica, and white and muscavado sugar from the West Indies. Colonial religion was nearly as entangled with the institution as was the colonial economy. Although some Quakers in the colonies and England aggressively opposed slavery, many Christian churches accepted and benefited from it. Maryland's Jesuit priests supported themselves from the labor of slaves, and Anglican pews and pulpits were filled with slaveholders too; Elizabeth Seton's maternal grandfather, the Anglican rector on Staten Island, owned several people.[8]

The Bayleys had a different connection to the plantation economy; Richard Bayley's mother had descended from a Huguenot settler who married a young woman from the island of Martinique and for a time sold sugar cultivated by slaves. (Both that settler, who was Bayley's great-grandfather, and his wife died of yellow fever, a plague that would in years to come send its tendrils through Richard Bayley's and Elizabeth Seton's lives.) Family legend has it that Richard's grandfather became betrothed to a young woman during a sojourn with his mother's family in Martinique; after returning to the island to marry her, he heard that she had married someone else. The young man sailed back to New York vowing to marry the first young woman who would have him. He did exactly that, only to learn that his fiancée in Martinique had not really jilted him.[9] Whatever its kernel of truth, that is an awkward family story, and one wonders how Richard's grandmother, the bride chosen out of mistaken pique, reacted to its telling. The grandmother's unknowability is the rule, not the exception, among women on both sides of Elizabeth Seton's family. Their lives were structured by the ambitions, choices, and migrations of fathers and husbands, and their thoughts must be left to the imagining.

EMPIRE IN CRISIS

William Seton had been in America for two years when the implementation of the Stamp Act roiled the colonies. Unhappy to feel the British bureaucracy reaching into their affairs and purses, more than two hundred of New York City's merchants signed a nonimportation agreement at the tavern known as Burns' City Arms. Seton and Curson cautiously joined in. They hoped to repair the bonds of empire, not unravel them, but others were more radical: a group called the Liberty Boys, boasting among its founders members of the Scottish St. Andrew's Society, heckled soldiers and erected Liberty poles, encasing one in iron after British regulars splintered several others. Most New Yorkers, however, were not ready to risk their comfort and profits in resistance to the empire. Families such as the Setons and Bayleys *were* Britons: they imported English fashions, read English books, and watched English plays, and as they continuously remade the island of Manhattan, they named their streets and squares King, Duke, Prince, and Queen. When in 1766 Parliament repealed the hated Stamp Act, many hoped (despite the stark declaration of Parliament's political authority that accompanied repeal) that colonies and mother country would settle back into their familiar ways.[10]

As the bonds of empire held for the moment, nineteen-year-old William Seton augmented the ties of business with those of family, marrying Rebecca Curson, a daughter of his business associate.[11] The young couple sailed to England to meet William's family. In 1768, with trade returned to its old patterns and Rebecca far along in her first pregnancy, the Setons were eager to return to New York. So it happened that William Magee Seton, Elizabeth's future husband, was born at sea, crossing the Atlantic as his father's merchandise so often did.

Once back in the city, the elder William steadily ascended. No longer did he piece together cargoes to sell on others' premises; he was now "William Seton, Importer of Dry Goods, European and India Goods. Store on Cruger's Dock."[12] In 1771, Curson formally took him on as a partner, and the newly formed house of Curson & Seton began to advertise wares ranging from "Florence oyl" (olive oil) to Madeira to flax, arriving on ships from London, Bristol, and Liverpool.[13] By 1773, after a decade in the colony, Seton was the father of three sons—James and Jack had joined William Magee—and sufficiently well placed to be included by the artist Henry Pelham Copley in a handful of "valuable friends" who treated him with "great civilities."[14] Around Seton, New York had settled into a disputatious but not radically disaffected relationship with England. The harbor was filled with ships, and a lead statue of George III, complete with gilding, rose on the Bowling Green.[15]

While William Seton ascended as a merchant, Richard Bayley advanced as a doctor. By 1766, he was a student of the prominent physician John Charlton, described in a nineteenth-century account of the city as "short of stature, with a florid face, of somewhat pompous manners," and possessed of a practice consisting of "fashionable clients, whom he leisurely attended."[16] Married to a daughter of two great New York families, Dr. Charlton ministered to the wealthy and was pleased to find himself grow wealthy in return. Working with Charlton placed Bayley in the company of genteel New Yorkers such as John Jay, a rising young lawyer who, like Bayley, hailed from the Huguenot community of New Rochelle. It also placed him in the company of Charlton's sister Catherine. He married Catherine in 1767, the same year that Seton married his business associate's daughter. Within a year, Richard and Catherine had a daughter, whom they named Mary Magdalen. But Bayley was not content. While Mary was still an infant, he sailed for London to continue his medical education.

Bayley thrived in London, staying for two years. At last, he returned to New York; his second daughter, the child who would grow up to become Elizabeth Seton, was born in August of 1774. Bayley rejoined John Charlton's practice, but rather than simply tending genteel patients he investigated two diseases that plagued the city's youth: croup and "putrid sore throat." Bayley peered into the throats of sick, gasping children around the city and recorded what he saw. When permitted, he dissected the corpses of children who had succumbed. It was a controversial practice in an era when many believed dissection was desecration, but Bayley had no interest in keeping to the expected path when his real quarry, truth, led him elsewhere.[17]

"EXCEPT PAPISTS"

When she wrote about New York after her conversion, Elizabeth Seton portrayed the city as profoundly anti-Catholic; those who've written about her have tended to follow suit.[18] The truth is more complicated. Manhattan was home to both daily tolerance and bursts of vitriol. In the colonies as in Europe, men and women disagreed over how to worship God and over whether they should regulate each other's faiths at all. New Yorkers opted for a fractious comity more often than they strove to enforce orthodoxy of any kind. At the time of Elizabeth's birth, the Dutch Reformed Church, whose black-clothed ministers known as dominies once held sway, maintained some of the privileges it had known under Dutch rule, but England's official church had been the established faith for many decades, and both the Bayleys and the Setons were Anglicans. The faith's largest New York church was Trinity, which then—when the southern end of Manhattan Island was more slender than it is now—stood a few blocks from the Hudson River. Through its trustees, Trinity parish controlled huge tracts of land, one of which it donated to start the city's first college, King's, on condition that its presidents all be Anglicans and that the Book of Common Prayer be used in daily services.

New York was also home to many other forms of Protestantism, and followers of those denominations increasingly resisted Anglicanism's cultural and political sway. Members of the powerful Livingston clan were Presbyterian; in 1754, Peter Livingston, along with John Morin Scott and a third lawyer, William Smith, founded the New York Society Library as an ecumenical institution intended to counter the Anglican influence of King's College. Evangelical Protestantism also found a voice; the charismatic Methodist preacher George Whitfield visited Manhattan twice, and Methodists built a chapel on John Street. A Baptist congregation met not far away on Gold Street, and other evangelicals convened prayer meetings in improvised spaces across the city. Amid religious change and new imperial regulations, simmering disagreements over England's power became entangled with resentment of the Anglican Church's claims of authority. In spring of 1766, trustees of the First Presbyterian Church petitioned the crown for a charter of incorporation. The petition was denied, as were similar ones from Lutherans and Huguenots, but skirmishes broke out again and again. The formal establishment of the Anglican Church remained, but the faith's cultural power ebbed by the year.[19]

If Anglicanism seemed, to some colonists, too closely tied to mother England, Catholicism offended in the opposite way. Elizabeth's depictions of antipopery were exaggerated but not invented. At the time of her birth, Catholicism was for many colonists the religion of priest-ridden wretches in the service of a Roman conspiracy to destroy liberty and the British empire; they believed that Catholicism must be suppressed if liberty were to thrive. New York's small number of Catholics tended to live at the margins, whether they were poor Irish immigrants or wealthy slaveholders from the French sugar colonies. But it was the idea of Catholicism, more than the presence or power of actual Catholics, that chafed; anti-Catholicism united Manhattanites when little else did. "Perfect freedome of conscience for all," explained a Dutch Reformed dominie in 1741, "except Papists."[20] Well-heeled New Yorkers such as New Rochelle's John Jay argued that Catholics lacked independent judgment and were loyal only to the pope. A more festive antipopery thrived too: each year on Guy Fawkes Day, Manhattanites created effigies of the pope and the devil, paraded them through the streets, and burned them.

Nonetheless, burning effigies is quite different from burning people, and throughout the latter half of the eighteenth century, the rhetoric and pageantry of New York's antipopery outstripped true persecution. Neither William Seton nor Richard Bayley resented Catholics. For Seton, profits mattered more than theology: trading with Catholics in the West Indies and Europe was an unremarkable fact of his life. Bayley, for his part, was as immune to the religious animosities of his Huguenot family as he was to their religious allegiances. Both men saw more value in cooperation than in orthodoxy, and many of their fellow Manhattanites agreed.

WAR

While acts and protests corroded the colonial relationship, pragmatic New Yorkers continued to seek grounds for compromise. But in the year of Elizabeth's birth, Boston, that pricklier city to the north, pulled Manhattanites toward war. The protest that became known as Boston's Tea Party provoked Parliament to dramatic retaliation: four acts, passed from March to June of 1774, closed the city's port, crippled its popular assemblies, empowered the appointed governor to remove trials from Massachusetts, and filled the city with regulars whom Boston's resentful inhabitants were told to billet. Following close on the heels of those acts, the Quebec Act negated Virginians' and New Englanders' claims to Canadian territory and offered protection for Roman Catholicism in the region, further convincing colonists that the cords of empire must be cut. News of the offending legislation arrived in Manhattan aboard the inaptly named *Concord*. "This intelligence was received with Great abhorrence & indignation by the Sons of Freedom," wrote a member of the St. Andrew's Society.[21] Sons of Liberty vowed to convince New York's merchants to end the city's trade with the British West Indies. As the crisis deepened, Seton, Curson, and other merchants tried to support resistance while avoiding revolution.[22] Then, in April of 1775, came more news from Boston.

Elizabeth was not quite a year old—and William Magee Seton barely seven—when regulars and Massachusetts men fought at Lexington and Concord. The news quickly reached Manhattan, where Liberty Boys seized muskets and gunpowder from City Hall. As a growing crowd disrupted courts and markets, protesters demanded the keys to the customs house, and an angry New Yorker denounced George III as a "Catholic" who intended to force his faith on the American colonies.[23] With some of its members leading the Liberty Boys and others loyal to the Crown, the St. Andrew's Society disbanded. The distance between those hoping for compromise and those favoring rebellion grew starker, and religious division accompanied political. Presbyterian ministers leaned toward radicalism, while most of the region's Anglican pastors deplored what seemed to them an "unnatural rebellion." Elizabeth's grandfather, rector of Staten Island's Anglican church, demanded "a Speedy suppression to insulting Mobs, and a restoration of Loyalty and obedience to our Parent State."[24]

Yet as the imperial crisis deepened, domestic life continued. By 1774, William's wife, Rebecca Curson Seton, had given birth to four sons. William kept a home close to the East River neighborhood where Curson & Seton did business, and he acquired a lease on a small farm in a part of rural Manhattan that still went by the old Dutch term for orchard, "bouwerie." In 1775, as the colonies thrashed toward rebellion, the couple's first daughter was born. The Setons named her Anna Maria, a name shared by Rebecca's younger sister. The infant thrived, but Rebecca, in fragile health even before this fifth pregnancy in eight years, weakened. On October 4, 1775, she died at the age of twenty-seven. A brief notice in *Rivington's New York Gazetteer* called her "a lady that was highly respected, and whose death was much lamented."[25] Rebecca's oldest child, William Magee, was eight years old.

Not far away, the Bayley family faced a different kind of loss. Even as the fabric of city and empire frayed, Richard Bayley left his wife and two small daughters to sail for England to continue his medical studies. Soon afterward, rumors spread of an imminent British invasion, and thousands of frightened New Yorkers, Patriots and Loyalists alike, fled the city. With her husband far away, Catherine Bayley took her children and followed her physician brother, John Charlton, to Long Island. By the next spring, the British had been driven from Boston, and a fleet sailed toward New York. On the twenty-ninth of June, ten ships of the line, almost 170 transports, and more than thirty-two thousand British and Hessian soldiers entered the Lower Manhattan Bay near Sandy Hook.[26] "I . . . spied as I peeped out the Bay something resembling a wood of pine trees trimmed," one New Yorker marveled of the ships' masts that suddenly bristled in the harbor. "I declare I thought all London Afloat."[27] Some New Yorkers donned red ribbons, raised the British flag, and predicted the speedy defeat of the rebels.[28] Others chose rebellion. In early July, a fast rider from Philadelphia brought a copy of the newly signed Declaration of Independence. Rebel troops cheered its public reading,

then joyfully brought down the gilded statue of George III that had
been erected on the Bowling Green just six years earlier. "The Lead we
hear is to be run up into musket balls for the use of the Yankees," jested
one young Patriot, "when it is hoped that the emanations of the Leaden
George will make as deep impressions in the Bodies of some of his red
coated and Torie subjects."²⁹

Bravado did not prevent New York City from falling to the British
in August. Those still resident had choices to make. Richard Curson
and his son Samuel made their way to Baltimore: they had cast their lot
with revolution.³⁰ William Seton stayed in New York, remaining loyal
to the Crown. The families would endure the war on opposite sides of
the political divide. Yet their faces remained turned toward each other,
so much so that it seems possible that agreement, rather than difference,
led to their separation: one side had to win the war, and either way, the
house of Curson and Seton would have a foothold. Whatever the reasons
for the partners' political configuration, the families grew only more
entwined. On November 29, 1776, the widowed William Seton remarried. His bride was Anna Maria Curson, another of Richard Curson's
daughters.

The Anglican communion forbade marriage to a sibling of one's lost
spouse, and although the Setons and Cursons were happy to overlook
this rule, the ministers of Trinity Church proved less open-minded. Seton
solved the problem by traveling to New Jersey. There, in the opening
months of the American Revolution, the Anglican Loyalist married the
daughter of a Patriot in a Presbyterian church. Seton's second marriage
was a testament to both flexibility and determination, and he set the
same qualities to work throughout the occupation. In July of 1777,
he accepted an office in the Superintendent's Department established
by General Sir William Howe, and as the conflict wore on, he rose to
become assistant to Andrew Elliott, the Crown's superintendent of New
York's great port.³¹ Seton's marriage to Anna Maria Curson, moreover,
proved as bountiful as his marriage to Rebecca. His young wife bore
her first child, a daughter named Eliza, in 1779; two more daughters
followed. Quietly, the relationship between the Loyalist Setons and the
Whig Cursons also continued. In late 1778, a well-connected former
congressman named William Duer sought permission for "Mr. Saml.
Curson Junr. Son of Mr. Curson whom you must have known in New
York . . . to meet his Brother in Law Mr. Seton upon the Lines in Case

the Enemy will permit him to come out."[32] Not even war could thwart William Seton's talent for connection.

Like Seton, Richard Bayley declined rebellion; when he arrived back in New York after the war's start, it was as a surgeon in the British army. A brief account written in 1825 to honor Bayley's medical accomplishments suggests that he joined the British army in order to support his family. Practicality dictated little in Bayley's life, however, and joining the army offered the opportunity for large-scale observations of disease and wounds and extensive practice in trying to heal them. The military chain of command permitted Bayley to enforce treatments and hygiene practices in a way impossible in civilian life. War was a laboratory, and Bayley intended to use it. Stationed as a military surgeon in Rhode Island, the physician became the subject of rumors that he was in the habit of "cutting up" prisoners in his care, an accusation likely sparked by his performance of autopsies.[33]

While Bayley served in Rhode Island, his daughters Elizabeth and Mary, along with their mother, Catherine, stayed with the Charltons. Long Island was the site of raids and counterraids among Loyalists and Patriots, and all households lived amid uncertainty and danger. Bayley visited when he could, and in spring of 1777, Catherine gave birth to a third daughter. Not long after, she fell gravely ill. Bayley rushed to New York, but his hard-won medical skills could not save his wife. Catherine Charlton Bayley died in May of 1777, leaving behind nine-year-old Mary, three-year-old Elizabeth, and a newborn who bore her name.

The motherless girls remained with relatives on Long Island. Soon, their maternal grandfather, the Reverend Richard Charlton, also died. The girls' losses were agonizing but not uncommon. Infants, elders, and women in childbed were always at risk; war, its traveling armies bearing disease as well as arms, increased everyone's peril. Slaves faced additional threat. The death of Elizabeth's grandfather meant that the people he owned were sent to live in other households, with no guarantee that their families would stay together. Richard Charlton's will distributed his seven slaves among his relatives. To Elizabeth and baby Catherine, he left "my negro boy, formerly named Brennus." To his older granddaughter, Mary, Charlton bequeathed "my negro girl, Bett."[34]

Elizabeth was accustomed to slavery from her earliest days, but it is possible that some of the enslaved people given by Reverend Charlton to his family—like many others during the war—escaped their bonds.

New York's wartime newspapers contained hundreds of advertisements for the return of runaways. Richard Bayley took the time to place one of them. "Runaway from the subscriber, a few days ago, living in the city, a mulatto fellow who lately had the small pox, named Jessemy, about 25 years old," reads the advertisement.[35] This may have been the "boy" given to Elizabeth and Catherine, whom Richard Charlton identified as the slave "formerly named Brennus." The historical record is silent on the young man's fate.

STILL AT WAR

When New York's Loyalists first donned their red ribbons, they expected the mighty British army and navy to quickly crush Patriot resistance. Instead, the war dragged on, and in October of 1777, General Burgoyne's surrender of his army at Saratoga, New York, left the city exposed. The Hudson River pointed like an arrow toward Manhattan, and the harbor was vulnerable as well. That was worrisome enough, and then (following reasoning that canny Loyalist merchants like William Seton could hardly have gainsaid) British strategists moved naval forces away from the northern colonies to protect the more valuable West Indian sugar colonies. Things only got worse: France entered an alliance with the rebellious colonists, and Loyalists found themselves fighting against an empire as well as for one. For some Patriots, France's involvement unsettled the traditional association of Catholicism with tyranny. Loyalists saw it as proof that both Patriots and Catholics were even more dastardly than they'd presumed. "Cursed be the Archbishops, bishops, Priest, Deacons and other dignitaries of the [Roman Catholic Church]" went one exuberantly hostile toast; "cursed also be their congregations; may they go to sea in a high wind, leaky vessel and a lee shore, to ferry them over the river Styx."[36] Tradition has it that New York's small group of Catholics held Mass in a private home, shutters drawn.[37]

As the war dragged on, Richard Bayley remained a Loyalist, but after Catherine's death he left the British Army, collected his daughters from the Charltons, and returned the family to Manhattan. There, he worked as a doctor and quickly found a new wife. Nineteen-year-old Charlotte Amelia Barclay was the daughter of Andrew Barclay, a successful merchant (and founding member of the St. Andrew's Society), and Helena Roosevelt, daughter of a proud old Dutch family. Charlotte's uncle had been rector of Trinity parish, and several of her older brothers and sisters married into prominent Loyalist families, including the most powerful of all Tory clans, the Delanceys.[38] Yet vulnerability as well as privilege trailed Elizabeth's new stepmother. Her family's connections to the Crown were assets only if the British army prevailed over the rebels, an outcome that seemed increasingly in doubt. Moreover, both of Charlotte's parents were dead—her mother when Charlotte was only thirteen –and she would have to tend her three stepchildren without their guidance. Then, not long after Richard and Charlotte's marriage, tragedy struck: baby Catherine died.

Late in her life, Elizabeth wrote a brief, impressionistic memoir that she called "Dear Remembrances." The first memory she offers is of the day of her sister's funeral. "At 4 years of age sitting alone on a step of the door looking at the clouds," Elizabeth wrote, "while my little sister Catherine 2 years old lay in her coffin." "They asked me did I not cry when little Kitty was dead?—no because Kitty is gone up to heaven." "I wish I could go too with Mamma," she thought.[39] When Elizabeth wrote "Dear Remembrances," she was eager to shape the twists and turns of her life into a straight path toward the Catholic Church that others might follow. Because she did not intend it to be a full accounting of her thoughts and experience, "Dear Remembrances" is a source best used with caution. This moment on the stoop, however, sounds a believably forlorn note: the little girl who remembered no time before the war, whose father was often absent, and whose mother, sister, and grandfather were dead imagined heaven as refuge and reunion.

The stoop on which Elizabeth sat was a tiny perch of sorrow in a vast landscape of destruction. Swathes of lower Manhattan had burned in a catastrophic fire soon after the occupation began; late in the war, almost one-quarter of the housing stock still lay in ruins. British commanders governed New York under a martial law that managed to be both oppressive and careless. Wallabout Bay contained prison ships on which hundreds of captured rebels lived in wretched conditions; the city's non-Anglican churches had been commandeered to hold still more. "We never drew as much provisions for three days' allowance," one prisoner wrote after the war, "as a man would eat at a common meal." Every day carts carried off the bodies of the dead.[40]

William Seton and Richard Bayley were uneasy at the callousness of their chosen side, and each responded in his own way. The genial Seton came to the aid of a young Frenchman named Hector St. John de Crève-coeur. Patriots resented Crèvecoeur's Loyalist ties, but when he traveled to Manhattan in search of safety, the British imprisoned him as a rebel. Moved by the Frenchman's plight, Seton helped raise bail so that he might leave the colonies.[41] When a grateful Crèvecoeur later published a set of essays about America, he dedicated them to "William Seton, Esq." Crèvecoeur's *Letters of an American Farmer* are still celebrated as a brilliant contemplation of a society at its birth; Seton's kindness had guaranteed him a footnote in American literary history.

Bayley was as prickly in his benevolence as Seton was amiable. The physician vociferously complained about the lack of barracks for sick soldiers, and one day, after helping a drunken regular who had gotten himself run over by a carriage, Bayley was jailed as a troublemaker. "This man is enraged," a Loyalist diary keeper wrote, "and told me today he would demand satisfaction, or leave to go home or leave to quit the British lines, averse to continuing any longer under military govern-ment."[42] For once, however, Bayley stood down. He, Charlotte, and his surviving daughters stayed grimly in Manhattan, prospects of a British victory growing dimmer and the city more squalid.

William Seton stayed too, but late in the war, he sent his two old-est sons, twelve-year-old William Magee and ten-year-old James, to his mother and sister in England. A surviving letter suggests just how uninterested in the struggle for American independence young William Magee was. "Mr. Mann was so good as to take me to see the House of Lords," the boy wrote, "Where I saw the King sitting upon the Throne with a crown upon his head, & I saw all the Lords dressed in their Robes & heard the bill read over to the King. . . . I saw that famous man lord North; but I think of all the lords I ever saw he was shabbiest, he had on a nasty old brown coat."[43]

While William Magee placidly contemplated the dress of English lords, Elizabeth remained in the war-torn city. Writing in "Dear Remem-brances," she recalled that her "poor" stepmother was in these months "in great affliction" but managed to teach her "the 22d Psalm: The Lord is my Shepherd, the Lord ruleth me. . . . Though I walk in the midst of the shade of death, I will fear no evil, for thou art with me." Charlotte Bayley Seton did walk amid shadows. The birth of two healthy infants, Emma in 1779 and Richard Jr. in 1781, did not steady her; on the con-trary, the challenges of life in an occupied city and something in her own temperament—an unhappiness that grew more pronounced as the years passed—left her struggling to nurture her stepdaughters and even her own children. Still in her early twenties, Charlotte bore her burdens while commanding only a small fraction of her husband's attention. As battles raged and his family grew, Richard Bayley was writing an analysis of croup.[44]

In the spring of 1781, George Washington's army lurked near New York City. In the South, a frustrated Lord Cornwallis, his army beset by armed rebels and malaria, moved his men north from the Carolinas toward Virginia. Learning of the movement and confident of French naval support, Washington marched his troops rapidly toward Yorktown. There, in October of 1781, the Americans were victorious. Peace negotiations lurched and faltered for two more years, but when Cornwallis surrendered his army, the British surrendered the fight.

Showing his customary contrarianism, Richard Bayley grew more content with the occupation once the prospects of British success ended, openly admiring the newly appointed commander in chief of British forces in North America, Sir Guy Carleton. William Seton, always more practical, turned his attention to adapting to the coming order. As the war ended, he had eight children, public ties to the defeated regime, and debts no honest man could pay. Seton wrote to his mother asking that his sons William Magee and James be sent home, but it was unclear what else could be restored to him. He would begin his life in an independent New York as he had begun his life in the colonial city, richer in connections and determination than in cash.

2

BETSY BAYLEY

WHEN THE TREATY OF PARIS formally ended the American Revolution, much of Manhattan's population had fled, and makeshift barricades littered its hillocks and shores. "Close on the eve of an approaching winter," one Patriot later recalled, "we took possession of a ruined city."[1] West of Broadway and south of Barclay Street (named for the once powerful Loyalist family of Elizabeth's stepmother, Charlotte) impoverished New Yorkers sheltered in shacks pieced together from ships' canvases and spars.

As New Yorkers began to rebuild, Elizabeth Bayley—Betsy to her family—was nine years old. William Magee Seton was fifteen. The two had not yet met in these years immediately after the Revolution, and in some ways seemed ill suited for friendship, let alone marriage. Elizabeth loved reading and thinking, while William took little interest in his studies. "I am very sorry that sweet William has profited so little in England," the boy's blunt English aunt Barbara wrote. "It was what I much fear'd, as he did not seem fond of application."[2] William Magee was of a mild temperament, while Elizabeth observed that as a child she had been "ungovernable."[3] And although religion held scant charm for William Magee, the young Elizabeth took "pleasure in learning anything pious," or so she recalled later in life, and there's no reason to doubt her.[4]

Despite their differences, the two young people shared an inward turn. "He is a good boy with a good heart," William Magee's grandmother gently observed, "& I am persuaded his manners will much improve as he grows older, sees more of the world."[5] Elizabeth hinted at her own sense of remove in her "Remembrances." Explaining that she loved to look at birds' eggs as a child, she wrote that one day she "Cried because the girls would destroy them, and afterwards always loved to play and walk alone."[6]

It was in her father's childhood hometown of New Rochelle that Elizabeth often walked and played alone. Charlotte chafed at having her stepdaughters in her home, so the two girls passed long stretches of time with their aunt and uncle. William and Sarah Bayley's household was well ordered, and during her stays amid New Rochelle's Huguenot descendants, Elizabeth attended school and learned passable French, a skill that brought her pleasure the rest of her life. Yet when she later alluded to these childhood years, Manhattan and not New Rochelle was "home." She wanted to live in her father's household, whether or not she was welcome. "Home again," Elizabeth later wrote of a time she and Mary returned to Manhattan. "Pleasure in reading prayers. Love to nurse the children and sing little hymns over the cradle." Elizabeth's recollection of caring tenderly for her half siblings is borne out by the deep affection the Bayley children showed her throughout decades of correspondence. Yet nothing healed the rift between Charlotte and her stepdaughters. A cryptic phrase in "Dear Remembrances" hints at the resentment Elizabeth felt: "Foolish, ignorant, childish heart."[7]

William Magee Seton's stepmother was also his aunt, and Anna Maria Seton did not mark the divide between her sister's children and her own. The Setons were short not on affection but on cash. After years of war, their affairs were in disarray: William wrote in distress to his father-in-law, Richard Curson, that a mortgage document "cannot be found," that accounts had gone missing—"for the life of me [I] cannot find the papers relating to the Money paid"—and that he was being aggressively pressed for funds by people ranging from his own kinsman James Farquhar to a professional debt collector. Personal shame and financial ruin loomed. "Many have delivered in their accounts," Seton wrote, "which I only wish to God I could pay." He was even sued under the 1783 Trespass Act, a law that allowed returning Patriots to sue Loyalists who had occupied their businesses or homes during the war. (Seton had worked out of a Patriot family's confiscated house.) Most distressingly of all, a 1782 law prohibited Loyalists from collecting debts. "To those few who owe us here," Seton wearily wrote Curson, "It would answer no purpose for me to send in the accounts. They know I cannot demand it or enforce payment; everyone who has been within the lines is in the same situation."[8]

Yet Seton made his way in his unchosen new world. The Cursons helped him to rebuild his reputation and the lines of credit that came with it. Wartime kindness bore fruit: Crèvecoeur was named French consul and helped Seton become deputy agent of a packet service between New York and France.[9] Seton proved as adroit as ever at piecing together cargoes and connections. An early postwar advertisement reads as if he looked around his warehouse, cheerfully jotting down the motley items he had managed to collect for sale. "Florence oyl," he advertised, and Italian and French brandy, marble, souchong tea and indigo, "a few bits of coal suitable for home use," "Straw and chip hats and coarse cotton stockings," and, from somewhere, "deerskins."[10] Each item bought and resold, each bit of credit achieved or extended, brought the Setons closer to the standing they'd enjoyed before the war. Expertly lacing people into his commercial network, William strengthened the ties of interest with bonds of affection. "So much for business," he wrote at the end of a long letter to his father-in-law: "We are in full hopes of seeing you and Mrs. Curson here with my [Anna] Maria this spring. . . . It will give the most hearty pleasure and satisfaction to all the family and brighten the chain of friendship and affection between us all."[11]

At a time when Loyalists feared reprisals, Seton's sunny amiability was its own form of courage. "The Whigs take the liberty to prognosticate," read one menacing little newspaper item, "that the calm which the enemies of Columbia at present enjoy, will ere long be succeeded by a *bitter and neck-breaking hurricane*."[12] Yet Seton turned even the trespass suit against him into a tie of cordiality and usefulness. Hiring Alexander Hamilton as his attorney, he began a fruitful association with that rising young lawyer and politician. When Hamilton created the Bank of New York, Seton was appointed cashier; before long his teenaged son William Magee was given a position as clerk. A few years after fearing ruin, Seton was cashier of an institution important to the nation's growing economy and once again a successful merchant. When the bank moved to Hanover Square, site of New York's most powerful firms and home to many of its wealthy merchants, Seton took the rooms adjacent for his home and business.[13] He began to regain the luxuries

FIGURE 2.1.
Anonymous, *William
Seton*, after Gilbert
Stuart. National
Gallery of Art,
Washington, DC,
Gallery Archives.

he'd been proud to claim before the Revolution, eventually acquiring a summer home—Cragdon, the family dubbed it—near the Bloomingdale Road on Manhattan's western side. In an ambiguous episode, Seton also purchased an enslaved woman and child, then allowed a man named Cato—apparently their husband and father—to buy them from him. Cato painstakingly offered what money he could from wages he was allowed to earn, Seton keeping careful track of the payments. Had Seton purchased the slaves with the intention of allowing Cato to earn their freedom? If so, his tidy columns of sums tally both kindness and its limits.[14]

Early national New York attracted many ambitious traders, and in keeping with the city's focus on profits over doctrines, enterprising Catholics found an open field. Two of the era's successful immigrants were Don Thomas Stoughton and Dominick Lynch, members of Catholic merchant clans with roots in Ireland and brothers and sons across the world. Stoughton arrived in New York in 1783 and Lynch, bearing cash, in 1785; soon Seton was selling goods from a wharf the Catholic merchants owned.[15] William Magee and his brother James listened and watched as merchants created commercial routes that disregarded not only sectarian difference but also the old rules of empire. New Yorkers dreamed of opening trade with Russia and Madras, and some of an even more spectacular possibility, China. Others began to trade with Italy, often through the port of Livorno on the northern Mediterranean. As he grew to manhood, William Magee Seton toiled faithfully within a web of optimism, profit seeking, and friendship that merchants such as his father energetically spun.

Richard Bayley was reclaiming his future too, his contrarianism as unchanged as William Seton's amiability. Three years after the war ended, Bayley named a newborn son Guy Carlton, honoring the former commander in chief of British forces in North America. Bayley was unfazed by the challenges this moniker would pose a boy in the newly independent nation, and he pursued his interest in scientific medicine with the same single-mindedness. Bored at the thought of resuming a genteel medical practice, he set up shop in buildings known as New York Hospital. The name was optimistic: the hospital's facilities had served as a barracks during the war and afterward stood neglected and unused at the northwest fringes of the city.[16] Bayley confidently announced that he would offer lectures and "chirurgical demonstrations" in them, using profits from the events to found an "anatomical museum."[17] Dissection, let alone the public display of bodies and body parts, provoked horrified rumors and even riots, and Bayley knew that he'd already faced whispers about "cruel experiments" during the war. But the advancement of knowledge required the collection of facts, so he carried on with his plans.

PIOUS INSTRUCTION

As William Seton and Richard Bayley rebuilt their careers, the scarred Loyalist city around them was transforming itself into a bustling American metropolis. It might have seemed inevitable that the Anglican Church, the religion of the Bayley and Seton families, would disappear along with the wartime barricades. The faith's long chains of authority led across the Atlantic to a now-repudiated king, and Anglican ministers such as Elizabeth's grandfather had preached Loyalism from their pulpits. Trinity Church had burned during the great conflagration of 1776, and after the war its charred walls jutted up from lower Manhattan like an old-world ruin. Yet Anglicanism was not doomed. George Washington was a member of the communion, and so were many other Patriots; rather than disavow the faith, such men wanted to refashion it for the new nation. New Rochelle's John Jay helped engineer the removal of Trinity's discredited Loyalist rector and write oaths that did not require American clerics' loyalty to Parliament or king.[18] Not everyone was pleased: close to four hundred members of Trinity Church, William Seton and Richard Bayley among them, petitioned the New York Assembly for the right to create a separate parish, arguing that the changes proposed to their faith converted religion into yet another spoil of Whig victory.[19] It was a futile gesture, and the legislature denied it. Soon, what had been the Anglican Church in the colonies was reborn as the Protestant Episcopal Church in the United States of America. Seven years after a revolution some thought would destroy the faith, the spire of a rebuilt Trinity Church stood as the highest point in Manhattan.

Elizabeth almost certainly attended Episcopalian services in both Manhattan and New Rochelle, but she offers no such reminiscences in "Dear Remembrances." Her silence on the subject accords with her purpose in writing: to draw readers to the Catholic Church. Nonetheless, it is plausible that she truly was unmoved by the Episcopalianism she knew in those postwar years. Trinity's ministers were not celebrated for their preaching, and her beloved father displayed little interest in organized religion. If her aunt and uncle in New Rochelle were conventionally devout, that may simply have been one more element of a household in which she did not quite feel herself at home. Whatever the reasons, Elizabeth's interest in pious lessons did not draw her childhood self toward the church in which she was raised.

Catholicism is also absent from the early pages of "Dear Remembrances," but there no speculation is required. Elizabeth would not set foot in a Catholic Church until many years later, and then not in New York but in Italy. Yet like Episcopalianism, Catholicism was making a place for itself in the new American nation. The challenges were many. New York's state constitution, adopted during the war, required officeholders to forswear "all foreign ecclesiastical authority" and required immigrant Catholics to renounce allegiance to the pope before attaining citizenship. Throughout the nation, suspicion of Catholics remained: one writer argued against adoption of the Constitution because it would allow "a Papist, a Mohamatan, a Deist, yea an Atheist" to ascend to the "helm of Government," and another demanded religious tests for office, in part to prevent "Papists," who "acknowledge a foreign head," from serving.[20] Yet Catholics had fought honorably in the Revolution, and a French Catholic king had come to the Patriots' aid against an English Protestant one. George Washington attended a Catholic Mass as well as Quaker, Presbyterian, and Anglican services when in Philadelphia during the First Continental Congress, and after his inauguration, replied to the well wishes of American Catholics with a letter thanking them for "the patriotic part which you took in the accomplishment of [the Revolution]." "I hope ever to see America among the foremost nations in examples of justice and liberality," the new president wrote.[21] Principles aside, many in New York saw more profits and votes in cooperation than in exclusion. Yet not everyone agreed. In 1784, when the New York legislature gave Protestant denominations such as Presbyterians, Baptists, and Methodists standing equal to that of the Episcopalian communion, John Jay argued against removing civil disabilities on the Roman Catholic Church. Religious liberty, he insisted, required Catholicism's suppression. This time the old argument failed. As long as parishes elected trustees to control property and manage business transactions—as Protestant congregations did—New York's Catholics were allowed to legally incorporate their churches.[22]

From Baltimore, the nation's most prominent Catholic cleric observed New York's expansion of religious liberty with pleasure. John Carroll was a scion of a prominent clan from Maryland, home to the country's oldest and largest Catholic settlements; his kinsman Charles Carroll of Carrolton had signed the Declaration of Independence and accrued massive wealth as a plantation owner, and other relatives enjoyed political, social, and economic success as well. As a young boy Carroll had been sent to Europe for the Catholic education Maryland did not allow. There he grew to manhood and entered the Society of Jesus; he taught at the Jesuit colleges of St. Omer and Liège, served as chaplain to an aristocratic British family, and was ordained a priest. Carroll returned to the colonies only because his life took a shocking turn: in 1773, when Carroll was thirty-eight years old, Pope Clement XIV suppressed the society in an effort to appease Bourbon monarchs who believed Jesuits undermined their sovereignty. Carroll, who deeply resented the suppression but remained loyal to the Church, supported American independence because he hoped a new nation might foster both political justice and a dignified Catholicism beholden to no monarch. In the years immediately following the Revolution, he and his allies—many of them also members of the suppressed Jesuit order—worked to convince Rome to create an American See and appoint a bishop who understood the country's distinctive circumstances and possibilities: John Carroll himself.[23]

Carroll heartily approved as New York's elite Catholics took advantage of their new civil liberties. Truth be told, those confident Manhattanites needed no one's approval but their own. Determined to end the days in which Catholics held Mass in secret—or, as happened after the Revolution, in a building in the city's pleasure gardens—they legally incorporated themselves and secured a lease from Trinity Church for land on which to build a church. The Catholic merchants Stoughton and Lynch proudly hired the architect of New York's much-admired Federal Hall to design St. Peter's Church and began raising funds. Not all went smoothly: the same savvy confidence that spurred the building of St. Peter's often led the trustees to buck the moral and clerical authority John Carroll attempted to exert, and St. Peter's priests proved unruly too. But the church where Elizabeth would one day worship was built, and the comity that had led the Episcopalian parish of Trinity Church to lease land for the construction of a Catholic church held steady. St. Peter's celebrated its first Mass on the feast of San Carlos in order to honor the church's greatest donor, King Charles of Spain. No one seems to have minded that a foreign king—from the land of the Inquisition, no less!—had financed an American church, and although the feast of San Carlos fell just before Guy Fawkes Day, when New Yorkers had traditionally burned the pope in effigy, everything proceeded peacefully.[24] The young Elizabeth Seton—still Betsy Bayley—paid it absolutely no attention, but an American Catholic Church was being born.

AT HOME AND ABROAD

In 1786, William Magee Seton was eighteen years old. By nineteen, his father had crossed the ocean, embarked on a life of trading, and married. It seemed high time for his oldest son to venture forth. The death of a young Curson relative in a pointless duel may have heightened Seton's eagerness to see his son leave youthful idleness behind, and there was a second troubling matter: William Magee complained of pain in his chest. The Cursons were plagued by pulmonary complaints, and

William Magee's symptoms worried his family. So when an Italian merchant named Filippo Filicchi proposed that everyone might benefit if William Magee worked for a time in his enterprise in Livorno—a city that boasted, along with its port, a climate that attracted travelers in search of better health—it was decided that young Seton should go.[25]

Filippo Filicchi was just five years older than William Magee, but his ambition and confidence left him more akin to William the elder than to his son. Proficient in Latin, Spanish, French, and English, he had boldly announced himself as "Philip Filicchi, merchant" on his arrival in the United States and shortly thereafter had begun a profitable association with the Seton house.[26] William hoped that in Livorno, his son would not only learn to oversee the family's European interests but also acquire some of Filippo's drive. In late 1786, the two young men sailed for Italy.

A town of over thirty thousand when William Magee Seton first saw it, Livorno had remained a tiny walled village until well into the sixteenth century, when the Tuscan grand dukes designated it a free port in which merchants "of all nations" could trade. Offered civil and religious liberties, Jews, Greeks, Armenians, and English Protestants made their way to the town, and a famine in the seventeenth century heightened the port's importance as a grain depot; like New Yorkers, Livornese believed that one man's loss was almost always another man's profit. At William Magee's arrival, the city's busy docks and multilingual population made it a closer cousin to Manhattan than to Florence.

William Magee worked dutifully in the Filicchis' merchant house; his letters home to his brother James carefully describe the value of the Filicchis' cargoes and explain how to purchase tobacco and naval stores for the ships' return. The elder Seton's advertisements began to bear the name "William Seton & Co." as into New York's harbor sailed ships bearing luxuries William Magee had selected for the city's tastes.[27] Despite these successes, the young man preferred Italy's museums, theaters, and concert halls to its docks and counting houses. "There was opera three times a week," he happily wrote his stepmother, "and I generally went every evening." He decided that Italians "understand cooking much better" than Americans, and although he stoutly declared to his stepmother that Italian women were less lovely than New Yorkers, he offered a different and perhaps more sincere line to James. "Beauty is so predominant in this country," he marveled, "that if one did not shut their eyes (as I do) when they meet an Italian Lady it would be impossible not to fall in love." When William Magee sailed home to New York, family tradition has it that he brought a Stradivarius violin, the first in the United States. He also brought something else. What he called the "weakness at my breast" had not gone away.[28]

During William Magee's time in Italy, Filippo Filicchi almost certainly tried to interest him in Catholicism. The confident young merchant was a devout Catholic who conversed and corresponded with cardinals and believed his faith was the one true Church. Convinced that the United States' lack of an established religion offered an opening for Catholicism to gain adherents, Filicchi had once volunteered to write a Catholic catechism for use in the new nation. (Ever the astute merchant, he suggested downplaying the Church's claim that it offered the only path to salvation, fearing it would alienate choice-loving Americans.)[29] Filippo's proposed catechism went nowhere, however, and so did any efforts he made to convert William Magee. The New Yorker was not offended; he simply had no interest, unless one counts his rueful observation that the beautiful Italian women he saw around him would never marry a "Heretick."[30]

A persistent man, Filicchi found other ways of advancing the Church's interests in the United States. While in Baltimore, he met John Carroll and offered to gather gossip from Rome, to transport Catholic books and documents, and to secure lines of credit for the fledgling American Church. Filicchi's help was welcome, and in these logistical matters, William Magee Seton also proved happy to oblige. By 1789, a close associate of Carroll trusted Seton "to acquaint Mr. Filicchi with the whole state of the affair," meaning the clerics' efforts to convince Rome to lay the groundwork for an American bishop. When the see of Baltimore was created—the first in the United States—it was William Magee Seton who brought word from Europe.[31]

INSIDE THE BAYLEY HOME

Like William Magee, Elizabeth Bayley lived amid a family business. When she and her sister Mary were not in New Rochelle, they inhabited a Manhattan household filled with their father's scientific treatises and discussions of patients and procedures. Shortly after the war ended, Richard Bayley had taken on a student, a young Long Islander named Wright Post, who proved as devoted to ferreting out the cause

of diseases as Bayley was and who helped the physician create his anatomical museum at New York Hospital. The two men considered the
collection an obvious contribution to the city's well-being, but rumors
spread that they and other physicians and medical students obtained
corpses by commissioning grave robbery. In early 1788, a group of black
freedmen petitioned the city's Common Council to prevent "the practice
of a number of young gentlemen in this city who call themselves students
of the physic . . . [and] Under cover of the night, in the most wanton sal-
lies of excess . . . dig up bodies of our deceased friends and relatives."[32]
Most residents of the slave-holding city were unmoved by the freedmen's
petition, but when rumors spread that the bodies of white New Yorkers
were being dug out of private graveyards, matters grew tense. Bayley,
Post, and the other physicians continued to collect and dissect. Confident that his specimens did not come from plundered graves, Elizabeth's
father took no heed of the fact that his work, as one newspaper later put
it, "wrought up the passions of the populace to a ferment."[33]

In April of 1788, thirteen-year-old Elizabeth witnessed the consequences of her father's single-mindedness. The trouble began when a
small group of New Yorkers thought they saw body parts obscenely
hanging out of New York Hospital's windows. Perhaps human specimens had been hung to dry, as one newspaper later suggested, or maybe
perceptions were distorted by rumors of wicked doings in the mysterious buildings on the edge of the city. Whatever New Yorkers saw or
thought they saw on that April morning, it was enough to turn simmering mistrust into outrage. "A mob of four or five hundreds immediately
collected," wrote a man who took part in the melee, "broke open the
hospital and made a search, wherein I was witness to finding several
Anatomies or Skeletons, and many parts of bodies just dissected, with
the flesh remaining on the bones."[34] As word spread of the discoveries
in the hospital, mobs ransacked doctors' homes, determined to find the
corpses that they thought lay broken and befouled within. New York's
mayor bundled physicians into the city's jail, hoping the building's stout
walls would keep out their pursuers. The Bayleys' home is not included
in a nineteenth-century list of those ransacked, but Elizabeth and her
family feared the worst. "A night passed in sweat of terror," she wrote
decades later, "saying all the while the Our Father."[35]

The next day dawned no quieter. Appalled at what he viewed as
an assault on reason and good order—and perhaps aware that Bayley,

his fellow New Rochellite and an acquaintance, was at risk—John Jay grabbed his sword and set off to try to disperse the mob. Jay was quickly felled by a thrown rock; a beloved figure from the Revolutionary War, Baron von Steuben, was also injured when he tried to intervene.[36] At last, someone ordered the militia to fire on the crowd. Three were killed. Surly but vanquished, the mob melted away.

Richard Bayley must have been shaken by the violence of what became known as the Doctors' Riot, but his convictions were not. Expressing his willingness "to submit his conduct to [the] candid and impartial examination" of his "fellow citizens," Bayley took to the newspapers to insist that there had been no body snatching or desecration. Had there been dissections? Yes, he acknowledged, and his fellow New Yorkers should be grateful. "In the pursuit of science," Bayley declared, "[my] views have been ever directed to the interest of mankind."[37] The physician was willing to risk his life to improve New Yorkers' health. He had no intention of abiding by their judgment.

Figure 2.2. *Richard Bayley.*
Print Collection, Miriam
and Ira D. Wallach
Division of Arts, Prints,
and Photographs, The
New York Public Library,
Astor, Lenox, and Tilden
Foundations.

The Doctors' Riot cost Bayley his meticulously collected anatomi-cal specimens, and the hospital's board of governors charged him "22 pounds 12 shillings 10 pence" for the mob's damage to the buildings.[38] Nonetheless, Bayley's determination to share truth as he saw it—as one nineteenth-century memoirist put it, "contrary to public opinion and in the teeth of professional disapprobation"—never faltered. Later that year, he publicly accused a fellow doctor of incompetence, starting a chain of events that led to Wright Post's (now a colleague rather than a student) being challenged to a duel. Post politely declined the summons. As for Bayley, he decided that it was time to pursue his medical inves-tigations elsewhere.[39] Just as he had done when rumors of war swirled through Manhattan's streets, Bayley sailed for England.

Once more, Elizabeth and Mary's father had left them behind. Again, the girls were sent to New Rochelle. Mary was by then twenty years old, and a suitor presented himself: Wright Post. Whether or not it was a passionate match, it was a plausible one, and Mary was pleased to think she might soon leave behind the unease of her childhood for a household of her own. At fourteen, Elizabeth had no such hope. In New Rochelle, she attended school and waited for letters from her father. They did not arrive nearly often enough, and she wondered just how much she mattered to the man who, despite his elusiveness, stood at the center of her life. She began to find solace in nature and in fleeting, vivid intimations of God's love. One day she walked through a meadow graced by a chestnut tree, saplings clustered around. "Here then was a sweet bed," she recalled years later, "the air still a clear blue vault above, the numberless sounds of Spring melody and joy—the sweet clo-vers and wild flowers I had got by the way." When she began her walk, Elizabeth felt miserable and alone, but now she was "filled with even enthusiastic love to God and admiration of his works." The pain of her father's absence faded. "I thought at that time my Father did not care for me," she later recalled. "Well God was my Father—my All."[40]

"At uncle B.'s, New Rochelle," she wrote of another moment in which she felt overcome by God's love. "The Bible so enjoyed, and Thomson and Milton. Hymns said on the rocks, surrounded with ice, in transports of first pure enthusiasm." God came to her in nature and in books. "Gazings at the stars—Orion," she recalled in another passage. "Walks among cedars singing hymns. Pleasure in every thing, coarse, rough, smooth, or easy, always gay. . . . Delight of sitting in the fields with Thompson, surrounded by lambs and sheep, or drinking the sap of the birch, or gathering colored stones on the shore."[41]

Elizabeth painted these moments as part of a providential journey toward Catholicism. Yet even her carefully curated account makes clear the Protestant influences of her culture. Her beloved Milton and Thomson were Protestant poets celebrated throughout the English-speaking world, the former for his searing explorations of truth, death, sin, and divinity, the latter for his gentle celebration of God's work in everything from meadows to microscopes. Elizabeth's sense of God in nature, for its part, resonates with both the past and the future of Protestantism. It harks back to Jonathan Edwards, the great Protestant theologian who a few decades before her birth celebrated earth as the canvas of God's revelation. "I am not ashamed to own that I believe that the whole universe, heaven and earth, air and seas, and the divine constitution and history of the holy Scriptures," Edwards wrote, "be full of images of divine things."[42] It also brings to mind the lyrical ebullience of a Protestant poet just becoming known in the late eighteenth century: William Wordsworth, who remained faithful to his Anglican upbringing while celebrating an individual connection to divinity felt most sharply in the open air. "But in the mountains did he *feel* his faith, / All things, responsive to the writing, there / Breathed immortality, revolving life," read lines from Wordsworth's "Excursion." "There littleness was not; the least of things / Seemed infinite."[43]

As she walked the woods of New Rochelle, Elizabeth knew nothing of Wordsworth, whose first major work was published in 1798. She may have read the poet by the time she wrote "Dear Remembrances," but their connection, if any, is that of kindred spirits rather than influence. The Elizabeth who felt God's presence as she gathered colored stones by the shore did know of others who celebrated ecstatic individual relationships with God, however: evangelical Protestant preachers. Their influence on her, though unproven, seems likely. The series of revivals known as the Second Great Awakening was just beginning in the late 1780s and early 1790s. Methodists and Baptist preachers held services outdoors, urging listeners toward an immediate, emotional commitment to God and promising rebirth into a life of joyful faith. A Methodist preacher named Thomas Ware traveled through New Rochelle in 1786, and a second Methodist minister, a convert from Catholicism named Peter Moriarty, preached in the area in 1788 and 1789. Catherine Livingston, a daughter of New York's prominent Livingston family, shocked her parents by converting from Presbyterianism to Methodism after being moved by Methodist preachers near the family's summer home in Rhinebeck.[44] Did Elizabeth also hear such a preacher? Revivals often had at their centers young people weeping and trembling at the enormity of God's power and mercy, and her use of the words "enthusiasm" and "enthusiastic" to describe her experiences offers indirect but suggestive evidence that she was touched by evangelicalism: when evangelical Protestants decried traditional denominations as dryly formalistic, their defenders retorted that evangelicals were "enthusiasts" who wrongly imagined that they communed directly with God.[45] When Elizabeth chose to use the words "enthusiasm" and "enthusiastic" to describe her youthful self, she knew the signal she was sending.

In a reminiscence she penned in 1803, Elizabeth placed a New Rochelle spiritual experience more directly within the template of evangelical conversion. "I prayed—sung hymns—cryed—laughed in talking to myself of how far He could place me above all Sorrow," she recalled of a girlhood afternoon. "Then," she continued, "[I] layed still to enjoy the Heavenly Peace that came over my soul."[46] Intuitions of divinity are part of many, if not most, faith traditions; when Elizabeth became "Mother Seton," such fervent worship would be understood within a Catholic rubric of mysticism, a partaking of the "contemplation, ecstasy, rapture, liquefaction, transformation, union, exaltation . . . jubilation of the spirit" described by, among others, the medieval theologian Jean Gerson.[47] But in 1789, as she collapsed praying in the woods outside New Rochelle, Elizabeth would have seemed to anyone who came across her like an evangelical Protestant in the throes of rebirth. Elsewhere in the "Remembrances," she offered a direct acknowledgment that evangelical Protestantism had moved her. Recalling that she'd overheard Methodist girls singing, she wrote that "their continual hymn, 'And am I only born to die,' made a deep impression." The hymn, more Milton than Thomson, portrays life as a war against sin, a war whose only victory lay in death.

And am I only born to die?
And must I suddenly comply
With nature's stern decree?
What after death for me remains?
Celestial joy or hellish pains
For all eternity?[48]

"What after death for me remains" became a central question of Elizabeth's life, one she pursued as relentlessly and unconventionally as her father pursued medical knowledge. She would ultimately seek its answer within the doctrines, liturgies, and hierarchies of the Catholic Church, but she first heard it posed in the cadence of a Methodist hymn.

"TO PLEASE MY FATHER"

In 1789, Manhattan was no longer the burned-out shell into which Patriot troops had marched. Beginning to overtake Philadelphia as the nation's largest city, it was now the federal capital; at George Washington's inaugural ball, members of former Tory families danced with old Whigs, while the city's many faiths mingled peacefully.[49] New York's port filled up with the era's deeper-keeled ships, and settlers pushed into the state's hinterlands, carving out farms from which to send agricultural products toward Manhattan's docks. Some of those same merchants, organized into syndicates, bought up tracts of Iroquois land, the original inhabitants leaving for Canada in the tragic aftermath of wartime allegiance with Great Britain. William Seton was among those who acquired property upstate, near the Black River that ran west out of the Adirondack Mountains and into Lake Ontario.[50]

When in 1790 Richard Bayley sailed home from England to this bustling city, Elizabeth and her sister Mary returned to Manhattan as well. Bayley turned his attention to his medical practice and investigations, Mary was courted by Wright Post, and Elizabeth helped tend her half siblings: twelve-year-old Emma, ten-year-old Richard Jr., eight-year-old Andrew Barclay, five-year-old Guy Carlton, and three-year-old William Augustus. In June of 1790, Charlotte gave birth to another daughter, Helen.

Amid this crowded household, Elizabeth began to command her father's attention. It was not her budding interest in religion that won him, nor the kind care she gave her half siblings. It was her mind. Richard Bayley had eight children, including four sons; it was Elizabeth who most passionately shared his love of learning. Bayley shared with her a practice begun in his youth, that of copying passages from works of history, literature, and science into "commonplace books." In the sixteenth century, the humanist scholar Erasmus recommended that readers collect extracts under headings such as piety, fidelity, and beneficence, and in the centuries following, individuals on both sides of the Atlantic turned ledgers and journals into, in the words of one practitioner, "a storehouse from which to draw an abundant supply of excellent material . . . for any matter on which they are required to speak or write." George Washington kept commonplace books filled with descriptions of virtuous behavior, and in Revolutionary Philadelphia, a Quaker woman named Milcah Moore copied poetry and prose exploring subjects from faith to war. When peace came and many Americans hoped educated wives and mothers would help create a virtuous, stable republic, girls at newly founded "female academies" took up the practice of commonplace books.[51] In Manhattan, Bayley shared with his daughter a book of extracts he'd begun during his New Rochelle youth, and as Elizabeth added to the book and commenced two others, the shared work of reading and writing fostered a mutually respectful companionship.

"This book was began when I was fifteen and written with great delight to please my father," Elizabeth later wrote in one of the large note-books that, marbleized covers faded but intact, reside in the Daughters of Charity's Emmitsburg archive. She drew passages from a wide variety of texts, and although her writing slurred as her hand tired, she always began a new copying session neatly and, somehow, she never doodled. In one ledger, Elizabeth transcribed selections from Charles Rollin's *Ancient History*, a work that the New York Society Library had recently pur-chased and that prominent New York men such as John Jay borrowed in the same months that Elizabeth read it.[52] Elizabeth neatly copied out Rol-lin's description of "the discoveries hateful and horrid" made by Oedipus as well as the claim that in Egypt, the "marriage of Brothers and Sisters was not only authorized by their laws, but was even in some measure a part of their religion." She also copied the story of Artemesia, who had her dead husband ground into a powder that she mixed with liquid and drank every day.[53] In Rollin's *Ancient History* and in the Bayley house-hold, the range of human possibility was not hidden.

While she read and extracted, Elizabeth came across claims about women's capacity to think and do. In one of the commonplace books appears Thales's expression of gratitude "that he was born a reasonable creature & not a beast, a Man, & not a woman, a Greek, & not a barbar-ian." Neither she nor her father offered a comment on that set of oppo-sites, but another extract bears an intriguing annotation. Copying the tale of Semiramis, Elizabeth included Rollin's remark that "the glorious

reign of this queen, might partly induce Plato to maintain in his common-
wealth, that woman, as well as men, should be admitted in the management of public affairs . . . and trained up in the same exercises as men, as
well for the forming of the body as the mind." At the end of the passage,
Elizabeth wrote a single word: "Wollstonecraft." In 1792, Mary Wollstonecraft published her *Vindication of the Rights of Women*, arguing
that women possessed the same natural rights as men and should receive
commensurate educations. By the end of the century, Wollstonecraft was
vilified as corrosively radical, her views blamed for her own difficult life
(after she died of childbed fever in 1797, her husband, William Godwin,
published a memoir recounting Wollstonecraft's unconventional sexual
history and a suicide attempt) and for the social and political transformations her critics feared might overtake Britain and the United States.
But Wollstonecraft's *Vindication* was read with interest and admiration
when first published, its argument that women's rights were human rights
avidly discussed among educated New Yorkers.[54] Elizabeth must have
read or at least known of the book, and she quietly noted the connection
between its arguments for women's capabilities and Rollin's musings.
What more she thought, in these early years, about Wollstonecraft or the
possibility of women's leadership is impossible to know.

The commonplace books also offer the first contemporaneous evidence of Elizabeth's views of organized religion, and there it is easier to
gain a sense of her thinking. She found no form of organized religion
superior to others. On the contrary, extracts portray Christianity as
simply one way of worshipping God and describe organized religion
as sets of rules, rituals, and habits that were just as subject to circumstance and taste as cuisine or fashion. "Our thoughts, our morals, our
most fixed belief" begins the first passage in the notebook that originally belonged to Richard Bayley:

> Are consequences of our place of birth:
> Born beyond Ganges; I had been a pagan
> In France a Christian, I am here a Saracen
> tis but instruction.[55]

Christian "instruction" was not necessarily preferable to any other kind.
"Should a person who has resided a few years in a Chinese family remove
at once to some firesides in England," reads another extract, "I fear he
would seem to have exchanged a civilized society for a confusion of

savages. And this is laid to the charge of Christianity by the pagans who judge of the principles by the practice of its professors."[56] It was likely Richard Bayley who chose to copy these lines, but Elizabeth grew up within the intellectual framework they limned. It is clear from her own later correspondence that as a young woman, she thought of institutional Christianity less as a divinely inspired way of worshipping God than as an ethical system, one that was perhaps imperfectly conceived and that was without question imperfectly carried out. The descriptions of institutional religion to be found in her commonplace books stand apart from the moments when, roaming the woods outside New Rochelle, Elizabeth felt the presence of God. Nothing and no one had yet bridged these two understandings of religion.

As Elizabeth and her father grew closer through sharing the commonplace books, Charlotte Bayley grew more estranged. "Sixteen years old," Elizabeth wrote tersely of this period of her father and stepmother's marriage, "Family disputes." In the third of her commonplace books, one she filled with bits of poetry and fiction chosen according to her own taste and interests, Elizabeth copied out one poem describing a happy marriage and another describing a failed one. In all of the books, she underlined the words "concord" and "union," feeling their importance because she was growing up in their absence. Neither Elizabeth nor her older sister Mary ever described the true nature of their father and stepmother's unhappiness, but both later alluded to the household's disorder. There were, Mary recalled, "very very painful events" and "circumstances" that "drove" the sisters "into situations that we must ever regret being attached to the life of any young person."[57] Family members began to refuse to speak to the girls, siding with Charlotte against Richard.[58] Another hint of the couple's deepening estrangement comes from Charlotte's pattern of childbearing. In the first six years of Richard and Charlotte Bayley's marriage, Charlotte gave birth to three children. Four years passed between the arrival of the third, Guy Carlton, and the fourth, Helen. After Helen's birth in 1790, when Charlotte was thirty-two years old, six years passed without a baby.

Despite witnessing the miseries of this fragile union, Mary did not imagine adult life outside marriage; no vision of an independent existence could be summoned. The way to escape life as an unhappy stepdaughter was to become a wife. When Wright Post proposed, Mary accepted. Yet she did not escape the Bayley disorder. Not long after the wedding, Post set sail for London to continue his medical education. A wife without a household, Mary continued to spend her time in Charlotte and Richard's uneasy home.

FEVERS

William and Anna Maria Seton's household was free of the strife that plagued the Bayleys. Content in his marriage and busy at the bank, Seton wanted his two older sons to take over the family's merchant house; they willingly obliged. By late summer of 1791, William Magee and James traded through Livorno and other ports in the Atlantic world; in September, whether out of coincidence or sentiment, they advertised charter of a ship called *The Two Brothers*.[59] Seton's other children by his first wife were also making their way in the world: fifteen-year old Anna Maria married a congressman from Delaware and moved to his home state, and William's third and fourth sons, Jack and Henry, were learning the merchant life from their father and grandfather. As his older offspring established themselves, William continued to sire more children. In 1791, Anna Maria gave birth to Cecilia, who became baby sister to twelve-year-old Eliza; eleven-year-old Rebecca; Mary, whose birthdate is unknown; five-year-old Charlotte; four-year-old Harriet; two-year-old Samuel, and one-year-old Edward Augustus.

For all its fecundity—in part because of it—a shadow lay over the Seton home. Anna Maria's constant rounds of pregnancy, labor, and nursing would have strained even the most robust woman, and Anna Maria Seton was not robust. William's sister had sent sharp advice from England: "If she be a delicate frame you ought to take the more care of her, and not wear out her Constitution by having so many Children."[60] William did not obey, and now everyone worried that it was too late. They knew Anna Maria did not simply have a "delicate frame." She suffered from the complaint that had probably killed her sister (William's first wife Rebecca) and that stalked other Cursons too: tuberculosis. In letters otherwise filled with commodity prices and lines of credit, Richard Curson inquired anxiously after his daughter's health. "I was impatient to hear of Mrs. S's return," he wrote, "and more so as you mention the old complaint not being eradicated, and still keeps hanging about her. I tremble for a relapse in her weak state."[61]

Tuberculosis truly is an "old complaint": skeletons from ancient Egypt and Greece bear its marks, and so do the dead from pre-Columbian America. A whimsical predator, the disease spared some exposed to it, killed a few quickly, and toyed cruelly with others. Its array of manifestations—from fluid-filled lungs and fevers to grotesquely swollen glands, skin abscesses, and collapsed spines—left tuberculosis with a variety of names, including phthisis and scrofula. In England and America, it was known most often as consumption; in their correspondence, the Cursons and Setons tried to avoid calling it anything at all.

Consumption's cornucopia of devastation emerged from one tiny source, the *Myobacterium tuberculosis* bacillus. Most people who inhale the organism possess immune systems that quickly encapsulate it and render it harmless. Some, however, probably because of mutations in a gene, become involuntarily welcoming hosts, and in their unlucky bodies the organism reproduces relentlessly.[62] Observing that the disease seemed to run in families and lacking a theory of contagion, eighteenth-century English and American physicians thought consumption emerged from some unfortunate constitutional delicacy in the sufferer, perhaps exacerbated by climate, sedentary habits, or childbearing. No one objected when Anna Maria continued to tend her children and husband as her health failed. When she coughed—even when she talked—invisible, disease-bearing bacilli escaped from her mouth into the air, to be breathed in by relatives who shared her genetic predisposition to the disease.

The unpredictable course of tuberculosis both tormented and tantalized. The flushed cheeks brought on by tubercular fevers could seem deceptively like the glow of health, and sometimes the progression of the disease really did slow. When that happened, sufferers credited whatever it was they had last done—a sea voyage, horseback rides, the decision to eat less meat or more—for their deliverance. Usually, however, brief improvement gave way to decline. When Anna Maria Seton went on a "water jaunt" in 1791 (a version of the mineral baths prescribed to consumptives for millennia), William Seton told his father-in-law that the trip had benefited her. "Let us hope all will go well," came Curson's cautious response.[63]

As he feared for his wife, William faced a second worry: New York's economy was suffering from a fever of its own. All around Hanover Square, where Seton lived and traded, risky speculation competed with more sober commercial endeavors. One man stood at the overheated center: William Duer. Seton had known Duer for years; it was he who had brokered the wartime meeting between the Curson and Seton families. Now, however, as cashier of the Bank of New York, Seton found himself anxiously trying to manage a crisis of Duer's making.

Duer had briefly served as an assistant secretary of the treasury and counted Alexander Hamilton among his friends. He possessed an extraordinary combination of access, energy, and avarice, and in an era in which public interest and private enterprise commonly mingled, Duer proved singularly able to suck the marrow of profit from the newly knitting bones of the national government. Throughout 1791, he and a group of collaborators informally known as the Six Percent Club gobbled up stocks held in Boston, Philadelphia, and New York, hoping that eventually all purchasers of securities and bank paper would have to pay whatever price the club asked. The scheme required Duer to borrow large sums, and New Yorkers of every social level, from wealthy merchants to laborers and even, one unhappy observer claimed, "the noted bawd, Mrs. McCarty" proved willing to lend Duer money in the hope of quick return.[64] Yet the plan to control the securities market proved unachievable, and when Duer and the Six Percenters were unable to pay back their loans, New York's overheated economy threatened to collapse. Confronted with the possibility that Duer's schemes might destroy the Bank of New York and the city's commerce as a whole, the amiable William Seton at last lost his temper. "These madmen," he wrote heatedly to Hamilton, "have aimed too deep a strike at our existence to be forgiven or forgot."[65] Matters grew worse as creditors unsuccessfully pressed Duer for payment. In the spring of 1792, the frightened speculator took refuge in the only place in New York that would have him: debtors' prison.

While stock prices plunged and New Yorkers desperately called in loans, Seton orchestrated informal public demonstrations that credit was still to be found. His connections and social wisdom augmented Hamilton's technical brilliance, and in May, securities prices began to stabilize. In the end, what became known as the Panic of 1792 passed without grave damage to the republic's fledgling economy. But it marked the Seton family. Realizing that his role as cashier of the bank brought more responsibility than profit, William pondered setting it aside and devoting himself anew to the merchant house. William Magee had never thrilled to the merchant life; in him, the Panic inspired a permanent dread of debtors' prison. James simply felt impatient. Unlike his older brother, he was eager to establish his own enterprise and form his own household, and while the Panic still threatened, he combined his two ambitions. Rumors had traveled through New York society that William Magee Seton would propose to Mary Gillou Hoffman, the sister of an enterprising auction house owner. When William Magee demurred, James offered her his hand. In early April, he and Mary Hoffman wed. Not long afterward, the Seton brothers dissolved their partnership, and James began business with his new brother-in-law.[66]

Amid worries over the Panic and preparations for James and Mary's wedding, thirty-six-year-old Anna Maria Seton descended into the final ravages of consumption. There are as many ways to die from tuberculosis as there are to suffer from it; lungs fill with fluid, skin and bones break down, and fevers grow unrelenting. Eventually, amid the cascade of insults, the body gives out. In August of 1792, Anna Maria Seton's did.[67] Her children and stepchildren sincerely mourned her. William allowed himself only the briefest absence from the bank—and apologized to Alexander Hamilton even for that—before returning to his labors. Although he was in his midforties and had a household full of children, he never remarried.

While the Panic claimed the attention of New Yorkers high and low, Richard Bayley had no time for commercial speculation and no interest in those who did. He continued to devote himself to medical investigations and practice, and despite the controversies of earlier years, his reputation was on the rise. In 1792, he was appointed professor of anatomy at Columbia College (its name the patriotic replacement for "King's College"), and his partner and new son-in-law Wright Post was appointed professor of surgery.[68] Post, however, continued to spend long periods of time in London pursuing his studies. This often left Mary in the Bayley household, and there was also a new arrival: Wright Post's dyspeptic younger brother Jotham, who had come to Manhattan to study medicine. The diary in which Jotham recorded his hopes (occasionally) and his frustrations and anxieties (often) offers a glimpse of the complicated household in which Elizabeth was growing to young womanhood.

Jotham's diary reveals that Richard Bayley treated everything from venereal disease to broken limbs, discussing the day's cases in his crowded home.[69] The teenaged Elizabeth learned of the innumerable forms human suffering took and witnessed her father's conviction that much of that suffering could be blamed on New Yorkers' own bad choices. Bayley also believed it fell to man to alleviate suffering through fearless investigation of its causes and relentless effort to root them out. Neither his worldview nor his daily schedule left much room for religious observance. "Did not go to church all day," Jotham wrote one late September Sunday. "The neglect however is not unpardonable, not being absolutely my own master, but in some measure under the direction of Mr. Bayley, and it is his wish that I should be in his way as much as possible and if I am not I lose many good and valuable opportunities for improvement."[70] As Bayley saw it, devotion to science and medicine improved the world; attendance at Trinity Church, did not.

When not working, Jotham fished in the Hudson River with the Bayley boys and whiled away evenings with Elizabeth, Mary, and their friends. Across the six months of his diary, he mentions Elizabeth's stepmother only once, as if Charlotte figured but little in the household's life. One diary entry hints at disorder in the Bayley home. After an encounter with Elizabeth's sister, Jotham angrily wrote that "[Mary] behaved villainously." "More like a drunkard than like a person in her senses. The reason is best known to myself. It is a shame to insert it here."[71]

Mary Bayley Post was far from the only woman to attract Jotham's criticism; he disapproved of loquacious girls and of the "most horrid custom" of women strolling on the Battery "without some man to accompany them."[72] Jotham's excoriation of Mary, however, was vehement even for him, and years later, Mary alluded to misdeeds she and her stepmother Charlotte shared. "Happy those who have an affectionate Mother to advise and maintain their own respectability by observing her precepts," she wrote, contrasting such happy respectability with her own youth.[73] What was it that so appalled Jotham and that Mary herself lamented? Jotham's phrase "like a drunkard" suggests it was not drink itself in which Mary indulged, but it could have been another substance whose effects he recognized: laudanum.

Laudanum was an opiate that Richard Bayley, like many doctors of his era, kept at hand, mixing small amounts into remedies for ailments ranging from diarrhea to the pain of late-stage tuberculosis. At times, Bayley even dosed himself with laudanum to relieve discomfort.[74] Laudanum produces euphoria when consumed in sufficient quantity, and it is highly addictive. Did laudanum cause the "scenes" to which Mary alluded, leaving her acting "out of her senses" and contributing to Charlotte's estrangement from the household? The opiate disrupts the menstrual cycles of women who frequently consume it. Charlotte Bayley's childbearing slowed dramatically in these years. Mary, for her part, wed Wright Post in 1790 but bore no children until 1798, after which she bore four children in ten years, a set of facts explained neither by Post's occasional sojourns in England for medical study nor by an underlying infertility in either partner.

Whatever its causes, the derangement in the Bayley household affected not only Mary but the younger children as well. Several years later, when Richard and Charlotte's sons were struggling through adolescence, Elizabeth remarked that "two of my brothers" "have already shewn the most unquestionable marks of unsteady dispositions." "We cannot Wonder," she added sadly.[75]

Although Elizabeth was slow to acknowledge it, another factor may have unsettled the Bayley home in these years: Richard Bayley's burgeoning friendship with a woman not his wife. Mary Fitch was in her forties during Elizabeth's late adolescence; married to a planter in Jamaica, Fitch had left her husband and moved to New York City, where she lived by herself and became Bayley's close friend. Elizabeth called her "Mama Fitch" and once remarked that the woman "fought many battles for me." Yet she came to mistrust the intense friendship between her father and Fitch. In addition to the effects of disparate temperaments, Richard's single-minded devotion to his career, and Charlotte's possible laudanum use, the relationship between Richard Bayley and Mary Fitch may have eroded a fragile marriage.

Whatever choices those around her made, Elizabeth maintained an unimpeachable respectability. Even Jotham Post liked her: his mentions of pleasant conversations with Elizabeth are among the few warm notes in his diary. Yet beneath her calm surface, turbulence roiled. In "Dear Remembrances," she summed up these years in five words: "folly-sorrows-romance-miserable friendships." The "romance" was nothing more than a brief courtship and the "miserable friendships" brought no scandal. It was her painfully intense emotions that Elizabeth believed had brought her to the edge of danger.

Once again, the commonplace books offer a glimpse at her thinking. In one, Elizabeth wrote out lines from the poet Mark Akenside, whose *Pleasures of the Imagination* celebrated an exquisite sensibility. But she mistrusted her passionate nature even as she treasured it, and she also extracted passages celebrating calm detachment. "Serene and master of yourself," she copied out, "prepare for what may come; and leave the rest to heaven." Richard Bayley prided himself on his imperviousness to both physical discomfort and others' opinions, and Elizabeth admired him for it, fortifying herself with his example and snatches of classical stoicism. After copying the Greek philosopher Epictetus's declaration that "I took no other notice of one who insulted & endeavored to irritate me than coolly to say to him: I withdraw," she added simply: "True philosophy."[76]

Yet "true philosophy" often failed Elizabeth, and years later she recalled her frustration. "Thousand reflections after being at publick places," she wrote in her "Remembrances," "why I could not say my prayers and have good thoughts as if I had been at home wishing to Philosophise and give every thing its place—not able though to do both." Although she still had little interest in institutional religion, individuals' intense faith held out the promise of peace. She envied the Methodist girls whose hymns she overhead and looked wistfully at the "Quakers in their pretty plain hats," so quiet amid Manhattan's clamor. Sometimes she imagined escaping the city entirely. "Fine plans of a little country home," she recalled, "to gather all the little children round and teach them their prayers and keep them clean and teach them to be good."[77]

In one passages of the "Remembrances," Elizabeth claimed that as a girl she dreamed of the religious life she would one day build: "Passionate wishes that there were such places in America as I read of in novels where people could be shut up from the world, and pray, and be good always—Many thoughts of running away to such a place over the seas, in disguise, working for a living."[78] Novels circulating in Elizabeth's youth were more likely to portray convents as places of oppression and degradation than of refuge; it seems likely that she superimposed a longing for a life "shut up from the world" on a girlhood where such a thing was still unimaginable. It is easy to believe, however, that the young Elizabeth dreamed of escape and seclusion and that she shared her dream with no one.

The commonplace books and "Dear Remembrances" together offer a glimpse at one particularly dark moment during these unsettled years. Elizabeth transcribed lines from Edward Young's famous *Night Thoughts*: "No bliss has life to boast," she wrote, "'till death can give /

Far greater, Life's a debtor to the grave. . . . / When shall I die?—when shall I live forever." The page bears small discolorations that Elizabeth later labeled "Tears the night of the little bottle." She told the story in the "Remembrances": one night she wept over Young's lines and contemplated taking her life. "The little bottle" was filled with laudanum, the opiate Richard Bayley kept with his medical supplies, the opiate that could kill as well as addict. New York's newspapers related the sad tales of young people who killed themselves with laudanum, and that night, at least for a moment, Elizabeth wanted to join them.[79]

She never dismissed the event as youthful melodrama. Years later, Elizabeth still shuddered at the "wretched reasoning" that had led her to eye the laudanum, deeming her thoughts a "Horrid subversion of every good promise of God in the boldest presumption." She unhappily recalled her logic: "God had created me," and because she "was very miserable," God "was too good to condemn so poor a creature made of dust" for taking her life. She also recalled her feeling of deliverance. When Elizabeth set the laudanum aside, she was flooded with "praise and thanks of excessive joy not to have done the 'horrid deed'—thoughts and promise of eternal gratitude." Her brief contemplation of suicide had brought Elizabeth first to a profound sense of her own sinfulness and then to a rebirth in God's mercy. Amid the Catholic melody of "Ðear Remembrances," notes of evangelical Protestantism once again faintly sound.

TOWARD A NEW LIFE

Elizabeth hid the night of the little bottle and the turbulence that birthed it behind a bright mien. In 1793 she was nineteen. Well-read, a lively conversationalist, and fond of dancing, she possessed a competence and outward calm that promised domestic tranquillity. She was also a beauty; years later, her sister Mary compared her own adolescent daughter to Elizabeth in her youth: "her full figure, expression & peculiarly fine Eyes were once yours entirely," she wrote admiringly.[80]

William Magee Seton turned twenty-five in 1793. He had become a competent and hard-working merchant, though not an inspired one. He sometimes suffered from coughs and "pain in the breast," but he was tall and possessed a handsome, gentle countenance.[81] Desultory in his religious observances, he loved music and theater, even if Manhattan's offerings could not compare to those he'd enjoyed in Italy.

FIGURE 2.3. William Magee Seton wedding portrait, attributed to
Francis Rabineau. Courtesy of the Sisters of Charity of New York Archives,
Bronx, New York.

Although Elizabeth and William Magee had spent much of their
lives within a half mile of each other, their paths had never crossed.
Manhattanites sorted themselves by professions and clans; the Setons
lived among merchants, the Bayleys among physicians. At last, however,
their intricate social and familial webs brought the two young people
together. The introduction could have happened in any number of quiet
ways. Mary Fitch was just one of the people with ties to both the Bayleys
(through affection) and the Setons (through business). Whoever did the
deed, in 1793, it was done, and a courtship began.

William Magee called Elizabeth not Betsy but Eliza. She welcomed
the name and the suitor, offering herself with a cheerfully flirtatious
confidence. "It is my intention to pass an hour with Mrs. Wilks in the
Evening where you may have the honor of seeing me if you please," reads
one merry note. "Mrs. Sadler is not going to the Concert and wishes

very much to see us there this Evening—do not be too late" comes a command from another day. The two shared a pleasure in music and theater, and Elizabeth proved a rapt audience for William Magee's reminiscences of the art and landscapes of Italy.[82] She did not find in him a companion for the intense religious affections she sometimes felt, but she was not seeking one. Those experiences had always been hers alone, and she withheld nothing from William Magee that she imagined sharing.

The courtship brought into contact two complicated families. William Magee's grown brother Jack did not like Elizabeth, but he was alone and unheeded in his view. The elder William Seton soon referred to Elizabeth as "my child," and William Magee's young half siblings grew fond of the young woman who knew how to talk to children. Charlotte Bayley may have been relieved that her stepdaughter was leaving the household or sorry to lose her help; in this as in most things, Charlotte is a cryptic figure. As for Richard Bayley, it is hard to imagine he was in any way impressed by his new son-in-law. William Magee Seton had received a practical rather than an intellectual education, and even in his chosen career he lacked the single-mindedness Bayley possessed and admired. Yet if Bayley conveyed less than wholehearted approval—and he was not one to keep his thoughts to himself— Elizabeth was unmoved. The most dramatic evidence of William Magee and Elizabeth's desire for each other is the uselessness of their union to the families they loved. A dutiful eldest son, William Magee had been expected to do as his father and brother had done: marry into a merchant clan and acquire useful new connections. Elizabeth Bayley brought the Setons only herself, but William Magee chose her. Elizabeth, for her part, could have won the love of a physician or medical student and remained, as her sister had done, within her father's orbit. She knew that marrying William Magee Seton would take her away from Richard Bayley's world, and she went eagerly.

3

A HOME OF ONE'S OWN

ELIZABETH AND WILLIAM MAGEE SETON wed in late January of 1794, their small ceremony presided over by the rector of Trinity Church.[1] The couple lived first in the elder William Seton's home on Stone Street, where the merchant house did business on the first floor and a flock of children roamed upstairs. Soon, though, they moved to a row house on Wall Street. When Elizabeth stepped outside, she saw brick buildings whose sober Federal façades exuded wealth and confidence; her neighbors included Alexander Hamilton toward one end of the street and Aaron Burr down the other.

Inside their cozy home, Elizabeth and William Magee had each other to themselves. She called him "my beloved treasure"; "These arms heart and bed are all forlorn without you," she once wrote her traveling husband. William Magee called her his "darling wife" and took along her portrait when he traveled: "I often ask it many questions, & I always fancy it beckoning me to return." Having learned self-sufficiency as a child, Elizabeth reveled in girlish dependence. "I think I never was in my life more pleased with a stranger," she wrote, than she was with a visitor who told her that she must learn to let her husband make all the decisions. She was happy to be "a poor little weak Woman" and her husband's "dear little girl."[2]

In fact, as worldly as William Magee seemed to Elizabeth, he still relied on his father in all matters commercial. The elder Seton had given

FIGURE 3.1. Elizabeth Seton wedding portrait, attributed to Francis Rabineau. Courtesy of the Sisters of Charity of New York Archives, Bronx, New York.

up his position at the bank, and now worked with his beloved oldest son and their new English business partner, David Maitland. From Italy, Filippo Filicchi urged greater attention to "the Leghorn [the Anglophone name for Livorno] trade." "For these two years past," he had written the winter before, "we have not done the tenth part of what we might."[3] He and Seton engineered Filicchi's appointment as American consul in Leghorn.[4] The two loved arranging deals and making connections, and it mattered little that William Magee did his part more through duty than pleasure. He was a competent worker and had his wife's sympathy for the "fatigue and vexations" the trading life brought.[5]

Elizabeth lived in a web of intermarried friends, relatives, and Seton business associates; a cousin might also be a sister-in-law and a creditor also a brother-in-law and friend. Just about everyone was connected to everyone else, and sometimes the clan's expectations chafed.

"I went [to] your aunt Farquhar's because I knew you would wish it," she ruefully wrote William Magee one day. James Farquhar was the flinty kinsman who had dunned the Setons for money after the war, and Elizabeth was less than pleased to discover that Farquhar's wife—another Curson sister, Elizabeth Curson Farquhar—demanded her own social tribute.[6] More often, however, the Setons' circle offered cultured companionship that Elizabeth deeply valued. She and William Magee entertained friends in evenings of conversation and music, he at his violin and she at her piano, and they attended plays at the city's John Street Theater. Members of the Ogden family, an influential clan of merchants, lawyers, and politicians, enlivened Elizabeth's day, as did men and women of the Hoffman family, into which William Magee's brother James had married. Old connections produced new associates, and new associates became friends. When a land company connected to Hector St. John de Crèvecoeur drew a Frenchman named Nicholas Olive into the Setons' orbit, William Seton entered into a business venture with him while Elizabeth and William Magee delighted in Olive and his wife's urbane company.[7] So did Richard Bayley: he took pleasure in his daughter's cultivated friends, and his son Guy Carlton—understandably styling himself simply Carlton—would one day be taken into the Setons' merchant network and sent to Livorno as a clerk in the Filicchi countinghouse.

Within this shared world, Elizabeth made particular friends and kept some from her earlier life. She was always pleased to see Aquila Giles, a kindly merchant who as a daring Continental army major had courted his wife right out from under her Tory family's gaze. She loved Abraham Ogden, gentle member of that powerful clan, and she appreciated the attentions of her godmother, Sarah Clarke Startin, a wealthy and childless widow whose portrait, painted by her brother-in-law John Singleton Copley, reveals a woman looking out at the world with a frankly appraising gaze. Elizabeth also remained close to a young woman she'd known since childhood, Juliana Sitgreaves Scott. Nine years older than Elizabeth, Julia was a Philadelphian who moved to New York to marry Lewis Allaire Scott, son of the Revolutionary-era Presbyterian reformer John Morin Scott. Julia's brother-in-law was a physician, and it may have been through Richard Bayley that Elizabeth first met her. Whatever the friendship's origins, Elizabeth sometimes marveled at its persistence. "Julia is a little vain shadow," she once wrote of the woman who took frank delight in creature comforts, "and never Interests me but when she is in sickness or sorrow." At those moments, Elizabeth mused, she would "fly to her [and] hold her in my bosom till the storm is past." It hardly seemed the makings of a strong friendship, but it was enough "to hold the chain together until it comes round again," and Elizabeth realized to her surprise that the chain was proving durable.[8]

Elizabeth shared her blunt assessment of Julia with the woman whose friendship she valued most of all, Eliza Sadler. The Irish-born wife of a sea captain and merchant, Sadler was well traveled and well read. The two women shared thoughts on books and friends, Sadler remaining calmly analytical even when discussing her heartfelt Protestant faith. A keen observer, she spied in Elizabeth a self-sufficiency the devoted young wife tried to disavow. Elizabeth confessed that her friend was right to see her as more independent than she let on. "You Eliza S. are the only person to whom I could commit the guidance of my conduct in preference to the impulse of my own Judgment," she told Sadler.[9]

At the age of twenty, Elizabeth Seton had a husband she loved, companions of all kinds, and a friend whose judgment she entirely trusted. It was a long way from the loneliness of her childhood, and she recalled her joy decades later: "My own home at twenty—The world and heaven too, quite impossible!"[10]

SICKNESS AND HEALTH

Nothing demonstrated the changed circumstances of Elizabeth Seton's life more clearly than the fact that her father now pleaded for her attention. "Never was I more vexed or disappointed than this evening," the physician pouted. "Why did you not write by the post—you said you intended it." Absent during much of Elizabeth's childhood, Bayley had little moral authority on which to draw, but she delighted in her father's newly felt need. She would apologize for not writing, she consoled him, but "An Apology is useless when the person who is to offer it is convinced of the fault committed."[11]

When they saw each other, Elizabeth and her father discussed his work, as they had done since her adolescence. Bayley was convinced that the city's dirty streets and water threatened New Yorkers' health. Kennels—open ditches through which waste and water flowed—ran down the middle of Manhattan streets, and maggots collected on the animal fat that chandlers hung in preparation for making candles. Filth literally underlay the city's growth: as they hurriedly made room for more docks and profits, New Yorkers used anything that came to hand for landfill, including rotting wood and animal carcasses. In accord with the medical science of his day, Richard Bayley did not know that viruses and bacteria carried disease; instead, he believed that garbage and stagnant water created miasmas, or disease-producing air. Cleansing the city would save its citizens.

Bayley was particularly concerned about one illness that had not yet struck New York with force: yellow fever. Yellow jack, as it was known with grim jocularity, had made occasional forays in the colonial era, with one visitation killing Bayley's own great-grandparents. But the disease did little real damage in the United States until 1793, the year it laid waste to Philadelphia. The first cases appeared in August; by mid-September fifty people were dying each day, most of them men and women in their prime. Sufferers endured blinding headache, raging fever, and the jaundice that gave the disease its name. About half of those afflicted died, many of them bleeding from every orifice. Terrified Philadelphians fled the city; others shut themselves up in their homes. Victims were brought to a hastily established fever hospital, often transported by members of the city's African Society, who were said incorrectly to have immunity to the disease because of their race. Only when the nights grew chillier did the cases stop. By late October, more than three thousand Philadelphians, roughly 5 percent of the city's population, had died.[12]

Horrified New Yorkers waited for this killer to arrive. Ministers and congregants prayed for deliverance, while Richard Bayley and other scientifically minded physicians pondered ways to prevent an epidemic through more earthly means. No one knew, nor would anyone know for another hundred years, that mosquitoes spread yellow fever, injecting a virus into the blood of those whom they bit. Some argued that the disease entered port cities on ships bearing damaged cargoes—rotting coffee a favored culprit—that emitted miasmas. Others believed it to be of local origin, bubbling up through the filth and fetid water that clogged the streets. Bayley thought both means of transmission were possible (and they were; disease-carrying mosquitoes thrived in areas of standing water, and ships transported sick passengers whose infected blood could, with the help of an insect, be passed to a healthy local).[13] As Manhattan's weather warmed in the spring of 1795, he was alert for signs of the disease's arrival.

FIGURE 3.2. One of four plates showing the development of yellow fever. From M. M., *Observations sur la fièvre jaune, faites à Cadix, en 1819* (1820). Courtesy of the digital collections of the Wellcome Library, London.

Elizabeth's mind was on a happier matter: she was about to give birth to her first child. She left no record of her pregnancy or delivery, but the child, a daughter, was born hale and hearty. The couple named her Anna Maria, honoring the stepmother and aunt who had raised William Magee to adulthood, and Elizabeth saw that she was baptized at Trinity Church. Richard Bayley and William Magee (who once wrote to tell Elizabeth that he'd thought about going to church but instead decided to pass the time staring at her picture) dutifully stood as sponsors. Elizabeth's stepmother did not join the little group. The infant's third sponsor was instead Bayley's close friend Mary Fitch.[14]

Elizabeth delighted in baby Anna Maria, tending her with the help of a free white servant named Mammy Huler.[15] But as spring turned to summer and mosquitoes buzzed, the dreaded yellow fever arrived. New Yorker after New Yorker suffered the tell-tale symptoms, and a young physician named Elihu Hubbard Smith estimated that at least twelve thousand fled. "It is the subject of every conversation, at every hour, and in every company," he wrote.[16] Richard Bayley and Wright Post stayed in the city to treat patients and investigate the disease's cause. Elizabeth, William Magee, and Anna Maria stayed too, the parents perhaps unwilling to make the short trip to the countryside with such a young baby. Like most of the city's merchant families, they lived near the docks, where the majority of cases appeared. But they and everyone in the Seton and Bayley clans survived that summer unharmed, and as the weather grew colder, the disease vanished as mysteriously as it had appeared.

New York's Health Commission declared the epidemic over, expressing gratitude to God.[17] Richard Bayley believed that yellow fever was not an act of God but a public health crisis. He wrote an analysis of the unhygienic conditions that he thought spread the disease, including a bleak portrait of living conditions among the city's poor that he drew from an account by a priest at St. Peter's Catholic Church.[18] Bayley found a willing ear in the governor of New York, his old associate from New Rochelle, John Jay. In February of 1796, as Bayley prepared his pamphlet for publication, Jay appointed him Manhattan's first "health officer." Elizabeth's father now had an official perch from which to attempt to save the city. Whether the city wished to be saved remained to be seen.

While Bayley prepared to do battle, William Magee and Elizabeth lived in peace. Little Anna Maria thrived, and in spring, Elizabeth was again pregnant. After a childhood in exile, she had made a home. Both the unhappiness and the "curiosity to see the world" that she had felt as a girl were willingly "laid aside." What she might once have seen as a circumscribed existence, she saw now as a charmed circle. "A half a dozen form my World," she wrote Sadler.[19] It was a world she was determined to protect, and when the next summer brought fears of another fever season, Elizabeth and Anna Maria decamped to Long Island, sharing a rented house with Mary and Wright Post. Her father's reports meant that Elizabeth never forgot the lurking threat of illness. But she loved her quiet weeks on the island, writing Sadler that she was "enjoying every comfort of the country without a single Interruption of visitors, servants, or any other difficulty"—a set of "difficulties" that suggests how privileged Elizabeth's life now was. William Magee stayed behind on Wall

Street to see to business, but he crossed to the island as often as he could, preferring his family's company to the strategic socializing at which his father excelled. "My Will comes three times a week," Elizabeth wrote happily, "and when the moon shines every evening."[20]

Having tended her many half siblings, Elizabeth knew that if she continued to bear children every year or two, she would have little time to herself. She wholeheartedly accepted that she would "accustom that [self] to yield to affection for my Will."[21] For now, she made time to read the Bible, as she had done throughout her life, and she perused the sermons of Hugh Blair, a Scottish minister and belletrist whose widely read essays eschewed doctrinal controversies in favor of urging Christians toward lives of virtue and social usefulness. Elizabeth also read works of secular philosophy. She loved Rousseau, whom she called "dear J. Jacques," and she and her father shared *Candide*, neither of them scandalized by Voltaire's mordant satire of the view that because God made everything, everything must be good. The view Voltaire mocked was not one Elizabeth held; she neither flinched at ugliness nor sought divine justification for it. Religion was not meant to explain the world and its sorrows; like many other educated citizens of the new nation, including statesmen such as Thomas Jefferson and John Adams, Elizabeth believed that religion's central purpose was to produce ethical, happy individuals. Although she enjoyed reading Blair's sermons more than attending "balls or amusement," she considered her choice a matter of taste, not virtue. "I think," she wrote in 1796, "the first point of Religion is cheerfulness and Harmony." If "the gayest" of European bons vivants achieved those attributes with their wigs and dancing rather than through prayer, "the effects of their manner may be as useful as ours."[22] Aware that safety was an illusion and her own temperament could betray her, Elizabeth was determined to stay within the compass of her contentment.

She failed. Although she and William Magee were delighted to welcome their first son (named, inevitably, William), Elizabeth's gratitude slowly became tinged with fear. Her husband was coughing more and often fatigued, and so was his gentle half sister Rebecca; everyone feared that the family curse of consumption menaced them. Elizabeth felt her old foe return: "I never view the setting sun or take a solitary walk," she confessed to Sadler, "but melancholy tries to seize me." Richard Bayley had neither remedies nor reassurance to offer, and Elizabeth did not expect God to intervene either. Instead, she summoned the informal stoicism she'd relied on in her youth. "Every hour I pass," she wrote Sadler, "shows me the instability of every expectation which is not founded on reason." She put Christianity to the same task; for Elizabeth, reason and faith coexisted as easily as Rousseau and her Bible, and the point of all of it was to find peace. "It is my fixed principle both as a Christian and a reasonable being," she wrote, "never to dwell on thoughts of future events which do not depend on myself." As dangers crept closer, she resurrected the self-sufficiency she had repressed since her marriage. "I have learnt to commune with my own heart," she told Sadler, "and I try to govern it by reflection."[23]

Elizabeth's new understanding of what it meant to fear for a marriage left her pondering the companionship between her father and Mary Fitch. In April of 1796, an odd event had made their relationship impossible to ignore: after six years in which Richard and Charlotte Bayley had grown increasingly estranged, Charlotte gave birth to a baby. Rather than signaling the restoration of their marriage, the child was christened Mary Fitch Bayley. The man who ten years before had given his son the name of a British occupying official now gave his daughter the name of the woman he had come to esteem more than his wife. Charlotte accepted the choice, but her estrangement from her husband deepened, and the event seems to have accelerated Elizabeth's alienation from Fitch. "Be assured I never will forget that she is in Years [that is, elderly] [and] A Stranger," she wrote Sadler, but she could not ignore the destructive effects of her father's long friendship with Fitch. "I am Irrecoverably lost to her and where Esteem does not exist how can I express friendship," she wrote, adding, "The moon might as well meet the Sun."[24]

Bayley did not agonize over his daughter's relations with Mary Fitch or over his marriage. Nor did he suffer, as his daughter did, from dread. Life's fragility kept Richard Bayley busy, not anxious; presiding as New York's health officer and possessed of the full confidence of Governor Jay, he worked tirelessly to prevent the return of yellow fever. His new campaign proved almost as controversial as his anatomical museum had once been. Bayley angered merchants by ordering that ships suspected of bearing disease be quarantined, and he angered businessmen by shaming them for their swampy, filthy properties.[25] "The Soap boilers and Tallow chandlers talk of petitioning the Legislature for a removal of the Health Officer," Elizabeth informed her father, knowing he loved a good fight.[26]

Bayley was in his element, determined to persuade his fellow citizens that they controlled their fates. Yellow fever, he told them firmly, was a "murderer of our own creating."[27]

Unlike some of their fellow merchants, William Magee Seton and his father did not oppose Bayley's quarantining of ships. The Setons eschewed open conflict of any kind, and they had a different kind of peril on their minds: although their merchant house was busy and its credit sound, they knew they stood just a few bad decisions—or a few unlucky waves—from disaster. The French Revolution that had begun in 1789 was transforming Europe, and the consequences for trade were uncertain; the high seas seemed as filled with privateers as New York's streets were with garbage. No one despaired; on the contrary, at a hale fifty years old, the elder William was as jovially enterprising as ever. He had recently overseen the marriage of his daughter Eliza to a business associate, James Maitland, and he was opening negotiations with a Canadian firm in order to skirt British law and participate in the China trade.[28] Yet even William sometimes fretted. "In short it is tough and tough," he wrote his son on a day that a financially pressed sea captain "cooly blew his brains out." "Our portion for this month of June, makes my hair stand on end."[29]

William Magee had lived in dread of debt since witnessing the Panic, and as he worried over business, Elizabeth worried over him. When she and the children once again left Manhattan for a summer sojourn in the country, anxiety went along. She watched her husband for fevers and coughs. A friend's death saddened her. Her father's visits brought vivid descriptions of peril and suffering. Then came the worst of it: baby Will fell frighteningly ill, tormented by an "inflammation in the bowels" from which Bayley warned the infant "could not recover." Will did get well but not before Elizabeth's stoicism abandoned her and she questioned her fitness as a parent. "Could I speak to you in the language of my feelings," she wrote Sadler, "should I attempt to express what passed in my Heart in any moment of that time whilst his recovery was uncertain, you would lament that Heaven had allowed me the privilege of being a Mother." The memory of her terror still fresh, Elizabeth questioned whether the motherhood she treasured truly was a privilege. "What is there in the uncertainty of human happiness," she demanded, "to repay the agonizing convulsion of those twenty-four hours in which I witnessed his sufferings"?[30]

Happiness brought dread. Elizabeth tried to hold her emotions at arm's length, witnessing them rather than being possessed by them. She willed herself to accept that loved ones would die. The price for self-protection was steep: steeling herself against sorrow, Elizabeth refused herself joy. "My bosom is yet trembling," she wrote after her infant son's recovery, "and takes the pleasures of the present hours with the same silent submission with which it has endured the past."[31]

That summer two ships in which Seton & Maitland held an interest were seized by French privateers, the losses in quick succession deeply unsettling. The house filed claims totaling almost $60,000 with French consuls at Barcelona and Cadiz, but no one held much hope of payment.[32] William Duer, accidental architect of the Panic, still moldered in Manhattan's debtors' prison, and while William Magee worried over his lost ships, another terrifying example of failure's toll presented itself. An impoverished New York musician desperate not to be returned to debtors' prison shot and killed the sheriff's deputy sent to take him into custody. Despite considerable public sympathy, the musician was put to death. A law passed after the Doctors' Riot decreed that the bodies of executed criminals be donated for dissection in order to prevent the desecration of "respectable" New Yorkers. The unfortunate man's remains—thrown hastily into the East River by physicians' assistants fearing a mob—floated grotesquely to the surface.[33] A more disturbing specter of debt's consequences can scarcely be imagined.

Because of their upbringing and experience, William Magee and Elizabeth Seton possessed sophisticated understandings of debt and disease. But no Manhattanites were strangers to them. Risks of all kinds, from fire to fever to fraud, threatened, and those who'd come to the city from elsewhere fought their battles without the help of family and friends they'd left behind. New York City had an almshouse and a Common Council that distributed clothing, food, fuel, and occasionally cash in an effort to keep the poor in their homes. But many Manhattanites struggled, and widows faced the constraints of gender as well as the burden of poverty and ill luck.

Some New Yorkers turned to religion for solace, companionship, and succor; between 1790 and 1810, two dozen churches were founded in the city, many of them evangelical.[34] Religious faith inspired one New York woman, Isabella Graham, to found a society dedicated to aiding women who'd succumbed to the perils all women feared. Graham's Society for the Relief of Poor Widows with Small Children was among the nation's first female-run groups devoted to charitable works, and Elizabeth Seton joined it in its earliest days.

Born in Scotland, Graham had married and emigrated to the West Indies, only to find herself left a pregnant widow with small children and limited funds. After returning to Scotland and founding a successful school, she became part of an influential transatlantic circle of Scottish evangelicals. She and her collaborators believed that the United States was "the place where the church of Christ"—in their view, an evangelical form of Presbyterianism—"would preeminently flourish." Arriving in New York in 1789, Graham founded a school that quickly gained favor with the city's elite, and she became part of the Setons' social world of merchant families and St. Andrew's Society members. Moved by the city's indigent women and children, Graham and her daughter Joanna Graham Bethune conceived the idea of a charitable organization unconstrained by the bounds of ethnicity. They made clear that all poor white women fell within the circle of their benevolence. That no poor women of color did was a fact that seemed so natural as to go undiscussed and unremarked.[35]

Women such as Elizabeth Seton could do little to avoid the risks of the commercial economy. They could, however, help those who had already fallen victim to it, and Graham inspired Elizabeth and others to do so. Although Graham recalled that the society at first faced "ridicule" and "opposition," her confidence and connections triumphed. The society boasted connections to the families of Alexander Hamilton, Albert Gallatin, and federal judges; Episcopalians and Presbyterians contributed resources, time, and prestige. In 1802, members had the society incorporated, affording its female leadership the legal right to manage its resources.[36] Elizabeth worked diligently on its behalf, serving as a manager and treasurer. Her godmother, Sarah Startin, and members of the Ogden family also joined, and in years to come, Eliza Sadler contributed her efforts, as did William's half sister Rebecca and another friend of Elizabeth's, a sea captain's wife named Catherine Dupleix.

Society members visited widows in their homes, hearing firsthand of their struggles to buy firewood and to feed and shelter their children. This intimate style of charity was born of a sense of authority, as well as a desire to console. The society's managers evaluated those who sought their help, meeting to review widows' applications and interviewing their neighbors in order to determine worthiness. The society's constitution makes clear that its members believed themselves the best judge of the poor widows' needs: they resolved to give women only items essential to their households, no luxuries. Despite this assumption of authority over beneficiaries' lives, members of the society did not evangelize the widows during the years of Elizabeth's participation. That was a reticence Graham would later rue, but it accorded with the women's sense that religious beliefs were matters of conscience.[37] Accepting charity brought many obligations but not the obligation to alter one's creed.

Elizabeth's work with the widows' society looms large in both hagiographic and historical accounts of her life. For Mother Seton's followers, these labors foreshadow the work that the Sisters of Charity undertook throughout the nation and the world. For secular historians, Seton's participation in the society places her within a familiar template of active benevolence; she is to be grouped with the nineteenth-century American women whose piety and skills drew them to social reform when conventional political and economic activities were closed to them. Each view has merit, but like her husband in his father's merchant house, Elizabeth in the society was a faithful laborer rather than an architect. She felt compassion for New York's destitute women and found in Graham's society a way to turn her fears for her own family into useful action. Yet she was never the society's driving force; on the contrary, left to herself, she was more inclined to read and contemplate than to organize a reform movement. Although Simon Bruté, a priest who became Elizabeth's close collaborator, would one day be fascinated by the parallels between Seton and Graham, Elizabeth herself felt no particular kinship with the older woman.[38] Graham's active Presbyterian piety had little in common with Elizabeth's idiosyncratic mixture of nondenominational Christian belief, philosophical inquiry, and stoic detachment. Elizabeth's model of public charity was not the pious Graham but her iconoclastic father.

Thus even when she was a Protestant, Elizabeth did not fit neatly into the mold of American female benevolence workers. It's also true that such benevolent work itself is less distinctively American and Protestant than is often assumed. Although unusual in the United States, Isabella Graham's society would have been recognizable to centuries of European Catholic women (consecrated and lay) who served poor people, used otherwise suppressed abilities, and found sisterhood by forming communities devoted to good works. Elizabeth's founding of the American Sisters of Charity emerges more directly out of that European Catholic tradition, conveyed to her by French clerics, than out of her experience with the society for poor widows. And her busy life within the expansive, socially engaged institution she founded never came easy; Isabella Graham was more temperamentally suited than the contemplative Elizabeth Seton to the sisters' life of active benevolence, and if there was a woman in Manhattan who seemed likely to found a charitable community of international reach, it was Graham.[39] But Elizabeth was the mother of young children, not a candidate for cloister, and Graham was a contented Protestant.

Two centuries after their deaths, Catholicism's apostolic communities and its culture of saints have made Mother Seton known to millions, whereas Graham has faded from view. Yet through the workings of history and memory, Seton has become a figure more kindred to Graham in death than she was in life. Elizabeth Seton has a shrine; Isabella Graham haunts it.

THE DREADFUL '98

In the earliest days of her marriage, Elizabeth's blissful absorption in her husband had drawn her away from her father. The birth of Anna Maria and Will drew them back together. His limitations as a father notwithstanding, Bayley confidently offered child-rearing advice and Elizabeth happily received it. Neither believed in corporal punishment; children should be reformed through the application of reason, not force. Such views accorded with Rousseau's, and they reflected Bayley's belief not only in the general power of reason but in the specific capacities of his daughter. Both accepted that it was in child rearing that Elizabeth would use her powerful mind. "Look up," Bayley told his daughter, "and urge forward your claims to preeminence—your children are to give you immortality, this is neither the world nor the age for you to enjoy it in."[40] In another letter, Bayley directly acknowledged the constraints of gender; Eve, he jauntily wrote his daughter, "surpassed Adam in Enterprise," "but she is a woman and ill treated."[41] Despite such observations, and despite a delight in defying tradition, Bayley never advocated upending gender conventions. Neither did Elizabeth. She confidently exerted her judgment and read and thought whatever she pleased. But she did so within the confines of a domestic world she willingly inhabited.

That fragile domestic world remained intact through the summer and fall of 1797. Anna Maria and tiny William were well, and Elizabeth was again pregnant. The house of Seton & Maitland stood ready to finalize arrangements with the Canadian firm of McTavish, Frobisher, in a deal the elder Seton hoped would unlock the riches of the China trade. William Magee's health, though not perfect, seemed stable, and Richard Bayley carried on making plans and enemies. Then, on a winter's day in January of 1798, there came a sudden blow.

Walking out of his home on Stone Street, Elizabeth's father-in-law slipped and fell heavily on the ice. When he tried to rise, he could not. Helped back into his house, the merchant took to his bed and stayed there. It seems likely that he had broken a hip, and when an ambitious young agent for McTavish, Frobisher arrived to conduct his business, the Seton family turned him away. "Sunday I waited on Mr. Seton," Alexander MacKenzie wrote a business associate, and "found him very unwell from a fall he had in his own passage the day before. This day I again called, he was so unwell I could not see him." William Magee eventually met the Canadian on the firm's behalf, but the Setons lacked ready cash, and when MacKenzie asked William Magee "to make out our account current," the thirty-four-year-old merchant replied that "he would mention this to his father."[42] As days passed, the elder merchant grew no better, and the younger no more confident. MacKenzie fussed and fumed.

Elizabeth knew that her father-in-law was in peril, and with him her world. If William died, her gentle, urbane husband would have to run the house of Seton & Maitland. And what of William's sprawling family? His children by Anna Maria—William Magee's much younger half siblings—would be orphans in need of a home. Throughout that troubling winter and spring, Elizabeth worked to stifle her dread. The Sadlers were traveling in Europe, and when Elizabeth learned they might be delayed in their return, she allowed her friend a glimpse at her fight for self-mastery. William Magee was "perfectly sick" at the thought that the Sadlers might be delayed, Elizabeth wrote, but she did not allow herself to "ponder" the possibilities. She encapsulated her struggle in a single line. "A state of Uncertainty is terrible indeed."[43]

Should Elizabeth have needed further proof of life's perils, it arrived: her friend Julia Scott's husband fell acutely ill. Elizabeth stayed with the Scotts during what soon became a deathwatch, horrified to see her friend undone by grief. "Such scenes of terror I have gone thro' as you nor no one can conceive," she wrote Sadler.[44] Soon after Lewis Allaire Scott died, Julia and her children moved to Philadelphia. Elizabeth wrote imploring her once lighthearted friend to cultivate the detachment she herself sought. "What I most desire and wish for you now," Elizabeth told Julia, "is *Peace* that first and most perfect of all earthly attainments."[45]

Elizabeth also hoped for "Peace" for William Magee, but none came. Fearful for his father and his future, the young merchant irritated his already impatient Canadian visitor by announcing he had developed qualms of "conscience" about the China deal. "I know not what to think of the Setons," MacKenzie wrote heatedly to his business associate. "They are lowered in my opinion, both with respect to their candour and understanding, as men of business they are never two days in the same mind."[46] Seton's qualms were no match for MacKenzie's implacability, and in the end the two men came to terms. But William Magee's unreadiness to head a merchant house had been revealed, and McTavish, Frobisher hoped never to do business with the Setons again.[47]

While those negotiations lurched along, the elder William had rallied, then failed, failed, then rallied. Recovery seemed always possible but never quite in reach. It was the kind of extended unease that Elizabeth most loathed, and she called on all her powers of self-governance to endure it. "You must learn the severe lesson of submission," she wrote Julia, articulating the lesson she herself was trying to learn: "That [lesson] once gained, all that follows becomes Easy—to resign our dearest Hopes, and console ourselves with *reason* in the hours when anguish rends the Heart—to rouse from the torpor of grief, and enter into scenes in which the Heart has no concern, or at best can receive no comfort, is the lot of Virtue, and Superior minds."[48]

Elizabeth relied for her composure on a brew of self-governance and fatalism, compatible with Christianity but stripped of most of its consolations. Occasionally during that difficult spring, she longed not only to escape life's miseries but to escape life. "If reason and the best Affections of this World did not withhold, and draw back with more than common force its flying propensities," she wrote Julia, "I should have renounced every other desire and aim long ago."[49]

As her troubles compounded, Elizabeth struggled to tolerate people less capable of self-governance than she. She confided that unhappiness in Julia too, their friendship blossoming now that they were correspondents rather than neighbors. Mary Fitch, Elizabeth told Julia, tried her patience. "The poor old Lady's passions are irritated," she complained after agreeing to a visit, "and she does not try to calm them."[50] The merchant Aquila Giles's sister-in-law became comic foil to Elizabeth's sharpest judgments. "Poor Miss Shipton" boasted a flighty self-absorption that drove Elizabeth to distraction, yet Elizabeth's increasingly acerbic remarks somehow convinced the woman they were true friends. Thrilled when Shipton at last sailed for England, Elizabeth was horrified to hear a rumor that her ship had been attacked by privateers; rather than worrying she might be harmed, Elizabeth feared she might somehow find her way back to Manhattan.[51]

Julia, to whom Elizabeth recounted the story, appreciated her friend's humor and understood that anxiety was withering her patience. By late spring, her father-in-law despaired of his life. Heavily pregnant, Elizabeth could no longer master her fears. "I think I have never in my life suffered so much from the Anticipation of Evil (as it is a source of uneasiness which I never indulge) as during the last fortnight," she wrote Julia. "My poor William," she added, "has been lost I may say in mute anguish, his disposition is of that kind which does not admit of the soothings of sympathy but wraps its grief in the stillness of despair." "Human life and sorrow," Elizabeth mused, "are inseparable."[52]

Six days later, Elizabeth's father-in-law was dead. Hundreds of New Yorkers joined the procession that bore William Seton to his grave in Trinity churchyard, a testament to the man's lifetime of making friends and money. "He was," an anonymous eulogist wrote, "long a respectable, and valued inhabitant of this city, whose general integrity of conduct, benevolence of heart, and philanthropy of temper, had endeared him to a numerous circle of friends and acquaintance." His family "have lost the best of fathers and the best of friends," a "fond, indulging, and affectionate parent."[53] A second effusive obituary ended with a stark, capitalized declaration: "WILLIAM SETON IS DEAD!"[54] The transformations Elizabeth and William Magee Seton had for months feared were upon them.

4

Courage Flies

S INCE HE WAS NOW head of the family and the house of Seton &
Maitland, William Magee's first responsibility was to sort through
his father's debts and assets. That would not be easy; the father to
thirteen had never made a will. His failure to do so, Elizabeth wrote in
understated fashion, "places my husband in a difficult and uncomfortable situation with respect to his property." Furniture, land near the
Black River, townhouse, country house, carriage: none of it had been
allotted. As what Elizabeth delicately called "disputes" threatened to
break out, William Magee and his siblings agreed to sell their father's
furniture for cash and divide his plate.[1] That was only the beginning of
the challenges. So respected had the elder William been that New Yorkers, some of them scarcely known to the family, had left deeds under
his name, confident that their property was safe in his keeping. Now
those deeds lay interleaved with Seton's own papers. Then there was the
largest challenge of all: running the house of Seton & Maitland. William
Magee's reluctance to take up that charge had likely contributed to his
father's inability to plan for his death. Yet by dying intestate, William
removed any chance of guiding his son from beyond the grave. It was as
if he had simply vanished.

In addition to his complex business affairs, the merchant left behind
a family large even by the standards of the day. Seven children were still
dependents. At seventeen, Rebecca was the oldest of them, and despite

suffering from consumption, she faithfully tended her younger brothers and sisters. Everyone knew, however, that this flock of children could not live on their own in the Stone Street house. Mary and Charlotte were in their early teens, Harriet (called Hatch) was eleven, and Sam, Ned, and Cecilia, whose births had so exhausted their consumptive mother, were aged nine, eight, and seven.

Several of William's children by his first wife had households of their own (only Henry, a would-be naval officer with a taste for drink, was struggling), but it was on William Magee and Elizabeth that the responsibility for the young half siblings fell. At twenty-four, Elizabeth was mother to two children and pregnant with a third. Now she became guardian to the six youngest Setons. Elizabeth enjoyed children generally and loved these children specifically; they were, she stoutly assured their great aunt Isabella Cayley, of "good and amiable dispositions."[2] Yet the thought of tending so many people—the thought even of living with so many people—brought her near despair.

She and William Magee (whom we will now simply call William) gave up their Wall Street row house and took up residence at Stone Street, its rooms brimming with merchant business and William's half siblings. "To be sure," Elizabeth confessed to Julia, "for me who so dearly loves quiet and a small Family to become at once the Mother of six [additional] children and the Head of so large a number is a very great change." She then abandoned all effort at understatement. "Death or Bread and Water," she admitted, "would be a happy prospect in comparison when I consider *Self*."[3]

The Stone Street house stood about a half mile from the Battery, the waterfront area New Yorkers had since colonial days fortified when fearing attack. As the Setons tried to settle into the rhythms of their new life, the sound of construction once again rang out. One month after the elder William's death, the United States abrogated its treaties with France, beginning an era of hostilities known as the Quasi War. While reports of French privateering proliferated, fearful New Yorkers erected barricades on the Battery. "Besides our family sorrow," Elizabeth told William's English aunt, "the situation of our affairs with the French and the constant preparation for war makes every one uncertain how long they may be permitted to enjoy their homes or what their future prospects may be."[4]

A hesitant merchant in the best of times, William shouldered greater responsibilities amid growing risk. "His mind," Elizabeth observed, "is in a state scarcely to be endured."[5] William turned for help to a newly hired clerk, a young Englishman named Thomas Masters. Masters had come into the house the way everyone seemed to, through a family connection, but he felt no great loyalty to the stricken Setons; when Manhattan began to swelter, he decamped for the countryside without remorse. ("It is so intolerably warm," he blithely explained, "that one is scarcely able to exist.")[6] With Masters gone and her husband beset by worry, the heavily pregnant Elizabeth took up a new task. She helped her husband run the merchant house.

"My poor William," Elizabeth wrote Julia, "has kept me constantly employed in copying his letters and assisting him to arrange his Papers, for he has no friend or confidante now on Earth but his little wife." Elizabeth had always delighted in her husband's love of home, so different from her father's restless ambition. Now the bill for William's domesticity had come due. "Most men," she reflected, "have the resource in an event of this kind either of particular friends, or habits to dissipate sorrow, but my Husband has neither." Mothering eight children and pregnant with another, Elizabeth found herself "woefully fatigued and . . . unwell."[7] William refused to see his wife's growing exhaustion, and so she stayed in the city working as his scribe while the other women of her circle (and it seems, the Seton children) left for summer homes.

Word soon came that despite Richard Bayley's efforts to protect the city, yellow fever was again loose near the docks. Elizabeth calmly prepared to stay and give birth in her Stone Street home. The upstairs rooms of the house were so hot that she laid a sleeping mat on the floor of a drawing room. "There I may comfort myself, and happy I am it is no worse," she told Julia resolutely.[8] She also put up mosquito netting. Although she did not know it, that one act offered more protection than all her father's campaigns.

When Elizabeth's labor began, William was in Philadelphia pursuing a deal. She had had straightforward deliveries with her two earlier children, but as the hours passed it became clear that this birth, perhaps because of her weariness, was different. "My illness was so severe," she wrote in a draft of a letter to Julia, "that both Mother and child were some hours in a very doubtful situation." When her father was summoned, the physician thought he might have to sacrifice his grandchild in order to save his daughter. At last he managed to deliver the baby whole, but the infant, a boy, neither breathed nor moved. While a spent

Elizabeth watched, Bayley blew air into the infant's lungs. The child stirred and began to breathe. Elizabeth ruefully credited God for her own survival—"Heaven," she wrote, had "again denied" her wish for rest—and more joyously credited Richard Bayley for saving the baby. He had "given the breath of life."[9] Despite his harrowing arrival in the world, the infant thrived, and his grateful parents named him Richard Bayley Seton.

Once back in Manhattan, William must have seen his wife's exhaustion. Still he could not bring himself to insist she leave the fever-ridden city. Elizabeth and the baby remained during what she called "this season of horrors." All around the Setons' home, houses stood empty, deserted when residents heard of neighbors falling ill. "Several have died in this street," Elizabeth told Julia, "one person three doors off." Bayley reported from the city's new fever hospital, Bellevue, that the disease was so virulent it was "more like the Plague than Fever." Elizabeth willingly shared the danger with her father and husband, her stoicism a hair's breadth from despair. "Ah Julia," she told her Philadelphia friend, "this Life is not worth one half the anxious moments that I suffer in one single day."[10]

When autumn chilled New York's evenings, fever cases slowed to a halt. Elizabeth took down the mosquito netting, and the clerk Thomas Masters cheerfully returned from his country sojourn. He was determined, he wrote his family, "to exert myself to make up the great length of time that I have spent in idleness here." A season of trading began.[11] "I am writing at the counting house from nine in the morning till ten at night," Masters wrote that November. "Mr. Seton and all his family treat me with peculiar kindness, and I find myself very comfortable near him."[12] William lacked the gregarious and decisive nature that underlay his late father's success, but it seemed that connections, civility, and diligence might be enough to keep Seton & Maitland afloat.

Freed from her role as unpaid clerk, Elizabeth returned her full attention to the children. Life at Stone Street was proving as hectic as she'd feared, and although she did not allow herself to complain to William, she divulged her sorrows to Julia. "I am so entirely occupied with [children]," she wrote her friend, "having only Mammy Huler to assist me, that I have no time to indulge reflection." If she sneaked away for a moment to think or read, "I hear a half dozen voices calling Sister, or Mamma."[13]

FIGURE 4.1. *William Magee Seton*, 1797. Courtesy of the
National Portrait Gallery, Washington, DC.

Elizabeth had the help of a servant and was sheltered, well clothed,
and well fed. Because of her father's reports and her own work with the
poor widows' society, she knew that she lived a privileged life. Nonetheless, her lack of solitude brought a constant ache. "We are, and are likely
to be in a state of confusion," she told Julia, "and where there is not
Peace, the mind loses all those delightful communications and Reflections which mine so much delights in."[14] The pain sharpened when Elizabeth visited her Wall Street home, now occupied by Wright and Mary
Post. When she crossed the threshold, she fell to her knees and wept,
hardly able to believe that she would never again be mother to a small
family. Once again, it was to Julia that she confided her unhappiness, her
friend's unembarrassed recounting of her own sorrows and dissatisfac-
tions freeing Elizabeth to reveal her own. "Oh Julia, Julia *never again,*"
she wrote after seeing her old Wall Street home. "Those hours are past
which tho' I enjoyed them, I never knew their value."[15]

FIGURE 4.2. *Mrs. Wm. Seton*, 1797. Courtesy of the
National Portrait Gallery, Washington, DC.

As she struggled to reconcile herself to a changed life, Elizabeth
found herself again imagining death as a release. A wife and mother, she
permitted herself no second night of the little bottle. Yet she sometimes
told close friends that she would be happy to escape life's uncertainties
sooner rather than later. Almost imperceptibly, her informal stoicism
was also becoming more richly colored with Christianity: she wrote not
only of death but of Heaven. "Julia," she asked wearily in late October,
"when shall we meet in a State of Certainty"?[16] Amid the vicissitudes of
accident, commerce, and consumption, a state of certainty seemed like
paradise, and thinking of it made the hectic days on Stone Street endur-
able. "[I] am jogging on Old style," she told Julia, "trying to accomplish
every duty, and *hoping* for the reward—without *that* in view heaven
knows this life would be a scene of confusion and vexation *to me*, who
neither values nor desires it."[17]

When death seemed too enticing, Elizabeth recalled her struggles
as a motherless child. "Think of your Daughter, my love," she urged

Julia when she feared her widowed friend cared for life as little as she herself did. "You never knew the want of a Mother's tender care, or you would tremble at the thought that *your child* should ever want it."[18] Two weeks later, Elizabeth set aside her own counsel. "I have no enjoyment so great as to induce me to remain Here" among the living, she confessed. "Even as the Mother of my children I would not stay if I were sure they would not be deprived of the Protection of their Father. Why do I tell you all this?" she mused.[19] Why indeed? One answer is that Elizabeth told Julia things she scarcely admitted to herself. Another answer is that Elizabeth, who had always loved poetry, sometimes used language like a poet. The death-turned self that she depicted in such moments was authentically felt but also a rhetorical creation. There is also a third answer to the question of why Elizabeth wrote to Julia wistfully of death. She believed it was not morbid but simply rational to prefer heaven to earth. How could one not long for a refuge beyond loss? Elizabeth had no answer, and she did not believe one existed. Several decades later, another spiritually ambitious American woman, the poet Emily Dickinson, penned lines that expressed a similar view. "The heart asks pleasure first / And then, excuse from pain; /And then, those little anodynes / That deaden suffering, / And then, to go to sleep; / And then, if it should be / The will of its Inquisitor, /The liberty to die."

KEEPING AFLOAT

Whatever the attractions of the next life, Elizabeth Seton believed in the importance of crisis management in this one. Within a few months of her father-in-law's death, she and William arranged for four of his young half siblings to be sent away to school. Mary and Charlotte were dispatched to Miss Hay's establishment in New Brunswick, New Jersey. "Girls of twelve and fourteen," she observed to Julia Scott, "are much more difficult to manage than at any other time of Life." Sam and Ned were sent to school in Connecticut, leaving just Hatch and Cecilia, whom Elizabeth took pleasure in teaching at home. The children's dispersal fostered peace and order inside 61 Stone Street, and Elizabeth's lot further improved as Rebecca, basking in the glow of Elizabeth's attention, revealed herself to be a helpmate. "Until I was under the same roof with her I always thought her an uninformed Girl," Elizabeth wrote in her usual frank manner, "with many good qualities, but very much neglected." Now she found William's oldest half sister to be "without any exception the most truly amiable estimable young woman I ever knew."[20]

Rebecca shared Elizabeth's capacities for clear-eyed judgment and warm sympathy; the mild young woman could also be endearingly partisan when the need arose. Indirectly acknowledging that her brother Jack still did not like Elizabeth, Rebecca reassured her sister-in-law that she knew her worth. "Let who will endeavour to prejudice me against you," the young woman wrote stoutly. "My opinion will ever be the same."[21]

With Stone Street less chaotic, Elizabeth stole moments to read. She admired Jane Bowdler's *Poems and Essays* and copied their gentle moralizing into one of her old commonplace books, intending to pass the ledger on to her daughter as her father had passed his on to her. Bowdler (whose brother Thomas famously removed what he considered the offending bits from Shakespeare) offered a sentimental didacticism that would have left the teenaged Betsy Bayley cold. The young matron Elizabeth Seton found it comforting.[22] She also enjoyed the works of James Hervey, an Anglican minister widely read since the middle of the century. Elizabeth copied out a long passage in which Hervey urged acceptance of all "Divine Dispensations" and admired the intricate workings of nature. "Does not that allseeing eye which preserves so exact a harmony among these pretty toys, maintain as watchful a care over his rational creatures?" the passage reads.[23]

The extract now bears a large X drawn across the page. After her conversion, Elizabeth or Simon Bruté, the priest who became her spiritual director, may have heard a whisper of deism in Hervey's depiction of divinity as an "allseeing eye" and have recoiled at the suggestion that Elizabeth, like many of her educated contemporaries, had once envisioned an abstract divinity who did not intervene in human affairs. Despite the reproving X, Hervey's counsel, like her reading of Blair and Bowdler, was leading Elizabeth toward Christianity, not away from it. Her Christian faith was still free-form rather than doctrinally grounded; like her informal stoicism, it promised tranquillity through detachment from earthly hope and fear. Yet the change in her thinking is clear. In the past, she had consoled herself with the idea that in the end nothing mattered. Now she contemplated the possibility that one thing did matter, and it mattered very much: God's love. Elizabeth kept reading.

At last 1798 lurched to its end, Elizabeth hoping turmoil would end with it. "The last year has been to *us* the reverse of our dearest hopes and the Grave of every enjoyment," she wrote Julia. "The first pleasant thought I enjoyed in the opening of this year was that the terrible ninety-eight was past." Then 1799 got under way. As the Quasi War continued, Congress passed legislation forbidding vessels arriving from France to unload their cargo, and Seton & Maitland was forced to leave valuable merchandise at the wharves. President John Adams authorized American ships to capture vessels sailing into and out of French ports, but French privateers continued to prowl the Atlantic. Some merchants turned risk into profit, but uncertainty seemed as hostile to William Seton as he was to it. Word came that another of the house's ships had been captured.[24]

While William labored grimly to keep Seton & Maitland afloat, Richard Bayley joyfully battled Manhattan's dirt and disease. In addition to its usual satisfactions, his work now offered an excuse to absent himself from Charlotte. Having agreed to oversee and live at the new quarantine station John Jay had authorized, Bayley decided that his wife and children should not accompany him there. "He is building a Hospital and dwelling House," Elizabeth wrote Julia, "but I fear not to receive his family."[25]

Bayley's youngest children ranged in age from Mary Fitch, three years old, to Carlton, thirteen, and Elizabeth delicately questioned his decision to move away from them. Bayley justified his choice with a nod to civic duty. "Staten Island, yes, it's more than probable," he wrote his daughter. "And then? Private considerations must be made, or ought to be made, to yield to the more interesting one, the public welfare."[26] The unhappy marriage of Richard and Charlotte Bayley had ended in all but name.

Having left his wife, Bayley insisted that his daughters Mary and Elizabeth shun her too; like a pool of standing water in the heat of summer, Charlotte had been deemed a threat to the family's health. Although the teenaged Betsy Bayley might have been triumphant, Elizabeth took no pleasure in the exile of the woman who had often exiled her. Both the joys and the anxieties of her married life left her sympathetic to Charlotte's years of unhappiness, regardless of Charlotte's own role in them. On a practical level, Charlotte was entangled with the Seton circle: Eliza Sadler's son was engaged to Charlotte's daughter Emma, and Elizabeth wondered how she might possibly avoid the woman at the wedding, not to mention during the years of dinner parties and casual gatherings sure to follow. Yet Elizabeth did not countermand or criticize her father. She worried for his children and doubted the wisdom of shunning her step-mother, but she had never asked Richard Bayley to change his course, and she did not do so now.

While her father's household fractured, Elizabeth assiduously cared for her own. Her youngest child, Richard, was just beginning to walk. "Your sweet Dick for the first time, stept this day," she delightedly informed Eliza Sadler, "and you cannot conceive a sweeter expression than When he [reaches my arms and] finds the danger over."[27] At two, William answered to "Bill" and was, Elizabeth fondly reported, "quite a Man, and very much improved."[28] She took pleasure in William's young-est half sisters, Harriet and Cecilia. Even Elizabeth's strong-willed first-born, Anna Maria, now "comes down every Morning after Breakfast with the clean hands and Frock."[29] Possessed of a tempestuous nature mingled with a desire to please, Anna Maria reminded Elizabeth of her own younger self. When the girl was still only three, Elizabeth wrote a New Year's message urging her to improve her moral character: "The blessings and attentions of the tenderest Parents and most affectionate friends are constantly yours, and by your conduct you will confer the gratification of our fondest wishes, or inflict the most bitter disappoint-ment." "In you," she continued, "I view the Friend, the Companion, and Consolation of my future years."[30]

Elizabeth's message hints at an unspoken truth: as William's con-sumption worsened, she feared her "future years" would not include her husband. More and more, happy moments gave way to foreboding. "How much we have both to fear," she wrote after one lovely family afternoon, "is terrible to think of."[31] Elizabeth told Rebecca—whose own coughing worried her—that she had "determined never again to allow myself the enjoyment of any affection beyond the bounds of *mod-eration.*" But Elizabeth's theory outstripped her practice, and she loved her family beyond the bounds of caution. When the French merchant Nicholas Olive praised her as a "Specimen of Philosophy," she observed to her father that her stoic mien was "dearly earned."[32] In a letter to Julia, she was more straightforward. Only "apathy" (a term from stoic philosophy connoting indifference to all things) could defeat the ties of nature, and apathy was "a blessing I fear I never shall attain."[33]

As she beat back fear and bitterness, Elizabeth began to entertain an idea akin to that which had prompted Voltaire's satire in *Candide:* all events, even the most painful, reflected the workings of providence. Two of her most valued confidantes, Richard Bayley and Julia Scott, had no patience for such thinking, and it had recently seemed laughable to Elizabeth as well. But she was discovering in Christian texts the peace she had long pursued; ugliness was not to be merrily welcomed (she had not become Voltaire's Pangloss), but perhaps it could be accepted as part of a larger, invisible beauty. "I have passed one of the most Elegant Evenings of my life," she wrote her father in early February of 1799. "Part of my Family are asleep and part abroad—I have been reading of the 'High and lofty One who inhabits Eternity.'" (That was a quote from the Book of Isaiah, though Bayley was unlikely to recognize it.) "How the world lessens and recedes," Elizabeth went on, "how calm and peaceable are hours spent in such Solicitude."[34] With Julia, Elizabeth was as usual direct. Asking her friend not to dismiss her as a "Preacher or Moralizer," she presented Christian worship as a cure for what ailed them both. "From experience I can declare that it will produce the most Peaceful sensations and most perfect enjoyment of which the Heart is capable."[35]

Elizabeth's increasingly rapt reading of the Bible and Christian sermons placed her in good company. The cosmopolitan inquiry and deism of the immediate post-Revolutionary era were fading, and Christian worship—vibrant and multiform—was on the rise.[36] As Americans listened to charismatic preachers and read the religious tracts printing presses turned out in ever-growing numbers, they repudiated authors such as Voltaire as prophets of political disorder and atheism. Thomas Paine's two-part attack on revelation and institutional religion, *The Age of Reason,* was greeted with enthusiasm when published in the early 1790s; by 1802, Thomas Jefferson urged him not to publish a third part for fear of reprisals. Yet neither Elizabeth's deepening Christianity nor her rejection of Voltairean satire drove out her interest in contemporary philosophy. She read and reread Jean Jacques Rousseau's *Emile,* which Eliza Sadler had recommended to her. "Your JJ," she told Sadler, "has awakened many ideas which have long since been at rest, indeed he is the writer I shall always refer to in a season of sorrow for he makes me forget myself whilst reading, but leaves the most consoling impression on every thought." Part novel and part philosophical treatise, *Emile* gave eloquent voice to the informal stoicism Elizabeth cultivated, but that was not its deepest appeal. She sometimes felt as if the responsibilities of motherhood and wifehood left her "clogged and shackled, without the power of one free act of the Will, in a narrow path from which I never expect to step until I arrive on that blest shore 'where weary travelers rest.'" *Emile* offered an escape into thought, and what *Emile* provoked Elizabeth to think about was faith. In a section entitled "Profession of Faith of a Savoyard Vicar," Rousseau portrays a Catholic priest who questioned each aspect of his faith in order to separate the essential from the inessential. The man was left with a divinity in whom he unquestionably believed but whose attributes he found unknowable. Rather than producing a chilly and remote God, this reasoned discernment filled Rousseau's vicar with a sense of God's immanence. "I perceive the deity in all his works, I feel him within me, and behold him in every object around me."[37] Elizabeth was enraptured. "Every half hour I can catch goes to Emilius—," she wrote Sadler, "three volumes I have read with delight and were I to express half my thoughts about it particularly respecting his religious Ideas I should lose that circumspection I have so long limited myself to and be EAB"—Elizabeth Ann Bayley—"instead of EAS."[38]

Decades later, Elizabeth and her confessor, Simon Bruté, shivered at Elizabeth's fascination with *Emile*. After her death, Father Bruté penned a pious annotation to a letter in which she praised "dear JJ." "O read at the end," the priest wrote, drawing attention to the passage, "o providential 1799–1805–1821." The dates were meant to plot the narrative of Elizabeth's deliverance: a young woman immersed in Rousseauvian infidelity in 1799, a Catholic convert in 1805, a soul arrived safely into the arms of the Lord in 1821. Elizabeth had come to understand her own story, lacking only the date of death, in the same way. But the Elizabeth Seton of 1799—still EAB as well as EAS—would have laughed at the thought that reading Rousseau put her soul at risk. The Savoyard vicar stirred a remembrance of her once overwhelming sense of God's presence. *Emile* sparked the hope of finding her way back to God and to her own buried self. Drawing on the diversity of her upbringing and her city, Elizabeth was piecing together a spiritual life made of Christian teachings, stoicism, a dash of scientific method, and a large helping of contemporary French philosophy. What she came to see as a deliverance—1799–1805–1821—felt then like a discovery.

SINKING

Throughout 1799, Elizabeth Seton drew on her full store of intellectual and spiritual resources. Summer brought another fever season: "My mind is in a state of anxiety and distress," she told Rebecca, "which does not admit of any calculation respecting the enjoyment of this Life—in one short week sisters, friends, and the whole world may be nothing to me."[39]

William worried for his business (another brig fell victim to privateers despite his paying to have it armed), and Thomas Masters again decamped for the countryside.[40] This time William did not ask his wife to stay in the city and serve as his amanuensis, but Elizabeth's summer respite brought little peace. William's visits revealed his frailty, and his mental state was as delicate as his physical health. "You know how extremely timid he is," Rebecca told Elizabeth, "his feeling the least ill would alarm him beyond any thing."[41] Even that fall, when the fever season had passed and the family was reunited at Stone Street, Elizabeth could not set aside her worries. "If he does not [survive]," she wrote to Rebecca, then tending her brother's children in Baltimore, "the greatest probability is that you and I will never meet again, for never can I survive the scene."[42]

As William grew more fragile, Elizabeth, once his "little girl," became his protector. With Julia Scott she allowed herself moments of rueful humor. Asking her widowed friend whether she might marry again, Elizabeth declared that "the very best of these men (one is writing opposite to me) are so unruly and perplexing that nothing should induce a reasonable Woman to wear the Chains of two of them, and that is the plain English of Matrimony, Julia."[43] Matrimony spoke in other languages, as well, though, and the same letter contained a casually intimate bit of news: Elizabeth was pregnant for a fourth time.[44]

This pregnancy, like her third, offered Elizabeth no shield from worry and work. New York's merchants reeled from the combined effects of privateering and a new Spanish decree that closed the fading empire's colonial ports to all but their own vessels. Thomas Masters, alert as ever to the call of self-preservation, announced that he had found a new position in Philadelphia and would not return to Seton & Maitland.[45] In December fell the sharpest blow yet: Seton's London associates suffered the loss of a ship, this one carrying coin. A cargo literally worth its weight in gold had sunk to the bottom of the sea. The London house could not sustain the loss and announced that it would no longer honor its debts. To "stop payment" in this way was to send a shock down the whole length of the sinuous chain of credit linking merchant to merchant and country to country. William Magee Seton's business associates drew back in alarm, no longer able, as Masters had recently written of another merchant's failure, to "feel that confidence in each other which is so necessary in business."[46]

As Seton & Maitland reeled, Elizabeth laid the trouble at the feet of her husband's London associates. "No part of the blame is attached to him," she insisted to Rebecca.[47] Elizabeth was eager to exonerate her husband because she, like many others, thought of financial ruin as a personal failing, even a sin. Although merchants such as the Setons and their friends accepted debt as a practical necessity—it was the necessary companion to credit—it bore a tint of recklessness or impropriety. When debts could not be paid, that tinge turned to stain. The consequences of this moralistic view of debt were more than rhetorical: in 1799, those who could not pay their debts still faced indefinite confinement. William Duer had died in debtors' prison that very year, his fate William's nightmare. "You know Willy's disposition," Elizabeth told Rebecca as her husband's finances grew ever more precarious, "sometimes he says he will work it out, at others Nothing but State prison and Poverty."[48]

The highly personal nature of the era's merchant life meant that William's creditors were in the main his relatives and friends, and although that intimacy offered a degree of protection, it also magnified the shame. He knew that he must figure out his complicated account books and pay at least some of his debts; as Elizabeth put it, "his personal honor and the satisfaction of his friends" depended on it. Yet the specter of ruin threatened to paralyze him. "My Seton is in a distress of mind scarcely to be imagined," she told Julia.[49]

Elizabeth's insistence that William had had no warning of impending failure is directly contradicted by the evidence of his accounts, which show mounting loans and losses throughout 1799.[50] Elizabeth had not seen those accounts: William may have decided not to use her as his clerk after Masters's departure because he wanted to hide the fragility of Seton & Maitland. If, as seems likely, she had nonetheless gleaned that all was not well in the commercial world, Elizabeth set that knowledge aside. She also refused to contemplate what the family would suffer if Seton & Maitland failed. Instead, she cultivated peaceful resignation and found solace in worshipping the kind of abstract but benevolent divinity Rousseau's Savoyard vicar described. "Sitting on a little Bench before the fire," she wrote one day on a fragment of paper, "the head resting on the hand, the Body perfectly easy, the Eyes closed, the mind serene contemplating, and tracing boundless Mercy and the source of all excellence and Perfection."[51]

Amid calamities large and small, Elizabeth drained her mind of words and images until she felt only God. "How pure the enjoyment and sweet the transition of every thought—," she wrote, "the soul expands all Earthly interests recede." As her family faced ruin and her husband shuddered with fear, the next life seemed more real than the current one. "Might not these mortal bonds," she mused, "be gently severed, loosed more easily than untying the fastening of a fine thread, at this moment without any perceptible change, to find the Soul at Liberty." Elizabeth did not desperately wish to die, but she found herself uninterested in life, her whole self fixed on "boundless Mercy." As she continued writing, she turned to more conventionally Christian language, God becoming "my Father-Friend" and her prayer becoming one for aid. Still, she did not ask for an end to William's commercial difficulties nor for the restoration of his health. She prayed only to continue in the selfless serenity she had just experienced. "Preserve me but this Heavenly peace," she wrote, "continue to me this priviledge beyond all mortal computation, of resting in Thee, and adoring Thee . . . for this alone I implore."[52]

In 1814, Simon Bruté annotated this passage in a way that marks it as more evidence of her ignorance during these years. "1814 How different," he wrote, "O praise and Eternal Gratitude!—help to love and praise you who have all in your own hands."[53] Elizabeth's description of her relaxed posture and her sense of impersonal communion with God is indeed "different" from the way she would learn to pray as a Catholic. Yet this fragment reveals Elizabeth working to reduce herself to a vessel of God's love. That quest, as ambitious as it was self-denying, underlay her conversion to Catholicism and all that followed.

Moments for contemplative prayer were rare and precious in those anxious weeks. No longer able to hide Seton & Maitland's vulnerability, William once again turned Elizabeth into his amanuensis. "For one entire week we wrote till one and two in the morning," she wearily informed Rebecca.[54] She did not allow herself to voice or even to feel criticism of her husband, but she worried that William's lack of self-mastery would strip her of her own. "To see my William's struggles and hear his constant reflections on what is to become of *us* and that us such a number," she wrote to Rebecca, "at times courage flies."[55]

Throughout the crisis, family friend Abraham Ogden, always a favorite of Elizabeth, offered what assistance he could. "A. Ogden has been more than ten Brothers to my William," Elizabeth observed gratefully. The comparison may have been more pointed than she cared to admit: in the same letter, she observed that William's actual brother, James, "has bought a handsome three story house in Greenwich Street, so thank heaven we are not all sinking." While James prepared to move to grander quarters, William vowed to his pregnant wife that he would if necessary sell all the family's possessions. Fighting off despair, she turned to pious effect a phrase her father had used in secular fashion, the year before. "We must look up," she wrote, adding, "and trust to the best director."[56]

Richard Bayley had little interest in "the best director," but he knew his daughter was suffering and tried to help. He paid off some of the couple's household debts and, equally important, distracted his daughter with philosophical questions. Elizabeth was delighted to think rather than brood. "My Father's redoubled attentions and affection keep my mind more anxious to please him than to attend to itself," she wrote. In February of 1800, with the wolf at the door, Elizabeth questioned her father about the purpose of thinking about misfortune. Bayley was happy to take the question on, although not in the way Elizabeth expected. "What is the purpose of it, a curious question truly," he wrote. "Shall we be compelled to assign the correct motive to every impulse of the mind, to every expression of a heart that feels?" "Calculations, cautions, intentions are all entitled to their place," Bayley continued, but he himself chose not to be guided by them. "The most heartfelt pleasure I have ever experienced," he told the daughter whose family faced ruin, "came from incautious commitment, and I would not be deprived of the result of such accidental commitment, for all the exclusive enjoyments I have derived from entering into contracts, or all the good bargains I was made."[57]

As advice went, it wasn't much use. Elizabeth was guardian to eight children and the loyal wife of a man whose body and finances were failing. She could no more abandon caution than she could fly, and she had good reason to rue the very thought of "accidental commitments." Yet she loved her father's letter. Bayley wrote his daughter as one unconventional mind to another, and although his words reminded her of the constraints under which she lived, they also reminded her that she was more than the sum of them. "You did not consider in your reflections or calculations," she gently teased him, "that you were indulging one of the most incorrigible failings of your Daughter": her tendency to unfettered intellectual inquiry. She had, she reminded him, "no right to the privilege as a Woman, pardonable [though] the active unrestrained mind of man may be in his errors." Content to mark this unfairness without lamenting it, Elizabeth went on to explain that since she could neither subdue her will nor change the circumstances of her life, she was learning to ignore both. "Nature's characters can never be erased," she told her father. "The next best choice is to keep cool and be satisfied with events."[58]

As she wrote her father, Elizabeth may have reflected on the distance between the convention of woman's weakness and the reality of her life. Helpmate to her husband and intellectual companion to her father, she also found the energy to take a lively interest in the troubles of her friends. When Catherine Dupleix endured some unexplained crisis—muffled descriptions suggest a struggle with depression or laudanum—Elizabeth tended her solicitously, worrying only that "we are too much inclined when together to indulge sympathy."[59] She also continued to participate in Isabella Graham's benevolent society, determined not to let her own ill luck blind her to the greater misfortunes of others. Elizabeth's ability to disregard her own troubles was impressive—and she was herself impressed. Although modest about her intelligence and her beauty, she did not hesitate to draw attention to her hard-won equanimity. "I have never expressed suffering when I have the choice of Silence," she told Julia."[60] Elizabeth's confidence in her own serenity, like her intellectual curiosity, met its match in her father. "What would afford the most inconsolable affliction to another person," Bayley wrote, "that which would afford to most people an aching heart, is to me a matter of amusement. Steady temper go on, and hail to the period when I will be at rest."[61] Father and daughter believed they sacrificed themselves for a greater good, civic in Richard's case, familial in Elizabeth's. Neither saw anything wrong in claiming a little credit for it. "It is easy for me," Elizabeth wrote to Rebecca, "for I never have thought of my own comforts when there was any other persons depending."[62]

THE LIMITS

Spring came and Seton & Maitland's prospects grew even gloomier. No one accepted William's "bills"—written promises to provide cash on demand—as payment, and his signature on others' bills now proved a taint. His ability to trade his way out of ruin was slipping away. New York newspapers that in 1799 bore 182 advertisements from Seton & Maitland in 1800 bore only seven.[63] As his prospects dimmed, William unashamedly leaned on his wife's equanimity and labor. "I am most truly his all," Elizabeth told Julia.[64]

In spring of that desperate year, there arrived a stroke of dark good luck: Congress passed the nation's first federal bankruptcy statute. Across the 1790s, more and more elite Americans involved themselves in complicated financial transactions, and the number of those who failed owing large sums of money—often to people who, as a result, faced ruin themselves—grew. Some still saw financial failure as moral failure and opposed any law that tacitly acknowledged debt had become essential to American life. But political will to contain the consequences of failure grew. In April of 1800, as Seton & Maitland teetered on the brink, Congress passed the Bankruptcy Act by one vote. Designed to protect the once-wealthy, the act required those seeking its protections to have debts of at least $2,000. William unquestionably qualified. If he were declared a bankrupt under its provisions, a commission would be established to evaluate his assets and debts. If two-thirds of his creditors (by number and by amount of debt) agreed, William would be immune from the threat of prison, left free to try to pay off the creditors who had registered under the act's provisions.[65] If he placed himself under the protection of the new Bankrupcy Act, William's would be a grim fate. But it would not be William Duer's.

When news of the act spread, imprisoned debtors in New York City raised glasses in an amazed toast. Most did not meet the requirements of the new law, but they cheered its spirit. The merchants whom the act protected hailed it more soberly—at least in public—but with equal sincerity. A congressional representative named Robert Goodloe Harper explained the act's usefulness in a letter reprinted in New York's newspapers. "To a trading people," Harper wrote, "a bankrupt law is highly beneficial, if not absolutely necessary."[66] William could not quite believe the law's promise. "He has been talking to me this morning," Elizabeth confided to Rebecca in the summer of 1800, "of *the limits*"—meaning debtors' prison—"in next October."[67] But as of April 4, 1800, luck and Christianity were not the Setons' only resources. The commercial economy and its allies in Congress offered their own tender mercies.

In June came a simpler piece of good fortune: Elizabeth gave birth to their fourth child, a daughter whom the couple named Catherine Charlton, after Elizabeth's long-lost mother. William announced the birth to Julia Scott with a grace that neither consumption nor impending ruin had defeated. "At the dawn of the day your little friend presented us with another Daughter," he wrote, "if possible more lovely than the first, but as you are acquainted with my sentiments with respect to what is mine, I will forbear all description at present."[68]

Catherine was a peaceful baby and like all the Seton children instantly received several nicknames—Kate, Kit, and Queen of Quiet among them. Elizabeth cultivated the serenity her "little cherub" effortlessly possessed. "Peace—Peace—Peace," she wrote Rebecca just before Catherine's birth, exhorting her sister-in-law and herself to achieve it. "If peace is your companion," she told Sadler a few weeks later, "the whole beautiful universe can bestow nothing more precious." "May Peace," Elizabeth wrote to Catherine Dupleix, "be yours my own Darling."[69]

When she wrote "Dear Remembrances" decades later, Elizabeth recalled that as a young wife she'd found it "impossible" to believe she could have a happy home and "Heaven too." The feeling that she must choose between happiness and heaven appears clearly in this summer of 1800. "We are not always to have what we like best in this world, thank Heaven!" she wrote Rebecca, "for if we had how soon we should forget the *other*, the place of endless peace."[70] A few days later, she elaborated on her view. "[You] will find that it is the happiest beings who are most apt to become careless of Religion and forgetful of their God."[71] Just a few years earlier, Elizabeth had written to Eliza Sadler that "Cheerfulness and harmony" were the purposes of religion. Now cheerfulness was a hazard, and religion was not the means to an end but an end in itself.

Seton & Maitland now seemed less like a thriving enterprise than a carcass circled by hungry dogs. Skirmishes broke out among its anxious band of creditors, and only the Bankruptcy Act offered William and his creditors hope of redemption. Elizabeth understood her husband's situation perfectly. "Julia Julia," she wrote, "when you come how will it be with us, for the *House* is to be declared Bankrupt . . . or Seton must go to Prison."[72] In December, out of credit and out of time, William chose bankruptcy over ruin.

Much had changed since the days seven years earlier, when Elizabeth gloried in living as William's sheltered little girl. "I have this last week watched and attended the street door to keep out the Sheriff's Officers with as cheerful a Countenance as ever you saw me with," she wrote Julia. Years of controlling her emotions served her well. "I have cause to sigh and weep from Monday to Saturday," she declared. "And yet viewing this World but as the passage to my Home it all goes by."[73]

The first meeting of William's bankruptcy commission and creditors took place the day after Christmas. Under other circumstances, they might have made a dinner party. In addition to all the friends and relatives present, one of the commissioners, John B. Church, was married to the sister of Alexander Hamilton's wife; the elder William had for years helped to manage his finances. Now, Church oversaw the younger Seton's unraveling. After taking the key to William's countinghouse, he and the other commissioners explained that the merchant must lay bare all his debts and assets. The ritual of bankruptcy included one more intimate humiliation: the inventorying of the Seton family's possessions.

Nothing more poignantly expresses what Elizabeth called "the changes of the last few years in my lot" than this inventory. By the alchemy of the Bankruptcy Act it transformed evidence of the Setons' wealth—pictures, handkerchiefs, linen shirts, silver—into markers of their loss.[74] Elizabeth countered with her own hopeful effort, deciding to write out the inventory herself in a bold clear hand. "I have given up my list to the Comissioners of bankruptcy of all we possess," she told Julia, "even to our and the children's clothing."[75] She headed the letter to Julia, "Stone Street (for the last time)," but she did not regret the losses. Law might deem it a confiscation; Elizabeth considered it a renunciation. That dark December, she inventoried something still in her possession. "I have," she told Julia, "as bright a hope and a faith as strong as ever animated a mortal."[76]

5

KNOT OF OAK

THE SETONS PUT THE Stone Street house up for sale, detailing for potential buyers its kitchen and wine cellar and the lovely fireplaces that Elizabeth confessed to her father she would miss. The newspapers carrying the advertisement also bore notices from the court-appointed assignees of William's bankruptcy; if anyone in the Setons' world had been unaware of their troubles, they were ignorant no longer.[1] Throughout the winter, William's creditors made their way through Manhattan's narrow, icy streets to present their claims to the commission, while William tried to present a clear accounting of all that he owed and all that he had any hope of earning. His book creditors—those with the best-documented claims on Seton & Maitland's assets—presented daunting sums: Richard Curson, William's grandfather, claimed $7,000; his brother James, the accounting muddled by sibling loyalty and anger, "about 6500"; Richard Bayley, who had done what he could to pay off the family's debts to tradespeople, $254.83. McTavish & Frobisher, the firm whose agent had been so frustrated by William's hesitancy, had reason to rue that their deal was ever done: they were the largest creditor in the house's books, owed $11,095.[2] William himself was owed money, but much of that came under the category—literally, a column in his accounts—of "bad, dubious debts." Many of those were sums from merchants flailing like William himself amid lost ships and useless promises to pay.

The pages of the Seton bankruptcy file are a study in bleakness, but one page is bleaker than most. It contains a list in William's hand of the contents of his storehouse, compiled so that every last scrap of property might be shown to his creditors. Twenty years earlier, his father had rebuilt his merchant life after the Revolution by piecing together odd cargoes. Like his father's old advertisements, William's description of his storehouse is a portrait of randomness, but rather than the scattered seeds of a growing enterprise, it offers up the scattered bones of a lost one. "11 busts of Washington and Franklin," reads the list of items held for Filippo Filicchi, "4 pieces of black lace." "Part of a box of feathers."[3]

As awful as it was, though, it did not always seem all that bad. Elizabeth had feared ruin for months and William for much longer. Now the calamity had arrived and it had not dragged the family under. William was allowed to trade in hopes of bringing in money that might satisfy his creditors. James Farquhar disapproved of failure—he'd badgered William's father after the Revolution and more recently driven a New Yorker named James Pintard to debtors' prison in New Jersey.[4] Yet in the end, no one in the Setons' circle treated the couple unkindly. New York families far more illustrious than they had faced dramatic reversals over the years, and the Setons' associates understood just how easy it was to falter. Even the sale of Stone Street did not exile them from gentility: the family moved to 8 State Street, an elegant brick home on the Battery that had until very recently been occupied by Mary Fitch. It is unlikely that Richard Bayley's old friend had happened to move out just when the Setons were dispossessed.[5] Instead, Mama Fitch helped break Elizabeth's fall, despite the fact that she herself had fallen from the younger woman's favor.

The family could not afford much domestic help—"I have but one Nurse for my four children," Elizabeth observed, in a complaint that suggests the privilege to which she'd grown accustomed—and the days in which William could unthinkingly purchase the shirts and handkerchiefs that filled out the Setons' household inventory were gone.[6] Elizabeth dwelled on what remained. Harriet Seton had been sent off to school like her older siblings before her, but Elizabeth enjoyed teaching her own children and Cecilia their lessons, and she continued to serve as a manager of the poor widows' society, happy to help women facing the penury that she and her children had so far escaped.[7] By rising early and going to bed late, she also managed to serve as informal clerk to her husband. Labor freed her from rumination. "I rise up early and late take rest,'" she told Julia, turning the words of Psalm 127 to her own purposes, "never before 12, and oftener one. Such is the allotment and as everybody has their *Pride* of some sort, I cannot deny that this is mine."[8]

William shared her diligence, putting together cargoes and deals and traveling to Philadelphia and Baltimore in search of credit and allies. His grandfather Curson remained loyal, and others were sympathetic too: visiting Baltimore the summer after his bankruptcy, William was feted at the elegant brick home of Margaret Carroll, widow to a member of the clan that had produced Bishop John Carroll and Charles Carroll of Carrollton. William was sure that anyone who blamed him for his bankruptcy was a fool—it "only shows . . . the man to be an idiot and influenced by passion," he wrote hotly of one critic—but he was unsure about most other things. "I shall enter on nothing decisive until I see you yourself with my friends at N[ew] Y[or]k," he wrote his wife.[9]

Elizabeth was still, as she'd once told Julia, William's "all." His courage sometimes thinned to an anxious bravado, but hers never did; William took to calling her his "Knot of Oak." When he mused aloud about what his prospects might be if he were unencumbered by a family and able to make "a voyage to the East India," Elizabeth took no offense (although when she recounted the episode to Julia, she noted wryly that her friend might be well advised to remain single, since "the consequences" of union could turn out "so different from our calculations").[10] Mordant observations aside, Elizabeth continued to delight in her husband. The couple found moments to read Shakespeare together as well as to ponder the fate of Seton & Maitland, and Elizabeth still loved any day spent, as she once put it, with "Peace and Willy."[11] "*All* the scene changes when he is here," she told her sister-in-law Rebecca, "*Countenances*, everything wears the Smile."[12] After seven years of marriage, Elizabeth still urgently loved her husband. "Is it possible that I am not to see you again for so long a time?" she wrote as he embarked on a business trip. "Dear Dear William farewell."[13]

Elizabeth treasured her happy marriage for any number of reasons, among them the fact that in her father's household she'd seen the alternative. Not long after William's bankruptcy, she witnessed the chaotic dissolution of another union. William's business associate and brother-in-law James Maitland had, like William, declared bankruptcy. Far less diligent than William ("not a worthy," was Elizabeth's terse assessment),

Maitland quickly fell afoul of the act's requirements, and one day Rebecca brought startling news: Maitland had been sent to debtors' prison. Although he managed to extricate himself, he had no intention of resuming his responsibilities as a merchant or husband. The St. Andrew's Society proudly records the accomplishments of members in its *Biographical Register;* of James Maitland it offers only this laconic note: after his 1801 "reverses," he "disappeared to parts unknown, leaving his family to be taken care of by relatives and friends."[14]

James Seton, William's younger brother who had recently purchased a new home, offered Eliza Seton Maitland and her children no help. Nor did Jack. Another Seton brother, Henry, was that summer himself threatening to become a deadweight: the family had used their social connections to secure him a naval appointment, but Henry proved such a wastrel that the navy released him during the first reduction of force following the Quasi War's end.[15] The bankrupt William knew that if his sister and her children were to have help, he must provide it. "My William is obliged to supply [them] from our own store room, and every day marketing," Elizabeth told Julia. "No other part of the family will keep them from starving, nor even in fire wood."[16]

It was the kind of observation Elizabeth shared with Julia but kept from others; the friend she'd once called a "vain shadow" had become a true confidante. So had William's oldest half sister, Rebecca. Now in her late teens, the young woman loved her family but recognized their flaws, and Elizabeth was relieved to hide nothing from her. She also relied on Richard Bayley's company. The needy adoration of her adolescent years having long since mellowed, Elizabeth understood both that her father took "little pains to show" his affections and that he felt them deeply.[17] To her satisfaction, there were now a few people on whom Bayley did shower love: his grandchildren. "Little Kit . . . doats on her Grandfather, dances even at the sound of his voice and when he takes her in his arms," Elizabeth told Sadler, "looks as—her *Mother* would wish to look."[18]

Richard Bayley, Rebecca Seton, Julia Scott, Eliza Sadler: each had for years offered Elizabeth Seton companionship, and each continued, amid the disruptions of the bankruptcy, to do so. There was also someone new. In the same month that William was declared a bankrupt, a man entered Elizabeth's life and quickly became a spiritual companion of a kind she had never known. His name was John Henry Hobart, and he was the controversial assistant rector at Manhattan's Trinity Church.

A year younger than Elizabeth, Hobart possessed an upbringing and temperament that marked him as kindred. The well-educated son of a merchant, he had married the daughter of a Loyalist and like Elizabeth had known sorrow early: his father died when Hobart was just two, leaving the boy to a loving but pinched childhood in the care of an anxious mother. As a teenager, Hobart had lost close friends to Philadelphia's terrible yellow fever epidemics, and like Elizabeth, he associated love with pain. "It seems as if I love with tenderness only to be made miserable by the loss of those I love," Hobart wrote his sister after one friend's death. He left no account of a crisis such as Elizabeth's night of the little bottle, but Hobart, too, possessed a melancholic temperament that he strove to conceal. "My mind . . . has generally been so depressed that I have not had the resolution to take up my pen," he confessed to a friend not long after his arrival at Trinity.[19]

Institutional religion had never been the animating force of Elizabeth's spiritual life. That changed after Hobart's arrival. Sitting in her pew at Trinity, she saw an unprepossessing young man—"middling size, sallow complexion, features somewhat irregular, a countenance obscured in its expression by the use of glasses to correct the deficiency of short sight," reads a contemporary description—who gave sermons alight with spiritual passion.[20] Although traditionalists accused the young minister of "enthusiasm and extravagance," Elizabeth tried never to miss a service that he celebrated, whether at Trinity or at St. Paul's chapel.[21]

Hobart admired the English romantic poets—managing later in his life to meet both Wordsworth and Coleridge—and his sermons appealed to Elizabeth by being both elegantly crafted and frankly emotional. There was charismatic preaching to be heard in the city's growing number of evangelical churches, but Hobart's expressive piety was accompanied by an insistence on the forms and hierarchies of the Episcopalian Church. Elizabeth, who had shown no interest in such teachings before, was moved by Hobart's confidence that the Episcopalian Church's prelates and liturgy connected believers to the pure religion of the apostles. His Church, he explained, bore the authority and truth of Christ's first gatherings.[22] More appealing still was Hobart's claim that by offering the sacrament of Communion, Episcopalian priests interceded with God on behalf of their sinning flocks. Hobart did not think that the rite transformed bread and wine into the literal body and blood of Christ; that was a barbarous superstition of the Catholics over on

Barclay Street. Instead he believed that by reverently commemorating Christ's sacrifice, the Episcopalian Church brought its members God's redemptive grace.[23]

Throughout her life, Elizabeth's desire to feel God's presence and her experience of institutional religion had existed independently. Listening to Hobart, she felt for the first time that these two elements of religious life could and should be united. Hobart's sermons combined a reverence for church structures with the promise of divine immanence, and intellectual confidence with a sorrowful awareness of sin. Rather than simply one man-made system among many for producing ethical behavior, Hobart's Episcopalianism was offered as a singular vessel of God's mercy. "Language cannot express the comfort the Peace the Hope," Elizabeth wrote.[24]

Richly satisfied by Hobart's offerings, she began to pity those who relied on what she now considered the thin broth of genteel Christianity. When Mary Wilkes, wife to one of William's longtime business associates, fell fatally ill, Elizabeth tended her generously but observed her critically. After she died "a hard and dreadful death," Elizabeth told Julia that she had learned she must herself be better prepared, lest she approach death "without the comfort and support of the Father." "My Soul shudders at the thought," she wrote. "*Think of it Julia*," Elizabeth urged, as she described the terror of facing death unprepared.[25]

Julia recognized the lesson and declined to learn it. She told her friend to stop contemplating death and keep her mind on the living, especially her children. Now it was Elizabeth who declined to heed advice. "You say you are a Mother," she responded. "I am a Mother too and am far from being so selfish as to wish to leave my Charge while my cares are required, but as the time of being called is so little known, and the prospect is so sweet a solace and so strong an assistance to the discharge of all our Duties—to keep it before me is the prayer of my Heart, and should be the prayer of yours."[26] The two women ignored each other's instructions as unhesitatingly as they shared their confidences.

Richard Bayley was impermeable to evangelization too, and there Elizabeth did not even try. Her pursuit of truth led her to read works of Christian devotion, her father's to read scientific tracts. That's all there was to it. Father "says I am such a hum-drum," Elizabeth once told Rebecca, entirely unfazed.[27] But when her husband continued to show only a polite interest in Christian teachings, Elizabeth was less sanguine. William lacked the internal resources her father possessed, and she believed only a deeper Christian faith could sustain him through bankruptcy and ill health. Yet she did not press, instead quietly hoping he would one day feel differently. "Willy did not understand," she observed after describing her own joy in a Hobart sermon. "That happy hour is yet to come."[28]

Elizabeth did find some who were willing to join her. Catherine Dupleix, often beset by troubles real and imagined, listened eagerly to Elizabeth's descriptions of God's peace. Eliza Sadler had long mixed a taste for philosophy with a more conventional piety, and she approved of Elizabeth's burgeoning interest in Episcopalianism. It was William's half sister Rebecca, however, who proved Elizabeth's most whole-hearted spiritual companion. "There is no distance for Souls," Elizabeth told her young sister-in-law, "and mine has surely been with yours most faithfully."[29] The two read and prayed together and so craved the sacrament of Communion that some Sundays they sought it out at the city's Episcopalian chapels as well as at Trinity itself.[30] Rebecca felt none of Julia's disapproval toward Elizabeth's longing for heaven, and Elizabeth confided in her unreservedly. "Oh Rebecca if I dared to wish, how gladly would I drink the cup," she told her sister-in-law, adding reluctantly, "but my God knows best."[31] Only twenty-one, Rebecca understood weariness. The cough and fatigue that plagued her grew more enfeebling by the year, and she spent her days caring for other people's children, whether her brother Jack's in Baltimore or Elizabeth's in New York. Heaven seemed a refuge to her no less than to Elizabeth, and when she attended services, discussed sermons, and read Christian texts with Elizabeth, she felt solace and inspiration. Rebecca also felt the rare pleasure of pursuing an interest that was, though shared, her own.

QUARANTINE

Elizabeth Seton's contemplation of death was not unique to her; mortality was the soil from which theologies and philosophies had always grown, and in the eighteenth century death remained as common as dirt. Women sickened and died in childbirth; men slumped home from work at the docks yellowing with a fatal fever; hearts failed, cancers grew, horses threw riders, and wounds suppurated. The possibility of death lay everywhere, whether one longed for it or feared it, so why not put it to use? Such was already Elizabeth's view when, in the summer after William's bankruptcy, she and her children made their country home at the city's new quarantine station.

As New York's health officer, Richard Bayley had taken up residence at the quarantine on Staten Island, living in the house built for him by the state, the house to which he had refused to bring Charlotte and their children. In June, Elizabeth and her own children joined him, happy to have a rent-free summer home and undaunted by the station's grim purpose. Still desperately trying to revive the merchant house, William remained in the city and made the short trip by boat when he could. During visits to the island, he stood watching the vessels sailing into New York's harbor, literally waiting for his ships to come in.[32]

At summer's start, Elizabeth's father spent his time examining cargoes and certifying that ships posed no threat to public health. Then, in late June, a ship from Ireland arrived laden with desperately ill men, women, and children. Bayley diagnosed them with ship's fever, an illness we now call typhus. Elizabeth and her children had happily roamed the grounds of the station. Now Bayley feared exposing them to a disease whose transmission he did not understand and that he could not cure (only in the early twentieth century was it discovered that typhus is carried by lice, and only after the development of antibiotics was it effectively treated). "We are not suffered to go further than the Gate," Elizabeth wrote Julia, and from that remove she witnessed the passengers' agonies and her father's unstinting efforts to treat them.[33] "The scenes of misery here are past all description," she told Rebecca. "There are ten large tents and other buildings fitting up as fast as ½ dozen Boatmen, and all hands, spurred up continually by my Poor Father can do them."[34] Death lay in all directions.

Bayley worked tirelessly to change the passengers' fate or at least improve their odds. Had Isabella Graham traveled to the quarantine station, she, like Bayley, would have been moved to action, perhaps raising money for the passengers or organizing reading lessons for the children. Elizabeth was stirred instead to contemplation. Her developing Christian ethos partook of the ancient tradition of memento mori—remember death—in which the world is a place to be endured rather than remade. Having tutored herself to bear her own misfortunes stoically, she proved placid in the face of others' suffering. "To me who possesses a frame of fibers strong and nerves well strung," she wrote Julia, the dying Irish were "but a passing scene of Natures Sufferings which when closed will lead to happier scenes."[35] Had she been challenged over the coolness of her response, Elizabeth might have pointed to the fact that the immigrants also seemed to accept their fate and that she admired them for it. The belief that everything that happened was somehow ordained by God was not absurd but wise. "Come what will, *'He is above'* therefore it must work for good," she insisted.[36]

June came to an end, and so did the typhus outbreak. The quarantine station had made literal Elizabeth's sense of the world as a theater of suffering, yet within its ambit she felt more lighthearted than she had in years. Her children spent so much time outside that Kit's brown hair bleached red in the sun, and Elizabeth thrilled to the toddler's joy. "She held up her little hands with such delight at the beautiful sky last Evening that I could have ate her up," she told Rebecca.[37] When the inevitable rubs of running a household were compounded by the challenges posed by living at a quarantine station, Elizabeth only laughed. Asking Sadler's help in finding a "decent woman" to serve as cook, she conceded drily that "a really decent one would hardly come to our Quarantine."[38] Occasionally Elizabeth even managed a young mother's version of solitude. "Father went to bed," she wrote one night in mid-July. "Seton to Vanduzurs—the Boys and Anna to walk and Kit to the cradle." It was, she wrote contentedly, *"my* hour."[39]

Another disease-ridden ship could arrive any day, and her husband's health and business continued to decline, but the twenty-six-year-old Elizabeth was serene. "Everything goes on so peaceably and with so much regularity, and particularly with respect to the *little* ones," she told Rebecca, "that if I could find a *Home* this side the blue-Vault, I should only wish for you and my Willy and set down without a sigh."[40] Finding a home had been Elizabeth's quest in childhood and her delight as a new bride. Now, she believed, in the words of a verse from Hebrews, that this world was not her home. That meant she could not lose it.

Sure that only Christian faith brought peace, Elizabeth urged her meek sister-in-law to skip family events rather than miss Sunday Communion. "It can never be a breach of civility, or seem unkind even to a sister of the dearest friend," she told Rebecca, "if you say it with the firmness of one who has been at *his* table."[41] Rebecca knew that this was advice Elizabeth gave but did not take: despite her love of Hobart's sermons, she often missed Sunday services to stay home with William. Elizabeth lamented her inconsistency. "Why should any one be more earnest in prevailing with me for a trifle or a thing of no consequence in itself than *I*, in maintaining the thing I know to be right, and that touches the interests of my Souls peace?" she wondered.[42]

Elizabeth had no answer to the question of how to reconcile intimate obligations with spiritual duties, but she had a lot of company in the asking. During the revivals of the Second Great Awakening, those who were born again felt a spiritual urgency that separated them from friends and family. That division deepened when evangelicals' newfound beliefs led them to condemn activities their circle considered harmless amusements. One disappointed evangelical recorded his friends' complaint that he had "'overshot the mark.'" "We all ought to be good," the friends told him, "but surely there can be no harm in *innocent mirth,* such as dancing, drinking, and making merry."[43] Elizabeth did not urge asceticism on the worldly Seton and Bayley clans, but her growing belief that things she knew to be right, such as church attendance and earnest piety, mattered more than cheerfulness and harmony, subtly set her at odds.

When Methodists and Baptists alienated family with their passionate convictions, they found consolation in the vibrant fellowship of their new communities. But Elizabeth still worshipped at Trinity Church, drawn to Hobart but not to most of the parishioners, who seemed content with the kind of faith she no longer found meaningful. Her relationship with Rebecca was the kind of spiritual friendship through which Protestant women of the era sought to deepen their faith and improve their characters, but Elizabeth craved a wider arena in which to work. Once happy to allow each soul to find her own way, whether through attending balls or reading sermons, Elizabeth now urged Christian reading on others and coaxed Rebecca to do the same. Some, such as Eliza Seton Maitland, demurred, but when Catherine Dupleix expressed a wish to join in Elizabeth and Rebecca's fellowship, Elizabeth welcomed her. First, though, she evaluated Dupleix's request, as she and other members of the poor widows' society might have judged the worthiness of an applicant for aid. Confident of her own sincerity and authority, Elizabeth was creating an informal spiritual sisterhood with herself as leader and gatekeeper. It was an intimate devotional world, vibrating with intensity behind the veil of genteel Episcopalian society.[44]

ALL THE HORRORS

In late July, another ship bearing desperately sick immigrants arrived at the Staten Island quarantine station. "I cannot sleep," Elizabeth wrote Rebecca in Manhattan, "the Dying, and the Dead, possess my mind." Once again, she looked through the fence that divided her healthy family from the ill migrants. This time, she found it harder to abstract the misery into moral lessons. "Babys perishing at the empty Breast of the expiring Mother, and this is not fancy—but the scene that surrounds me." Still nursing her youngest, Elizabeth imagined offering the babies her own milk, "Kit's treasure." But that thought was a wish, not a plan, and it was again prayer to which Elizabeth felt called. "Rebecca," she explained to her sister-in-law, "they have a provider in Heaven who will smooth the pangs of the suffering innocent." On earth, they had Dr. Richard Bayley, who went from patient to ragged patient, hoping to soothe what he could not cure.[45]

One evening Elizabeth delighted in the high spirits her father showed despite his labors. Bayley marveled at "the different shades of the sun on the clover field before the door" and fed Kit from his spoon, demanding the child call him Papa before each bite. As the evening ended, he sang along while Elizabeth gaily played the piano. The next day, fever slipped through the fence. Looking out her window, Elizabeth was startled to see her energetic father sitting by a wharf, head in hands. She rushed a servant out with an umbrella and burst into tears when her father came back to the house in unmistakable distress. Helped into bed, Bayley sank into delirium. He had contracted typhus.[46]

Day after day, Elizabeth and Bayley's assistants, including a man identified only as "Young Bayley," who was likely enslaved, tried and failed to bring down the physician's fever and ease his suffering. Wracked with nausea and pain, Bayley writhed in bed, able to be still only when he held onto his daughter's arm. In moments when his mind cleared, he was tormented by his knowledge of what the fever would bring. "All the horrors are coming," he told Elizabeth, "I feel them all."[47]

Young Bayley carried out every treatment the ill physician proposed; his enslavement, if that was indeed his status, curbed neither his skill nor his generosity. All was in vain. "Neither opium or any remedy whatever could give him a moment's relief," Elizabeth later recalled, and he vomited everything he consumed. "Cover me warm," Bayley said. "I have covered many, poor little children." "I would cover you more," he told the daughter whom he'd always loved but not always tended, "but it can't always be as we would wish."[48]

On the night of August 16, Richard Bayley continued to struggle "in extreme pain," and Elizabeth realized that little Kit felt warm to the touch. Then her young son Dick began "vomiting violently." There was nothing to do but carry on. Elizabeth placed Richard on a mattress by her feet, nursed the feverish Kit, and counted her father's weakening pulse. As morning turned to afternoon, the children's frightening symptoms melted away. Richard Bayley never rallied. Elizabeth sought no deathbed declaration of faith from him, although she may have taken some comfort in the fact that he cried out in his agony, "May Christ Jesus have mercy on me." Nor did she see in his suffering a moral lesson, as she had at Mary Wilkes's deathbed. He was her father, and he was dying; there was no other meaning. She observed his final moments with a precision of which he would have approved. He died at half past two.[49]

Days of worry and exhaustion gave way to confusion and frustration. Elizabeth wanted her father buried in a churchyard, but victims of ship's fever were not to leave quarantine even in death. Just when it appeared that Richard Bayley must be laid to rest in the station's grounds, bargemen with whom he'd worked offered to row his body to a nearby town. No one else, including the sexton, would touch the body, so the boatmen and Young Bayley buried him. While a local minister performed a short service, "two wagons full of relatives and friends paid the last respect" from a distance.[50]

Richard Bayley's absences had shaped Elizabeth's childhood. His presence gave form to her adolescence and adulthood. She revered her father's intellect, understood and respected his controversial crusades, and gladly tolerated the self-absorption that formed the correlate to his benevolence. Bayley treasured his daughter's keen mind and forceful will and encouraged her to use them. Elizabeth knew that with his death a companionship had been extinguished, never to be replaced. As she had done when a child, she turned in her father's absence to God. Months after his death, she wrote to Julia Scott that her heart "very seldom can unburthen itself since Poor Father is gone except when humbled before Him who made it."[51]

Bayley was also mourned by the city he had so doggedly and controversially served. Newspapers praised him for his "promptness and vigour" in fulfilling the "very responsible and difficult" role of "physician of the Port of New-York." "He had that one quality, that passive courage, that more than Nemean hardihood of nerve, without which all others could but be of little avail, and which disease and death in their worst forms, could not appal or affright," one author wrote, comparing the physician to the Nemean lion, a mythical beast whose fur was like armor and claws sharper than swords. The obituary concluded with a gentler sentiment that Elizabeth wholeheartedly shared. "Light lie the earth on the ashes of his faults."[52]

Another shock followed on Bayley's death when his will was read. It was dated 1788 and left all his worldly goods to Charlotte. In the intervening years, Bayley had left his wife and insisted Elizabeth and Mary refuse even to see her; he'd doted on the Seton and Post grandchildren and watched Elizabeth's family fall into bankruptcy. Yet he had never revised his will. Elizabeth and her sister Mary received not a cent and not a keepsake.[53]

Although neither Elizabeth nor Mary seems to have complained, there is evidence that Bayley's oversight did not go unremarked. On the day his will was formally recorded, Elizabeth's husband filed his own. William's father had died intestate, and his father-in-law had failed to make provision for two beloved children. William left nothing to chance. After setting forth every kind of property he could imagine possessing, he wrote firmly, "I do hereby give, devise and bequeath the same and every part and parcel thereof unto her, the said Eliza Ann Seton her heirs and assigns forever.[54] If only, William must have thought, he could be sure to have something other than debts to leave behind.

EQUAL TO ALL THINGS

Her father's companionship was a foundation of Elizabeth's life. When that foundation was wrenched away, she marveled to find she still stood. "[I] now review with wonder, and with grateful praise," she told Julia, "that I live, much less that I have lived thro' it."[55] Julia knew as well as anyone what Bayley had meant to his daughter, and she too marveled at Elizabeth's serenity. "What a mind is hers!" she wrote Aquila Giles. "Her character rises upon every Trial. She appears equal to all things."[56]

Adamant that her new sorrow not lead to self-pity, Elizabeth pointedly contrasted her situation with that of the women she and other poor widows' society members tried to help. "No work—no wood—child sick etc.," she wrote after a two-hour visit to one widow. "Should I complain with a bright fire within—bright, bright Moon over my Shoulder and the Darlings all well hallooing and dancing"?[57] Her faith fortified her, and as the weeks passed, it consumed more and more of her attention. Her father's crisp rationalism no longer sounded in her ears, and she began to write less often to Julia. It was a different voice Elizabeth now listened for: John Henry Hobart's.

Elizabeth felt "unbounded veneration, Affection, [and] Esteem," for the minister who had entered her life just months earlier. "HH in the pulpit," she wrote one day after services, "such fervent prayers I ever heard before . . . [my soul] had its Peace perfect as can be received in this world."[58] Not content simply to listen to Hobart's sermons, Elizabeth sought his personal counsel. He was, she wrote, "the soother and comforter of the troubled Soul" and "one of those who after my Adored creator I expect to receive the largest share of happiness from in the next." Astonishingly, of all those Elizabeth knew and loved, Hobart was now "the friend most my friend in this world."[59]

Elizabeth modestly suggested that the minister had no "consciousness" of his importance to her, but Hobart's respect and affection are unmistakable. Like Richard Bayley before him, he appreciated the powerful mind of the woman who claimed she needed his guidance. Hobart shared with Elizabeth his sister's devotional poetry, and as he adapted English works of Anglican devotion for American use, he showed her drafts of his work.[60] Hobart also encouraged Elizabeth's interest in the Psalms, giving her his copy of George Horne's *Commentaries*. The volume, now at the Cathedral Library in Vincennes, Indiana, bears the marks of her intense contemplation. "0 that I could escape from the Sorrows and Sins of this world to Heaven my eternal Home where immortal Glory and bliss await me," she wrote on the left front flyleaf, "where imperfection and affliction shall no more embitter my enjoyments, where my wearied soul weighed down by sorrow and sin, shall be at rest forever."[61]

In one of their increasingly rare exchanges, Julia again warned Elizabeth that by turning her gaze so fixedly to heaven, she overlooked those who needed her on earth. Elizabeth was unmoved. "Religion," she replied, "does not limit the powers of the affections, for our Blessed Saviour Sanctifies and approves in us all the endearing ties and connections of our existence." But she also argued that all earthly ties *should be* secondary. "I will tell you the plain truth," she wrote her friend, "that my habits both of Soul and Body are changed—that I feel all the habits of society and connections of *this* life have taken a new form and are only interesting or endearing as they point the view to the next."[62]

This was not the young woman who had called herself her husband's little girl and claimed to give up her judgment to his. Her love for William never wavered, nor his for her; when Elizabeth again discovered herself pregnant, the couple worried for her health and William's but delighted in the thought of another baby. Yet William stood outside the devotional world Elizabeth was making, and that world felt more real to her than anything else. It was a common position for husbands. Some men of Elizabeth's acquaintance, such as Isabella Graham's son-in-law Divie Bethune, were fervent Christians. More commonly, however, the women in Elizabeth's circle were more involved in religion than their husbands: a list of those who took Communion at Trinity in 1801 shows that nearly 65 percent of them were female.[63] Elizabeth believed that William was too overwhelmed by practical concerns to "look up." He was, she wrote Rebecca, "near distracted at the times." "When I talk to him of our hope," she explained, he says that "he is too much troubled." "Oh—oh—," Elizabeth sighed, "[God] alone can set him right."[64]

William's worries were well founded. Stronger merchants than he were faltering, and not only in New York; his former clerk Thomas Masters watched as the Philadelphian for whom he had left Seton's employ began to sink too. "Let other speculators embark on the wide sea of uncertainty," the once cocky clerk wrote, "and let me keep safe in port."[65] But William could not keep safe in port; only new ventures held out the hope of paying old debts. Desperate and ill, he dreamed of escape, proposing that the family abandon Manhattan for his late father's parcel of land near the Black River. Elizabeth knew that her frail Manhattanite husband could never carve out a living in rural New York, but she had learned to treat William's anxious musings with detachment. "What will you think of Willy's 'serious thoughts,'" she asked Rebecca, answering, in an affectionate variation on her usual theme, "They do not trouble me [.] Where he is, is my *present Home,* and our God is everywhere."[66]

All of it—her father's death, her husband's fear and illness, the threat of real poverty—remained bearable because of Elizabeth's faith. And then, in August of 1802, heavily pregnant in Manhattan's summer heat, she found herself unable to pray. God had turned His face. "My soul is sorrowful," Elizabeth wrote. "My spirit weighed down even to the dust, cannot utter one word to Thee my Heavenly Father."[67] "My soul is very very very sick," she mourned several days later. "I call to my physician every moment from the bottom of my heart—but find no Peace."[68] The sense of being isolated from God was new in her prayer life and extraordinarily painful. If prayer did not bring peace, what would? Desolate days passed. Then came a bounty as sudden as the drought. "My cup has indeed run over," Elizabeth told Rebecca. "Never would I have thought of such enjoyment in this world[.] Last night was surely a foretaste of the next."[69]

From the evidence of Elizabeth's extant correspondence and "Dear Remembrances," Elizabeth's most intense spiritual experiences had in the past been solitary. No longer. The sudden joy she felt that August followed one of Hobart's services. Newly reassured of the power of Episcopalian worship, she allowed herself an unaccustomed sharpness at her husband's different choice. "Willy regretted very much he did not hear [Hobart]," she told Rebecca. *Regrets are idle things.*" But it was not William's loss but her own gain that most interested Elizabeth, and she vowed to commemorate the day. A period of despair ending in a blessed assurance of God's love was a familiar Protestant experience, one that the revivals of the Second Great Awakening sought to evoke. Member of the Episcopalian Church and a stranger to camp meetings, Elizabeth too felt reborn. "Yesterday," she told Rebecca, "shall while I have any birth days to keep always be considered the *Birth day* of the *Soul.*"[70]

Five days after her "Birth day of the Soul," Elizabeth felt the pangs of earthly labor. The delivery progressed quickly; no doctor or midwife arrived until fifteen minutes after she'd given birth. "I have the satisfaction to tell you," William reported to Julia with his usual charm, that "our dear Eliza" "was safely delivered of a girl, *Great and Beautiful,* equaled, but not excelled by any of our others."[71] The Setons had named their first daughter after William's stepmother and their second after Elizabeth's mother. They gave this third daughter the name of William's mother. It seems certain that Elizabeth also had in mind her beloved companion and "soul sister": the child was called Rebecca.

Part 2

A Crisis of Faith

6

THE OTHER SIDE OF THE FENCE

IN THE WAY of all Seton children, baby Rebecca was adored and nicknamed, but she'd been born into a changed family. The grandfathers who would have doted on her were dead, the father her older siblings had known was faded, and her mother, by her own account, was reborn. By Bec's first birthday, the family had been further transformed, and her parents were laying desperate plans. Details are difficult to recapture: few letters survive from this period, and Elizabeth's spiritual reflections are undated and lacking in external referents. Yet a few moments emerge from the fog.

Late 1802: The Reverend John Henry Hobart thrills Elizabeth by visiting her at home. "I went down quietly as possible," she tells her sister-in-law Rebecca, "but *trembled* rather too much even for a Christian." The young minister treats Elizabeth as a valued spiritual companion, telling her about a sister who has recently died and encouraging her joy in her "Birth day" experience of God's presence. "Said a great deal about *my happy day*," she writes.[1]

Late 1802 or early 1803: William grows sicker and begins to share his wife's interest in Christianity. "I think our Willy will go [to church]," Elizabeth tells Rebecca.[2] "Willy's heart seemed to be nearer to me for being nearer to his God," she writes in another undated note.[3]

March 1803, *Daily Advertiser*: "The creditors who have proved their debts under a commission of bankruptcy issued and awarded against William M.

Seton are requested to meet the assignees, at a meeting of the commission-ers, to be held at their Office at No. 5 in Nassau Street."

April 1803: William's young half sister Cecilia, who along with Harriet had spent much of her life in Elizabeth's home, joins Catherine Dupleix, her older sister Rebecca, and Elizabeth in their prayer circle. "Where He is there shall we be also," Elizabeth encourages her. "We must keep our Hearts fixed on Him and try with all our souls to pleasure our dear and blessed Lord . . . then when he calls us 'Come up hither,' we will fly with joy to our heavenly home."[4]

May 1803: The *Morning Chronicle* bears notice of the arrival of the "Brig Ann . . . from Leghorn via Gibraltar" bearing "silks, marbles, hats, &c. to Wm. M. Seton (owner)."[5] There is no large advertisement like the one Seton & Maitland had taken out in its heyday, but William is still trading.

August 1803: Elizabeth writes a letter to her daughter Anna Maria, aged eight, reminding her to keep herself prepared for death, as the biblical par-able of the wise and foolish virgins requires.[6]

Undated, 1803: Elizabeth shares with Anna Maria one of the commonplace books she kept as a girl but cautions her daughter that the book does not contain enough Christian devotional reading. Elizabeth tells her daughter that she can add secular extracts on her own, but devotional reading is what matters; it is "as necessary to the well ordering of the mind as the hand of the gardener to prevent the weeds destroying your favourite flower."[7]

Then, after months in which there are few or no letters, September of 1803 produces a flurry, and they reveal a startling development: "The vessel is chartered," Elizabeth writes Julia Scott, "freight procured—and the 25th appointed for departure." She, William, and Anna Maria were to set sail for Livorno, Italy.

Why Livorno, and why then? Italy's climate was thought more healthful for consumptives than Manhattan's, but sailing from New York in late September would bring the trio to the Italian port as winter approached—not so extreme a winter as Manhattan threatened but far more bitter than that to be found in the West Indies, where consumptives also traveled and where both the Setons and the Bayleys had connections. Cold was not the only peril. Tripolitanian corsairs attacked ships en route to the ports of southern Europe, and Americans had been warned that pirates disguised as English sailors plied the waters.[8] Throughout the summer of 1803, yellow fever also pillaged the Mediterranean, terrifying

Europeans who had not previously witnessed its deadly power. So far Livorno was spared, but ships had been quarantined and merchants and port officials were on edge.

Yet the Setons booked passage. Livorno offered what the West Indies did not: Filippo Filicchi. William had begun his merchant career under Filippo's tutelage. Now he hoped to revive it there. Among the possessions he packed for the voyage was a cabinet filled with business papers.

The four younger Seton children were to stay behind. Will was six years old, Richard five, and Catherine—still known as Kit—was three. At fourteen months, Bec was barely weaned. Rebecca, Elizabeth's "soul sister," was to tend the older three, and Eliza Seton Maitland, despite being in frail health herself, was to keep Bec. William's half sisters Harriet and Cecilia, who had been raised since their father's death among the Seton children, would help to keep them company. Only Anna Maria, aged eight, would come with her parents to Italy. Elizabeth believed that the child's passionate nature, so like her own, needed a mother's careful curbing. And even now, something of Elizabeth's girlhood desire to see the world, remained; she hoped that a European voyage would broaden and inform Anna Maria's mind. "Tho she is so young," Elizabeth told Eliza Sadler, "the voyage will have its use to her in many ways and probably will be strongly remembered by her thro' life."[9]

Elizabeth delighted in her children—"marvels of perfection," she called them, only half joking—and dreaded leaving. "It seems now to me like my last hour with all that I love," she mourned, and she penned wistful notes as she prepared to sail.[10] "If you love me," she wrote Richard, shamelessly wielding a mother's sharpest weapon, "do not plague your sweet Kate for that would make your dear Maman very unhappy."[11] Cecilia also got a note, hers recognizing the fact that Elizabeth considered the twelve-year-old a spiritual companion, albeit a junior one; Cecilia should "rejoice to bear your share in the Cross which is our Passport and Seal to the Kingdom of our Redeemer." The girl also got a nudge toward high-minded rebellion: Elizabeth told her to follow the pious rules of conduct the little prayer circle had developed, even if her family laughed. "All who love you will respect and esteem you the more for persevering in what you know to be your duty," Elizabeth insisted.[12]

As it happened, Elizabeth and William were themselves persevering despite others' doubts. Friends and family questioned the wisdom of the Atlantic crossing; the scarcity of letters from this period may reflect a couple turning away from unwanted advice. "All say it is presumption and next to madness to undertake our Voyage," Elizabeth told Sadler, "but you know we reason differently."[13] Elizabeth trusted in God, and William trusted in Elizabeth. One other person showed confidence in her judgment: John Henry Hobart. The minister gave Elizabeth hand-written sermons to take with her, told her he knew she would "meet the trials that are before you" with "serene and more than human resignation," and signed himself "your pastor, your friend, your brother." His approval outweighed others' doubts.[14]

The Setons planned to leave on September twenty-fifth, but the day came and went. William wanted to travel under a British passport, whether because of loyalty to his father's birthplace or because of an ill-conceived hope of business advantage, and it seems not to have arrived. Days passed. "My Seton's decline is so rapid that there can be no hope of his recovery in the view of MORTAL HOPES," Elizabeth wrote Julia on October 1. Not long before, she had felt unable to bear the thought of her husband's death. Now she faced even that, as well as the prospect of being an ocean away from her children, with serenity. Believing that she had mastered melancholy and dread, she felt calm and proud. "My soul reposes on that Mercy and now feels the full force of those consolations I have so often wished you to know the value of," she told Julia pointedly.[15]

At last, all was in order, and William, Elizabeth, and Anna Maria boarded a ship called the *Shepherdess*. William brought his business papers, Anna Maria carried a doll, and Elizabeth saw to what she called her "treasure": her Bible, Hobart's sermons, Thomas à Kempis's *Imitation of Christ*, and other works of Christian devotion. She also brought little bottles of currant jelly and soothing syrups, hoping to relieve her husband's fevers and cough aboard ship.[16]

The *Shepherdess*'s route from harbor to sea retraced Elizabeth's married life. The first hours brought the ship around the southern tip of Manhattan Island, where the Setons' home stood blocks from the water. Passengers waved their handkerchiefs to those watching from shore, but William was too distraught to join in. The *Shepherdess* next passed through quarantine on Staten Island, where the Setons were greeted by Elizabeth's cousin Joseph Bayley, who had succeeded his father at the station. Looking at the house where she and her children had passed happy hours and where she had held her dying father's hand, Elizabeth wept.[17] "The Pangs of Parting Nature would press," she wrote resolutely to Eliza Sadler, "but He over rules all."[18]

After clearing quarantine, the *Shepherdess* sailed through Long Island Sound, giving passengers a glimpse of the countryside in which the Setons and Posts had passed happy summers. Rather than reminisce, Elizabeth kept a watchful eye on William. Love and hope mixed with the precisely analytical style she'd learned from her father. "Sweat as much as usual, but slept very well from 7 to eleven, and from ½ past eleven until ½ past three—He has more appetite than I wish as it brings on fever invariably," she recorded.[19]

The family's mortal battle with consumption was briefly sidelined by a skirmish: the *Shepherdess*'s pitching and rolling left William and Anna Maria miserably ill. Elizabeth was as immune to the tossing of the waves as she felt to fortune's strokes and contentedly ate her breakfast. To her green-gilled husband and daughter, she must have seemed invincible. She seemed so to herself.

THE RISING AND SETTING SUN

At last the *Shepherdess* was through the sound and into the open sea. William and Anna Maria got over their seasickness, and, spared for the duration of the voyage from trying to obtain credit and cargoes, William found his mind quieter than it had been for months. Elizabeth discovered that the circumscribed wooden world of the ship suited her perfectly. Her domestic duties shrank to just a few, and she had time to read and think. She also discovered that she loved the sea. Despite living on an island, she knew no more of the ocean than could be imagined from the waters off the Battery or the beaches along the sound. Now she stood on the deck of a ship in the middle of the wide Atlantic, surrounded by sea and sky. "If I dared indulge my Enthusiasm and describe . . . my extravagant Enjoyments in gazing on the Ocean, and the rising & setting sun, & the moonlight Evenings," she marveled to Julia, "a quire of Paper would not contain what I should tell you."[20] As the days passed and the *Shepherdess* sailed eastward, Elizabeth gloried in her strength.

A month after its departure from New York, the Setons' ship floated into the Bay of Gibraltar. Elizabeth began a spiritual journal she meant to share with Rebecca. The journal was later copied by friends and admirers; existing versions are largely consistent with each other and entirely consistent with the content and style of Elizabeth's writings from the time. Through these documents, we can witness what became of the family's hopeful trip to Italy.

"Can I ever forget the setting sun over the little Island of Yivica [Ibiza]"? Elizabeth marveled as they neared the coast of Spain. Dreaming, she saw herself climbing "a Mountain of immense height and blackness" and heard a voice tell her that "an angel waits for you." The lovely dream was interrupted by William calling for her: "Now we will part no more in time nor in Eternity," he told his wife.[21] The family trio had become a prayer circle, and although William's conviction waxed and waned, little Anna Maria was as fervent a participant as Rebecca or Cecilia. The girl who shared Elizabeth's passionate nature threw herself into sharing her mother's beliefs. Elizabeth watched with satisfaction as the child wept at the thought that she "offended God every day."

Anna's tears flowed from her mother's teachings: Elizabeth meditated often on what she now saw as her "corrupt and Infirm nature." As the ship neared Italy, she came to a decision. She would, she wrote in her journal, never again expose herself "to the Smallest temptation I can avoid." "If my Heavenly Father will once more reunite us all," she promised, "I will make a daily sacrifice of every wish even the most innocent."[22] Despite her humble belief in her own corruption, Elizabeth was trying to strike an ambitious bargain: she would give up everything else if God allowed her the only thing she truly wanted, her family's reunion after death. She was confident she could hold up her end.

In mid-November the *Shepherdess* sailed into Livorno's harbor. At the dock stood Filippo Filicchi; his wife, Mary; and Elizabeth's half brother Carlton Bayley, who was working in the Filicchis' merchant house. A band struck up American tunes as the *Shepherdess*'s Yankee passengers danced with delight and Elizabeth ran toward Carlton. Then two things happened at once. Carlton backed away, and Elizabeth heard a guard say, "'don't touch.'"[23]

Don't touch. A rumor had arrived in Livorno that there was yellow fever in New York City. Elizabeth knew the *Shepherdess* had passed New York's quarantine; she had stood in the room where her father died the day the boat was inspected. But the Livornese had lived anxiously through the summer's yellow fever epidemic in the Mediterranean, and the port's worried officials found the ship's health certificate insufficient. Word came that the *Shepherdess* was to be searched and the pilot who had guided it into the harbor punished, perhaps executed. The frantic activity ended as quickly as it had begun. No one showed the yellowed skin and fevered brow of the dreaded disease, so passengers were allowed to disembark. But the scare had drawn port officials' attention to coughing, feverish William Seton. The only physicians in the Western world who believed consumption was contagious were Italian. The Setons were to be sent to Livorno's quarantine.

The serenity Elizabeth had thought unassailable cracked. "I was glad to hide in my berth the full heart of sorrow which seemed as if it must break," she confessed. (One copy of the journal includes the plea "do not judge me," and it is entirely plausible that Elizabeth, shocked to be faltering, should have written such a phrase.) William openly despaired. He'd survived the voyage only to be locked away from his friends' help. "You can never have an idea of the looks and tears of my poor Willy," Elizabeth wrote in her journal. He "seemed as if he would not live over the day."[24]

In the waters below the *Shepherdess*, a large rowboat appeared towing a smaller craft, so that quarantined passengers could be kept separate from the crew. Ordered into the little boat, the Setons were rowed out "out to sea again . . . over the waves." An hour later, they found themselves in a high-walled canal, an austere stone building rising before them. This was the quarantine station, known in Italy—in honor of St. Lazarus—as a lazaretto. Chains barred the boats' way. A bell sounded and someone sent out a message; the boatmen lit a fire and held the message in the smoke to ward off sickness that might cling to the paper. A guard pointed with his bayonet toward the lazaretto. There, waving at the family through a fence, stood Filippo Filicchi's wife. Elizabeth had stood behind the gate at her father's quarantine and looked with pity on wretched migrants. Now she'd become one.[25]

GOD IS OUR ALL

Italy had been home to lazarettos since the fourteenth century; the travelers who brought the region trade and culture carried plagues as well, and port cities such as Livorno worked hard to contain the risks. Like quarantines in the United States, lazarettos were part inspection stations for cargo and part holding cells for unlucky travelers.[26] The drafty stone building to which the Setons were sent was the latter, used to confine suspect passengers for thirty days. Passengers who survived were released.

If Elizabeth thought that the quarantine would be run as her father's was, like a field hospital, she immediately learned her error. Its director was not a physician but a member of the military, whom the Setons were directed to call "Monsieur le Capitano." No one helped as William "tottered along as if every moment he must fall." Had her husband stumbled, Elizabeth wrote bitterly, "no one dared for their life to touch him."[27]

The little family struggled up stone steps to a room with bare stone walls, its "high arched ceilings" incongruously reminding Elizabeth of St. Paul's chapel in New York.[28] The capitano ordered mattresses laid on the floor and a small supper brought in. Determined to help, the Filicchis arranged to have more food sent, and that too was brought up. These courtesies extended, the door to the room was shut and the Setons left alone.

In her journal, Elizabeth described the scene that followed in the third person, not quite believing she was the woman who sat in a cold stone room with her sick husband and young daughter, the wind sounding through the chimney like thunder. "You could not rest in your bed," she told Rebecca, "if you saw her as she is sitting in one corner of an immense Prison bolted in and barred with as much ceremony as any monster of mischief might be." William coughed so hard he brought up blood, and Elizabeth retreated to a closet to cry and pray. She soon forced herself out to console her husband and daughter. "Mama if Papa should die here—but God will be with us," Anna Maria said stoically. The child unwound a rope from one of their bundles and started "jumping away to warm herself."[29]

Elizabeth's shipboard vow to guard herself against temptations, taken just days earlier, seemed laughable. In the lazaretto, there was no need to resist desire or thwart whims. She wanted only to withstand the circumstances in which she found herself and to help William and Anna do so as well. "[God] is our all indeed," she wrote that night by candlelight. "My eyes smart so much with crying, wind and fatigue that I must close them and lift up my heart." "If sufferings abound in us," she added, turning to the Bible for words of comfort, "his Consolations also greatly abound, and far exceed all utterance."[30]

The next morning she awoke to the sound of church bells. When she prayed, she felt nothing. Staring out at waves lashing the rocks, Elizabeth willed herself to feel God's care. To suffer another period of spiritual dryness, as she had when pregnant with Bec, would be unbearable. To her immense relief, she found that "pleading for Mercy and Strength brought Peace."[31] From that moment, she devoted herself to easing the pain and fear of what she was sure must be her husband's final weeks.

The lazaretto's cold and damp wrecked any improvement the sea voyage had brought William. Lighting the fire brought warmth, but the primitive fireplace belched smoke, oppressing the merchant's ragged breathing. The most extended version of Elizabeth's journal contains occasional bursts of indignation. "My Husband on the old bricks without fire, shivering and groaning lifting his dim and sorrowful eyes, with a fixed gaze in my face while his tears ran on his pillow without one word," reads an entry. Yet Elizabeth tried, even in her most private moments, to maintain the serenity that Rebecca, Hobart and she herself expected. She read and reread scripture, the words and images offering frames through which she viewed each harrowing day. ("Be still and know that I am God," reads a line from Psalm 46, offering no comfort but the one she coveted.) She also imagined herself at Trinity Church. Correcting for the time difference between Italy and New York—"It was 9 o'clock with us—3 at Home"—she "imagined what I had so often enjoyed and consoled myself with: the thought that tho' separated in the Body six thousand miles—my Soul and the Souls I love were at the Throne of Grace at the same time, in the same Prayers." Without hesitation and with no deference to gender, she led William and Anna Maria in an imaginary church service.[32]

Filippo and his wife Mary did what they could for the trio, some days appearing at the foot of the lazaretto to wave at them, some days sending food, and one day having a bed brought in to replace William's mattress. Perhaps as a result of their efforts, the quarantine was reduced from thirty days to twenty-five. When the capitano made the cheerful announcement, the Setons simply wept. Five days would not save William.[33]

The capitano was disappointed by their tears. He was a kind man, sharing chestnuts and fruits from his own stores and offering sympathy in a mixture of Italian and French. His tendency to finish his thoughts with a fatalistic "que voulez-vous, signora" caught Elizabeth's fancy, and she occasionally leavened the sorrowful piety of her journal with gently humorous descriptions of his visits. Once, however, the capitano elicited her stern rebuke. "'All religions are good,'" the Italian had said. "It is good to keep one's own, but yours is as good as mine, to 'do to others as you would wish them do to you' that is all religion and the only point." It could have been a line from Betsy Bayley's commonplace book, but Elizabeth Seton deplored it. John Henry Hobart taught, and she agreed, that religions did *not* exist just to make people good and happy. They existed to help people worship God and to do so as God intended. "Well, Monsieur le Capitano," Elizabeth responded, "He who commanded your excellent rule, also commanded in the first place 'love the Lord your God with all your Soul'; "do you not give that the first place Capitano?" The capitano's diplomatic response, "Ah Signora, it is excellent—mais il y a tant de choses," did not mollify her. "Poor Capitano," she observed sharply. "Sixty years of age—and yet to find that to give God the Soul interferes with 'so many things.'"[34] On the page, Elizabeth seems sanctimonious. Yet the capitano took no offense; in the freezing lazaretto, her charisma burned bright.[35]

None of the three Setons was allowed to leave the room in which they were held. Enclosed with her coughing father—"the fever comes hot—the bed shakes even with his breathing"—Anna Maria fell ill. Elizabeth did not want her daughter to be afraid, and she believed that everything that befell the family lay within God's plan. So she encouraged the eight-year-old to see her sickness as a gift. Anna obeyed wholeheartedly. "'Sometimes I think when this pain comes in my Breast,'" she told her approving mother, "'God will call me soon and take me from this world where I am always offending him.'" Rather than question the mercy of a God who left her to watch her father die while herself falling ill, Anna Maria was grateful God "'gives me a sickness that I may bear patiently.'"[36]

Anna was quickly over the worst of her fever and cough, but William grew weaker. Business papers forgotten and hope lost, he took comfort only in his wife. Elizabeth encouraged him to pray not for his recovery, which she thought impossible, but for his salvation. "We pray and cry together, till fatigue overpowers him," she wrote in her journal to Rebecca, "and then he says he is willing to go."[37] "Dear, dear William," reads another entry, "I can sometimes inspire him for a few minutes to feel that it would be sweet to die."[38]

Elizabeth's observations of her husband were precise; when she wrote that she could get him to welcome death "for a few minutes," that is exactly what she meant. William felt flashes of Elizabeth's conviction and willingly read and prayed with her, but he did not share his wife's impatience with life. He loved art and music, good dinners and white linen shirts. Elizabeth had found a new way to be happy and a new home, but William had not. The thought of their son Will celebrating his birthday without his parents made him weep. "He is so weak that even a thought of Home makes him shed tears," Elizabeth observed. "How gracious is the Lord who strengthens my poor Soul," she added.[39]

Elizabeth's language of weakness and strength is unmistakable; her gratitude for her faith was mixed with a sense of accomplishment. She had worked hard to distance herself from temporal concerns and wishes, and she maintained a constant vigilance. "That thought did not do," she wrote one morning when, watching gulls fly by, she imagined them flying toward her children. She quickly replaced it with an image of the birds "Flying towards Heaven—where I tried to send my soul."[40] This was not just belief but discipline, and she knew it. "If I could forget my God one moment at these times," she mused, "I should go mad."[41]

Elizabeth had felt flashes of God's presence since a child, but now she did not simply wait for such a moment to come. She had developed her ability to feel steadily close to God through ambitious prayer—a kind of practice. She was becoming a spiritual virtuoso, and the days in the lazaretto afforded endless hours to hone her skills. "William at rest—Ann playing in the next room—alone to all the World," she wrote one day, "one of those sweet pauses in spirit when the Body seems to be forgotten." Writing of the sensation, Elizabeth remembered the first time she had felt it: the day in New Rochelle when she fell to the ground in rapture. In such moments, she felt as if "the Body let the Spirit alone."[42]

One night, the sound of voices and feet ascending the stairs echoed off the lazaretto's stone walls. There had been a shipwreck, and thirty or forty of the crew—"Turks, Greeks, Spaniards, and Frenchmen"—were brought to a room near the Setons. Elizabeth wrote sympathetically of their lack of clothes and mattresses and disapproved when the Capitano said "he can do nothing without orders—'Patience—que voulez vous Signora.'" But when Anna Maria contrasted the crew's tendency to "quarrel, fight, and holloo" with her family's "Peace," Elizabeth quietly agreed. She didn't remind her daughter that the Setons should be expected to do less fighting and hollooing than a shipwrecked crew, nor did she share her family's provisions. The crew's misery, like most strangers' misery she'd witnessed, prompted her to reflection rather than action. "Dear Ann," she told her daughter, "you will see many more such mysteries."[43] Her father had treated suffering as a foe; Elizabeth welcomed it as a mentor.

"SO ASSURED"

As day followed difficult day, Elizabeth felt unexpectedly blessed. "Sometimes I feel so assured that the guardian Angel is immediately present that I look from my book and can hardly be persuaded I was not touched," she wrote. Her "days of retirement and abstraction from the world" felt like liberty. In genteel Manhattan, Elizabeth had reluctantly curbed her spiritual urgency. In the stone quarantine, she felt unconfined. "When I thank God for my 'Creation and preservation,'" Elizabeth wrote in mid-December, "it is with a warmth of feeling I never could know until now. To wait on him my W., Soul and Body, to console and soothe those hours of affliction and pain, weariness and watching which next to God I alone could do."[44]

In the lazaretto, Elizabeth's life as a wife finally became one with her life as a Christian. She spent her days teaching her husband to see that the life they'd lovingly made together was not his real home. William struggled toward agreement, telling Elizabeth that he too missed "dear HH," and speaking hopefully "of meeting, ONE family in Heaven." "To strike up the cheerful notes of Hope and Christian triumph, which from [William's] partial love he hears with the more enjoyment from me because to me he attributes the greatest share of them—to hear him in pronouncing the Name of his Redeemer declare that I first taught him the sweetness of the sound . . ."[45] Elizabeth trailed off, contented.

As December began, the bleak conditions in the lazaretto seemed almost cheerful. The capitano sent wood and hand irons for warmth, Elizabeth lessened the smoke with a cleverly hung curtain, and the Filicchis faithfully sent provisions.[46] Then, on December 5, William awoke in agony, scarcely able to breathe through the phlegm that clogged his lungs. A doctor summoned by the capitano said he could do nothing; what William needed was a minister. "My husband looked in silent agony at me and I at Him," Elizabeth wrote several days later, after she'd gathered herself enough to resume her journal, "each fearing to weaken the others Strength." Morning turned to afternoon, then evening. Elizabeth spent the night listening for her husband's breath and "kiss[ing] his poor face to feel if it was cold," while Anna Maria lay a few feet away.[47] In the morning, William clung to life.

The day ended and more days passed. A storm lashed the stone walls of the lazaretto. On the fourteenth of December, impatience flashed through Elizabeth's usually serene journal. "You need not always point your silent look and figure there [toward heaven]," she imagined telling the capitano. "If I thought our condition the Providence of man . . . you would find me a lioness willing to burn your Lazaretto about your ears if it were possible that I might carry off my poor prisoner to breathe the air of Heaven in some more seasonable place." She had watched her father die from an illness contracted while tending a quarantine's inmates; now she was watching her husband die in a quarantine with no physician to tend him. What shame, she wrote angrily, "to keep a poor Soul who came to your country for his Life, thirty days shut up in damp walls, smoke and wind from all corners blowing even the curtain round his bed, which is only a mattress on boards and his bones almost through."[48]

With death now truly upon him, William suddenly took up his wife's lost serenity. "He very often says this is the period of his life which if he lives or dies he will always consider as Blessed," Elizabeth wrote, "the only time which he has not lost."[49] William felt "like a person brought to the Light after many years of darkness." Elizabeth steadied, but when she regained her bearings, William lost his. "Melancholy days of combat with nature's weakness," she wrote tersely.[50] She prayed with her husband, directing his eyes where the capitano pointed, toward heaven.

At last, the nineteenth of December arrived. Twenty-five days after they had sailed into Livorno's harbor, the Setons were released from the lazaretto. No longer able to walk, William was carried down the stone steps to the Filicchis' carriage, dispatched to bring the Setons to lodgings in Pisa, fifteen miles away. Elizabeth had long since resigned herself to her husband's death, but the thought that the exertion of the trip might kill him there and then made her "heart beat almost to fainting." Instead, in the odd way of tuberculosis, the air and motion briefly revived William, and they reached Pisa safely. Soon after, Elizabeth stopped writing in her journal. When she resumed, it was to tell the story of her husband's last days.

"Let me stop and ask myself if I can go thro' the remainder of my memorandum with that sincerity and exactnesss which has so far been adhered to," she wrote. Could "the crowd of anxieties and sorrows" "be suppressed and my Soul stand singly before my God"? "Yes," she answered. "Every moment of it speaks his Praise and therefore it shall be followed."[51]

Elizabeth described the Filicchis' generous care, the lazaretto's naked stone walls and smoky fire giving way to an apartment of "taste and elegance," "every necessary comfort within . . . reach." Yet nothing comforted William. He was beset with the "disorder of the Bowels" that the lazaretto's visiting doctor had warned Elizabeth signaled the final stage of the disease. Elizabeth had never prayed for her husband's miraculous restoration, and she did not do so now. Nor did she tell William what this new complaint meant. Alone with her knowledge, she listened sadly as her husband insisted on being taken for a ride in the Filicchis' coach, only to return after five minutes, carried helpless to his bed. On Christmas, William became so violently ill that he thought he would die that night, and he wanted to. The next day, the captain of the *Shepherdess* visited. William knew Elizabeth would sail home without him, and he commended her to the captain's care, taking up his old mantle of protector just long enough to pass it on.

Elizabeth spent the days and nights weeping and praying, gently urging William to join her "whenever he had the least cessation from extreme suffering." In William's weakness and incontinence, she "did for him like a Baby." He could bear no one's presence but his wife's, insisting the door to their room be kept closed. Sometimes he imagined Elizabeth could die with him, confusing her assurances that everyone would one day reunite in heaven with the promise that he would not have to die alone. "When the cold sweat came on," Elizabeth wrote, he "would reach out both his arms to me and said repeatedly 'you promised me you would go, come, come, fly.'"[52]

In her journal for Rebecca, Elizabeth described only William's sufferings and faith in God. But in a letter written a few days later, she recounted a desperate thought that seized him in his last hours. "He took a strange fancy in his mind," she wrote, "that he had received a letter from the letter office in London telling him that my ticket which he had renewed there had drawn the Royal prize." Agonized over leaving his wife and five children without resources, William imagined that he'd won the lottery. Nor was that his only sweet delusion: he raved that he was no longer a bankrupt and "that he had not a single bill out in the world."[53] Elizabeth took bittersweet pleasure in his hallucinatory relief.

Finally, at four in the morning two days after Christmas, William's dehydrated and breathless body failed. "The hard struggle ceased," Elizabeth wrote, "Nature sunk into a settled sob." He murmured, "My dear Wife and little ones" and "My Christ Jesus have mercy and receive me" until after dawn. At "a quarter past seven," Elizabeth wrote, "the dear Soul took its flight to the blessed exchange it so much longed for."[54] Her husband was dead. Elizabeth opened the door of the room and told the others.

7

THESE DEAR PEOPLE

ELIZABETH HAD NOT RESTED for three days and had eaten only once. In the months since her family had boarded the *Shepherdess* in New York's harbor, she'd exhausted herself caring for her suffering husband—"always watching," she once described the nerve-racking work.[1] Through it all, a tragic simplicity of purpose had sustained her: tend William "body and soul." William was gone, and so was the simplicity.

Of all the people who hovered in the Setons' lodgings at Pisa, only one, a servant, was willing to help Elizabeth with William's body. Whether moved by compassion or by a servant's lack of choice, the Filicchis' washerwoman helped lay out the corpse, William's bones ridging against his skin after months of consumptive wasting. Only laborers had been willing to help Elizabeth tend her father's body, too, but there was no time to ponder the connection. William was to be laid to rest in the English cemetery in Livorno, and Italian law required that his burial take place within twenty-four hours of his death. And so, Elizabeth wrote, "I must wash, dress, pack up, and in one hour be in Mrs. F[ilichi]'s carriage and ride fifteen miles to Leghorn."[2]

As William's body lay in "the burying house" of the English churchyard, word of his fate spread through the expatriate community. American and English residents of the bustling port gathered to pay their respects to the unlucky merchant who had sailed to Italy to save his enterprise and life, only to waste away in the lazaretto. Elizabeth wrote without elaboration that her husband was buried "according to his own directions." Far more important to her than either the manner of the burial or the sympathy of Livorno's expatriates was her private confidence in William's eternal fate. "My William often asked me if I felt assured that he would be accepted and pardoned," she wrote Rebecca. "I always tried to convince him that where the soul was so humble and sincere as his, and submission to God's will so uniform as his had been through his trial, that it became sinful to doubt one moment of his reception through the merits of his Redeemer."[3]

After exhausting months and harrowing days, Elizabeth had no more offices to perform. Filippo brought her to the home of his younger brother Antonio. Antonio "gave me the look of many Sympathys as he helped me from his carriage," Elizabeth observed in her journal, and "his most amiable lady . . . looked in my face as if to comfort me." She appreciated their kindness, but they seemed very far away. "My poor high heart was in the clouds," she wrote, "roving after my William's soul and repeating my God you are my God."[4]

Elizabeth expected to spend a few days or weeks with the Filicchis, then sail home with Anna Maria. Despite her hosts' kindness, she was desperate to leave. Her urgent mission to save William having failed, she allowed herself to miss her children, as well as Rebecca and Cecilia, the young sisters-in-law who had become her spiritual companions. "We have not heard one word from Home," she wrote anxiously. In his dying moments, William had hallucinated the presence of tiny Bec, and Elizabeth worried his delusion meant her youngest had died. Nor were her children the only ones she missed. After months of reading John Henry Hobart's sermons, she longed to be once more within the sound of his voice.

Yet four months passed before Elizabeth and Anna Maria boarded the ship that took them home. In that time, the two grew to love what Elizabeth called "this strange but beautiful land."[5] When she finally sailed for New York, Elizabeth was still sustained by faith. But it was a different faith, and it left nothing in her life unchanged.

What happened in those four months? Elizabeth told some of the story to Rebecca Seton in the journal that she began aboard the *Shepherdess*. As she learned of ships sailing for America, she also wrote letters. Aboard ship to New York, she wrote a brief journal.[6] That last account, a fragment, was translated into French, lost, and then translated back into English. Despite that provenance and despite the fact that both versions of the fragment display somewhat more formal language than Elizabeth habitually used, the story the shipboard account tells and the themes on which it touches accord with what we know from original documents; moreover, some of its details—"Philip Filicchi and Carlton waited for us at the Health Office"—are things no one but Elizabeth would have thought to record.[7] Thus the shipboard fragment, together with the letters and journal, form a bundle of papers from which we can try to reconstruct the story of how a woman who sailed for Italy with a "treasure" of handwritten Episcopalian sermons sailed for home a Catholic in all but name.

Even with those sources, Elizabeth's transformative months are visible only in odd flashes: a question posed, a sign of the cross made, a Mass attended. It is possible that she, one of her Catholic confessors, or a later descendant intentionally destroyed some writing. It is more likely that Elizabeth withheld from Rebecca and even from herself a full account of her initial movement from Protestant faith to Catholic. It was impossible until it was happening, and by then it was too astonishing to describe.

THE FILICCHIS

Before William's death, the Filicchi family had hovered at the edges of Elizabeth's vision. Immediately after, they became central actors in her disorienting new life. At forty, Filippo was a commanding figure still possessed of the commercial and spiritual ambitions that had led him as a young man to sail for America, develop an alliance with William Seton, and propose a catechism for American Catholics. He and his wife, Mary Cowper Filicchi, an American from either Boston or New York, had no children. Mary, who left behind few traces in the historical record, appears in Elizabeth's writing as kind but often ill. "Mrs. F. has been in bed ever since our arrival," Elizabeth noted one day.[8] Filippo's brother Antonio, three years his junior, had studied philosophy and practiced law before joining his brother as a merchant.[9] He and his Italian wife, the pious and vibrant Amabilia, had young children whom Elizabeth and Anna Maria quickly came to love. Antonio lacked Filippo's excellent English and his expertise in Catholic doctrine, but "the look of many sympathies" he gave Elizabeth as he helped her from his brother's carriage marked the beginning of an intense mutual affection.

Elizabeth was grateful for the Filicchis' kindness as she found herself "crowded with the whole sense of my situation."[10] She'd been transformed from an observer of quarantined migrants to a quarantined migrant and from the benefactor of poor widows to a poor widow herself. "When I look forward to my unprovided situation as it relates to the affairs of this life," she wrote wryly to Rebecca, "I must often smile at [the Filicchis'] tenderness and precautions."[11] She would have been even more moved had she known that in the large bankruptcy file marked "William M. Seton" lay not only accounts listing William's known debts to the Filicchis but also a letter in which the brothers explained that out of confusion or illness, William had failed to register yet another large sum due them.[12] William Seton died as he had lived: among creditors.

If Elizabeth had scant intimation of the Filicchis' financial affairs, she had even less sense of the complex political and religious arena through which they moved. Since Napoleon's triumphant northern Italian campaign began in 1796, the Italian states had been the site of struggle both between France and Italy and between the power of nations and the influence of the Catholic Church. In 1798 Pope Pius VI refused the demand of a French general that he give up all claim to temporal authority. Taken prisoner in retribution, Pius died in exile the next year. By the time Elizabeth found herself in the Filicchis' home, Livorno had seen the local French commander hastily evacuate—the Filicchis helping to negotiate the fate of men and materiele left behind when he did—but French domination of the region continued. The brothers neither hid the turmoil nor explained it, and Elizabeth felt no inclination to probe. She calmly wrote Rebecca that she saw a "lovely part of the country" where Filippo had taken shelter in a convent "during some political revolution."[13]

The daughter of a Loyalist, Elizabeth was content to imagine political revolution as something to be endured as best one could, but the literal and figurative battles between Napoleonic France, the Italian states, and the Catholic Church were ongoing. Much of Tuscany had been renamed the Kingdom of Etruria and granted to the Bourbon dukes of Parma as compensation for their displacement by French troops elsewhere in northern Italy. Political realignment begat religious when the 1801 Concordat between Napoleon and Pope Pius VII laid the groundwork for a French Catholicism intended to complement the empire. In the French-controlled Italian states, as in France itself, Catholicism was meant to become a harmless realm of feasts and rituals, its once powerful ecclesiastical hierarchies subordinate to the bureaucracy of the state. The Filicchis had no desire for Italian Catholicism to follow this path; they preferred Bishop John Carroll's vision of a church that claimed no temporal authority but maintained its ecclesiastical hierarchies and was independent of state control. Filippo still hoped to help Carroll plant Catholicism in the United States, beyond the reach of Europe's ancient animosities and new radicals.

The Filicchis' long-standing interest in American Catholicism was as unknown to Elizabeth as the intricacies of Italian politics and the extent of her husband's indebtedness. Elizabeth's character—her searching intellect, her strong will and passionate nature—was equally mysterious to the Filicchis. From this happy ignorance emerged a plan that tickled Elizabeth with its utter improbability. Tell "dear friend J H H," she wrote Rebecca, "that I am hard pushed by these charitable Romans who wish that so much goodness should be improved by a conversion."[14] The Filicchis wanted Elizabeth to become a Catholic.

The Filicchis' understanding of the situation emerges in a letter Filippo wrote to Bishop Carroll. After dispensing with the death of his friend and associate William Seton in a sentence or two, he turned to Elizabeth; the normally brusque merchant was giddy with a sense of providential possibility. Elizabeth possessed "a very pious and religious disposition in a degree far superior to what I ever had remarked in people of her persuasion," Filippo wrote. She fulfilled with "exactness" "the duties of wife and mother" and showed "in her character an uncommon docility." (Elizabeth would have laughed at that one too.) "I was struck with the idea," he told Bishop Carroll, "that Providence had arranged the plan of her voyage to Italy for the particular purpose of giving her an opportunity of rectifying the prejudices entertained against our Religion, of enlightening her mind and of granting her the blessing of discerning the true Church and being made a Member of it." There it was: through Elizabeth Seton, God had given Filippo Filicchi the chance to plant Catholicism in the United States. "I indulged this hope," he wrote, "and considered in discreet silence all these things."[15]

Elizabeth's account of these days makes clear that what Filippo viewed as a discreet silence was more of a full court press. She had no idea her kind Italian host was writing a bishop about the state of her

FIGURE 7.1. A view of Livorno, dated after Seton's visit. APSL 1–3 #102.
Courtesy of the Daughters of Charity Province of
St. Louise Archives, Emmitsburg, Maryland.

soul, but she immediately understood that Filippo wished her to abandon the Episcopalian faith she loved. She was confident she would not be swayed. Telling Rebecca that the Filicchis had "even taken the trouble to bring me their best informed priest," she explained that she listened politely while fending off their efforts as gently as she could. (Since "learned people like to hear themselves, best," she wryly observed, her reticence was much appreciated.)[16] Filippo's efforts to convert a grieving widow would have offended many, but Elizabeth took them with good humor. For the past few years she had herself been an evangelist. The proselytizing had the ironic effect of pushing her back toward the gentle ecumenism she'd once embraced. The kind and generous Filicchis were Catholics, she thought to herself, she was an Episcopalian, and everyone was doing the best he could.

FLORENCE

When it became clear to everyone that Captain O'Brien and the *Shepherdess* would not sail for some weeks, the Filicchis decided that Elizabeth and Anna Maria should see Florence, the Tuscan city that for centuries had enchanted travelers. The family set off, Elizabeth and Anna

Maria in tow. Elizabeth's journal entries from her week in Florence are in some regards the kind of travelogue many an educated traveler has made before and since. "Four days I have been at Florence lodged in the famous Palace of Medicis," she wrote at its commencement, then dutifully admired the view.[17] Yet a dawning interest in Catholic worship gleams through her descriptions of the sights.

The marvels began in one of Florence's most beloved churches, La Santissima Annunziata. Walking up to the Annunziata, Elizabeth saw a fairly restrained façade, its pillars and columns not inconceivable in Federal Manhattan. On entering, she found herself in an immense vaulted space ringed with lavish chapels built by Florentine clans competing to give glory to God. The Annunziata was to Trinity Church what the wide Atlantic had been to the Long Island Sound. The ornate riches of Italian churches would have troubled many American Protestants (John Adams was horrified by such sights), but Elizabeth thrilled to it. She did not believe the money that had built and bedecked the chapels should have been used to relieve the poor, and she did not worry that the representations of saints, patriarchs, and the Holy Family encouraged an idolatrous worship of images. It was beautiful, and it was done to honor God, and she loved it.

Filled with worshippers and gentled by candlelight, the Annunziata's interior was both sublime and intimate. To Elizabeth's surprise, all the worshippers seemed as enraptured as she. "Old men and women, young women, and all sorts of people kneeling promiscuously about the Altar as inattentive to us or any other passengers, as if we were not there," she recorded. "Every one is so intent on their prayers and Rosary that it is very immaterial what a stranger does." Wandering eyes and minds were undoubtedly to be found in the Annunziata just as they were in Trinity Church, but Elizabeth was as blind to them as she was to the country's political and religious unrest. She saw a faith whose vibrant solidity gleamed from floor to ceiling. Yet she had no desire to join the Florentines in their faith. Moved by the Annunziata's beauty, Elizabeth "fell to her knees" and "said our dear service"—the Episcopalian service—"with my whole soul."[18] The Annunziata offered a sacred ambience within which she prayed as a fervent Protestant.

As she toured Florence, Elizabeth mourned William. The Uffizi Gallery left her painfully missing the company of her art-loving husband. "[I] felt the void of him who would have pointed out the beauties of every object, too much to enjoy any perfectly," she wrote."[19] (She found one flash of amusement amid her loneliness, remarking of the gallery's bronze male nudes that "being only an American [I] could not look very straight at them.") A carriage ride through Florence's spring-like weather left her hiding her face while she wept. Anna Maria grieved too. She had watched her father in the lazaretto, spared not a moment of his suffering until the final few days in Pisa. Elizabeth's journal depicts her daughter as preternaturally pious and obedient; exquisitely attuned to her mother's thoughts, the little girl recognized that Elizabeth did not want her to dread or resent her father's death. Now her mother's grief freed Anna Maria to feel her own. "She says," Elizabeth wrote Rebecca, "my dear Papa is praising God in Heaven, and I ought not to cry for him, but I believe it is human nature, is it not Mamma?"[20] Anna Maria knew her mother agreed, or she would not have asked.

Tears at night gave way to tours in the day, and Elizabeth and Anna Maria usually shared those too. Elizabeth recorded their opinions of the city's sights. (Boboli Gardens: impressive. Maria Luisa of Parma, the woman known as Etruria's "Queen": less so.) One visit, to the city's natural history museum, Elizabeth made on her own. With its anatomical rooms and exhibits of disease and deformity, the museum was inappropriate for a child. But because it was a monument to scientific inquiry, Elizabeth would not have missed it any more than she would have missed the monument to God's glory that was the Annunziata. Walking through the museum, she wanted Wright Post's company, and although she could not bring herself to mention him in her journal, she missed her father too. Bayley and Post would have left the museum newly determined to combat the ills exhibited within. Elizabeth did something different. "I passed through most of the rooms uninterrupted in the sacred reflections they inspired," she wrote, and "received more than I could have obtained in years, out of my own Cabinet of precious things."[21] She thought the natural history museum revealed God's will and power, not the need for man's.

In a city in which the sacred and the secular sent Elizabeth into raptures, one thing failed to delight: the opera. William had spoken warmly of the art form and so, wearing a "hat and veil" rather than the traditional Florentine mask, Elizabeth set off with Anna in tow. They hated it. "Ann thought the singers would go mad," Elizabeth wrote afterward, "and I could not find the least gratification in their quavers." The Filicchis knew better than to try again.[22]

The opera was a rare failure in a week of pleasure. Wearing a sober black flannel gown and bonnet, Elizabeth walked the city, an enchanted American in Italian widow's garb. She admired the church known as Santa Maria Novella and the frescoes of Pitti Palace, marveling at immense paintings filled with the faces and bodies of biblical figures such as Mary, Jesus, Abraham, and Isaac. Elizabeth had reveled in Rousseau's description of a divinity beyond human imagination. Now, surrounded by images that limned divinity in profoundly human ways, she was moved to tears. "A Picture of the descent from the Cross nearly as large as life," she wrote in her journal, "engaged my whole soul." In another fresco, the suffering of the Virgin—looking as if "the iron [of the nails] had entered into her"—touched her. The paintings' melding of human emotion with divine love left her with "dropping tears" and "shaking frame." Yet Elizabeth felt no urge to adopt the Catholic faith that underwrote the paintings' creation.[23]

The week came to its end, and Elizabeth, Anna Maria, and the Filicchis returned to Livorno. Florence had opened a new realm in which Elizabeth felt God's presence, but the city's beauties had not convinced her of Catholic doctrines. The same was true of Francis de Sales's *Introduction to the Devout Life*, which Filippo had given her. "How many times I was on my knees from strong impression of its powerful persuasion," she wrote, but the little book displaced none of the Protestant writings that were her "treasures."[24] Then Amabilia took her to church back in Livorno, and Elizabeth found herself contemplating what it might mean to become a Catholic.

Livorno's church boasted none of the glories of Florence. Instead, Elizabeth was moved by the Latin Mass, which was murmured by the "tall pale meek heavenly looking man" who stood as priest. A lover of clarity felt the stir of mystery. What the priest did, Elizabeth wrote, "I don't know . . . for I was the side of the altar, so that I could not look up without seeing his countenance on which Many lights from the altar reflected, and gave such strange impressions to my soul that I could but cover my face with my hands and let the tears run." At the center of the Catholic Mass lay its greatest mystery: the priest's transformation of bread and wine into the body and blood of Christ. Elizabeth believed that this transformation—transubstantiation, in the language of the Church—did not really happen: Episcopalians like her understood the moment to be symbolic, not literal. Yet as she knelt in church beside

Amabilia, she could not shake off the thought that she had witnessed a miracle. "I don't know how to say the awful effect at being where they told me God was present in the blessed Sacrament," she wrote.[25] She craved God's presence; now she was told it could be had each Sunday, told God could be put in her mouth and swallowed. Although she did not believe the doctrine of transubstantiation to be true, she found to her surprise that she did not, that day at Mass, feel it to be false.

Elizabeth expected the Mass to become an exotic memory, fondly recalled once she'd settled back into her real life. "Oh my the very little while we were there will never be forgotten," she wrote Rebecca. "These dear people are so strange about Religion."[26] Yet she was more drawn to Catholicism than she admitted. Accounts she and Filippo wrote of a conversation they shared about faith reveal her ambivalence.

In Elizabeth's journal, the conversation appears as a casual discussion that turned into an unwelcome lesson. "I asked Mr. F. something, I don't know what, about the different religions," she wrote, and he "began to tell me that there was only one true Religion and without a right Faith we would not be acceptable to God." Elizabeth describes her reply as polite but pointed: "Oh my Sir, then said I, if there is but one Faith and nobody pleases God without it, where are all the good people who die out of it"? Filippo replied that their fate "depends on what light of faith they had received."[27]

In the catechism he'd proposed for the United States, Filippo specifically suggested hiding from Americans' view any suggestion that the Catholic Church offered the only path to salvation. In this conversation with Elizabeth, he did the opposite. "I know where people will go who can know the right Faith if they pray for it and enquire for it, yet do neither," he told her ominously. Perhaps he was frustrated with Elizabeth's imperviousness to his evangelizing efforts. Perhaps he sensed that she was *not* impervious and thought that presenting Catholicism as sinners' lone hope of redemption (which he believed it to be) would speed her progress. Whatever Filippo's motives, his remarks drove Elizabeth further toward the ecumenism that had characterized her beliefs as an adolescent and newly married woman. "Not that I can think there is a better way than I know," she wrote, "but every one must be respected in their own." She quoted Alexander Pope's couplet: "If I am right, thy grace impart, Still in the right to stay; / If I am wrong, oh teach my heart/ To find a better way." The lines are from Pope's "Universal Prayer," and

Elizabeth may also have remembered the couplet that immediately pre-
cedes them: "Let not this weak, unknowing hand Presume thy bolts to
throw, / And deal damnation round the land, On each I judge thy foe.[28]

In short, having stumbled into Filippo's harsh catechetical embrace,
Elizabeth danced quickly away. Or so she told both Rebecca and herself.
But here is Filippo's account of the same event:

> [Mrs. Seton] discovered to me that I was not deceived in my imagination
> [that she was interested in Catholicism] by putting several questions to me
> on the subject of Religion and asking me to give her every information in
> my power. . . . I was encouraged by the consideration that Providence often
> employs feeble instruments that her own power and glory may shine the
> more. I gave her all the information I could, my words seem'd to conquer
> her natural prejudices, and to enlighten her understanding.[29]

Filippo may have exaggerated the earnestness of Elizabeth's questioning
and the impression his answers left. But when she wrote in the journal
intended for her devoutly Protestant sister-in-law, Elizabeth may have
understated them. Hope for heaven animated her Christian belief; it
made a painful world bearable and turned death into a blessing. She
would have inquired about Catholic views of salvation if she inquired
about anything at all. And could she really have laughed off Filippo's
stern suggestion that because she had been exposed to the light of Catholic teachings, she was obligated to open her eyes to it? There was another
terrifying implication of Filippo's remarks. If Filippo was right, where
was William's soul?

Elizabeth may have wanted nothing more than to dismiss the possibility that only Catholics reached heaven. Yet she found she did not
want to dismiss a second Catholic teaching, the doctrine of transubstantiation. Attending another Mass, she had recoiled when an Englishman
whispered to her, at the moment the priest elevated the Host, "this is
what they call their real PRESENCE.'" "My very heart trembled with
shame and sorrow," Elizabeth wrote, "for his unfeeling interruption of
their sacred adoration for all around was dead Silence and many were
prostrated." With his whisper, the Englishman had turned a sacred ritual
into a tourist spectacle. But wasn't Elizabeth also a tourist rather than
a participant? The Englishman thought so, but he was wrong. She tells
the story as an offense against "their" beliefs, but she too felt she was
in the presence of God. "Involuntarily," she wrote, "I bent from [the

Englishman] to the pavement and thought secretly on the word of St. Paul with starting tears, 'they discern not the Lord's body.'" Filippo had presented the verse as evidence for the Catholic teaching that during Mass, the priest turns bread into the "Lord's body." Elizabeth felt that he—and the Catholic Church—might be right.[30]

By telling the story of the whispering Englishman, Elizabeth edged toward telling Rebecca—and herself—that she believed priests turned bread into the body of Christ. She immediately took a step back, questioning the plausibility of transubstantiation. But she followed that question with a chain of others. "How did he breathe my soul in me, and how and how a hundred other things I know nothing about," she demanded.[31] Her meaning is clear: Was transubstantiation really more improbable than a hundred other things Christian teachings, and life itself, daily proposed?

Elizabeth cut off her unspooling thoughts with a sudden turn toward New York: "I lost these thoughts in my babes at home," she wrote, "which I daily long for more and more."[32] Any dalliance with Catholicism's stern demands and beguiling mysteries must remain just that, a dalliance. She was a widowed mother who would soon sail home to her children. She might sometimes find a moment to think of Florence and the "dear people" who were "so strange about Religion." But it would all seem very far away. Not long after she penned these musings, Elizabeth and Anna Maria said goodbye to the Filicchis, boarded the *Shepherdess* "with gold and passports and recommendations," and went to sleep "ready to sail next morning."[33]

THEY POSSESS GOD

That night a storm swirled around the *Shepherdess* and sent it crashing into a vessel moored at the same wharf. When the Setons disembarked to await repairs, Anna Maria confessed that she'd felt sick for days. Bright "iruptions" were the telltale marks of an advanced streptococcus infection: scarlet fever had set in.[34] Elizabeth was so desperate to reach home (and to leave the increasingly confusing environs of Italy) that she tried to reboard the repaired *Sheperdess* with her sick daughter a few days later. Knowing he risked quarantine, the captain refused the Setons passage. Elizabeth and Anna Maria remained with the Filicchis in Livorno.[35]

Six days passed before Elizabeth took up her pen. When she did, Anna was well and Elizabeth was again contemplating the Catholic Eucharist. "My Sister dear," she mused to Rebecca, "how happy would we be if we believed what these dear Souls believe, that they *possess* God in the Sacrament and that he remains in their churches and is carried to them when they are sick." What had a week earlier been a reluctant contemplation of the possibility that God was present in the Eucharist now was open desire. "The other day in a moment of excessive distress," she wrote, "I fell on my knees without thinking when the Blessed Sacrament passed by and cried in an agony to God to bless me if he was there, that my whole Soul desired only him."[36]

The Virgin Mary beckoned too. As intercessor and granter of miracles, Mary had long helped Catholicism gain converts. Men and women professed allegiance to Catholicism for all kinds of reasons: the appeal of doctrine, the advantage of alliance, the threat of the sword. But Mary, the merciful and powerful mother, was embraced by cultures throughout the Old and New Worlds, her shrines visited by Muslim women in Lebanon and Syria and by indigenous peasants in Mexico. In Italy, Elizabeth saw images of the Madonna and Child everywhere, and they added a female and maternal dimension to a Christian faith she had known as centered on Father and Son. Finding in one of Amabilia's books the Memorare, a prayer "of St. Bernard to the Blessed Virgin," Elizabeth felt that "really I had a Mother which you know my foolish heart so often lamented to have lost in early days." Like the promise of transubstantiation, Mary offered a presence that Elizabeth had sought throughout her life. "From the first remembrance of infancy I have looked in all the plays of childhood and wildness of youth to the clouds for my Mother," she wrote as she meditated on the Madonna, "and at that moment it seemed as if I had found more than her, even in tenderness and pity of a Mother—so I cried myself to sleep in her heart."[37]

Filippo urged Elizabeth on. Just as Hobart had taught that the Episcopalian communion brought Elizabeth the faith of the apostles, Filippo instructed her that the Roman Catholic Church had descended from that first, intimate circle. Antonio was an admirer and friend rather than a guide, but he, too, passionately wanted Elizabeth to adopt his faith. Antonio proved as gallant as Filippo was stern, and Elizabeth was drawn to him and the vision of herself—brave, soulful, Catholic—that she saw in his eyes. Raw from William's loss, Elizabeth found comfort in Antonio's presence, and in March was happy to tell Rebecca that when she and Anna Maria sailed for New York, Antonio would go with them. Doing so, Antonio explained, suited the Filicchis' business purposes and allowed him to honor William's memory. After praising Anna Maria's newfound maturity—"in understanding and temper the five months past are to her more than years," the proud mother wrote—and telling her sister-in-law that she "had wept plentifully over" "my dear Seton's grave," Elizabeth signed off.[38]

There are no extant letters or journal entries for a month. When Elizabeth next writes, it is to Antonio, and her affection for him bears a startling undercurrent. "My most dear A," she wrote, "We often receive blessing from the hand of God and convert them into evils [,] this has been my fault in respect to the very sincere and uncommon affections I have for you." Elizabeth had enjoyed many friendships with men. This note reveals that her affection for Antonio unsettled her; she had considered shunning him in order to avoid temptation. She shook off her worry. "I am determined with God's help no more to abuse the very great favour he bestows on me in giving me your friendship and in future will endeavor to shew you how much I value it by doing all I can to contribute to your happiness," she wrote. After urging Antonio to "behave to me with Confidence and affection" and assuring him that "the more you confide in me the more Careful I shall be," she signed off with a dash of her old spiritual confidence. "Trust me and the Angel," she wrote.[39]

Antonio probably found the whole episode confounding. He understood his attentions to Elizabeth as harmless gallantry, although his admiration for her was real. The Italian custom of *cisisbeismo*, in which a married woman conducted an intense friendship with a man, flourished in the eighteenth and nineteenth centuries; some partnerships were romantic in their language and gestures but entirely chaste, and Antonio likely understood his relationship with Elizabeth in this way.[40] Like his brother, he believed Elizabeth's soul would be saved through conversion, and if charm and affection enabled him to escort her along the sacred path, where lay the harm?

Elizabeth was more ambivalent. She was drawn to Antonio and to his Catholic faith. But she wondered whether these were God-inspired loves or infidelities. She decided that she was not being unfaithful—to

FIGURE 7.2. Antonio Filicchi. APSL 1–3–5, box 42, folder 12. Courtesy of the Daughters of Charity Province of St. Louise Archives, Emmitsburg, Maryland.

William's memory, to John Henry Hobart's guidance, to her family's faith—but rather was finding a new path to God. She resumed her intense friendship with Antonio and wrote more directly than ever before about the beauties of Catholicism.

As she left caution behind, Elizabeth told her soul sister Rebecca that she preferred the literal, Catholic experience of fasting to "Mr. H"'s elegant explanation that biblical language was figurative.[41] Having spent a lifetime trying to transcend emotional pain and fear, Elizabeth also praised the Catholic teaching that suffering could be offered to God. Less transactional than her shipboard promise to avoid pleasure if God would one day reunite her family in heaven, the Catholic teaching, in Elizabeth's eyes, gave suffering a transcendent purpose. "O my," she wrote, "—I don't know how any body can have any trouble in this world who believe all these dear Souls believe. . . . Why they must be as happy as the angels almost."[42] Elizabeth had drawn Rebecca with her into a circle of devoutly Protestant devotion. Now she hinted that she wanted Rebecca's company in a different kind of sisterhood.

The portrait Elizabeth painted for Rebecca, of dear people happy in their simple but exotic world, is a romantic traveler's view. She saw Italy as the gorgeously simple opposite of her home. Manhattan's landscape was spiked with churches of all kinds and loud with arguing inhabitants. Florence seemed a place with a single purpose, a unified people, and a palpable truth. Elizabeth wanted that wholeness as much as she wanted the Catholic faith. She was not content simply to sample Catholicism, taking from it what might be useful, as she had done with other intellectual and spiritual traditions. Instead, she wanted to live inside it as she believed Italians did. Symbol and referent, God and man, individual and community: all that was separate in Manhattan seemed united in Italy.

Catholicism also offered Elizabeth something completely unexpected. Although Protestants had argued for centuries that Catholicism rigidly confined the sacred to the bounds of churches and the rites of priests, Elizabeth felt she had discovered the opposite to be true. Catholicism enabled divinity to penetrate life. "All the Catholic Religion is full of those meanings which interest me so," she wrote. Even making the sign of the cross seemed momentous. "Dearest Rebecca I was cold with the awful impression my first making it gave me. The Sign of the Cross of Christ on me." Elizabeth's journal reveals her approaching a decision unimaginable weeks earlier. "If I don't believe [what Catholics believe]," she wrote, "it shall not be for want of praying."[43]

If that sentence suggests certainty, its placement shows lingering hesitation. It appears in the middle of a paragraph, and the paragraph itself comes in the middle of a meandering discussion of Catholic fasting and Communion. The entire passage, moreover, appears in a journal Elizabeth intended to give Rebecca on her return, not in letters that might arrive in New York before Elizabeth herself did. Yet even if it was all somewhat muffled and hesitant, and even if Elizabeth could in the end decide not to give Rebecca the journal at all, she was starting to draft an appeal that the young woman join her in an astonishing decision. "How often you and I used to sigh and say *no more till next Sunday* as we turned from the church door which closed on us," she wrote, reminding her soul sister of their shared craving for services. "Well here," Elizabeth declared, "they go to church at 4 every morning if they please." In New York, she and Rebecca were "laughed at for running from one church to the other Sacrament Sundays, that we might receive as often as we could." In Italy, hunger for Communion was readily sated: "They can go *every day*."[44]

Even now, Elizabeth did not reveal to Rebecca the extent of her attraction to Catholicism. She confided instead in the thrilled Filicchis. Filippo insisted—whether against Elizabeth's wishes or in accord with them, is not clear—that she make no formal change before returning home. The conversion of this genteel Protestant woman would be a marvelous advertisement for the Catholic faith, and Filippo did not want to jeopardize its effects by having it appear Elizabeth had been coerced in a foreign land. It was a reasonable worry; contemporary novels contained such tales, and a forced conversion to Catholicism figures in Rousseau's *Emile,* a book Elizabeth herself loved. Instead, Filippo wanted Elizabeth to sail home, explain her decision to her friends and relatives, and adopt her new faith under circumstances that made her free will clear. Antonio would accompany her and bolster her courage. Filippo would in a way accompany her too: he prepared a long document defending Catholic doctrine and practice on all points at which he expected Americans to attack it. Having sailed to Italy treasuring Hobart's elegant Episcopalian sermons, Elizabeth would sail home with a tract declaring Roman Catholicism the one true faith.

Elizabeth, Anna Maria, and Antonio bade loving farewells to Amabilia and the other Filicchis. As their ship, the *Pyamingo,* sailed out of Livorno's harbor, Elizabeth was a Catholic believer. She understood her change in creed to be a necessity rather than a choice. "To be brought to the light of thy truth," begins one unfinished sentence, "notwithstanding every affection of my heart and power of my will was opposed to it . . ." There were a number of reasons for her reluctance. Although the Setons knew elite Catholics in New York, Elizabeth realized the faith was thought primitive by some in her circle. New York's lone Catholic parish was populated more by artisans and laborers than by merchants such as the Stoughtons and Lynches; her father had included an account of St. Peter's wretched poor in his pamphlet on yellow fever. There were more personal pains too. Elizabeth would complicate her children's lives by raising them in a Catholic household amid a Protestant clan.

Rebecca and Cecilia Seton, along with Catherine Dupleix, Eliza Sadler, and others with whom Elizabeth had shared her Protestant faith, would be shocked by her change of heart.

There was another haunting ramification of Elizabeth's decision to convert, one that emerged from Filippo's belief that Catholicism offered the only safe path to salvation. "Most dear Seton," she wrote, "where are you now?" Four months earlier, Elizabeth was sure her husband's gentle soul rested in heaven. But William had learned of Catholicism during his sojourns in Italy and declined to accept its teachings. If Filippo was right, his soul was not at rest. Elizabeth imagined her husband in purgatory, the realm in which, according to Catholic teachings, souls were cleansed by literal or figurative fire before entering heaven. Prayers for the dead were thought to speed their passage and lessen their pain, and Elizabeth was left to hope she might still prove her husband's helpmate. "Does he pass this birthday in heaven?" she wondered. "Oh, my husband, how my soul would rejoice to be united with yours—if rejoicing before his throne, how joyful—if in the bonds of justice, how willingly it would share your pain to lessen it."[45] Elizabeth's decision to convert distanced her from William. In doing so it brought pain and her old foe uncertainty, as well as hope.

As the ship sailed westward, Elizabeth prayed for William and for her own soul. Then, shocking herself, she felt a resurgent, dangerous affection for Antonio. In oblique and agonized fashion, Elizabeth recorded her struggle.

21st of April, 1804:

> "Ye shall not be tempted above what ye are able, but with the temptation there shall be a way to escape." . . . Since we cannot fly the monster, we must face him, calling on thy name, Jesus! Jesus! Jesus! . . . When a soul whose only hope is in God, whose concern and desires are so limited that it would forsake all human beings, and account the dearest ties of life as foolishness compared with his love—when this soul sincerely desirous of serving and obeying him, is beset by the lowest passions of human nature, and from tears and prayers of earnest penitence can, by the apparently, most trivial incitements, pass to the most humiliating compliances to sin . . . this can only be the work of the enemy of our souls.[46]

What had happened? Was it a touch, a kiss? In the tight quarters of the *Pyamingo* and within the strict confines of Elizabeth's conscience, it was unlikely to have been more. To Filippo, it may simply have been another

moment of harmless gallantry. But Elizabeth felt shame. She thought she
had mastered herself; she was wrong.

It seems extraordinary that within a few months of her husband's
agonizing death, Elizabeth found herself drawn to any man. It was more
extraordinary still that the man should be married. Not only did Elizabeth believe infidelity to be a sin, but she knew it to be a marriage's
killing frost. Yet it may have been precisely Antonio's marriage and her
own grief that led Elizabeth to leave her emotions unguarded: it was
impossible that anything untoward could develop. And then her affection for Antonio threatened to escape its bounds.

"Until the effects [of the lowest passions] are experienced," Elizabeth
wrote, "it would be too incredible that the commonest affections and
unintentional actions should produce a confusion and disturbance in the
mind that is exalted to the love of God, and destroy every impression
but momentary gratification." "Confusion and disturbance in the mind"
could have been taken from Richard Bayley's descriptions of patients,
but later in this headlong passage, Elizabeth suggests that the attraction
could "only be the work of the enemy of our souls"—Satan. Discordant as those two interpretive schemes seem, in both of them Elizabeth
casts the problem as something external—illness, the devil—that she
could combat. She set herself to the task. Once again, she vowed that
her friendship with Antonio would remain chaste, and once again she
decided that because the friendship could be purified, it need not end.
She went further: the very temptation each posed to the other became a
struggle they could offer God. Elizabeth would not give up this friendship. And she would not give up her Catholic faith.[47]

The rest of the voyage passed peacefully. Near its end, Elizabeth
addressed herself to the task she dreaded more than any other, telling
Reverend John Henry Hobart that she wished to become a Catholic.
"The tears fall fast thro' my fingers at the insupportable thought of being
Seperated from you," she wrote her minister. Elizabeth knew Hobart
felt absolute confidence in her Protestant piety, and she insisted that
she had not betrayed him lightly or at all. She laid the secret pain of her
conversion at his feet. "You have certainly without my knowing it been
dearer to me than God," she wrote in a startling phrase, and she told
him that only her belief that Hobart wanted her to do as her judgment
instructed allowed her to make a decision she knew he'd loathe. Her difficulty in choosing between Episcopalianism and Catholicism, she told

the minister, had been "destroying my mortal life and more than that my peace with God."[48]

The letter exists only as a draft. It is unclear whether she sent a final version. One way or another, Elizabeth had resolved to consider Hobart's "dear friendship and esteem" as "the price of my fidelity to what I believe to be the truth."[49] She believed that converting to Catholicism was the way to submit to God's will. In order to achieve that submission, she was now willing to defy everyone she knew.

8

THE BATTLE JOINED

"ARRIVED THIS MORNING," reads a June 4, 1804, notice in New York's *Daily Advertiser*, "ship Pyomingo, [Captain] Blagge from Leghorn, with Mrs. Seton, widow of the Wm. Seton, Esq. a passenger." Elizabeth stepped from the wooden cocoon of the *Pyamingo* onto the docks of a city that had clattered on in her absence. As she, Antonio, and Anna Maria disembarked, merchants traded their goods, physicians tended their patients, and newspaper editors proffered news of an intensifying feud between Alexander Hamilton and Aaron Burr. But all of that could wait: when the Seton clan reunited, all five of Elizabeth's children were there to greet her. "Do I hold my dear ones again my bosom," she wrote in relief. "Has god restored all my Treasure—even the little soul [Bec] I have so long contemplated an angel in heaven[?]"[1]

Yet sadness lapped at the edges of the reunion. Bec had been barely weaned when her mother and Anna Maria sailed away and could not have recognized them on their return. Will, Richard, and Kit grieved their father's death. And although Harriet and Cecilia welcomed Elizabeth home, the young woman Elizabeth called her soul sister, was not there to greet her. Rebecca's consumption had dramatically worsened over the months of Elizabeth's absence, and she lay bedridden at the Farquhars'. Brought to see her, Elizabeth knew immediately that she was looking at a dying woman. "Only the shadow remaining," she mourned.

The journal she'd expected to share with Rebecca became the record of a new grief. "The Society of Sisters united by prayer and divine affections," Elizabeth mourned, "the Evening hymns, the daily lectures, the sunset contemplations, the Service of holy days, the Kiss of Peace, the widows' visits—all—all—gone—forever."[2]

That was the first blow. There was soon a second: Elizabeth learned that she was entirely destitute. Her brother-in-law Wright Post, as well as family friend John Wilkes and Elizabeth's godmother, Sarah Startin, promised to provide money to keep Elizabeth and her children housed, clothed, and fed. But rather than living in a stately (if rented) home on the Battery, as they had done even after William's bankruptcy, they would inhabit the upper story of what Elizabeth described as a "small, neat house half a mile from town"; there were to be lodgers on the floor below. Elizabeth was to have one servant, an older woman named Mary, but the days of cooks and nurses were gone, and when little Bec was old enough, the family expected Elizabeth to contribute to her own upkeep. Although she did not fear deprivation or work, she dreaded the thought of living on others' sufferance. She had spent her childhood housed but homeless, and it was to that unpleasant half-exile she had returned.

Elizabeth wanted to offer up her new sorrows to God. To do that, she believed she must pray as a Catholic. And to do *that*, she believed she must become a Catholic. So, not long after her arrival, she told her friends and family of her decision to convert. No one left an account of the conversations, but it seems from later evidence that Elizabeth's announcement was greeted with some of the surprise and concern she'd expected. The Farquhars and one of William's half sisters, Charlotte, thought Catholicism a primitive faith and looked with particular suspicion on Antonio, whose presence turned out to evoke the very fears of coercion Filippo had hoped to avoid. Yet it's also clear that surprise and concern did not become cruelty. Mystified but loyal, Elizabeth's friends and family hoped that her fascination with Catholicism would fade with her grief.

One person was both less tolerant of her decision and more respectful of its seriousness: John Henry Hobart. Elizabeth gave her minister her Italian journal and Filippo's tract on Catholicism, hoping the texts would persuade him of the reasonableness, if not the desirability, of her conversion. She thought that the worst that could happen was that the young minister would end their friendship. She did not imagine he would launch a bitter fight for her soul, but that's what Hobart did.

He proved well armed for battle. Hobart loved Elizabeth and believed Catholicism unworthy of her; he also understood that her conversion might become a public embarrassment to Trinity and to himself. His recently published *Companion for the Altar* was already proving controversial; his insistence that Episcopalian priests were uniquely the inheritors of Christ's relationship with the apostles had left members of other denominations furious, with at least one critic publicly accusing Hobart of being "popish."[3] There could hardly have been a less opportune time for a socially prominent member of his flock, one known to have been particularly moved by his sermons, to actually convert to Roman Catholicism.

Hobart enlisted the aid of Trinity's rector, Bishop Benjamin Moore, to argue Elizabeth back into the Episcopalian fold. The two launched a withering assault on everything she loved about the Catholic faith. The beauty of its churches, the promise of saints' intercession between heaven and earth, the unbroken path back to apostolic days, even—especially—the doctrine of transubstantiation: Hobart and Moore rejected every teaching and countered every claim. The joyful certainty Elizabeth felt as she left Italy was gone before they finished speaking. With "the decided testimonies that are given me by the clergy of the Protestant Episcopal Church that they are a True Church," she later wrote, "I acknowledge that the foundation of my catholick principles is destroyed."[4]

Hobart and Moore had achieved exactly what Filippo had tried so hard to prevent. Yet the ministers' victory, though stunning, was partial. When the freshly laid foundation of Elizabeth's Catholic faith crumbled, her Episcopalian beliefs did not reassemble themselves beneath her feet. Instead, she fell into uncertainty, and out of uncertainty grew resolve. In Italy she had listened to Antonio and Filippo. On her return to New York she listened to Hobart and Moore. Now Elizabeth vowed to make no decision about her faith until she had compared claims and evidence by the light of her own reason.

First, however, she had to watch her soul sister die. In the days after her return from Italy, Elizabeth sat with Rebecca, saying "our usual prayers, the Te Deum, the fifty-first psalm, and part of the Communion Service." Love and uncertainty filled the sickroom. Years later, writing "Dear Remembrances," Elizabeth hinted that she shared something of her experience in Italy with her sister-in-law. "A thousand pages could not tell the sweet hours now with my departing Rebecca," she wrote, "the wonder at the few lines I could point out (in her continually fainting and exhausted condition) of the true faith and service of our God." Those "few lines" about "the true faith," no matter how gentle and tentative, must have unsettled the desperately ill Rebecca. The young woman had not dreamed that the companion who'd so confidently beckoned her toward heaven would now, as Rebecca faced death, hint that she'd been wrong about the path to take. Rebecca gracefully but firmly turned their conversations away from doctrine and division. "'Your people are my people,'" she told Elizabeth over and over, "'Your God my God.'"[5] Elizabeth did not press her further.

Over the next several days, tuberculosis toyed with Rebecca as it had with William, her strength briefly returning only to fade again. At last, after declaring "All is ready," twenty-four-year-old Rebecca died. "He who searches the heart and knows the spring of each secret affection," Elizabeth wrote, "He only knows what I lost at that moment." She mourned not only a friend but also a sounding board; Elizabeth had developed her Episcopalian faith in conversation and correspondence with Rebecca, and now, desperately needing her spiritual companionship, she had to carry on alone. She vowed not to fear or lament. "The Soul presses forward towards the mark and prize of her high calling in Christ Jesus."[6]

The busy Seton clan paused at Rebecca's death. A notice in Manhattan's *Evening Post* celebrated the young woman as a model of piety that did not disrupt: her faith was "humble and unassuming," the obituary read, and "ardent without enthusiasm."[7] If Rebecca's beloved minister, John Henry Hobart, had a hand in writing the notice, the lesson he hoped to teach was not one Elizabeth wished to learn.

Scant days after the family laid Rebecca to rest in Trinity churchyard, they and the rest of Manhattan awoke to shocking news. The hostility between Alexander Hamilton and Aaron Burr had flamed into violence; the two crossed the Hudson to duel in Weehawken, New Jersey, and although Hamilton aimed his pistol harmlessly toward the branches above him, Burr shot his rival through the gut. Hamilton died after two days of agony. As bells rang throughout the city, a somber procession took Hamilton's body to Trinity churchyard, where the dirt on Rebecca's grave had not yet settled.

Hoping to turn the grotesque event into a lesson for the stunned city, Trinity's rector, Benjamin Moore, took to the newspapers to detail Hamilton's deathbed scene. Like William Seton and many other men of the congregation, Hamilton had not taken Communion at Trinity, although his wife did. As he lay dying, he wanted to receive the sacrament so summoned Bishop Moore. As Moore recounted the event, he elicited Hamilton's denunciation of dueling, then posed straightforward questions: "Do you sincerely repent of your sins past?" "Have you a lively faith in God's mercy through Christ; with a grateful remembrance of the death of Christ; and are you disposed to live in love and charity with all men?" When the dying man agreed to it all, Moore offered him Communion. "The strong, inquisitive, and comprehensive mind" of the statesman, the Episcopalian bishop wrote, embraced a simple creed "as the truth from Heaven," and all New Yorkers should be satisfied with the same.[8] Like the obituary of Rebecca that had appeared days earlier, this was counsel Elizabeth had no intention of heeding. Her "strong, inquisitive, and comprehensive mind" believed the truth was more complicated than Moore let on.

A CAVE OR DESERT

The city sweltered, and the women of Elizabeth Seton's circle decamped for country homes. Elizabeth remained in her rented rooms. She took pleasure in her children, with whom she shared music and Bible stories, and in Harriet and Cecilia, to whom she remained something very like a mother. Otherwise, she was miserable. "It appears to me . . . that a cave or a desert would best satisfy my Natural desire," she wrote.[9] Manhattan embodied choice as Florence embodied Catholicism, and Elizabeth no longer felt at home within its cacophony of possibility. Grieving her husband and unsettled in her faith, she also chafed at life as an impecunious, widowed mother of five. Used to having her judgment respected, she had become the object of constant well-meaning advice. The same assumptions that led members of the poor widows' society to evaluate the worthiness of those they helped left Elizabeth's family confident they should offer judgment along with their charity. Whether because the irony of her situation was too acute to endure or because she had even less in common with their religious sensibilities than before, Elizabeth avoided Isabella Graham and her godmother, Sarah Startin. It was her irreverent old friend Julia Scott who cheered her.

Their correspondence had faltered as Elizabeth burrowed deeply into her Episcopalian faith, but Julia had no interest in their past religious differences. Nor did she question Elizabeth's tentative Catholicism. She offered sympathy and neither took nor gave advice. "The tenderness and affection of your expressions," Elizabeth wrote in response, "brought many quick and bitter tears from my very heart. I find so many changes and reverses in my singular fate that I did not look for your kindness or value your friendship as I ought." She described her straitened circumstances to Julia as cheerfully as she could. "We eat milk morning and evening and chocolate for dinner, always with a thankful heart and a good appetite," she wrote, adding that she was pleased to see her children "without those pretentions and indulgences that ruin so many."[10] Julia had no doubt that Elizabeth was pleased to raise her children without indulgences. But chocolate for dinner? She made plans to travel to New York.

Grateful for this sturdy friendship, Elizabeth nonetheless longed for a spiritual companion; Rebecca was gone and in this role Julia would not serve. Cecilia Seton had become an ardent member of Elizabeth's prayer circle before the Italian trip, but she was still in her early teens, and Elizabeth did not want to drag the girl into her crisis of faith. She had expected to have Antonio's companionship, but he, aware that Elizabeth's relatives mistrusted him, kept a distance. ("[I] was so unhappy as to lose you in the crowd this Morning dear dear Brother," reads a plaintive note from Elizabeth. "Why did you not look for me as I did for you?")[11] In order to share and organize her thoughts, Elizabeth tentatively began a new journal. Her intended reader was a surprising choice: Amabilia Filicchi. Antonio's wife knew nothing of Manhattan society or Protestant teachings, and her English was likely imperfect at best. But Elizabeth admired the Italian woman's faith, and writing to her served, consciously or not, to guard against attraction to Antonio. She took up her pen.

Elizabeth began the journal by deftly sketching herself as a coveted customer in Manhattan's marketplace of religion. "Old friends come to see me," she wrote. "One of the most excellent women I ever knew, who is the Church of Scotland [likely Isabella Graham], said to me, 'oh do dear Soul come and hear our J. Mason and I am sure you will join us.'" Others came too, she told Amabilia: a Quaker "coaxed . . . with artless persuasion, Betsy I tell thee thee had best come with us," an Anabaptist made a pitch for regeneration, and Elizabeth's servant, Mary, a Methodist, groaned over her lack of "convictions."[12] The cheerful, witty lines, with their acknowledgment of friends' steady (if meddlesome) love, stand in contrast to Elizabeth's anxious and unhappy letters. But after one entry, she laid the journal aside.

One New Yorker was trying far harder than any other to influence Elizabeth's choice: John Henry Hobart. Amid the press of his duties at Trinity and the claims of a growing family, Hobart found time to write an eighty-page tract answering Filippo's claims (he also found time to borrow from the New York Society Library a volume on the Council of Trent, the better to do battle). He had no money for a clerk and no time for corrections, so in contrast to Filippo's elegantly produced document, Hobart's text is spotted with strike-outs, its lines uneven. There is another difference: Filippo's missive was intended to command Elizabeth's obedience. Hobart wrote as a man who feared not rebellion but betrayal.

"When I see a person whose sincere and ardent piety, I have always thought worthy of imitation," the minister began, "and an honor to the church in which it was quickened and cherished, in danger of forsaking it and connecting herself with a communion which my sober judgment tells me is a corrupt and sinful communion, I cannot be otherwise than deeply affected." Hobart could not understand how Elizabeth's "pious and holy ardour" could turn against its source, her Protestant faith. His wounded affection darkened into warning. "When I see one too from whose friendship myself and many others have derived [benefit] . . . in danger of taking a step which in its consequences may separate her from our society, a society which in times past was her solace and enjoyment—it would be strange indeed if my anxious sensibility were not awakened."[13]

Hobart's missive appealed to Elizabeth's reason and loyalty in prose both elegant and impassioned. It was an amalgam that had until recently formed the language in which Elizabeth spoke to God and the language in which she listened for a reply. But in Italy, Catholicism offered a new language: the seven sacraments, the intercession of the saints and the Virgin Mary, the paintings and sculpture of Florence. Hobart had read Elizabeth's Italian journal and understood this, so he scathingly attacked Catholicism's offerings and directed particular venom at the doctrine of transubstantiation. The doctrine that so moved Elizabeth was "abhorrent to reason, to our senses, and to our feelings."[14] The ritual of Communion was figurative, Hobart insisted, using a form of that word three times in a single paragraph. The mind, not the body, consumed God. Surely a woman such as Elizabeth Seton, brought to her faith by a man such as John Henry Hobart, understood this.

Hobart's phrases caught in Elizabeth's mind like scripture. Yet they did not win her back. The Protestant apologetics Hobart and Moore recommended failed in the same way, their harsh condemnations of Catholicism alienating Elizabeth from both faiths. Her Episcopalian guides had combated Filippo's every claim, but they quietly agreed with him on one central matter: some faiths pleased God, and some did not. Elizabeth was left with one certainty: the eternal fate of her soul and her children's souls rested on her choice of religion. Her spiritual life brought not peace but dread.

The more Elizabeth struggled, the more she coveted Antonio Filicchi's companionship. His faith in Elizabeth had made her conversion seem possible, and she missed both her confidence and the man who'd inspired it. Antonio admired Elizabeth, but he was eager to leave for Boston. He understood more clearly than Elizabeth that her merchant clan looked on him with suspicion, and he found their distaste not only unpleasant but financially damaging. In Boston his reputation and thus his credit were sound. Hoping to find Elizabeth some local Catholic guidance so that he could leave Manhattan in good conscience, Antonio turned to the priests of St. Peter's parish.

They were, he quickly discovered, a complicated lot. The most senior, William O'Brien, had in earlier years earned the confidence of Bishop John Carroll; now he did so little that St. Peter's business-minded trustees resented his salary. In 1799 O'Brien had been given an assistant, Matthew O'Brien. Known as "the little Doctor," or "the young gentleman," this new O'Brien quickly gained a reputation as an effective preacher. The two O'Briens seem to have been relatives, but shared blood and pastoral duties did not make them allies; in letters to Carroll, they referred to each other with bristling contempt. Busy with their own small wars, neither wanted to involve himself in an Episcopalian widow's spiritual struggle.[15] Bishop Carroll had recently sent a third Irish priest, John Byrne, to the growing parish, but Byrne was both dour and zealous, and within months of his arrival, Carroll instructed him to try harder to adapt himself to his new countrymen's expectations.[16] Antonio did not see Father Byrne as Elizabeth's guide either.

Drawing on his brother's connections, Antonio decided to appeal directly to Bishop Carroll. Telling Elizabeth to prepare an account of her spiritual state, he intended to bundle it together with Filippo's statement of doctrine and Hobart's eighty pages of counterarguments and let the bishop sort it all out. Elizabeth wrote a draft, and Antonio prepared a cover letter. "As soon as I shall be relieved through your better interposition from my present responsibility and anxiety, I propose to leave this town for Boston and Eastward," he wrote Carroll. All Antonio needed was Elizabeth's final draft. Instead, she sent a message demanding that Antonio return Hobart's and Filicchi's texts to her. Hobart had convinced her "not to enter into any more discussion."[17]

His plan disrupted, Antonio brought Hobart and Filippo's texts, along with an account of his dilemma, to Father Matthew O'Brien. The priest was at first confident but after reading the dueling missives, had nothing to offer beyond a copy of *England's Conversion and Reformation Compared,* a tedious set of dialogues ostensibly between "a young gentleman and his preceptor," which spent considerable energy heaping scorn on Henry VIII and Anne Boleyn. That would clearly not do, so Antonio decided to send Carroll the draft of Elizabeth's letter and hope for the best. "I must beg you with all my soul," he wrote the bishop, "to hasten to come to my relief with the proper direction and answer."[18]

Elizabeth's draft did all that was needed. She must have known that sending it allowed her to obey Hobart's wishes without sacrificing what she wanted: John Carroll's advice. In it she described her profound attraction to Catholic teachings and her painful doubts. She also made a practical point: "as the Mother and Sole parent of five children," she needed to make a decision. She had no church at all now, she told the bishop, so "it will be an act of the greatest charity to forward your sentiments as soon as your leisure will permit."[19] Antonio sent the draft and his cover letter to Carroll in Baltimore. When three weeks had passed without a reply, he wrote again. He was the guardian of "the eternal salvation of 6 souls," and he should "have been already in Boston." He needed help right away.[20]

Soon after receiving Antonio's second urgent letter, John Carroll replied. He knew of the widow Seton from Filippo's letter months earlier and realized that the merchant brothers saw her as a compelling and respectable face for American Catholicism. Carroll's own training as a Jesuit left him with an appreciation for the role of elite converts; the Society of Jesus had evangelized powerful and educated individuals as they sought to plant the Church throughout the world. Yet Carroll proceeded cautiously. Optimistic about the future of the American Church, he was also vigilant about overstepping, convinced that legal and cultural backlash threatened. In his first sermon as bishop of Baltimore, Carroll told his flock that they must "preserve in their hearts a warm charity & forebearance towards every other denomination," "& at the same time" avoid "that fatal & prevailing indifference, which views all religions as equally acceptable to God & salutary to men."[21] Both were essential; both were difficult. Carroll believed Elizabeth's soul—like everyone's— was safer within the Church, and he, like Filippo, prayed that Catholicism would take root within the new nation; it was the purpose for which he had willed and maneuvered the Baltimore see into existence. But he had no wish to antagonize New Yorkers by intervening ham-fistedly in the conversion crisis of a genteel Episcopalian matron. In his letter, he suggested Elizabeth continue to read scripture and works of Catholic devotion, but he made no effort to turn her against Hobart's counsel.[22]

Elizabeth held Carroll's letter "to my heart, on my knees beseeching God to enlighten me to see the truth, unmixed with doubts and hesitations."[23] She wanted the bishop to persuade her, to urge her; instead he'd offered gentle instruction. Her doubts and hesitations continued, and now no visit from Antonio could lighten her mood: after delivering Carroll's letter, Antonio left for Boston.

Trying to gather her thoughts, Elizabeth took up her journal to Amabilia. She confessed a profound heaviness of spirit, an "unworthy dejection" and "sad weariness now over life I never before was tired with." Her "lovely Children" still brought her joy, but everything else had collapsed into the hopeless choice between Episcopalianism and

Catholicism. On that choice hinged her soul and those of her five children, but each religion attacked the other without proving its own merit. The one thing they agreed on—that the other's congregants risked their salvation—saddened her. "It grieves my very Soul," she wrote of Hobart and Filippo's claims, but she believed they were right. She could no more recapture her confidence that there were many paths to heaven than she could recapture her Episcopalian or Catholic faith.[24]

The Elizabeth who wrote in her journal to Amabilia was saddened but contemplative; as she began to write to Antonio in Boston, a different woman emerged. Antonio gently discouraged her from sending him too many letters, so Elizabeth combined frequent, urgent notes into a single letter before mailing. "I have thought of you incessantly," she wrote a week after the merchant left New York. "Indeed I cannot think of my Soul without remembering you." The preternaturally calm matron turned back into the eager dependent she'd been in the first months of her marriage. "I begin now wishfully to watch for J[ames]," she wrote Antonio, "every evening hoping that he will bring me a letter from you." When at last a letter arrived, Elizabeth was not sated. "I can find but one fault in your letter," she wrote, "which is that a whole side of it is blank."[25] Elizabeth was desperate for a home, literal and spiritual, and Antonio was its image.

MY CONTEMPLATIONS

Elizabeth Seton wanted to think about God and Antonio. Friends and family wanted her to think about gaining her bed and board. Her benefactors felt they could not support her forever, and Elizabeth showed no interest in remarrying, a traditional means through which a widow regained her footing. Antonio had held out a promise of assistance but offered no details.[26] Having worked as treasurer for the poor widows' society and informal clerk to her husband, Elizabeth possessed valuable skills, but they brought her no gain. Since the colonial period widows had successfully taken over their late husbands' businesses, but William's transatlantic merchant house was a different kind of enterprise and bankrupt to boot, and the era's gender conventions made the idea of Elizabeth's working for pay in someone else's merchant enterprise unthinkable. Family friend John Wilkes proposed that she run a school, and while teaching offered the possibility of a respectable (in every sense of the word) living, Elizabeth feared the work would steal her time for reflection just when she most needed it. Then came a minor deliverance: Julia Scott and her daughter arrived for a visit, and along with good cheer, Julia offered money— money that Elizabeth was to use precisely as she chose. Her problems remained—Julia's money supplemented her benefactors' but could not replace it—but Elizabeth delighted in Julia's company and was relieved to have a sum that was her own.

When Julia left, Elizabeth closed herself back up in her rented rooms. Eliza Sadler faithfully visited but did not, Elizabeth wrote, "share our cause." Elizabeth's agonized indecision mystified her pious but practical friend; Elizabeth, in turn, had no use for Sadler's cool analysis, which in the past she'd so admired. The teenaged Harriet and Cecilia visited, and Elizabeth greeted them warmly but did not confide in them. Days passed without any visitors at all, and when John Henry Hobart discovered his tract had not convinced Elizabeth to return to Trinity, he proved "entirely out of all patience." "He says 'the Church was corrupt, we have returned to the Primitive doctrine and what more would you have when you act according to your best judgment,'" Elizabeth explained, capturing the minister's eagerness to close the question. Two weeks later, she realized all the city's Episcopalian ministers had "left me to my contemplations."[27]

For much of her life, Elizabeth had been content to be a solitary seeker. Yet when she immersed herself in John Henry Hobart's Episcopalianism, she had ceased to be—as a twenty-first-century American might say—spiritual but not religious. She wanted fellowship and a chalice of shared belief. She'd begun to find these things through Trinity Church. In Italy, Catholicism offered them in abundance. Now her desire to find the true communion left her standing entirely alone.

Weeks passed, evenings cooled, and women and children returned from their summer refuges. Still Elizabeth deliberated. In Italy, art and ritual had been the primary vessels of religious persuasion; back in New York, that vessel was books, and Elizabeth found a companion in Augustine of Hippo, whose *Confessions* she read and reread. The fourth-century African had taken a reflective, halting path toward Christianity, for years unwilling to embrace a religion whose teachings he found naive and unpersuasive. He at last converted to Christianity at thirty-one, the age Elizabeth now approached. "When I read that St. Augustine was long in a fluctuating state of mind between error and truth," she wrote Antonio, "I say to myself, be Patient, god will bring you Home at last."[28]

While she deliberated, Elizabeth welcomed the melancholy she'd suppressed throughout her adult life: until she discerned God's will, feeling miserable reassured her of her sincerity. She wept often, and her children worried. They say "'poor Mamma,'" she told Antonio, "and really are better than they were that they may not add to my sorrow."[29] A year earlier, Elizabeth would have shielded her children from her disquiet, but now she needed them to bear witness to her efforts. She knew she'd changed. "I am ashamed of my own letters," she wrote. "They are all Egotism." But she was *not* ashamed. "My Soul is so intirely engrossed by one subject," she continued, "that it cannot speak with freedom on any other."[30] As a child, Elizabeth had watched her father subordinate everything and everyone to his career. Now, although she lovingly tended her children, her own attention and purpose lay elsewhere.

While Elizabeth's soul was engrossed by the question of her faith, her heart remained engrossed by Antonio Filicchi. There, too, she was unembarrassed. "I can say with perfect truth at all times," she told him, "I prefer my Solitude to the company of any human being except that of my most dear A."[31] In a startling image, she told Antonio that just as her dying husband had called out for her, she found herself calling out "Antonio Antonio Antonio." "[I] call back the thought," she wrote, "and my Soul cries out Jesus Jesus Jesus." It was astonishing to place Antonio in the role of either spouse or savior; Elizabeth unabashedly did both. "In order to disclose to you the interior," she wrote Antonio on another day, "I must speak to you as to God."[32]

Elizabeth believed that her longing for Antonio was really a longing for Jesus. Was it instead the case that her longing for Jesus was a longing for Antonio? Her earlier affection for John Henry Hobart—which also contained exhilaration as well as admiration—has sparked such suggestions. After reading Elizabeth's letters to the Episcopalian minister, her grandson, Monsignor Robert Seton, concluded that she was infatuated with him. A modern historian, although carefully avoiding the monsignor's condescending tone, suggests that Elizabeth and Rebecca's relationship with John Henry Hobart had "another, nearly sexual dynamic in its intensity" and that Elizabeth was "flirtatious" as a congregant.[33] The collaboration was indeed highly charged, but there is no evidence Elizabeth was physically attracted to Hobart and no hint that she worried about the nature of their friendship. Not all intense relationships are really sexual in nature; there are other powerful animators of human passion. Elizabeth's excitement emerged from Hobart's role in her own transformation from a casual Christian to a devoted worshipper; he was witness and guide to her thrilling metamorphosis.

Elizabeth's friendship with Antonio was more complex. She worried over it in a way she did not over her love for Hobart, and although she and Antonio called each other "brother" and "sister," they wrote in tones of courtly love. Unlike her friendship with Hobart, Elizabeth's yearning for Antonio left her unsettled, nearly unable to think of anything else. Yet as she wrote her impassioned letters to Boston, Elizabeth did not imagine Antonio as an earthly romantic partner. She *did* turn to him as the dying William had turned to her and as she turned to Jesus: Antonio was the receptacle for her anxious yearning for God, for unconditional love, and for certainty in the face of death. In her letters to Antonio, she allowed full voice to the hope and dread that threatened daily to overwhelm her. Yet even in those letters, she did not cede independence in the one thing that mattered most: her faith. She would make that decision how and when she chose. Elizabeth painted herself as a fragile, clinging vine, but the oak remained.

IN SPIRIT AND IN TRUTH

John Henry Hobart was impatient but hopeful. Surely Elizabeth Seton's love of scripture and intellectual inquiry would return her to the Episcopalian communion. Like many Protestants, Hobart believed that the Catholic Church limited the flock's access to the Bible and shackled them to clergy. With its commanding tone and constant invocations of the Church's authority, Filippo Filicchi's missive seemed to fit that ugly pattern. "Judge you whether a piety founded on such a basis could have been enlightened and satisfactory to your own mind," he urged Elizabeth, and "whether it would have been acceptable to that infinitely perfect Being who requires his worshippers to 'worship him in *spirit* and in *truth*' . . . with 'the *mind*' as well as with 'the soul and strength,' who requires you to be able 'to give a reason for the hope that is in you.'"[34]

This was an excellent argument to make to a woman who honored reason as well as God, and the local incarnation of the Catholic Church, St. Peter's parish, offered little to counter it. Its priests believed that questions were for catechisms: they came with answers. But Elizabeth knew that the stone-faced certainty of Filippo and the sullen silence of St. Peter's priests were not the only faces of the Church; there was St. Augustine after all. And as Antonio astutely pointed out, although Protestants claimed to advocate inquiry, New York's Protestant ministers hardly welcomed it. It was "your priests who call loud for investigation," and "who do not acknowledge any authority above private reason of any human being," Antonio sniffed, "who nonetheless try to persuade you as a sacred duty to decline examination."[35] He had a point.

There, for months, matters stood. No one convinced Elizabeth that Catholicism was an unreasonable faith, and she did not convince herself it was a reasonable one. Determined to find a way out of her impasse, she took up her journal to Amabilia. In her letters to Antonio, she wrote what she felt; in the journal, she tried to figure out what she thought. After attending an Episcopalian service in order to soothe her family, she reflected on her reaction: disheartened by the "naked altar," she imagined herself "twenty times speaking to the Blessed Sacrament" in St. Peter's Catholic Church.[36]

Months after Elizabeth's return from Italy, Catholicism's promise of God's literal presence still thrilled her, and so did the beauty of its churches and rituals. But did those promises and rituals allow God to be felt by mortal man, or did they throw up a cloud of superstition that hid God's true face? The question of how people should represent and appeal to the divine had ricocheted through the Christian world for centuries, dividing the Eastern Church from the western, Protestant from Catholic, Lutheran from Anglican. Such questions had helped fracture the Islamic world as well.[37] Now these questions were Elizabeth's intimate and demanding companions. In her journal she tried out the possibility that Catholicism, with its murals, gestures, saints, and sculptures, understood the human mind and heart more fully than Protestantism did. The Protestants' God, she wrote, seems not "to love us . . . as much as he did the children of the old law since he leaves our churches with nothing but naked walls and our altars unadorned with either the Ark which his presence filled, or any of the precious pledges of his care of us which he gave to those of old." Turning Hobart's use of scripture against him, Elizabeth declared she could not worship God "in spirit and truth" without "something to fix [my] attention."[38] She was beginning to think that thought was not enough. Yet still she could not decide.

9

THIS STORM

ELIZABETH'S RENTED ROOMS lay north of the dense old
streets of lower Manhattan, close to the Post Road that ran
from New York to Boston. Antonio had traveled that road in
July, following it as it curved northward through the farmers' fields of
northern Manhattan and across the Bronx River to Westchester County,
where, years after New York's slow emancipation began, slaves still
labored. With its northern climate, Puritan roots, and tightly knit
cousinages, Boston seemed an unpromising destination for an Italian
Catholic merchant. But Antonio and the city took to each other from
the start.

Boston boasted a brand-new Catholic church, the first building
ever erected for that purpose in the city. Its architect, a not-yet-
famous Charles Bulfinch, gave Holy Cross a design that led locals to
describe it as an Italian Renaissance building. That required some
imagination, but the building's façade unabashedly gestured toward
continental Europe even as its rectangular-windowed sides fit neatly
into Boston's Federal cityscape. The building required not only a confident architect but also confident parishioners, and Holy Cross had
them. Like New York, the city was home to successful Catholic merchants, and Boston's historic distaste for the Catholic faith was leavened by a new belief that the diverse and fragile American republic
was strengthened when Christian denominations—Catholics among

them—lived harmoniously. In service of that ethos, Holy Cross's building campaign had drawn financial contributions from some of Boston's leading Protestant citizens, including President John Adams himself.

Over Holy Cross presided two priests who proved as welcoming to Antonio as St. Peter's clergy had been cool. Jean Cheverus and François Matignon (who restyled themselves John and Francis) were refugees from the French Revolution; their elegance and piety impressed a city that had previously been sent priests prone to scandal and dissension. The Sorbonne-educated Matignon arrived in the United States in 1792 and Cheverus, the more dynamic of the pair, four years later. Serving first in northern New England, Cheverus observed settlers and natives with a keen eye, sending John Carroll descriptions laced with humor and undergirded by respect and affection for those to whom he ministered (his correspondence, begun in French, shifted within months to a graceful English). Sent next to Boston, Cheverus saw that American religion was a marketplace and began to compete. He bravely tended parishioners during a yellow fever epidemic and gave sermons so eloquent that Protestants turned out to hear them. Cheverus hoped someday to return to his native France, but like Elizabeth he had learned the futility of expectation. "We live in times where less than one year is enough to overturn not only individual projects, but even Empires and Nations," he mused to Carroll. "My only wish is to obey the voice of Providence and to go wherever it calls."[1]

Antonio delighted in Cheverus, Holy Cross Church, and the fact that Boston's merchants felt none of the mistrust for him that New York's had; across the city, homes and purses opened to him. Yet he took seriously his duty to escort Elizabeth into Catholicism, a duty he, like Filippo, felt was part of a larger mission to plant Catholicism in the new American nation. So how to help this woman, who was proving as obdurate as she was pious? For weeks, Antonio did not write her at all. At last he offered a mixture of gallantry and need. "You have perhaps been tempted to think that I must have forgotten you," he wrote, "perhaps that I had sunk at sea or had broken my neck on shore." He was safe, he assured Elizabeth, and could "pass no evening without seeing you, recollecting, and lamenting the actual privation of your edifying company." She must "pardon the vanity, the shortness, the insignificancy, the blunder of my Letters to you." Antonio would, however, forgive no failure of communication from her. "I want to know every thought, every thing of you," he commanded. "Your worthy Soul is mine. I shall call for it every where, from whomsoever." "Help me with your prayers," Antonio added, shifting in a moment from master to supplicant. "God must bless you in this world and in the other world, and I believe He blesses me for your sake."[2]

It was Antonio at his most irresistible, but Elizabeth resisted. She may have wished to punish his delay with a delay of her own. She may simply have been pressed for time. Whatever its cause, her failure to reply provoked Antonio to an outburst of courtly passion. "To this moment I have called in vain every day at the Post office for an answer from the best of Sisters," Antonio wrote. How could this be? Was Elizabeth ill? Her failure to write was intolerable. "Do not refuse him longer, I beseech you, your kind assistance," he implored, in a pitiful third person. "He would read [her letter] ten times in the day till learnt by heart." Like Elizabeth, Antonio was confident that the urgency of their friendship proved its godliness. His soul required her "interesting, edifying, holy society. In this side of water, you are highest in my esteem, nearest in my heart."[3]

Esteem aside, Antonio recognized what Elizabeth uncomfortably felt: her choice of religion had practical consequences as well as spiritual. Her family and friends made no threats, but they expected her to find a way to contribute to her upkeep, and her possible Catholicism complicated everyone's plans. Were she willing to remarry, she had fewer choices as a Catholic woman than she would as an Episcopalian. Should she take up John Wilkes's plan of keeping school, her interest in Catholicism might harm her prospects of attracting students. Antonio offered to save her from all such worries: he declared that he and his brother would transplant Elizabeth and her children to Italy. Antonio's letter has been lost, so the terms of his proposal cannot be known. Elizabeth's answer survives, however, and it was a firm no. She was lonely and unhappy but not weak: she would resolve her questions about Catholicism before going anywhere.[4]

Stymied, Antonio appealed again to Bishop Carroll. Perhaps, he seems to have reasoned, the bishop had not fully understood the ferocity of Elizabeth's spiritual hunger and the delicacy of Antonio's position. And really, who other than Antonio did? Not trusting his ability to explain the matter, he began copying intimate, expressive sections from

Elizabeth's letters in order to send them to Baltimore. Then he went one better and decided to send Carroll the letters themselves.

By early October, Antonio had prepared a new packet for the bishop and in a cover letter asked Carroll to write again to the anxious would-be convert.[5] When Antonio wrote to Elizabeth explaining what he had done, his letter was loving, respectful, and entirely lacking in urgent gallantry. He also offered Elizabeth a bit of news. "I am giving Italian lessons, in exchange for English ones to a young very genteel, good, pretty handsome Miss, a first daughter [perhaps a daughter-in-law] of Mr. Stoughton." "She is one of the new converts to the Roman Catholic Communion from the Presbyterian since about three years," Antonio continued blandly, and "she is very anxious to form your acquaintance."[6] After Elizabeth received this letter, she sent no more impassioned notes up the Post Road to Boston.

WHICH RELIGION, WHICH LIFE

"I do not get on, Amabilia," Elizabeth wrote in her journal, "[I] cannot cast the balance for the peace of this poor soul."[7] In the weeks that followed, she started and set aside letters to Antonio. "My heart has jumped almost out of me every time our street door opened," she told him in one, then in another repudiated the need she'd so freely expressed: "I ought only to thank God," she declared, "that by depriving me of confidence in any human affection he draws my Soul near to its only center of rest."[8] Antonio either failed to notice Elizabeth's silence or was relieved by it. When he wrote in early November, it was only to excuse his customary lack of letters, send love from Amabilia, and attribute his recent commercial successes to God's pleasure at Elizabeth's piety.[9]

Antonio was busy in Boston. The priests of St. Peter's left Elizabeth alone with her struggle. Yet her conversion remained of interest to men on both sides of the Atlantic who believed her allegiance benefited not only her soul but the reputation of their faiths. And now, Filippo Filicchi reentered the fray. Elizabeth had written asking for guidance, and Filippo, as always, had some. He excoriated Hobart and Moore, but he also criticized Elizabeth's "propensity to melancholy," which he believed fed a pointless anxiety. Satan "delights in trouble," the merchant warned. "He knows that he cannot catch fish in clear water." For all his sternness, Filippo had grasped the way Elizabeth's doubt and self-reproach begat doubt and self-reproach: "If you trouble yourself for being troubled," he wrote, "you will never find peace." He also realized that Elizabeth was trying to reason her way to the correct faith, and he wanted her to know that she would fail. She should no more attempt to debate points of theology than she would dare question a physician "on every point of medical science" before allowing herself to be treated.

Elizabeth felt perfectly capable of debating medical science. But Filippo's hectoring tone evinced no more impatience with Elizabeth than she felt with herself, and in two final injunctions, he offered advice well tailored to her mingled desires to ask and to be freed from questions. "Your submission [to Catholic doctrine] will be reasonable even if those points you may not understand," he reassured her, "because it is reasonable to trust in the word of a Church which is the Column of firmness." Filippo offered something closer to strategy than theology: "All your Divines admit that the Roman Catholic may be saved," he told her. "What risk do you run therefore in the change? To put oneself on the safer side is certainly prudence."[10] That was, at last, a new argument, and Filippo reiterated it in a second letter written just five days later. He also promised an end to the uncertainty Elizabeth loathed. "You cannot ask without something being given you," he assured her, "you cannot knock and find the door always shut, you cannot seek never to find."[11]

Filippo's arguments stayed in Elizabeth's mind as she prayed and read. When Antonio offered a burst of charm—"In vain I have called 20 times for your letters at the post office," he wrote, "scolding . . . 20 times the Post Officer for his cold answer, no letter for you"—she declined to be drawn in.[12] Two months earlier, she had melded her need for Antonio with her desire to feel Jesus's presence. Now she untangled the knot. Jesus, she told Antonio sharply, "never disappoints me, but repays every instant with hours of sweet Peace and unfailing contentment—and the tenderest interest you ever can bestow on me is only a stream of which he is the fountain." Antonio was no longer her "savior." If there was a man who did help, Elizabeth continued coolly, it was John Wilkes: he had arranged for her to take in boarders taught by an Episcopalian minister. Yet she'd used "every possible evasion" to avoid consenting to Wilkes's plan, vainly hoping that Antonio would return to New York.[13] This letter sat unsent, but Elizabeth was at last beginning to find indecision more intolerable than the thought of choosing wrong.

In the months since the *Pyamingo* docked at New York's harbor, Elizabeth's world had collapsed into prayer, reading, children, and Antonio. Now she willed herself to regain equanimity and independence. Taking up her journal to Amabilia, she noted that Eliza Sadler had gently questioned her love of the Catholic teaching that earthly pains could be offered to God. "That was very comfortable," Sadler had drily observed, and "she wished she could believe it."[14] Although Elizabeth did not directly engage Sadler's question, the act of recording it allowed a skeptical breeze through her overheated thoughts. She also turned to correspondents who, unlike Antonio, elicited the old, self-sufficient Elizabeth. She wrote more often to Julia Scott, joking that her old friend might have decided that "an intercourse with the mad Enthusiast [Elizabeth herself] is loss of time."[15] She also tried out a new correspondent, Madame Olive, widow of the French merchant Nicholas Olive.

"This is the first letter I have ever written in French," she told her friend, then made a surprising claim: Catholicism "has won me over, heart and soul, so much so that, were it not for my duties to my children, I would have gone into a convent as soon as my husband died."[16] Although this was not entirely true—Elizabeth still hesitated over the faith's legitimacy—it was a part of the truth that she'd confided in no one else. She loved her children but she sometimes dreamed of a life with and for God alone; Catholic religious communities, not Protestant ones, offered women that possibility. She was admitting that she agonized not only over her afterlife but over her life; French had freed her tongue.

Still, Elizabeth did not decide. Because she remained troubled by Hobart's disgust at the doctrine of transubstantiation and had found no counter to him in her reading, she tried her own hand at a reasoned defense. "Mr. H says how can you believe that there are as many gods as there are millions of altars and tens of millions of blessed hosts all over the world," she wrote in the journal to Amabilia. But "is it GOD who does it," she continued, "the same God who fed so many thousands with the little barley loaves and little fishes?" This was the line of thinking she'd begun in Livorno: Why was it that this one miracle was

FIGURE 9.1. Gilbert Stuart, *John Carroll,* oil on canvas, circa 1804. Gift of Judge Pacificus Ord. Courtesy of the Booth Family Center for Special Collections, Georgetown University, Washington, DC.

laughable and all the others in which Protestants believed reasonable? "I look straight at my GOD and see that nothing is so very hard to believe in it, since it is He who does it."[17] Reason, she was deciding, revealed the limits of reason. The rest was faith.

An earnest letter arrived from Antonio: "If ever . . . my expressions missed the proper line, of which I am not conscious of, you would judge me, I know, by my heart, and I should have been cleared."[18] Elizabeth, softening, began a reply in her old, confiding tone. But she laid it aside, her attention commanded by a stern letter from Filippo. Elizabeth was walking into "the labyrinth of controversies" from which there was no obvious escape, he warned her, echoing her own thoughts. "You will be neither Catholic, nor Protestant."[19] Still hoping Bishop Carroll had the answers she sought, she wrote that she would trade "the treasures of the World" for "one hours conversation" with him.[20] But when Carroll offered advice that winter, he did so indirectly and he posed unwelcome questions.

It was not long after Elizabeth expressed her desire for one hour's conversation that Antonio received a letter from the bishop. Carroll explained that he'd delayed writing because he had expected Antonio to visit Baltimore. (Elizabeth might have appreciated knowing that she and the nation's only bishop shared the fruitless pastime of waiting for Antonio Filicchi.) He found the subject of the "estimable lady" "very interesting" and recommended she read Thomas à Kempis. Then the bishop set aside generic advice. Remarkably, given the array of business he had conducted since receiving Antonio's letter, Carroll had been pondering the state of Manhattan's anxious convert. He thought it possible Elizabeth's unending misery might be self-indulgent, even strategic. "She ought," he told the merchant carefully, "to consider whether the tears she sheds, and the prayers she offers to heaven, are purely for God's sake, and arise solely from compunction for sin; & are unmixed with any alloy of worldly respect, or inordinate solicitude for the attainment of some worldly purpose." Carroll proceeded delicately. "A fear arises in my mind," he explained, "that God discovers in her some lurking imperfection, and defers the final grace of her conversion, till her soul be entirely purged of its irregular attachments."

Carroll may have been thinking of Elizabeth's reluctance to sever herself from the religion of her friends and relatives, or he may have suspected an "irregular attachment" to Antonio himself. Nothing in her letters shocked him: he had witnessed the moral struggles of congregants and fellow priests and faced his own, and he knew potential converts were often "tried by interior darkness and tribulation." Yet it was important, Carroll explained, for those trials to force converts "to explore "the entire state of their consciences[,] all their weaknesses, and even those imperfections, of which formerly they made no account." Carroll had recent, painful experience with a convert who had not subjected himself to such an examination. In the 1780s, a Boston minister named John Thayer traveled to Europe, converted to Catholicism, and, with the support of delighted officials in the Holy See, became a priest, returning to Boston determined to win his hometown to the cause of the true faith. Skeptical from the outset of Thayer's fiery self-confidence, Carroll watched in dismay as the priest engaged in dramatic public battles with Boston's Protestant ministers, feuded with fellow Catholic clergy, and finally warred with the bishop himself, convinced he, Thayer, was American Catholicism's best and perhaps only hope. The experience had heightened Carroll's conviction that impassioned converts must be treated with at least as much caution as sympathy, and he urged Antonio to make sure Elizabeth investigated her motives and emotions.[21]

Antonio seems never to have given this letter to Elizabeth. Beyond a reluctance to cause her pain, he may have feared that sharing Carroll's letter would frighten her into more months of self-doubt or even spin her back toward John Henry Hobart. Whatever his reasons, Elizabeth continued to contemplate her spiritual destiny without John Carroll's incisive advice.

WHERE IS MY STAR?

January 6, 1805, brought the feast of the Epiphany. In Christian tradition, the feast commemorates the visit of three kings to the newborn Jesus, bearing gifts and led by a marvelously bright star. Elizabeth did not attend services at any church that day. Alone except for her children, she celebrated the day by consulting yet another book. This time it was a work by the Catholic writer Louis Bourdaloue, a French Jesuit whose simple and direct sermons had been beloved since their delivery in the reign of Louis XIV. Struck by Bourdaloue's counsel that "when the star of faith is invisible" one should seek guidance, Elizabeth wondered, "Where is my star?"[22]

She decided to reread the books the Filicchis had first given her, and she also tried to contact Matthew O'Brien of St. Peter's parish. Whether through laziness, fear that he would fail, or a reluctance to evangelize a respectable Protestant widow, O'Brien refused to see her. His recalcitrance left Elizabeth contemplating the questionable reputation St. Peter's possessed among her New York friends and family. "Catholics are the offscourings of the people, somebody said their congregation [is] 'a public Nuisance,'" she wrote in her journal.[23] Until this point, Elizabeth had contemplated conversion mainly as a matter of her religious conviction. Now she thought about the declaration of allegiance it entailed. By becoming Catholic she would join a group for whom she felt little affinity.

St. Peter's parish contained a few wealthy merchants whose families Elizabeth knew, but they were not the ones she thought of when she imagined attending Mass. The pews were in the main filled with artisans, day laborers, and poorer folk, including enslaved Catholics brought from Saint-Domingue by owners fleeing revolution and, in greater numbers, refugees from Ireland. The increasingly visible population of Irish Catholics in the city had reinvigorated New Yorkers' old tradition of burning the pope in effigy on Guy Fawkes Day: journeymen and apprentices, unhappy at Irish competition for jobs, now carried straw-stuffed effigies of Irish laborers—"Paddies"—through Manhattan streets. The Seton and Bayley clans disdained such festivities, but they also felt distaste for the poor Catholics who inspired them. St. Peter's was filled with people who simply *were not like* Elizabeth and the people among whom she'd lived. "Dirty filthy red faced," her sister Mary Post called them.[24]

Elizabeth was not immune to her sister's trepidation. It was one thing to worship with the "simple folk" in Italy, but she did not look at Manhattan's Catholics with a traveler's romantic eye. In her journal, she defended the Catholic faith but did not quite defend New York's faithful—or its priests. "The congregation for a city, may be very shabby yet very pleasing to God," she ventured. "Should the priest himself deserve no more respect than is here allowed him, his ministry of the sacraments would be the same to me if dearest friend I shall ever receive them."[25]

But *was* St. Peter's "pleasing to God"? Where was Elizabeth's star? When Antonio Filicchi's latest letter arrived, Elizabeth was again ready to ask for help. She directed the merchant to "give a short history of your dear Sister" to John Cheverus or Francis Matignon, the "Priests of Boston" he so admired.[26] Unwilling to wait for a response—and perhaps realizing that no priest or minister could offer what she sought—Elizabeth went to St. George's, a chapel of Trinity Church, and demanded

God's own help. "I looked straight up to God," she wrote in her journal, "and I told him since I cannot see the way to please you, whom alone I wish to please, everything is indifferent to me, and until you do show me the way you mean me to walk in I will trudge on in the path you suffered me to be born in, and go even to the very sacrament where I once used to find you." Elizabeth was vowing—threatening—to remain an Episcopalian. Yet as she sat through the Episcopalian Communion, "said to be Spiritually taken and received," she recoiled. Hobart had expressed horror at Catholicism's claim that Communion offered the literal body and blood of Christ. Very well. Elizabeth felt disgust at Episcopalianism's insipid pantomime. Her journey to the chapel wrought an unexpected transformation. "If I left the house a Protestant," she wrote to Amabilia, "I returned to it a Catholick."[27]

The conviction that had approached with agonizing slowness overtook Elizabeth with vertiginous force. "I became half crazy," she wrote, "and for the first time could not bear the sweet caresses of the darlings or bless their little dinner. O my God that day." It was a brief disintegration. By evening, she took calm pleasure in the Catholic practices she had denied herself since her return from Italy. "[I knew] a renewed confidence in the blessed Virgin," she wrote, "whose mild and peaceful love reproached my bold excesses."[28] Elizabeth prayed to the Virgin as a daughter in need of reassurance and as a mother confident she had chosen correctly for her own children.

After months in which she'd written out her agonized confusion and doubt, Elizabeth triumphantly recorded her decision in large, clear lettering: "I will go peaceably and firmly to the Catholick Church." Done with poring over apologetics and parsing doctrinal claims, she was ready to place her bet. "If [choice of] Faith is so important to our Salvation I will seek it where true Faith first began, seek it among those who received it from GOD HIMSELF," she wrote. Filippo's closing arguments had hit their mark. "As the strictest Protestant allows Salvation to a good catholick, to the Catholicks I will go, and try to be a good one, may God accept my intention and pity me."[29] Episcopalians and Catholics had fought for Elizabeth's allegiance on the ground of frightening accusations, and she had cast her lot with the side whose accusations were most terrifying.

There was, of course, more to it than that. Elizabeth loved the saints and sacraments of the Catholic Church, gloried in the hope of the

Eucharist, and found sustenance in the writings of centuries of thinkers and mystics. She also found persuasive the Church's understanding of the limits of individual reason. Her months of uncertainty had convinced her that evidence-based inquiry could not help her decide between competing systems of belief. Protestantism's failure to understand the limits of reason threatened to unravel faith all together.

Elizabeth's thinking anticipated that of a later American convert, Orestes Brownson. Raised a Presbyterian, Brownson was a well-known author and editor who had sampled any number of the nation's Protestant denominations—and acted as both a Universalist preacher and a Unitarian minister—by the time he converted to Catholicism in the early 1840s. To him as to Elizabeth, "no-churchism"—the destruction of both faith communities and individuals' faith—was the logical result of Protestantism's endless fissuring, and the United States' vibrant pluralism made that end result immediately visible. "If we have a Church and cannot have one without going to the Roman communion," Brownson wrote, "then let us go to Rome."[30] Elizabeth Seton traveled that path before him.

"I am between laughing and crying all the while Amabilia," she exclaimed. She would take "my little ones [and] we will go to Judgment together." If after their deaths God told them, "You fools I did not mean that," she would retort that it was God's own fault for misleading her.[31] Abject uncertainty had given way to utter confidence.

THE CHURCH OF ST. PETER

Her decision made, Elizabeth's frustration with Antonio dissolved. She awaited his return to New York before formally adopting her new faith, happy to have the Italian merchant as her gallant escort. While she waited, she received a letter from Father John Cheverus. He suggested she read works of Catholic devotion, but it was his warm sympathy that she appreciated. "True, there are many good books," she wrote the French priest, "but directions personally addressed from a revered source most forcibly impress."[32] Cheverus offered counsel perfectly suited to Elizabeth's own thinking. "'We see as through a glass in an obscure manner,'" he reminded her, quoting scripture. "When doubts arise, say only: 'I believe, O Lord, help Thou my unbelief.'"[33]

Not long after her decision, Elizabeth attended her first Mass at St. Peter's. "Amabilia I have been—where—the Church of St. Peter with a CROSS on the top instead of a weathercock," she gloated. St. Peter's did not hold a candle to the churches of Florence or even of Livorno, but its altar contained a receptacle for the Eucharist and a Crucifixion painting, and that was enough. She found St. Peter's congregants—its "offscoured congregation"—unappealing, but she was so rapt that she did not notice them until after the Mass. She was even delighted by grim old John Byrne. ("[He] seems just come there," she wrote, surprised at the priest's existence.)[34]

Two weeks after her first New York Mass, Elizabeth made her profession of faith as a Roman Catholic, pledging allegiance to "what the Council of Trent believes and teaches." The Council of Trent: Filippo had emphasized the importance of it in his treatise, John Henry Hobart had borrowed a book from the New York Society Library in order to better refute it, and Elizabeth had fretted to Antonio that if she prematurely declared her allegiance to it, God would know her insincerity. Now she was "laughing with my heart to my savior, who saw that I knew not what the Council of Trent believed, only that it believed what the church of God declared to be its belief." Elizabeth would no longer investigate the nooks and crannies of religious dispute: "I cannot, being quite tired out, and I came up light at heart and cool of head the first time these many long months."[35]

When Elizabeth confessed her sins to Matthew O'Brien, she found that the priest who had been of no use while she hesitated between faiths now played the role of Catholic pastor to her perfect satisfaction. "IT IS DONE," she wrote Amabilia in large letters. "I count the days and hours," until taking Communion.[36] New York was still caught in its long winter, but "deep snow, or smooth ice, all to me the same I see nothing but the little bright cross on St Peters steeple." Anna Maria had already guessed at her mother's decision, Elizabeth's lightness of heart revealing to her attentive daughter that the crisis was at an end. Now Elizabeth told her four other children as well. They knew nothing of Catholicism but were thrilled by whatever had dried their mother's tears. "The children are wild with the pleasure of going with me [to St. Peter's] in their turn," she wrote.[37]

The night before she was to take Communion, Elizabeth barely slept. At last morning came, and she walked to St. Peter's. Her first experience of the sacrament—her first literal touch from God—was ecstatic. "It seemed to me my King had come to take his throne," she wrote Amabilia. "Let God arise [and] let his enemies be scattered." There was no more watching and no more fear. "At last Amabilia," Elizabeth wrote, "At last. GOD IS MINE and I AM HIS."[38]

PART 3

TRANSITIONS

10

A CONVERT IN NEW YORK

LIZABETH SETON WAS THIRTY years old, the widowed mother of five, and a Catholic. Setting aside her journal, she wrote Amabilia a happy letter. "The heavy cloud has given place to the sun shine of Peace," she exulted. After denying herself the consolation of church services for much of the past year, she loved going to Mass. "I have been three times to communion since you left me," she wrote Antonio in delight.[1]

Thrilled to feast on the Eucharist, Elizabeth still needed to think about her daily bread. She had finally accepted John Wilkes's plan that she teach; the very thought of it wearied her, but dependence was more wearisome still. Among her benefactors, only Julia Scott treated her like an adult capable of overseeing her own finances. "I could go almost mad at the view of the conduct of every friend I have here except yourself," Elizabeth wrote Julia in early March. "It would really seem that in their estimation I am a child not to be trusted with its daily bread lest it should waste it."[2] She found a cheaper set of rooms to rent, in a neighborhood of artisans' homes and shops. The move gave her more control over her finances and something else as well: it was an easy walk from St. Peter's, and she planned "to go every morning before breakfast to visit my Master."[3]

Receiving the sacrament of Communion compensated for a thousand irritations and worries. It also turned out that not all of St. Peter's congregation was offscoured: Elizabeth discovered that she'd moved from one transatlantic lattice of wealthy individuals and enterprises to another, overlapping one. Thanks to Antonio's introductions, she sat in a pew with Andrew Morris, a wealthy chandler and soap maker who had risen from artisan roots to become a civic leader and owner of a country estate.[4] She met the charming Barry family, recently arrived from Washington, D.C., who counted Bishop Carroll among their friends.[5] Irish-born James Barry was a successful merchant whose letters brim with acerbic judgments, self-deprecating wit, and pleasure in life: kings and emperors faced misfortune, Barry once observed to Carroll, so "why should an humble son of St. Patrick complain, particularly while whisky is at 50 cents the gallon?"[6] He and his wife, Joanna, doted on their two daughters and worried for them too: consumption stalked the Barrys as it did the Setons, and young Mary Barry seemed to be slipping toward an early grave. Despite their sorrows, the Barrys welcomed Elizabeth into their home, feeding her lunch between the two Masses she attended each Sunday.[7]

Immensely relieved to have chosen a faith, Elizabeth found pleasure and comfort at St. Peter's. She even insisted that she was "More and more . . . satisfied with my Director," Matthew O'Brien.[8] Yet she soon realized that the priest offered none of the spiritual companionship she'd known with Hobart nor even the stern, learned direction she'd received from Filippo. And unlike Italy's churches, which had seemed to her sacred spaces, St. Peter's fit all too easily into Manhattan's familiar clamor. An air of mundane disorder emanated from both priests and congregation. "It requires indeed a mind superior to all externals to find its real enjoyment here," Elizabeth mused. "I am forced to keep my eyes always on my Book, even when not using it."[9]

She thought wistfully of the Church beyond St. Peter's. Having received one letter from Cheverus, she wanted another, and she hoped Bishop Carroll might send guidance from Baltimore too. Her New York clan sustained businesses, friendships, and families through extensive webs of correspondence; Elizabeth decided to sustain her religious life using the same tool. St. Peter's parish need not be the center of her Catholic world.

Elizabeth's relationship to St. Peter's was complicated; her relationship with Antonio Filicchi, now freed from its cosmic weight, had become wonderfully simple. When Antonio failed to write, she neither stewed nor scolded but informed him that if he wished to be forgiven he must "open your cause as a Plaintiff" and she would serve as judge. "You men when once convinced of your consequence," she added jauntily, "are saucy mortals, that is well known."[10] She'd once disliked the thought of Antonio's befriending other American women. Now she playfully asked, "Do you meet any Elegant Friends in Philadelphia, any Pupils for the Italian language, any Sirens?—God preserve you."[11] Her spiritual confidence restored, Elizabeth urged Antonio toward prayer and good conduct, and he was delighted to be commanded, offering himself as part penitent acolyte, part bumbling brother. "Though I have no letters from you," begins one missive, "though lazy, though diffident, though quite an infant, or rather an ignorant old fellow in your language, here is a short English letter from your true, firm friend & Brother."[12] All awkwardness in their friendship removed, Elizabeth dared to imagine an afterlife with Antonio and Amabilia. "Tonino, Tonino, how I long to meet you in your state of perfection, where I shall receive the transfusion of your affection without your exertion," she wrote, portraying her friend as worthy of paradise even as she mocked his lackadaisical correspondence.[13]

Her husband, William, had no place in these imaginings. He appears but seldom in Elizabeth's letters and journal, her conversion having brought with it a decision to cordon off the life that came before. The Filicchis insisted that the Catholic Church offered the only safe path to salvation, and though she prayed for William's soul, the question of his fate—and what her choice of faith implied about it—was too painful to contemplate. His disappearance from her writing is as complete as it is remarkable. When Elizabeth thought now of heaven, she thought of the Filicchis. She told Antonio that she hoped to "enjoy the blessing of being one of your inseparable companions forever."[14]

"TELL ME CANDIDLY"

Elizabeth's agony over conversion had been born of her own desperation to find salvation, not provoked by others' cruelty. True, Hobart had condemned her, and some friends and family thought Catholicism was beneath her. But genteel Manhattanites believed in choice, and Elizabeth had at last made one. John Wilkes gently criticized what he called her "imprudence in offending" her wealthy uncle, Dr. John Charlton (who the family hoped would leave Elizabeth and her sister Mary money in his will), but he reassured her that her "sentiments made no difference to him." Mary Post asked that Elizabeth "tell me candidly if you go to our church or not," then accepted that the answer was "not." Eliza

Sadler proved grateful for her friend's return to equanimity, whatever its doctrinal grounds.[15] In short, Elizabeth's conversion demonstrated the weakness of antipopery among her circle, not its strength. From her friends' and family's point of view, affection, respect, and simple habit mattered far more than doctrinal differences.

Yet Elizabeth no longer felt at home in Manhattan. Her friends' and family's efforts to help her vexed rather than soothed, and an incident in June laid bare the divide. John Wilkes's plan had not come to fruition, so Catherine Dupleix introduced Elizabeth to an Englishman named Patrick White, who along with his wife wished to open a school for girls. The Seton clan was politely skeptical of the Whites, but Elizabeth—possessed of "so great a desire to taste a bit of bread of my own earning"—brushed off their concern and agreed to the proposal. Even if something went wrong, she observed, she could not "be more dependent than I am now."[16] All looked promising until John Henry Hobart learned of the plan; he decided he must protect the city's Protestant children by warning parents about Elizabeth's faith. Dupleix and Sadler rushed to tell the minister that Elizabeth did not wish to proselytize; they assured him that she wanted only to "be at Peace with all the world."[17] A chastened Hobart promised to speak well of the school to anyone who asked.

It was not the happy ending it appeared. Hobart had behaved intolerantly, but he had also understood Elizabeth better than those who defended her. Unbeknownst to her friends, Elizabeth had asked Matthew O'Brien whether she had a duty to share her faith with children in her care; she was disappointed to be told she did not. O'Brien's caution accorded with the expectations of Elizabeth's friends and with John Carroll's vision of a Catholicism that was internally orthodox but inoffensive to those who did not share it—a Catholicism that accepted its position as a minority faith in a pluralist polity. But Elizabeth had agonized for months over her conversion because she believed that the fate of her soul depended on the choice. How could she politely allow others to fritter away their hope of salvation? The rules of a dinner party did not apply when eternity was at stake.

Elizabeth was alone in her view; even Antonio counseled her not to evangelize. "In each Country as America in particular," he wrote, "this mutual forbearance is quite to the advantage of the true cause of Catholicism, since the propention of its inhabitants and its schools and institutions is so much against us."[18] She obeyed, but unhappily. Hobart's intolerance had felt like persecution, but everyone else's tolerance felt like dismissal.

Matters came to a head when neighbors visited Elizabeth with diplomacy on their minds. The visitors, a "Miss Ludlow" and Elizabeth McElway Livingston, belonged to influential clans of Protestant merchants and lawyers. Livingston, a friend of Antonio Filicchi, believed religion was a matter of private conscience; her own sister-in-law, Catherine Livingston Garrettson, had converted in the 1780s to Methodism, and when some in the family objected, her husband had helped bring about a reconciliation. Now Livingston and Ludlow wanted to smooth Elizabeth's way as she began her school. Elizabeth was having none of it. "I found one object of [the visit] was to ascertain if I had really resolved on not interfering in the religious principles of those committed to my charge," she sniffed to Antonio. "I told them plainly that if I had not taken the advice of my Director on the subject, and felt that I was not to be considered a 'teacher of Souls,' I would not for any consideration have subjected myself to the necessity of returning ingratitude for the confidence reposed in me."[19]

Elizabeth, in short, told her neighbors that she would like to convert Protestant children to Catholicism but refrained from doing so because her priest told her not to. It's hard to imagine a reply better calculated to unsettle her well-meaning visitors. When Miss Ludlow and Mrs. Livingston tried again, venturing that "the heart only was required by God," Elizabeth summarily dismissed the ecumenism she once embraced. "I believed the heart must be given," she told the women, "but if other conditions were required too, the Master certainly had a right to exact them." By the time Elizabeth scoffed at the women's query about whether Catholics believed reciting prayers washed away sins, Miss Ludlow and Mrs. Livingston were ready to flee. They "begged that the subject might not be mentioned between us," and left.[20]

Had they witnessed this awkward encounter, New York Catholics such as Andrew Morris and the Barrys would have sympathized not with Elizabeth but with her visitors. They, too, believed that religion was a private matter and that polite silences made good neighbors. It was a belief Elizabeth no longer shared.

Reluctantly obeying O'Brien's instructions not to evangelize students, Elizabeth devoted herself to teaching her own five children as she pleased. She brought them to Mass, told them stories of the saints, and spoke glowingly of the Virgin Mary's love. Her boys, Will and Dick, at first seemed "mad with Joy at going where they can see the cross at St. Peter," but their attention soon wandered.[21] Catherine and Anna Maria, however, eagerly partook of their mother's faith, writing notes festooned with crosses and the initials "J.M.J." for Jesus, Mary, and Joseph. For them and for tiny Rebecca, love of their mother became inseparable from love for the Holy Family and the saints whom Elizabeth made into intimate companions.

The same principle that led Elizabeth's circle to insist she not evangelize students meant that no one questioned her right to bring up her children as Catholics: children should share the faith of their parents. But what of the children to whom Elizabeth and William had stood guardian? Sam, Ned, Charlotte, and Mary had quickly been sent off to school, but for Harriet and Cecilia, Elizabeth had been more mother than sister-in-law. At eighteen, Harriet imagined marriage and a household of her own; in the entangled way of the clans, she was being courted by Elizabeth's half brother, Andrew Barclay Bayley. But Cecilia, fourteen, still looked to Elizabeth for her happiness. She lived with William's brother James and his growing family, but she listened eagerly to Elizabeth's prayers and instructions during frequent visits to the Setons' rented rooms. A grim realization heightened her interest: Cecilia suffered from the consumption that had killed her mother, aunt, sister, and half brother. If this world was not to be her home, Cecilia must find her way to the next, and the woman she trusted most told her that Catholicism offered the only safe path.

Elizabeth kept Cecilia's interest secret. Her family accepted Elizabeth's free will and her control over her children's faith, but they would be angry if she tried to influence other young people. As important as any distaste for Catholic teachings was a practical question: Cecilia's hopes of marrying, and so of escaping a life dependent on aunts, uncles, and siblings, might be harmed were she to declare herself a Catholic.

Elizabeth blamed friends and family for the subterfuge. Despite the tolerance with which she'd been treated, she felt she faced a kind of persecution, one whose instruments were pity and raised eyebrows rather than crosses and lions. "I have passed thro' a fire today in the number of people I accidentally encountered," she once wrote. Her next line revealed that the fire was nothing anyone else could see or feel: "Every one smiled some with affection, some with civility." Yet she felt afflicted. "When I get alone again," she continued, "I recollect with delight how 'gently He clears my way' and say with Blessed David 'Tho' I walk thro' the Valley and Shadow of Death I will fear no evil, for thou art with me.'"[22]

Elizabeth often reminded herself that her family showed her charity. But in that letter to Antonio, she told her story the way she wished to read it. She was not an eccentrically single-minded woman who frightened off neighbors and secretly proselytized a vulnerable child; she was a servant of God bravely making her way through the harrowing landscape of the Twenty-Third Psalm. Antonio wholeheartedly shared her vision, and in these months, the two began to create the story of social martyrdom that would color Elizabeth Seton's portrayal, in devotional and historical literature, ever after.

SUMMER'S HEAT

Elizabeth spent weeks waiting for the Whites to recruit children for their school, and she waited as well for guidance from clergy more congenial than those of St. Peter's. When at last a letter from John Cheverus arrived, he offered sympathy, encouragement, and something even better: he sent it in the care of a priest who he believed would help Elizabeth find her way in her new faith.

Cheverus's letter bearer was Jean Tisserant, a French cleric who, like Cheverus himself, had fled the French Revolution. Napoleon was now emperor and Pius VII had blessed his coronation, but the fate of the French Church and its clergy remained uncertain, and Tisserant remained in the United States. Unlike Boston's priests, he neither learned English nor placed himself under Bishop Carroll's direction. Instead, he served as tutor to an Elizabethtown, New Jersey, family of French émigrés. Carroll believed he had "quitted . . . entirely all duties of the priesthood."[23] Cheverus and Matignon, however, found Tisserant "both learned and pious," and they were confident he could fulfill the role of Elizabeth's spiritual director more effectively than St. Peter's priests.[24]

They were right. Tisserant was educated and attentive, and the French language Elizabeth had learned as a child amid New Rochelle's staunchly antipapist Huguenots became the language of her new Catholic faith. Eliza Sadler was almost as relieved as Elizabeth herself. "My heart," Sadler wrote, "ascends in gratitude to the source of every good, from whom you have received the blessing of such a guide."[25]

Heartened by Tisserant's presence, Elizabeth tried to be both a good Catholic and a good Seton. That summer she nursed first her half sister Emma, who fell mortally ill after childbirth, and then her dying stepmother. Orphaned in her teens, Charlotte Amelia Barclay Bayley had married a man whom she could not please, raised stepchildren whom she could not love, and borne children whom she could not nurture. Now, having alienated those on whom she had greater claim, Charlotte turned for help to Elizabeth. She had at last made a good decision. Elizabeth willingly tended her stepmother, giving no thought to the woman's failings during her childhood. Quietly, however, she sought in Charlotte and Emma's difficult deaths evidence of the superiority of the Catholic Church. "When I see these poor souls die without Sacraments, without prayers, and left in their last moments to the conflicts of parting Nature without the divine consolations which our Almighty God has so mercifully provided for us," she wrote, she rejoiced at her own "different prospect."[26] Elizabeth had always had the capacity for sharp judgments, and her new faith heightened it. But she kept her thoughts to herself.

As August's torpor descended on the city, a sudden shock unsettled everyone: the Whites announced they'd given up on finding students for the school and would try their luck elsewhere. Elizabeth was left without work and, because she and the Whites had planned to share a house, with a rent she could not afford.[27] Just as she and her five children faced homelessness, word spread of the season's first yellow fever cases.

Weeks earlier, Elizabeth had told Antonio that she disliked feeling dependent on Wright Post and John Wilkes, "Philosophic spirits" who lacked religious conviction. But it was Post who came immediately to her aid, bringing her and the children to the summer home he and Mary kept in Greenwich Village. Elizabeth was grateful but disoriented: no longer could she walk to Mass at St. Peter's, and no longer could she run her own household. She and her sister had seen each other through difficult childhoods and remained loyally affectionate, but they shared neither temperament nor interests. More acutely than ever before, Elizabeth's single-minded desire to worship God set her at odds with those around her. Her singing of hymns, her family's prayers and lessons and cross-festooned notes lodged awkwardly in the Post household. Catholic duties such as purchasing and eating fish in order to follow fasting rules were a pleasurable burden when Elizabeth herself had to bear it. Now, as she watched Mary try to assemble the Setons' weekend meals, she felt less like a Christian pilgrim than like a troublesome boarder.

Elizabeth wanted to find other lodgings, but both Sadler and Tisserant urged her to remain where she was. Submit to God's will, Sadler told the woman who so often gave others that advice.[28] "You find yourself where God wants you to be," Tisserant wrote, "we should judge God's will in connection with our situation in this world, in accord with what circumstance suggests." "Ties of blood, friendship, and charity" mattered, the priest reminded her, and she could always ask permission from Father O'Brien to break the fasting rules.[29]

Sadler simply wanted to preserve Elizabeth's domestic harmony; Tisserant had a broader goal. Believing Elizabeth's social prominence as a convert would either harm the American Church or aid it, he warned her not to present Catholicism as "more inflexible than It is."[30] Knowing this was unwelcome advice (as the demand for moderation had throughout the history of the Church often been unwelcome counsel from priests to spiritually ambitious women) Tisserant cast it in a way brilliantly suited to Elizabeth's spiritual imagination: he compared her need to curb her Catholic observances to Job's suffering. A summer home in Greenwich Village might seem laughably different from a dung heap, but Tisserant understood that Elizabeth would moderate her desire to give up everything for God, only if she understood moderation itself as a sacrifice. His counsel found its mark. She stayed in her sister's home, obtained a dispensation from Father O'Brien, and ate meat on the weekends.

Weeks passed, Manhattan remained beset by fever, and Elizabeth remained uneasily at the Posts'. In early October, Cecilia came to visit. She had grown more and more devoted to Elizabeth's new faith, and now the two began to speak of the possibility that the girl might formally convert. No one told James and Mary Seton, the Farquhars, or any of the other adults on whose charity Cecilia and Elizabeth herself depended. "In that little secret we mentioned," Elizabeth told the girl, she should confide only in God and Elizabeth.[31]

While Cecilia courted trouble with her interest in Catholicism, Elizabeth's sons courted trouble with their indifference to it. "My saucy Boys almost Master me," she'd confessed to Julia in the spring, and now she worried that they were influenced by the "ridicule" and "mockery" of the Catholic Church she believed they heard around them.[32] In the exhilaration that flooded the family after Elizabeth's conversion, William had told his mother, "I would rather be [a priest] Mamma than the richest greatest man in the whole world."[33] Now the contrast he had innocently voiced—priest versus rich and great man—limned the threat. The boys' Protestant friends and family made money and went to dances and the theater; Harriet and Cecilia's brother Sam, only sixteen years old, would soon sail to China as a supercargo.[34] Elizabeth feared that with such models before them, Will and Dick would leave her world of prayers and hymns behind.

Willing to send her sons away in order to keep them within the faith, Elizabeth asked for Antonio's help in finding a boarding school in which they might grow to Catholic manhood. He was impressed by a school and seminary in Montreal, where he traveled on business, but the Seton boys had little French, and the Filicchis exerted little influence in the Canadian city. So Antonio's attention turned to two other possibilities: Georgetown College in Washington, D.C., and St. Mary's College in Baltimore.

Although they were called colleges, Georgetown and St. Mary's—like other colleges of the day—were boarding schools that regularly admitted boys as young as eleven; at nine and seven William and Richard were young for admission but not impossibly so. The schools were young too: Georgetown had admitted its first student in 1791, its existence owed mainly to the efforts of John Carroll, who wrote that on the success of the institution "is built all my hope of permanency and success to our holy religion in the United States."[35] That same year members of the French order of St. Sulpice founded St. Mary's seminary in Baltimore; the college at St. Mary's followed in 1803. Despite being tiny Catholic institutions in a sea of Protestants, the schools lived in a state of mutual enmity. The Anglophone members of the suppressed Jesuit order who staffed Georgetown mistrusted the French Sulpicians and mistrusted them even more after John Carroll briefly placed one Sulpician, an energetic and ambitious priest named Louis-Guillaume-Valentin Dubourg, in charge of Georgetown itself.[36] Elizabeth knew nothing of the rivalry between the schools, and Antonio knew little. Each simply hoped that one or the other might offer a place for Richard and William, and Antonio pledged to help with tuition at either institution. The Filicchi brothers understood themselves to be guardians of the family's faith, and whatever Antonio's distractions, he was determined not to disappoint.

The fever epidemic of 1805 at last slipped into the realm of dread and memory. But the problem of Elizabeth and her children's maintenance remained. Hopes rose when a Protestant minister named William Harris dangled the prospect of Elizabeth's employment, but that came to naught, and the family cast about for other ways she might earn money. Perhaps "a Tea store—or china shop," Elizabeth wrote wryly, "or a school for little children (too young I suppose to be taught the

Hail Mary.)"[37] Then John Wilkes reported that there was once again a possibility that Elizabeth could take in the students of St. Mark's school as boarders. "This plan so much dreaded before I had drank deep of my cup," Elizabeth wrote frankly, "was now embraced with eagerness." She would "Board, Wash and mend for" the students, and thanks to Julia's charity, would pay "a good old Woman whom I have known for many years to take a great part of the burden off me."[38] It was a long way from the luxury she'd known as a young wife. But even now Elizabeth was shielded from the poverty many New Yorkers knew, and even now Episcopalian parents were willing to entrust their children to her.

Elizabeth left the Posts' Greenwich Village home and once again rented rooms close to St Peter's. In her absence, the parish had acquired a new priest, a Philadelphia-born member of the Augustinian order named Michael Hurley. In his midtwenties in 1805, Hurley had studied for the priesthood in Italy with the financial assistance of the Filicchi family.[39] Initially assigned to serve under Father Matthew Carr in his home parish in Philadelphia, Hurley chafed under Carr's direction; a cryptic letter from Bishop Carroll suggests that both he and Hurley believed Carr habitually violated his vow of celibacy.[40] Hoping to forestall conflict and strengthen the growing parish of St. Peter's, Carroll removed Hurley from Philadelphia and sent him to Manhattan.

Hurley had arrived during the fever season, and he found himself among ill parishioners in a parish that seemed itself in questionable health. His letters, filled with level, tidy handwriting and intricately constructed sentences, suggest that he was a meticulous man. St. Peter's was not accustomed to meticulous men. Hurley forced himself to overlook irregularities such as the congregation's failure to stand at appropriate moments of the Mass. But, he later wrote Bishop Carroll, "I observed many gross abuses which I thought it my duty to reform," including parishioners' habit of traipsing through the sacristy and the priests' practice of entrusting "the blessed sacrament enclosed in a small case . . . [to] the hands of the school boys."[41] Hurley's criticisms profoundly offended Father Matthew O'Brien; St. Peter's had gained another unhappy rivalry even as it had gained a priest.[42]

Elizabeth, who should have been an excellent audience for Hurley's reforms, took no notice. She probably found the young priest cold, even arrogant; Hurley "appears proud, without being so," James Barry once explained to Carroll.[43] Rather than seek guidance from any of St. Peter's clergy, she waited for letters from Tisserant and Cheverus and dreamed of making her way to Montreal and its centuries-old Ursuline convent. Perhaps the nuns might accept her as a lay associate or teacher, and her daughters as students. She did not ask for New Yorkers' tolerance. She wanted to make a passionately Catholic life somewhere else.

ADVICE AND DECISIONS

Elizabeth shared her dream of a life among Montreal's Ursulines with Cecilia. She also began to draw two other girls into her clandestine prayer circle, Cecilia's older sister Harriet and their cousin Eliza Farquhar, daughter of the wealthy couple who had long presided, usually with a faintly disapproving air, near the center of the clan. For Harriet and Eliza—dubbed, by this nicknaming family, Hatch and Zide—the dream of Montreal was like Catholic worship itself: beautiful but exotic, something to be savored secretly and then set aside. Cecilia, however, was absorbed by the possibility of formally converting and following Elizabeth wherever she might go. Yet she worried that doing so meant betraying her fond brothers Ned and Sam, her aunts and uncles, and the young cousins whom she tended at James and Mary Seton's home. For Cecilia as for Elizabeth, worshipping God and behaving well had parted ways, and the strain told. "Oh that I could take the Wings of the Angel of Peace and visit the heart of my darling darling Child, pain and sorrow should take their flight," Elizabeth wrote, assuring the girl that her unhappiness could be offered to God. She promised the orphaned girl every kind of love she needed. "My Cecilia," she wrote, "my Sister—my friend—my dear dear child."[44]

Elizabeth was creating a secret world of devotion. In these same months, Father Michael Hurley pursued a different goal: ensuring that Catholics required no secrecy at all. The energetic young clergyman wanted to overturn the New York requirement that officeholders forswear allegiance to all foreign powers, including ecclesiastical ones. The requirement was a descendant of British oaths intended to bar Catholics from office by making them choose between loyalty to the nation and loyalty to the pope. To its supporters, the oath was a defense against Papists who might replace the laws of the republic with the terrors of the Inquisition. To Hurley and St. Peter's confident trustees, the oath was a relic of an unenlightened past, an assault on liberty rather than a safeguard. They, like the Barrys, Miss Ludlow, Mrs. Livingston, and just about everyone else Elizabeth knew, believed that religion was a matter of private conscience and should neither make claims on one's neighbors nor require the sacrifice of one's own civic rights. Hurley held meetings of the congregation and gathered two hundred signatures on a petition to have the oath abolished.[45]

Elizabeth showed no more interest in this than in Hurley's other campaigns. The very premise on which Hurley demanded full political inclusion for Catholics—that religion was a private choice that could be set off from social and political life—was alien to her. In fact, as winter fell, she was questioning whether her convictions could be reconciled even with the conventions of family life. The physical and emotional chores of mothering five children—augmented by the similar but less joyful chores of caring for the young boarders from St. Mark's—eroded the life of religious devotion and observance she wanted to lead. As she had done when unhappy in her sister's home, Elizabeth confided her discontent to Jean Tisserant. Once again he told her to cut her devotion to the pattern of her life. "You must entirely dedicate yourself to the duties of the mother, and to the gentle tasks with which you are charged," the priest directed. True, he acknowledged, those tasks "don't permit you to undertake that which you would perhaps be advised in a Cloister."[46] But they, not the heroic sacrifices and monastic seclusion to which Elizabeth felt called, were her duties. She must carry them out.

Similar advice arrived from Cheverus in Boston; suddenly everyone was telling Elizabeth to be reasonable. Elizabeth had asked Cheverus whether she should encourage Cecilia to convert, and Cheverus, delicately, said no. He'd thought and prayed, he explained, contemplating Cecilia's physical frailty and her family's likely opposition to her conversion. "Here is the result, which however I propose to you with the utmost diffidence," he wrote. "Neither the obstacles you mention, nor the sickly state of the dear child permit to instruct her in the points of controversy." If Cecilia dreamed of "living one day in a convent & there to become a member of the Church," Cheverus continued, that was wonderful. If she grew healthier, anything was possible. But for now, Cecilia should be told that "it is enough to know Jesus & him crucified, to put all her trust in him, to suffer with him &c . . . to wish to become a member of His Church." This was closer to Bishop Moore's advice to the dying Hamilton than to anything the Filicchis might have written, and Cheverus also offered a surprisingly inclusive vision of the Catholic communion. Elizabeth should not despair of Cecilia's eternal fate, he insisted, even should the girl die as a Protestant. Given Cecilia's desire to join the Church and her "singular innocence of mind and ardent piety," she might well reach heaven, although being "a member of the triumphant Church would render her salvation more secure."[47]

Cheverus intended to soothe and reassure. But Elizabeth had chosen Catholicism over Episcopalianism because it claimed to be the only sure path to salvation. Cheverus's optimism, even narrowly tailored to Cecilia's circumstances as it was, threatened to reopen questions Elizabeth had emphatically closed. And so she set the priest's counsel aside. She did not acknowledge, even to herself, that she was refusing Cheverus's guidance. Instead she begged forgiveness for displeasing him on a point so minor he had not considered it a correction (he asked her not to praise him so effusively). Her abject apology left Cheverus remorseful. "I am sorry if my letter made you suppose for a minute that I was angry with you," he soothed. "Never have I had any other sentiments towards you but those of the most sincere respect & friendship & with these I do & always shall remain."[48] Whether she willed it or not, Elizabeth's apology left her with the upper hand.

As Elizabeth chafed at her inability to create a fully Catholic life for herself in Manhattan—and chafed at others' insistence she not try—St. Peter's parish grew quietly more unsatisfying. Unsettling rumors rippled through the congregation. John Byrne had come upon Matthew O'Brien and a young woman named Catherine McLennan standing near each other in the vestry and had not liked what he saw. McLennan was likely the daughter of an Irish immigrant and almost certainly a young woman of modest means. But she was not afraid to tell Father Byrne that Father O'Brien had laid hands on her against her will. Not long after, a French parishioner wrote to Bishop Carroll accusing O'Brien of misconduct with a second young woman.[49] Such allegations had plagued the Church throughout the history of the celibate priesthood; Carroll knew that priests in the new nation had already been accused of misdeeds ranging from long-term relationships with their housekeepers to fumbling gropings in the confessional. He tended to cautiously investigate such allegations while offering accused priests the benefit of the doubt, and that was his response to the disturbing letters from New York. But he found the situation alarmingly ill timed. The accusations against O'Brien fed Protestants' darkest views of the priesthood just as Father Hurley and the city's Catholics pressed for full political rights.

The next weeks and months brought a flurry of outraged denials from O'Brien and an obviously coerced statement from McLennan recanting her accusation. Carroll was unconvinced by O'Brien's protestations but reluctant to punish the priest without proof of wrongdoing. Elizabeth must have heard the rumors and witnessed parishioners shunning O'Brien, but not a word of the scandal appears in her correspondence. It's possible a letter has been destroyed or lost, but it is more likely that Elizabeth chose not to put her thoughts to paper. Protestants already considered the Church the scene of corruption, and she had no wish to add evidence. The priests of St. Peter's had long been imperfect representatives of the universal church. They were proving more imperfect than she'd realized, but she would not comment on their troubles.

That spring Elizabeth instead contemplated her own frailty. Unusually for her, she was persistently ill, and her thoughts turned to mortality. Tisserant found her self-indulgent. "I advise you," he wrote with unusual sharpness, to "fight" any tendency to dwell on death. "Imagination," he continued, can be "a source of temptation, of torment, and of inquietude." Elizabeth apologized so profusely that Tisserant begged her forgiveness. It was what priests seemed to do after criticizing her.[50]

Poor health also prompted Elizabeth to worry that her children would be orphaned and raised by Protestant relatives. After she pressed Antonio on the point, the merchant renewed his effort to place her sons at a Catholic college.[51] On a business trip to Baltimore, he sought out John Carroll to settle once and for all the question of where young Will and Dick should go. The bishop remained reluctant to correspond with Elizabeth, her intensely emotional piety holding none of the appeal for him that the Barry family's quieter faith did. But Antonio convinced Carroll that Elizabeth was sincere and her relatives hostile. The bishop agreed that the Seton boys should be sent to a Catholic school, and he went one step further, offering to contribute to their tuition from his own funds.[52]

Carroll preferred that the boys be sent to Georgetown rather than St. Mary's, but he left the final decision to Antonio and Elizabeth. A lay instructor at Georgetown wrote urging Elizabeth to choose his institution for her sons. Georgetown, he informed her, boasted superior purity and "order." "There are no protestant boys or boys of other denominations here," he claimed.[53] In fact, Georgetown's greater purity reflected its failure to attract Protestant students, not their principled exclusion. John Carroll, who had been instrumental in Georgetown's founding, directed that the school welcome "Students of Every Religious Profession" in order to promote the harmony he believed essential to Catholicism's survival in the early republic.[54] Nonetheless, purity was what Elizabeth sought, and the letter, Carroll's preference, and the fact that the Barrys still kept a home in Washington, D.C., made her choice clear. In late April, she wrote to Antonio to tell him that she wished her sons to be sent to Georgetown.

An impecunious widow who'd joined a suspect faith, Elizabeth was proving remarkably capable of remaking the circumstances of her life. There was, however, one immovable object equal to her irresistible force: Julia Scott. Ablaze with her new faith, Elizabeth repeatedly urged Julia to contemplate her own mortality, even cautioning her that her indifferent Christian practice risked her children's souls as well as her own. "Ah Julia Julia," she urged, "when you see the tears of your dear children you will then feel that you have been only as the Mother of their Bodies while the divine image in their souls has been disfigured if not sullied by a mistaken Education."[55] Elizabeth pillowed that warning with a profession of love—"how can I write without showing my heart—" but it remained a shocking accusation for one mother to levy against another. Julia neither took offense nor obeyed. She was determined to remain Elizabeth's friend without becoming her follower.

RASH JUDGMENT

Elizabeth Seton was hoping for a richly Catholic life beyond Manhattan's compromises; Michael Hurley was trying to create an orderly and confident Catholicism within them. Both, for the moment, were thwarted. In early spring Hurley reported to Bishop Carroll that the parish was still roiled by rumors of Matthew O'Brien's indecency toward Catherine McLennan; he also made clear that he believed the rumors to be true. Declaring the young woman "a devout and pious Christian, and an exemplary member of our Confraternity," Hurley offered a coolly ironic description of O'Brien's headlong campaign to regain his reputation. "On Sunday last," he reported, "Dr. M. O'Brien committed himself to the congregation by preaching an inflammatory sermon on *Rash judgment*, which occasioned much talk."[56]

The Catholic Church's location of institutional authority and sacramental power in a celibate male clergy throws Catholic men and women together even as it separates them. One result was the intense, collaborative relationships Elizabeth developed with Jean Tisserant and John Cheverus. A different result was Catherine McLennan's apparent abuse at the hands of Father O'Brien. Yet McLennan held more power than O'Brien realized. For a time, all of St. Peter's parish seemed to center on the young woman: throughout February and March, Matthew O'Brien worked to discredit her, while Hurley promoted her cause and Carroll, from Baltimore, tried to discern the truth of the situation.[57] Fearing that the scandal was "in the mouths of some of the Congregation," Carroll hoped to keep word of it from spreading still further, but he was loath to tolerate a corrupt priest.[58] When his attempt to use Father Matthew Carr (himself accused of misconduct in Philadelphia) to investigate resulted in Carr's brazenly trying to force McLennan to retract her allegations, Carroll was at a loss.[59]

Then, unexpectedly, Catherine McLennan herself weighed in. On April 10, the young woman of modest means and challenged reputation wrote to her bishop. Elizabeth Seton was finding ways to assert her judgment and will within the hierarchical relations of the Church. So, facing much greater obstacles, was Catherine McLennan. In the letter, McLennan's handwriting is neat but her spelling poor; periods rather than commas separate clauses. Some words are skipped, then added above the line; others are squeezed in on the margin, as if the letter had been copied from a draft, then revised. Nonetheless, after months in which others had spoken for her, McLennan's own voice is tantalizingly present. "I do hear declare in the presens of Almighty God," she wrote, "And of the Blessed V Mary in whos Sacred order, I have the honour of being a member, and that if I was sure of going to eternity this minute. That, what I confessed, to the Revnd. Mr. Byrn, was abslutly true." MacLennan also offered to speak directly to the bishop.[60]

Elizabeth had for months hinted to the Barrys that she would love to hear from their friend John Carroll. She received nothing. It was Catherine McLennan, with her painful and unwanted power, who brought a bishop to New York City. Within a month of receiving Catherine's letter, Carroll arrived in Manhattan for a week-long stay. He seems to have interviewed O'Brien and McLennan, and in the end to have cautioned but not removed the priest. It was, Carroll later wrote, "business . . . of a nature so disagreeable."[61] (Not least for Catherine McLennan, whose life after the incident can't be traced.) During the visit, Carroll also found time to instruct Elizabeth in Catholic doctrine. She was grateful for his presence, and when he left felt ready to be confirmed in her faith. Elizabeth had joined the universal Catholic Church, not St. Peter's parish. The latter's scandals interested her little and changed nothing about her faith.

In Church teaching, the sacrament of confirmation binds Catholics strongly to the Holy Spirit and heightens their obligation to spread and defend the religion. By tradition, Catholics take as a confirmation name that of a saint to whom they feel a particular devotion. Elizabeth Ann Seton took the name Mary, in honor of the Blessed Virgin. It was the authority, not the vulnerability, of women within the Church that moved her; she proudly bore the names of three women the Church revered as mothers (of Jesus, of John the Baptist, and of Mary herself) and began to sign letters "M.E.A.S," asserting a new signature for the new woman she'd become.

Shortly after Elizabeth's confirmation, more good news arrived; Richard and William had been given places at Georgetown College at reduced cost, and Carroll and the Filicchis would pay the remaining expense. Within a week, Elizabeth sent the little boys on their voyage south. "My darling dear Julia," she wrote exultantly, "My heart is almost too happy to write you—My Darling Boys are on their way to Georgetown College."[62] She would miss her boys, but that was immaterial. The influence she exerted so readily over her daughters was lost on her sons, and she was grateful to send them to what she hoped was a place of greater spiritual safety.

Throughout these months, Elizabeth's new faith had not severed her friendships or cost her her family's support. The boys went off to Georgetown without anyone's objecting, and no one seems even to have noticed Elizabeth's confirmation. When Elizabeth and Mary's wealthy uncle, Dr. John Charlton, died and failed to leave the sisters the immediate inheritance some in the family had hoped for (instead bequeathing each $1,000 to be paid after the death of his wife, an act motivated by a desire to leave his estate in his wife's hands rather than by animosity toward Elizabeth's new faith), Elizabeth's benefactors stepped in to help. Antonio Filicchi organized and headed a small list of "subscribers"—Protestants as well as Catholics—who pledged annual sums in order to "mitigate as much as we can the distress of [Mrs. Seton] and children."[63] Months after Elizabeth's conversion, her Protestant friends and family believed that nothing in their unspoken agreement with Elizabeth had changed. They were wrong.

11

DUTY OR OBEDIENCE

O N JUNE 20, FOURTEEN-YEAR-OLD Cecilia Seton abjured her family's Episcopalian faith and became a Catholic. Father Michael Hurley, who presided over the ceremony, must have contemplated the outcry a young woman's secret conversion might provoke. But he believed that the frail girl's salvation rested in the Catholic Church, so the young priest with the high standards and awkward manners received her into his faith. Cecilia's sister Harriet and cousin Eliza Farquhar knew what she had done, but other than Elizabeth, no adults—not James and Mary Seton, with whom Cecilia lived, and neither the Farquhars nor John Wilkes—realized what had happened. The sprawling merchant clan valued harmony and trust above devotion to any cause; harmony and trust in the face of a dangerous world *was* their cause. No one imagined that unselfish Cecilia, who could always be counted on to mind a child or cheer a sibling, had secretly set her face against her family's faith.

In the days that followed, Cecilia tended James and Mary Seton's brood and waited to be found out. Sometimes Elizabeth tried to tease the girl out of her fears. "How silly to set your little brain to work and threaten it with a storm that may never come," she wrote. But Elizabeth did not really think the storm would pass over, so at other moments she urged Cecilia to welcome it. "If it reaches you," she told her, "it may drive you still further in your interior castle." Cecilia would instantly have recognized the image: the seventeenth-century Spanish mystic Saint Teresa of Avila had described humanity's relationship with God as an interior castle whose innermost rooms were known only to the rarest of souls. Elizabeth was suggesting that by braving her family's anger, Cecilia ventured toward the heart of that beautiful dwelling. It was a lovely thought, but Cecilia lived not only in God's castle but in her uncle's house. She worried over what her family might do when they learned of her dramatic choice, and the fact that Elizabeth spoke ever more longingly of leaving with her daughters for Montreal made matters worse. Elizabeth, so often left behind by her own father, understood Cecilia's fears. "Do you think I would leave you without seeing the coast is clear, that is your situation established in some way or other?" she soothed. "Death alone can take your Sister from you while there is the least probability you may want her sheltering heart."[1] Cecilia hoped it was true.

Two weeks after Cecilia's secret conversion, James and Mary Seton sent her to stay with her older sister Charlotte. Charlotte had recently married an ambitious young lawyer named Governeur Ogden, and Cecilia likely thought she was being sent to help set up housekeeping. But while she was away, Mary searched her things. She may have noticed Cecilia's worried face, or perhaps Aunt Farquhar overheard some whispered confidence between Cecilia and Eliza. Whatever her reasons, Mary went through Cecilia's few belongings. Among them she found a Catholic prayer book.

She sent an urgent note to Cecilia at the Ogdens' home: "Are you a Roman Catholic?" she demanded. Mary assured her young sister-in-law that whatever the answer, "My love will ever be the same."[2] It was a gentle start to a bitter conflict. Unlike Mary, Charlotte Ogden and Elizabeth Farquhar felt sure there was nothing simple or sincere about Cecilia's conversion. They blamed Elizabeth. Charlotte, quickly sent off to school after her father's death, had never felt the warmth toward her sister-in-law that her younger siblings did, and now she was a new wife whose socially prominent husband considered Elizabeth's Catholicism an embarrassment. As for Aunt Farquhar, she disliked Catholicism, and she disliked challenges to her authority even more.

The storm had come. Elizabeth and Michael Hurley counseled Cecilia to avoid trouble where she could but to refuse to apologize for her choice. When she replied to Mary, Cecilia denied she was a fragile child under Elizabeth's sway. "The books you have seen I purchased myself," she wrote firmly. She insisted that she would not exert her own spiritual influence over Mary's children, declaring that doing so "would be the height of ingratitude," and she asked that Mary keep her conversion "secret as far as is possible."[3] Like Cecilia, Michael Hurley hoped the girl's decision could be kept a private matter. But the outraged Seton family believed that keeping religion private was precisely the principle Elizabeth had overthrown.

"I will be very explicit," came Mary's response. "If [Elizabeth] had never been a Roman, neither would you. I decisively say, I firmly believe, that she has acted towards me both cruel & unjustifiable." She vowed to tell everyone of Cecilia's conversion so "that others may not trust to Mrs. Seton's liberality of principal as I have done." She also expressed dismay that Cecilia believed Catholicism a requirement for salvation; did the girl really think her own family damned? When she closed her letter, Mary's bitter tone turned sad. "My feelings are overpowered," she wrote. "I can only add, your happiness will ever be my first wish, for I love you tenderly."[4]

Cecilia countered with a complaint of her own. "I am mortified that my drawers should have been open," she observed. "It would have pleased me better had you acted more candidly." But Cecilia did not really want to trade accusations. She wanted to tuck her faith into her own life, where it could please God and harm no one. When it came to Catholicism, "I am fixed and firmly fixed and nothing but death can break the bonds." But she would teach James and Mary's children the principles of "your religion": Episcopalianism.[5]

It was too late. The clan threatened and raged; someone suggested Cecilia be sent to the West Indies and that the New York legislature somehow curb Elizabeth's influence. Those wild threats evaporated as soon as they were uttered. But the family also discussed cutting off Elizabeth's support and vowed, as she told Antonio, that if Cecilia did not recant, "they would consider themselves individually never to speak to either of us again or suffer her to enter the House of either of them."[6] Elizabeth was outraged, but her family believed they had supported her generously and in return asked just one thing, the thing Cecilia now claimed as a right: that Elizabeth keep her faith to herself. Instead Elizabeth had evangelized Cecilia and perhaps—because who now knew what their children believed—others. The clan told Cecilia she must recant by a date in August or leave their homes for good.

Shocked by the ferocity of the family's anger, Elizabeth appealed to the woman whom long experience had taught her to see as their decision maker: Aunt Farquhar. Elizabeth made no promises about Cecilia, but she assured Farquhar that she would stay away from Zide, Hatch, and Emma (the last, one of James's young daughters, thought to be at risk).[7] She did not mention that she'd already shared Catholic prayers and teachings with Hatch and Zide, and Aunt Farquhar did not ask.

The day before the family's deadline for Cecilia, her older sisters Charlotte and Mary repeatedly asked the girl what she would do. When evening fell, they were confident she had chosen to remain a Protestant; trying to avoid confrontation, Cecilia allowed her guardians to believe her will far weaker than it was. But before daybreak, she silently left the Ogden home. Elizabeth's rented house was too far for the consumptive young girl to walk, so she made her way to Catherine Dupleix's home and waited for the next storm to arrive.

Agonized notes once again crisscrossed lower Manhattan, Cecilia pleading to be allowed simply to practice her faith and family members accusing her of cruel deception. "My dear Cecilia," Charlotte Seton Ogden wrote from her Wall Street home, "I can scarcely express my astonishment at receiving your note yesterday morning. How different it was from the language you held the day before your departure." Charlotte and her husband, Gouverneur, felt particular distaste for Catholicism, which they, like John Jay, considered primitive and unsuited to the American republic. They also felt betrayed. Charlotte hoped her sister would change her mind and return "to our arms and religion" but warned her that if she did not, she would be forever cast out. Even in this missive, hurt glimmered through the anger. "I cannot believe but what you will return to us, Dear Cecilia!" she exhorted her younger sister. "Can you expect to find that parent you lost in her to whom you have flown?" "Farewell," Charlotte closed, "with a heart overflowing with pity, and affection for you."[8]

Citizens of the new American nation enjoyed considerable religious liberty. There was no national religion to which all must adhere, and many states, including New York, lacked an established church. As the Revolutionary taste for inquiry and deism faded, the years surrounding Elizabeth's and Cecilia's conversions saw a spreading conviction that myriad forms of Christianity, including even Catholicism, strengthened the republic and its citizens. Thus the support of Protestant Bostonians for Holy Cross Church, and thus in 1806 the success of the campaign to remove the oath restricting Catholic New Yorkers' ability to hold public office. Across the nation, new religious societies were founded and churches planted, and New York City itself saw an ever-growing number of congregations, some meeting in elegant new buildings, others in storefronts and attics.[9] But within this flowering of expression lurked the seeds of pain. Legal protection and even social tolerance did not dull the sting when friends and relatives chose differently from the profusion of possibilities, especially when their choices implied condemnation of one's own. In the minds of the Seton clan, Cecilia's conversion to a faith that claimed it was the only true church turned tolerance against itself. Both passionate faith and religious liberty were desirable. But together they brought heartache.

A VISITOR FROM BALTIMORE

Cecilia regretted her family's anger but was not swayed by it. Their punishment, forcing Cecilia to live with Elizabeth, felt like a reward. In Elizabeth's rented rooms, Cecilia was free to read Saint Teresa's *Interior Castle*, pray a rosary, and go to Mass at St. Peter's, where Father Hurley greeted her with affection and admiration. She even found moments of rest: Elizabeth had three children at home to James and Mary's seven. A few years earlier, Cecilia's older sister Rebecca had been Elizabeth's beloved companion, and John Henry Hobart their "blessed JHH." Now, Elizabeth and Cecilia were spiritual collaborators, with Father Hurley their faithful "St. M." The chilly young priest warmed to the satisfaction of being needed. Since his arrival in Manhattan, he'd been surrounded by quarrelsome priests and arrogant trustees. In their ardent piety, Elizabeth and Cecilia harked back to the brave converts of Christianity's earliest years. Your "heroic conduct," Hurley told them, "convinces me that the powerful grace of God does yet occasionally produce in the world, degenerate as it is, effects as [in] worthy apostolic days."[10]

James and Joanna Barry, though faithful Catholics, were less sure than Hurley about the ethics of Elizabeth's conduct. They had not encouraged Cecilia's conversion nor even invited the girl to dine. "We thought it prudent (as strangers here, and only barely knowing the young lady, and family)," Joanna told Bishop Carroll, "in no way to encourage her acquaintance."[11] The family did not need to court trouble: they had lost daughter Mary to consumption in December, and now both their remaining child Ann and James himself were seriously ill. But the Barrys also believed this life mattered, and not just the next. "The unpleasant consequences to her interest would probably exceed any good," Joanna wrote, invoking just the kind of practical calculation Elizabeth disdained.

Elizabeth realized that only Antonio would share her understanding of what had happened. He had returned to Italy, so it was there that she sent him the story of her "sea of troubles." "The anger and violence of the Setons, Farquhars, Wilkes etc. when they found Cecilia was not only a Catholic but as firm as the Rock she builds on, cannot be described," Elizabeth wrote, simplifying a story of warring emotions and principles into a parable of persecuted faith.[12] Antonio responded as she hoped. "Courage and perseverance," he urged. "The crown of everlasting glory awaits only, you know, those who persevere to the end." Elizabeth's family were "persecutors," Antonio declared, but "God and I are your Protectors. Of whom shouldst thou be afraid?"[13]

The merchant offered not only gallantry but money. Putting down his letter to Elizabeth, he wrote to his New York banker, John Murray. Describing Elizabeth as the image of "virtue in distress" and those around her as her "Persecutors . . . her Relations, her pretended Friends," Antonio explained that he would supply Elizabeth with any funds she required, should others be withdrawn because of Cecilia's conversion.[14] It was not at all clear that people such as Sarah Startin and John Wilkes *had* withdrawn their support.[15] The truth was that Elizabeth herself could no longer bear to take money from anyone but the Filicchis, who shared her faith, and Julia Scott, who cared nothing about it.

Elizabeth found it painful to admit that friends and family remained willing to help her, despite their unhappiness at Cecilia's conversion. She did not want to think she'd betrayed people who were fundamentally reasonable, preferring to understand herself as a martyr to intolerance. "Upon my word," she told Antonio, "it is very pleasant to have the name of being persecuted and yet enjoy the sweetest favours, to be poor and wretched and yet to be happy, neglected, and forsaken, yet cherished and most tenderly indulged by God's most favored servants and friends."[16] This was not a lie but a story, one told through centuries of Catholic saints and martyrs, one into which Elizabeth now wrote herself.

While Elizabeth and Cecilia openly defied the family's wishes, Zide and Hatch quietly rebelled. Although the girls were not allowed to see Elizabeth, they wrote notes to her at all hours of the day and night, filling tiny squares of paper with pet nicknames, phrases of Catholic devotion, and declarations of love. Cecilia and Hatch's brother Sam had not yet returned from his voyage to China, but Ned, their other brother, obligingly ferried notes back and forth, sometimes dropping them at secret spots where they could be picked up later.

Over the centuries, the Catholic Church had seen innumerable formations of laywomen drawn together by fervent piety. Some, such as the St. Peter's confraternity to which Catherine McLennan belonged, received Church sanction and were led by priests. Other groups, such as the Beguines, who flourished in the twelfth and thirteenth centuries, rejected institutional authority in favor of the authority of the charismatic women who led them. Still other circles, such as the tiny group of Iroquois women surrounding Catherine Tekakwitha in seventeenth-century Canada, existed under the partial control and in the partial view of priests, animated by a spirituality that overflowed expected bounds.[17] Elizabeth's informal circle of prayer and devotion was closest to the last kind. Michael Hurley heartily approved of her prayer and reading with Cecilia and may even have known of Harriet and Eliza's involvement. But he was not included in their impassioned correspondence, and Elizabeth, not Father Hurley, was the young women's spiritual guide. She did not want to join a confraternity; she wanted to lead a sisterhood.

The girls followed Elizabeth's counsel ardently, both chafing at and thrilling to the need to hide their newfound faith. "O! My soul sister how long must duty yield to obedience," Zide wrote one day, neatly sketching the tension they all felt between obligations to God and those to family.[18] "Do not carry your resignation too far," Elizabeth counseled the girl. "Tho' a Heavenly virtue in itself, in your situation it must be limited."[19] She knew the girls' defiance of their family carried risks, to Harriet most of all. The orphaned young woman had become engaged to Barclay Bayley—then trying to establish himself as a physician in the West Indies—and marrying him promised to free Hatch from a life dependent on relatives. A conversion might put the betrothal at risk. Elizabeth understood better than most how much was at stake, and she never insisted Harriet throw everything over for her faith. But she urged her not to forswear her interest in Catholicism. "Take care how you deny [your beliefs] by word or letter," she wrote. "We are not always obliged to declare, but always on every penalty forbid to deny, which to our dear Barclay I know you will find difficult."[20] She signed the letter "MEAS."

Despite her delight in the little prayer circle, Elizabeth longed to leave Manhattan. She still dreamed of Montreal, but in the fall of 1806, a different possibility suddenly emerged, in Baltimore, a city not two hundred miles away. Its bearer was Father Louis-Guillaume-Valentin Dubourg—now styling himself William—past president of Georgetown College and current president of St. Mary's College and Seminary, Baltimore. The charismatic Sulpician priest entered Elizabeth's life the way he'd entered the United States, full of more ambition and ideas than he could reasonably pursue.

Born into a planter family on Saint-Domingue, Dubourg left for France to study for the priesthood. He joined the order of Saint Sulpice, which had emerged in response to the Council of Trent's call for a less corrupt secular clergy. Although by the late eighteenth century the order's Parisian seminary prepared aristocratic men for positions within the Church hierarchy, its superior-general, Jacques Emery, strove to create a community known for piety, rectitude, and a rejection of worldly pleasures, and the Sulpicians also maintained their original purpose of training humble parish priests. Proponents of the distinctive nature of the Gallican Church, the Sulpicians nonetheless understood themselves to be defenders of Catholic orthodoxy. The order, in short, was classifiable as neither radical nor conservative, its members neither servants of power nor its critics.[21] Creative and ambitious, Dubourg quickly found a home in it.

While Dubourg entered into life as a priest, revolution crept toward him and the family he'd left behind. An uprising against Haiti's brutal slave regime sent Dubourg siblings fleeing to the United States, where slavery still flourished. In France itself, the Constituent Assembly at Versailles confiscated the Catholic Church's property and required that clergy take an oath of allegiance to the new French constitution: revolutionaries believed that the Church no less than the monarchy upheld the old order. When Jacques Emery instructed his priests to refuse to place themselves under the control of the state, Sulpicians saw their seminaries and churches closed. Their lives in danger, many crossed the Pyrenees into Spain, but Emery had also laid the groundwork for a different emigration: he corresponded with Bishop John Carroll about sending a small group of Sulpicians to the United States. Both men hoped that the United States—dominated by Protestants but free of an official church-state alliance—would provide a harbor for this fragile ark of French Catholicism. Dubourg made his way to Baltimore, where the tiny Sulpician seminary of St. Mary's had just been founded.

Carroll deplored the anticlericalism of the French Revolution and its subjugation of religion to the state; it seemed to him that the corrupting state power that had years earlier led to the suppression of his beloved Society of Jesus had taken on a new and more dangerous form. In addition to sympathizing with the Sulpicians' plight, the bishop hoped that well-trained French priests could do the work the United States' aging former Jesuits and motley collection of immigrant priests (more than one of whom had arrived scant steps ahead of ecclesiastical law) could not. Dubourg showed himself to be particularly energetic, learned, and optimistic, and before long Carroll placed him in charge of Georgetown College. In France, Jacques Emery was thrilled—"You are truly in your place," he wrote the young Sulpician; "God has given you an affection for the young, zeal, and an attitude for teaching"—but his appointment shocked the former Jesuits.[22] That may have been part of the point: the immigrant Dubourg embraced the need to compete for students and believers, and Carroll believed Georgetown's becalmed American clergy and teachers should learn from him. But Dubourg ran up debts and ruffled feathers, and in the face of ever-increasing indignation from the Jesuits, he was soon removed.

Sent next to Baltimore, Dubourg started a college to accompany the Sulpicians' tiny seminary. Although Carroll had advised Elizabeth to send her boys to Georgetown, it was becoming clear that St. Mary's under Dubourg was by far the more dynamic institution. The Sulpician confidently added faculty and fields of study to the school, counting on tuition from wealthy Americans and West Indian planters to meet his rapidly rising costs. The students arrived, but tuition monies lagged, delayed by the cash shortages and business failures that merchant families such as the Setons knew all too well. In an effort to raise money, Dubourg traveled to New York seeking subscribers for a lottery. There he met Elizabeth Seton.[23]

Dubourg knew of Manhattan's devout convert from Fathers Cheverus and Matignon and soon found himself near her at a dinner party. He offered a characteristically bold suggestion: Elizabeth should take her daughters to Baltimore, where with Dubourg's help she could open a school for girls. There was more: Dubourg told her that her sons, William and Richard, could be brought from Georgetown to St. Mary's College.[24]

Grateful for Dubourg's interest and intrigued by the possibility of reuniting her children, Elizabeth was nonetheless ambivalent. This was yet another plan that left her a schoolteacher. Baltimore was home to John Carroll and the nation's oldest Catholic families, but it was not Montreal; to Elizabeth it had always been just a place her husband went to do business. Cheverus and Matignon, however, soon sent word from Boston that Dubourg's suggestion pleased them. They doubted that an American widow with five young children could find a place among Montreal's Ursulines. More than that, they actively wanted to keep Elizabeth in the United States and Baltimore seemed the only realistic possibility. There was a tiny Carmelite convent in Port Tobacco, Maryland, and a community of Irish women living as the Order of the Visitation of the Blessed Lady near Georgetown, but the clergy never considered those viable options for Elizabeth and her daughters. Nor did anyone imagine their traveling to the Ursuline convent in New Orleans, which since the Louisiana Purchase of 1803 had stood within the borders of the United States. Dubourg's plan seemed the only hope of giving Elizabeth an American field for her spiritual ambition. "You are, I believe, called to do a great deed in the United States," Matignon wrote, "and it is there that you should stay, before all other places."[25] Cheverus added his voice. After evasively claiming that he was unable to "procure the Rules of the Nunneries in Canada," he praised the Baltimore scheme. "It would do better for your family," he wrote, and "would be very conducive to the progress of Religion in this country."[26]

Elizabeth voiced her mixed emotions in a letter to Antonio. The Sulpicians, she told him, do "not leave me any hope to their consent to my Canada Scheme," but they offered a bright promise: she was "destined to forward the progress of his holy Faith (such is their opinion)." "The very idea is enough to turn a stronger brain," she confessed. Perhaps she could be a schoolteacher *and* an instrument of God's will.[27] The Seton clan saw her as a deluded and meddling woman. In the eyes of Antonio and the Sulpicians, she was a heroine of the American Church.

When he learned of the plan, Carroll had his doubts. He had at last begun to take a real interest in Elizabeth after turning to her for news about the Barry family. Her compassionate letters about their struggles with illness won what fervent accounts of her own spiritual state never had: Carroll's affection.[28] After months in which the bishop knew Elizabeth only as an overwrought correspondent of Antonio, he saw the calm and competent woman others admired. Despite his wariness of fervent converts, he began to think Elizabeth was truly aflame with love for God, and that her devotion rather than her ego unsettled conventions. It was inevitable, Carroll told her now, that one who placed "a higher value on . . . salvation than all earthly things" would face opposition.[29] He also gave her a subtle warning about William Dubourg. When she wrote asking the bishop what he thought of the priest's Baltimore plan, Carroll told her that Dubourg had said nothing of it. He was delicately cautioning Elizabeth against placing her trust in a man whose dreams outstripped his resources. Elizabeth wondered whether she would ever leave New York.

CRUELLY PAINFUL

The winter of 1806–7 found New Yorkers nervously reading of hostilities between England and France. In May, the British had blockaded much of the European coast. Now, in December, Napoleon demanded that neutral nations stop trading with Great Britain; Great Britain responded in kind. The dueling proclamations signaled a real and growing threat to transatlantic trade, and New Yorkers—from merchants to sailors to the artisans who sold them wares—worried. December also brought a sudden jolt of violence to the city. On Christmas Eve, a group of apprentices and journeyman butchers jeered worshippers leaving midnight Mass. The next day, Irish Catholics stood at St. Peter's armed with cudgels and rocks. In the fight that followed, a watchman was killed.

Elizabeth showed almost no interest in any of these events. She briefly described the riot in a letter, then never mentioned it again; she seems to have decided, as have most historians, that alcohol and street rivalries rather than antipopery were the riot's true fuel.[30] Nor did she worry about transatlantic trade, although the fortunes of her benefactors depended on it. Instead, she brimmed with a sense of spiritual fullness and the essential rightness of things. Writing on the second anniversary of her conversion, she asked Antonio, "Do you remember when you carried the poor little wandering sheep to the fold? And led it to the feet of its tender Shepherd?" She gave him credit for the decision she herself had made: "Whose warning voice first said 'my sister you are in the Broadway, and not in the right one?' Antonio's. Who begged me to seek the right one? Antonio! Who led me kindly, gently in it? Antonio. . . . And who is my unfailing Friend, Protector, Benefactor? Antonio Antonio."[31] It was a return to the days in which Elizabeth's affection for Antonio and her love for the Church flowed together, but now she was as content as she'd once been uneasy.

Cecilia was happy, too, her regret at her family's anger overshadowed by the joy that life with Elizabeth and her daughters brought. But elsewhere in the clan misfortune struck: Elizabeth's impoverished sister-in-law, Eliza Seton Maitland, fell mortally ill. While Elizabeth and Cecilia nursed her, they inadvertently reminded the family of their usefulness. James and Mary Seton, the Farquhars, and even Charlotte and Governeur Ogden missed Cecilia's good cheer and willing hands, and Mary was heavily pregnant with her eighth child. Practicality overcame division. Cecilia was welcomed—summoned, really—back into the family, her plea that she be allowed to practice her new faith as she wished honored on condition that she help Mary in the final weeks of her pregnancy. In late April, Cecilia packed her few things and returned to James and Mary's house.

"My precious merry little Cis is gone," Elizabeth wrote Julia, "and I may truly say I am lost." Grief soon overtook wistfulness: after giving birth to a healthy child, Mary Hoffman Seton inexplicably sickened. She died in May. Others in the family had been in worrisome health for years, but Mary went from healthy childbed to the grave in a month. Even Elizabeth struggled. "Every power and faculty of my mind," she admitted, was "completely covered" "with the veil of Sorrow."[32] James Seton was left with eight stunned children and his own grief, and there was more disruption to come. Within months of his sister's death, Martin Hoffman dissolved the partnership of Hoffman & Seton. At his beloved home, which he had grandly dubbed the Wilderness, James contemplated a changed world. A decade earlier, he was a confident young merchant impatient at his older brother's hesitancy. Now he was a widower facing his own uncertain future. James turned to fourteen-year-old Cecilia for help in running his household, caring for his children, and calming his fears.

Cecilia did her best, but if being sent to live with Elizabeth was no punishment, being welcomed back to the Wilderness was no reward. No one openly criticized her faith, but Charlotte and Aunt Farquhar needled her about the manner of her conversion, and others considered the young Catholic convert, as she unhappily told Elizabeth, "a perfect wonder." Cecilia was pained and embarrassed. "You know it is not a very difficult thing to raise my blushes," she confessed.[33] Yet when James's young daughter Emma showed interest in Catholicism, Cecilia answered her questions. Despite her promises, the logic of her faith led her to share it. It was the family, and not the frail girl, who gave way. Rather than again confront her, the Setons decided that there could be no Cecilia without her faith, and that without Cecilia, the James Seton household and perhaps James Seton himself would fall apart. The Wilderness became the site of the kind of practical religious tolerance the city around it had known for centuries. James even reconciled with Elizabeth. "James walked in my room the other morning, took me in his arms like one of the children, asked some questions about a bundle at the Custom House, and seemed to have met me every day of the twelve months I have not seen him," a surprised Elizabeth told Sadler. The unfussy reconciliation suited her perfectly. "I like that," she observed, "so all the world should do."[34]

Despite her pleasure at these reconciliations, Elizabeth was convinced that she must leave Manhattan. Casual tolerance was as threatening to her vision of a God-directed life as persecution was, and perhaps more so. Having despaired of Dubourg's Baltimore scheme, she again hoped that somehow she and her daughters could live among Montreal's Ursulines. Cecilia desperately wanted to go along. Marooned at the Wilderness, she joined Zide and Hatch in writing Elizabeth urgent notes. A frail fourteen-year-old with the responsibilities of a matron, Cecilia imagined a convent as the essence of liberty. "My imagination has often carried me to the *little cells at Montreal*," she told Elizabeth, "—*tho' accompanied with sighs—they ascended—knowing full well—God will work it his own way.*"[35] Elizabeth commanded Cecilia to find meaning in her suffering; "The Heart will sometimes sink," the girl replied. Reminding Cecilia that in comparison with the engaged Harriet she lived "in perfect freedom," Elizabeth instructed her to "do your part to get rid of all depression."[36]

Despite her fears, Cecilia valued her spiritual liberty. So did Zide and, although she felt she must honor Barclay Bayley's views, Harriet. Little lay within the young women's control, but participation in this secret prayer circle—and, as Elizabeth told it, their eternal fate—did. As Zide had put it, they could choose "Duty" to God over "obedience" to man, and duty felt like liberation. The girls' family considered Catholicism the enemy of independent thought, but the Church had for millennia celebrated rebellious women. Young female martyrs who defied their families' orders to marry pagans are venerated as Roman Catholic saints, and in both the medieval and modern eras, female spiritual athletes rejected their families' and societies' claims on them.[37] Elizabeth's small circle combined the solace of a refuge with the thrill of an adventure.

FIGURE 11.1. Notes. APSL 1–3–3–4 159. Courtesy of the Daughters of Charity Province of St. Louise Archives, Emmitsburg, Maryland.

Some were willing to help with that adventure. When Sam Seton returned from his voyage to China, he happily took up the task of transporting the circle's clandestine notes. Witty and affectionate, Sam had no objections to his sister's new faith; he bridled only at unbroken seriousness. Near a cross drawn piously on a note, he wrote "Sam's Cross," and then "Sam's Crossness exceeds all." Elizabeth was delighted; Sam reminded her of William in the years before illness and failure grayed his spirit. "Our much loved makes us all alive again," she wrote after the young man's return.[38]

Michael Hurley was another helpmate to the circle and one who expected and received far more reverence than Sam. As a priest, he offered Elizabeth and Cecilia what lay at the heart of their faith: the sacrament of Communion. "When the clock struck 7 was on the knees to St. M. receiving the dearest consolation this world can afford," Elizabeth wrote Cecilia of one Mass.[39] As he celebrated that Mass, Hurley knew something Elizabeth did not: his position at St. Peter's was precarious. Despite the priest's scrupulous observance of his vows and successful participation in the campaign to abolish the resented oath, he'd fallen afoul of his parish's demanding trustees. Andrew Morris believed that Hurley tried to exert political influence over his parishioners; while that might have been forgivable, the fact that Hurley's politics differed from Morris's own was not. James Barry, half amused and half despairing, tried to explain the tangled situation to his friend the bishop. Hurley was almost surely innocent of wrongdoing, he wrote, but his crusty manner upset the trustees. "The low & nonlettered spalpeens are the greater number of our dignitaries of the church," Barry declared, and the clergy "are literally viewed and treated by them as a master taylor or shoemaker to their journeyman."[40] Barry suggested Hurley's name should be cleared through an investigation, but a Philadelphia priest named John Rossiter offered Carroll a starker view. He agreed Hurley had done nothing wrong but warned that the "young and unsuspecting and unexperienced" priest could not "remain in safety in New York in the present deplorable, critical, and alarming situation of things."[41]

Rossiter's startling assessment reflected the fact that the situation in St. Peter's parish was spiraling from disorder into chaos. Carroll desperately wanted to find "a priest of the most respectable character . . . to prevent the explosion of dreadful scandals" at St. Peter's, but priests were scarce in the new nation, and so far he'd failed.[42] In late 1806, a new priest, an Irishman named Matthias Kelly, had been assigned to the parish at the trustees' request, but he'd soon sniffed to Carroll that the congregation lacked "docility."[43] That it surely did, but the bishop needed a priest who could manage New Yorkers rather than complain about them. Reading Rossiter's grim accounting of Manhattan's clergy—"jealous of each other, suspecting each other," some "addicted to drinking" and others simply incompetent—Carroll agreed that he did Michael Hurley no favors by making him stay.[44] He directed the young priest to return to Philadelphia.

When she heard the news, Elizabeth immediately wrote to Cecilia. "St M never known till lost," she lamented, "nor did we know our love and value for him until the blow is struck—He leaves US on Monday to return NO MORE."[45] A final Mass, an affectionate farewell, and St. M. was gone.

No one told Elizabeth the reason for Michael Hurley's hasty departure; it may have seemed an excess of candor to tell the fervent convert that yet another of St. Peter's priests had run afoul of the congregation. Elizabeth believed that Hurley was simply needed in Philadelphia, and although she regretted his removal, she felt no fear. Confident in her faith, she enjoyed Hurley's guidance and companionship without relying on it.

Hurley's departure was far more devastating to Cecilia, and from Philadelphia the priest sent a heartfelt letter. Like "primitive Christians," Hurley counseled, Cecilia must make good conduct her defense against criticism and turn to "that fount" that brings "life everlasting," for nourishment. Urging her to "Remember the 17th of June"—the day she decided to convert—he told the girl that her choice made him value his own life. Gone was the cold reserve James Barry thought essential to the priest's nature. When he and Cecilia were "called upon," Hurley wrote, he hoped they might "be found side [to] side." "Pray for me, my dear child," he implored in closing, "and believe me with affection, your's, M. Hurley."[46]

The letter, Elizabeth wrote the priest, "has changed the tone of [Cecilia's] mind and harmonized it like a message from the skies."[47] Elizabeth herself had not read it; Cecilia did not give it to her. She may have been embarrassed by Hurley's effusive praise, or she may simply have wanted something in the world to be hers alone.

WHAT NEXT?

Elizabeth Seton's days churned along, filled with events that could not quite catch her interest. "Every body is talking of War here," she told Julia Scott in high summer, "and it has seemed impossible for me to feel an interest in the subject."[48] She felt equally removed from the rambunctious schoolboys to whom she served as housemother. Although she had once thought it would be tempting to evangelize them, she discovered it was trying enough simply to keep them decent and fed. Far from suspecting Elizabeth exerted a nefarious control over her charges, the boys' parents began to complain that she seemed to have no influence over them at all. "Roasted," she confessed to Julia Scott.[49]

Half-heartedly trying to render the schoolboys more presentable, Elizabeth dreamed of escape. Cheverus and Matignon still believed she should go to Baltimore rather than Montreal, but they now understood that she made her own decisions. "I know not what she has determined upon," Cheverus wrote Antonio in early October. "It is some time since I have been favoured by any letter of hers."[50] Elizabeth had determined only that she must leave New York one way or another. In a frank moment she mused that her critics were right to think she no longer had a place within genteel society. "My friends have so much distrust of my character," she wrote John Carroll, "considering, and justly that every Action is involved in my religious principles that they would certainly rather consider it as a relief if they knew I was in a situation conformable to my own Peace."[51]

Unable to leave New York, Elizabeth decided to signal through her wardrobe that she was nonetheless not really there. As a child, she'd admired the bonnets that distinguished Quaker women from everyone else. In Italy, she'd seen nuns in their habits. Now she fashioned a distinctive garb based on the sober black dress and bonnet she'd first worn as a new widow in Italy. Two years after William's death, the black garments had begun to signal her status less as William Seton's widow than as a self-made woman of religion.

Before her conversion, Elizabeth had contained her keen mind, incisive judgments, and burgeoning spirituality within genteel forms. Now the sharp, single purpose of her life—God's worship—was a blade slicing through convention and harmony. Or was it? She told Antonio that she still tried "to take every event gently and quietly, and oppose good nature and cheerfulness to every contradiction." "This succeeds so well," she continued ruefully, "that now it is an acknowledged opinion that Mrs. William Seton is in a very happy situation. . . . But Mrs. William Seton is obliged to watch every moment to keep up the reality of this appearance."[52] "Mrs. William Seton" was who others thought Elizabeth was and who, while in New York, she must remain. To live an authentic life without slicing her family to bits, she had to leave the city. She perfectly understood the pain she would cause Cecilia if she left her behind. She was willing to cause it, believing her duty to God and her children's souls outweighed even Cecilia's claims.

Elizabeth asked John Carroll for help in trying yet again to resuscitate the Montreal scheme. The bishop was distracted; in addition to his myriad duties throughout the nation, he was still trying to extricate St. Peter's from scandal (Matthew O'Brien was again accused of sexual misconduct, and now so was the recently arrived Matthias Kelley), and Carroll could no longer turn to the Barrys for help. James died of consumption in January, and Joanna and Ann sailed south, desperately hoping to improve Ann's health. So unsettled was the parish that when in spring Rome created New York as one of four new American dioceses—raising Baltimore to the status of an archdiocese and Carroll to archbishop—Carroll could think of no one to recommend as New York's bishop.[53] In short, New York did not need more drama from its Catholic denizens, Elizabeth Seton included. Carroll bade her take no rash action.

Just when Elizabeth felt truly thwarted, she found herself again under the bright gaze of William Dubourg. On a second visit to New York, the Sulpician revived his proposal that she start a girls' school in Baltimore. This time he followed up. After returning to Baltimore, Dubourg offered her "a formal grant of a log of ground situated close to the college which is out of town and in a very healthy situation." He promised that her boys could attend St. Mary's for a pittance, leaving her free to use the Filicchis' money for other purposes.[54] His attention for the moment fixed, Dubourg also reenlisted the support of the Boston clergy.[55] Cheverus left no doubt about the priests' united guidance: "We infinitely prefer [Baltimore]," he wrote, "to your project of retreat in Montreal."[56]

Elizabeth could not resist the firm and direct request of so many clergy, at least not when no other hope of leaving New York remained. She made plans to take her girls to Baltimore as quickly as possible, deciding Carroll's injunction against haste applied only to Montreal.

It did not: Carroll doubted sufficient groundwork had been laid for a school in Baltimore, and he questioned Dubourg's diligence. But the archbishop knew nothing of Elizabeth's sudden decision, and it was not he but Dubourg himself who wrote with doubts. "Do pray for me," the Sulpician implored Elizabeth, all at once uneasy. "My intentions, to be sure, are pure . . . My devotedness to the cause of Religion invariable. But that is not all; I am so slack, so irregular, so tepid, alas!" Perhaps, he offered, Elizabeth was "destined by His goodness to operate a salutary reformation of [me.]"[57] Elizabeth did not think her purpose lay in reforming Dubourg or any man. But she had made her choice and did not turn back.

At least her fortunes did not rest entirely with Dubourg: the Filicchis assured her, via a letter to Cheverus, that "*Money shall not be wanting.*"[58] In fact, Elizabeth suddenly had more financial stability than those around her. In late 1807, President Thomas Jefferson shepherded through Congress acts designed to keep the United States out of war by ending its trade with warring France and Britain. The embargo—"O Grab Me," angry merchants called it—immediately laid waste to American commerce. An English visitor who returned to New York after a brief absence was startled by the city's decline. "The coffee-house slip, the wharfs and quays along South-street, presented no longer the bustle and activity that had prevailed there five months before," he wrote. "The few solitary merchants, clerks, porters, and labourers, that were to be seen, were walking about with their hands in their pockets."[59] James Seton was one of those whose fortunes were failing, and Cecilia was left trying to cheer him while facing her own worst fear: Elizabeth was leaving. Elizabeth reassured the girl that she would send for as her soon as the Baltimore school was under way. Cecilia hoped and prayed.

Three years after returning from Italy aboard the *Pyamingo*, Elizabeth Seton had made it both necessary and possible for her to leave New York behind. As she and her three daughters prepared to depart, the family whom she'd believed unsympathetic—whom she'd *needed* to believe unsympathetic—proved both tender and generous. Wright Post paid for passage to Baltimore, and family members gathered to see them off. Learning of Elizabeth's decision, John Carroll wrote a quick letter to alert Georgetown's president that the Seton boys would be removed from the college. "I presume that Mr. Dubourg, when he was there last Easter persuaded her with his promises of protection," the archbishop wrote wearily. "Her embarrassments of fortune and the suggestion of her French Director at N.Y., closely connected with Dubourg, may have induced her to form some plan of which I shall fear bad consequences, if carried into execution." But Carroll exonerated Elizabeth. She could not be expected to conform herself to expectations. Elizabeth Seton, he told his correspondent, was "a Saint."[60]

12

A NEW BEING

ELIZABETH WATCHED from the deck of the *Grand Sachem* as the landmarks of her life glided by. "I saw once more the windows of State Street," she told Eliza Sadler, "passed the quarantine, and so near the shore as to see every part of it." She had watched her father die at that quarantine, then seen the station again at the start of her desperate voyage to Italy. "Can a heart swell so high and not burst?" she mused as the boat passed. The answer was yes.[1] Staten Island seemed like a rock "battering the waves of my changeable life," but Elizabeth believed she too was a rock, her faith as immovable as her life was variable.

Although the *Grand Sachem* should have taken two days to reach Baltimore, the sea turned against it, and the boat rocked and pitched in place. After three days of squalls, it finally neared Cape Henry, and two days later it docked at a wharf in Baltimore's busy harbor. From the deck, Elizabeth and the girls looked onto a scene not so different from what they'd left behind. Baltimore had grown dramatically since the end of the American Revolution, and it was now the nation's third-largest city. Laborers unloaded cargoes, merchants and their agents pointed goods toward warehouses, and street vendors—hucksters, the Baltimoreans called them—sang out their wares. French as well as English sounded through the city's busy streets: the slave uprising on Saint-Domingue that forced William Dubourg's family from the island had led thousands of other slaveholders to leave as well, and many made their way to Balti-more. There the slaveholders were warmly welcomed as coreligionists by the city's Catholics and their slaves coolly absorbed into the city and state's economy.[2]

Elizabeth and her daughters climbed into a carriage and were soon at St. Mary's. They arrived in the midst of a rainstorm and a ceremony: the *Sachem*'s unexpectedly slow voyage meant that they got to Baltimore on the day the Sulpicians consecrated a new chapel. From the wet street, Elizabeth stepped into a vaulted space of high arched windows and delicately wrought ornamentation. Sulpicians in their vestments gath-ered while seminarians and attentive worshippers filled the pews; even Michael Hurley was there, visiting from Philadelphia. Some in atten-dance knew that the chapel's false front rose above a roofline lowered as a result of scant funds and that a tower, statuary, and stained glass windows had been struck from the architect's plans.[3] But the chapel that rose from those compromises was beautiful, and Elizabeth was over-whelmed.[4] "The Glory of the Scene, all I have told you of Florence," she marveled to Cecilia, "is a Shadow."[5]

The chapel was surrounded by four stately brick buildings in which the Sulpicians ran St. Mary's Seminary and College. Just past their gate, on Paca Street, stood the house in which Elizabeth and her daughters were to live. After she had spent two years moving to ever-smaller and shabbier rooms, the newly erected, two-story brick building seemed to her like a "French mansion." Better yet, no one in Baltimore would scold Elizabeth or pity her or expect her to nurse sick relatives while holding her tongue. Instead, the Sulpicians and seminarians greeted her courte-ously, and William Dubourg's elegant sister Victoire helped her settle in. Elizabeth took a busy mother's delight in being tended to rather than tending. "I find the difference of situation so great that I can scarcely believe it is the same existence," she wrote Catherine Dupleix. "In every respect my condition is like a new being."[6]

It was as if the *Grand Sachem* had delivered Elizabeth from the city of man to the city of God, her home steps from a seminary, her open windows letting in the sound of a Catholic chapel's bells. "Mass from day light to Eight—my dwelling the most compleat—almost joining the chapel—Vespers and Benediction every Evening," she marveled. Amid her contentment, she did notice that Dubourg had found only two stu-dents for her school, one of them his niece. But the priest assured her

FIGURE **12.1.** *St. Mary's Seminary Chapel, North Paca Street & Druid Hill Avenue, Baltimore,* from the *Historic American Buildings Survey* by Maximilian Godefroy et al. Courtesy of the Library of Congress, Washington, DC.

that more pupils would come, and in the meantime, she had a happy task: collecting Will and Dick from Georgetown.[7] Leaving her daughters in the care of Victoire, Elizabeth embarked on a two-day carriage ride. Father Michael Hurley traveled with her, and so did a former sea captain named Samuel Sutherland Cooper.

FIGURE 12.2. Paca Street House. Courtesy of the Saint Mary's Spiritual Center and Historic Site, Baltimore, MD.

Elizabeth knew that Cooper and a merchant's wife named Rachel Montgomery had separately converted to Catholicism in Philadelphia, but her mind had been on her own choices, and she'd given neither much thought. Now, as the carriage rolled toward Washington, she met Cooper and was fascinated. Born in Virginia to a well-to-do family, Cooper was uninterested in religion until the night he heard a disembodied voice say, "Jesus, the water and the spirit."[8] Deciding to become a Christian, he investigated various denominations and became as convinced as Elizabeth that the Catholic Church was the true faith. As they conversed, Elizabeth found someone who shared both her taste for inquiry and her hunger for God. She also found a man marked by strangeness: Cooper had no teeth. Whether he'd pulled them to combat vanity, in despair over a woman, or in an inexplicable fit—all stories told about him—is not clear. Whatever its cause, Cooper's toothlessness did not repel Elizabeth. "From the involuntary attraction of certain dispositions to each other," she told Julia, "there was an interest and esteem understood." For the length of a carriage ride, Elizabeth contemplated what marriage to this passionate believer might bring.[9] "If we had not devoted ourselves to the heavenly spouse before we met," she mused to Cecilia, "I do not know how the attraction would have terminated." But they each *had* devoted themselves to God, and when the carriage arrived at Georgetown, they parted ways. "I fear him not nor any other," Elizabeth told Cecilia, and she turned her attention to her sons.[10]

Will and Dick, aged twelve and ten, were thrilled to see their mother and to learn they would now live a short walk away from her and their sisters. "The children are in a dream of delight on being once more united and so much caressed," Elizabeth wrote after the reunion.[11] All that remained was to make a place for Cecilia, and Baltimore would fulfill her hopes.

ST. MARY'S

"Placed between two orchards, and two miles from the city," St. Mary's seemed to Elizabeth like a world apart. It was not. St. Mary's lay not in the city of God but in the environs of Baltimore. While Elizabeth settles into the peace and beauty of her new surroundings, we'll take several steps backward and survey the world that surrounded and supported her.

Crucial to St. Mary's was a genteel merchant cousinage of the kind Elizabeth knew in New York. At its center stood the Carroll clan, and at that clan's center stood the wealthy planter Charles Carroll of Carrollton. William Dubourg turned to him for loans while he built St. Mary's college, and the Sulpicians also courted the support of Carroll's daughters, Polly and Catherine. Vivacious Polly had charmed William and slightly unsettled Elizabeth during a long-ago visit to New York, and in the years since, she had married an English merchant named Richard Caton and borne four daughters. Caton's business failed, but his father-in-law paid his debts and the family lived luxuriously. Polly's sister Catherine had married a lawyer and politician named Robert Goodloe Harper, and the couple had five living children. Like Caton, Harper was raised Protestant (mixed marriages were common among Maryland Catholics, though they saddened the archbishop), but he converted to his wife's faith. Hardworking and ambitious, Harper was the man the family turned to when calm advice was required. Yet like his brother-in-law Richard Caton, Harper borrowed large sums from Charles Carroll (it was he who had written the defense of the Bankruptcy Act of 1800 that appeared in New York's newspapers while William Seton's fortunes hung in the balance).[12] The Catons and Harpers offered Elizabeth entrée to Maryland society, and the Catons' two younger daughters, Louisa and Emily, spent time with Elizabeth and her daughters. Louisa had barely extricated herself from a disastrous near engagement, and neither she nor her sister was an obvious candidate for Elizabeth's pious influence. But the girls, Elizabeth, and Anna Maria quickly grew fond.[13] By fall, the fledgling school still had only a handful of students, but with the support of elite Catholic families, Elizabeth and Dubourg were hopeful.

The boarding students lived with Elizabeth and her daughters in the snug brick house on Paca Street, studying together on the second floor and sleeping near each other under the building's eaves. Despite her reluctance to be a schoolteacher, Elizabeth felt happy to be "stuffing her brain with dollars, cents, and fractions" in order to teach the children math. Within the sound of the seminary's bells, each moment seemed consecrated and "congenial to all my ideas of happiness."[14]

Elizabeth's new life, like St. Mary's itself, relied not only on families such as the Catons and Harpers but on the institution from which those families—and Maryland's Catholic Church—drew their wealth: slavery. The former Jesuits still owned plantations that their brethren had begun in the seventeenth century, and the Sulpicians struck an agreement to draw on the profits of one of the plantations to support St. Mary's. Many priests, including John Carroll, believed that clergy were gentler in their extraction of labor and less willing to divide families than were other slaveholders. While there is scattered evidence for that position, there is also evidence of the inevitable brutality of the institution. A priest in charge of a Jesuit plantation during much of the early nineteenth century complained that he was restrained from extracting more profit not by Christian charity but by slaves' determination to defend themselves from the lash. And when in 1805 the Jesuit corporation found itself facing a financial shortfall, Bishop Carroll wrote coolly that "the sale of a few unnecessary Negroes, three or four, and stock would replace the money."[15] While Elizabeth settled into her new life at St. Mary's, Jesuit managers were arranging to sell a family of eight, and the labor of enslaved people continued to support Georgetown College.[16]

St. Mary's reliance on profits from a Jesuit-owned plantation was its most direct link to slavery but not its most financially important. Charles Carroll's great wealth was the fruit of slavery's poisoned tree, and the

Sulpicians willingly reached for it. The planter loaned Dubourg thousands of dollars for the running of St. Mary's, and some of the money he bestowed on the Catons and Harpers (Charles Carroll's meticulous records suggest he gave the latter over $85,000 in cash alone) found its way to Sulpician coffers.[17] The Sulpicians also borrowed money from William Duboug's brother, Louis, now a Louisiana planter, and parents paid tuition with money extracted from the plantations of Maryland, Cuba, and Guadeloupe.

Throughout Europe's New World empires, Catholic orders did just as Maryland's Jesuits and Sulpicians had done, drawing sustenance from stolen labor while understanding themselves to offer the gift of Christian guidance and charity. Nonetheless, the circumstances of the British colonies and the United States distinctively shaped the American Church's use of enslaved labor: having no state support or aristocratic patrons, the American Church, John Carroll once explained to Rome, was "supported . . . by the farms which the first missionaries acquired by purchase and transmitted to their successors."[18] Those who owned slaves on the Church's behalf insisted that they had no choice but to accept the evil of slavery in order to do good. Although their conception of the good was distinctively Catholic, this argument from necessity placed Catholic clergy squarely within an American school of self-exculpation. "I sincerely regret that slaves were ever introduced into the United States," one Jesuit priest wrote, "but as we have them, we know not how to get rid of them."[19] Americans had "the wolf by the ear, and we can neither hold him, nor safely let him go," Thomas Jefferson similarly declared. Robert Goodloe Harper made the same point: "Necessity indeed, that iron law, to which all others must submit, renders unavoidable a deviation from the maxims of justice," Harper wrote. Harper came closer than most to admitting that this was a law made not of iron but of gold. "Slaves," he explained, are "the foundations of our wealth."[20] Yet like many of his countrymen, Harper believed that that wealth and slavery itself were necessary to the United States' ability to defend and spread liberty. Nation and Church had each sunk their roots in slavery's soil.

Elizabeth gave no thought to the institution that supported the Catholic society to which she'd moved. Her mind was on her school, her family, and her soul. Living cozily within St. Mary's bucolic grounds, her five children thrived. William and Richard were happy if uninspired students. "Neither of [the boys] appear to me to show any distinct marks of genius," Elizabeth told Julia straightforwardly, but "their progress in their classes is superior to that of most Boys of 10 and 12." At eight, Catherine was pretty and "sweeter every day," and although six-year-old Rebecca was "not so handsome," she was "so wise and full of expression you would not wish her to be lovelier." Elizabeth had been far more interested in learning than were her half brothers, and now she thought her girls brighter than her sons. She herself read almost exclusively devotional literature, but she'd brought with her to Baltimore the commonplace books she'd kept as a teenager, and she planned to share them with her younger daughters, as she had with Anna Maria.[21] The girls were to pray, and they were also to think.

When it came to Anna Maria herself, Elizabeth did not know quite what to think. The girl who had first been ungovernable and then been preternaturally obedient now seemed ever so slightly alien. She kept her thoughts to herself and at twelve suddenly no longer looked like a child. "The woman is so marked in her appearance and manner that indeed you would scarcely know her," Elizabeth told Julia. "Her chest is very prominent and the shoulders quite in their right place." Anna wanted to dress like her Baltimore friends, and she adored a white beaver hat that Julia sent, not least because another girl had one "exactly like it."[22] Hopeful that Anna would remain pious and discreet, Elizabeth realized she must nonetheless let the girl dress more fashionably than she had in New York. Baltimore's genteel Catholic clans expected the Paca Street school to create polish as well as piety, and Elizabeth's daughters were to be proof of her own good sense.

Elizabeth was in fact beginning to wonder whether her new life was a bit too polished. She could not help but notice that Baltimore's wealthy Catholics often married outside their faith, and some even wandered outside their marriages; Maximilien Godefroy, architect of St. Mary's beautiful new chapel, was openly conducting an affair. More to the point, elite Baltimore Catholics' practice of religion seemed more like the polite Episcopalianism she'd known in New York than like her own single-minded passion. Educating the daughters of these worldly families was, while pleasant, far from a heroic mission. She did not admit to discontent. But while her daughter happily wore the white beaver hat that left her indistinguishable from other girls, Elizabeth "dressed for the grave" and with surprising speed began to once again imagine a different and purer life.[23]

NEW YORK

Reading Elizabeth's Baltimore letters to Antonio, one would think friends and family in New York had happily washed their hands of her. "Mrs. Startin has excused herself from contributing. . . . Mr. Post as you know made no advances," she told the merchant.[24] In fact, Wright Post assured Elizabeth that "I am always ready to render you any service which may be in my power"; John Wilkes so admired her that he asked her to send a copy of any spiritual journal she might keep; and if Sarah Startin sent no money, the reason may have been her own hurt feelings: Elizabeth never wrote. She still needed to understand her departure from New York as a necessary escape from persecution, so ties of family and friendship lay unmended.

The only New Yorker she wanted to think about was Cecilia. Elizabeth assured the girl that she was safe from "the beating storm," but Cecilia demurred. "The storm is heavy and my little bark is weak surrounded by rocks, I tremble lest it dashes against them," she wrote.[25] Yet Cecilia never wavered in her faith, and Hatch and Zide continued to imagine they, too, might convert. The Seton clan had hoped that with Elizabeth gone, the young women would quickly lose interest in Catholicism, but the trio remained devoted and defiant. "[Zide] gets into more scrapes than you can possibly imagine," Hatch wrote Elizabeth, "for whenever a discussion of religion takes place (which is very often and I believe intentionally too) she defends your dear Faith with more than enthusiastic ardour."[26] Desperate to stop the contagion, the Hoffmans and Farquhars agreed to pay for two of James Seton's younger daughters to go off to boarding school. "Uncle Ogden and Uncle Martin are to pay for me—any thing you see to get me out of the hands of Precious Cicil," one of the girls laughingly wrote Anna Maria. Her uncles, she explained, "do not know the more they strive to set me against it the more I shall love it."[27]

Lacking the will for open conflict—and needing Cecilia's help—Charlotte Seton Ogden and Aunt Farquhar needled the young woman but did no more. James remained desperate to keep her, berating the girl when he heard a rumor that she meant to leave for Baltimore. "I could scarcely persuade him that so far from preparing to leave him that I had not even thought of it," Cecilia wrote wearily.[28] Her family needed her labor; so, it now turned out, did her faith. A new priest had arrived at St. Peter's, a young Alsatian named Anthony Kohlmann, and he was as adamant as James that Cecilia remain in the city. Kohlmann was beginning to wrestle the chaotic parish into good order, and he wanted Cecilia to help him start a girls' school. Aware of the many demands on her, Elizabeth urged Cecilia to see herself not as a helpless drudge but as a Catholic heroine. "Yes my Cecilia favoured of Heaven, Associate of Angels, beloved Child of Jesus," she wrote, "You shall have the Victory and he the Glory." Cecilia found meaning in her misery. "Angry words and cross looks are all I meet with," the girl wrote, "but how sweet is it to feel that we suffer with and for Jesus. My Soul truly rejoices."[29]

When Elizabeth wrote to Cecilia about St. Mary's and its people, she singled out one priest for praise: Pierre Babade. A Sulpician in his early forties when Elizabeth met him, Babade had been very young when he and his confreres were driven from France by the Revolution. After joining those making their way to safety in Spain, he sailed for Cuba. With its faithful but doctrinally ignorant population, Havana seemed a perfect setting for a Sulpician school and seminary, and Babade convinced William Dubourg, just then ending his controversial term as Georgetown's president, to join him. Dubourg arrived with a nephew, two former Georgetown students, and a fellow Sulpician named Benoit Flaget in tow, but he quickly realized that Babade's plans would come to naught: Dubourg, master of the grand but impractical scheme, had been taken in by one. When he abandoned Havana for Baltimore, Dubourg brought Babade with him.[30] In the decade that followed, Dubourg served as president of St. Mary's college and Babade as a professor of languages under his direction.

When Elizabeth and her girls arrived that first rainy day, Pierre Babade greeted them with an original poem in French and English. Its rhymes turned on the fact that "Seton" could be rearranged to spell "Stone"—Pierre in French, and Peter, as in the Rock of the Church, in English. Its charming intricacy struck Elizabeth as marvelous.[31] The three Seton daughters immediately loved Babade, and Rebecca and Catherine, who barely remembered their father, offered their hearts without reserve. "My dear father I love you very much," Kit wrote on a square bit of paper, "but I love my dear dear savior best of all and my dear mother and you both and I hope that we will live happy forever."[32] Elizabeth was nearly as enraptured. Although Babade was just eleven years her senior, she thought of him as her "venerable Patriarch who is always instructing me."[33]

Babade's was a baroque spirituality, far removed from Archbishop Carroll's reserved piety. Carroll wanted to create a style of Catholicism akin to the cathedral being built under his direction in Baltimore: sober and republican in its exterior, identifiably Catholic within. Respectful of Catholic tradition but convinced that adaptation was desirable, Carroll advocated the use of English in the Mass, sure it would improve Catholics' piety and reduce Protestant mistrust. He believed Catholicism offered the safest and best path to salvation but rejected the idea that those outside the Catholic communion were damned. The bishop was also hopeful that sincere religious faith produced ethical beings and optimistic that mankind could improve, the latter reflecting both his Jesuit formation and his interest in Enlightenment philosophy. He cooperated with a Philadelphia publisher named Matthew Carey to publish an English-language Catholic Bible so that the laity might have direct access to scripture.[34]

Pierre Babade took a different view of just about everything. He complained to Rome about Carroll's favoring of English and could not have cared less whether Protestants mistrusted him; Protestants had no hope of salvation unless they accepted the one true church, and their ministers were "ravenous wolves."[35] Carroll avoided ostentatious displays of devotion; Babade loved dramatic gestures and insisted on praying the Angelus "always on the knees because there is a particular indulgence annexed to it." He did not oppose Bible reading, but it was the liturgy, feast days, and material culture of Catholicism that Babade thought carried the faith. He wept as he said Mass and thrilled to sacred pictures and richly decorated altars.

Carroll's and Babade's differing spiritualities easily coexisted in the loosely organized and heterogeneous American Church, and both offered things Elizabeth valued. Carroll's linking of the ethical elements of faith to the devotional, his quiet insistence that believers constantly examine their interior life, and even his sometimes disappointingly moderate opinions on ascetic practice and pious display appealed to Elizabeth's lifelong respect for reason and harmony. Babade, with his delight in gesture, pictures, saints, and feasts, wove together heaven and earth in the way Elizabeth had longed to experience since her months in Italy. She respected Carroll's optimism about human beings' ability to learn and become virtuous, but she was profoundly drawn to Babade's sense of man's moral frailty and helplessness. And whereas Carroll's crafting of a respectable Catholicism appealed to Elizabeth's mind, Babade's defiance of everyone's demands but God's spoke to her heart.

Elizabeth had no idea that the traits she loved in Babade—along with some she had not yet seen—had for years unsettled his fellow Sulpicians and his bishop. His surveillance of liturgical practices, alert for any hint of laxness or change, irked brethren and superiors. His frequent trips to Philadelphia, which Elizabeth saw as evidence of Babade's selfless zeal, were unauthorized. Brethren suspected that his judgment was impaired by drink. Father Nagot, the dignified elderly priest who served as the superior at St. Mary's, once asked Jacques Emery to remove Babade from Baltimore.[36] But the Sulpicians seem to have hoped his attention to the Setons offered a harmless outlet for his energies, and Elizabeth was left free to make of him the spiritual director she'd sought since her conversion.

Not long after her arrival, Babade encouraged Elizabeth to imagine herself becoming something other than a schoolteacher. His urging strengthened her existing desire. It was true that her prayer life was rich; since her arrival on Paca Street she rarely felt "the enthusiastic delight . . . I once experienced" in the Eucharist, but she lived in contemplation of Jesus's love and sacrifice, as if she were "living in Christ's wounds."[37] She might have decided life on Paca Street was all that she needed. Instead, the slight dissatisfaction she'd begun to feel, grew. "Rectifying [girls'] tempers and giving them good sentiments" was worthy and pleasant, but it was not enough.[38] Elizabeth understood that a widow with five young children could not easily join a convent in either the Old World or the New. But Cheverus and Tisserant had encouraged her to believe she could play an important role in the American Church, and Babade added a thrilling new voice. Elizabeth had been unable to enter an existing community. Perhaps a new one could be founded.

This hope was in some ways quintessentially American: Elizabeth was to be a self-made nun, shaking off the constraints of tradition. Yet her vision took shape under the tutelage of French clergy who had seen women in France live a consecrated life outside conventional cloister and so believed American women under Elizabeth's direction might do the same. Those French sisters—to whom we will return—were themselves part of a long tradition of Catholic women who found creative ways to serve others and live their faith in community. Centuries earlier, the Beguines of northern Europe and the beatas of Spain lived in poverty and celibacy, devoting themselves to prayer and good works outside convents and without the sanction of monarchs. When Rome suppressed communities, others sprang up. Widows were prominent among founders and participants. One reason was that in medieval and early modern Europe, there were simply a lot of widows, but it was also true that widows faced challenges and opportunities that made life in a religious community enticing. Some needed to support themselves in eras when women's occupational choices were few. Others, perhaps because they had known a particularly bitter marriage or a particularly sweet one, sought a different kind of companionship and household. Still others had married only because their families commanded it, and widowhood offered a second chance at the consecrated life they'd coveted.[39]

Historically, female devotion outside cloister bore an uneasy relation to the institutional Church, and in the sixteenth century the Council of Trent sought to end it. Eager to neuter Protestant criticism of women who lived beyond the control of husbands or priests, the council decreed that professed nuns could not leave their cloisters; two subsequent rules extended the Tridentine decree to female lay associates and prohibited visitors within convents. These rules were neither immediately nor uniformly enforced; female religious communities in Munich remained uncloistered more than half a century after Trent, and an Englishwoman named Mary Ward founded a women's community, inspired by the Jesuits, which gained the favor of three popes. Yet in the end, Ward's "English Ladies" were suppressed and the communities at Munich cloistered, and there is no denying that the sixteenth-century rules ushered in a new era of inward-turned Catholic female monasticism.[40]

Tridentine cloister was a decision made by men about women, but some women willingly laid the bricks of cloister, and some men questioned the wisdom of the construction. For some nuns, cloister offered a satisfying life of worship and contemplation, a near-miraculous opportunity in eras in which women's lives were consumed by domestic labor. For some clergy, that was the problem. Women at prayer were not women at work, and the Church had a lot to do. John Carroll himself held that view, and he engaged in a long struggle with the tiny community of Carmelites near Port Tobacco, Maryland. The Carmelites (several of whom had been born in the colonies, joined their religious community in Belgium, then sought refuge from Europe's wars back in the new United States) saw cloister as a precious expression of their spirituality and adamantly defended it; Carroll thought the women "would be far more useful if . . . they undertook the education of girls." The bishop received approval from Rome to urge the community to break their cloister and teach; the Carmelites ignored him.[41] Seven years after beginning his campaign, Carroll conceded defeat. "I doubt not of the efficacy of their prayers in drawing down blessings on us all," he wrote of the Carmelites, "but their utility to the public goes no further."[42]

In a different life, Elizabeth's love of prayer, contemplation, and reading might have led her to a cloistered order such as the Carmelites; as a widowed mother of young children, she had to look elsewhere. And there *was* another model of vowed life: the Ursuline order, the very community she'd learned of in Montreal. Angela Merici had founded the Company of St. Ursula in Italy in 1535, but it first flourished in France, where Protestantism claimed the allegiance of much of the countryside. The Ursulines were female soldiers of the Counter-Reformation, determined to recapture Europe for God by teaching the principles of Catholic orthodoxy. Yet the new cloister rules banned the women's practice of traveling in pursuit of their mission. One Jesuit cautioned an Ursuline leader that their lives were "pure temptation, and that it was absolutely necessary for a young girl to have either a husband or a cloister."[43] But the Ursulines attracted supporters, too, not least clergy who saw their educational work as essential to the Church's survival. As John Carroll might have put it, "their utility to the public" was considerable.

Over the course of decades, Ursulines reached a compromise with clerics and the Holy See and knit themselves into the fabric of aristocratic Catholic France. Gone were the days when an Ursuline named Anne de Vesvre traveled from town to town teaching clergy how to catechize children and chastising the nobility. Instead, the Ursulines fulfilled their mission within schools for girls. Poor children were taken in as day students for little or no tuition, while wealthy families paid to have their daughters board.[44] Pupils were taught within clearly designated sections of houses equipped with grilles, turnstiles, and multi-keyed doors, so the Ursulines argued that they lived in Tridentine cloister despite being in regular contact with students.[45] This architectural and doctrinal ingenuity received papal approval, and the Ursulines were declared a religious order in compliance with the Council of Trent's demands. Women could belong to a vowed Catholic religious community while leading lives of active benevolence.

John Carroll thought Maryland would benefit from the presence of Ursulines, and William Dubourg came to the same conclusion not long after his arrival from France. The order, however, was decimated and scattered during the French Revolution, and no community existed in the United States outside New Orleans (that community was founded in the early eighteenth century, when the region lay under Spanish rule). Now Elizabeth, Babade, and Dubourg pondered an American version of the Ursulines. It would not be exactly like the French order, since even the Ursulines' modified cloister posed challenges to American sensibilities and to Elizabeth's family. But perhaps a community could be created that served poor and wealthy children and spread Catholic teachings in a land where priests were scarce and—as St. Peter's parish in Manhattan painfully demonstrated—often unreliable.

Nothing was certain, but Elizabeth hoped she would not remain a Baltimore schoolteacher for long. "It is expected," she had confided in Cecilia months earlier, that "I shall be the Mother of many daughters."[46] She and Cecilia urgently prayed that the expectation would soon come to pass and that Cecilia would be one of Elizabeth's first spiritual daughters.

13

SOME CHARITABLE PERSONS

ON HIS FREQUENT, mysterious trips to Philadelphia, Father Pierre Babade had a new purpose. Believing that an American sisterhood centered on Elizabeth Seton would improve the orthodoxy and reputation of American Catholics, he decided to find young women to join it. Others were just beginning to ponder a sisterhood's possible funding and configuration, but Babade was recruiting members. In early fall of 1808 Elizabeth learned that he had found "two of the Sweetest young women" to join her still hypothetical community.[1]

Cecilia O'Conway, aged twenty, and Maria Murphy Burke, aged about sixteen, were the daughters of Irish immigrant families in which education flowed more freely than money. Cecilia was not just the older but the more daring of the two, and before Babade redirected her attention, she had planned to sail to Spain to become a Carmelite. It was not as improbable as it sounds: Cecilia's father, Matthias, made his living as a translator, and he'd moved his growing family from Pennsylvania to New Orleans to Havana during Cecilia's childhood. Fluent in French and Spanish, the young woman knew of Europe's monastic traditions and was confident that her true home lay in the Reformed Carmelite cloisters founded by Teresa of Avila.

Maria Burke decided to go along. Her father had died of yellow fever in 1798, and her mother, Margaret, had married an impecunious sea captain, who had recently died as well. The family boasted one prominent member: Matthew Carey, the well-known Philadelphia printer, who was Margaret's brother (and Maria's uncle). But money was scarce, and Margaret skittered from one disastrous endeavor to the next, including a doomed effort to run a strawberry farm. Maria wanted a different kind of life, and she had decided to sail for Spain with her friend when Pierre Babade made his surprising proposal.[2]

Babade told the Philadelphia families that a marvelous sisterhood would soon open its doors in Baltimore, and the girls could be among the first to join it. Matthias O'Conway was delighted; the thought of his daughter a day's journey rather than an ocean crossing away was a gift. Maria's mother saw matters differently. She seems not to have known of her daughter's intention to join the Spanish Carmelites, and she firmly rejected this new plan. Perhaps she had disliked the Ursuline school where she was educated during her Dublin childhood; perhaps she thought her daughter too young to make such an important decision. What is certain is that Margaret Burke said no. Babade did not see fit to share that detail when he told Elizabeth of the "two sweet girls" he'd found to join the sisterhood.

Back in Baltimore, serious questions remained about the viability of a sisterhood built around Elizabeth. Spiritual motherhood lay at the root of her authority, but literal motherhood threatened to circumscribe her vocation. The challenges were several. Establishing a house modeled on the Ursulines would resolve the problem of Elizabeth's daughters, who could live among the boarders. But Will and Dick would have to remain at St. Mary's College, seeing their mother and sisters less often than they wished, if at all. Nor was it clear how Elizabeth would reconcile her children's expectation that she be *their* mother with a religious community's expectation that she be everyone's mother. Years earlier, Jean Tisserant had told her that convent life was impossible because of her responsibilities to her children. Now John Carroll quietly wondered how Elizabeth would manage. Mary Post put the question of competing duties and desires most directly. "It seems almost incredible," Elizabeth's sister wrote, "surrounded as you are by dear little children that you can familiarize yourself to the contemplation of any change that must incur the necessity of separation from them." Like Elizabeth, Mary had suffered when their father put work before family. Now she gently asked how a woman she knew "to be one of the most affectionate of mothers" could have "the power . . . of divesting your mind of such cares as one attached to every situation of which [your children] make a part." Having stated the problem, Mary declined to press. "It can only be that you have a perfect reliance on the care of him who is the ruler of all things," she concluded.[3] Mary's answer was the one Elizabeth herself settled on. Confident that if it were God's will that she found a religious community, all problems would melt away, she put aside her sister's letter and the questions it posed.

Elizabeth understood herself to be leaving the sisterhood's fate to Providence, simply waiting to see whether anything came of it. In reality, she remained what she'd always been, a woman who analyzed and acted. Whatever else the establishment she already thought of as "my house" would need—rules, sisters, a divinely sanctioned purpose—it would also need money, and she pondered where that might come from. It was difficult to imagine any girls' school bringing in enough tuition to cover expenses, support a sisterhood, and teach poor girls for free. Elizabeth had no funds of her own; years after her husband's death, his bankruptcy case ground on, the payment of occasional dividends heartening creditors but offering Elizabeth and her children nothing.[4] She knew that there was wealth in Catholic Baltimore; the Catons and Harpers were proof of that. Unfortunately, it tended not to be liquid; the Catons and Harpers were proof of that too. Merchant finances were growing more straitened. "The Embargo has deprived [New Yorkers] of half their work," Elizabeth's cousin Joseph wrote, "and I am apprehensive that after the last of February it will completely deprive me of my present resources of living."[5] Matters were no better among the Caribbean planters who sent sons to St. Mary's College. Charles Carroll of Carrollton remained rich, but the Sulpicians were already deeply in his debt.

There was one family who seemed able and willing to help: the Filicchis. John Wilkes told Elizabeth that the Italian clan, unconstrained by Jefferson's embargo, had "made a mint." So Elizabeth sent each brother a letter explaining her desire to found a religious "establishment" capable of "instructing children in our religion." She delicately inquired whether they might pledge money. Each letter was crafted for its recipient: she told Antonio of "favours and consolations" she enjoyed while assuring Filippo "it is not a self-gratification I seek." She also suggested Filippo could lessen the risk of investment by purchasing a building for the sisterhood to use; if the women failed, she pointed out, Filippo would still own the building.[6] To both brothers, she emphasized that Providence, and not her own will, would decide the sisterhood's fate.

While Elizabeth awaited a response from the Filicchis, Matthias O'Conway arrived from Philadelphia, bringing Cecilia with him. At St. Mary's, the peripatetic Irishman found a place unlike anything he had seen in the new nation. "Ah, my Rebecca," he wrote his wife, "If you were here you would see everything carried on precisely as you have seen in the Catholic countries. You would hear the heavenly music and the High Mass performed in a manner that would raise your soul above the thoughts of this world and make you forget that you were in it." O'Conway agreed to let Cecilia remain with Elizabeth, believing his daughter was "placed where she may be happy, if one can be happy on earth."[7]

When her father returned to Philadelphia, Cecilia O'Conway quickly settled into life on Paca Street, teaching French and Spanish to the boarders. (She would later adopt the name Veronica, to avoid confusion with Cecilia Seton, and we will begin to call her that now, for the same reason.) "I have had everything that could do me good and no less than three of the priests see me every day," she wrote her father, adding that Babade was "as tender as the most loving father could possibly be."[8] The pleased O'Conways decided to send another daughter, Isabel, to be prepared for her first Communion at the Paca Street school.[9] Maria Burke remained unhappily in Philadelphia, Margaret steadfastly refusing her consent.

Cecilia Seton, for her part, struggled along in Manhattan, tending children, soothing James, and sending meals over to her brother Sam, now working at the Bank of New York. ("I think more of you all, than you can imagine," Sam found time to scrawl on a letter to Baltimore, "although I do not take the trouble of telling you of it.")[10] As Cecilia weakened, even Charlotte Ogden and Aunt Farquhar quieted their criticism of her conversion. Still, James Seton and Father Kohlmann insisted the girl must not leave New York. The latter, Cecilia mourned, went "so far as to tell me I cannot go unless in opposition to his advice & the will of God." In the midst of Cecilia's unhappiness, a family friend began awkwardly to court her. "What a world!!" she wrote Elizabeth. "Always inventing something new to harass the soul that wishes to disengage herself from it." Thinking of Baltimore was like "thinking of Paradise."[11]

Cecilia knew where she wanted to go but could not achieve it; her sister Harriet did not know in what direction her hopes lay. Harriet's fiancé, Barclay Bayley, had gone to the West Indies to make his fortune (or at least his living), and he rarely wrote. Nor did he return, nor did he send for Harriet. Both she and the Seton clan began to doubt his intentions. Worried for her future, Harriet craved Elizabeth's charismatic insistence that nothing mattered other than God. Memories of the prayer circle came to her "like a vision." "Can it be possible," the young woman asked, "I should ever feel a heart so light so cheerful so contented so replete with every pleasurable sensation again. Alas! I never can."[12] Elizabeth worried and prayed for the girls she'd left behind.

CHARITY

Elizabeth Seton had lived her life in port cities. Into those ports came the letters and money, the good news and bad, that shaped her world. She expected that support for her proposed sisterhood would come from port cities too—Livorno, perhaps, or New York, Boston, or Philadelphia. That winter, however, a person profoundly important to her future was hauling wood and breaking rocks in a place far from any ocean. For the rest of Elizabeth's life, that person, Father Jean Dubois, would be essential to the working out of her vision. For almost all of that time, he would also be occluded from her sight. It seems fitting to introduce him now, while Elizabeth's attention is elsewhere.

Jean Dubois was born into middling obscurity in Paris and by dint of talent and luck educated as a scholarship student at the famous Collège Louis-le-Grand. Dubois shared the halls with Jean Cheverus, a class behind, and with two young men a class ahead: Camille Desmoulins and Maximilien Robespierre. When some of the college's professors began to explore revolutionary ideas, Dubois cleaved to faculty loyal to the Church. When he left Louis-le-Grand, it was to enter the seminary, and he was ordained a priest at the age of twenty-four.[13]

Dubois's first assignment was to the parish of St. Sulpice, from whence the Sulpician order had emerged and where many of its priests still studied and served. Dubois, however, was a diocesan priest rather than a member of the order. Nor was he assigned to St. Sulpice itself, the massive church whose confidently mismatched towers proclaimed the power and wealth of the Church. Instead, he served as chaplain at an asylum run by a female apostolic community known as les Filles de la Charité.[14]

Like the Ursulines, the Daughters of Charity had at their inception challenged Trent's demand for cloister. The community's origins lay in the collaboration among three seventeenth-century French Catholics: Vincent de Paul, Louise de Marillac, and Marguerite Naseau. Born to a peasant family in Gascony, Vincent de Paul was a young, ambitious priest when he found himself troubled by what seemed the spiritual and material poverty of French peasants. De Paul embraced a mission of evangelization and charity, establishing confraternities in rural parishes through a community of priests and brothers, the Congregation of the Mission. He also organized a company of aristocratic women to raise funds and prepare meals for the unfortunate at the Hotel Dieu in Paris. "God gave me this thought," he later wrote, "could . . . good women not be brought together and persuaded to offer themselves to God to serve the sick poor?" When Louise de Marillac was introduced to de Paul, she recognized him as the spiritual director God had promised her in a vision. The illegitimate daughter of an aristocratic father who acknowledged her but did not live with her, and possessed of a stepmother who wanted little to do with her, Marillac, like Elizabeth Seton, led a privileged but unsettled childhood. She applied to enter a cloistered order but was denied, perhaps because of ill health, and eventually she married and bore a son. During her marriage, she joined in the efforts of wealthy women in her parish to serve the poor—Catholic predecessors to Isabella Graham's society for poor widows—then watched as her husband's health failed. While caring for him, Marillac met Frances de Sales, author of *Introduction to the Devout Life*, and drew sustenance from his counsel.

When her husband died, Marillac vowed to dedicate herself to God. It was in this period that she met Vincent de Paul, and after several years of sharing in his charitable projects and seeking his spiritual counsel, decided that she was called to live in community and devote herself to service of the poor. Realizing that the wealthy women whom de Paul had organized were awkward and often reluctant servants to France's poor people, Marillac organized peasant women, who proved far more effective. One of these women, Marguerite Naseau, helped Marillac and de Paul transform the circle of wealthy Parisiennes into an ambitious, interlocking set of benevolent organizations.

Hundreds of women allied themselves with the Compagnie des Filles de la Charité. They rose before dawn, practiced daily devotions, and observed silence at specific times between evening and morning prayers. They also performed spiritual retreats and read aloud their "petite reglement" each week. "Your vocation," Vincent de Paul told them, "is one of the greatest that I know of in the Church." Yet the Daughters were not nuns: they were not cloistered, and their essential purpose—serving the suffering poor wherever they were found—precluded the kind of creative accommodation the Ursulines had made. Determined that the Daughters not be disbanded or cloistered, de Paul forbade them to wear veils, put up grilles in their houses, or even ring bells to mark devotions. The Daughters' vows of poverty, obedience, and service to poor persons lasted only one year, and rather than being celebrated in the gorgeous public ceremonies of France's cloistered orders, the vows were taken silently, during parish Masses. The price of the Daughters' consecrated life was a denial that it was a religious congregation. "Your monastery is the house of the sick," reads the formulation from 1659, the Rules for the Sisters in Parishes, "for cloister, the streets of the city; for enclosure, obedience . . . for grille, the fear of God."[15]

By the time Dubois worked alongside Daughters of Charity, the company founded and staffed hospitals, orphanages, and other institutions tending the old, sick, and poor; Daughters negotiated contracts and administered complex programs as well as offering physical and spiritual solace to individuals. Any threat the women posed to the Church or the social order was outweighed by the undeniable fact that the Daughters did work on which the French Church and state relied.[16]

The young Dubois was deeply impressed by the Daughters' management of the Hospice des Petites Maisons, where he stayed as chaplain for five years. When word first spread of political unrest, he hoped that social change might mitigate the aristocratic excess that left Paris's poor so in need of the Daughters' work. Quickly, however, he realized that some revolutionaries (his schoolmate Desmoulins prominent among them) saw the entire French Church as a problem in need of eradication. When the Sulpicians collectively refused to take the oath of allegiance to the new order, Dubois refused along with them. He fled France (a fellow priest later claimed, without proof, that he was protected by false papers prepared for him by his schoolmate, Maximilien Robespierre).[17] Not long after, Dubois had made his way to the United States, and the massive church at St. Sulpice had been rededicated a revolutionary Temple of Victory.

By 1808 Jean Dubois had become John Dubois, diligent priest to the scattered Catholics first of Virginia and later of western Maryland. He found American antipopery far less pernicious than what he'd seen in France, and he tended his flock—many of whom had lived without pastoral attention—rather than proselytizing his Protestant neighbors. Dubois learned an idiomatic English—aided, he explained, by "many friendly lessons" from Patrick Henry—and purchased two horses so that he could tend Catholics dispersed from Harpers Ferry through the valleys of the Monocacy River to the crests of the Blue Ridge Mountains.[18] Surviving letters reveal a pastor who sympathetically pondered the challenges of his flock and was not afraid to press Bishop Carroll when he thought the prelate's regulations too exacting. "She threw herself at my feet the other day all in tears, begging me to save her from despair," he told Carroll of a young woman who'd married a Protestant. "Some allowance must be made for the youth and ignorance of the girl."[19] Dubois was often less than deferential. "Have you been kind enough as to promote the subscription for the elevation of the Soul to God, a sheet of which I left in your hands," he once wrote Carroll, "or did you forget it altogether?"[20] The work of the Lord was work, and someone had to make sure it got done.

Dubois first visited the place that would become so important to Elizabeth Seton's life in 1797, when Carroll asked him to resolve a simmering problem in a western Maryland hamlet called Emmitsburg. Lying just a few miles south of Pennsylvania, Emmitsburg was as bucolic as Manhattan was urban, yet it too was a landscape of pluralism, peopled by Catholics (the Carroll family was granted land in the area and settlers considered calling the town Carrollton), Scotch-Irish Presbyterians, and German-speaking Lutherans.[21] Comity prevailed among the denominations, but the same could not always be said of relations among Catholics themselves: Dubois was sent to resolve a dispute between an Irish priest and his flock. The area's Anglo-Catholic families may have been quick to find fault with an immigrant priest, but Father Ryan brought much of his trouble on himself. Parishioners found him "queer, violent," and prone to drunkenness; Ryan retaliated by forcing them to stand at the back of the church with African Americans, a punishment that revealed that he had made himself at home in Maryland's racial regime, if not in his parish.[22]

Sent to clean up the mess (Ryan was eventually removed), Dubois found himself captivated by the area's beauty. He conceived an ambitious plan to build a church outside Emmitsburg and dedicate it to the Virgin. The small church already in the hamlet would be dedicated to St. Joseph, "and the two congregations," the priest later explained to

FIGURE 13.1. Mirza Vizzala, *John Dubois*. Courtesy of the Rhoads Memorial Archive, Mount St. Mary's University, Emmitsburg, MD.

Carroll, "incorporated into one under the name of Mary and Joseph." By 1807, with the help of local Protestants as well as Catholics—and thanks to the labor of "three colored men," a participant recalled years later, perhaps some of the enslaved people Dubois had purchased along with the land—a hillside near Emmitsburg had its St. Mary's church, and Dubois was busily enacting another plan. He bought seventeen acres of land near Emmitsburg, explaining that "I wish to keep them in my hands as a refuge in my old age." John Carroll made clear his preference that Dubois grant the land to the Church. But Dubois had lived through the near destruction of French Catholicism and would not leave his fate to chance. "As I know not what may happen," he explained to the archbishop, "I think the best is to keep it in my hands."[23]

Not long afterward, Dubois came up with yet another plan, one that took the land out of his hands and brought him a step closer to Elizabeth: he wanted to trade his Maryland acreage for a place among Baltimore's Sulpicians. By contrast with the community life he'd known in France, Dubois lived and often prayed alone in the United States. He had turned to the Sulpicians for spiritual companionship, riding the miles from St. Mary's, Emmitsburg, to St. Mary's, Baltimore to perform retreats. When Dubois first applied to join the society, the practical priest was refused on practical grounds: no more Sulpicians were needed in Baltimore, and the Sulpicians did not wish to supervise a country pastor. The matter might have ended there, but William Dubourg learned of Dubois's property and the lovely hillside chapel. He believed the area might make a good spot for a "petit seminaire," a school for young Catholic boys destined for St. Mary's of Baltimore. The Sulpicians wanted Dubois's land, and Dubois wanted to be a Sulpician. Practicality dictated what it had once prevented, and within months, Dubois signed his land over to the Sulpicians and was accepted as a member of the order.

To prepare the land for the petit seminaire, the former Parisian cut terraces and conjured building plans that could accommodate the "uneven and queer logs" he scavenged from an abandoned distillery. Meanwhile, Dubourg decided still more land was needed and agreed to purchase a plantation owned by a local Catholic family. For $200 up front and $800 paid each year, as well as other ongoing accommodations for the former owners, the Sulpicians were to own the plantation's land, movable property, and enslaved people, who numbered eleven at the 1800 census. Dubois thought the scheme wildly impractical and implored Dubourg to cancel what he viewed as a ruinous bargain. Dubourg cheerfully dismissed his worries, and the other Sulpicians agreed. The purchase was made. It fell to Dubois, as he brusquely recalled, to "buy provisions and clothing for the negroes" while Dubourg dreamed up a "house of education 96 feet long by 90 wide."[24]

While Dubois labored to bring Dubourg's vision to reality, another actor unexpectedly entered the stage: Samuel Sutherland Cooper, the convert and former sea captain who had ridden with Elizabeth in the carriage to Georgetown. Cooper knew of Dubois from the latter's visits to St. Mary's and, it seems, knew also of Elizabeth's desire to found a religious community. Cooper came to a dramatic decision. Emmitsburg should be home not only to the Sulpicians' petit seminaire but to a charitable religious establishment for women organized around Elizabeth Seton. He, Samuel Cooper, would donate the funds.[25]

Two decades later, William Dubourg wrote a dramatic account of how the plans for Emmitsburg and those for Elizabeth Seton came together. As Dubourg recalled it, Elizabeth came to him one morning and declared that "'our Saviour had just commanded in a clear, intelligible voice, after her Communion. 'Go. . . . Address Mr. Cooper; he will give you all that is necessary to begin the establishment.'" That same evening, Dubourg wrote, Cooper presented himself and offered money for the establishment, with the provision that the sisterhood "would be at Emmitsburg." When Dubourg asked whether Cooper had spoken with Elizabeth, he replied, "Never."[26]

By the time Dubourg wrote his account, the sisterhood had blossomed in a manner that to him seemed divinely inspired. Elizabeth herself never told the story in this way. God did not speak to her in declarative sentences, for one thing, and if God *had* told her one morning to ask Samuel Cooper for money, she certainly would have done so by evening. Elizabeth believed God played a providential role in the founding of the sisterhood at Emmitsburg, but she knew human effort and relationships did too. She had likely told Cooper of her hope to found a sisterhood and would have seen no reason to keep her need for funds secret from him. At the edges of this origin story, moreover, stands another quite human actor, John Dubois. Cooper had not only fixed the establishment in the countryside that Dubois loved but decided it should serve the poor as did the community Dubois admired, the French Daughters of Charity.

Elizabeth gratefully accepted the plan in all its dimensions. Her own spirituality was more contemplative than activist, but she had enjoyed working with the society for poor widows, and Cooper's offer held out— at last—the promise of a life lived wholly for God. She happily wrote Filippo that Cooper wanted to found an "institution for the advancement of catholick female children in habits of religion and giving them an education suited to that purpose—he also desires extremely to extend the plan to the reception of the aged and also uneducated persons who may be employed in spinning knitting etc. etc. so as to found a manufactory on a small scale which may be very beneficial to the poor."[27] It went unremarked by everyone that the labor of the slaves Dubourg had purchased along with the plantation would contribute to the support of the establishment. The new religious community would be able to aid the poor in part because Sulpicians expropriated the labor of the poorest. The city of man would support the city of God.

In early spring, the Sulpicians discussed the details of Elizabeth's suddenly viable religious establishment. It was to be "a community of daughters, *a peu près sur le même plan que les filles de la Charité*, de St. Vincent de Paul; who join to the care of the sick, the instruction of young girls in all branches of Christian education." "Some charitable persons" would purchase the plantation near Emmitsburg and see to repairs "in the name of the Gentlemen of the Seminary."[28] Elizabeth wrote to ask Filippo for support, once again insisting she had been entirely passive as the plan was worked out. "I have invariably kept in the back ground and avoided even reflecting voluntarily on any thing of the kind," she wrote, "knowing that Almighty God alone could effect it."[29]

Plans for a petit seminaire near Elizabeth's new Emmitsburg community solved the problem of her sons. They could attend the boys' school on the hill while their mother and sisters lived close by, in the valley. Will and Dick Seton still did not excel in their studies—they "do not seem to have either talents or application which is a great cross to me," Elizabeth confessed to Antonio—but they were "innocent in their conduct" and she hoped life at the petit seminaire might inspire them with a desire to become priests themselves.[30] Veronica O'Conway hoped rural Maryland would offer the serenity she'd once thought to find among the Spanish Carmelites; Emmitsburg would be, she told her parents, a "sweet Retreat" "far from the noise of passion and pleasure."[31] Then, amid the happy preparations, came a bit of drama: Babade's second Philadelphia recruit, Maria Burke, unexpectedly arrived.

Margaret Burke had not dropped her opposition to her daughter's plan. Instead, taking matters in her own hands, Maria left her mother's house for the O'Conways'. There, Matthias reported, she "sits up . . . to two and three o'clock reading the 'Spiritual Combat, Temporal, Eternal,' etc." Convinced Maria should lead the life she chose, Matthias brought the young woman to Baltimore. When she presented herself at Paca Street, Maria presented a dilemma. Elizabeth sympathized with the young woman whose determination to live a consecrated life outstripped her obedience to family. The Sulpicians did not believe a mother's opposition sufficient grounds to turn a young woman away. But an American Catholic sisterhood could not begin haunted by rumors of a girl kept against her family's will. And this family in particular must not be crossed: Maria's uncle, the printer Matthew Carey, could readily spread any story about the sisterhood that he wished. So Elizabeth and Dubourg set about winning over Margaret. They soon realized that financial negotiation, not spiritual exhortation, was the way to proceed, and discussions of how the Sulpicians might help Margaret educate and support her other children began.[32]

Although he offered no opposition to Elizabeth and the Sulpicians' preparations for the new community, John Carroll remained gently skeptical. He no longer doubted Elizabeth's motives or the depth of her faith. But he remained unsure how she would reconcile her children's needs with those of her religious daughters, and he wondered how a woman who had never belonged to an apostolic community would lead one. Nonetheless, Carroll consented to the establishment, hopeful that Elizabeth's piety and intelligence would outweigh her inexperience and eager to see the nation benefit from the creation of a teaching sisterhood. In late March, he witnessed the moment in which Elizabeth took private vows of obedience and chastity. In the tradition of the French Daughters of Charity, they were to last one year.

In extant letters, Elizabeth has almost nothing to say about this vow taking. Her uncharacteristic silence shows Carroll's sobering influence. The archbishop saw such rituals as prompts to reflection, not moments of transformation, and his presentation of the vow to Elizabeth focused on its contractual nature: the day before the simple ritual, he sent "for your perusal and consideration a formulary of the act intended for tomorrow," adding that he'd left "a blank . . . for your name and another for the word, *poverty,* if it is to be inserted." That last was a nod to Carroll's sense that Elizabeth's motherhood prevented her from adopting all the conventions of religious life; he had "a doubt," he explained, "whether and how far you can take or keep that vow in your present circumstances."[33] Elizabeth agreed not to take a vow of poverty and in a letter to Filippo dutifully adopted Carroll's understated view of the whole event: "I have long since made the Vows which as a religious, I could only renew."[34]

Such matter-of-factness was nowhere in evidence when Elizabeth described her future to others. "To speak the joy of my soul at the prospect of being able to assist the Poor, visit the sick, comfort the sorrowful, clothe little innocents, and teach them to love God!" she marveled to Julia Scott in late March.[35] She was sure that in the community outside Emmitsburg, God's will and her own would at last be one. Others were equally effusive. John Cheverus had recently received word that he was to become bishop of the newly created see of Boston, but he was far more gratified at Elizabeth's news than at his own. "How admirable is divine providence," he congratulated her. "I see already numerous choirs of Virgins following you to the Altar, I see your holy order diffusing itself in the different parts of the U.S., spreading everywhere the good odour of J.C., & teaching by their angelical lifes & pious instructions how to serve G. in purity & holiness."[36]

In Emmitsburg, Dubois saw visions of a different kind. Buildings were unfinished and debts daunting. He was locked in a complicated set of disputes with Carroll over the literal and figurative boundaries of his jurisdiction and over whether Sulpician or diocesan priests should preside over the petit seminaire—now turning into simply a boys' school or "college"—the congregations, and the religious institutions. Elizabeth would have been slack-jawed to read the priest's worried, hectoring letters; she imagined her new community was to join a harmonious Catholic enclave like St. Mary's of Baltimore. While Dubois worried over governance and funding, Elizabeth serenely wrote to the wealthy Philadelphia convert Rachel Montgomery, asking whether she might send black flannel to make the sisters' habits.

YOUR NEW SCHEME

Although she was happily unaware of Emmitsburg's simmering conflicts, that spring Elizabeth faced a governance issue of her own: how to manage her oldest daughter. Since her arrival in Baltimore, Anna Maria had maintained the "even and independent spirits" that left her mother admiring but slightly unsettled.[37] Now Elizabeth learned that beneath Anna's cool exterior there still beat a warm heart. The thirteen-year-old had a suitor. Her admirer was a St. Mary's student named Charles duPavillon, a planter's son from the island of Guadeloupe. While her little sisters were exchanging notes with Father Babade, Anna had been exchanging billets-doux with Charles. Babade approved of the boy and may secretly have encouraged the courtship; a Caton sister may also have helped the romance along. Elizabeth, however, told Julia Scott that she was deeply unhappy to have known so little of her daughter's heart. Julia had a daughter of her own, and she responded with worldly good sense. "Anna if I mistake not, is not yet fourteen," she soothed. "An attachment formed at so early an age, is not likely to leave a durable impression on the mind tho' felt with violence at the time." Julia urged Elizabeth not to expect to play spiritual director to a teenaged daughter: "I believe we expect too much from human nature if we hope unlimited confidence from our children."[38]

In fact, Anna Maria soon vowed to do anything her distraught mother asked. "It seems as if the moment she was made sensible of the uneasiness and sorrow she occasioned me," Elizabeth wrote, "the terror and alarm of her mind banished every fancy and imagination which has blinded her, and she became docile and attentive to my will as if it was not opposed to her own." Gentle and loving with her daughters, Elizabeth nonetheless expected them to obey her instructions and share her judgments. Since the long-ago trip to Italy, Anna Maria had for the most part done just that. At least for the moment, she felt more terror at the thought of division from her mother than she felt desire to make her own way. As for Elizabeth, on reflection she saw a welcome kinship in the girl's flare of affection for Charles. Her oldest daughter, she observed to Julia, "had the milk of an *inflammable* Mother."[39]

Julia worried more about Elizabeth's impetuosity than about Anna Maria's. When Elizabeth told her of the proposed sisterhood and delicately asked whether Julia might loan her money, Julia declined. Instead, she interrogated Elizabeth with all the straightforwardness their long friendship, more than any other relationship in Elizabeth's life, allowed. "What shall I say of your new scheme," Julia demanded. Not only was the sisterhood "uncertain," but what few specifics there were worried her. "You are to be the . . . Mother of probably a very large family," Julia wrote, "rich and poor, a heterogenous mixture, which will only increase your difficulties, and render your duties more arduous." Her solitude-craving friend would have "no peaceful hours, no peaceful moments." And could she even do the job? No one seemed to have figured out exactly how the poor were to be helped, and Julia believed her friend did not know enough of "the ways of the World to be aware of the difficulties attending the care of a large Establishment." She had one more concern. Elizabeth's three daughters must one day reenter society. What kind of education and polish could they receive in rural Maryland?[40]

Elizabeth took no heed. Nor did she take offense. The pair loved each other despite their incompatibilities, and even, in ways neither woman could explain, because of them. "Twenty five years I have known you the same dear elegant slave of the world," Elizabeth once wrote her old friend. "Believe me not unthinking think me not ungrateful, or hard of heart," Julia offered in response to one of their many points of contention. "Continue your prayers for one who loves you most truly most sincerely."[41] Elizabeth was as content to let Julia raise objections as Julia was happy to let Elizabeth pray. But she did offer her friend one bit of reassurance. "It is true that I shall be the head of a community which will live under the strictest rules of order and regularity," she wrote, "but I shall not give those laws, nor have any care of compelling others to fulfill them." It would be up to their ecclesiastical superior, she explained, to "rectify or dismiss the person."[42] Elizabeth imagined the sisterhood as an extension of the informal prayer circles she'd guided in the past, a set of interlocking friendships grounded in Bible reading, prayer, and mutual exhortation. Because she saw the making and enforcement of the laws as extrinsic to the community's true life, she was happy to delegate those tasks to a priest, and she showed little interest in which clergyman would undertake them.

The Sulpicians thought clerical governance mattered quite a bit, and after discussion they formalized the procedures by which the community's male superior was to be chosen. Samuel Cooper wanted "some connection" between the community he was funding and the Sulpicians, so the order decided they would present their choice for the male superior of the community to Bishop Carroll, if necessary continuing to present choices until the bishop approved of one. In this inaugural instance, they proposed William Dubourg, and John Carroll immediately accepted.[43]

Content to see Dubourg entrusted with matters she considered purely technical, Elizabeth expected Pierre Babade to serve as her spiritual director and confidante. The man who thought nothing of traveling to Philadelphia could surely make the trip to Emmitsburg as often as he and Elizabeth wished. Her confidence in their partnership deepened as the two prepared girls at the Paca Street school for their first Communions. Most of the girls had been brought up to think of Communion as a slightly awkward duty; in Baltimore as elsewhere, few parishioners received the sacrament at any given Mass. Together, Babade and Elizabeth made the sacrament thrilling. "Is it true, is it possible, my dear and every day dearer child," Babade wrote Kit, who was among those making her first Communion, "that . . . you will see, you will embrace, you will receive and lodge in your heart him whom so many kings and prophets have longed to see & could not see, have longed to hear and could not hear?" He promised that the sacrament would connect the girls not only to God but also to Babade himself: "You will be in possession of him! And I will give him to you; convey him to your breast! Oh!" In a series of urgent notes, he exhorted young Kit toward spiritual and physical purity. "Let your innocent tongue never be defiled by any word contrary to truth and honesty," he wrote. "Let your body be altogether hallowed by such a contact such a receiving let it be hence forth a consecrated temple." In Babade's pages of exhortation, purity is sensual and chastity a consummation. "Let his love inflame your tender loving heart, consume it, fill up its vast capacity, transform it in a new one, in his own," he commanded Kit.[44]

Babade's pages of breathless phrases in tiny handwriting now seem overwhelming, even off-kilter. But Elizabeth saw in them only the emotional urgency she believed true worship must contain. Although she respected Archbishop Carroll's restrained approach to ritual, she gloried in Babade's passionate dramaturgy, as well as his gift for infusing the forms of the Church with secret intimacy. When the day for the first Communions arrived, she dressed the girls "all in white as modest as angels," and brought them to the chapelle-basse, or lower chapel, where Babade celebrated Mass. "We had liberty to sob aloud unwitnessed by any," Elizabeth wrote, "as no one had an idea of our going there."[45]

John Carroll would never have arranged such a spectacle, but he was pleased by the results: soon after that secret first Communion came a display of public devotion he himself had never inspired. The archbishop noted with satisfaction that at Easter Mass, "Mrs. Harper, Mrs. Patterson and her three Sisters [together, the four Caton daughters] edified us and the Congregation by receiving the Holy Communion publicly at Highmass on Easter Sunday. Mrs. Caton promises to perform soon the same duty."[46] For a moment, the emotion-drenched Catholicism nurtured by Babade complemented Carroll's careful institution building.

The moment quickly passed. Not long after Easter, and still thrilled by her first Communion, Louisa Caton announced she intended to join the sisterhood at Emmitsburg. "One of the most elegant and highest girls in Baltimore," Elizabeth proudly wrote to Cecilia Seton, "refuses the most splendid matches to unite herself to our Lord."[47] Elizabeth's and Babade's ability to conjure a Catholic world of love and ritual had attracted the flower of Maryland society. Maryland society wanted its flower back. Louisa's father angrily confronted Dubourg, demanding to know how his daughter had been coaxed into such a shocking step. Caton was a Protestant, but his Catholic wife was no more thrilled than he, and unlike Margaret Burke, who was still negotiating terms with the Sulpicians, the Catons had nothing to gain from allowing their daughter to join the sisterhood. On the contrary, to the extent that Louisa might make a marriage benefiting the Catons, her decision to join a celibate sisterhood constituted a social and financial blow. When Caton berated Dubourg (in language, the indignant priest reported, "profuse with indecorous elements"), Dubourg turned to Robert Goodloe Harper, the girl's even-tempered uncle, for help.

"How . . . can I be accused of having infused those notions into her mind?" the flustered president of St. Mary's demanded of Harper. "What did I say to her?" "What more could I do?" Gathering himself, the priest explained that Elizabeth's "Institution" was modeled after the Daughters of Charity, whose worth was proved by the fact that even ravening French revolutionaries appreciated their usefulness to "the Poor of every description." (Harper had been moved to enter politics in part because of his horror at the French Revolution, and Dubourg knew he would appreciate the point.)[48] Surely, Dubourg implored, he could not be expected to disavow the worthy institution proposed by Mrs. Seton. "God forbid!" he exclaimed. Dubourg's letter was a pottage of denial and defense, but he concluded with an astute observation. "They say she is very ardent in her wishes and obstinate in her notions," he wrote of Louisa. "Such dispositions are generally fired and hardened by open contradiction."[49] Harper agreed, and with his counsel, the Caton family and the Sulpicians decided that Louisa would not be directly forbidden from joining the sisterhood. She would pass the summer with her own family, during which, the Catons hoped, she would turn her ardent imagination away from white dresses and convent life and back toward earthly romance.⁵⁰

During the same weeks that Louisa Caton caused such consternation, other young women also announced their desire to join Elizabeth. She received two earnest letters from a young Emmitsburg woman named Eleanor Thompson, who had decided, with John Dubois's encouragement, to join the religious community forming near her home. "Revd mother inexpressible was my joy when I heard that I was to have the happiness of becoming one of your children," Eleanor wrote in a crabbed and meandering hand.⁵¹ Elizabeth wrote the young woman that she looked forward to beginning the institution, and she may also have suggested Eleanor work on her handwriting. "Oh my reverend mother," Eleanor responded in a newly tidy script, "I cannot tell you what an effect that sweet letter had on me it seems it has enkindled, in my breast flames which I hope with the grace of God will never be extinguished." She addressed the letter to "Mrs. M. E. Seton," and formed one of the letters into an angel's wing.⁵²

Margaret Burke remained as steely eyed as Eleanor Thompson was adoring. Others might draw angel wings; she demanded return on her investment, tirelessly negotiating with the Sulpicians over her daughter's entrance into the community. Elizabeth was sympathetic, seeing the widow as a fellow "child of affliction," determined as was Elizabeth to navigate by the light of her own judgment. In the end, Margaret won a promise that her three boys and a daughter would be educated at the Emmitsburg schools for reduced tuition and that Margaret herself would work for John Dubois at a reasonable salary.⁵³ "Miss Burk has had another letter from her mother," Elizabeth wrote Matthias O'Conway that spring, "who I believe will leave her at liberty without much further trouble, as our interest for that excellent child has induced us to smooth every difficulty as much as possible."⁵⁴ Maria Burke would join the sisterhood.

As the little band of sisters grew, Elizabeth's very first Catholic follower, Cecilia Seton, remained trapped in New York.⁵⁵ The consumptive young woman's health was visibly failing, and everyone but James Seton—his anxieties augmented by a looming bankruptcy that required him to auction his possessions and sell the Wilderness—and Father Kohlmann agreed she must be allowed to leave. Finally, after Elizabeth asked Carroll to intervene with the priest, Kohlmann removed his opposition.

Now it was only her loyalty to James that pinned Cecilia in place. She was trying, the girl told Elizabeth, to get "brother settled in town. As yet I have said nothing to him being so uncertain of the time I shall leave him. I thought it was best to be silent until I heard again from you and perhaps it would at this present period seem unkind."[56]

The distressing auction of James's home came and went. Sam tried to distract his sister with a witty letter, his admiring love breaking through its light-hearted surface as he praised her for bearing all with her "usual fortitude and resignation."[57] Still Cecilia hesitated. She worried about Sam: "His tender love for me daily increases," she confided in Elizabeth, "he often tells me he finds no pleasure when away from me." She feared that Harriet, still miserable over her uncertain future with Barclay, depended on her company. And she knew she was the closest thing to a mother James's children had. "I must not be in a hurry," she wrote Elizabeth one day. "When I think of the dear children of the change it will be for them when I leave them I know not what to think of it."[58]

Like Elizabeth, Cecilia knew what it was to be left behind. She was loath to cause others that pain. Yet, also like Elizabeth, Cecilia in the end placed her duty to God—and her desire to lead a consecrated Catholic life—above family obligations. She told everyone that she wanted to go to Baltimore, and as her health completely collapsed, everyone, even James, agreed that she must leave. "You cannot think how much it grieves me to part with my own Cecil, what would I give to go with her, and what shall I do without her?" James's daughter Ethelinda wrote to Anna Maria. But even Ethelinda agreed Cecilia must go.[59] The family arranged for Sam and Harriet to accompany her to Baltimore. All three would be briefly reunited with Elizabeth and her children, and then Harriet and Sam would return to New York.

"How ever sick you may be," Elizabeth wrote Cecilia on hearing the news, "I cannot but expect you with an anticipation of joy which you alone can conceive who knows how much my happiness is connected with you." She urged the girl not to grieve too deeply over leaving her relatives but rather to "look up." She also told Cecilia what she should bring. "Do not put up any other clothes but a black gown (if you have it) and your flannels," Elizabeth wrote happily.[60] She was dressing the young woman for her new life. The Seton family were less confident. In Cecilia's trunk, they packed a "few yards of black silk to make a dress in case she would live." They also packed a shroud.[61]

PART 4

A SISTERHOOD AT EMMITSBURG

14

HALF IN THE SKY

IT WAS A BITTERSWEET reunion. Harriet and Sam caught up with the Seton children and admired St. Mary's, while Elizabeth brought a painfully frail Cecilia to be examined by a Baltimore doctor. Pierre Chatard suggested Emmitsburg's country air might revive the girl, and the faint hope seized the Setons' imaginations. Nothing was ready for the sisterhood and Cecilia might not survive the journey, but it was decided that a small group must set out immediately for western Maryland.

Sam said goodbye to his sister; according to the family's plans, Harriet should have accompanied him back to New York. Instead, she prepared to travel to Emmitsburg, wanting to settle Cecilia in before returning to Manhattan. Elizabeth decided that Anna Maria should come with the first group while Kit and Bec would stay for a time with a Catholic Baltimore family, the Weises. Will and Dick were to remain at St. Mary's until sent for. A wagon was found, black flannels packed, and in late June, Anna Maria, Cecilia, Maria Burke, Harriet, and Elizabeth set off.

Writing to William Dubourg from the inn where they stopped overnight, Elizabeth portrayed the journey as a comic pilgrimage. "The dogs and pigs came out to meet us and the geese stretched their necks in mute demand to know if we were any of their sort," she wrote cheerfully. "We gave assent."[1] The next day, the travelers passed through woods of chestnut, poplar, oak, and ash. Creeks cut through the soil on their way to the broad silver band of the Monacacy River. Hills appeared, and

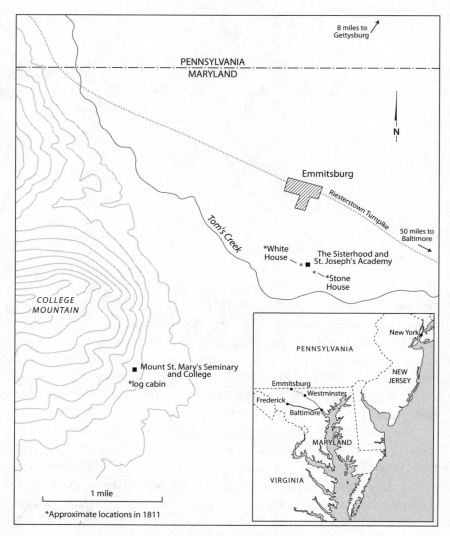

FIGURE 14.1. Emmitsburg and environs. Map drawn by Bill Nelson.

then, toward the horizon, the form that gave the region its name, the Blue Ridge Mountains. They had arrived.

An energetic priest in his forties greeted them: John Dubois. He was kind and respectful, and he'd done what he could to make a small cabin intended for Emmitsburg's recently appointed pastor, the Reverend Duhamel, suitable for these sudden arrivals. But John Dubois was not

Pierre Babade. There was no poem in French and English prepared for the Setons' arrival, no effusive congratulations for commencing their sacred mission. Dubois saw the newcomers quickly settled and got back to work.

There was—and is—no denying the beauty of the hillside where Elizabeth found herself. "We are half in the sky," she wrote Matthias O'Conway.[2] Like the nearby chapel, the cabin on St. Mary's Mountain looked out over forests brightened by patches of farmland. The hill itself was dense with trees. Large rocks jutted through the earth, stark notes in a peaceful melody. One such spot, where the sunlight glinted through thick foliage and caught the silver of a waterfall, struck all who saw it as an avenue for prayer, and it was soon dubbed "the grotto." "Woods, rocks, walks," Elizabeth wrote later of those first days.[3]

As startling as the area's natural beauty was its effect on Cecilia Seton. The young woman who in Baltimore had barely been able to walk found her strength returning. When Margaret Burke arrived, hoping to explore the premises and sweeten the deal she'd struck, she was moved by Cecilia's improvement and the change in her own daughter. Maria, the practical Margaret mused to her brother, seemed "as much abstracted from the world as tho' she never lived in it."[4]

Amid this tranquillity, one person secretly struggled: Elizabeth Seton. She immediately missed the cocoon of ritual and meaning she had found at St. Mary's. She wondered how she would create such a place in the rough countryside, alongside a priest who seemed more interested in overseeing construction than in weeping over the Mass. As the days passed, the cordiality of Seton and Dubois's first meeting never failed but did not deepen. The two puzzled each other, Elizabeth frustrated by the Sulpician who had little time for Catholicism's beauties, Dubois mystified by the woman who wanted to lead a religious society yet knew nothing of life within one. As she tried to turn herself into the Mother she'd confidently imagined, Elizabeth looked to Pierre Babade for help and encouraged the others to do so as well.

Letters to Babade soon flowed down from the little cabin and east on the turnpike to Baltimore. In return, Babade filled page after page with his spindly handwriting and idiosyncratic mixture of English and French. He depicted the fledgling community as sacred, heroic, and essential to the future of the Church. Elizabeth took solace in his vision—her own, to her astonishment, having fled. Her disorientation is evidenced by two silences: she wrote neither to Julia Scott nor to John Carroll. Both had warned that life at the sisterhood would be harder than Elizabeth imagined. She could not bring herself to tell them that within days they'd been proved right.

Harriet Seton was also unsettled, not by discontent but by happiness. When she'd set out from Baltimore, twenty-one-year-old Hatch had intended only to see Cecilia safely to her new home. She'd done that, and in the days and weeks that followed, she watched as her sister grew happier and stronger than she'd been in months. Still, Harriet made no plans to return to Manhattan. When Elizabeth and the others attended Mass in Dubois's mountain chapel, Harriet walked alone through the woods or perched on a rock outside the little church, fearing to become any more attached to the community. She did not mean to stay but could not bring herself to leave.

Understanding Harriet's ambivalence, Elizabeth did not press. Babade felt no such constraint. The priest had met the young woman only briefly in Baltimore, but he was enchanted. Renaming the betrothed Harriet "the Magdalen" (inspired by her middle name but also, perhaps, by what he perceived as her fallen state) he set out to save her soul. Her fiancé, Barclay Bayley, had written a handful of pages during the years of his absence; Pierre Babade sent handfuls each week. "I will . . . begin to speak to you the true language of a spiritual father," the priest wrote in early July, and he exhorted her to rid herself of anything that threatened her immortal happiness, not least Barclay Bayley. "If your right hand, if your eye be a scandal, a stumbling stone for you," he urged, "that is to say an obstacle to your eternal salvation, cut if off and cast it away." Babade promised a direct substitution of divine love for earthly: "Would you regret the capricious caresses of inconstant man, when you secure to you the eternal embraces and caresses of Jesus?"[5] He offered his own love too. "Thousand blessings I send you every day," the priest closed one letter, "Day and night. P.B."[6]

Harriet sent Babade letters and tokens of affection—"souvenirs," he called them, as he promised to keep them close—and was grateful for his attention. Yet she still wanted to marry Barclay, and she continued to stay outside the chapel during Mass. Finally one day, Elizabeth asked her to come in: "If you cannot perceive the sweetness of his presence as we do, at least you might say Your prayers."[7] Harriet obeyed, and just as she had imagined, felt irresistibly drawn to the serene community she witnessed within. On a late July day, she learned that Masses were being said for her soul both in Baltimore and in the mountain church. That evening, Harriet asked Elizabeth to walk with her up to the chapel. In a scene that would have delighted Louisa Caton's romantic sensibility, they made their way "by the light of a full moon" and in silence. Reaching the chapel, they prayed together. "It is done my Sister," Harriet said as they descended the mountain together afterward, "I am a Catholic."[8]

"Saint Mary's Mountain," she wrote on a bit of paper, "a night *ever to be remembered*."[9] But the romance of evening gave way to the worries of day. Harriet wrote Barclay an account of her spiritual state, hoping he would still want to marry her. To her family in Manhattan, she sent nothing at all.

NEW ARRIVALS

As Elizabeth, Harriet, and the others began life in western Maryland, the Catholic Church received a shocking blow: another pope was made prisoner. The chain of events had begun that spring, when Pius VII excommunicated Napoleon; the enraged emperor told subordinates that the pontiff must be locked away. Eager to please, a French general brought men and ladders to the papal palace tucked inside the Holy See and spirited the astonished pope off to Savona. Napoleon also professed astonishment, swearing that he had not meant to order such a capture. Once in possession of the pope, however, Napoleon proved loath to release him, and the pontiff remained in captivity and under guard.

It was a stunning development; as stunning, perhaps, is how little effect it had on American Catholicism. John Carroll had long relied less on Rome than on his own judgment and network of correspondents, often waiting years for instructions from the Holy See; the Sulpicians looked for guidance to their superior in Paris and to Carroll. Everyone prayed for the pope's deliverance, but no one waited around for it. The work of the American Church, including the plans for the new sisterhood, rolled on.

More women made their way to the house on Paca Street. Susan Clossy arrived from New York and Mary Ann Butler from Philadelphia; both were Irish women in their early twenties, Mary Ann the sister of a priest. Kitty Mullen came from Baltimore, and so did Rose Landry White. Born into Catholicism, far from wealthy, and young, Rose in some ways resembled the other women. Unlike them, however, she was a widow and mother: she had married a sea captain when she was just thirteen and had borne a son and daughter before learning that her husband was lost at sea, killed, it seemed, by the pirates who ruled the waters off North Africa. Not long after, Rose's tiny daughter died. A Sulpician named John David directed the bereaved woman to the house on Paca Street. He believed that the petit seminaire at Emmitsburg could educate her little son Charles and that the sisterhood offered Rose the opportunity to attain holiness in widowhood.[10] Rose was grateful for his counsel and determined to seize her chance.

That other determined widow, Margaret Burke, had in the meantime finalized her arrangements with John Dubois. She had secured appointment as "Superintendent of Necessities" at what was now a boys' boarding school that also accepted Protestants. Margaret sent her brother, the printer Matthew Carey, a long list of possessions he was to collect from her house and failed strawberry farm (the latter of which, she told Carey with some asperity, had been a success "but in the one article of the strawberries"). Eager to start her new life and unabashed in her demands for help, Margaret also informed the printer that she was "without a cent" and would appreciate his sending her fifty dollars and "a couple of suits of Black which is the dress the Ladies wear."[11]

One more enterprising woman made her way to Emmitsburg that summer. Like Margaret Burke, she went not to join the sisterhood but to make a life on her own terms, and Charlotte Melmoth could set those terms more or less as she wished. Born in England, Melmoth had made a living as an actress and married (or perhaps not quite married) an Anglican clergyman who abandoned his rectory to join her on the stage. After converting to Catholicism, she emigrated to America and became a celebrated presence in the New York theaters Elizabeth and William once enjoyed. When her advancing age and increasingly sturdy figure—"well past embonpoint," one theater manager observed—robbed her of leading roles, Melmoth took up character parts. At some point, though, as parts dwindled and her dissatisfaction grew, she met William Dubourg, who urged her to take up a life of peaceful prayer in the orbit of the new sisterhood. After visiting Paca Street several times, Melmoth made the journey west. She had no wish to live cheek by jowl with other women but was intrigued by the community and its clergy and decided to lease a little home in Emmitsburg. Dubourg was delighted, and so, when he met her, was John Dubois.[12]

In late July, Dubois declared that Elizabeth and the others could move from their hillside cabin to a dwelling more appropriate for the sisterhood, an old farmhouse that stood in a valley less than two miles from the mountain chapel. It was unplastered and bare, but Elizabeth and the others dubbed it the Stone House and moved in. Veronica O'Conway, the other would-be sisters, and the Seton sons set out from Baltimore to join them. Victoire Fournier waved from her window as the group set off, the passengers packed tightly among their belongings. The group rode in silence but that evening found shared amusement. An innkeeper who'd been instructed not to serve the group meat, since it was Friday, gave them chicken. "Chicken," explained the serving woman, "is not meat."[13]

They arrived at the Stone House late the next afternoon. Everyone marveled over Cecilia Seton's improved health; "She was one of the first who ran down the lane," Veronica O'Conway recalled years later. Dubois and Dubourg went off to Emmitsburg to buy more cups and chairs, the Seton boys were sent to the boys' school on the mountain, and the newly arrived sisters laid their mattresses on the floor. The next day, William Dubourg said Mass, then returned to Baltimore. Eleanor Thompson, the local woman who'd been so thrilled by Elizabeth that

FIGURE 14.2. Stone House. Courtesy of the Seton Shrine, Emmitsburg, Maryland.

she'd decorated her name with an angel's wing, soon presented herself at the Stone House, and so did her cheerful sister Sally.[14] The community at Emmitsburg had begun.

So had its first crisis. William Dubourg learned of the many letters traveling between Babade and the Emmitsburg community; Elizabeth suspected Charlotte Melmoth had reported the missives' quantity. Dubourg questioned Babade's judgment and stability; beyond that, he thought the sisters must learn to accept Dubourg's guidance sooner rather than later. He, Dubourg, was the community's superior, not Pierre Babade. On his return to Baltimore, Dubourg sent word to Elizabeth that she and her companions must stop writing to the effusive French priest.

It was the first real directive Elizabeth had received as Mother, and she bridled at it. Although Kitty Mullen and Rose White had little interest in Babade, everyone else loved him. Believing Dubourg commanded her to "eradicate as far as possible from the minds of the Sisters that confidence and attachment they all have for" the priest, Elizabeth decided she could not in good conscience obey.[15] The peace and good order of her community *depended* on Babade's participation. Suddenly the clerical governance she'd imagined of little consequence threatened the very nature of the sisterhood.

Dubourg knew Elizabeth was dissatisfied, and he was unfazed. Disagreements over confessors and just about everything else were endemic to the religious life. Orders relied on spiritual retreats and on demanding regulations—the latter known as "the Rule"—to soothe the frictions of life in community. The Sulpicians were confident that as the fledgling Emmitsburg community settled into rhythms of work and prayer, the women's individual desires would meld into a collective purpose and Babade would recede to a memory.

To that end, Dubourg returned to the valley to conduct a spiritual retreat and provide a preliminary set of rules. Everyone attended: all the would-be sisters, Elizabeth's daughters, Harriet, and even Charlotte Melmoth, although she continued to maintain her own snug home in the village. Dubourg brought copies of Alonso Rodriguez's *Christian Perfection*, a centuries-old guide to the practical virtues essential to life in community, and he presented the women with "provisional regulations," a copy of which still exists in Veronica O'Conway's hand.[16] The regulations were descendants of St. Benedict's sixth-century guide to monastic life, and like Benedict's original, they displayed both enormous spiritual ambition and hard-boiled common sense. Life was to be orderly, the women's attention directed to God and community rather than to self, their living conditions ascetic but not punitive. Under the provisional regulations, the Emmitsburg sisters were to rise at five and spend their days in prayer, pious reading, and household labor; there would also be periods of recreation that might occur "out of the house in the grove or wherever the Mother may find it most agreeable." Morning "manual labor" was to be done "in silence" except for the sound of one sister reading to the others, but the silence could be interrupted "by singing together at intervals under the direction of the Mother or the presiding Sister such spiritual songs as they may know by heart." The regulations were precise in their choreography of prayer—each morning sisters would "walk two and two to church saying one-third of the Rosary in going and another in returning"—and equally precise in their assignment of shared housework. "The one appointed to prepare the Dinner, will have nothing to do with the Breakfast and supper."

In the regulations, Elizabeth appears as "Mother." Her authority extends from choosing readings (although she was to avoid the glowingly sensual Song of Songs) to reviewing the other women's correspondence, a provision that made clear both her preeminent position and the fact that she'd joined a community that rejected the privacy she'd valued all her life. (The community's male superior also had the right to review correspondence, causing Margaret Burke to warn her brother not to write her anything that "you or perhaps I would not choose to make public, as it is no uncommon thing for the Superior to open the letters addressed here when he thinks fit." Elizabeth would for years reassure others that her letters were not intercepted, accepting the superior's right to surveil but aware that her friends and relatives would find it oppressive.)[17] A figure of authority in a community that eschewed individualism, the Mother did not govern alone. In addition to the male superior, there was to be an elected council of sisters, a structure that reflected Catholic tradition rather than American innovation. So small was the sisterhood that the council was for the moment essentially congruent with it. Rose White, who had already displayed decisiveness and competence, was named Elizabeth's assistant.

Dubourg gave the community a bell to regulate the prayers and spiritual exercises that were to govern their days (Vincent de Paul's fear that bells would seem to imitate cloister long since set aside). Just before returning to Baltimore, he invited the women to choose a site for the community's graveyard. Everyone knew death could come at any time, and the thought of burial in what felt like the sacred beauty of the valley was more consoling than dreadful. Even Harriet cheerfully pointed out a spot under a large oak that she said would make a peaceful grave.[18]

After the retreat, Elizabeth felt hopeful enough to write to Archbishop Carroll. In the last weeks, "So many things occurred to disappoint and distress me," she told him, "that it was impossible to say any thing that would not give you more pain than pleasure." Now, however, "we begin to get accustomed to" Dubois, "and we also have the consolation of observing in some degree the System which is hereafter to govern us." Yet as she wrote, Elizabeth began to complain, without quite admitting she was doing so, about Dubourg's directive regarding Pierre Babade. Although she found the rule he eventually settled on reasonable—sisters could write one letter in two months "to the Director they prefer, on subjects of direction which are designated"—she criticized Dubourg's handling of the affair and lamented the damage done when the sisters believed he acted "like a tyrant." She reported that the episode had also alienated the community from "the excellent Mr Dubois," and she even took a swipe at "some very busy persons making exaggerations to our superior" about the number of letters going back and forth on the turnpike. (It had quickly become clear that Elizabeth Seton and Charlotte Melmoth did not easily inhabit the same space.) Amid the complaints, she assured Carroll that she herself accepted the deprivation but added that Babade was the only priest "to whom I ever yet had opened my heart or been able to draw the consolation and instruction so necessary in my situation."[19]

On the surface, Elizabeth asked for nothing other than Carroll's prayers and understanding. "Forgive all this detail," she wrote. Yet she also wanted her judgment affirmed. Her vow of chastity challenged her not at all, and though she hadn't taken a vow of poverty, she was content with little. Obedience was the gauntlet. Elizabeth confessed to a thought she could not have imagined just six weeks earlier. "If I were to indulge myself," she wrote, "instead of rejoicing in the delightful prospect of serving and honoring God in a situation I have so long earnestly desired, death and the Grave would be my only anticipation."[20]

Carroll did not scold Elizabeth. Nor did he offer the reassurance she craved. He knew that life in community demanded the subjugation of

personal preferences and desires. At the same time, he did not believe
religious life required the abdication of judgment, and he shared Elizabeth's distaste at anything that smacked of tyranny. Carroll had seen
Rome suppress the religious order to which he'd pledged his life and
had found a way to be loyal to both the society and the Church that
destroyed it. He hoped that Elizabeth would work, as he did, to integrate
analysis, principle, compassion, and faith. Her strong will had brought
her to the foothills of the Blue Ridge. Time would tell whether it would
keep her there or drive her out.

The sisterhood settled into its daily cycles of work, recreation, and
prayer. Each morning Dubois walked down to the farmhouse to say
Mass in a small room designated a chapel. Council minutes find the
women "resolved to unite in breaking the two [sic] natural propensity of
us all to forming private parties, and to watch over the general good."
With its rustic conditions, the Blue Ridge sometimes seemed to make its
own rule. The women hauled their washing to and from Tom's Creek,
and at Dubourg's instructions cultivated "plenty of carrots, in order to
make use of for coffee." To travel from the Stone House in the valley up
to the mountain chapel, the women in their black dresses and bonnets
went "one by one on horseback" or, when the water was low enough,
"walk[ed] over the creek on stones."[21] Sometimes after services they
fried meat over a fire and ate it directly out of the pan. The landscape
felt sacred. For these Catholic women, as for the evangelical Protestants
gathering for revivals in fields and clearings across the new nation, God
filled the raw American air.

The sisterhood fit into the new nation in a second way: the Emmitsburg women lived amid slavery. Despite their austere lives and hard work,
they were significantly supported by the work of others: Joe, Kitty, Mon-
ica, Clara, Nace—a few partial names survive, traces of the people whom
the Sulpicians had purchased along with the land. There is no evidence
enslaved people did domestic work for Elizabeth and the other women, and
it was the Sulpicians, not the sisters, who served as owners. Yet enslaved
people labored on the institutions' farm and for the schools, and the austerity of the bondsmen's lives was forced rather than chosen. Dubois and
the local pastor, Charles Duhamel, took seriously their obligations to offer
Mass and the sacraments to enslaved people and to the free people of color
who in that border region were often their family members. But pastoral
care came with a master's power: Nace had to ask Dubois for permission

to marry a free woman of color, and Dubois's consent required that the couple's children be bound to the Mount until the age of twenty-one. Rules written later in the institutions' history make clear that Mass attendance was required of the enslaved, and when African Americans entered Emmitsburg's chapels, they knew to stand at the back.[22]

INGREDIENTS OF HAPPINESS

Margaret Burke had gone to Emmitsburg reluctantly. So it was to her surprise that she discovered herself almost content. Her instructions to her brother were growing less urgent (although in February she sent a note requesting that Carey pack up Maria's "parrot and cage" and ship them to Baltimore) and her previously surly thanks gentling to sincere gratitude.[23] Life on the mountain agreed with her, and that was largely due to Dubois. The priest Elizabeth found cool and not kindred was for Margaret "every thing to me my warmest heart could wish." They shared a "friendship," she wrote, like that between "Brother and Sister," with Dubois speaking of her children as "'nos petits enfans.'" Margaret Burke could never be completely satisfied as an employee, but contrary to both her own and Elizabeth Seton's expectations, it was she who found the Blue Ridge an arena in which to exercise her abilities. Margaret wrote contentedly that she had "the entire management of all but the [girls'] school." With Dubois's support, "My word passes as law."[24]

Among those whose well-being Margaret oversaw were William and Richard Seton. The former city boys rambled over hills and valleys, enjoying the camaraderie with which Dubois enlivened the school's strict order. ("As for my little gang at Mount St. Mary," the priest told Charlotte Melmoth, "they are as hardy as the mountaineers in Scotland.")[25] Every Wednesday, the boys walked to the Stone House to be doted on. Kit and Bec, still young children, also readily adapted to life in St. Joseph's Valley. Moving to an isolated religious community seemed no odder to them than anything else that had happened, and they loved living cozily with their mother and the sisters.

Then there was Anna Maria. Her initial horror at displeasing her mother had faded, and Julia's warning that a mother should not expect to know her child's heart proved apt. As Anna "grows up," Elizabeth observed, "and looses herself from that blind obedience exacted from a child under thirteen, she takes many varieties of temper." The girl who had a year earlier seemed a model of cool reserve now possessed a "disposition so unequal" that "it is very difficult to make her happy." (Sam would have been less surprised than Elizabeth at the change. "How is Anna and what does she do among the woods," he inquired of Cecilia. "I have some idea that from the wildness on display when in civilized society, that she will become perfectly savage when she gets in the mountains.")[26] Confronted with Anna's renewed willfulness, Elizabeth blamed herself, believing she'd "made her my friend and companion too soon."[27] Anna had indeed been her mother's confidante since her earliest years. But she would have looked beyond the isolated farmhouse no matter what Elizabeth did. She'd socialized with the Catons and Harpers wearing a white beaver hat. Now she lived among quiet sisters in dark dresses, while back in Baltimore, Charles du Pavillon pined for her. Or worse, got over her.

Anna Maria was not the only one who found no easy place to alight; Harriet was also neither child nor sister. She still wore a miniature of Barclay Bayley around her neck, and as she worked and prayed with the other women and tenderly cared for Cecilia, whose health was again failing, Harriet expected to leave the mountain and marry. But when a letter arrived from Barclay, it was jarring. She should try a "different" kind of "letter writing than your last," Barclay warned in response to her account of joining the mountain Mass, "or else I shall turn to Goad and to Scold at a terrible rate." Barclay affectionately imagined Harriet in "a neat little bonnet & russet gown," able to "pass very well as a little fairy" when she someday joined him in a "cottage" in Jamaica. But his mockery of her religious experience stung, and he offered no sense of when that cottage might become real.[28]

Back in Manhattan, the Seton clan waited for word of the little Emmitsburg band. "We wish for you a thousand and a thousand times but at the same moment feel contented and happy because you are so," Sam wrote gracefully. Everyone inquired anxiously after Cecilia's health, James sent best wishes, and Ned promised to keep a journal that would "contain every thing useful and interesting to the enlightened inhabitants of St. Mary's Mountain" (a promise he promptly broke.)[29] The urbanites also wondered what life was like "among the woods." "Anything that partakes of polite life or civilization must be quite a rarity among the mountaineers," Sam teased, "and perhaps, my letter may be looked on with astonishment—wonder and admiration by you wild people!"[30] Elizabeth's young half sister Mary Fitch Bayley quizzed Anna Maria: "How do you spend your time?" she demanded. "What pieces are you learning in music? Where are the mountains?"[31]

Amid the flurry of good wishes, it was Sam who noticed that Harriet had fallen silent. "I will not write her another letter till she writes me," he told Cecilia, adding astutely, "I think we have reaped very little information from all your letters from the mountains."[32] When rumors flew that Cecilia was, as one of Harriet's friends put it, "taking the veil," Sam insisted to the family that he knew from Cecilia herself that this was false. If Cecilia said she took no veil, however, she was relying on the fact that the Emmitsburg women wore black bonnets rather than veils, to forestall conflict. She had found contentment in the community and wanted never to leave.

It was Elizabeth who remained unsettled. She confided in Archbishop Carroll that her prayer life felt barren—"it pleased our Lord to withdraw from me all comfort in devotion and deprive me in a manner of the light of his countenance"—and she told Baltimore friend George Weis that she had not yet found her way as Mother. But she did not share her troubles with her family or old friends, and when Julia worried over Elizabeth's reticence, she responded with a glowing vison of contentment. "Never was I more at liberty or in a happier state of mind to answer and make every communication to the dear ones of my heart," she insisted. Elizabeth was as conscious as John Carroll of the need for Catholics to present a respectable face to suspicious Protestant countrymen. Aware that the sisterhood—Catholic, celibate, female—provoked curiosity, she urged Julia to heed only her accounts. "You will hear a thousand reports of nonsense about our community which I beg you not to mind," she wrote, "the truth is we have the best ingredients of happiness—order, peace, and solitude."[33]

In fact, the community *was* for the most part peaceful and orderly. Frequent Masses and communions, along with the arrival of rosaries, medals, and a sacred picture or two, added to the women's sense that they lived close to God and the saints. Maria Burke, whose manner had once prompted Babade to insist she accommodate herself better to others, was now so mild that Elizabeth called her "la petite Colombe."[34] Veronica O'Conway was less content; the Stone House was far in every way from a Spanish Carmelite convent, and she worried her parents with her unhappy letters. But she loved Elizabeth and stayed on. Sally Thompson proved a skilled procuratix, using her good nature and familiarity with the locals to provision the sisterhood handsomely.[35] Before long, people were coming to see the institutions so unexpectedly rising in the Blue Ridge. "This little town is constantly thronged with visitors," Margaret Burke wrote, "who come from all parts to see the wonders working here: a Nunnery, a Seminary, & a chapel on top of a mountain, and a mountain that at a distance seems to touch the clouds."[36]

Beneath the sisterhood's success lay Elizabeth's unacknowledged dependence on Pierre Babade's counsel. She kept a journal for him, a testament both to her familiar practice and to Dubourg's prohibition against sending him frequent letters. She used the fact that Harriet and the Seton daughters were not bound by Dubourg's rules to sanction their passing of messages to and from the priest. Elizabeth believed herself to be obeying the letter, if not the spirit, of Dubourg's instructions. Babade enjoyed flouting his brethren's commands. He examined letters for broken seals and routed notes through George Weis so that the Sulpicians would not realize the extent of the correspondence. "If this regime were known, if it were public, how many good souls who are called to join you would be hindered and turned away," he wrote, deploring Dubourg's governance. He scoffed when a Sulpician warned that he "inserted himself into work that does not concern me and which Providence had given to another." "I explained to him the difference between the exterior in which I have never interfered and the interior in which no one but myself could intervene," Babade sniffed.[37]

So heartily did Babade enjoy his role as Emmitsburg's secret counselor that after announcing he would "fly on the wings of zeal" to St. Joseph's Valley to preside over Harriet's conversion, he instead dawdled for weeks, writing more letters. Through it all, Elizabeth saw nothing to criticize. Babade made her feel chosen and brave rather than misguided and struggling. When she learned that Babade was at last preparing to come to the Stone House to receive Harriet into the Church, she pleaded with John Carroll to allow the priest to hear her confession and that of the other sisters. Cecilia was again desperately ill, Elizabeth wrote, and "the only consolation I can give her is the promise of writing you to beg in her name and the names of four other Sisters" for permission to confess to Babade. She too was desperate for his guidance. "I assure you that if it is not granted to me you will leave a Soul so dear to you in a cloud of uneasiness which can be dissipated no other way," Elizabeth wrote. When she closed her letter, she indirectly acknowledged her struggle to accept clerical direction from anyone but Babade. "[God's] ever blessed adorable will be done," she wrote, "but as [God] permits us to desire and express that desire to you as our Father you will not be displeased with me for again troubling you on a subject on which you seemed already to have made known your intentions."[38]

Dubourg spent much of his time in Baltimore seeing to his duties at St. Mary's, and he did not grasp the extent of the women's preference for Babade. John Dubois did—though Elizabeth was sure the priest did not understand her—and in his way tried to find a practical solution, proposing that Babade become his assistant at Emmitsburg. Babade furiously refused. He preferred his secret authority to serving in an official capacity under Dubois's or anyone else's direction.[39]

And so the first summer at Emmitsburg sweltered on, the not-quite-sisters doing their best under their not-quite-rule, Dubourg not quite realizing that the sisterhood lived in a state of not-quite-rebellion, Harriet not quite believing she would marry and not quite believing she would not. Then, in a matter of weeks, simmering conflicts burst into view.

First came a letter from Barclay Bayley. After hinting that he might remain in Jamaica for many more years before his fortune could be secured, Barclay recounted the story "of a young man who left his mistress lovely and youthful and was so long separated that he found her old and ugly." Had Harriet "lost her bloom?" Barclay inquired. Having kept Harriet waiting for years, he apparently wondered whether she was still worth having.

Stricken, Harriet burned the letter and vowed to stay forever with the sisters. All she wanted was peace, she told Elizabeth, and peace was to be found only in St. Joseph's Valley.[40] At last writing to her family, she told them of her conversion to Catholicism and her despair over Barclay. Harriet dreaded her family's anger but could no longer let them think she was the same young woman who had left Manhattan five months earlier.

Then came more news: William Dubourg was no longer to be the community's clerical superior. Elizabeth and the other sisters—excluding only Rose White and Kitty Mullin—had made painfully clear that they did not turn to Dubourg for spiritual counsel. The Sulpician had innumerable other plans and little reason to fight endlessly for the women's attention and confidence. Yet Elizabeth was stunned by his resignation and also by the next bit of news. The women's new superior would be a clergyman she knew barely if at all: John David, the priest who had encouraged Rose White to go to the house on Paca Street.

Elizabeth had wanted the sisterhood to have the benefit of Babade *and* Dubourg. Now the women would have the counsel of neither. "It seems but a dream that things are as they are," she wrote Dubourg. Could she not repent and be given one more chance? Her "perverseness" was all in the past. "The mother is worthless," she wrote abjectly. "Pity [the sisters], pity her and if she ever vexes you again, quit her forever."[41]

This was not the first time Elizabeth had felt rebuked by a priest and not the first time she'd apologized. But whereas Fathers Tisserant and Cheverus were so moved by her repentance that they themselves begged forgiveness, Dubourg did not change course. He was convinced that Elizabeth would never open her heart to him; more to the point, he could not reappoint himself to the role of superior, even had he wished to. The process was clear: the Sulpicians as a body must recommend a superior, and it fell to John Carroll to approve or deny their choice.

So be it. Elizabeth decided to persuade Archbishop Carroll and the Sulpicians' aged superior, Father Nagot, to undo their decision. Lamenting her failure to obey clergy's previous instructions, she threw herself into an effort to subvert the current one. Knowing that it was possible John David would soon be sent to the newly created diocese of Bardstown, Kentucky, Elizabeth pointed out that his departure would require yet another change in direction, leaving the sisters with "three changes in one year." She implored Carroll to let her undo the damage she'd done. "Since it is our first Superior I have offended," she wrote, "I ought to be permitted to make the reparation, if it may be allowed." Elizabeth was as sure of her errors as she had recently been of her judgment. She also newly shared Carroll and Dubois's old worry: she had "been made a Mother before being initiated" into the ways of religious life. But now "you will see how good a child I am going to be," she promised Carroll, "quite a little child, and perhaps you will have often to give me the food of little children yet."[42]

It was not Carroll but Father Nagot who would nominate a superior, so Elizabeth wrote to him too. Unsure what tone to take, and realizing that her earlier notes had wreaked unintended consequences, she showed a draft of her letter to John Dubois. Although she did not find the industrious French priest a kindred spirit, she realized that he wished the best for the sisterhood. Dubois gently tried to prevent Elizabeth from once again overstepping expected bounds, but he also encouraged her not to abandon her own judgment. Offer "no immediate answer" to a letter from Father David, he counseled; ponder "what yr own reflexions will suggest to you." He included with his letter Elizabeth's draft, "having underlined what I consider rather too harsh, coming from you," and he closed humbly. "You know not," Dubois wrote, "with how great affection & respect I am with all my oddities yrs for ever."[43]

Perhaps Elizabeth ignored Dubois's underlinings. Or perhaps Father Nagot found even a gentle request to rethink his decision offensive. In early November he wrote Elizabeth a letter whose opening lines must have stopped her breath. "Madam," the old priest began, "I am persuaded that it is God's holy will that M. David be the Superior of your house. Perhaps it will prevent me sending you a letter as impertinent as the one which you have sent." The honored correspondent of Bishop Cheverus and Archbishop Carroll felt the slap of true rebuke, and as she read on, she found nothing to soften the blow. "I have great confidence," Nagot told her, "that you will submit yourself completely to the wishes of Divine Providence as you sacrifice your own pride." His meaning was unmistakable: Elizabeth had not opposed Dubourg's instructions out of love for the sisterhood but out of arrogance. "I hope that you will have the fairness and goodness to agree this time with my command," Nagot instructed, "as I see it as my task to at times agree to yours."[44]

It was done. Elizabeth stopped protesting the appointment of Father David and ended forever her unauthorized correspondence with Babade. "Separating us from Our own Father," she told her friend George Weis, was the Lord's decision, made "to trust and prove our Submission and love for his Adorable Will."[45] She had taken a vow of obedience; now she would learn to keep it. Babade, for his part, turned away from Elizabeth as quickly as he'd turned toward her. He was still allowed to write to Harriet. More important, his admiration for Elizabeth had never burned quite so brightly as his love of himself. "I am always with my poor ones in all the streets," he'd written excitedly that summer, "I go on my way blessing and receiving a thousand blessings."[46] On his way Babade now went, leading man in every drama he conjured. Elizabeth would have to find a way to play her role as Mother—to *be* Mother—without him.

"CRUEL GIRL"

Leaves were turning on Saint Mary's Mountain and the shock of Dubourg's resignation still resounding when letters from Manhattan began to arrive for Harriet. The first came from Aunt Farquhar, and she was not pleased. In Harriet's announcement that she wished to stay at Emmitsburg, Aunt Farquhar sensed a rebuke, and she had no intention of letting it stand. "Surely my dear girl," she wrote Harriet, "your society [in Manhattan] must be equally select, with *that* you at present enjoy." Aunt Farquhar took up the language of eighteenth-century sensibility: "Nature formed us for the society of each other," she wrote. Life in a remote nunnery—for that is how she saw the sisterhood—was unnatural. So was a woman who gave up on her fiancé. "The kind and affectionate letters I receive from dear Barclay expressive of his tenderness for you, merit more of your approbation, than your last letter *to me* gave him credit for," she scolded. The Seton clan had tormented Harriet by doubting Barclay's intentions and prospects, but Aunt Farquhar swept all of that aside. "From whence have you this information of his extravagance, and habits of dissipation?" she demanded. "I . . . must insist on your giving me your author, or I shall punish you as the propagator, *cruel girl* to destroy his peace of mind."[47]

Harriet's resolve fled. *Had* she unjustly turned against Barclay? Was she not the brave Magdalen of Babade's letters but a "cruel girl"? She wrote to her aunt asserting her devotion to her fiancé, then spent days drafting a letter to Barclay.[48] Alerted to Harriet's anxious sorrows, Babade wrote from Baltimore. "You must drive out from yr mind any idea of either joining again yr relations, or marrying," the priest urged.[49]

Another letter arrived. This one was from Sam, and his gentle expressions of dismay at his sister's "fatal letter" were no less painful than Aunt Farquhar's scolding. "You will find nothing but a fond recapitulation of all that tender affection I have and ever shall possess for you," he wrote, but "I cannot tell you half the anguish, half the pain and anguish, I felt on perusal of your last letter." Harriet must not take "a little room in the Big House"—must not join the sisterhood. If she did not want to return to the Farquhars, she could live with Sam himself. He had his job at the bank, and he would take a "little cottage" a short distance from town where they both could live. "What a *nice housekeeper* you would make!"[50]

Her brother's housekeeper: Sam's loving offer confronted Harriet with the dependent future she was desperate to avoid. But she had little time to contemplate his mixture of insight, affection, and obliviousness. Governeur Ogden, her sister Charlotte's husband, also sent a letter. Harriet, Cecilia, and Elizabeth had seen confusion, anger, and hurt from their relatives; now came fury.

Back in Manhattan, Elizabeth had shaped the story of her conversion into a martyr's tale. Now Ogden told the story as he, Charlotte, and the Farquhars saw it. Elizabeth had always been "a warm enthusiast in religious matters," he wrote, and in Italy, the Filicchis "so far prevailed over her judgment, that she embraced the catholic faith." After briefly regaining her judgment, Elizabeth succumbed to "the importunities of Mr. F" and to "interest." Now, Ogden concluded, she is "abbess at Emmitsburgh over the *Sisters of Charity!!*" Her new faith consisted of "senseless addresses to wooden images or imaginary saints"; it was a hodgepodge of "superstition, ignorance, [and] misguided zeal" fit only for "the most ignorant . . . part of Europe." He urged Harriet to come back to Manhattan. Surely, away from Elizabeth's poisonous influence, she would choose "union with our rational and established religion."[51]

There was more. Like Sam, Ogden understood Harriet's constrained choices: she must either stay at the sisterhood, marry, or live as a dependent on her birth family. Choosing the first option might forever destroy the latter two. And if Elizabeth and Cecilia died, Harriet would "find yourself immured in the gloomy recesses of your Mountain, dependent on the scanty provision of the sisterhood." "Let me also remark," Ogden wrote, his pen biting into the paper, "that the establishment at Baltimore & St. Josephs are novel things within the U. States—& would not have been permitted by the populace many other places than in the democratic, Frenchified state of Maryland." Through much of the letter, Ogden wrote as much to Elizabeth as to Harriet. Now the lawyer seemed to address a legislative assembly—or a mob. The Catholic religion, he wrote in a slashing hand, "is uncongenial to the habits, manners, and nature of Americans and ere long I predict from many causes, the demolition of every building in that state in any wise resembling a convent or Catholic hospital."[52]

The letter was meant to wound and surely did. Yet for Elizabeth, it was also reassuring. Beneath the good will expressed by so many of her friends and relatives lay this boiling cauldron. She had done right to leave Manhattan, and Harriet would do well to stay away. Elizabeth's story of Manhattan as a place of martyrdom was true.

In fact, when Harriet read Ogden's letter, she was in no condition to leave Emmitsburg, even had she wished to. "Harriet . . . is not well," Dubois reported to Charlotte Melmoth in late November. At the time, many of the women were indisposed—"colds and slight fevers . . . a consequence of their exposing themselves too much to hardships to which they are not inured," Dubois observed—but when the others recovered, Harriet did not.[53] She began to spend her days in a bed next to Cecilia, who was now nearly as ill as she'd been on her arrival in Baltimore. Elizabeth slept near them on a mattress on the floor. When in early December another letter from Manhattan arrived—Charlotte Ogden, telling Harriet, "I love you as a sister, but I have felt for you as one that was unworthy of the title"—Harriet may have been too ill to read it.[54]

Rather than agonize over her family's hurt and anger, Harriet joined Cecilia as an exemplar of patient suffering. During the Advent season, "The door of the chapel would be left open," Sister Rose White recalled years later, "so that the two dear sisters could hear Mass, and often partake of Holy Communion." Learning of Harriet's extreme illness, Pierre Babade sent congratulations: "I rejoice at hearing of your sufferings because I know you say with the saint of the day, let me die with him."[55] In a second letter, he transformed Cecilia into a heroine at once saintly and erotic. "I seem to see you here, stretched on a bed of pain, like a dear wife on her nuptial bed," feeling the "delicious" pains "from the august and tender husband," Babade wrote.[56]

Elizabeth could not quite believe all that had transpired. Cecilia, once restored, lay dying. The robust Harriet was bedridden. Even her sturdy son William had been desperately ill, though he was now recovered. Her efforts to undo the replacement of Father Dubourg with Father David had failed, and she was left with nothing but Dubourg's sympathetic letters, equally painful for their kindness and rebuke. "Oh! That we could cling to none but God and equally love him in all things and in all persons!" Dubourg observed pointedly. Yet the life of the sisterhood continued. "Buy sugar at Mr. Hughes'," Dubourg counseled. "It is but as dear as in Baltimore, but buy a barrel at once."[57] Staggered, Elizabeth carried on as Mother.

The week before Christmas, Harriet was "burning up with fever," and Elizabeth, veteran of many sickbeds, feared the young woman suffered from an "inflammation of the brain." In her delirium, Harriet spoke of neither Barclay nor her family in Manhattan. Instead, she asked "in the most plaintive sweet voice" for Communion and begged to be brought anything that carried with it the touch of Pierre Babade—"his towel his cake his handkerchiefs his letters." Babade had blessed water for the sisters, and Harriet drank it "in the night by stealth."[58] Three days before Christmas Harriet lost the ability to speak. She died the next day.

"Our Harriet is gone without my even knowing she was in danger," a dazed Elizabeth wrote to friends in Baltimore. Harriet was buried under the large oak tree, where a few months earlier she had pointed to a spot she had not really thought would become her grave.

15

ENDEAVOR

ARRIET WAS DEAD, Harriet was free. That is how the community at Emmitsburg saw it and the Sulpicians too. "How mercifully our good Lord has treated our Harriet," Dubourg wrote to Elizabeth, "and what congratulations can be equal to her happiness!'"[1] Harriet's Manhattan friends and relatives also believed that she was in heaven, but they were heartsick. In the choice between life and death, surely one chose life, for others and for oneself. A New York friend neatly captured the clan's feelings: as a Christian the woman knew she must accept Harriet's death, but she could hardly bear to write of it.[2]

Elizabeth was not sure what she felt. She told George Weis that although she had moments in which she "felt happy, contented, embracing my lot with . . . joy," she more often was "stupefied." "I . . . have not the power," she confessed, "to wish or care for anything but heaven and eternity, every other thought is troublesome."[3] Not six months earlier, she thought that serving as Mother to a religious community was itself a matter of caring for "heaven and eternity." Instead, the sisterhood was an endless source of troublesome thoughts and emotions.

Harriet was barely in the ground when Elizabeth realized that John David would be a far less congenial superior than Dubourg. The two priests wrote her on the same day, Dubourg informing her that he'd told David "your ideas concerning the school and many other reflections of mine concerning the latitude" the Sulpicians should allow her to "direct with your own council what is to be done in your own house." David made clear that he intended to rely more on his own judgment than on Elizabeth's.[4] Phrases such as "Take care, dear Mother," "You would do well to," and "Let also the Sisters of St. Joseph remember" studded David's letter. Elizabeth had exchanged a superior she found unsatisfying for one she might well find unbearable.

Into this swirl of grief and remorse walked an unexpected visitor: Ned Seton. He arrived from Manhattan just weeks after Harriet's death, on a trip the clan must have planned as a reconnaissance mission rather than a condolence errand. He found Harriet in her grave, Cecilia bedridden, and a group of women living in a drafty stone house. For all that, what Ned most found, or thought he found, was peace. When he returned to Manhattan, he brought sketches begun during his visit: the Stone House in its quiet valley, Cecilia lying serenely in her little room, serene sisters in sober black dresses. As he added to the sketches after his return, the Manhattan clan watched the mysterious world to which their relatives had disappeared take comforting, even enviable, shape. "When Unkle Edward came back we asked him a thousand questions how the place looked and everything we could think of," one of James's young daughters wrote Anna Maria. "I think you must be very happy at St. Joseph how I should like to [be] with you." It was not only the children who were moved. "It never fails to draw a tear & a smile in the same moment," Ned wrote of his drawing of "the little dear cottage." Mary Seton Hoffman had tried to stay out of the conflicts caused by Elizabeth's and Harriet's conversions, but after Ned's visit, she no longer restrained her affection. She and Zide, Mary told Cecilia, would "often very often sit and talk of Emmitsburg—shall we ever be there, we exclaim together, and then the silent tear drops." "Surrounded by my family and much bustle," Mary loved to think of the sisterhood while she was "striving to keep peace within."[5]

After Ned's return from the Blue Ridge, even Charlotte Seton Ogden lay down her arms. Whether Harriet's shocking death softened her resentment, or Ned's sketches drove out uglier visions, Charlotte wrote gently, even humbly, to Cecilia. "Ought I not to be ashamed of myself, for never having written you a line since we parted on board the ship," she wrote. "Indeed, I am truly so. But know that I love you as much as ever." Charlotte could not stop herself from offering

FIGURE 15.1. Edward Augustus Seton, painting of the sisterhood (made from sketches). APSL 1–3 #48. Courtesy of the Daughters of Charity Province of St. Louise Archives, Emmitsburg, Maryland.

one bit of criticism: "Soon after you left us," she told her sister, "I went to the Willow, and found [your clothing] in an open trunk in the garret, tumbled & exposed to the view of every body." She did not really want to scold. In a line that must have astonished Cecilia and Elizabeth, Charlotte wrote that she wished she could visit. But she and Governeur had made their own dramatic decision: they were leaving Manhattan for upstate New York, "to settle ourselves on the St. Lawrence," and Charlotte wanted to leave with a clear conscience. "Heaven only knows when we shall meet again," she wrote Cecilia, "but let us trust it to Him, who orders all things for the best. . . . Adieu my darling girl."[6]

There would be no more scathing missives from Manhattan. But Elizabeth had a letter of her own to write, to Barclay Bayley. She expressed sympathy while making clear he had caused Harriet great pain. Barclay wrote back, sorrowful and surprised, but he did not have long to repent. He died less than two years later.[7]

THE SCHOOLS AT EMMITSBURG

Not long after Ned's departure, while winter still cloaked the valley, another change arrived for the sisters: a new and larger house, quickly dubbed St. Joseph's House, was deemed ready for their habitation. St. Joseph's was to be the permanent home for the sisters and the boarders they hoped to attract to their school, and they and Dubois infused the move with ritual solemnity. "The Blessed Sacrament brought in procession," Rose White recalled, "Sister Veronica walking before with the bell and the cross, the Rev. Mr. Dubois carrying the Blessed Sacrament next, the Mother and Sisters following." Cecilia Seton, spitting blood and feverish, was too ill to walk, so hearty Sally Thompson wrapped her in a blanket and carried her. The new house was still unfinished (seemingly a requirement for any dwelling into which the sisterhood moved), but it promised a permanency neither the hillside cabin nor the old farmhouse provided. Through a large window, the women looked out onto the oak tree and Harriet's grave.

That spring, families began to send their daughters to the sisters' new school, conducted in St. Joseph's House and called St. Joseph's Academy, and their sons to the boys' boarding school now known as Mount St. Mary's College. The Harpers sent young Mary Diana and Charles Carroll (the latter named, inevitably, for his wealthy grandfather), and Baltimore's Dr. Chatard sent a son and daughter too. Catholics in Maryland had long moved between townhomes and plantations. Now their ecosystem included a mountain and valley. Far enough from Baltimore that their location seemed an unsullied realm, the Emmitsburg institutions were nonetheless a day or two's travel at most; once there, children were taught by Catholic sisters and clergy but remained surrounded by the sons and daughters of their social stratum. In June of 1810, Elizabeth wrote John Carroll that "our school is very respectable and has increased to *forty*, including Boarders."[8] So rapidly did the numbers expand that the sisters slept in the garret. Animal hair used for plastering the unfinished building was stored there, so the women spent nights moving their mattresses from place to place searching for a respite from fleas. The boys' school grew even faster, and Margaret Burke was determined to keep it in good order.[9]

Despite his initial rumblings, John David left the running of the schools to Elizabeth and Dubois. Dubois in turn left the running of St.

Joseph's Academy largely to Elizabeth. A document in his handwriting entitled "Schools at St. Joseph" begins with this note: "This department is chiefly under the sole control and inspection of the mother in all its branches."[10] Augmenting Dubois's respect for Elizabeth's judgment was the fact that the two agreed on the schools' ethos. Regulations for both Mount St. Mary's and St. Joseph's sought to instill strict order. The rules of Mount St. Mary's note that "the children will get up at six o'clock, say prayers so as to begin their study at half past six until half past seven, then go to Mass when it is to be had, then breakfast. Then follows the arrangement of classes."[11] On Sundays, girls and boys attended catechism and Mass, during which strict silence was expected. "Any laughter not rendered unavoidable by some accident, any whisper, any attempt to disturb another shall be punished severely and particularly in church," reads one rule.[12]

The natural entropy of children inspired pointed regulations at each school. During spiritual reading times, St. Mary's boys were to "behave decently without leaning on benches, putting their elbows on the tables or pews."[13] At St. Joseph's Academy, girls were not allowed to "loll, sit where they please, stoop too low, sit cross legged [or] leaning upon one another, talking or whispering to one another, pushing or making faces to one another."[14] When students inevitably did sit cross-legged or show "a spirit of contradiction," corporal punishment was not allowed. Elizabeth, like her father, had never endorsed it, and "Mr. D does not approve of such," Margaret Burke noted. "He thinks it debases the mind."[15] Dubois and Elizabeth relied instead on surveillance, praise (the archive at Emmitsburg contains yellowing certificates of good behavior), and criticism finely tuned to each student's temperament. They also sought to reduce opportunities for misconduct: the girls of St. Joseph's lived under the eye of sisters dubbed "angels," the intensity of whose surveillance rendered the romantic name slightly comedic. No girl was to go "up stairs without permission of the Angel, who is to grant it only in a case of necessity," reads a typical rule.[16] The angels were to watch each other as well as the boarders, alert to hints of favoritism or laxness.

Rather than summoning unpleasant visions of an oppressive European nunnery, these rules appealed to many parents—including the Protestant families who began to send their daughters to St. Joseph's—as an excellent way to instill character and refinement. Dubois and Elizabeth also leavened the strict regimes with affection.[17] "He seems like the

Father of the large family," Margaret Burke wrote of the priest, "is fond of all, kisses & plays with the boys, but has the happy art of making himself beloved and dreaded by the little folks."[18] After the first flush of contentment, Margaret herself was sometimes unhappy in what she dubbed "this wilderness." But she never doubted the schools' effectiveness. "My boys have commenced the Latin language, and advance very well," she wrote her brother, "if ever so prone to mischief they have no time to put it in execution for they are never suffered to go anywhere without the attendance of one of the teachers."[19] As for Margaret's young daughter, "My former scabby sickly little Cecilia is as smart lively sensible a Child as I ever saw, and much more so than any of my children has ever been."[20]

The schools' rural setting offered opportunity for adventure and play. Mary Diana Harper asked her parents to send potted geraniums and seeds "because I have a little garden"; her brother Charles wrote that he and his friends set snares and caught "rabbits, rackoons, possums, and another kind of animal called a pole cat."[21] Men, women, and children constantly traversed the countryside between Mount St. Mary's and St. Joseph's House, both inhabitants and visitors marveling at the area's beauty. "The solitude of our mountains," Elizabeth rhapsodized to Catherine Dupleix, "skipping children over the woods which in the spring are covered with wild flowers."[22] "Oh!" she told Sadler, "if [you] could breathe our mountain air and taste the repose of deep woods and streams."[23] "The grotto" was a favorite place, especially in summer, and although boys and girls were not to meet unsupervised, tradition has it that St. Joseph's girls scratched their names into laurel leaves with a pin, leaving them for the besotted boys of Mount St. Mary's to find.[24]

The schools' rustic location did not make them inexpensive. Tuition for boarders at St. Joseph's was initially $100 and by 1815 stood at $125; the Mount's tuition was similar. The cost was comparable to that for colleges such as Harvard and Yale as well as female boarding academies such as Massachusetts's Greenfield High School for Young Ladies, and it was a significant financial burden at a time when a farm laborer in the Middle Atlantic states might earn $10 a month, a sea captain $40.[25] Parents were also expected to reimburse the Sulpicians for countless small items ranging from candy to medicine to stationery. A sharp little note records a charge to a boy for "1/4 yard blue cloth and tailor to mend pantaloons torn as soon as put on."[26]

No one had forgotten the sisterhood's pledge to educate the poor as well as the wealthy, and in February, the women took in their first two nonpaying students. (The Mount also had "externs," or day students, sometimes as many as twenty at a time, who in the school's early years paid a small fee: $10.66 per year and $2.00 more if they wished to use a desk.)[27] A tradition developed celebrating the local girls' arrival as the start of the parochial school system. In fact, St. Peter's parish in New York had for several years educated children without charge.[28] Nonetheless, the sisters considered the education of local girls an essential part of their mission, and there were always at least a few day students on the rolls, their parents asked to pay what they could.

The day students were to be taught, the regulations held, "as much as possible, separately from the other boarders with whom they shall not be permitted to have much intercourse in order to prevent them from contracting habits of idleness, pride, and forming notions above the sphere of life in which they may have to live if one day they return [to] the world."[29] This segregation followed French Ursuline practice but accorded with Maryland's own unwritten rules. Families such as the Harpers and Chatards did not expect their daughters to share a classroom with poor girls. Elizabeth, for her part, agreed that disappointment and bitterness would result should the children of local farmers feel themselves indistinguishable from Baltimore's wealthy daughters. "I think it the worst of plans to put a *poor* girl among the rich," she once mused.[30] Nonetheless, at a time when fewer than 20 percent of white children in the southern Atlantic states went to any school at all, the creation of the sisters' day school was a notable event, and the women took seriously their responsibility to educate all their charges. The school's 1812 plan specified that although the "poor orphan children" would spend part of their day in "manual labor," the sisters "will . . . be scrupulous of taking any of the time allowed to them for their education by requiring of them services which would take their attention from their studies."[31]

Just as she did not believe that poor girls should share the lives of the Harpers and Catons, Elizabeth expected that girls would pursue paths distinct from those of boys. Mount St. Mary's boys were marched through higher math and classical languages; St. Joseph's girls were kept to arithmetic and the modern tongues. She was preparing girls to enter society, not to upend it, and she saw two paths open to them: marriage or the sisterhood. "A Woman Unmarried," she mused to Julia, "unless she is all all all for God is to me one of the most pitiable beings in the world[,] living for no purpose to be desired."[32] Yet Elizabeth did not consider the boarders' educations mere adornment, and this was a latent point of contention with Father David. "Remember," he instructed the sisters, "altho' profane learning must enter into the plan of education intrusted to their care, the principal part of it is to form the tender minds of their pupils to piety and sound morals."[33] Elizabeth cultivated the boarders' piety, but she also cultivated their minds, an ethos that accorded with that of celebrated female American educators such as Sarah Pierce and Mary Lyon. Although some of Elizabeth's contemporaries—like later historians—associated a respect for literacy with the Protestant tradition of scripture reading, St. Joseph's Academy was an early and ambitious participant in the effort to educate American girls. Enough convent schools followed that in 1834, the editor and reformer Sarah Josepha Hale warned fellow Protestants that "the convents are now considered the best and most fashionable places of education."[34]

At St. Joseph's Academy, Elizabeth ensured that the curriculum was presented rigorously, and thanks to Veronica O'Conway, the boarders could study French, Spanish, and Italian. (Elizabeth's daughters penned notes to each other in schoolgirl French and once in a Spanish that looks amusingly like schoolgirl French.) Elizabeth took pleasure in lively intellects, telling one set of parents that their daughter displayed "a clearness of ideas that delighted me, not for the value of [the] attainment, but as a proof of the intelligence and application of her mind."[35] Domestic training was subordinate to other pursuits. "You know my old notions . . . about the needle," she explained to Julia Scott one fall, "if girls are once turned to a reasonable cultivation of the mind, their good Sense and Pride will afterwards make them needle women."[36]

St. Joseph's Academy thrived under Elizabeth's direction. Yet the community bore little resemblance to what Samuel Cooper had envisioned when he pledged his fortune. The focus was less on poor than on wealthy girls, there was no "manufactory," and sisters rarely worked with the truly destitute. Cooper's insistence on placing the sisterhood in rural western Maryland was in no small measure to blame: "Every Occasion to visit the sick is embraced," Elizabeth wrote Sadler, but "the Villages round us are not very extensive."[37] Despite his own role in shaping the institution, Cooper was dissatisfied. He embarked on a series of disputes with the Sulpicians—their outlines only murkily visible in surviving documents—and may have contemplated withdrawing his support from the sisterhood in order to fund a Pierre Babade scheme to create exclusively Catholic rooms at the Baltimore poorhouse.[38]

That plan faded away, but Cooper's increasingly erratic thinking and extreme views—he declared Georgetown an unacceptable site for the training of priests, since people in its vicinity drank—began to unsettle everyone but Babade. Carroll thought him the victim of a "disordered imagination" and cautioned Georgetown's priests to think twice before admitting him to their community. With Elizabeth, Carroll was more circumspect, but his worry was unmistakable. "You have surely heard of the apprehensions entertained of the soundness and stability of Mr. Cooper's mind, which however, in its perfect state, is a strong and magnanimous one," the archbishop wrote. He told Elizabeth to let the Sulpicians cope with Cooper; she must fix her attention on the sisterhood and school.[39]

Elizabeth easily tolerated Samuel Cooper's passionate eccentricities. Her unhappiness arose from a different source: Father John David. David offered neither Babade's expressive spirituality nor Carroll's astute judgment nor Dubois's humble practicality. Dwelling on man's sinfulness, the priest believed that control of the passions was the central act of Christian devotion and warned the sisters to avoid error.[40] Rose White adored him. Elizabeth found him utterly uncongenial. "Sincerely I promised you," she told Archbishop Carroll, "and really *I have endeavored to do everything in my power* to bend myself to meet the last appointed Superior in every way." She engaged in "continual reflection on the *necessity of absolute conformity*" with Father David's guidance and begged God's help in achieving it. Everything failed. Despite her efforts, "the *heart is closed.*" "The Soul selects her own Society / Then—Shuts the Door," Emily Dickinson would later write, and Elizabeth's had. Because of her "unconquerable reluctance," David "*remains now as uninformed in the essential points as if he had nothing to do with us.*"[41] In scarcely six months, Elizabeth had found three priests—Dubourg, Dubois, and now David—unsuitable.

Elizabeth's struggles with directors place her in an illustrious tradition. Teresa of Avila observed the challenges of working with uncongenial clergy; an oafish or inexperienced spiritual director, the Spanish mystic wrote, "can be greatly mistaken and lead a soul without understanding it nor allowing it to understand itself." Such an experience "will be no small cross, especially if the soul is unwilling to submit to one with poor judgment." "I haven't been able to submit in this way myself," Teresa noted, "nor do I think such submission is fitting."[42] It's not clear whether Elizabeth drew sustenance in these months from Teresa's observation, but when Father David insisted, "We must always rest contented when we have followed the advice of those who are to direct us," Elizabeth silently answered, No, we must not.[43]

It did not help matters that David found in Rose White the obedient sister Elizabeth would not become, nor that Rose felt all the confidence in David that Elizabeth lacked. To her astonishment, Elizabeth realized that she felt like an unwelcome and divisive presence in her own home, just as she had as a child at her father and stepmother's house. Increasingly convinced that David preferred Rose as Mother, Elizabeth decided not to fight for her position. The whole idea of a battle for "Motherhood" seemed comical, and if the battleground was to be obedience, Elizabeth had already lost. There was a deeper reason for her passivity. Her struggles with superiors and dry spiritual life made her question her fitness to be Mother.

Estranged from David and inclined to treat Dubois as more of a comanager than a spiritual director, Elizabeth turned to Archbishop Carroll for advice. Over months of watching her struggle, Carroll had become more, not less convinced of her spiritual power. "It would be a triumph for heterodoxy & irreligion," the archbishop wrote with unusual forcefulness, "& what is of much more consequence, the disappointment of pious and admiring Catholics, should anything happen to shake the stability of your holy establishment." The sisterhood's "ultimate success under God, depends on your sacrificing yourself."[44] Carroll's analysis emerged in part from his determination that the sisterhood, like the larger American Church, avoid public disarray. But he genuinely admired Elizabeth's faith, judgment, and intellect. In his sober way, he offered her the greatest possible encouragement: she mattered to the faith and her unhappiness was not in vain.

"SIMPLE AS A CHILD"

Word of the Emmitsburg community continued to spread, and as winter ended, two young women, Ann Gruber and Elizabeth Boyle, arrived from Baltimore to join the sisters. They had been recruited by the French pastor of St. Patrick's, Father Moranville, and both quickly settled into St. Joseph's House. The foreword to a nineteenth-century memoir praises Boyle with this line: "Through all the years of her religious life, Mother Elizabeth was as simple as a child." In fact, however, the young woman arrived at Emmitsburg only after several years of questioning and a painful rebellion against her mother. In 1806, sixteen-year-old Boyle and a young Methodist friend had decided to visit as many of Baltimore's churches as possible, becoming a member of the one they preferred. It was a kind of spiritual inquiry advocated by some evangelicals, but for Elizabeth Boyle it had an unexpected outcome. The plan to attend a large number of churches fell through, but Boyle attended a Catholic Mass and found herself unexpectedly moved. It was not her first experience with Catholicism; when she was a child, an enslaved woman had taught her to say her "beads," or the prayers of the rosary. Now she decided to convert, doing so secretly to avoid her mother's displeasure. When she learned of Boyle's choice, her would-be partner in religious exploration disapproved; their exploration had not been intended, in her view, to lead them toward a faith believed to suppress freedom of thought. Boyle's mother asked only that her daughter not "go to religion" and isolate herself from her family. She was right to worry. When Father Moranville told her of the little community forming at Emmitsburg, Boyle set out despite her mother's objections, another rebel for God.[45]

In the decades after the founding of St. Joseph's House, Americans created utopian communities such as Brook Farm and Oneida, reconfiguring labor and gender in pursuit of a higher purpose. Women such as Elizabeth Boyle, Elizabeth Seton, and even quiet Maria Burke were companions to such adventurers, even as they were also companions to the Catholic laywomen who over the centuries created communities in which to worship as they saw fit. Convents, although portrayed by critics as places of captivity and oppression—and although unquestionably being such for some inhabitants—had always attracted women who saw them as places of spiritual and intellectual liberty. In seventeenth-century Mexico, a brilliant young woman entered a Hieronymite convent rather than see her studies curtailed by domesticity. Sor Juana de la Cruz thrived for years as an ambitious scholar and poet before opposition from local prelates silenced her. In Reformation England, Catholic women risked their safety to found and join secret nunneries, and an Anglican woman, the protofeminist author Mary Astell, proposed a plan through which Protestant women could live in community and devote themselves to thought and prayer, a plan that seemed to many, including Jonathan Swift, a convent by another name. When Elizabeth Boyle arrived at St. Joseph's House, one more devout Catholic sought God, one more quietly rebellious woman joined a community whose third pillar was obedience, and one more American sought to remake her life.

BALTIMORE

When spring came to the Blue Ridge, the sisters and boarders decorated Harriet's grave with wildflowers. Too ill to join them, Cecilia knew that the residents of St. Joseph's House would soon have another grave to tend. To her surprise, she was afraid to die. "Why is it so?" she wrote Pierre Babade. She immediately answered her own question: her short life had been filled with sin. Clinging to the thought of God's mercy, she found that "often-times I behold nothing but darkness and gloom before me."[46] A month later she had regained her courage. Even if some sins were "yet unexpiated," she told Babade, "I trust our Jesus will shed a ray of His divine light in my unworthy bosom." "Death has no longer a frightful appearance," Cecilia wrote. "I can now meditate on it with the greatest composure."[47]

Not quite ready to let Cecilia go, Elizabeth arranged to take the young woman to Baltimore to consult with Dr. Chatard. Anna Maria, she decided, would come along. The daughter who had once wanted nothing more than to please her mother was now a malcontent; in a house filled with prayer books and devotional art, Anna Maria painted a cabinet with "Calypsos and Telemachoses." Sometimes she felt like a different species from those around her, by her own account the possessor of a "little stony heart," a "poor, solitary butterfly" who "could only converse with the ancient or fictitious ones, since the silent sisters would not answer me."[48] Elizabeth began to think that Charles du Pavillon's courtship might be a good thing after all. Anna Maria was very young for marriage, but one of William's sisters had married at fifteen, and Elizabeth now thought of her daughter as a woman. Anna had no interest in staying in the sisterhood, so Elizabeth thought marriage to a Catholic offered her the only route to spiritual safety; it would also bring Anna a secure home. "[Charles's] fortune is very large," Elizabeth wrote Sadler, "and his education of the first kind with superior talents.

His family only a very tender Mother who resides in Guadeloup and I am told very amiable."[49]

So in the spring of 1810, Elizabeth set off for Baltimore with two young women, one thinking of marriage and the other of the grave. Sister Susan Clossy came along to help. On arrival in the city, Anna Maria was placed in the care of a branch of the Barry family. Louisa Caton—who, just as her family hoped, had quickly lost interest in joining the sisterhood—urged the girl to spend time with the Caton circle instead; Charles du Pavillon might impress the Setons, but Louisa favored the young military officers who gathered in the city as tensions over Atlantic shipping mounted. "We will get a much better match for you," Louisa gaily told Anna as a horrified Elizabeth looked on, "you don't know the enchantment of cockades and epaulets."[50] Elizabeth needn't have worried. Anna Maria had wanted to leave St. Joseph's House, but she had no taste for adventure. She stayed quietly with the Barrys and hoped for a marriage proposal from Charles.

Cecilia's fate was already clear; Dr. Chatard had no remedies to offer, and Elizabeth and Susan Clossy settled in to tend the dying girl. Yet even now, Elizabeth faced distraction; visitors passed along a rumor that the Sulpicians might remove her as Mother, and she believed Rose White would and perhaps should replace her.[51] She had not renewed her annual vows and in her discontent asked Archbishop Carroll to make sure she was no longer bound by them.[52] Years of prayer and struggle, her willingness to uproot her children's lives and rend the fabric of her family, had led only to this.

Cecilia Seton died at April's end. Ill for much of her eighteen years and mild by nature, she had chosen others' happiness over her own at almost every turn. Yet when she believed her soul to hang in the balance, Cecilia did as she believed duty, rather than mere obedience, required, and left her family behind to join the sisterhood. More than Elizabeth herself, Cecilia had found contentment in religious life. "A happier more consoling departure than she made you cannot imagine," Elizabeth told Sadler. "She was innocence and Peace itself."[53]

Elizabeth and Susan Clossy prepared Cecilia's body for the journey back to Emmitsburg. Expected to visit St. Mary's to bid farewell to the Sulpicians, the women instead slipped quietly out of Baltimore. They "set out alone with Cecil in the coffin as cheerful and gay as two filles," Elizabeth wrote, and when a priest caught up with them on the road,

"We could hardly look at [him] with proper gravity." She grieved for Cecilia and dreaded what lay ahead. But they were two would-be nuns traveling through a country that did not know what to make of them, toward a community at risk of falling apart. They had a corpse in the carriage and a bewildered priest chasing behind. The only thing to do was laugh.[54]

16

TRIALS OF THE PASSAGE

ALL THAT SPRING, Rose White had wanted to do something about the state of St. Joseph's House. Ongoing construction left wood shavings everywhere; the debris attracted hogs, and the hogs attracted bugs. "We were literally eaten with fleas," Rose wrote years later, the memory still sharp. When Elizabeth, Anna, Cecilia, and Susan Clossy left for Baltimore, Rose "took occasion of their absence to clean the yard."[1] When Elizabeth and Susan arrived home, the evidence of Rose's confident competence stood before them.

Elizabeth admired Rose's practical hard work. Rose, for her part, knew she could not teach the boarders as Elizabeth did or offer the spiritual guidance on which the sisters were coming to rely. Yet rather than complementing each other, the two women were locked in unacknowledged competition. In the weeks after Cecilia's death, Rose and Elizabeth grew increasingly awkward around each other.

Much in Elizabeth's new life was turning out to be unexpectedly difficult. Yet the aspect some had insisted would be most difficult, reconciling her Motherhood and motherhood, was proving manageable. At eight, her daughter Bec was a pet of all the sisters. Eleven-year-old Catherine was calm and diligent. "Kit rules books, sets copies, hears lessons and conducts herself with such grace," Elizabeth wrote Catherine Dupleix, "that girls twice her age show her the greatest respect."[2] Up at the Mount, William and Richard flourished, too, although not quite in the way Elizabeth hoped. She watched eagerly for one or the other to show some sign of wanting to become a priest. "A man may be a very good man in the pursuit of any other profession," she once wrote, "but certainly that of a clergyman is the easiest, surest road to God, and the first, the highest, and the most blessed that can adorn human being."[3] Nothing. Asked "if his business in the world was to make money and gain reputation or to serve God and use all his endeavours to please him," Will declined to give the expected answer. "'My business is to do both Sir,'" he declared firmly.[4] Will even knew what he wanted his "business" to be: the navy. Dick thought he might one day live on a farm near his mother and sisters. "They are two beings as different as sun and moon," Elizabeth mused of her sons, Will dreaming of making his mark and Dick, though only two years younger, "still as much in love with Mother as when hanging on the breast and always happier with his little Sisters than all the companions in the world." Elizabeth was not charmed by her younger son's sweet dependence. "William most interests poor Mother," she straightforwardly told Sadler.[5]

Will and Dick were still boys, and their future could be safely put off. Anna Maria stood at the threshold of adult life. The moodiness and distance she'd shown at St. Joseph's House had evaporated somewhere on the road to Baltimore, and she wrote often and affectionately to her mother and the St. Joseph's sisters, keeping her mother apprised of Charles's courtship. Something at first went wrong, but soon "the Reconcilement," as Anna romantically deemed it, was complete. Babade urged the courtship onward, and with surprising speed it was arranged that Charles du Pavillon would sail for Guadeloupe to dispose of family holdings, then return to Baltimore and marry Anna Maria.[6] The couple would live in the United States, perhaps among other West Indian planters in the recently acquired Louisiana Territory. Anna Maria saw Charles off on his voyage home and in her upstairs room at the Barry house waited for her new life to begin.

That Anna was to be a planter's wife troubled neither the young woman nor anyone she knew. Mount St. Mary's owned slaves—between ten and fifteen people in a given year—whose labor benefited both Emmitsburg institutions, the men working the land, cutting wood, and serving as wagoners and the women working in the kitchen and washhouse.[7] Dubois's name appears both in the records of sacraments he offered to slaves as their pastor and in tuition accounts settled in

FIGURE **16.1.** Structure identified as a "slave cabin" at Mount St. Mary's University. Courtesy of the Rhoads Memorial Archive, Mount St. Mary's University, Emmitsburg, MD.

human lives. The Taney family of nearby Frederick (whose most famous member, Roger, served as lawyer to the Sulpicians before becoming a Supreme Court justice and authoring the infamous Dred Scott decision) sent children to the Mount and was credited $300 toward tuition "par un negre"; another family paid its bills with "a horse, a slave, and five hundred dollars worth of grain."[8] There is no record of harsh physical punishment at the Blue Ridge institutions, but documents demonstrate Dubois's determination to keep slaves obedient, control their domestic lives, and render them profitable.[9]

The Mount's slaves are hazily visible, glimpsed through the scrim of others' sentiments and self-justifications. Bruté made a note to write "a few little anecdotes" of the enslaved Joe: "his Christmas, Epiphanies, little books, so great affection and respect to the Sisterhood"; an unnamed slave's expressions of Catholic devotion (perhaps also Joe, but it is impossible to tell) moved the priest to envy what he believed to be his pious simplicity. "Shoeless, in rags . . . black, ignorant; without mother, without father, without friend," the priest wrote, both sincere and patronizing, "but he is baptized, his heavenly father is infinitely good, Heaven will open for him."[10] Bruté wanted to believe equality before God ennobled earthly inequality; a reminiscence from a student at the Mount suggests an enslaved man named Pompey thought differently. Two boys (one of them a Taney) asked Pompey whether he thought their Latin studies were useful. "'Twouldn't, of course, be no good to me," the man answered. "But I'm only a poor nigger, and you may be an archbishop someday.'" Deaf to Pompey's sorrow and to his analysis, the boys laughed and called their school mate "Archbishop" for months.[11]

If we cast our net wider, beyond the confines of rural Maryland, we still draw in painfully little of enslaved Catholic life. Diocesan archives contain letters from priests inquiring of bishops what to do when slave marriages were broken by sale, the priests' eyes more on canon law than on justice. A slave laments that French priests prohibit the exuberance of evangelical Protestant services; another man escapes from his Catholic master and becomes a Protestant minister. Others, such as the enslaved woman who introduced Sister Elizabeth Boyle to the rosary, found sustenance in Catholic teachings. Still another bondsman recalled that his Catholic mistress used to lock him and her other slaves in a closet; when this man thought of his mistress's faith, it was that closet that came to mind.[12]

Like many a master before him, John Dubois felt his own captivity rather than that of the slaves whose labor he oversaw. He believed that he worked as hard as those he owned and considered himself the victim of injustice: he resented that the debts Dubourg had blithely taken on fell to him to repay through his own labor and extracting that of others. That Baltimore's Sulpicians believed the sisterhood and seminary to be inefficiently run infuriated Dubois. He seethed when, in July of 1811, his brethren "thought it wise" to remind him of "the fundamental object of the institution, which is to train Daughters of Charity, following as much as possible the very Constitutions of St. Vincent de Paul."[13]

Yet the question of the sisterhood's purpose and rule quietly worried Dubois and the sisters themselves. The women spent most of their time on the boarders and still lived under the provisional regulations Dubourg had set forth two years earlier. Thus when the Sulpician father Benoit Flaget was given permission to travel to France before taking up his role as bishop of the newly created see of Bardstown, Kentucky, the Sulpicians decided that he should bring back a copy of the Rule of the Filles de la Charité. They planned to present this rule, with whatever revisions proved necessary in the American setting, to the Emmitsburg women; the hope was to create a stable community knit into the fabric of the European Church. The priests also hoped that a few French Daughters might be sent across the Atlantic to join the Emmitsburg community. No longer an idiosyncratic American experiment, St. Joseph's House was to become a well-ordered outpost of the universal—and the renascent French—Church.

Told of this plan, Elizabeth did not know what to think. The French rule might enable the sisters to serve the poor more effectively and live in greater harmony. It might also explode the intricate compromises on which the American sisterhood and Elizabeth's role as Mother relied. That summer, Elizabeth still questioned her future; one day she heard rumors that she was to be sent with a detachment of sisters to Baltimore, on another that she would be reduced to director of St. Joseph's Academy. Archbishop Carroll patiently reassured her. The Sulpicians had not presented a plan for her removal, he told her, and he would oppose such a plan if they ever did. It was true, Carroll admitted, that he had "once thought that [a division of duties] might be attended with some relief of your present disquietude."[14] Elizabeth was after all so unsettled that she had not renewed her vows, even writing to George Weis that she was "casting about to prepare for beginning the world again."[15] But Carroll no longer favored such a division; Elizabeth should remain Mother Seton.

More directly than ever before, the archbishop addressed the source of Elizabeth's pain: in the place she'd expected to feel God's presence and find her life's purpose, she felt alone and barren. This trial, Carroll observed, "must naturally disappoint your expectations, more than any preceding one; that is, you are destined to be tried by disapprobation and where you expected to meet confidence and tranquility." By laying bare this wound, Carroll sought to heal it. He told Elizabeth her unhappiness was not failure but suffering, the kind needed "to perfect your other Sacrifices, and to operate in your heart an entire disengagement from human things and expectations; even the consolations of religious retirement."[16]

Carroll was offering Elizabeth a lesson from the Jesuit tradition in which he had been formed. Ignatius of Loyola instructed his followers that seasons of spiritual dryness and uncertainty were necessary seasons of prayer: they taught Christians to love God with no expectation of return and to realize that delights of the spirit were unearned gifts. A similar idea appears in texts ranging from the Psalms to the writings of Teresa of Avila and Juan de la Cruz. "As the deer pants for streams of water, so my soul pants for you, O God," read the plaintive lines of Psalm 42. "My tears have been my food day and night, while men say to me all day long, 'Where is your God?'" Juan de la Cruz wrote famously of the "dark night of the soul" that generated light. Rather than a sign that God was far, "this dark night," the Spanish priest explained, "is an inflowing of God into the soul."[17] Carroll urged Elizabeth to discern the workings of God in what seemed like the moments of God's absence. She held fast to the instruction and the hope it offered.

"NOT LIKE THE WHOLE EXPANSE OF HEAVEN"

Anna Maria Seton had not found the sisterhood to be a dark night of the soul: she'd simply found it dull. Baltimore, at least, was not dull. Yet after Charles du Pavillon's departure, the city felt as unsatisfying as St. Joseph's House had been. From her room at the Barrys', Anna Maria looked out the window at "the tops of houses . . . and two or three poplars shining in the rain." "Not like the whole expanse of heaven from the great window at St. Joseph's," she mused, "the beautiful view of the Mountain."[18] Rather than delighting in the social engagements the Caton girls offered, she found herself watching the clock and joining in prayer with her mother and the sisters—an echo of what she'd watched her mother do during those long-ago days in the lazaretto. Anna's letters home became a jumble of her mother's teachings and her own insistence that she could not live up to them. Learning of the Sulpicians' plan to bring the French Daughters' regulations to Emmitsburg, Anna wished the women "joy on your rule" and added ruefully, "perhaps I have need of one."[19]

Although Babade exhorted her to stay in Baltimore, Anna Maria implored her mother to send for her. "I am as unhappily here almost as I used to be at the Mountain," she confessed, and a recurrent pain in her side and shortness of breath, symptoms grimly familiar to the Seton family, left her uncertain what her future held.[20] "Oh! My Mother— pray for me when you receive this," she wrote one day. "I am no longer *the Nun*—I am much worse than I ever was." "You know," Anna observed, "I was always a wicked piece of furniture."[21] Elizabeth sent for her.

Back at St. Joseph's House, Anna became as participatory as she'd once been distant, studying, joining in the sisters' prayers, and teaching a "decury," or group of ten little boarders. The worrisome symptoms she'd felt in Baltimore grew no worse, but her newly minted marriage plans wavered: Charles wrote from aboard ship, then fell silent. Anna Maria remained serene. "We are all all well," Elizabeth wrote Julia. "Anna as quiet as puss in the corner, keeps her sensibilities all in order—has not [received] letters since I wrote you [but] takes the matter coolly."[22] Then stunning news arrived, and Elizabeth told her friend the tale: when Charles arrived home in Guadeloupe, a young woman "nabbed him on the spot."[23]

In less than three months, Anna Maria had gone from a young teen-ager at a remote boarding school to the fiancée of a planter and back. She absorbed the blow with remarkable composure. Whatever the depth of her feelings for Charles, she knew what she'd been spared: years of uncertainty such as Harriet had suffered. "It cannot but be a good escape," Elizabeth observed, "to lose a heart which does not know its own inconstancy."[24] The whirlwind courtship over, Anna Maria rededicated herself to what had been her occupation most of her life: serving as boon companion to her mother. She "mixes the attention of a friend with the duty of a child," Elizabeth wrote happily, and "makes more progress in the formation of her character than any one could believe who did not observe her con-tinual advancement."[25] Possessed of her mother's strong will and intelli-gence, Anna rapidly transformed herself from dissenter to exemplar, from "wicked piece of furniture" to "Nun." Rose White admired the girl's sud-den efforts to observe the sisterhood's rules, and her conduct was praised all the way to Baltimore. "I will not make Annina vain," Archbishop Carroll told Elizabeth, "by repeating all I hear of her merit."[26]

Carroll and the Sulpicians were also pleased when, at summer's end, Benoit Flaget returned from France with the rule and constitutions of the Daughters of Charity. John Dubois set to work translating the docu-ments and contemplating revisions. Elizabeth was at first less interested in the rule than in a piece of news Flaget brought with him: he'd decided to take John David along to Bardstown. Carroll made explicit what Eliz-abeth quietly thought: should David, whose authority she still could not accept, go to Kentucky, "some change must ensue in the government of St. Joseph's."[27] But Flaget and David postponed their departure for Kentucky, and Elizabeth realized she would have no quick deliverance. Worse, David announced he would hold a fall retreat for the sisters during which he might determine the house's permanent rule.

Elizabeth found David's announcement willfully perverse. "Why," she demanded of Carroll, "should [regulations] be made by a Superior on the point of leaving us?" Obedience, she was sure, did not require capit-ulation to injustice; knowing that traditional Catholic practice offered women religious the ability to debate their proposed rule, Elizabeth warned that if David insisted on proposing regulations "to us without going thro' the necessary discussion and approbation, I can never give the example of Accepting them."[28] To Father David himself she was even more direct. "What use can it be to discuss those rules with any other than the one who is to take your place?" she asked brusquely.[29]

Whether by his own choice or at the urging of Carroll, David in the end declined to press regulations on the sisters. Nonetheless, Elizabeth continued to hear rumors that before leaving for Kentucky, David would name Rose White her replacement as Mother or that he would take sisters with him when he left. Margaret George, a widow whom Elizabeth had befriended in Baltimore, found herself at dinner with clergy in that city and spent the evening eavesdropping, determined to glean news.[30] This was hardly how a mother superior and her clerical partner were supposed to communicate.

Turning yet again to Carroll, Elizabeth for the first time found her concerns brushed aside. Rose was "candid," the archbishop soothed, and had no expectations of replacing Elizabeth. "She assuredly is liable to failings, for who is without them?" he asked mildly.[31] This was too much: Rose was not only wresting Elizabeth's role as Mother from her but had apparently insinuated herself between Elizabeth and her most trusted adviser. In response, Elizabeth bitterly told Carroll that Rose was an insubordinate woman who provoked factions and unhappiness.[32] She strove to regain a gentler tone. "Every one is so bent on serving our Lord" that the sisters lived in relative peace despite their troubles, she assured Carroll, adding that Rose showed "affectionate kindness" to Elizabeth's children. But there was no hiding the fact that Elizabeth thought the community at St. Joseph's house was at risk, nor that her composure was slipping.

At last, a change: Father John David left the valley, headed to Kentucky to assist Bishop Flaget at Bardstown. He wished the sisterhood well, continued to think the world of Rose White, and turned his attention to his next duties. It was Elizabeth who could not move on. She would have been sorry to see David stay but felt no joy when he left. She still had not renewed her vows, and she once again demanded Carroll's reassurance she was not bound by them. "I intreat you," she wrote him, "to relieve me from them if you think any obligation remains." Nothing brought peace. When Carroll paid tribute to her judgment by asking whether she thought John Dubois should be named superior or perhaps Dubourg reappointed, she hardly cared. "Rev. Mr. Dubois an economist and full of details dictated by habits of prudence," she replied, "Rev. Mr. Dubourg all liberality and schemes from a long custom of expending." Feeling obligated to express some preference, she came to a decision that would have surprised her just a year earlier. Despite her regret at having once opposed Dubourg, she preferred Dubois. His dogged work and quiet respect for the sisters' judgment were undeniable. Yet the final point she found in Dubois's favor unintentionally revealed just how distant from him Elizabeth still felt. Dubois "always and invariably . . . recommended me to refer constantly to you," she told Archbishop Carroll, "which is not only in the order of Providence but the only safety I can find for the peace of my mind."[33]

When Elizabeth's thoughts turned to the French rule, she was equally unenthusiastic. "How could you have expected my Reverend Father that the regulations of the house would have been concluded before the departure of Rev. Mr. David?" she demanded in response to Carroll's inquiry. In her fear and exasperation, she voiced the concern that had haunted her for months: French sisters might finish the dispossession that John David and Rose White had begun. "How can they allow me the uncontrolled priviledges of a Mother to my five darlings?" she demanded. "Or how can I in conscience or in accordance with your paternal heart give up so sacred a right?"[34] Not long before, Elizabeth had confidently insisted she could nourish both her literal and her figurative children. Now she was not sure she could persuade the French Daughters of this. She was not even sure it was true.

Elizabeth did not know that clergy shared her worry over the French Daughters' arrival. It's not clear when the change had occurred, but a significant number of Sulpicians believed that the American community should be allowed to develop separately from the French; Flaget, who had sought the Filles de la Charité, had gone so far as to try to intercept the French sisters before they left Europe.[35] The universal Church thrived in the new nation through adaptation, not transplantation. John Carroll summed up everyone's thinking when he reflected on events a few years later. The "distance, different manners, and habits of the two countries, France & the U.S." he wrote, meant the Emmitsburg congregation could not be "entirely conformable & the same with the institute of St. Vincent of Paul." A transformation in thinking had quietly occurred, its implications forced to the surface by the prospect of French Daughters descending on St. Joseph's House. The community's departures from European precedents did not make it less Catholic. They made it more likely to succeed.[36]

It's not clear what would have happened had French Daughters arrived once they were no longer wanted. But the Atlantic conflicts that so often disrupted Elizabeth's life this time offered respite: the Daughters were denied passports and so could not leave France. Yet Elizabeth remained unsure whether she should be Mother and whether she should lead a consecrated life in community at all. Her clerical antagonist was gone and her potential French critics vanished, but her own will, which she could neither trust nor forswear, remained. She hinted at her weariness to George Weis—"I am so worn out now that it is almost a matter of indifference how it goes," she told him—but in the main, Elizabeth revealed her unhappiness only to John Carroll and God.[37] Julia, she knew, would tell her to pack her things and come to Philadelphia. She no longer allowed herself to pour out her troubles to Babade, and when a letter from Antonio managed to cross the turbulent Atlantic, Elizabeth responded to her benefactor with blank-faced contentment. "No wars or rumors of war here," she told him, "but fields ripe with harvest; the mountain church St. Mary's, the village church St. Joseph's and our spacious log-house, containing a private chapel (*our Adored always there*)."[38]

Two people other than Carroll might have understood Elizabeth's troubles in these difficult months, but she hid her troubles from them too. The first was a young priest named Simon Gabriel Bruté de Remur, who had accompanied Flaget on the latter's return from France. Four years younger than Elizabeth, Bruté had been an adolescent when revolution shook the foundations of French Catholicism, and he and his mother remained faithful Catholics throughout the danger. After studying mathematics and medicine, Bruté entered the order of St. Sulpice when it reasserted itself in Napoleon's France. Dreaming of life as a missionary to Asia, Bruté met Flaget during the latter's visit to Europe and decided to come to the United States, which he imagined offered a similar field for heroic evangelizing.[39] When the young priest came to Emmitsburg, Elizabeth was immediately struck by his cultivated mind and expressive piety, the former reminiscent of her father, the latter of Babade. "Sometimes I am tempted to tell him *all*," Elizabeth mused to John Carroll, surprised at herself. But she did not.

The second person with whom Elizabeth sensed a closeness was Margaret Burke. Despite her love for Dubois, the prickly widow was finding it increasingly difficult to conform her will to her circumstances. Burke tried to laugh at herself for being "like the proud favourite of the Eastern king who pined because poor Mordecai would not worship him," but she confessed that "I still feel within me pride which whispers . . . I am a dependant." Like Elizabeth, Margaret loved the works of Teresa of Avila, a saint who desired to submit to God's will—and to no one else's.[40] And like Elizabeth, Margaret bridled at being the object of charity: "The idea of obligations conferred always sat a heavy burden on my mind," she told her brother.[41] Sensing Margaret's desire for self-sufficiency, Elizabeth secretly gave her money to purchase clothing for her daughter, rather than simply offering clothing from the school's charitable supplies. And when Margaret apologized for some bit of churlishness, Elizabeth offered understanding, insisting pardon was not needed. I "only . . . observed in you the effects of sorrow and misfortune which are so familiar to myself and often are the occasion of so many peculiarities of conduct that when I meet with them in others they occasion no surprise," she told Margaret. "Let us in future understand each other and be true friends."[42] Instead, the two women kept to their separate paths.

ROUGH AND BLEEDING FROM WORK

Summer again. Boarders left for their families' plantations and townhomes. In July, William Dubourg appeared in the valley, bringing with him three would-be sisters he'd met during travel to the island of Martinique. Like those who had joined the community earlier, each woman had her own reason for coming to St. Joseph's House and each found a slightly different place within it. The "gentle and docile" Louise Rogers sought a peaceful life, the fact that she was a "capital hand at the needle" making up for the fact that she brought no money to contribute to the house's management. Second was a Frenchwoman named Adele; having as a young woman been unable to join the French Daughters of Charity, she saw in Emmitsburg a second chance to follow "the first impulse of her heart." The third woman was Adele's sister, and it was she, a widow who Dubourg suggested had been "long the sport of the world and the dupe of its wiles," who captured the imaginations of the St. Joseph's sisters. Madame Guèrin wished to renounce the world and its pleasures, and in her "spirit of mortification" the sisters saw and quietly celebrated their own.[43]

Guèrin arrived at St. Joseph's wearing a brown dress and cap in honor of the Virgin Mary, her natural elegance heightened by her plain clothing. Rose White noticed that the new arrival "delighted in the dirtiest work," eager even to scrub chamber pots. Her hands bore witness to her penances. "Very soft and beautiful" when she arrived, they were soon "so rough and bleeding from work and exposure, that they would be purple." Rose White and Elizabeth Seton disagreed about many things but not about Madame Guèrin. "She is making fine progress in the paths of penance, and drinks carrot coffee with as good grace as if she had been used to mortification all her life," Elizabeth noted approvingly. She "takes dry bread at breakfast, as if it was really her choice."[44]

Strapped finances and a rural setting made some austerity inevitable. But as Rose's description of Madame Guèrin makes clear (and as Elizabeth herself would have quietly agreed) the women also sought out sacrifice in order to suffer for God. These two strands, of sacrifices accepted and sacrifices sought, thread through Elizabeth's life, through the early years of St. Joseph's House, and through the history of Christian monasticism.

In the third century CE, Christian believers walked into the deserts of North Africa seeking to leave behind earthly pleasures and judgments. Living sometimes singly, sometimes in single-sex communities, and sometimes in communities of both men and women, these Christians—whose numbers grew so large that one contemporary claimed the desert had become "a city"—placed fasting, silence, and austere living at the heart of their religious practice. The desert dwellers believed that disdain for pleasure liberated the soul from vice and opened a window onto the realm of the spirit. The conviction that Christianity must not dwell comfortably within the world deeply influenced first Eastern and then Western Christianity, including the Rule of St. Benedict, the framework for much of monastic life.

Asceticism also lies at the heart of reforms that have again and again remade religious communities. Teresa of Avila repudiated the luxuries that her community of Spanish Carmelites accepted, founding convents graced by bare walls and cells empty of everything but a bed. The rough sandals Teresa's spiritual daughters wore gave the reformed order its moniker, the Discalced (Unshod) Carmelites. Renunciation of worldly comforts and appetites, Teresa and other reformers taught, freed the soul to devote itself to God.

What, however, does renunciation of worldly comforts and appetites require? And can renunciation become its own form of self-indulgence? Catholics who share a respect for ascetic tradition have disagreed ferociously over whether they should simply avoid rich foods or should fast strenuously, over whether to wear plain linens or a hair shirt. Some have cautioned that asceticism deteriorates into barter: the penitent promises to give up A only so that God will grant her B. And some have argued that by constantly guarding against pleasure, ascetics unwittingly place the body—and thus the self—at the center of experience.

Cistercian monks sought to separate asceticism's wheat from its chaff by renouncing both luxury and heroic self-mortification.[45] Their great abbot Bernard of Clairvaux wrote that one must move from "love of self for one's own sake" through "love of God for one's own sake" to "love of God for God's sake."[46] Ignatius of Loyola recommended mortification through fasting, disruption of sleep, and self-flagellation but cautioned against extremes and came to think his own youthful practices were excessive. John Carroll, formed in this tradition, saw no place for physical mortification or severe asceticism in the lives of clergy or sisters; the faithful should live simply and offer spiritual struggle, not physical agony, to God. The Sulpician order likewise mistrusted mortification, advocating in its stead interior devotions and discipline instilled by orderly rounds of work and prayer.[47] Far from exhorting the Emmitsburg women to acts of heroic physical sacrifice, Dubourg and Dubois exhorted them to make sure their windows were snug and to buy as much flour as they could at the best possible price; accounts show the sisters consumed meat as well as carrot coffee. John David differed from his brethren in many things, but he shared their belief that physical mortification had no place in Emmitsburg. "The love of penance" must "yield in our dear infirm sisters to the voice of obedience," he wrote Elizabeth one Lenten season, "for better is obedience than sacrifice."[48]

Elizabeth and the sisters did not quite share this ethos. They nurtured a more passionate spirit of self-denial, one that emerges in glancing comments in Elizabeth's letters, in Rose White's reminiscences, and in Margaret Burke's fear that her daughter—whom Veronica O'Conway admired as "truly victorious over the powers of the flesh"—"hurt her health by her abstinence & mortification."[49]

Like asceticism itself, the struggle between religious women and clerical superiors over the limits of sacrifice courses through both Elizabeth's own life and the history of the Church. In Manhattan, Father Jean Tisserant had told Elizabeth not to abstain from meat if doing so disrupted her sister Mary's household; now, at Emmitsburg, clergy sought to moderate what they saw as a zeal that might harm not only the women but also the fragile standing of the Catholic community in the United States. Despite the distinctive circumstances, disagreement over the proper use and limits of asceticism placed Elizabeth and the Emmitsburg community squarely within a transatlantic tradition. In seventeenth-century France, ascetic Daughters and Ursulines struggled against clerical superiors who feared their weakened bodies would be unable to work and might attract the condemnation of outsiders. Medieval female spiritual seekers struggled with families and confessors over the limits of fasting and self-flagellation.[50]

Throughout her life, Elizabeth contemplated the purpose of suffering, seeking its meaning as diligently as her father had sought its alleviation. As a child and young woman, she struggled to accept that she could not protect anyone she loved from disease and death. As an adolescent, she made an effort at detachment through her homemade stoicism; as a young wife, she followed John Henry Hobart's Episcopalianism, which promised that earthly miseries were ephemeral and heaven was her true home. On the ship to Italy, Elizabeth turned to barter, offering to lead an ascetic life if God granted the Setons reunion after death. The Filicchis' Catholicism offered something less transactional and more appealing, something that not even Eliza Sadler's disapproval could tarnish: the promise that suffering could be offered to God as worship, as a way of expressing humility and love. In Baltimore, Elizabeth came to understand suffering in a slightly different way, as a kind of union—partial, fleeting, but precious—with a suffering Christ. Now, as she thought about what kind and degree of physical sacrifice the sisters should offer, she drew on the writings of Vincent de Paul, Teresa of Avila, and Bernard of Clairvaux, as well as on her own rich life.

A notebook preserved at the Sisters of Charity of Cincinnati's Motherhouse contains a long reflection on the subject of asceticism; like much of Elizabeth's writing intended for use at the sisterhood, it is both ruminative and instructional. At its start Elizabeth assumes a practical tone—"generally we may remark that those in religion as well as people of the world who keep always going on simply and quietly without stopping for occasional indispositions are the very persons who reach the greatest old age." Then she sets practicality aside, acknowledging the appeal of the kind of severe mortification both the sisters' way of life and their clerical superiors forbade. She counseled that the sisters could partially satisfy their longing for self-sacrifice simply by following their rule exactly, seeking no rest beyond what it allowed and giving up even some of the plain food they were granted. She also searched Catholic teachings for justifications of austerity the way a lawyer hunts precedents that favor his client. "St. Bernard requires some of his religious to moderate their austerity but what was this moderation[?]" she demanded. "It is well known that this consisted only of badly prepared vegetables, and in the first years of his order they used only wild fruit and leaves as were to be found in the deserts they inhabited." In the end, however, Elizabeth agreed with Carroll and the Sulpicians: regulation of the will was the most perfect sacrifice, the "continual mortification" that one should offer God. She offered the sisters an echo of Tisserant's long-ago counsel to her: moderation could be its own Jobian suffering. "Where . . . we are forbidden the use of complete and intire abnegation," she wrote, "at least let us be able to take our God to witness that we are willing to do more and lament to him that we cannot." [51]

This ethos of renunciation was as much a part of St. Joseph's House as the religious pictures and the furniture, and the Academy students responded to it in different ways. Some boarders avidly imagined themselves suffering with Jesus as they knelt on the hard chapel floor. A student named Mary Jamison stitched the phrase "Live Jesus live and let it be my life to die for love of thee" into her sampler, her beautifully rendered depiction of St. Joseph's House limning also the white gate that marked the sisterhood's cemetery.

FIGURE 16.2. Mary Jamison sampler, 1812. Courtesy of the Daughters of Charity Province of St. Louise Archives, Emmitsburg, Maryland.

Others were more ambivalent. Charlotte Smith, one of a pair of sisters sent to the school on the charity of John Carroll in order to escape the consequences of their mother's blistered reputation, could not quite forswear a world she'd barely been allowed to enter. Charlotte recognized "the vanity and nothingness of the world," she told Elizabeth, "yet I cannot have the courage to renounce it or the strength to despise its vanities which I fear I keep too close to my heart."[52] Then there was Anna Maria Seton. Not long before, she'd forcefully resisted the sisterhood's ethos and ventured out into the world. Now she turned her will against her own body and vowed to renounce the smallest pleasure. She rose at 4:00 a.m. for prayers, oblivious to the lack of a fire in the grate. The girl who had taken pride in her white beaver hat now walked two miles to the mountain chapel without cloak or shawl. When Anna Maria again felt a pain in her side and her breath grew short, she does not seem to have told her mother.

RULE

In the months since Benoit Flaget had brought the rule and constitutions of the French Daughters of Charity to Maryland, John Dubois had found time, amid his constant labors, to translate the documents and decide what amendments seemed necessary. In the fall of 1811, he shared his efforts with the sisters and the other Sulpicians. Dubois had made some noticeable changes: he acknowledged the "secondary aim" of educating girls and wrote an appendix setting forth the specific regulations of St. Joseph's Academy, he specified that the sisters would follow the fasting and abstinence rules of the American Church, he established procedures for appointing "extraordinary confessors," and he indicated that small changes to daily schedules were acceptable if circumstances required.

In the end, however, what is most striking about Dubois's modifications is how minor they were. The regulations retained the French congregation's language of serving the poor (expanding it to include the insane), and in most regards, the Regulations for the Society of the Sisters of Charity of St. Joseph's were duplicates of the French Règles.[53] The Emmitsburg women would take private, annual vows and actively serve God and man. Thanks to Dubois's skillful translation, Vincent de Paul's exhortation to the women of seventeenth-century France now sounded in the Blue Ridge. The American Sisters of Charity would have "no cloister but public streets or hospital rooms, no enclosure but obedience, no grate but the fear of God, no veil but that of holy modesty."[54]

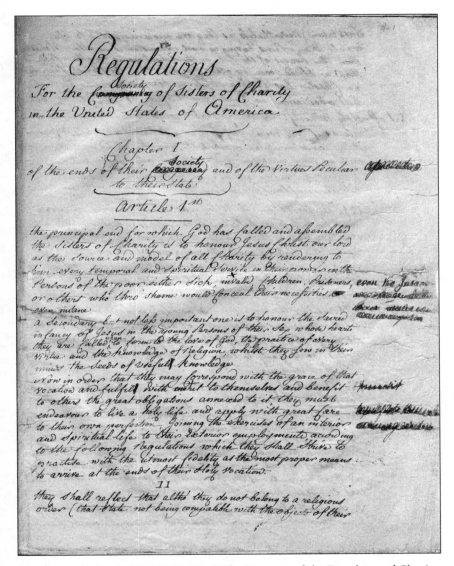

FIGURE 16.3. Rule of 1812. APSL RB #29b. Courtesy of the Daughters of Charity Province of St. Louise Archives, Emmitsburg, Maryland.

Despite all the worry and muffled disagreements over the shape and governance of the sisterhood, Dubois's proposals quickly satisfied all who read them. Elizabeth told John Carroll that she "never had a thought discordant with" the proposed regulations. Carroll, too, was pleased. "I shall congratulate you & your beloved sisters" when the regulations are adopted, the aged archbishop wrote. "It will be like freeing you from a state in which it was difficult to walk straight, as you had no certain way in which to proceed."

Because Dubois had not spelled out all "the rules of detail & particular duties of the Sisters," Carroll realized the women retained significant powers of self-governance. He heartily approved. "They being matters of which yourselves & your Rev. Superior will be the best judges," he told Elizabeth, "I commit you & them with the utmost confidence to the guidance of the Divine Spirit."[55] Like Elizabeth, Carroll and Dubois had found David's heavy-handed rule over the sisters inappropriate. "I am exceedingly anxious," the archbishop explained, "that every allowance shall be made not only to the sisters generally, but to each one in particular, which can serve to give quiet to their conscience." Carroll "rejoiced" to see that only the "immediate Superior residing near you" would "share in the government or concerns of the Sisters," and that the Constitution would "confine the administration of your own affairs & the internal & domestic government as much as possible to your own institutions once adopted."[56] The women were in the main to govern themselves.

The sisters discussed the regulations before voting. That vote, like the existence of an elected council, was part of Catholic tradition. The Sisters of St. Joseph's could not vote in the nation's elections, but they could vote on the rule by which they lived in Catholic community. One sister voted no, almost certainly a New Yorker named Jane Corbet who had joined the sisterhood at Anthony Kohlmann's suggestion and who left the community soon after the vote. Everyone else voted in favor and stayed.

Eight years earlier, Elizabeth Seton had been a Protestant matron. Now she was Mother of a formally sanctioned Catholic community for apostolic women, the first to be created in the United States. When he wrote to approve the regulations, John Carroll nodded, in his understated way, to the importance of the occasion. "I am deeply humbled," wrote the archbishop, "at being called on to give a final sanction to a rule of conduct & plan of religious government, by which it is intended to promote & preserve amongst many beloved spouses of Jesus Christ, a spirit of solid and sublime religious perfection."[57]

The women became novices, expected to take their vows as Sisters of Charity (or Sisters of St. Joseph's; the two terms were used interchangeably) after a year of preparation. Elizabeth planned to be among them. It was a fact unremarkable to those around her; none understood the depth of the uncertainty and discontent she'd suffered. There had been no miraculous deliverance or even a transformation: Elizabeth still found her prayer life drab and strained, still worried she was not the Mother those around her believed her to be. But she wholeheartedly committed herself to a life lived within Emmitsburg's rule.

PAIN

Amid the discussions of the rule and the serene bustle of the sisterhood, Anna Maria's illness at first seemed a passing trouble. She sat "in the chimney corner, worn out with bilious fever," while over at the Mount her brother William was sick too. But when Will was back to his lessons and rambling the countryside, Anna Maria remained ill. By November, she was "worn out with cough and fever [and] pain between her shoulders," and as the month wore on, a swelling appeared under her arm. When Advent approached, Elizabeth forced herself to tell Julia what she had slowly come to see. "Anna my sweet and precious comfort and friend," she wrote, "is undergoing all the symptoms which were so fatal to our Celia and so many of the family."[58] Consumption was hunting another Seton.

This, too, was suffering that must be accepted, and Elizabeth refused to question God's will. "All is in the hands of him who gives," she told Julia resolutely. Yet as she had always done when confronted with loved ones' illnesses, she also drew aggressively on the era's fledgling medical science; accepting God's will did not require setting aside human intellect and endeavor. She consulted with Dr. Chatard, fussed over Anna's diet, and set the girl to horseback riding. When Mary Post learned of Anna Maria's illness, she sent a barrage of questions. "How has this happened," she demanded, "has she taken cold—are her spirits affected—does the climate disagree with her?"[59] No one knew the answers. They were riveted by something else: the horrifying speed with which Anna's consumption was advancing.

Cecilia, Rebecca, and William Magee Seton had lived with tuberculosis for years before finally succumbing; that winter, Anna Maria grew weaker by the day. Her newly womanly figure wasted away. "My darling daughter's complaint is so much increased that it is no longer prudent Diana should be her [room]mate," Elizabeth wrote Robert Goodloe Harper, worried not that Mary Diana would contract the disease—no one understood contagion—but that she would too closely witness her friend's destruction.[60]

Tuberculosis bacilli burrowed into Anna's lymphatic system and bones. Elizabeth thought she knew consumption's weapons, but she saw her daughter endure a terrible new assault. A wound opened on Anna's side, a bedsore or the kind of abscess the disease itself sometimes caused. When it refused to close, a local physician recommended a procedure—known, in a meaningless coincidence, as a Seton—by which a cord was inserted into the wound and each day pulled through the broken flesh to clear it of pus. Elizabeth allowed her daughter to decide whether to undergo the painful procedure; Anna welcomed it as a mortification. "I do not believe it will do my body any good," she explained, "but let me pay my penance for so often drawing in my waist to look small and imitate the looks of my companions, let the ribs now draw with pain, for having drawn with Vanity."[61]

As a little girl in the lazaretto, Anna Maria had watched her father's misery and willed herself to become her mother's perfect child. Now, desperately ill herself, she became the perfect young woman, and her mother again took heart. Despite her renewed determination to act as Mother, Elizabeth still felt her spiritual life to be lacking. It was, she told George Weis, as if "there is a death like silence between me and all I love best." She felt "no love of Vocation—no *pure* charity—no assimilation with holy Poverty—no pliancy of spirit."[62] Everything Elizabeth lacked, she saw in Anna Maria. Everything her mother needed and admired, Anna Maria wanted to give. Elizabeth eagerly wrote down her daughter's pious sayings and gestures. Through it all, John Dubois watched and worried. He thought Elizabeth looked to her daughter for solace only God could provide. But he said nothing.

As Anna's health declined, the young woman made a dramatic announcement: she wanted to take vows as a Sister of Charity. Clergy wrote to encourage mother and daughter. "May the Prince of Peace continue to calm the emotions of your soul," John Carroll told Elizabeth, adding, in an odd turn of phrase, "How happy for you and your blessed companions to be removed from [the world's] contagious breath!"[63] Dubourg wrote, too, abandoning the cool politeness he'd recently shown in favor of a truer accounting of his feelings. "You are too good to put some value on my friendship," he told Elizabeth. "I wish you could know what your apparent suspicion of its Sincerity, and your unmerited reserve have inflicted on my heart." They had both suffered over their estrangement, Dubourg continued, but perhaps this crisis could restore their friendship. As for Anna, she would soon be free from earthly troubles, and Elizabeth should rejoice in her daughter's liberty.[64]

In mid-January, when John Carroll and Jean Tessier, the archbishop of Baltimore and the superior of the seminary at St. Mary's, formally approved the sisterhood's rule, it was agreed that Anna Maria would be allowed to take vows. Too ill even to go to the tiny chapel that lay within St. Joseph's House, she made her vows from her sickbed, laughing with her mother at Dubois's earnest explanation of their importance. Neither felt any need of Dubois's counsel; Anna's vow taking, Elizabeth wrote, was "communion for the child and the mother."[65]

The young woman's sickroom became the center of St. Joseph's House. She urged her friends, "Let my weakness be a lesson to you," and turned her gaunt frame into a memento mori; at the top of a list of pious instructions to her decury, she sketched a skull and bones.[66] Little Bec watched in wonder. When one winter day the little girl fell hard on ice, she hid the limp that followed, determined that nothing distract from her sister. William, too, was called to witness. "Be good, be good, be good," Anna told her brother. "Oh when you come to y[ou]r death bed as I am how you will wish you had been good, that you had never offended our dear Lord." Since the colonial era, Americans had sought to create "good deaths," peaceful departures marked by prayer and calm farewells. Anna Maria's bedside teachings—"which had a good effect on me," one boarder wrote—drew on that cultural tradition as well as specifically Catholic imagery, but there was also more than a hint of the dramatic graveyard poetry the girl had read in Elizabeth's old commonplace books. When Anna Maria pulled up a sleeve to "show her bony arm to one of the boarders" or told her young visitors "You come to look at what the worms will soon devour," she enacted a lesson she had learned in the languages of both religion and poetry. There is also a self-conscious theater in these scenes, as there had been in Anna's painting of Calypsos and her mournful declaration that she was a "solitary butterfly." But the young woman's agony was real, and so was her courage.

Days passed, the wound around the Seton stitch suppurated, and Anna's lungs filled with phlegm. She lay in bed holding a crucifix and speaking to Jesus. "Oh how I wish I was good enough to help them," she said of souls who refused God's call, "poor souls see how they fall into Eternity how I wish I could help them." Sometimes, Anna imagined she *did* suffer not only for her own sins, but for others'. No one—except perhaps Dubois, who held his tongue—questioned the young woman's immense spiritual ambition. Elizabeth worried only when she thought her daughter's heroic resignation might falter. "Don't you see how my tears run and I can hardly help groaning?'" Anna once gasped out to her mother. "But my darling in your heart you are not impatient with your pains," Elizabeth urged, and her daughter composed herself.

By mid-March, the teenager was nearly blind, and bones broke through the skin of her back. Her chest turned purple and black overnight. "Mother what does this mean?" she asked. Elizabeth told her it meant God "is now going to receive you." Determined to offer one final lesson, Anna had her friends and decury brought to her bedside, showing them "her poor little breast, nothing but a skeleton and so discolored." Summoning the sisters, Anna asked pardon for having offended them; when boarders she'd never met trooped past her, she told them graciously, "I do not know you, but I love you in my Jesus, be good." Amid the sobbing, the sisters asked Anna Maria to assign them a penance; the girl who'd once lived sullenly among them had become a folk saint.[67]

In her last hours, Anna Maria tucked money from Julia Scott into a "little pocket book" to be given to her brothers. She asked that her sisters, Bec—still secretly limping—and Catherine, be brought to her, and the girls knelt by her bed to sing a hymn.[68] Rose White came, and as she said Jesus's name over and over, Anna gaspingly repeated it. When the girl's mind wandered, Elizabeth knelt at the foot of her bed, holding a crucifix high and willing her daughter not to falter. "Unite yourself to your suffering Jesus in the divine sacrifice," she urged. A Mass was said in the chapel, Anna Maria kissed a crucifix held to her mouth, and she died.

Realizing that her daughter lay with her hands gripping each other, Elizabeth commanded that the prayerful gesture not be disrupted. The sisters cut off Anna's nightdress and made a shroud to slip over her arms, hands still clasped. "The dear spotless beloved Soul is gone," Elizabeth wrote Sadler a few days later. "[I] left her with Harriet and Cecil in the sacred wood."[69]

PART 5

BECOMING MOTHER SETON

17

Death, Judgment, Hell, Heaven

ELIZABETH SETON HAD KNOWN grief intimately all her life, but her child's death staggered her. She prayed. She reminded herself that Anna Maria had "Departed for heaven." She even copied out lines from Young's *Night Thoughts*, a poem she'd loved as a melancholy teenager in Manhattan. "Nothing is Dead but wretchedness and pain," she wrote, "Nothing is Dead but what encumbered, galled, Blocked up the pass, and barred from real Life." Nothing helped. "The Separation from my Angel has left so new and deep an impression on my mind," she told Sadler, "that if I was not obliged to live in [my other children] . . . ." Elizabeth left the thought unfinished. "Never by a free act of the mind would I ever regret his Will," she wrote firmly.[1]

She did not resent God's will, and she did not doubt God's existence. What plagued her, beyond sheer sorrow, was an overwhelming sense of sinfulness. Everyone's sinfulness including even Anna's. When Anna lay dying, Elizabeth had taken comfort in the finitude of her suffering, compared with the mercy of eternal life. Now the logic turned against her. Had Anna paid *too* small a price? Elizabeth wondered how any human being could reach salvation, given the immense distance between human nature and God's. This was a new question in her long contemplation of the meaning of suffering, and she had no answer to it. She drifted through her days in a stupor. "To tell you the truth," she later wrote George Weis, "for three months after Nina was taken I was so often expecting to lose my senses and my head was so disordered that unless for the daily duties always before me I did not know much what I did or what I left undone."[2]

When word reached Manhattan that Anna Maria had died, Mary and Wright Post set out for Maryland. There had been too many losses, and it was time to mourn together. They wanted to comfort Elizabeth, but on their arrival she hid her distress, unwilling to reveal that she felt bereft of God's peace. So successful was Elizabeth's performance that Mary marveled at her happiness. "It seem'd to me that I had actually seen an order of beings who had nothing to do with the ordinary cares of this life," she wrote after returning to New York, "and were so far admitted to the society of the blessed as to take pleasure in the same employments while they were at the same time exempt from the solicitude for, from having ceased to have a value for what actually occupy the attention of Mortals."[3]

From the evidence of surviving documents, the sisters and boarders were as unaware as Mary Post of Elizabeth's profound distress. But her surviving daughters, Kit and Bec, watched her closely, fearing their mother might slip from their grasp and take the known world with her. "If only a head ache is discovered," Elizabeth wrote, "the countenance of both is changed in a minute." When Kit saw a fleeting sadness cross her mother's face, she jumped into her arms and wept.

One anxious guardian hovered just beyond Elizabeth's view: John Dubois. Dubois thought she had taken "exaggerated pleasure" in Anna's pious suffering and had felt "excessive fear" that the girl might "say or do something too human when in the presence of others." What others had seen as proof of a magnificent spiritual life, Dubois saw as evidence of a disordered one. He did not confide his worries to John Carroll or William Dubourg, whose admiration for Elizabeth he knew. He turned instead to Simon Bruté, the young priest who'd come with Nagot from France just months earlier.

At heart a steward, Dubois knew which fields lay unterraced and which buildings unplastered, and he found tools, time, and labor to attend them. Believing that the woman all called Mother lacked a well-ordered religious life, he set about remedying that situation too. Dubois coolly judged himself unsuited to the task; Bruté, more contemplative and effusive than he, was the workman he wanted. So he requested that the Baltimore Sulpicians assign Bruté to Emmitsburg. The valley, mountain, and surrounding parish were short-handed, Dubois explained. It made sense for Bruté to be dispatched to teach at the Mount and help Father Duhamel tend the parish; while he was there, he could also direct Elizabeth Seton.

Dubois wrote to Bruté on Maryland's eastern shore, where the young priest was preaching and trying, as he put it, to "force this dreadful English into my backward head."[4] He described the pain and confusion he saw in Elizabeth: "A hundred times I wanted to probe this wound," he wrote, "it is only lately that I dared to touch it." He explained that Bruté could help, but only if he refused to succumb to Elizabeth's charisma: "For many years she has been flattered too much." "Do not flatter her," he commanded. Bruté must instead "try to make her explain herself on such points as humility, obedience, detachment from all things even from her children in God and out of love for God, renunciation of one's own will, the love of discipline, of uniformity, of the rule—in a word [to make herself clear] on the religious life."

Dubois felt Elizabeth's charisma no less than other clergy did. But he believed her powerful spirit and mind were not yet formed to their purpose. Devotion to God, courage, knowledge of Catholic teaching: these she possessed, but these were not enough. The key—the key to everything—was following the rule in letter and spirit. He did not think Elizabeth lacked inspiration, but rather that she needed to be guided toward self-reflection and self-regulation; her brilliance and strong will required a brilliant and strong-willed director. "How great a soul this work would demand!" Dubois exclaimed to Bruté. "God grant that you may know how to treat [Elizabeth's] soul," he continued, "what a fabric! But like gold brocade, rich and heavy indeed, but hard to handle." Dubois's criticism was born of humility and admiration. "It would take a saint of the highest caliber, a St. Francis de Sales," he mourned, "and I am so insignificant."[5]

The Sulpicians did not fully understand Dubois's passionate desire that Bruté direct Elizabeth, but they agreed to assign him to Emmitsburg since there was much work to be done, and the priest cheerfully agreed to go. Opposition came from an unexpected source: John Carroll. The archbishop worried that the sisters might turn Bruté into their "advocate" against other clergy, and he thought the work Dubois proposed beneath Bruté's capabilities. Bruté should be training priests at the seminary in Baltimore, not sent "to fill the office of a director of some devout

FIGURE 17.1. Fritz Hoelzer, *Simon Bruté*. Courtesy of the Rhoads Memorial Archive, Mount St. Mary's University, Emmitsburg, MD.

women."[6] That was a startlingly dismissive phrase, and Carroll quickly gentled it, insisting that he was "far from meaning to deprecate" the women's work. But that was just it: the sisterhood was women's work. Sisters could not say Mass, offer Communion, or absolve Catholics of their sins. Only priests could animate the vast spaces of the new nation with Catholic sacramental life. Therefore Bruté should go to Baltimore and train young men to the priesthood. But the Sulpicians disagreed, and Carroll did not press the point. Bruté left Maryland's eastern shore for the foothills of the Blue Ridge.

Arriving at St. Joseph's House, he found a still stupefied Elizabeth. Unexpectedly, he encouraged her to plunge into her grief without embarrassment or restraint. Likely at Bruté's direction (he was a lifelong collector and chronicler), she began to gather every note and letter of Anna Maria's that she could find; their evidence of piety began to renew her hope for her daughter's soul. "Eternity was Anna's darling word," she wrote excitedly to Eliza Sadler, "I find it written in every thing that belonged to her, music, books, copys, the walls of her little chamber, every where that word." By the time of Anna Maria's birthday, Elizabeth's terror had faded and she again thought of her daughter as a paragon: "It appears to me I never saw or shall see any thing to be compared to her."[7] Dubois mistrusted this kind of adulation. But Bruté saw Elizabeth's belief in God's mercy returning, and for the moment that seemed enough.

As the fog of anguish lifted, a new worry glimmered: Elizabeth noticed the limp Bec had hidden since winter. How, she wondered, could a simple fall on the ice have so damaged a healthy child? Robert Goodloe Harper, always attentive to Elizabeth and the Emmitsburg institutions, helped bring the little girl to the Chatards' home in Baltimore; despite the physician's efforts and his wife Marie-Francoise's tender care, Bec's painful hip did not improve. "Unite all your pains to the pains of our dearest," Elizabeth urged her, reminding her youngest daughter that she was a "child of Eternity."[8] Rebecca had witnessed her sister's months of patient agony. She had no intention of complaining about a painful leg.

WAR AND STRUGGLE

Although Bec did not realize it, the Baltimore she'd visited was a city gripped by rumors of war. France, Great Britain, and the United States had been locked in an unhappy triangle since Elizabeth's own girlhood, but through years of conflict, the United States had never been drawn into open battle. In the spring of 1812, that seemed about to change. Baltimore's merchants anxiously pondered possibilities, and in Washington, D.C., citizens (the Caton sisters among them) crowded the Senate's galleries to hear Henry Clay and the other war hawks exhort the nation to action. Most of the Carroll clan, including Robert Goodloe Harper, believed that the English were no more troublesome, and far more kindred, than the French. Better to arm privateers and work for compromise, they argued, than go to war with America's powerful cousin. But the war hawks' vigorous confidence carried the day, and in summer Congress narrowly voted to declare war.

The denizens of Mount St. Mary's and St. Joseph's House followed the debates, the summoning of troops, and the first hints of war on the high seas through public gazettes and urgent letters from well-connected family members. When a critic of the war and associate of Robert Goodloe Harper, the Baltimore publisher Alexander C. Hanson, was attacked by a mob—and one of his supporters left for dead—an outraged Charles Carroll of Carrollton made noises about leaving the state.[9] The moment passed, but no one doubted difficult days lay ahead.

Now sixteen, Elizabeth's older son, William, wanted nothing more than to join the navy. He obeyed his mother's command to continue his studies, but his days of contentedly rambling the mountain were over. Margaret Murphy Burke's son Charles Murphy left the Mount and signed on with the crew of a privateer.[10] For a third young man of different ambitions, the school proved a refuge: Dubois observed that he entered Mount St. Mary's in 1812 "to escape the necessity of military service."[11]

In St. Joseph's House, the women followed news of the war, but their own greatest danger remained illness; that year there were a startling number of casualties. Elizabeth suffered from coughing and shortness of breath. Mary Diana Harper, who had shared a room with Anna Maria long into the latter's illness, was in delicate health. Ellen Thompson was sick. So was Maria Burke, and as fall progressed, her health broke entirely. Once again, a young woman, in pain and scarcely able to breathe, fixed her eyes on Elizabeth and held tight to a crucifix. "I have him—will not let him go," Maria gasped. On an October morning, not long after Dubois gave the young woman last rites, Margaret Burke and Elizabeth watched as Maria pressed her crucifix to her heart, dropped her head, and died.[12]

"What delight," Elizabeth wrote later that day, "to have been and to be still her Mother—the natural one was present but the spiritual one who had all her dear little Secrets of the Soul was the dearest."[13] Had she read Elizabeth's claim, Margaret Burke would not have taken offense. Her daughter had come to seem far more a Sister of Charity than she was a Burke. Margaret herself, by contrast, no longer felt at home at Emmitsburg, having become increasingly unhappy in her role as a "dependent." With Maria dead and Charles off chasing British ships, she decided it was time to move on. After ensuring that her younger children could continue their education at St. Joseph's House and Mount St. Mary's, Margaret moved her few possessions to Emmitsburg, determined to start her own school. The valley and mountain would in the future be one strong-minded widow short.

Although she had not at first realized it, Maria Burke's death unsettled Elizabeth as well as Margaret; the equanimity she'd regained faltered. The wood where her daughter lay buried alongside Harriet and Cecilia had always seemed a welcome reminder that the afterlife lay just beyond the window of St. Joseph's House. But one day that fall it became for Elizabeth a place of horror. She knelt at Anna's grave, once again fearful for her daughter's soul. "Did She? adored, did she know?" she implored, agonized. Just then, she heard a strange "rattling sound" and looked down to see a "large and ugly" snake slithering over her daughter's grave. Elizabeth had begged for reassurance and been sent a serpent.

She lunged for the creature, dragging it toward a gate in the fence that enclosed the graves and hurling it away. She started to run but imagined herself leaving the gate untied and wild hogs digging her daughter from the earth. "My darling shall not be rooted by the hogs for you," she thought wildly. Even after fastening the gate, she could not throw off her terror and disgust. "Oh, my dear ones," she thought, "companions of worms and reptiles—and the beautiful Soul Where?"[14]

This was not blessed eternity but sin and decay, the snake in the garden, dirt and hogs and worms. Human suffering seemed endless but insufficient; it could never make up for sin, never earn God's grace. Yet without that grace, suffering and life itself were unbearable. Elizabeth would never have revealed such desperate thoughts to Dubois and perhaps not even to Archbishop Carroll. But she wrote an urgent, jagged account for Bruté. He neither scolded her for her lurid imagination nor patted her hand and told her not to worry. Instead, the French priest and the American Sister of Charity urgently conversed and prayed, and their friendship deepened into a true collaboration.

Beginning in those first difficult months, Bruté shared with Elizabeth a Catholicism that—perhaps for the first time since her conversion struggle—fully engaged her mind. He owned hundreds if not thousands of books, and as the two pondered suffering and grace they read and discussed centuries of Catholic writing. They also read the Bible; Elizabeth had underlined and annotated her Matthew Carey–printed Bible since Antonio Filicchi gave it to her, and in early 1813, Bruté presented her with a new one so that he might take the first and learn from its markings.[15] Their scholarly inquiries were of a distinctive kind: both Elizabeth and Bruté thought that the highest use of the human mind lay in worshipping God, and both believed that for all their reading and reflection, God was ultimately unknowable. This was the argument Elizabeth had loved in Rousseau's *Emile*; now she found it voiced by an orthodox Catholic priest who shared her love of the liturgies and traditions of the Church. Bruté's Catholicism, like Elizabeth's, engaged the emotions and senses as well as the mind. Saints' pictures and holy relics did not diminish God's immensity and otherness but rather acknowledged that people needed help to turn their finite minds toward infinity.[16]

Elizabeth and Bruté collaborated as equals. Pierre Babade had been "Père," but Bruté was "Frère," as eager that Elizabeth counsel him as he was willing to counsel. "I entreat you help me by all advices, and an utmost freedom of every remark," he told her once, and on another day offered a list of his reform efforts. (Number three was "Again and again I will watch my light French manners, even this morning too much of them.")[17] Other clergy, Protestant as well as Catholic, had coveted Elizabeth's prayers; they possessed ecclesiastical authority but turned— as had clergy throughout the centuries—to a spiritually gifted woman for charismatic inspiration. Bruté, however, was the first to request not only Elizabeth's blessing but her criticism. His respect never faltered, even when Elizabeth offered sharper commentary than he might have expected: "I seldom see you but in such wild enthusiasms of your own particular impression of the moment," she once wrote him, "that you can see nothing, hear nothing, but that one object."[18] Bruté's humble openness inspired Elizabeth's.

Bruté's humility was more than an ethical stance; it was linked to the intellectual and emotional dimensions of his faith. Formed in a French school of spirituality that outlined human insignificance against God's greatness, the Sulpician believed joy came from realizing that one was purposeless except as a vessel of God's love. "Our nothingness, and His goodness—our nothingness made so great by His goodness,—our nothingness made so great!" reads one of his many notes to Elizabeth.[19]

Trained as a physician, Bruté envisioned man's insignificance with an image sprung from science: the atom.[20] John Dalton had proposed the modern theory of the atom less than ten years earlier: tiny, indivisible particles formed the building blocks of all matter. Some saw, and see, such theories as incompatible with traditional understandings of the cosmos; two centuries after Dalton, the French biologist Jacques Monod declared that "the ancient covenant is in pieces; man at last knows that he is alone in the unfeeling immensity of the universe, out of which he emerged only by chance." Bruté saw in atomic theory something entirely different: the perfect expression of the gulf between God's immensity and the fragile finitude of earthly life. Man was infinitesimal but *not* alone. Contemplation of God revealed one's individual insignificance but also one's profound purpose: to be loved. Rather than eroding Bruté's faith, atomic theory offered a new way to understand and express it. "Ah! This world, atom disappears," he wrote in one of many passages inspired by the theory. "What then? O immense Eternity! Beautiful Eternity! Glorious." Elizabeth also found the language of atomic theory spiritually expressive; it conveyed the relational nature of spiritual life, not the coldness of a mechanistic universe. In a meditation on the necessity of feeling God's presence, she wrote that when a soul is able to "taste the joy" of God, it marvels at having ever attended to anything else, "all that we so value like atoms and nothings." "O God immense God," Elizabeth wrote of a moment of spiritual communion, "will your atom ever forget this Epiphany 1815."[21]

Bruté's humility and erudition deepened his collaboration with Elizabeth. So did his irremediably poor English. He simply could not command the language, so when he needed to instruct his English-speaking flock, he turned to Elizabeth. "Where you see two translations proposed blot out the worse," Bruté suggested one day, adding cheerfully, "except you may be obliged to blot out both, and contrive a new."[22] This was far from the first time Elizabeth had undertaken "man's work": she'd been her husband's secret clerk and served as sounding board for her physician father. Like those labors, her work with Bruté went publicly unacknowledged. But she knew that as a growing number of Emmitsburg's Catholics began to come to the Communion rail, it was to her own words as well as to Bruté's that they responded.

COMMUNITY

Through her work with Bruté, her translations of devotional literature and reflections on spiritual challenges, and the daily labor of the sisterhood and school, Elizabeth—Mother Seton—was refining her views of life in a community of prayer, service, and worship. Dubois had wanted just this. But she had been forced by personal and national circumstance to refine those views in a busy, outward-facing household rather than in a quiet cloister, or even in a community exactly like the Ursulines or the

French Daughters. Just as St. Joseph's House was distinctive, Elizabeth was beginning to produce a distinctive vision of religious life. At its heart lay not the detachment Dubois expected but attachment.

The sisterhood's Vincentian spirit and the demands of the academy drew Elizabeth away from the contemplative, socially passive spirituality to which she'd been inclined toward a more active engagement in the world. She embraced what she would not have chosen, and the daily work of school teaching gained a deeper meaning as she attended to those who struggled. Among them was Robert Goodloe Harper's daughter Mary Diana, who found it nearly impossible to comply with St. Joseph's rules, and whose intransigence was highlighted by her brother Charles's eerie perfection ("Send me a New Year's gift big enough for me to share it with my friends," Charles wrote in a characteristically virtuous letter to his parents, "for you know I would have no pleasure in enjoying it alone.")[23] Elizabeth disciplined Mary Diana, often sternly, but also felt a particular tenderness for the girl who found the world so difficult to navigate. Similarly, although she believed some of the young women who arrived at the novitiate were not suitable candidates for a religious life, she never exiled them from her affections. "You will be forever dear to me in Him who died for us," she wrote one such woman, "be sure of the unchangeable affection of EA Seton."[24]

Since her arrival in St. Joseph's Valley, Elizabeth had learned that she was more willful than she'd believed, less able to "look up" than she'd imagined, and more often deprived of a sense of God's presence than she'd hoped. In the place of her lost confidence grew a greater capacity for sympathy. Her letters to Julia Scott, always affectionate, grew more so. Julia's daughter was about to marry and set off for Europe, and Julia dreaded the loss of the young woman's companionship. Elizabeth might once have reminded her friend that such a thing was hardly a tragedy and perhaps even pointed to her own greater sorrows. Now she offered only tenderness. Your circumstances "are my near concern and interest me more than any thing in this world except the first ties of Nature," she told Julia.[25] Elizabeth was nearly as effusive with her old friend Eliza Sadler. "My own and dear Eliza," she responded when Sadler apologized for being a poor correspondent, "never had [I] one thought of you but love and dear remembrances." "Far from cooling," she assured Sadler, her love was "softened and endeared by every thought of the past."[26]

Elizabeth's acknowledgment that she thought fondly of the past, like her casual acknowledgment that she had first ties and near concerns, directly contradicted Dubois's belief that the religious life required "detachment from all things even from her children in God and out of love for God." Dubois had considerable Catholic teaching on his side. Teresa of Avila insisted that the women of her Carmelite order free themselves from all ties, even those they might form with each other. "Let no sister embrace another or touch her on the face and hands," she instructed. "The sisters should not have particular friendships but should include all in their love for one another."²⁷ Elizabeth knew these teachings but chose to create a different kind of community, one rooted in a different theory of the relationship between earthly affections and worship of God.

Elizabeth reunited ethical and spiritual elements of Catholic thought that had over the centuries tended to diverge.²⁸ She believed that contemplation of Christ's sufferings produced an awareness of the brokenness of all creation and the abundance of God's love, and that this awareness was the wellspring of both worship and compassion. In one sense, her views resemble those of contemplatives such as Julian of Norwich and Teresa of Avila. They believed that God's love in the face of humanity's sin should not just break hearts but break them open. "I desire to suffer, Lord, since you suffered," wrote Julian from the tiny cell in which she, a fourteenth-century anchorite, had voluntarily walled herself up. "Let your will be done in me in every way." Contemplating Christ's suffering and humanity's sinfulness eroded the boundaries of the self; only then could one be united with God and only through that union could one feel true compassion for others. Yet Elizabeth was no anchorite or even a Discalced Carmelite. She cared for her children, disciplined the boarders, wrote anxious letters to friends, and gave nicknames by the dozen. This was not simply because her life as a widow and mother made detachment impossible. She actively cultivated connection at every turn, and she did so knowing she departed from a central tenet of the monastic tradition. "I am not enabled as Jesus Christ to do miracles for others," she wrote, "but I may constantly find occasions of rendering them good offices and exercising kindness and good will towards them." Such offices were not sufficient without specific, loving attention to the people she helped. "Am I interested for [others]," she demanded, "sharing in their sorrow, compassionating their pains or rejoicing in their joy—for Christian charity requires all this of me." "How can I hope that God will bestow on me his graces and benefits," she continued, "if my heart is shut up from his members and children?"[29]

This ethos departed not only from tradition but from the self-protective detachment Elizabeth herself once cultivated. Closing off her heart had seemed the way to protect herself from loss. She no longer allowed herself that tactic; nor did she allow herself to close the door against those she found uncongenial. Love of the kind Elizabeth now advocated was less an emotion than a skill. In recent years, neuroscientists have used magnetic resonance imagery to demonstrate that practices such as Buddhist meditation leave physical traces in the brain; quite literally, they change the way practitioners think. Elizabeth believed that constant attentiveness to God and others would remake a person from the inside out. The substance she wished to remodel was not the brain but the soul, and what she was determined to enlarge was its capacity to love. "Your first step in this heavenly way," she wrote in one reflection, "is to contract a habit of the presence of God and the spirit of recollection—and let Divine Love cast out Fear. Fear nothing so much as not to love enough."[30]

John Dubois realized that Elizabeth and Bruté were fashioning a different theory and practice of spiritual life than the one he treasured. He also knew that the two found him as alien as they found each other kindred; Dubois counted minutes while Elizabeth and Bruté watched the sun. He accepted all of it, grateful to see Elizabeth creating a sustainable religious life, even if not the one he had expected. A low-grade irritation appears in Bruté and Elizabeth's accounts of Dubois, but they respected and loved him too. "I see plainly it is like changing an Ethiopian to pretend to preserve the spirit of detail which the charity and natural disposition of [Dubois] has made the Spirit of our Community," Elizabeth observed one day. "Long may our Lord spare him to it for who could ever be found to unwind the ball as he does and stop to pick out every knot—too happy I to break the knot and piece it again."[31]

In fact, Elizabeth's willingness to improvise depended on a deep respect for the sisterhood's rule and Dubois's meticulous maintenance of it. She relied on the serene rhythm of days and seasons, especially in months when she felt "like the dry and barren tree."[32] She marveled at the emergence of harmony in a house filled with women of diverse backgrounds and temperaments, not least hers and Rose White's. Had she lived long enough to see the hopeful start and quick demise of utopian communities such as Brook Farm, Elizabeth might have smiled in recognition. Virtue was nearly as unruly as vice. The rules of Catholic religious life took as their starting point human fractiousness, pettiness, and distraction and by doing so offered a framework in which self-restraint, gentleness, and love might emerge. When she'd first left Baltimore for the Blue Ridge, Elizabeth had thought that good people would create a good community. Now she believed as Dubois did: good communities created good people.

A year after Anna's death and months after the awful day in the garden, Elizabeth sat by the window, looking out onto the little wood and writing to Julia. "The white pailings appear thro' the trees," she told her friend. "Oh Julia my Julia if we may but pass our dear Eternity together—are you good, do you try to be good—I try with my whole heart I long so to get above this blue Horizon."[33] Sin, decay, ugliness—snake, worm, hog—were still real. But she could again feel the merciful pull of eternity.

18

WAR AND BUSTLE

WHILE THE SISTERHOOD and seminary continued their peaceful rounds of work and worship, the United States pursued its war with Great Britain. After a disastrous effort to invade Canada, Americans won important victories on the Great Lakes and in the Old Northwest, and Stephen Decatur became a naval hero with his capture of a British frigate, the *HMS Macedonian*. By spring of 1813, however, the British had strengthened their blockade of the Chesapeake, and a British fleet seemed poised to sail up the Patapsco River. Thousands of green troops assembled to defend Baltimore. The ships glided away but reappeared off Maryland's eastern shore, where the priests who managed St. Inigoes plantation uneasily eyed the waterways, expecting attack. Enslaved people sought freedom by joining the British lines or simply fleeing the plantations on which they labored; planters in Maryland's eastern regions sent slaves to the Blue Ridge and Frederick to forestall rebellion and escape.[1] Uneasiness grew there, too, and from Emmitsburg, where she was trying to make a go of her new school, Margaret Burke wrote her brother that "there have been serious apprehensions obtained here for some time of a revolt of the Negroes, so many of our Men being absent." A "Patrol," Margaret explained, had been established. It seems likely that the men and boys of St. Mary's participated.[2]

The aspirations of the enslaved make no appearance in documents of the sisterhood. Other consequences of the war do: when disruptions in trade strapped the finances of tuition-paying families, the sisters began to reduce the use of sugar and substitute coarse cotton for linen.[3] The turnpike to Baltimore, always rutted, grew rougher as travelers avoided the newly dangerous waterways. Elizabeth found such deprivations trivial and the war a distant concern. "[I] now [have] some apprehension," she wrote Julia one day, "that all this war and bustle I hear is going on in the world may have troubled you in some particular manner."[4] Most days, the world troubled Elizabeth herself only in one "particular manner": it was to the world that she must soon release her sons.

It did not seem long since Will and Dick had been little boys. Now William wanted to join the navy, and Mary Post reminded her sister that both sons must "learn to make their way through this world of care & business."[5] Elizabeth was not accustomed to taking counsel from Mary, and she thought that Richard, at least, could be kept at the Mount a while longer. Although he was growing tall, as the Seton men did, her younger son looked backward, not forward. "Mother," he said one day, after noticing that the sisters now kept a polite distance, "when I look at the Sisters and think of the happy days when we were little and we could run in their arms, I am obliged now to turn away I feel so sorry we are grown big and they do not treat us as children."[6] Elizabeth wasn't quite sure what to make of this determined boyishness, but she was pleased that it offered time for Richard's future to be decided. The opposite could be said of William. Elizabeth admired his eagerness to make his way in the world but found his insistent wish to join the navy profoundly upsetting. Not only was the navy dangerous in wartime, but her brother-in-law Henry Seton's wrecked and alcohol-sodden life suggested it was hazardous even during the peace.

Determined to keep William from a life at sea, Elizabeth encouraged him to pursue a career as a merchant, as his father and grandfather had done. But how? The Seton clan could no longer arrange junior positions. (James's son Alfred, unable to work in the family business, had the year before signed on as a clerk with John Jacob Astor, whose fortunes had risen as the Setons' fell.) Robert Goodloe Harper was a faithful and well-connected friend, but he was a lawyer and politician rather than a trader, and the war's slowed economy made all clerkships scarce. Elizabeth tried not to care about her sons' earthly success, claiming to Julia that she was a "hard hearted mother" who told her children their happiness lay only "beyond the grave."[7] But she worried that William's eternal fate might itself be put in jeopardy if he joined the navy. Anxiety clawed at her heart.

Unlike their brothers, Catherine and Rebecca still fit seamlessly into Elizabeth's world. Kit quietly excelled at everything she tried, her proud mother reporting that she was "excellent at reading, writing, spelling and the needle, and above all arithmetic almost without my knowing it." Kit was happy to do most things without other people's knowing it, and in a family who offered and demanded effusive declarations of love, the thirteen-year-old practiced a less demonstrative affection. "Since you desire it so much I will write to you," she wrote her sister one day. "The reason generally . . . I write to the other girls is they write to me and I answer it. But you see you don't write to me. You know whenever you write to me I answer it."[8] What, one can almost hear the girl thinking, could be easier to understand than that? Like John Dubois, Catherine was more inclined to do than to say; also like Dubois, she nevertheless felt deep love for those around her. The pain in Rebecca's hip horrified Kit. I hope your leg is not "paining you much," she wrote her sister in Baltimore, adding that whatever happened, "I dare say you will be resigned to it." "I feel quite lonely without you," Catherine also reported, sounding the slightest bit surprised.[9]

Rebecca was as effusive as her sister was reserved, and where Catherine excelled at studies, Bec devoted herself to becoming the "child of the Cross" her mother wished her to be. Her fall on the ice had left her permanently lamed. She walked with a crutch and was sometimes carried by an enslaved man named Joe.[10] Elizabeth assured her youngest child that her misfortune came "from the hand of our dear compassionate Master who no doubt intend[s] to take more care of this darling and bless her more than the rest." Some children might have asked what kind of God gave little girls gifts such as this. Having grown up within the compass of her mother's faith and resignation, Rebecca did not. Her deepest fear was that she might be *too* healthy and outlive her mother and sister. "*If I should be left behind*," she fretted after Anna's death.[11]

Rebecca was surrounded by people who suffered without complaint, even joyfully. Sisters including Benedicta Corish, Ellen Thompson, and Agnes Duffy were often ill, and Elizabeth herself coughed and wheezed through the summers. No one seemed to fear death: on the contrary, so welcome a guest was it that Simon Bruté once turned from his elegant descriptions of the nothingness of human life to remind the women that they must nonetheless appreciate it. "Let us turn," he exhorted the sisters, "from this amiable view of death, of Eternity, of thoughts of heaven, towards this life in which we are detained." "Let us not refuse to live," he commanded.[12] If she heard Bruté's exhortation, Bec paid it little mind. Instead she wrote of her determination to ponder "Death, Judgment, Hell, heaven," and to fight "Pride, distraction in my prayers, and attachment to my own opinion & will."[13] "Oh this leg," Bec told her approving mother, "it will carry me to heaven."[14]

"THE SUN IN THE HEAVENS"

In July of 1813, four years after the first band of would-be sisters arrived at a mountainside cabin and one year after the formal adoption of their regulations, eighteen women pronounced their first annual vows as Sisters of Charity. Before the ceremony, they undertook a spiritual retreat. Elizabeth encouraged them to "promote [God's] interest in every other soul and to cherish it first in each other . . . united to him together by the bands of our common love and service."[15] The next day, the women quietly took vows to live in poverty, chastity, and obedience for one year.

Rose White, the woman who had once seemed at risk of pulling the sisterhood in two, was there, now living peacefully, if still awkwardly, under Elizabeth's direction. Cecilia O'Conway (who had stopped using the name Veronica after Cecilia Seton's death) still longed for a more contemplative life than St. Joseph's House provided, but she too took vows, grateful to live within Elizabeth's direction and determined to conform herself to the Vincentian rule. Elizabeth Boyle, the young convert who had defied her mother's wishes by making her way to Emmitsburg, took vows, and so did Margaret George, the Baltimore widow who had leaned in at a Baltimore dinner party to overhear news of the sisterhood's fate. Madame Guèrin, still eager to sacrifice her comfort for God, became a sister, and so did Susan Clossy. The little community contained women who had never married as well as widows, converts as well as lifetime Catholics, American born and Irish.[16] Each had exercised her will in order to arrive in this unexpected place, and each had agreed to constrain her will in order to live within its rule.

Elizabeth offered no more commentary on this vow taking than she had on her first. The vows mattered to her: at the nadir of her relations with Father John David, she had declined to renew them precisely because she took them seriously. Nonetheless, the woman who loved Church rituals took little interest in this one; even without Carroll's restraining influence, it wasn't the making of the promise but its keeping that commanded her attention. And in that keeping, in the daily work of living within the sisterhood's rule, Elizabeth felt increasingly sure-footed. When Julia asked her to describe her "present situation," she replied serenely. "Dearest Julia," she answered, "it is as uninterrupted as the sun in the heavens . . . health much mended and spirits generally pretty even."[17] Elizabeth habitually offered Julia only the rosiest view of her life, but even to Bruté, she now had little unease to confide. "I am so in love now with the rules," she wrote, "that I see the bit of the bridle all gold, and the reins all of silk."[18]

Governeur Ogden would have seen that line as proof of Catholicism's oppression; Elizabeth meant it as a description of liberty. Despite Ogden's conviction that Americans reviled "nunneries"—and despite Elizabeth and Dubois's own belief that Protestant animosity was an ongoing

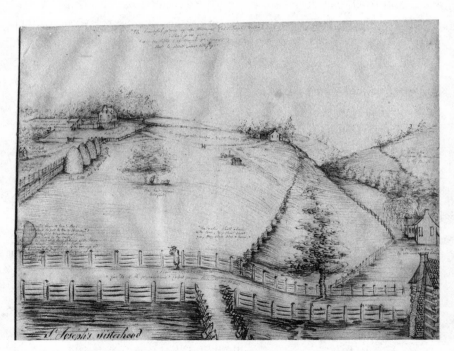

Figure 18.1. Bruté sketch of the sisterhood. APSL 1–3–3–13 152. Courtesy of the Daughters of Charity Province of St. Louise Archives, Emmitsburg, Maryland.

danger—the convent sparked more fascination than mistrust. The religious ferment of the Second Great Awakening had not inspired a resurgence of antipopery, and although Ogden predicted St. Joseph's House would be razed to the ground, it faced no obvious public disfavor. On the contrary, Protestant families sent girls to St. Joseph's Academy, and it was the French philosophes whom Elizabeth had once admired, rather than the pious Catholic women whom she now led, who were thought incompatible with the republic's good order. Pious women stood at the center of Second Great Awakening Christianity, and the black-flanneled Sisters of Charity were to many Americans a recognizable if exotic example. Rather than summoning a vision of oppression and depravity, the Emmitsburg "nunnery" exerted a romantic appeal. "Dear Lady Abbess," a young Baltimore woman named Henrietta Dukeheart wrote in carefully formed letters, "I wish to know the rules of your happy Convent. Dear lady I wish to be with you as I have heard so much of your goodness to your young ladys that is under your protection." Dukeheart's spelling was dubious but her intention clear. "O how happy I shold be to see you my dear Lady & for you to give me good instruct[io]ns to love my God, and then how happy I would be to have so good a friend as you."[19]

Henrietta did not enter the sisterhood, but in the months and years to come, many others presented themselves as candidates, nearly one hundred during Elizabeth's lifetime.[20] The reputation of St. Joseph's Academy also spread; Bruté was delighted to receive a letter announcing that the English consul and his Catholic wife had five daughters they wished to send.[21] Boarders vied for certificates of "good behavior" and "good lessons," their parents appreciating the keen-eyed attention Elizabeth and the other teaching sisters offered. Some, such as a young woman named Mary Egan, decided to stay on and enter the novitiate. Others left without regret but remembered St. Joseph's House as a place of unparalleled serenity. Former students wrote to Elizabeth seeking prayers and counsel. Even Louisa Caton, who thoroughly enjoyed her life in society (on coming to know Louisa, Julia Scott drily observed that it was probably best she had not become a nun) wrote and visited. The connection to Emmitsburg preserved a part of herself Louisa did not want to lose.

And then there was Mary Diana Harper, as devoted to breaking the written and unwritten rules of St. Joseph's Academy as other girls were to honoring them. Often ill, Mary Diana viewed her physical suffering as a nuisance, not a cross, and coughs and stomach pains did not rob her of energy to defy the "angels." Disdainful of punishment—Elizabeth confined her to her room and restricted her diet—and impervious to moral suasion, Mary Diana called St. Joseph's a "vile and bad . . . house" and insisted she found it easier to be good at home. By 1814, the girl had thrashed her way almost to expulsion, which may have been her goal all along. But Elizabeth was not quite defeated. Knowing that Mary Diana hated to displease her father as much as she loved to vex the sisters, she asked Robert Goodloe Harper to tell his daughter how he would feel should she be banished from the school. Harper did, and Mary Diana folded her tent. She would never be as docile as her brother—"I pray for your happiness every day of my life," Charles wrote his grandfather in yet another perfectly crafted letter home—but she agreed to do her lessons and end her outright war.[22]

Harper was deeply grateful for Elizabeth's attention to his unruly daughter and his compliant son. He also treasured something else: the opportunity to be benevolent. He answered Elizabeth's anxious questions about tuition—raise it, he advised, the parents would pay—and adroitly helped Dubois dun Charles Carroll of Carrollton for overdue payments.[23] Harper also hunted remedies for Bec's lameness and offered his home to Kit should she wish to leave St. Joseph's for school vacations.

Religion was not the source of Harper's diligence; he had long since abandoned the Presbyterianism of his family, and he adopted his wife's Catholicism more as a familial allegiance than as a creed. Instead, Harper believed that thoughtful engagement in civic life was a moral obligation. In addition to aiding the Emmitsburg institutions and pursuing elected offices, he worked with Baltimore's Washington Society to establish a "free school" intended to prepare poor children to take a dignified place in the world by both educating them and rigorously surveilling their conduct.[24] Harper's civic benevolence proved a secular counterpart to Emmitsburg's Vincentian spirit.

Despite his many services, Harper's attention was divided; the War of 1812 continued, and the United States' prospects rose and fell. Harper had eventually come to support the war against England, but like many of Maryland's elite Catholics, he remained most offended by Napoleon Bonaparte. If it were not enough that Napoleon had taken the pope captive and seemed poised to rule much of Europe, the emperor had also insisted his brother Jerome abandon a well-connected young Maryland woman whom he'd married and given a son. (That son, also named

Jerome Bonaparte, was now a student at the Mount.) Within the Carroll clan, Napoleon had his own nickname, PP, for "Perfidy Personified." So it was delightful when news came that he had been decisively defeated at the battle of Leipzig and was on the retreat. "God send that the disturber of the world may meet with his deserved fate & punishment," Charles Carroll wrote his daughter.[25] Yet it soon became clear that Napoleon's comeuppance had an unwelcome consequence: Great Britain was free to turn its full attention to making war on the United States.

William Seton was now almost eighteen, and his determination to join the navy grew as the conflict intensified. Family friends pursued the possibility of a commission for him. "If it was not for the boundless love for Mother and Rebecca and Kitty," Elizabeth conceded, "he would probably be off." Determined her son should not "follow the drum" in this dangerous moment, she seized on a suggestion from Pierre Babade: perhaps the young man could be sent to apprentice with the Filicchis in Italy.[26] Elizabeth wrote to Antonio, from whom, because of disrupted Atlantic communications, she'd scarcely heard in years, and tentatively broached the subject. While she waited for a response, war lurched closer: a British armada commanded by Vice Admiral Alexander Cochrane sailed up the Chesapeake Bay and into the Patuxent River. Troops landed thirty-five miles south of Washington and began to march on the capital. (Louisa and Elizabeth Caton were visiting a plantation along their path, and when the plantation's owner nervously invited a group of British officers to lunch, the Caton sisters patriotically declared they could not dine with their country's enemies.)[27] When the troops reached Bladensburg, Maryland, a town from which they could cross the Anacostia River and enter the capital, Americans engaged them in battle. Among the hastily assembled defenders was Robert Goodloe Harper. He had not seen military action since the Revolution, but he conducted himself bravely and emerged with an appointment as major general in the US Army. Harper's good conduct was one of the day's few bright spots: the Americans retreated so hastily that the battle was instantly dubbed the Bladensburg Races. Not long after, British soldiers strode through the halls of the White House, toasting the king with the president's wine. A fortuitous rain put out the fires the troops set, but when the British withdrew on August 26, the American capital lay scorched and humiliated.

Worse seemed to lie ahead: the British had their sights set on Baltimore, a city whose busy harbor and daring privateers made it of greater

strategic importance than Washington itself. Men and boys from Emmitsburg (though not, apparently, William) rushed eastward to help defend
the city, and Bruté went with them to offer his blessing. Weeks after the
near sacking of Washington, British troops bombarded Ft. McHenry.
Archbishop Carroll described the scene to an English friend. "The visit
of your countrymen," he wrote, "has nearly ruined several of my dearest connexions. . . . It was an awful spectacle to behold before us at
least 40 vessels great & small, and for about 25 hours five bomb ketches
discharging shells on the forts of upward 200 lb weight each. You may
suppose that we did not sleep much."[28] In the morning, Frances Scott Key
(whose family lived near Emmitsburg and whose sister Anna had married
Roger Taney in a ceremony presided over by John Dubois) was relieved to
find that the American flag still flew, and he began the poem that would
become the national anthem. Disaster was averted. Elizabeth hoped that
one way or another, her son William might yet escape the war.

MISSION

As the risk of invasion subsided, Dubois, Elizabeth, and Bruté turned
their attention to other news: an intriguing letter had arrived from
Rachel Montgomery in Philadelphia. The well-placed Catholic convert
was serving as "President of the Lady Managers" of the city's Catholic orphan asylum. Philadelphia had long been the home of ambitious
reform societies, and in recent years those efforts had come to include
more overt religious content; beginning in 1802, Presbyterians raised
funds to supply a chaplain for the city's hospital and jail, questioning
why Philadelphians had in the past been content to supply the poor's
"temporal wants" while overlooking their need for "the instructions and
consolations of the gospel."[29] The changing tone accorded with the rising
intensity of Christian expression throughout the nation, as benevolent
societies that, like Graham's poor widows' society, had once considered
others' souls beyond their purview became more explicitly evangelical.[30]

Philadelphia's Catholic orphan asylum differed in denomination but
not in ethos, its members concerning themselves with children's faith
as well as their earthly well-being. The asylum was among the first to
place children—many of whom had a living parent—in a central shelter.
There they were housed, fed, and offered Catholic religious formation.
This way of caring for and enclosing the poor would come to dominate

nineteenth-century poor relief efforts, but Philadelphia's asylum was in debt and poorly managed. Montgomery and Father Michael Hurley, now pastor of the city's St. Augustine parish, thought that the Sisters of Charity might do better. They proposed that a small mission be sent from St. Joseph's House to run the Philadelphia asylum, using $600 per year that the managers would provide.[31]

Elizabeth, Carroll, the council, and Dubois favored the plan as a welcome chance to more fully participate in the Vincentian tradition of service. The French tradition took on new meaning in the American context: a successful orphan asylum would demonstrate Catholicism's respectability by matching the benevolence of Protestant societies and by reducing the number of poor Catholic children visible on the streets.

While the British still prowled the Chesapeake, a decision was made to send a small delegation of sisters to Philadelphia. Elizabeth would remain Mother at Emmitsburg. It was Rose White who would lead the Philadelphia mission, bringing with her Susan Clossy and a third sister, Teresa Conroy. In September of 1814, the three women left the valley, traveling by land to avoid the danger still threatening the Bay. Diligent as ever, John Dubois accompanied the trio as far as Taneytown. He gave, Rose later recalled, "lessons of economy all the way."[32]

The women's arrival in the city was less than triumphant. Their carriage driver had no idea where the orphan asylum was, nor, it seemed, did anyone else. "You might as well ask a pig about a holy day as to ask those people where St. Joseph's Asylum is," Rose heard the frustrated driver exclaim. At last, the little group came upon St. Augustine's and Father Michael Hurley, who welcomed them to Philadelphia. The asylum proved to have few children, Rose later recalled, and those who were there were "lying three and four in a bed" and "running the streets like so many little ragged beggars."[33] Rose had at her command only the labor of three women and $600, a sum diminished by wartime inflation. She set to work.

At St. Joseph's House, Rose's inclination to fix the things she felt needed fixing had often left her at odds with Elizabeth. Although they lived in greater harmony after Father David's departure for Kentucky, the strain had never entirely left. Rose blamed herself, telling John Carroll that she possessed "an unhappy disposition of impatience, which has caused myself and others much pain in this blessed family."[34] In Philadelphia, Rose was free to put her temperament to use. Her decisiveness and frugality soon placed the orphanage on solid financial footing; before long, the sisters found bills forgiven and barrels of flour left at their door. As conditions at the asylum improved, more children were given into its care.[35] The Vincentian tradition born in ancien régime France was proving of ready use in the new republic, and the woman whom Elizabeth had feared might sunder the sisterhood was shepherding it into a new era of service.

The Philadelphia mission demonstrated the power of the Vincentian model, in which highly competent women, freed of the responsibilities to husbands and children that interrupted the benevolent labors of most Protestant peers, carried out the charitable work of the Church. In a nation with few priests (and some of those unreliable) and simmering mistrust of immigrant Catholics, the value of the Sisters of Charity seemed clear. Among those who admired them was Elizabeth's old nemesis, John David. David had never understood the unhappiness his heavy-handed direction caused her, so he saw no awkwardness in writing to Dubois and Dubourg with a request: he wanted to establish a band of Sisters of Charity in his new home of Kentucky.

David and Flaget had been laboring for the Bardstown see's Catholic population amid rugged conditions and competition from the evangelical Protestant revivals burning through the region.[36] Flaget put his hopes in a seminary, believing that only priests could save the Church from disorder and irrelevance. Despite having tried Elizabeth's patience with what felt like his disrespect for the women's judgment, David did not think priests could do the job alone; the frontier needed sisters. In 1813, David wrote Bruté that he and Bishop Flaget were establishing a women's religious community in Kentucky, and he'd like it to be united to the Sisters of Charity of St. Joseph's. Might he be sent the regulations the sisters had adopted? And might David also be sent Sister Rose White? She would, he explained, be the perfect person to set the sisterhood on its proper course.[37]

It's difficult to tell from the surviving documentation precisely what kind of union David and Flaget had in mind, and it is not clear how modestly or imperiously they made their requests. One thing is unmistakable: John Dubois's wrath. He found every last bit of David's proposal misguided and high-handed. Was the debt-encumbered Emmitsburg sisterhood to be financially bound to a fledgling organization on an even more remote frontier? Was David planning to establish a novitiate in Kentucky, thereby creating a situation in which two sets of women, formed under potentially incompatible principles, were part of the same religious community? And why on earth should David expect him to hand over the invaluable Rose White? The Philadelphia mission extended the sisters' community; Dubois feared that a Kentucky sisterhood under David's direction would dilute it.

Dubois discussed David's proposal with Elizabeth and the council. Their initial reaction is as difficult to reconstruct as David's precise proposal, but Elizabeth had been extricated once from David's oversight, and she felt no desire to come under his surveillance, even indirect and remote, again. Dubois wrote a series of urgent letters to John Carroll, insisting that the archbishop refuse David's request. David tried to counter, but neither he nor the aged prelate was a match for Dubois. Faced with the priest's indefatigable opposition, the obvious risk of uniting two fragile institutions separated by a great distance, and the sisters' own quiet opposition, Archbishop Carroll did not insist on a union between the Kentucky and Emmitsburg houses. After protesting that Dubois had misunderstood his plans, David abandoned his request. He continued to create a Kentucky sisterhood—known as the Sisters of Charity of Nazareth—but the communities remained separate.[38] Maryland's Sisters of Charity retained St. Joseph's House as their single motherhouse, and Elizabeth Seton as their only Mother.

"A GOOD AND UNEXPECTED PROSPECT"

Advent fell on the Blue Ridge. Rose and her companions sent encouraging accounts of their work in Philadelphia. Britain and the United States seemed likely to come to terms. Napoleon had been safely contained on Elba and John David safely contained in Kentucky. Richard Seton remained his sweet, boyish self, one day surprising his sister Rebecca, ill at the infirmary, with a bouquet of wildflowers. Bec's lameness had not improved, but her health seemed otherwise sound and her patient piety moved all who knew her. Catherine continued in peaceful self-sufficiency. She pored over her mother's commonplace books, intrigued by their messages from another, more cosmopolitan world, but she was content within St. Joseph's House.

The commonplace books were just one of the links connecting Manhattan to St. Joseph's. Elizabeth's female relatives and friends sent word of babies born, courtships formed and thwarted, and deaths sudden and slow. St. Joseph's was not an alien nunnery but a serene refuge they vowed one day to visit, although most suspected they never would. Elizabeth's young half sisters Helen and Mary Fitch Bayley created deeper relationships with her than they'd known before she left, sending her affection and news, such as that their inveterate bachelor brother Richard was now a happily married father preparing to purchase a farm in Yonkers and that Helen herself was engaged (in the way of the intertwined clans) to a relative of Eliza Sadler.[39] Family relations that had died down to their roots sent forth new shoots.

Peace seeming possible at home and abroad, Baltimore's Sulpicians decided that Simon Bruté should travel to France. There, in addition to seeing his mother and purchasing books, he would try to connect the Sulpicians in the United States with the reawakening French Society.[40] As Bruté prepared for the trip, men who had left France in a blind rush years earlier pressed lists of names on him, hoping to learn the fate of family members and to convey long-delayed expressions of love. Elizabeth saw a different possibility: the priest could bring her son William with him to Europe. She had not received a reply to her letter to Antonio and had no idea whether the Filicchis wanted William as a clerk. But she decided that Bruté's trip was providential. A "good and unexpected prospect for my poor William of going with Mr. Bruté to Europe" has emerged, she wrote John Carroll. The embarrassment of sending William to a family and business who weren't expecting him paled before the alternative. "The sad prospect of his entering the army," Elizabeth told the archbishop, "makes every thing desirable in comparison with it."[41]

All that was left was to tell Antonio. He had helped other relatives, she reminded her old benefactor, and her sons possessed a "tender claim on you as the Father of their true and eternal welfare." "Do not be angry but forgive and love your poor little bad Sister, but ever yours in true heart and soul of Eternity," she wrote. William was to sail for Europe and make his way to Livorno. "Dear Antonio right or wrong there it is."[42]

19

Our Meaning

WILLIAM SETON AND SIMON BRUTÉ left Emmitsburg in February of 1815, traveling by road and turnpike to Baltimore and then by clipper to New York. Eager to retain Elizabeth Seton's spiritual companionship, Bruté brought with him her much underlined and annotated Bible. William traveled with a set of instructions—neatly numbered and unmistakably tear-stained—from his mother. She cautioned him not to take on debt, to show gratitude to the Filicchis, and, more interestingly, not to disapprove of what he might find in Europe's cities. "I beg you so much," she wrote, "not to give way to National prejudices, but to allow for many customs and manners you will see." Elizabeth had set aside much that she'd believed as a young New Yorker but not her cosmopolitanism. "Why should not others have their peculiarities as well as we have ours?" she asked her son. There might be one best faith, but there was no best nation. She also reminded William that he was both her child and a child of God. "My stroke of Death," she wrote urgently, "would be to know that you have quitted that path of Virtue which alone can reunite us forever."[1]

William's eyes were fixed more on New York than on heaven. As conscious as his mother that he'd barely left the Blue Ridge since a boy, he was so determined not to say anything wrong that he said almost nothing. Eliza Sadler at first suspected he'd been commanded not to enjoy himself among New York's heterodox horde. "Wm has an exterior so grave," she wrote Elizabeth, "that one might be induced to think it not natural at his age and think him under some restraint." Bruté assured Sadler that William was simply reserved, and she and the Seton clan showered the young man with attention and presents.[2] William was in fact thrilled to see proof that his family still claimed a place in the New Yorkers' hearts, and he breathlessly detailed the largesse shown him: "shirts cravats handkerchiefs and all kind of underclothing all new."[3] But he offered only the tersest of thanks. "A true Mountain Boy—too timid even to acknowledge an obligation in a manly way," he later judged himself.[4]

Simon Bruté was not timid. He loved meeting Elizabeth's friends and relatives, even urging one of her old associates to save his soul by converting to Catholicism. The object of those exhortations was none other than John Henry Hobart, by then a bishop in the Episcopal Church. Bruté's proselytizing letter went unanswered. Despite its awkward moments, the visit strengthened ties between New York and Emmitsburg and sent William and Bruté off to Europe in good cheer. Back in the valley, Elizabeth, Catherine, and Rebecca traced the voyage on a globe Bruté himself had made. "Our separation was truly painful," Bec wrote her beloved older brother, "but yet we have a continual comfort in our hearts that you have not gone to the Navy."[5]

Elizabeth and Dubois prayed for William during days also filled with work and cordial disagreement. Dubois questioned Elizabeth's decision to admit Protestant girls to St. Joseph's Academy. This was a chapter in an ongoing argument: years earlier, the Parisian superior of the Sulpicians had worried that "mixing" of students at St. Mary's in Baltimore might lead to scandal and "religious indifference." Emery's objections were overcome by John Carroll's insistence that the benefits of good relations outweighed any risks, but in the years since, the Sulpicians in the United States had become convinced that admitting Protestants diluted the spiritual and educational atmosphere they wanted to create. John Dubois had originally admitted Protestant boys to Mount St. Mary's, but he decided in 1813 that the school could and should survive without them. As was often the case, Dubois's reasoning was distinctive from his brethren's: it emerged from his respect for the nation's pluralism, not distaste for it. He thought Protestant boys might take it upon themselves to convert to Catholicism, and rather than rejoicing in the conquest, he worried over the arguments with parents that would inevitably ensue.

"How would you like your Charles to become a Methodist because his ship's crew were all Methodists," he once demanded of Rose White.[6]

Elizabeth's thinking on the subject had changed over the years. Immediately after her conversion she'd told her startled neighbors that she wanted to evangelize any Protestant schoolchildren put in her care, and she'd chosen Georgetown for her boys in part because it was said to contain only Catholics. Now Elizabeth not only wanted her own school to admit Protestants, but she also declined to evangelize them. She believed with John Carroll that the ill effects of Catholic self-seclusion outweighed those of mixing, and she hoped that simply exposing Protestant children to the Catholic atmosphere of St. Joseph's might plant the seeds of the faith without sowing the conflict Dubois feared. Her judgment held sway. That spring, eleven Protestant girls were among St. Joseph's boarders, their parents seeing the school as a place of refinement and generic Christian teaching and Elizabeth content to let them think so.

Elizabeth and Dubois disagreed without acrimony, confident in each other's good intentions. Yet respect did not bring intimacy, and Bruté's absence drew them no closer. Instead, both planned to keep a journal in which to share their thoughts with the absent priest rather than with each other. No journal of Dubois's remains, but Elizabeth's survives, its entries marked by feast days rather than by calendar date, as if to honor the sacred world she and Bruté wished to inhabit. Because she also inhabited the mundane world of prying eyes, Elizabeth wrote the journal in a tiny hand, rendering it illegible to anyone who might walk by while she wrote.

In the absence of Bruté's ebullient sympathy, Dubois's practicality grated on Elizabeth. She lamented the priest's apparent indifference to feast days and to the sights, sounds, and smells of Catholic tradition. Even when she praised him, she kept an amused distance. Dubois is always "planning and laying out [the] future," she observed in the journal; "He lives in futurity, and I in *the past*." "To tell you how gay and cheerful he is is impossible," she wryly declared on another day, "it puts me out of patience almost."[7] Elizabeth blamed her own "bad heart" for her irritations. But the woman who saw and tried to heal the secret pains of so many remained oddly oblivious to those of Dubois. "I spare him all that depends on me," she wrote in her journal for Bruté, "You understand." Elizabeth's refusal to turn to Dubois—her obvious belief that only Bruté "understood"—was itself one of Dubois's burdens. "Your brother cried out to me what he had lost in [your] absence," she told Bruté, "and could hardly restrain his tears at my louder cry, "My God what then have I not lost."[8] She did not understand the blow she had struck or the man who resolutely absorbed it.

The journal also reveals Elizabeth's impatience with a second priest, the recently ordained John Hickey. She and the sisters doted on the young clergyman, even giving him homemade bitters and candy when they feared he was ill. But his careless sermons drove Elizabeth to distraction. A few months after Bruté's departure, she listened unhappily as Hickey gave an "evidently lazy" sermon to the full pews of the mountain chapel. When he afterward blurted out, "I did not trouble myself much about it Mam," Elizabeth gave him "a scolding he will remember," reminding him that "a priest holds the honor of God on his lips." When Hickey began to stammer out a defense—"But prayer—" Elizabeth gave no quarter. "Prayer and *preparation too*," she told him sharply.[9]

She blamed the young priest and his dreary sermons for the declining fervor of the Emmitsburg congregation: "5 or 6 communions only . . . where there used to be 70 and 80" she observed after Bruté had been absent some time. Dubois agreed that Hickey was inadequate: "pure as an angel but neither Judgment or intelligence," he declared. Concerned about the decline in Communions, and alert to competition from itinerant evangelical preachers, Dubois tried to solve the problem by writing more sermons himself.[10] Having no such outlet, Elizabeth resorted to shame. "If your subject is unintelligible for want of preparation and connection," she demanded of Hickey, "what becomes of Your grace and theirs?" Hickey's priesthood made him more accountable to her, not less.[11]

In such moments, the Church's gender hierarchy was unsettled by the moral and spiritual authority Elizabeth commanded. But it was not upended. As a sister, she possessed no authority over Hickey beyond moral suasion. That was the same authority women claimed and were limited to in the new nation's politics. Women in Protestant denominations were in the main absent from pulpits too; within the realm of religion as outside it, gifted women exhorted men to apply themselves properly to jobs the women themselves were not allowed to attempt. Two things were distinctive in these frustrating months. First was Elizabeth's belief in the cosmic importance of the priesthood. Transubstantiation lay at the heart of her Catholic belief and experience; it was given to the lazy young Hickey to perform that rite and to inspire others to partake of it. How could he fail to respect the privilege he, as a man, had been granted? Second was Elizabeth's certainty that she could write more effective sermons than Hickey: the sermons that everyone now missed had been her creations as well as Bruté's. Together she and the French priest had brought the area's laity to the altar rail, inspiring a Catholic revival amid the area's evangelical Protestant stirrings. Now Bruté was absent, and Elizabeth's voice was silenced.

GROWTH

On the last day of April 1815, John Dubois ran hatless toward St. Joseph's House. He bore shocking news: Napoleon had escaped his island prison and made for France. Unbeknownst to the loved ones following their progress on a wooden globe, William and Bruté had sailed straight into the Hundred Days. Disembarking at Bordeaux, the astonished pair learned that the would-be emperor was gathering troops and seeking to regain control of France. No one knew what would happen next, but it was assumed that Catholic priests might once again be in danger. The carefully laid plan for Bruté to accompany William to Livorno and settle him with the Filicchis was useless. Bruté traded his clerical garb for civilian clothes and tried to lie low, while William made his way alone, first to Nice, then Genoa, then at last to Livorno.[12]

"My heart when I approached the house of our friend," the young man confessed to Bruté, "beat very much." Finding Antonio Filicchi at home, William quickly explained that he was Elizabeth Seton's son. The merchant responded with all the warmth Elizabeth had hoped for. "A few moments conversation with him quickly dispersed all uneasy sensations and banished all disagreeable feelings," William wrote Bruté gratefully.[13] The young man had not wanted to be a merchant and still did not want to be a merchant. But he'd made his way across an ocean, traveled alone to a country whose language he did not speak, and announced himself at the home of a family he barely knew. Surely, he must have thought, he could now do whatever was needed to succeed.

Back in Maryland, Elizabeth and Dubois did not know for months what decisions Bruté and William had made or whether William had safely reached Livorno. Anxious notes arrived from worried Baltimore friends, but Elizabeth found herself able to "look up." "What is the worst and the worst that can happen to the dearest," she wrote in her journal for Bruté. "Death? And what of that?" She had meant it when she told William that she feared the loss of his soul more than the loss of his life.

That spring brought reminders that danger lurked everywhere, no escaped emperors required. From New York came news that Elizabeth's half brother Richard, who had not long before delighted Helen and Mary Fitch Bayley by giving up his bachelor ways, had fallen out of a wagon as it descended a steep hill, dying in front of his pregnant wife. More heart-breaking tidings arrived: Louisa Caton brought word that Julia Scott's recently married daughter had died on her wedding trip to Europe.

Losing a child had been Julia's worst fear, and it was Elizabeth's worst memory. Knowing that her friend was too distraught to read a long letter, Elizabeth compressed love and sympathy into a single urgent page. "Take courage at this moment look up think of our future blessed home where there will be no more separations do do my Julia," she wrote. If Julia was too overcome to write, Elizabeth instructed gently, she must have her son John let her friends know how she got on. She closed her letter simply: "May the God of all mercy bless and comfort you."[14] For years, Elizabeth had warned Julia that a trial would come and that when it did, she would regret her lack of a vibrant Christian faith. Now the trial was upon Julia, and Elizabeth sent love without reproach. As the months wore on, she shared with Julia her own long struggles after Anna Maria's death and coaxed her to persevere. Julia's responses were short, heartbroken, and grateful.

Elizabeth also did what she could to lighten John Dubois's labors; their lack of closeness did not reduce her sense of obligation. John Hickey had been called by the Sulpicians to Baltimore, depriving Dubois of help that was, though imperfect, nonetheless essential. (In Baltimore, Hickey proved himself no less disappointing: "You are too diffident on yourself," his Sulpician superior scolded. "You see how many things Mr. Dubois is able to do on account of the same good and courageous will. . . . Learn from him how to behave yourself.")[15] Dubois also suffered from the absence of Margaret Burke; since she left to start her own school in Emmitsburg, he'd found no local women to replace her. Concerned for the busy priest, Elizabeth and the council approved a plan to send a few sisters from St. Joseph's House to attend to the Mount's domestic needs. "One in charge of linen and clothing," as a pleased Dubois explained the plan, "the other of expenses, and the third who would be superior at the head of the entire economy, particularly put in charge of the infirmary." No one found the prospect menial. It was understood to be a "mission" as worthy as the one in Philadelphia: the sisters would help to promote the education of the boys, albeit from behind the scenes, and they would lessen the burden on the beleaguered Dubois. In order to avoid scandalizing the Sulpicians or the locals, Dubois prepared a little house in which the sisters would live apart from the men and boys of the Mount and he insisted that the women chosen for the mission be "old."[16] Those provisions made, three sisters of St. Joseph's set off to the mountain.

As that effort began, the mission in Philadelphia flourished. At the end of the first year, the orphan asylum had grown, but the sisters had used less than their allotted $600. Rose immediately reported to the board of managers that the women "cannot relinquish our claim" to the excess, but rather would put it toward the next year.[17] Founded in rural Maryland, the American Sisters of Charity were now a thriving presence in the urban northeast, and although Elizabeth herself had not traveled to Philadelphia, her ethos of attentive connection—bolstered by Rose's practicality—animated the Philadelphia mission.

In late July, the Emmitsburg community held its second election. Elizabeth was again chosen Mother, no more questions raised than when George Washington was reelected president. Margaret George was made both treasurer and secretary and Elizabeth Boyle assistant Mother.[18] One incident that fall briefly threatened the sisterhood's peace: a young woman named Martha demanded she be allowed to leave the novitiate, then insisted she wished to stay, then one night crept out through the cellar and disappeared. "Any publicity of this case can do no good, & may do much harm," Dubois fretted to Elizabeth. "I hope she did not throw herself in a fit of insanity in the open well which is in the potato field— or in Tom's Creek."[19] He and Elizabeth feared that lurking mistrust of Catholicism left the sisterhood vulnerable to public scandal. But Martha had not come to a bad end; "A true romantic spirit—poor child," Margaret George wrote sympathetically when it was clear she'd simply sneaked away.[20] The sisterhood sailed quietly on.

Almost quietly. Mary Diana Harper was still there. "Her dispositions unfold very fast and reason and good sense are always predominant when she takes time to reflect," Elizabeth observed to Robert Goodloe Harper, "but that is not often." The girl was also increasingly frail, and although the Harpers believed Elizabeth to be the best possible guardian (they sent two more daughters to St. Joseph's), they decided at last to pack Mary Diana off to France. There they hoped she could regain her health, finish her education in a Catholic country, and at last outgrow her tantrums.

Mother Seton's serenity in these months seemed as implacable as Mary Diana's temper. But in the tiny handwriting of her journal to Bruté lay a surprising truth: she was struggling through another season of spiritual dryness. "The poor little Atom in darkness, clouds, and continual miseries," she wrote, "going like a machine in the beautiful round of graces." Once again, she found herself suffering from a "stupidity and weariness of soul and body," a "state of torpor and abandonment" from which Communion could only temporarily rouse her. When she looked "to the clear Vault," she confessed to Bruté, "all is silent." Although this dryness pained her, she did not feel the terror and disorientation she'd known in the past. Instead, she continued reading and underlining her Bible, meditating on the Psalms and the writings of saints, and "praying and begging for the accomplishment of his will and the establishment of his Kingdom." She also found a true confidante in Cecilia O'Conway. The young woman had a rich and ambitious prayer life and did not hesitate to offer criticism and guidance. She "has taken my soul in hand," Elizabeth wrote, "and declares *it shall be perfected*, she will do violence to *his* heart she says, and every communion and prayer for that until her mother is a *true Mother*." Far from being offended at the younger woman's clear suggestion that she was not yet a "true Mother," Elizabeth found the prayers "of such a soul" "precious." Even so, it was still Bruté whom she considered her most valuable spiritual guide. When there was a "gathering of clouds," she wrote, "I read again the hundred direction papers of two years past with yet greater delight than the first reading."[21] Bruté's notes offered Elizabeth the balm that her own counsel gave others.

Elizabeth also withstood uncertainty over William's fate with less agony than she would have felt in the past, and in August, a letter at last arrived from Livorno. Elizabeth, Catherine, and Rebecca sat together on a trunk, the girls trying to break the letter's seal without tearing a single word of their brother's. (They succeeded.) Thrilled to learn that William was happily at work in the Filicchis' countinghouse, the Setons wrote back joyfully, Elizabeth imploring her son to confess his sins regularly.[22] With news and affection also arriving regularly from Manhattan—"Mysterious Sam, still walks about and round, and round, as large as life, absorbed in something which time I hope, will make manifest," Mary Seton Hoffman reported wryly—it seemed as if everything and everyone might be well.[23] Then the fragile truce with Rebecca's lamed leg came to an end.

The girl's hip had become less painful but never fully healed, and now a tumor appeared beneath the skin. Something more dangerous than a cracked bone threatened her little body, and no one knew quite what. Dr. Chatard had been unable to help her in Baltimore, and from New York, Wright Post offered no remedies. Hoping to help her friend's daughter despite her own grief, Julia Scott sent a ray of hope. Rebecca should come to Philadelphia, she insisted, and see the city's renowned doctors. Elizabeth agreed. She had never found the use of medical science incompatible with acceptance of God's will, and she did not now.

The fact of Rebecca's trip to Philadelphia was a testament to Elizabeth and Julia's friendship. The manner in which Rebecca traveled bore testament to something quite different: Elizabeth's reluctance to have her old friend visit St. Joseph's House. Others had come, including Catherine Dupleix, who was so moved by her visit that she eventually converted to Catholicism. But when the prospect of Julia's visiting had arisen, Elizabeth had always gently brushed it aside. "O yes Julia, come and see," she'd written once, then reminded her friend "that the accommodation in our Village is very bad and you could not probably remain more than one night." If Julia stayed at the sisterhood itself, she added, "you could not put up with my room [since it is] the resort of the whole community."[24] It's hard not to conclude that Elizabeth did not really want Julia there, and now, as Julia made plans to travel to Emmitsburg in order to accompany Bec to Philadelphia, Elizabeth arranged for Bec to travel by herself. One late September day, she saw her daughter off; Julia arrived in a carriage soon after, expecting to collect the girl. The two friends had not seen each other for years, but they could spend only a few moments before Julia climbed back into her carriage and hurried back to Philadelphia so that Rebecca would not arrive to an empty house.

Julia had always lamented the slightest inconvenience, but she forgave this wasted journey on rutted roads without complaint. It was Elizabeth who judged. "O when the beautiful coaches and horses went off so grand and gay," she wrote Rebecca, describing Julia's departure, "how Mothers Soul darted through the blue heavens to bless and praise that we are not numbered with the rich in this world, and to call down pity on them." It was an odd response to her friend's generosity and tolerance. Together with her reluctance to have Julia visit, Elizabeth's unaccustomed harshness suggests that she feared her old friend might unsettle the Mother she'd become, accidentally or intentionally unearthing the EAB that still lurked within EAS, even within MEAS. She distanced herself to avoid the risk, and told Bec to do the same, instructing her child to turn to Rose White, not Julia, for any advice she needed in Philadelphia.

Rebecca so carefully followed these instructions that she later lamented her awkward reserve. But the girl was never truly tempted to trade her mother's world for Julia's. She admired the sights Julia shared with her—"the museum, the bank of Pennsylvania, the bank of the United States," she reported—but was far more moved by the "poor house" to which Sister Rose took her. "I do not dare to think of my own sufferings," she told her mother, "now that I have seen theirs."[25]

Her sufferings never lessened. Although she stoutly assured her mother that she was mending, Philadelphia's doctors offered Bec no real hope. Nor should they have. Surrounded by consumptives her whole life, Bec had contracted tuberculosis. The wily disease had made a home in the cracked bone of her hip and now traveled through her lymphatic system. Realizing the child could not be cured, Julia sent her home.

Bec arrived more determined than ever to make herself St. Joseph's "child of the Cross." In Livorno, William also tried to fulfill his mother's hopes, writing to Bruté that he believed himself capable of succeeding as a merchant.[26] Immune to others' expectations, Richard was as carefree as ever, that fall gunning and frolicking his way through rural Charles County. That left Catherine. Although Elizabeth had once feared she too showed symptoms of consumption, Kit grew sturdier as Bec grew more frail. Despite the fact that she was not expected to earn her living, Kit had already begun to do so. "She earns her full 200$ a year for the sweet independence of a heart that wishes not through pride, but principle, to do its part," Elizabeth wrote approvingly.[27] Catherine still declined the gushes of affection her mother and sister delighted in: "I need not tell you how much I love you, you know it without my telling you," she once wrote William.[28] Yet where William's reserve left others wrong-footed, Catherine's made her only more appealing. "Kit," Elizabeth observed, "is really an elegant soul."[29] Whether she intended it or not, she was becoming the Seton about whom no one worried.

"A RIGHT FAITH"

Late that fall, news came that should not have startled but did: eighty-one-year-old Archbishop John Carroll was dead. Carroll had been a steady, nurturing presence since Elizabeth's earliest days as a Catholic. He'd offered neither the sustained collaboration of Bruté nor the effervescence of Babade. Yet Elizabeth had valued no one's guidance more. Carroll deeply admired her mind and soul, and although as an institution builder he believed resources must be devoted to the training of clergy, he'd relied more with each passing year on the prayer and good works emanating from the "devout women" of St. Joseph's House. Elizabeth did not lament that the old priest was released from his labors, and she hoped for good counsel from his successors (briefly Lonard Neale and then, beginning in 1817, Antoine Marèchal). But she knew that John Carroll's like would not come her way again.

News of Carroll's death arrived while John Dubois was in the midst of a battle. He often was, but this controversy was if possible more galling to him than most. The Baltimore Sulpicians now openly questioned his financial management of the Blue Ridge institutions, insisting that it was high time the institutions contribute to the order's coffers rather than deplete them. They also scolded Dubois for approving the sisters' mission at the Mount: if women were in any way caring for the boys and priests there—or making decisions about the school's operation—the Sulpicians believed Dubois risked scandal.[30]

Dubois was outraged. Financial irresponsibility? It was he who had strenuously opposed the agreement that left the seminary saddled with debt. It was he who labored—and directly extracted the labor of slaves—to pay that debt down. As for the sisters, Dubois found them frugal and diligent where local women were unreliable and demanding. Their help at the Mount reduced costs, just as the Sulpicians wanted. Indignantly, Dubois began another letter-writing campaign. Because he wrote in French and criticized the work habits of Maryland women, he can appear as an unhappy immigrant deploring his new surroundings. Yet at the heart of his efforts lay his belief that it was necessary to adapt European customs to American circumstances and to fully use the sisters' talents. "Most American women and girls," he explained, "can most certainly live on their own or with their parents. They sneer at such jobs as domestic help," but the sisters were competent and saw a higher purpose in their labor for the Mount. French customs, he believed, were one incarnation of the Catholic Church, but they were not the Church itself. If the Sulpicians' French expectations prevented American sisters from usefully serving the Church, those expectations should be modified.[31] Dubois was as sure he'd be ignored as he was convinced he was right. Unhappy and exhausted, he offered his resignation to the Sulpicians.

Dubois missed the sympathy of Simon Bruté in this latest struggle, and he and Elizabeth were thrilled when word came that the priest had returned from France. But Bruté was not returning to the Mount; instead, he was to be made president of St. Mary's Seminary, Baltimore. The Sulpicians' logic followed a familiar path: the United States needed priests more than it needed Sisters of Charity. Bruté had the intellectual capacity to train the men studying at St. Mary's, so that was what he should do. Although this might have seemed like still more evidence of the Sulpicians' depreciation of the Emmitsburg institutions, Dubois and Elizabeth resigned themselves with surprising equanimity to Bruté's new posting. After the uncertainty of his trip into Napoleon's Hundred Days, they were relieved he was only a day or two's ride away. Dubois may also have sensed an advantage: now that Bruté was president of St. Mary's, he began to address his complaints about the Sulpicians' demands to his friend. Whether because of affinity or relentlessness—what a weary John Carroll once called "Mr. Dubois' persevering importunity"—Dubois had his way. The sisters were allowed to keep their mission, and the Sulpicians for the moment stopped complaining about the Mount's spending. Although Dubois claimed that "I wish more than anyone in the world to be freed from the care of the Sisters," he doggedly and lovingly carried on.[32]

Elizabeth also commenced a correspondence with Bruté. She wanted to resume their spiritual collaboration, and Bruté was delighted to oblige. "If I preach you it is to preach me," he wrote one day from Baltimore, his English as expressive as it was off-kilter.[33] In fact, Elizabeth did want to discuss Bruté's tendency to preach, more specifically, his tendency to try to convert non-Catholics to his faith. Although her manner was far gentler than Dubois's, she, too, was determined to make her thinking clear.

Since his arrival in the United States, Bruté had exuberantly proselytized; in addition to exhorting John Henry Hobart, he tried to convert

Eliza Sadler to Catholicism ("I feel it impossible to subscribe to the belief that out of your church there can be no Christians," Sadler politely replied), as well as two Quaker girls he met in Baltimore.[34] In believing that the nation's religious liberty carried with it an obligation to shepherd others onto the correct path, the French priest agreed with many American Protestants. The Second Great Awakening witnessed impassioned believers evangelizing family, friends, and even strangers. Some were grateful for the efforts, but others were not. Elizabeth had once resented arguments that she should keep her faith to herself. Now she doubted that the good that evangelization sometimes achieved outweighed the discord it so often caused.

So when Elizabeth learned, after Bruté's return from France, that the priest had urged her sister to convert to Catholicism, she gently suggested he desist. Elizabeth explained that Mary Post would find Bruté's arguments against Protestantism hurtful and his depiction of a God who must be worshipped in one particular way absurd. Elizabeth limned the ecumenical views she herself had once held: "[Catholics] make God a merciful being indeed if he would condemn souls of his own creation for their Parents bringing them in the world on one side of it or the other." She assured Bruté that she believed Catholicism *was* the one true Church; God had saved her by rolling away the "big stone of darkest ignorance and indifference." But she knew that Mary, like most of her friends and family, believed sincerely in other forms of Christianity and valued (as she herself had once valued) "the dress and quiet of the Quakers, a sweet enthusiastic preaching among the Methodists, a soft melting music of low voices among Anabaptists." Not only did they believe in other faiths, but they believed there were many paths to salvation. "The thought of a right Faith or wrong Faith, true church enters the mind of one among a hundred," she explained to Bruté.

Although she believed that the Catholic Church was the true church, Elizabeth made clear to Bruté that she no longer tried to persuade others to agree. No one but God could roll away the stone of darkest ignorance. And if Bruté thought Elizabeth's own conversion was proof of the usefulness of Catholic evangelizing, he was wrong. "I tell you a secret hidden almost from my own Soul," she told him. "My hatred of opposition, troublesome enquiries etc. brought me into the church more than conviction." She saw her conversion as a vulgar fumbling, its happy outcome creditable neither to her nor to those who had sought to persuade her. No

Protestant, she told the priest, can "see our Meaning"—the meaning of the Church—"without being led step by step and the Veil lifted little by little."[35] Only God could lift the veil, not a priest, a charismatic preacher, or one's own judgment. This way of thinking melded a belief that safety lay within the teachings of the Catholic Church with one more familiar to Protestants: each individual must forge her own relation with God. Neither ecumenical nor evangelical, Elizabeth's ethos emerged from a profound spiritual humility. Amid the proliferating, competing religions of the early American republic, it opened the way to a social harmony she had once disavowed.

20

SWIFT ROLLING EARTH

WILLIAM, RICHARD, CATHERINE, and Rebecca shared a love for their mother and a dread of displeasing her. But their temperaments had always differed and their futures were about to diverge. William was ambitious, Richard carefree. Catherine was self-sufficient and sturdy, Rebecca pliant and increasingly frail. As Elizabeth found herself dwelling with ever-greater peacefulness within the Emmitsburg community, her children in their different ways contemplated life beyond it.

In Livorno, William was finding life as a clerk at the Filicchis' countinghouse less interesting than he'd expected, and he had not expected much. His work consisted almost entirely of copying letters, and the young man did nothing to convince Antonio and Filippo that he was worthy of a greater challenge. As the weeks and months passed, William realized that each day would be the same as the last, except on the days when there were no letters to be copied. Those days were duller.

Outside the countinghouse lay Italy, but as Elizabeth had feared, the culture and art that fascinated both of William's parents left their son unmoved. He looked around him with homesick ennui and spent leisure hours playing cards with expatriates who liked to "speak of America." "Emmitsburg has now more charms for me than any part of the United States," he declared. "It is very natural that one should love his country—but I am proud of mine." The Filicchis were at a loss to understand the young man who'd presented himself at their doorstep only to prove uninterested in their business and country. They also suspected he was not attending church or at least not taking Communion. William could not quite bring himself to offer his confession to priests he did not know. In the land where his mother had felt Catholicism's irresistible call, William skipped Mass; surrounded by artistic treasures, he envied his brother Richard's trip to Charles County. He'd always wished, he wrote Catherine wistfully, "to go there to shoot the ducks and squirrels."[1]

Richard, for his part, was finally ready to leave such adventures behind. The mountain was not the same without his brother, and day after day he wrote William sweet, chatty letters, confiding a newfound desire to make his way in the world. "Could words express how much I wish to be at something or other, I would tell you," Richard wrote, "but my tongue cannot express it."[2] Elizabeth was eager that Richard embark on his adult life but was dissatisfied by his prospects. Luke Tiernan, a Baltimore merchant whose daughter attended St. Joseph's Academy and who was a trustee at the cathedral, offered Richard a spot in his enterprise, but Elizabeth grew irritated as Tiernan wrangled over the terms. "Charity and friendship [are] so cold this side of the water," she complained to William, and she, "a poor Nobody," could do nothing without help. In fact, she had a great deal of help and might have had more had she not so hated playing the supplicant. Governeur Ogden was successful in his new home near the St. Lawrence River, and Elizabeth learned to her amazement that he no longer professed hostility to her faith; he "would have allowed his children to learn the Catholic catechism," Ogden told a mutual acquaintance, had his wife Charlotte only agreed.[3] Yet Elizabeth could not forget that the Ogdens "wrote the threatening letter that the house would be burned over my head, calling me Siren, etc. etc.," and she never asked them to help Richard.[4] She did try Sam Seton, but his response came in the form of a long, gracefully written apology. "The merchant finds his profits too small to allow of sinking any part of them in salaried clerks," he observed mournfully.[5] Finding no alternative, she and Dubois at last reached an agreement with Luke Tiernan, and in mid-May Richard set off for Baltimore, eager to follow his brother into the merchant life. He proved as lighthearted as William was morose and was soon penning his siblings witty accounts of his adventures and urging Catherine to find money for him without letting their mother know he'd asked.[6]

Elizabeth hoped for the best from her younger son, and she looked on approvingly as other young people she'd nurtured also ventured forth. Three of the Caton sisters sailed for Europe, "for . . . health and for fashion of the world to travel," as Elizabeth put it. The other Caton sister, Emily, had recently married a Canadian merchant. John McTavish was not only a well-educated, devout young Catholic but also an heir to the fortune amassed by the firm of McTavish, Frobisher. In the years since that company's impatient agent had found the elder William Seton unwell and William Magee Seton agonizingly indecisive, the Canadian firm had profited from expansion into James Bay and China. Emily's marriage pleased not only her but her family as well.[7] The irascible Mary Diana Harper, for her part, was in Paris, from whence she wrote her parents that she'd regained "perfect health" and would like to know "whether you would have any objection to me wearing corsets."[8] Even young Jerome Bonaparte, studying at Mount St. Mary's while his father and uncle gained and lost power in France, left for vacations, begging Elizabeth for an "Agnus Dei" to help him be good as he left.[9]

Elizabeth insisted that her daughter Catherine leave Emmitsburg too. Kit had always refused invitations to go to friends' townhouses and plantations, but that spring she found herself packed off to Baltimore; she had a worrisome cough and her mother thought a month at the Chatards might do her good. At first disoriented, Kit resolved to "dry my tears and look pleasant" and soon proved herself as quietly competent outside St. Joseph's House as she was within. Before long, she was writing to instruct her mother about hat purchases (cloth not straw, better in the long run), and matter-of-factly noting that "I do not think I will go to Confession till I come back," since she found it preferable to confer with her mother before confiding in a priest.[10] Intellectually curious and socially graceful, Catherine was pleased—and just a bit unsettled—to find herself enjoying town life. "Do unite with me and pray for me," she wrote her mother in mid-July, "I have so many things here to distract my mind, it is so different from St. Joseph's where the most we see are the mountains round us and such dear friends."[11]

THE TRAVELER

One young person did not leave St. Joseph's House: Bec. A few years earlier, she'd feared that her mother and sisters would die and she would be "left behind." Instead, Bec was left behind in a different way, ill and homebound as friends and siblings tried the world. The tumor in her hip grew relentlessly. In January, Elizabeth told Catherine Dupleix of the girl's quiet suffering and "fast rolling tears"; in February, she cut short a letter to William explaining that "Your Bec looks so pale and tired that I must finish."[12] By spring, Rebecca was too ill even to play with her friends. She did not complain. "Mother and I [are] left alone in Noah's ark," she wrote William one day. "Never mind one of these days we will have our enjoyment too."[13]

As consumption attacked her bones and more tumors emerged, Bec realized it was she, youngest and frailest, who would soon move beyond her friends' and siblings' reach. "Try to meet me in the world where there are no separations," she urged her brother, "and where my soul calls for no one so much as you next to mother."[14] Her misery mounted. "5 days and nights in groans and tears and agonies out of my power to give any least thought," Elizabeth wrote of the pain caused by her youngest child's diseased bones, "could not be believed if I had not seen."[15]

She held her suffering daughter night and day, seeking any position that might lessen the girl's agony. She consulted with doctors and even wrote to George Weis in Baltimore for oysters in case Rebecca might enjoy them. Yet she did not try to free her daughter from the burden of believing her suffering was deserved. When Rebecca explained that she thought "our Lord sent these sufferings for neglecting my little practices of piety since the retreat," her mother approved. "Dear simple heart," she wrote admiringly, "these her very words with such pure looks of sincere meaning."[16] After a week in which Bec was "unable to sit, stand or lie down," she felt her agony briefly ease and recoiled at the thought of more suffering. "O Mother," she exclaimed, "if all my pains should come back!" Elizabeth reminded the child of her duty: "My darling I only intreat you say thy will be done."[17] Rebecca did.

There are many such moments in Elizabeth's account of Rebecca's illness, all of them difficult to read. The humility and compassion Elizabeth displayed in other realms of her life seem virtuous and ethical; her insistence that a dying child bear responsibility for her own agony seems perverse and cruel. Yet everything flowed from the same fount: Elizabeth's sense of the immense gulf between God's nature and man's. She now found human life so ephemeral in comparison with eternity that her youngest child's months of misery were but a moment; she found humanity's sinful nature so alien from God's that mercy, rather than suffering, was inexplicable. Yet she also felt a deeper faith in God's mercy than she had during the terrible months before and after Anna Maria's death. Elizabeth encouraged Bec's resignation but did not fearfully demand it; her greater confidence in God's mercy left her less needful of a daughter's perfection. Serenely, she taught Bec to see herself "sitting on this swift rolling Earth—moments and hours passing so swiftly to our glorious happy Eternity."[18]

John Dubois, often critical, saw nothing to question. Bec is "melting away," he wrote William, "but amidst the ruins of her little frame, the soul appears to shine brighter than ever. Her eyes are clear and peaceful yet. . . . She talks of her going to Heaven just as you were talking of going to Italy."[19] From Baltimore, Bruté sent the girl encouragement; learning that her bone tumors left her unable to lie down, he gracefully compared her to "the knights of old" who bravely stood watch.[20] From New York came still more sympathy and concern. Mary and Wright Post had lost their son Edward that winter, and Mary mourned with her sister that it appeared "no mortal aid can reach Rebecca" either.[21]

Mary was right. Bec's coughing jolted joints that had grown swollen and painful, and tumors swelled relentlessly beneath her skin. "You can have no idea of my trial," the girl told her mother, but she unhesitatingly applied herself to the challenge of dying well. Suffering on her fourteenth birthday, she reminded herself of what she'd seen in Philadelphia's poorhouse and told her mother that she felt grateful for "the love of all around her . . . and her many comforts."[22] Still, Bec feared that she might somehow displease God. "I have begun to watch every action of [mother's] that I may imitate her," she wrote one day to Pierre Babade. "I spoke to her last night about correcting my defects, faults, and whatever she saw in me displeasing to our dear Lord or to her." Bec wanted Babade to criticize her too. "And you, my dear father," she urged him, "tell me twice or thrice a week what displeases you."[23] For once, Babade felt no need for drama or attention. "You are still but a child," he wrote soothingly, "our Lord loves you, and knows the infirmity and instability of mind to which your age makes you liable."[24] From Baltimore, Bruté offered an even simpler message: "Love is stronger than death."[25]

When William learned of his little sister's shattered health, his dissatisfaction with Livorno grew. Having abandoned all hope of advancement or satisfaction at the Filicchi countinghouse, he grew convinced he should return home and try once again to join the navy. But the same troubles that left him feeling he should return to Maryland—Bec's ill health and the fact that his brother was, in Dubois's telling, "a good child but a child yet"—also left William loath to burden his mother. He remained sullenly in Livorno.[26]

The Filicchis had grown as eager as William to see the young man returned to Maryland, but they were equally unwilling to disappoint Elizabeth Seton. At last, however, the impasse broke. In July, William hinted to his mother of his unhappiness. "Everything here is so dull," he told her. "I think more can be learned in an American Counting house than an Italian one."[27] Not long after came a startling development: Filippo, whose health had long been more fragile than his will, died. Expected to take Filippo's place in the family business, Antonio found himself harried and anxious. Feeling ever more acutely his own uselessness, William decided that honor now required he leave Livorno.

"SWEET BEC"

Elizabeth's attention was fixed on Rebecca. "I hardly know how to tell you your sweet Bec suffers more and more," she wrote William, and she sent word to Richard and Catherine in Baltimore that their sister was struggling. "Most of her time is passed in my arms or on my knees," she wrote, "we wet each other pretty often with tears."[28] Catherine immediately returned to St. Joseph's House, where she worked to alleviate the agonies around her. "She divides her time between the care of her education & the duty she owes to her mother and sister," a proud Dubois told William. One of the duties Catherine took up was that of writing Elizabeth's letters, including to Julia Scott. "[Rebecca's] sufferings are inconceivable," Catherine told her mother's old friend, "as she can never lie down, or stand; but with her arms around Mother's neck for a minute or two."[29] Julia wrote back immediately, sending a book she thought might distract Bec, a gown she thought Elizabeth could convert into a petticoat, and a one-sentence encapsulation of the women's decades-long friendship. "Love me and pray for me," Julia wrote, "and believe that I always sympathize in all your griefs, as I know you do in mine."[30]

Unlike Catherine, Richard remained in Baltimore after learning of Bec's decline; he was not ready to abandon his pleasures. Although he made one quick visit to Emmitsburg, he barely saw his dying sister before riding off again. Elizabeth tolerated a great deal from her younger son, but this failing she could not abide; in a letter since lost or destroyed, she chastised him for his coldness. Richard began his reply with petulant excuses but then gathered himself. He'd acted "like a blockhead," he confessed. He loved his "dear dying sister," and despite the press of his duties—"always writing writing writing"—he swore he would be more attentive.[31] Elizabeth prayed it was true.

Through it all, Bec kept to her task of becoming a child of the Cross. If Dr. Chatard "could say Rebecca you will get well," she declared one day, "I would not wish it—Oh no my dear Saviour I know now the happiness of an early Death and to sin no more." Life at St. Joseph's House had taught her to see her fate as desirable, not tragic. Yet she could not quite believe she *would* die. Heaven was real to her, but her own disappearance from St. Joseph's House? That boggled the child's mind. "O my Mother it seems so strange," she told Elizabeth, thinking of her burial. "You will come back dearest Mother, you will come back alone." It was "hard," Elizabeth wrote in her journal, "to familiarize the darling with hastening Death—we sit in tears together—hers she says so inexplicable for she knows how good it is to go." "The last struggles Mother," Rebecca said one day, "there is something in Death I cannot tell."[32]

Yet death approached. "Oh Mother how I suffer," Rebecca one day gasped, "every bone, every joint." On October 31, she was given extreme unction. She fixed her eyes on a crucifix set near a candle from her first Communion. As the candle burned, she waited. When the flame went out and she found herself still alive, she was disappointed but struggled on, uttering what prayers "her cough and continual choaking would permit." As another day passed and another night began, Rebecca feared she would become impatient. What if, after all her prayers, she failed now? What if she brought punishment on herself in these final, endless hours? Seeing the girl's distress and Elizabeth's exhaustion, John Dubois announced in his practical way that he would stay the night and see Rebecca through. He also quietly suggested she take more paregoric, a tincture of opium. Rebecca understood. "If I go to sleep," she said to the priest, her mother, her sister Catherine, and Sister Susan Clossy, all of whom sat by her bed, "I shall not come back[,] so good by to you."[33]

Despite the paregoric, neither sleep nor death came, and Bec's mind wandered. She imagined that she'd gathered a bag of apples, only to discover one had a black spot. Her brother Richard must see that it be removed from the bag, she called out, "for nothing defiled can enter

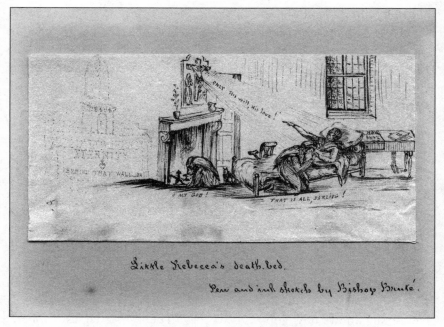

FIGURE 20.1. Bruté sketch of Rebecca's deathbed. APSL 13313 149.
Courtesy of the Daughters of Charity Province of St. Louise Archives,
Emmitsburg, Maryland.

heaven." By then, the spotted apple had himself come to St. Joseph's
House. Receiving word that his sister was dying, Richard this time came
at once. A letter arrived from William too, but after a few words were
read out, Bec said, "Tell him only to meet me," explaining that she could
not bear to hear any more.[34] Finally, on a November day after more
suffering and more prayer, Bec died, her head falling onto her mother's breast, and her life's purpose, as she understood it, fulfilled. "Her
death," Dubois wrote Bruté in Baltimore, "was as calm, as sweet, as
the fall weather which we have been having." He added, in a line whose
loving precision was pure Dubois, that despite her exhaustion, Elizabeth
held Rebecca "for more than eight minutes after her death."[35]

Cheverus and Matignon wrote, as they always did, to congratulate
rather than to console, confident Elizabeth felt more joy than sorrow.[36]
Bruté sketched a delicate scene of Elizabeth and Catherine receiving
Communion while Anna Maria and Rebecca floated nearby.[37] From

Mary Post and Julia Scott came letters bearing the love of women who knew this awful pain. "To say my dearest sister that I sympathize in your sorrow conveys but an imperfect expression of the feeling your trials have given me," Mary wrote. "The departure of dear Rebecca must leave an aching void in the heart that has treasured her with such affection."[38] Elizabeth did feel an "aching void," but she suffered none of the uncertainty and anguish Anna Maria's death had brought. "PEACE," she'd written to Bruté in the thick of Rebecca's agonies, "OUR GOD never my Soul in the quiet as now."[39]

For both Elizabeth and Dubois, Rebecca's suffering and death revealed the fundamental soundness of life at St. Joseph's, as Anna Maria's had revealed its fragility. Dubois wrote that he was "inundated with consolation and so have been for some time, in the midst of all my temporal trials." As for Elizabeth, "The Mother lives amongst the angels." She "goes her round of duties," Dubois observed humbly, "and seems to forget the unworthiness of the poor Superior, whom she treats with all possible cordiality."[40]

William, Catherine, and Richard, entering the world as their mother became increasingly abstracted from it, grieved their little sister and tried to figure out what their own next steps should be. William renewed his determination to leave Livorno. Catherine, intrigued by her forays outside the sisterhood, contemplated the choices she knew she would soon face. Richard simply settled back into Baltimore's delights. "Oh, my God," he wrote William, recounting his last visit with his little sister, "how I felt." "I can bear any trial on earth and say 'tis nothing to that."[41] But Bec's dying exhortations soon faded, and a few weeks after her death Richard wrote his mother complaining that his stockings didn't suit and that his hat, gloves, and handkerchiefs needed to be replaced. It was true, he admitted, that Catherine had sent him money from the pay she received for giving lessons, but that was all gone. "She thinks she has some money left," he observed jovially, "but when she sees the books she won't think so." Then came a line that both comforted and worried Elizabeth. "Pray," Richard wrote, "for your wild son."[42]

21

WRITTEN BY HERSELF

A S 1816 ENDED, John Cheverus made a trip to Maryland. He had business in Baltimore, but he also wanted to visit the sisters in their valley. A decade earlier, Cheverus had been a parish priest writing to a widow who could not decide whether to be Protestant or Catholic. Now he was bishop of Boston and the widow was Mother Seton, founder of the American Sisters of Charity. After his visit, Cheverus wrote admiringly of the "excellent Sisters, their happy and edifying pupils, the Mother with her children in heaven and on earth."[1] A few years later, arranging for Ursulines to come to Boston, Cheverus thought wistfully of the community he'd seen in the Blue Ridge. "Just between us," he told Bruté, "I would have preferred your Sisters, and above all the Mother."[2]

As Cheverus knew, Elizabeth had once wanted nothing more than to leave the United States, convinced she was ill suited to live amid its diversity and tolerance. Instead she had created an American Catholic sisterhood that thrived where others faltered. Port Tobacco's nuns remained a tiny group, and a community of Trappist sisters failed in 1814, a few of its would-be participants making their way instead to Emmitsburg. The Ursulines maintained their convent in New Orleans, which had been established long before the United States took possession of the territory, but an attempt by Irish Ursulines to plant themselves in New York City was disastrous. No women entered their novitiate, and although the nuns were pleased by "the docility of the Irish pupils" at the Manhattan school, they were horrified by "the assumption, pride, and petulance,

FIGURE 21.1. Gilbert Stuart, *Bishop Jean-Louis Anne Magdelaine Lefebvre de Cheverus,* 1823, oil on canvas, 92.07 x 72.39 cm (36¼ x 28½ in.). Courtesy of the Museum of Fine Arts, Boston. Bequest of Mrs. Charlotte Gore Greenough Hervoches du Quilliou 21.9. Photograph ©2018 Museum of Fine Arts, Boston.

which the name, and perhaps the reality of political independence were developing in the youthful character of America." The Ursulines had not even met Mary Diana Harper, and they'd seen enough. In 1815 the group returned to Ireland.[3]

At the time of Cheverus's visit to St. Joseph's House, the Ursulines' retreat from New York was opening a new field for the Sisters of Charity. The city now boasted more than one hundred thousand inhabitants; some lived opulently, such as the auctioneer Philip Hone—who declared his days as a businessman concluded at the age of forty—and the spectacularly rich Jacob Astor, whose sprawling empire traded in fur and flour, guns and opium. Broadway boasted elegant townhouses and its "neat awnings" and "well-dressed pedestrians" impressed even the critical eye of the English traveler Frances Trollope. Most New Yorkers, however, knew a different city, one in which men and women struggled to make ends meet in an unpredictable and rapidly changing economy. Some found work in the new manufactories springing up near the waterfront, but others, including artisans who might once have prospered from their trades, lost ground. The frigid winter of 1817, which saw horse-drawn sleighs crossing the thick ice between Manhattan and Governors' Island, threw into high relief the number of New Yorkers dependent on charity for firewood and food.[4]

It all seemed a long way from St. Mary's Mountain and St. Joseph's Valley. But the two worlds were connected by the kind of community—born of correspondence, kinship, and shared purpose—that had so often shaped Elizabeth Seton's life. A small band of elite Catholics, concerned by the suffering of poor Catholic New Yorkers, founded the Roman Catholic Benevolent Society (RCBS) not long after 1817's dreadful winter. In doing so they rejected a growing sense among New York's elite that the poor needed correction rather than charity; drawing on the ideas of British political economists such as Jeremy Bentham, that new breed of reformer argued that almsgiving encouraged "indolence, dissipation and consequent pauperism." The Society for the Prevention of Pauperism (SPP), begun at nearly the same time as the RCBS, even criticized Isabella Graham's poor widows' society; its aid to widows with children, the SPP insisted, encouraged childless women to become pregnant, which "ought not to be tolerated in a christian land." The women of the society disagreed, continuing to work on its behalf and on behalf of the city's orphan asylum, founded a decade earlier by women including Isabella Graham's daughter Joanna Bethune; Elizabeth's godmother, Sarah Startin; and her friend Eliza Sadler.[5]

Participants in the RCBS agreed that aid must be given, and they found the existing orphan asylum insufficient in more ways than one. Intended to keep children out of the city's almshouse, the asylum was hard-pressed to serve the city's growing population of needy children. Equally troubling to the Roman Catholic Benevolent Society's founders was the fact that the asylum offered children only Protestant educations and bound orphans out only to Manhattanites in good standing with a Protestant church.[6] Francis Cooper, a cathedral trustee and the state's first Catholic legislator, had witnessed Rose White's work at the Philadelphia orphanage and decided Manhattan needed a similar institution. RCBS members believed the children deserved compassion; they may also have been eager to prevent Catholics from becoming a larger and more visible presence among the poor, especially as the poor were looked on with increasing disfavor.

Francis Cooper found a valuable ally in Robert Fox, a well-heeled Catholic whose wife had befriended Elizabeth after her conversion and whose three daughters now attended St. Joseph's Academy. The two men arranged for the purchase of a cheap but roomy house near St. Patrick's Cathedral, which, consecrated in 1815, stood north of the city's dense old neighborhoods in an area still studded with farmers' fields. Cooper and Fox also spoke to Bishop John Connolly, an Irish-born Dominican who had arrived not long after the consecration of St. Patrick's and who was said to have a heart for the poorer members of his diocese.

Soon two letters arrived at St. Joseph's House. The first, from Robert Fox, personally appealed to Elizabeth to send sisters to New York. The second was a formal request from the bishop. "Madam," John Connolly wrote, "Many pious and zealous Catholics of New York [are] very desirous that we should have here for the relief and education of poor Catholic children such an Orphan Asylum as there is at Philadelphia, under the care of your Religious Society." Such was the coziness of this tiny Catholic world that the bishop specifically requested Sister Margaret George start the institution.[7]

It was another opportunity for the sisters to pursue their Vincentian mission, and Elizabeth, the council, and John Dubois quickly agreed to send three women to New York. Margaret George was deemed essential at Emmitsburg, so it was decided that Rose White should begin this mission as she had the one in Philadelphia. Elizabeth explained that Rose "will keep so well the dignity of rules and good intentions."

Dubois was as usual more practical: he told Bishop Connolly that Rose was "better calculated" than Margaret George "to guide the beginners of New York." She was a skilled manager prepared to train others in any setting to which she might be posted. The sisters' mission to New York followed on the heels of Isabella Graham's pioneering work, but it drew as well on the French Catholic tradition of the Filles de la Charité. That tradition fit with a turn toward institutional care, and it fostered a protoprofessionalization of charity that American female Protestant benevolence could not muster.[8]

There may have been a final, less acknowledged inspiration: Pierre Toussaint. Toussaint, now honored by the Catholic Church as "venerable," was a devout Catholic and former slave from Saint-Domingue who had for years single-handedly supported his widowed mistress through his work as a society hairdresser. Freed at his mistress's death in 1807, Toussaint used his money and social connections to Manhattan's elite to support Catholic charitable activities, and he and his wife took orphans of African descent into their home. Toussaint had been a parishioner when Elizabeth joined St. Peter's, but it is unclear whether she knew of him or whether his efforts directly inspired Roman Catholic Benevolent Society members. Nonetheless, Toussaint became an important fundraiser for the society and the sisters' work, his own generosity and his connections to Manhattan's Protestant and Catholic grandees proving invaluable. "Received from Toussaint the sum of $53.56 money which he collected from subscribers," reads an 1821 receipt signed by Cecilia O'Conway; in 1832, Toussaint collected one-third of all donations to the sisters' asylum.[9]

That lay in the future. In 1817, the orphanage was still just an imperfectly laid plan. Rose White prepared to leave Philadelphia, both her vow of obedience and her love of a challenge pointing her toward Manhattan. A second sister, Felicitas Brady, also set off for the new mission without apparent qualm. But the third sister was Cecilia O'Conway, and she struggled to resign herself to the instruction she'd been given. This was a woman who'd wanted to be a Carmelite; laboring in an orphanage in Manhattan would leave her even less time for prayer and meditation than she found at Emmitsburg. "If you suffer so much the better for our high journey above," Elizabeth reminded her. "The only fear I have is that you will let the old string pull too hard for solitude and silence." Elizabeth herself often felt mismatched to her sisterhood's active life, but "this is not a country my dear one for Solitude and Silence, but of warfare and crucifixion."[10] Cecilia went to New York.

The sisters discovered that the house purchased for their use had been an informal hospital during the Revolution. Still known as the Dead House, it had bloodstains on its floors and a boarder who declined to be dislodged. Rose realized that the $600 allotted her in Philadelphia was a princely sum compared with what she'd been given in New York: $36 per year for each of the sisters and a vague promise of more from the RCBS. Yet there was good will in abundance; the Fox family took in the sisters while the Dead House was rendered habitable, and Catherine Dupleix, now a Catholic herself, offered companionship. Soon the women took in their first five children. Cecilia clashed with Rose as she'd feared she might, but Rose took no offense. Everyone was "miserable enough" in their faults, Elizabeth reminded Cecilia, and the women carried on with their work.[11]

When Dubois and the council had agreed to send sisters to Manhattan, they'd made two demands: the asylum's trustees would be responsible for finances and a society of Catholic ladies would be formed, modeled on Philadelphia's "lady managers," in order to mediate between the trustees and the sisters.[12] The ladies' society was duly created, and along with the RCBS began raising funds, including by selling tickets to a discussion of the question "Are the intellectual faculties of women equal to those of men?"[13] The choice of subject signaled society members' confidence, not deference, and members were equally confident that their faith need not limit their civic role. Although the orphanage had been created in part to ensure that destitute Catholic children received a Catholic education and not a Protestant one, the society appealed for funds in the language of Christian harmony; members hoped that all "Ladies of New York . . . will cheerfully contribute towards the support of an institution, the object of which is to bring up in the principles of Religion and morality a number of poor forlorn creatures whose situation calls for the sympathetic feelings of the human heart."[14] No Protestant seems to have objected. The rhetoric and assumptions of antipopery lurked, and would one day, when Catholic refugees arrived by the thousands in Eastern cities, surge anew. But when the sisters began their New York mission in 1818, daily tolerance was more powerful than old animosities, and so was the desire to reduce, or at least to contain, the city's growing ranks of poor.

In fact, Elizabeth worried less about Protestant opposition to the orphanage than she did about misunderstanding between the Catholic members of the ladies' society and the sisters. Convinced that laywomen might look with distaste on the rule by which the sisters lived, she turned to a graduate of St. Joseph's Academy, a young woman named Ellen Gottesberger, to serve as cultural broker. "You know so much of the sacred principles of our rules which seem so odd to strangers," Elizabeth wrote her former student, "that you can take their part, and often show the truth in her beautiful colors." The black flannel habit, the strict schedule of work and prayer, and the celibate existence must be understood as evidence not of superstition or oppression but rather of a life freely chosen. Ask those unsettled by the sisters' regulations, Elizabeth counseled, "what would a life in the service of God be without rules?"[15] Ellen obliged, and the sisters and ladies worked harmoniously. The sisters' Vincentian rule, rooted in a French past, was drawing them seamlessly into an American future. In decades to come, Sisters of Charity would serve waves of immigrant Catholics, their skills and local knowledge proving essential as the Catholic Church's center of gravity shifted to the urban Northeast.

For now, the sisterhood and the American Church were still rooted in Maryland, and in early 1817 Robert Goodloe Harper, with Samuel Cooper's approval, helped to secure incorporation of the Sisters of Charity of St. Joseph's in that state. Decades earlier, former Jesuits had constituted themselves as the Roman Catholic Gentlemen of Maryland, turning to incorporation so that they, a group who persisted through generations but was not a family, might have "perpetual succession" and "powers and privileges for taking, holding, and disposing of property." Now the sisters incorporated themselves, their Vincentian spirit transposed into a civic key. As "unmarried women," the statute reads, they "have formed themselves into a religious association, by the name of the Sisters of Charity of St. Joseph's, and under the superintendence of certain clergymen, of their religious persuasion, for works of piety, charity and usefulness, and especially for the care of the sick, the succor of aged, infirm and necessitous persons, and the education of young females." Incorporation was even more empowering for the sisters than it had been for the Jesuits (here, in fact, they had more in common with Isabella Graham's society for poor widows, which also incorporated, than with the Society of Jesus). As individual women, they faced all the disabilities law and custom imposed. But the corporate body that was the Sisters of Charity could take its place in the nation "in as full and ample a manner as any person or body corporate"—although they might need the aid of a male lawyer to do it.[16]

"THE FAULTS OF THEIR CHILDREN"

As 1817 began, the complex and improbable experiment that was the Sisters of Charity had become a confident and competent actor in the world. The same could not yet be said of William or Richard Seton. First, William. Convinced that he should leave Italy and pursue a naval career, he complained to his mother that his hand shook when he copied letters, that Antonio offered him no real hope of advancement, and that he was miserable in "this line of life" he'd never wanted. "I should long ago have made this explanation," William wrote, "but knowing how much your wishes were bent on the course we at first pursued and how much our happiness (if I may be allowed the expression) depended on the success of it, I thought it but reasonable to take sufficient time for a fair trial." He believed that a fair trial had now been conducted, and the "impossibility of succeeding" in Livorno fully demonstrated.[17]

Elizabeth was moved by both her son's unhappiness and his resolution. She wrote Antonio that if William was indeed failing as a clerk, he should not stay.[18] Then she released her son from the prison of obedience in which he'd felt confined. She still feared what might become of William in the navy, but the choice was his. Her own terrors, she told him, "shall never bind you to any course of life you do not willingly embrace."[19] Antonio prepared a letter for William to carry back with him to his mother, and a grateful William made arrangements to sail home as soon as he could.

Elizabeth admired William's determination even if she regretted his goal. Although she had named her second son after her father, it was William who seemed to possess Richard Bayley's force of will. Richard, by contrast, seemed weak, a collection of whims held together by other people's money. "The destruction of all your grandfather's family . . . happened through their dependence on [their] Father," she was moved to remember, contemplating her younger son's conduct in Baltimore.[20] Nor was fecklessness all she worried about. Richard was living in the house of a cathedral trustee, but word of any number of misadventures ("scrapes," Dubois called them, with his love for American idioms) made its way back to Emmitsburg. When Richard reassured his mother that he passed his days at the Tiernans' "all alone, making out bills, entering notes, &c. all day . . . quite a man of business & respectability," she knew better than to believe him.[21] "He is a fine young man," Tiernan's son-in-law had reported, "but will be lost for want of employment, and by company."[22] Richard's determination not to appear "the Mountain Boy" meant he avoided all religious observance. "Here if you speak of Confession, or Communion, more of going to church, you are laughed at, and made fun of, by all the young men, Protestant as well as Catholic," Richard complained to Dubois.[23]

One person still believed in Richard: his sister Catherine. In the fall of 1817 a stunned Elizabeth told Julia that Richard had spent "all that poor Kit had saved by her piano lessons and your constant remittances."[24] She and Dubois were horrified; Catherine was not. Thanking Julia for sending another fifty dollars, the girl quietly warned her benefactor not to expect her to keep it to herself. "Mother has given it in my care," she wrote, "but I cannot bear to have anything without sharing it with Richard."[25] Catherine loved her brother's graceful wit and affectionate manner, so different from her own reserve. She also knew that he lived in his brother's shadow; William was their mother's favored son, and even Bec had felt "double the affection" for William.[26] In Baltimore, Richard was at last living at the center of his own life, and Catherine cheered him on.

Worried that her younger son traipsed toward debt, disgrace, or both, Elizabeth hinted to Antonio that perhaps Richard might find a place in an Italian merchant house.[27] John Hickey proposed an idea Elizabeth herself had reluctantly abandoned: the young priest wrote to ask Richard to consider entering the seminary in Baltimore. "I have not such a calling," Richard wrote, adding wistfully, "many a time do I wish I had, tried and (you may almost say) forced myself to it, I would not have experienced so many unhappy hours." Nonetheless, Richard insisted he was no longer "the wild rattlebrained fellow I was some months ago," adding that he was soon leaving Baltimore altogether.[28] A week after his letter to Hickey, Richard wrote to his mother and Dubois asking them to set him up as a tenant on a farm he'd happened across.[29] He wanted to leave the "wicked city," he explained, where a man had to face ridicule simply to go to Mass. He just needed some more money to make that happen.

Elizabeth and Dubois did not send money. But they allowed Richard to leave his Baltimore position, their hope of removing him from temptation outweighing their desire that he be gainfully employed. So Richard was back at the Mount when word arrived from Baltimore that brother William was home from Europe.

After the first exhilarated greetings, William handed his mother Antonio's letter. She must have found it painful to read. Although Antonio acknowledged that William's shaking hand made his work difficult, he laid the blame for William's failure squarely at the young man's feet. William "thoroughly disappointed my expectation in point of rendering him useful to my Countinghouse," not only because of his "physical weakness" but because of "his own moral indifference, if not aversion to trade in general." Antonio also reported that Italy had done nothing for William's Catholic faith.[30]

Elizabeth had once complained to Bruté that "American parents" were "most difficult" "in hearing the faults of their children."[31] Now she proved unwilling to contemplate her own son's faults, instead blaming herself for William's failure: she'd allowed him to suck his fingers as a child, and that had made his hand shake, and from thence arose all the trouble.[32] Rather than dwell on what Antonio might mean about William's unimproved faith, she took comfort in the merchant's assurance he was "of perfect character and most mild disposition." Elizabeth wrote resolutely that her beloved son had returned and was "the same dear amiable dutiful child" he had always been. She also seized on a welcome announcement buried in Antonio's stern letter. Despite William's failure, Antonio was willing to take on Richard as a clerk, as long as he had "a good will and a good handwriting."[33] Elizabeth began to make arrangements to send her younger son to the Filicchis.

Decades earlier, the Setons' merchant network had secured an appointment for Henry Seton despite his dubious character. Although she'd recently called herself "a poor Nobody," Elizabeth now had friends—some of them the same people who had financed the sisters' new mission to New York—who proved if anything more effective. Robert Fox arranged to meet the vice president of the United States, Daniel D. Tompkins, at Staten Island, and Francis Cooper asked the help of John Quincy Adams.[34] Such influence bore its expected fruit, and William received an appointment to the navy on the satisfyingly patriotic date of July 4.[35]

That left Richard, and with the help of the newly indispensable Robert Fox, he was soon ready to sail for Europe to replace his brother at the Filicchis' merchant house. Elizabeth did not give her younger son a long letter of loving advice, such as she'd written for William, and she was less than sanguine with Antonio. "With his quick temper and want of experience," she confessed, Richard "is in continual dangers which his Brother escapes."[36] But Richard resolved to surprise everyone, and as the ship embarked, he put his graceful prose to an uncharacteristically earnest end. "Mother, love and delight concentrate in three dear beings," he wrote, "tho' not a tear came when we parted, yet every one that was forced back, went down, deep to the bottom of my heart."[37]

Three beings: his brother, mother, and last living sister. Of the three, Catherine was sorriest to see Richard leave. She considered his every flaw the slight misalignment of a virtue and hoped that in Italy he would find his footing. Catherine herself seemed never to lose hers. Even her charges at St. Joseph's Academy loved her; when she spent time in Baltimore, a boarder named Biddy wrote pledging her undying (and slightly competitive) love. Calling the sixteen-year-old Catherine "Mother" and "dear Mother," Biddy reported, "One of the girls said she would take my place in being your child, and made me very angry, but I won't tell her name."[38]

Amid her teaching duties, Catherine also pursued the kind of reading and extracting her mother had long ago enjoyed. Deep in one of Elizabeth's old commonplace books appears the heading "Catharine Charlton Seton 9th January 1819, Extracts from Rollin's Roman History St. Joseph's House Maryland age 18." There followed paragraphs relating information about vestal virgins "buried alive" and the veneration of Roman gods.[39] Some of Catherine's contemporaries might have thought a teenaged girl who lived in a convent and was called Mother was herself buried alive. Catherine would have laughingly dismissed such a claim, but her mother, Dubois, and Bruté believed she must spend more time outside St. Joseph's. Elizabeth hoped her daughter might be suited for life in a religious community, but she agreed with Bruté and Dubois that the girl must not embark on it too early. "Fear infinitely to force by degrees her vocation," Bruté wrote in an undated note. "Leave her to her divine Master."[40]

So as her brothers left for Italy and the navy, Catherine was sent to spend weeks with Julia Scott, the Chatards, and the New York clan. She

enjoyed the visits but weighed each dinner invitation and article of clothing on the scale of her mother's judgments. "I am afraid to trust myself.
I have not you beloved to guide me. Do write soon," Catherine one
day pleaded. Visiting Philadelphia, she declined because of the Lenten
season to attend a ball, then agreed to please her hosts by viewing the
decorations and dancing from behind a curtain, clad in a plain dress.
"All was like a fairy scene to me," the young woman marveled in a letter
home. "Such a collection of beauty and dress astonished me." But had
she sinned? "I hope I was not wrong to go," Catherine told her mother.
"I did not dress or join the company but was merely a spectator."[41]

Elizabeth had once feared her old friend would lead Bec astray, but
Julia helped Catherine enter society without losing sight of her mother's
teachings. As had been the case throughout Julia and Elizabeth's long
friendship, differences formed not an abyss but a bridge: Julia's appreciation of fashion, for example, meant she understood the symbolic importance of dress, and she asked Catherine how she would like to present
herself. "Plain but not singular," Kit replied carefully, and Julia ensured
she had just the clothing she needed. Julia showed an interest in Catherine's beliefs but never demanded the girl defend them to her. "I never
hesitate to explain my sentiments when required on a particular subject—religion—and she never pressed me," Catherine told her mother,
adding, "I love and admire her for it."[42] Kindness and mutual respect
kept open the border between St. Joseph's House and genteel society, and
Catherine crossed it at will. The question of where she would make her
life, in the sisterhood or in the world, could for now be put off.

BEHIND THE CURTAIN

While her surviving children explored the world, Elizabeth was
pondering the distance she'd traveled in her own life. She wanted to lead
her daughter safely through the genteel world she'd once known, and her
reflections were also motivated by a shocking bit of news: a young printer
in New Jersey, a Presbyterian named Isaac Kollock, had published the
diary Elizabeth kept during her long-ago journey to Italy. *Memoirs of
Mrs. S: A Fragment of Real History Written by herself* appeared in
1817. Kollock's foreword praised the Catholic convert "Mrs. S." without reserve, comparing her favorably to famous Protestant female writers and predicting that "all her writings," when revealed, would "be

considered an acquisition to the Christian's library, and precious in the annals of American literature."[43] Kollock promoted the drama of Elizabeth's story and the strength of her Christian faith rather than praising or deploring her conversion to Catholicism. The printer wanted a paying readership, not a harvest of souls.

When Elizabeth learned that her journal had been published, she desperately tried to lay hands on a copy. Although she had for years circulated her writing to friends (one of whom, it seems, eventually shared the Italian journal with Kollock), the exposure of her thoughts to strangers wounded her. She also worried that something in the journal, which she'd begun as a fervent Protestant, might cast doubt on the legitimacy of the faith she'd chosen. But soon after the journal's publication, Catherine was shown a copy during a stay in Baltimore. "Do not be uneasy," she quickly wrote her mother. "There is nothing in it you need repent of not one single protestant expression, the only thing is that every disinterested person should be acquainted with your private feelings." A former student added further reassurance. "I do not think it has those pompous protestant expressions," she soothed Elizabeth, adding, "indeed dearest I believe any other woman but you would be proud of it."[44]

To Kollock's disappointment and Elizabeth's relief, the *Memoirs of Mrs. S.* faded quickly into obscurity. But the incident left her contemplating the trail of words she'd left in her journey from Betsy Bayley to Mother Seton. Notes, letters, and journals held vignettes from her girlhood in Manhattan, bulletins from her marriage, and rhapsodic mentions of Rousseau's *Emile*. Even once she had become Mother Seton, she'd written letters she was loath to have others read: complaints to Babade about Dubourg, to Dubourg about David, to Bruté, although more gently, about Dubois. Elizabeth also worried over what she saw as Americans' simultaneous fascination by and horror at convents and nuns. Someone who hated her work might shame her; someone who admired her might accidentally do the same. (In 1818 Pierre Babade wrote to announce that he planned to publish an account of Elizabeth's life, undoubtedly celebrating his own role within it.)[45] There were any number of ways that the letters and journals in which Elizabeth had thought through her complicated life might come to light. So she resolved to burn them.

Simon Bruté stopped her. The priest believed even more fervently than Elizabeth that her life before Catholicism was filled with error. But he was an inveterate chronicler and collector who thought that truthful history, like good science, taught God's lessons. He and Elizabeth may have destroyed some documents—letters from Julia Scott, for example, are notably scarce before the Emmitsburg years, there are fewer from William Magee Seton than one might expect, and Elizabeth's correspondence with Babade during her unhappy first months at Emmitsburg is thin. But Bruté made sure that much of her life's writings were preserved. His annotations occasionally lament Elizabeth's cosmopolitan, Protestant past: "Some older" letters, Bruté noted, "relate to the danger she was in for infidelity—seduced by reading Rousseau and Voltaire—many volumes of which she had yet and delivered to me."[46] For the most part, however, Bruté believed that Elizabeth's archive offered its own evidence of her deliverance from error into the truth of the Church. It is not without irony that his single-minded confidence preserved the story of Elizabeth's life of inquiry, struggle, and choice.

Bruté did more than protect existing documents; he also encouraged Elizabeth to tell him about her childhood and young womanhood: "Her father doted on her—she loved him so much," he scrawled on one page. Impressed by Elizabeth's connections ("Hamilton—Knox," he noted); he nonetheless believed that the woman herself was worthy of commemoration. Around this time, he likely encouraged her to write what became "Dear Remembrances," the impressionistic fragments in which Elizabeth depicted moments in her life as stepping-stones toward a rich Catholic faith.[47]

"Dear Remembrances" was conceived as a guide for strangers who might one day seek to understand Mother Seton. At roughly the same time, Elizabeth also began to fill a red notebook with reflections and advice for her daughter Catherine. The notebook's contents were not meant for the public eye, and they are as contradictory and spiky as "Dear Remembrances" is smooth and opaque. Some pages offer briskly sensible advice: Elizabeth deems dancing "good exercise," cautions Kit against marrying "an unprincipled man," and explains the usefulness of "simplicity" in dress ("it makes a lovely woman more lovely, and even an ugly one pleasing"). Other pages crackle with ambivalence about the social world through which Elizabeth had once moved. Catherine must have pure principles, Elizabeth warned, because once she fell in love, "Passion will soon blind poor reason and even a Mother's tears would have no power to save her darling." Despite Elizabeth's own happy marriage, nuptials for Catherine appears rather like the navy for William: a choice Elizabeth lamented but would not seek to undo. "Never will I abuse your love for me by such severity," she told her daughter, "so do do mind your first step as if it was for your whole life."[48]

Still other pages bear witness to a darker vision. Perhaps in response to Catherine's story of standing behind a curtain looking out at the "fairy scene" of a ball, Elizabeth urged her daughter to "look behind the curtain." She would discover that "a ball room" contains "a horrible massacre of souls . . . souls destroying souls, women with the form of angels rousing the Vilest passions of men." If that warning seems inconsistent with Elizabeth's calm observation that dancing is good exercise, it is: the red notebook reads in some parts like an advice manual from a widow who'd known happiness in the world, and in others like a broadside from an impatient cloistered mystic. Elizabeth counsels moderation and praises the "empire of reason" yet also writes that "'tis impious to be calm. Passion is reason." She demands a single-minded devotion to God that would place Catherine at war with American society; yet she also insists to her daughter that uniting one's life with God fosters gentleness and peace. To the extent Elizabeth offers Catherine a way to reconcile these directives, it is the cultivation of humility. Still troubled by the harshness of her own judgments, Elizabeth urges her daughter to consider herself no more worthy of God's mercy than anyone else and to seek the good in everyone. "Every object has two faces," Elizabeth tells her, "[and] we should endeavor to discover and adopt the best." If one loved God humbly as well as passionately, one would be ethical and happy as well as devout. "Communication with God," Elizabeth tells her daughter, "gives an unspeakable sweetness and joy to the heart, under its influence we feel light and gay, the temper is calmed and softened so that good humour and cheerfulness cost nothing; what we love, in this happy turn of piety, we love still better, every thing around us looks smiling, and we enjoy a foretaste of ETERNAL LOVE."[49]

The red notebook marked both Elizabeth's break with her past and her connection to it. Her father had shared commonplace books containing classical history, cosmopolitan affirmations of religious diversity, and descriptions of scientific advances. Elizabeth shared with her own daughter an impassioned exhortation to love God above all else. Yet share it she did. No less than her father had, she wished to know and guide her daughter's mind, and no less than her father had, she accepted that her daughter would use her mind in ways she could not predict or approve. In the book she created for Catherine, Elizabeth quoted a verse by Young, a favored poet of her youth. The lines celebrate the wisdom of the oracle at Delphi. "KNOW THYSELF," Elizabeth wrote in large letters. "ALL Wisdom centres there / To none man seems ignoble but to man." Elizabeth still believed in the need for self-knowledge; now that knowledge consisted of understanding that one's true purpose lay in relationship to the divine. Long plagued by her sense of the fragility of everyone and everything she loved, Elizabeth wanted Catherine to know that she would find permanence—eternity—in God. "We are but like grains of sand, with which the wind sporteth, if we do not attach

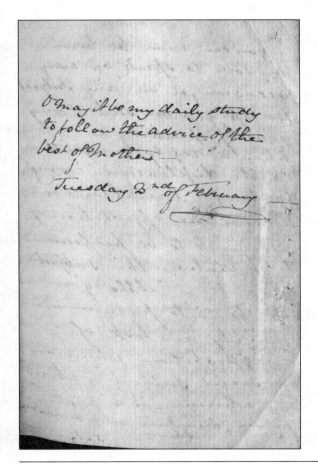

FIGURE 21.2. Catherine Seton's Little Red Book, inscription. APSL 1–3–3–25b. Courtesy of the Daughters of Charity Province of St. Louise Archives, Emmitsburg, Maryland.

ourselves immoveable to that point of support," she told her daughter. Man, she continued, "must perceive an infinite being whose image he is and in whose sight he is but—AN ATOM."[50]

THE SCHOOLS THRIVE

St. Joseph's and Mount St. Mary's had been receiving students for close to a decade, and by 1817 each enrolled more than fifty children. Focused on boarders but providing educations to locals at reduced cost, the institutions were important both to the region and to a larger web of well-heeled Catholic families (and some Protestant ones too). The Harpers, Carrolls, and Catons continued to be an important part of that web; Emily and Louisa Caton sent loving letters and donations to Emmitsburg, and when in January of 1817 Louisa married the English war hero Sir Felton Hervey-Bathurst, St. Joseph's House gained its first friend in the English peerage.

Dubois and Elizabeth stood together at the center of the linked schools, sharing a gift for loving but stern judgment that drew the respect of students and the confidence of parents. "It is a great comfort to perceive that my little darling is so affectionately attached to all the good Ladies and children," a satisfied father wrote, "and indeed I may say even to every rule and practice of that Holy institution."[51] A wealthy Protestant Philadelphian who had fathered a child out of wedlock sought to enroll the girl at St. Joseph's because he believed its quiet orderliness would ensure she received a good education and was spared "ever seeing the finger of shame pointed at her."[52]

Busy translating works of devotion, penning spiritual instructions for the sisters, and seeking to guide her own surviving children to adulthood, Elizabeth nonetheless remained the final arbiter of discipline for the boarders, and she calibrated her guidance, encouragement, and criticism to each temperament. "I think you are too anxious for the fruit of your dear little tree," she wrote one mother. "If there is a true danger for one of her turn, it would be to push her too fast, and force an exterior look without the interior spirit."[53] Like Dubois, Elizabeth considered criticism an essential tool of the teacher but one that must be grounded in intimate knowledge and in an appeal to the student's own conscience. "The faults of young people," she told John Hickey, maladroit in his efforts to reform a younger sister, "must be moved by prayers and tears because they are constitutional and cannot be frightened out—I have said much harder things to her than you do, but turning the tune in her own heart."[54]

Mary Diana Harper had heard more "hard things" from Elizabeth than almost anyone else, and although she'd once wanted nothing more than to leave St. Joseph's, she now wrote affectionately and respectfully from France. Elizabeth responded with the kind of counsel she'd always provided the girl. "The first step to happiness," she sternly reminded her, "is to subdue our feelings." She also urged the young woman to remember how much more fortunate she was than the lost Rebecca, but there Elizabeth's insight failed her: even as she wrote, Mary Diana's own fragile health was breaking. In January, a visiting Louisa Caton found her in need of last rites. Not long after, Mary Diana was dead.[55]

The Harpers had sent their troublesome, beloved daughter abroad to preserve her health and finish her education. Now she'd died far from home, on a date her parents did not even know. "Our darling child, our delight and our hope," Robert Goodloe Harper mourned. "How must her tender and affectionate heart have yearned for us." The distinguished lawyer and politician did what so many young boarders had done: he opened his heart to Mother Seton. Harper knew, he told her, that he should "rejoice that [Mary Diana] has been admitted after so short & happy a probation to that eternal reward." But he could not welcome his child's death: "I taste the full bitterness of the cup which I know that it is my duty to drink."[56] Elizabeth replied with delicacy and compassion, not instruction. "I hesitate much my dear sir," she began, "in daring to say a word to you at this moment, yet your Mary was my own, more than you can imagine." So well had she known Mary's "particular turn of temper" and "lovely Soul" that she felt "as if I too was losing again a dear darling child." Never imagining that Mary Diana had contracted her consumption at St. Joseph's Academy, the Harpers took comfort in keeping their younger daughters, Emily and Elizabeth, under Elizabeth's care, and she turned the memory of the turbulent young woman into an "angel" for her little sisters to emulate.[57]

Like Elizabeth, Dubois remained indefatigable and essential. He supervised the Mount's instructors, disciplined the boys, and communicated with their parents. "Religion, inconstant and neglectful . . . English reading, reads without method and application . . . Latin, pretty well lately" reads a blunt report card. Dubois also oversaw the institutions' building and grounds projects, and students' reminiscences attest to his

genius at harnessing children's energy to his own ends. "The amusements of the boys, besides marbles, tops, and some athletic games," one
later recalled, "were sometimes of a very practical character. On one
occasion we gathered up all the loose stones about the premises and filled
up a frog pond in the garden, which it was desired to obliterate; another
time we spent a whole day clearing the stones out of the roadway to the
church and with them filling in the roadway of the stone bridge." The
school's rustic, frugal nature is unmistakable in these reminiscences, but
Dubois made it seem born of a careful effort to build character rather
than of the school's chronic debts. Wealthy boys woke at dawn on winter mornings and filed outside to wash their faces in troughs of water,
frozen droplets slicking the ground. Boys accustomed to seeing slaves do
manual labor found themselves "furnished with small axes to prepare
the kindling-wood" and waited tables at meals.[58] Like the Seton clan in
Manhattan, parents of children at the Mount thought of Emmitsburg
as a different, purer realm. "I cannot indeed describe to you my feelings
and my sentiments," one father wrote, "on quitting Mt. St. Marys to
enter again into the unmeaning bustle of a world that has become dis-
gusting to me."[59]

Baltimore's Sulpicians took a different view. When they thought of
Mount St. Mary's, they thought not of purity but of debt. A letter from
the superior general of the Sulpicians in Paris, relating the good things
Simon Bruté had said of the Mount and hoping it would never "degenerate into a college," only made them more unhappy. Was it not already
just a college, its original incarnation as a petit seminaire abandoned
nearly at its start? And did the Mount not therefore lie outside the French
order's mission of training priests? Even if the Sulpicians agreed that
Catholicism must adapt to American circumstances, must they completely abandon the purposes for which they'd been founded? The crisis
of Revolution and emigration now past, the Sulpicians thought it was
time to reassert control, not least because the Mount still drained their
coffers. In the spring of 1818, Superior Jean Tessier asked John Hickey
to "take a very attentive view of current expenses" at the school and to
do so without telling Dubois.[60] Hickey, so often the one watched and
found wanting, willingly took up the job. Not long after, word reached
Dubois that his brethren were considering closing the Mount for good.

Dubois was furious and Bruté disheartened; although the latter was
president of the Baltimore seminary, it was the Blue Ridge that he loved.

The two priests let it be known that were the Mount to lose the Sulpicians' support, they might try to continue it on their own. "This disposition is in direct contradiction with the spirit of the society," wrote an astonished Tessier.[61] Unmoved by Bruté and Dubois's opposition, the Baltimore Sulpicians resolved to sever ties with the mountain school.

One set of supporters having stunningly threatened to depart, another set, equally stunningly, stepped forward. Locals had come to see St. Joseph's and Mount. St. Mary's as linked institutions bringing education and refinement to a place otherwise overshadowed by Baltimore, Philadelphia, and the District of Columbia. When news spread of plans to close the Mount, neighbors took action. A Catholic carpenter named Thomas Radford brought word that he and a few others were willing to provide financing in order to keep the seminary where it was.[62] "A most interesting scene took place here last week," Elizabeth wrote William. "The Sulpicians of Baltimore (except poor Mr. Bruté) solicited Mr. Dubois' suppression of the Seminary. . . . and lo our good Emmitsburgers came forward [and] offered Mr. Dubois 8 or 10,000 [dollars] in hand and to buy the Seminary for him if he chose, if only he would not leave them."[63]

Dubois later wrote to Paris describing the offer as an interest-free loan, but whatever its precise terms, it was a generous and dramatic gesture. The locals felt the Mount belonged in Emmitsburg and if it also needed to belong *to* Emmitsburg, so be it. The proffered loan helped convince Archbishop Marèchal to broker a compromise between the Sulpicians and the school. The Mount would remain affiliated with the order, and seminarians could continue to assist with its teaching; the official tie would be directly to Paris, however, not through Baltimore, and title to the property would be transferred from Tessier to Dubois. This was quickly achieved, and Dubois arranged for public notice to be given that the school was continuing as before.[64]

The Mount saved, Dubois, as always, looked forward. He saw the struggle as evidence of a fundamental structural problem that the Sulpicians must yet confront, and he explained the issue in terms Elizabeth had over the years come to appreciate: American circumstance and good governance. "Saint Sulpice has not yet any government in America," he wrote to a superior in Paris. "We need a constitution adapted to our local situation [and] to our distance from the central government." In the absence of such a constitution—and, Dubois warned pointedly, in the absence of local clergy who could carry out the French superior's will "without a constitution"—harmony and order would continue to be elusive.[65] A universal Church required local adaptation; adaptation, Dubois believed, could happen only when authority was clearly defined. He presciently believed that clear rules and hierarchies would make Catholicism in America more, not less able to thrive in the ever-changing landscape of the United States.

The contretemps had highlighted the complexities of the Mount's international, national, and local allegiances. More subtly, it also underscored the centrality of gender. Gender separated Mount St. Mary's from St. Joseph's House: the former had priests, seminarians, male boarders, and local boys; the latter had sisters, novices, female boarders, and local girls. Yet gender also brought the institutions together: the division of secular and religious labor meant that men needed women and women men. Sisters saw to the domestic arrangements of the Mount, while Dubois negotiated contracts and oversaw the labor of free and enslaved workers. Men performed the sacramental labor of the Church but coveted the sisters' prayers and relied on Elizabeth's spiritual guidance and charisma. So entwined were the institutions that when the Mount was saved, the sisterhood at St. Joseph's may have been saved with it.

MAKING MONEY

While the Mount's fate was being decided, Richard Seton was in Italy, absorbed by his own unexpected plight: tedium. "I'm surprised, Bill, that you never even hinted to me the consequences of my coming out when you knew them so well," he reproached his older brother. "Had you told me . . . why then I'd have considered matters and things before I came, but instead of that, you painted it in the liveliest colours, and told me all the sweet (if there be any here) and not one word about the sour." Bored nearly senseless, Richard was outraged to learn that William had told his fellow card-playing expatriates that his younger brother should never come. "Why did you not keep your word, when stamping in the square, you swore that Dick should never come out here?" he demanded. But Richard asked William to keep secret his discontent.[66] He would stay "ten years" before he disappointed their mother.

Had he been more like William, Richard would have settled into a stolid unhappiness, declining to complain to Antonio and cheering himself up by taking his brother's seat at the card table. But the outgoing nature that had drawn Richard near disgrace in Baltimore led him to explore his Italian surroundings with open eyes. He visited the Tower of Pisa and the Campo Santo, where he marveled at the "beautiful paintings of all kinds" (although "that much celebrated river the Arno," he found "not half as handsome as Tom's creek.")[67] Richard spent so much time with Italians that he wondered whether he was forgetting his English, and he quizzed Antonio directly about his future, coming away from the conversation optimistic that he would advance to earn $1,000 per year. Six weeks after his despairing letter to William, Richard had changed his view. He wrote to Catherine declaring that William "had been led astray" but that he, Richard, would not fail. He had visited their father's grave, he told her, and sat thinking about how he would take care of everyone. Catherine could stay with him in his flat. "You will find beautiful walks here, and oh would to God we had the happiness to be all together." The work in Livorno was hard, but Richard welcomed it. "Pleasure has often conquered me to lead me astray, but pain never shall," he wrote grandly. "I can bear a great deal in such cases, when I am spoken to as a man and not corrected as a boy." "I feel such a wish to be a merchant that I know I'll never wish for anything else."[68]

Five days later, Richard was bored again. But when his exuberance ebbed, his confidence remained. He would make his mark in Italy and care for the sister who had so often cared for him (and he would make extra money teaching English to French girls). I write to "ease a mother's heart, which I well know I have so often wounded," he told his mother," tho' as often been forgiven with love & kindness." Richard's witty letters bore some of Sam's old charm, and Elizabeth again hoped for the best.[69]

The letters also offered occasional glimpses of Antonio, and it was clear the merchant was a weary man. "Ah, these gentlemen are always troubling me with their orders, or something or other," he grumbled one day, on opening a note from yet another Maryland priest.[70] When Antonio found time to write to Elizabeth directly, his tone was less cranky but sober. J. Murray & Sons had gone bankrupt and owed the Filicchi house more than $30,000. Antonio explained that he would not take over Filippo's pledge of support to the Setons and that his own pledge was "more than absorbed by the expenses incurred for Wm. and maintenance of Richard." He assured Elizabeth that "should you ever really stand in need of my pecuniary aid," he would provide it, but this was far from the open-handed offer of support he had so often made.[71]

Elizabeth took Antonio's changed circumstances and tone in stride. Soon, she hoped, the Setons would cease to be a financial burden on anyone. Now in the navy, William was turning into a "solid old gentleman."[72] Catherine had a circuit of homes to which she could travel, as well as the assurance of the Harpers' protection. The sisterhood was on sound footing in Philadelphia and in Manhattan, where an agreement had been reached, in keeping with the custom of the day, to reduce expenditures by binding out the older children as apprentices to Catholic families. The sisters at the Emmitsburg community brought in tuition money and donations, and a confident Dubois had even commissioned a separate building for the free school.

If there was a remaining, essential benefactor of St. Joseph's House, it was in fact Robert Goodloe Harper, not Antonio Filicchi. Over the years, he'd offered advice, helped collect debts, and shepherded the sisters' incorporation. Elizabeth and Dubois were confident that he would continue to aid their institutions, and Harper had no intention of disappointing. Yet he had also embarked on a new benevolent project, one that quietly suggested his uneasiness with an important, if in the main indirect, source of his own and the Emmitsburg schools' money: slavery. Harper had joined the American Colonization Society.

Founded on the theory that slavery was wrong but abolition dangerous, the Colonization Society argued for gradual emancipation and for freed slaves to be sent to Africa. There, members argued, they would escape the racial prejudice endemic to American life. The society's goals and membership suggest a complex set of motivations. Some participants spoke in crudely racist terms and seemed intent only on protecting their own slaveholding purses; others were genuinely disturbed by slavery but convinced that the United States' racial hierarchy made simple emancipation impossible.[73] A member of the latter camp, Harper was disappointed when prominent African Americans strenuously opposed colonization and pointed out that they had just as much claim to life in the United States as those who deprived them of liberty. Harper decided such opposition was misguided and continued to devote time to the society.

As he worked on behalf of the Colonization Society, Harper did not request that Joe, Nace, or the other people enslaved at the Mount be freed; on the contrary, he advised the Sulpicians how best to negotiate slave ownership in a border region. When a slave was emancipated at the Mount in 1814, it happened because the man's son, who had gained his own freedom from a different owner, purchased his father from John Dubois.[74] Nor did Harper free his own slaves. Yet it's also true that Harper's remarks about race suggest discomfort over the society he was unwilling to upend. "There is no state of the union, where a negro or mulatto can ever hope to be a member of Congress, a judge, a militia officer, or even a justice of the peace," Harper observed. Even Paul Cuffee, a successful merchant of African and American Indian descent, harbored "no expectation or chance of ever being invited to dine with any gentleman of Boston, [or] of marrying his daughter."[75]

The Sisters of Charity offered sad evidence for Harper's belief that white Americans' circle of compassion did not take in people of African descent. Race did not create the only unexamined hierarchy at St. Joseph's House, which followed its French predecessors in assuming wealthy and poor girls would lead separate lives. But racial slavery most starkly revealed the bounds of Christian community. As Elizabeth contemplated compassion, sin, and love—and the torments and limits of obedience—she did not ponder slavery or ask others to do so. St. Joseph's students participated in the depreciation of black life that was a part of Maryland's culture; Mary Egan, a boarder who so loved the sisters that she entered the novitiate, once tried to cheer up the ailing Rebecca by telling her a gruesome joke about a "black woman being buried in a trunk." "I have a great many funny anecdotes to tell you about Monky tricks," she added cheerfully.[76] Such carelessness was the necessary handmaiden of racial slavery, and there, too, Elizabeth and the other sisters accepted the world as it was. The sisters' mission to the Mount drew the women into direct participation in the institution: a handwritten sheet of instructions makes clear that sisters supervised enslaved women at the Mount's washhouse. If "mild correction" of the slaves fails, the instructions command, "Scold them!" ("You can be angry without sinning even against Meekness," its author adds.)[77] The underlined exhortations suggest that whoever wrote the regulations—likely Dubois—found the sisters reluctant to treat the slaves harshly. Perhaps the women's spirit of charity undermined their willingness to directly expropriate others' labor. Whether or not the "Regulations for the Washhouse" hint at mercy, they unquestionably document exploitation. The regulations remind the sisters that workers were not to be allowed to have visitors without permission or to make their own decisions about their spiritual lives; their attendance at Masses was mandatory.

Elizabeth makes few mentions of the institutions' slaves, except to note Joe's kindness to the crippled Bec and, once, to mention her responsibility to catechize the "good blacks": "Excelentisimo!" she wrote, her tone indecipherable. The slim record of engagement offers its own evidence. Elizabeth had a gift for making others feel loved and seen, known in their human specifics. She did not often turn that gift toward the people of color who labored for the sisterhood, and when occasionally she did, she did so in a way that did not acknowledge the central, brutal fact of enslaved people's lives. Like the idea of American citizenship, the ethos of the Sisters of Charity contained within it a logic that would in the future be turned against racial hierarchy and human bondage. But Robert Goodloe Harper was correct about at least one thing: in 1817, that day had not come, and it showed no signs of dawning.

BRUTÉ

Amid the bustle of the Blue Ridge's schools, sisterhood, churches, and arguments, Reverend Charles Duhamel quietly took to his bed. He had long been aged and frail; now everyone realized he was dying. Ever practical, Dubois wrote to Tessier explaining his preference for a replacement. It was not Pierre Babade, whose instability was evident, or John Hickey, who though "a good child and a good priest" (Dubois did not hold his reports to the Baltimore Sulpicians against him) lacked skill. Only one man was qualified, and he was the only man, Dubois rather unfortunately wrote, "willing to come and share my slavery."[78] That man was Simon Bruté. No response came to this request, so when Duhamel died, Dubois resumed his campaign. Writing to Archbishop Marèchal, he pointed out the difficulties priests faced in the region: there were between 140 and 200 communicants, he claimed, but an annual revenue of only $90, so any priest who was expected to support himself solely through the parish "would starve." A priest had to serve a number of roles, including working with the sisterhood, and Dubois reminded the archbishop that as the male superior, he had the right to name the sisters' confessor. Dubois had one more arrow in his quiver. Aware of Bruté's quixotic efforts to convert Protestants, he noted that his friend possessed a "zeal towards the public . . . not always according to prudence."[79]

Perhaps, he implied, everyone would be better off if Bruté were tucked
away in the Blue Ridge.

To Dubois's surprise, Tessier readily agreed. He thought that Bruté
"discharged his duty" in Baltimore "very imperfectly"—"Not because
he was not quite capable of fulfilling the functions of president, but
because he did not like it." Tessier knew that Bruté was "sighing for
the Mountain" and that Dubois "had absolute need of help," so the
Sulpician superior decided to oblige them both. Westward on the pike
went Bruté.[80]

And so Bruté, Dubois, and Elizabeth Seton resumed the intercon-
nected lives and duties they'd shared before Bruté sailed with William
for Europe. Bruté's notes reveal his endless labors: terracing gardens,
teaching philosophy, saying Mass, serving as confessor, visiting the sick.
His energy and piety made him invaluable, just as Dubois had expected;
his exuberance and distractibility made him infuriating, as Dubois must
soon have recalled. The two men lived in a familial, fractious harmony.
Something of its character is captured in an account written years later
of a day on which Bruté proposed walking the sixty-five miles to Baltimore to do an errand. Level-headed Dubois insisted that he instead ride
and lent him a saddle he'd recently been given, a handsome one that bore
Dubois's name engraved on a silver plate. On his return from Baltimore,
Bruté found Tom's Creek swollen with water. Rather than wait until the
water receded, Bruté coaxed the horse onto a tiny log bridge meant for
people. The horse declined to cooperate, and as Bruté struggled to control him, the girths snapped and the saddle floated away. When Dubois
demanded to know what had become of it, Bruté answered with a mixture of remorse and mischief. "Alas! I know not," he said, "I watched
it hurrying down the torrent, and I could just see 'John Dubois,' 'John
Dubois,' 'John Dubois,' bobbing up and down from one wave to another,
bidding me adieu.'"[81]

Like Dubois, Elizabeth sometimes found Bruté exasperating; unlike
Dubois, she could keep the ebullient priest within bounds. Their collaboration had thinned somewhat during Bruté's time in Baltimore, and
not long after his return, she firmly explained to him how she expected
their work together to proceed. She and three other sisters—Margaret
George, Elizabeth Boyle, and Joanna Smith—were the "management."
They worked as a "Union." She and Dubois also worked in harmony,
she continued, because she knew "he is not to be pushed any where,"

and Dubois accepted that "if anything essential happens I always inform him of it." ("Inform," she wrote, not "consult.") If something was not essential, she and Dubois let it pass in silence. Her point was clear: Bruté must again learn to fit into this excellent arrangement. Nor was that the end of her instruction. In response to a complaint from Bruté that she did not now fully confide in him, she wrote, "You speak as if your Mother's confidence is deficient, but it is surely not." She admitted that she did have one concern, which was the fact that she allowed herself to become vexed at some sisters' conduct. But, she pointed out, Bruté had taken no interest in that, and she had no other "private concerns" to offer him. On the contrary, she assured him, she'd at last found the peace she had expected to achieve when first she came to St. Joseph's Valley, and she enjoyed a "willingness to live, so different from the past nine years dragging." Bruté should rejoice that she possessed "tranquil dispositions [as] my continual feast, instead of the war of Nature which was so long my daily Bread."[82]

A different priest might have taken offense. Not Bruté. He tried to fit into the management system Elizabeth described, and he accepted her rebuke. ("She had a great love for St. Theresa," the priest observed years later, astutely noting that Teresa's "liberty of spirit with her directors, her gayety, her contempt of what people called her sanctity and extraordinary graces, accorded more with Mother's own turn of mind . . . than the character of Saint [Jeanne] de Chantal, whose humble and faithful devotedness to Saint Frances de Sales probably pleased her less.")[83] Most important, Bruté continued to confide his own worries and faults. Humble self-reflection achieved what priestly instruction could not: before long Elizabeth once again opened her heart to him.

A new chapter in their collaboration began when Bruté confessed a new discontent. After the turmoil of the Revolution and Napoleonic eras, French Catholicism was experiencing a wave of missionary fervor, and Bruté was filled with a resurgent longing to be a hero for God. He lent Elizabeth volumes of the *Jesuit Relations*; he was inspired by their dramatic accounts of missionary work and martyrdom. Reading them, Elizabeth made clear that she'd no more wanted to be a schoolteacher than had Bruté. Together the two turned to Vincentian teachings to discern the grace of their own and others' daily labors. "He takes in time, to restore in Eternity," Elizabeth wrote in the margins of a Thomas à Kempis volume, "not the cross of our own choice—he only knows how to crucify."[84]

While she sympathized with Bruté's frustration, Elizabeth also turned his eyes toward the privilege he enjoyed. Even if he could not be a missionary, Bruté could at least be a priest, she reminded him, as could Samuel Cooper, who despite years of mental instability had recently been ordained. "I glance a fearful look at you and Mr. Cooper," she told Bruté, "and say secretly if I was one or the other . . ." Elizabeth did not allow herself to continue that thought. "I know nothing about it," she wrote. Safer to discuss their mutually thwarted desire to be missionaries than to question the gendered architecture of the Church. She told Bruté that if she could do as she wished, "I would not stop night or day till I reached the dry and dark wilderness," there to risk "a glorious Death."[85] She even shared her thinking with William. "If I was a man all the world should not stop me," she informed her likely astonished son. She would "go straight in Xavier's footsteps [on the] waters of the abyss, and expanded sky should be well explored." Of course, as she and her father had long ago observed, she was not a man, and from that fact was born the shape of her earthly life. "I must wait for liberty," she mused, "till I get higher than seas or skies."[86]

Inspired by her conversations with Bruté, Elizabeth imagined escaping both the constraints of womanhood and the polite hedges of life lived at close and diverse American quarters. Foreign lands filled with people possessed of their own beliefs seemed to her arenas for heroic, Catholic selflessness. "Oh . . . if I was light and life as you are," she told Bruté, "I would shout like a madman alone to my God and roar and groan and sigh and be silent all together till I had baptized a 1000 and snatched these poor Victims from Hell." Suspecting that Bruté would tell her to live passionately in the Blue Ridge—"why does not your zeal make its flame through your own little Hemisphere?" she imagined him demanding—Elizabeth explained that she found life within St. Joseph's as confining as he found life at the Mount. "Rules, prudence, subjections, opinions," she exclaimed, "dreadful walls to a burning SOUL wild as mine and *somebodys*."[87] If she could be a missionary, she could live out the passionate exhortations she'd offered Catherine in the red notebook while escaping the cautions and compromises she'd felt compelled to include.

To Bruté, Elizabeth confessed her sense of unfulfilled purpose without worrying she would be judged ungrateful to God. "I am like a fiery Horse I had when a girl," she told him, "whom they tried to break by making him drag a heavy cart, and the poor beast was so humbled that he could never more be inspired by whips or caresses, and wasted to a skeleton till he died." Briefly, she also returned to the central contrast between her life and his. "You and Mr. Cooper might waste to Skeletons to some purpose," she told him, "and after wasting be sent still living to the glories of the Kingdom."[88] She and Bruté shared a sense of constraint, but she wanted it acknowledged that womanhood limited sacrifice and service in ways manhood did not.

Elizabeth voiced this lurking frustration without suggesting any remedy existed. On the contrary, openly acknowledging the constraints of her role seemed to reconcile her to them. As a consequence, she revisited her impatience with the stolid young priest John Hickey. "I once told you how I wished to do as you have done," she told Hickey, meaning she had wished to become a priest. It was a wish that simultaneously honored the Church's teachings (Elizabeth saw the priesthood as the most desirable role for any person) and unsettled them (she imagined that she, a woman, could hold that role). She told Hickey that she had set her wish aside. Now, she claimed, "all the illusioning and spider web of earthly weaving is broken, and nothing now more bright and steady than the divine lamp he feeds and trims himself *because as I suppose I staid in Obedience.*" By honoring that most challenging of vows, obedience, she had found peace. But peace did not require blindness: she recalled to Hickey the contrast she saw between Hickey's service to God and her own. "Oh this master and Father we serve," she wrote him, "You in Your Glorious Embassy, I in my little errand!"[89]

In such moments, Elizabeth hinted that she saw the sisterhood as John Carroll and the Sulpicians did—as "some devout women" whose service to God was less important than the clergy's. The priesthood was an embassy, the sisterhood an errand: she drew the contrast ruthlessly. Yet she also believed that both errands and embassies were in the end missions, and that both priests and sisters were servants, frail in their humanity and powerful only through connection to their "master and Father." In this as in everything, Elizabeth reminded herself, no one chose her own cross.

22

I See My God

IN THE SPRING OF 1818, Catherine Seton visited Philadelphia and New York, reaching the latter city aboard one of the steamboats that had recently begun to ply the eastern waters. Increasingly confident in her judgments, when she found one household unwholesome, Kit simply refused to visit again, declining either to criticize its inhabitants or to apologize for avoiding them. ("I could not seem [sorry] Mama," she later explained, "for I was not sorry under the circumstances that took place.")[1] Such contretemps aside, Catherine and the New York clan delighted in each other, so everyone was surprised when Elizabeth suddenly wrote asking her daughter to return to Maryland.

She offered a variety of reasons. Writing to Eliza Sadler, Elizabeth laid blame on Catherine's "delicate" health. To William, she claimed to have taken umbrage at Julia Scott's casual suggestion that Catherine was "helpless," a remark that recalled her own "bitter experience" as a dependent. To Catherine herself, Elizabeth gave a truer accounting. The coughing and shortness of breath that had annoyed her in summers past was now severe, and she feared her daughter would wear out her welcome with family whose hospitality she might soon truly need. "Your way to secure a more welcome reception among our friends when you will have no mother (and you must look for that my darling)," Elizabeth bluntly declared, "[is] by being a shorter time with them now."[2] Catherine hurried home.

Elizabeth did not tell her sons that she was ill. Richard was too far away to respond, and she wanted William to focus on his naval career and his soul; rather than asking him to visit, she sent small sums to augment his pay and a flurry of anxious letters imploring him to attend confession. "DO DO LET ME HEAR FROM YOU," she wrote in late May, "and do do go to your voyage with the preparation your own would beg on her knees."[3] William made no promises.

Kit was as solicitous as William was detached, and for a time after her return, Elizabeth's health held. Death instead came for others at the valley and the mountain, and Elizabeth and the sisters greeted each departure as a blessed escape. One sickly girl, Cecilia Fenwick, challenged this ethos. When, following a boarder's death, a sister looked at the assembled children and asked, "And who will die next?" Cecilia snapped, "You need not look at me, Sister."[4] (She died not long after.) In April of 1818, Sister Ellen Brady died suddenly—"eating a full dinner reading in the afternoon," Elizabeth afterward noted, "senseless at 7 and gone forever a little after 9." A few days later, Elizabeth watched as the coffin and grave were prepared. "A grey headed carpenter whistling over the plank he measures for Ellen's coffin," she wrote Bruté contentedly, "just beyond the ground plowing to plant potatoes, just beyond again good Jo (I believe), making the pit to plant Ellen for her glorious Resurrection—beautiful life, the whole delight in God."[5]

Within days of Ellen's burial, Elizabeth herself was gravely ill. As she had suspected when she wrote Catherine, she at last had fallen victim to the tuberculosis that had dogged her family for so many years. Mary Post wrote worriedly for news, and Bishop Cheverus offered eloquent encouragement. "I envy your situation," he told her, "running now to the embraces of him Who is love."[6] Pierre Babade sent his patented mixture of affection and self-absorption. Noting that he was writing to Elizabeth "on your death bed," he observed that "if I had a vote" Rose White would succeed her as Mother. When she read Babade's explanation that he "would like very much to see you before you die but I foresee that the superior will not allow me to go to Emmitsburg in the present state of things," Elizabeth may have felt as much relief as disappointment.[7]

By early July, Elizabeth's voice roughened and broke when she tried to offer spiritual guidance to the sisters. Her worried letters to William slowed, and she felt herself sinking into a welcome rest. Taking pleasure in "the stillness and quiet" of her mind, she went to Communion nearly daily. "Death grins broader in the pot every morning and I grin at him and show him his master," she wrote with homely lyricism. "I see nothing in this world but the blue sky and our altars." Like Ellen Brady, she was simply another crop to be planted in the earth. "We talk now all day long of my Death and how it will be just like the rest of the housework."[8] Having often pondered the horizon between life and death, Elizabeth felt herself nearing it. One day, as the other sisters moved through the chapel, she "forgot for a good while kneeling by the altar railing what was doing or to be done."[9]

"I AM TO STAY"

Reelected that summer to the position of Mother, Elizabeth laughed to Eliza Sadler that it had been "an Election of the dead."[10] But to her surprise and everyone else's, her health stopped its precipitous decline. She remained short of breath and afflicted with what she called "an ulcer in my breast . . . which stops not night or day," but she slowly realized her life was not at its end. Catherine was enormously relieved; Elizabeth felt something closer to chagrin. "My health turns out a nothing," she wistfully told Sadler in August. "O Eliza, I am to stay. Very well."[11]

Resolutely, she turned back to the academy, the sisterhood, and her children. William was in Boston, assigned to the USS *Macedonian*. The frigate Stephen Decatur had triumphantly captured from the British near the start of the War of 1812 had since seen dramatic service against the Barbary pirates. Now, thoroughly overhauled and "admired by everyone who goes on board," in the words of a proud officer, the *Macedonian* floated in Boston Harbor under the command of a charismatic young captain named John Downes. Her orders were to sail to the Pacific coast of South America and help open the Pacific to American trade.[12] The cruise would take two or three years, and William was thrilled. But Elizabeth's fears for her son's soul had returned with her health; she sensed from his silences that he did not practice his faith away from St. Joseph's House and the Mount. Elizabeth's old friend John Cheverus, bishop of Boston, invited the young man to dinner and extracted a promise that he would fulfill his religious obligations. "I have confidence that he will one day be with you in heaven," Cheverus wrote.[13] But Elizabeth recognized the distance between her world and her son's, a distance like the one that had long ago separated her from her husband. She believed immersion in practical affairs was a cost of manhood, as the priesthood was manhood's privilege. "How strange to be a man and God but a secondary consideration, or no thought at all," she wrote as the *Macedonian's* day of embarkation drew near. She could only pray that her son not "enter an eternity of existence quite unprepared, though to prepare for it is the only end of our being here below."[14]

William knew everyone worried for him, and he thought wistfully of his mother and sister—"Tell Kitt to write me a long letter before I go," he instructed, "it will be so long before I hear from you after I sail." But he was eager to be off and proud of the life he'd finally achieved. "The *Macedonian* is a beautiful frigate," he declared, "carrying 48 guns, more completely and handsomely fitted out than any ship that has ever sailed from this or perhaps any other port."[15] As William recounted the number of barrels of powder the ship would need and the route it would take to the Pacific, the unhappy reserve of his merchant days gave way to delighted chatter.

On September 20, the *Macedonian* set sail, four hundred men on a ship built for three hundred, the hold packed so heavily with provisions that it plowed low through the water. Still frail, Elizabeth worried that she might not survive William's long cruise. It also seemed possible that the notorious waters off Cape Horn or the violence of the Latin American revolutions might claim William. No one worried that just six days out of Boston, the *Macedonian* would sail into a hurricane. But that is what it did.

No forecasts cautioned the frigate's captain about the storm that lay northeast of Bermuda, and only an eerie calm, noted in the ship's logbook, hinted that something was amiss. Suddenly, waves swept a man overboard, the crew watching in horror as he drowned yards from the ship. The rigging tore loose, and the *Macedonian's* huge masts became battering rams, threatening to dash the vessel to pieces with the rise and fall of the waves. Below decks, William, astonishingly, slept. Then a dream of his mother asking him "Are you prepared"? sent him jumping from his bunk. He landed in water up to his knees, thinking he might die just as his mother had long feared, his soul as unprotected as his body.[16]

As the storm raged, the crew daringly cut the rigging and controlled the pounding masts. The *Macedonian* stayed afloat. A few days later, it limped into port at Norfolk, so denuded that local officials who prided themselves on knowing the navy's most obscure ships had to ask who this famous frigate was.[17] The crew was given a brief leave while the ship was repaired, and a stunned William wasted no time making his way to St. Joseph's House. Elizabeth embraced the young man she called "my soul's William." He confessed his sins and received Communion from the priests of his boyhood, this second chance not to be wasted. Then he was off to rejoin his ship.

William's visit both comforted his mother and made clear he was truly beyond her grasp. Weeks later, she marveled to Marie Françoise Chatard that with her sons gone, she felt she lived "thousands and thousands of miles from a part of one's own self." If she could "help their salvation," she explained, she would wish to live with them, "but boys give a mother so little share in that comfort after early years are past."[18] Richard grew distant too, her younger son's letters from Livorno arriving less often. Perhaps Richard was simply busy, but his mother feared other possibilities.

Elizabeth herself had not traveled for years, not since the trip to Baltimore from which she'd returned to a Rose White–organized cleanup and an uncertain future. She had no wish to leave the valley again and gently made clear as much to Julia, who still hoped she might visit Philadelphia. Yet Elizabeth was not isolated; friends and family wrote and visited, and even John Henry Hobart, reconciled to her conversion, let Mary Post know of his reborn affection and admiration. Children who'd never met Elizabeth knew of her beautiful refuge in the mountains. So much a part of the Seton clan was she that a little boy named Henry, born years after Elizabeth left Manhattan for good, would pretend his stick was a horse and clop away to Emmitsburg to see "Aunt Seton."[19] Her young half sister Mary Fitch Bayley made a flying visit to Emmitsburg when she traveled. Now married to an Englishman (who, the family delightedly realized, possessed a title), Mary wrote after her departure that "the little glimpse that I caught of you when at Emmitsburg only increased my desire to know you better, and added you to the list of those that I love dearest."[20]

Elizabeth and the Sisters of Charity were also alive in the thoughts of Catholic clergy throughout the United States. Archbishop Maréchal visited in early fall of 1818, and although he was appalled by the travel— "Most dangerous and horrible road," he grumped in his diary—he was impressed and moved by the sisterhood. "Mrs. Seton" he found "in consumption, but far better than expected" and "still animated with a pious cheerfulness"; the sisterhood was a "fine and very precious institution."[21] Not long after, the archbishop reported to Rome that "if at some future time, with God's favor, I may be able to collect a large enough sum of money, I intend to erect another house, besides that at Emmitsburg and this house for girls I intend to erect at Baltimore."[22] As other clergy had long done, Marèchal coveted the sisters' prayers. "Since my consecration, my D[ear] and R[everen]d Mother, " he wrote Elizabeth that winter, "I have received many hundred letters. Very few, perhaps none, have given me so much consolation as yours." Other people, the archbishop observed, sent prayers out of mere politeness. "But ye, sisters of Charity, how much more enlightened you are!"[23]

At the time of Marèchal's visit, the Blue Ridge was also home to a priest who could not be accused of doing things through mere politeness: Samuel Sutherland Cooper. Having returned from travel to Rome, Cooper was sent in 1818 to Emmitsburg. He was an outlandish presence in that quiet realm; decades later, a sister recalled him as "'an uncommonly ugly man. Uncommonly ugly. Had red hair, wore a wig I believe, and had all his teeth taken out. Someone asked him if it was for penance and he said 'No.' He denied it.'" (The same sister had much fonder reminiscences of Dubois, recalling how as a very young woman she'd been so relieved to see him visit the New York mission that she'd run up and hugged him, prompting a stern rebuke from the fond but restrained French priest.)[24] It was impossible for the sisters or anyone else to overlook Cooper's strangeness, but his money had made the Emmitsburg institution possible, and he proved an eloquent preacher. Emmitsburg's priests tracked the number of Communions, keeping score in their battle against apathy and evangelical Protestantism. In Cooper's first weeks that number rose from 190 to 225.[25]

Quickly, however, Cooper's fervor flamed into something like mania. The same aversion to alcohol that had caused him to declare Washington, D.C., an unfit city to host a novitiate led him to point the finger of judgment at Emmitsburg. (In 1823, Bruté would write that the town had four taverns, "perhaps seven or eight tippling-shops," and "drams and whiskey" sold out of groceries and dry goods stores.)[26] Cooper announced that drinkers "who give public scandal" would have to "kneel or stand, or sit in some particular place in the Church" and hear their names disapprovingly read out from the pulpit. Exhortations to temperance coursed through the era's evangelical Protestant preaching, but it was unexpected in a Catholic setting, and the archbishop and Dubois worried Cooper would prompt rebellion rather than reformation.[27] Undeterred, Cooper did as he had planned. Afterward, he confidently told Marèchal that other than one recalcitrant parishioner who'd stormed out of the church, the public penance "meets with the unqualified approbation of the people," and Emmitsburg "looks a little like the primitive times." Cooper thought he had achieved the dream of many a reformer and returned a Christian community to the purity and zeal of apostolic days.[28]

Cooper was mistaken. Just as Dubois had predicted, many of Emmitsburg's Catholics were offended by Cooper's actions. The parishioner who had stalked off turned out to be Thomas Radford, the man who'd helped orchestrate the community's offer of a loan during the crisis over the Mount's suppression. Cooper may have struck the hearts of some of the faithful, but he was not an independent itinerant preacher who could gather his audiences from the willing. He was a Catholic priest who had disregarded his archbishop's advice and offended much of his flock. Cooper agreed he must withdraw from the congregation, and he left Emmitsburg in the summer of 1819.

Cooper was not the only one who failed to make a place for himself in the Blue Ridge. Over the years, a small number of women left the novitiate, including eight who entered between 1814 and 1817. It was a distinctive, demanding life; some decided on their own that they had no vocation, while Elizabeth and the council sent others away. One of the latter kind, Mary Kelley, had been sent to Emmitsburg by Archbishop Marèchal himself. "I assure you," Elizabeth wrote the prelate, "that the greatest care has been taken to turn this little wild head to some account but in vain, she cannot be depended on a moment nor remain half an hour in adoration without so much complaining and restlessness that we fear she should be seen by children or strangers."[29] Elizabeth's compassion still did not preclude stern judgment.

Most who chose to come stayed, however, remaking themselves within the rule and taking the sisters' purposes as their own. There were more than fifty novices and sisters in 1819, and sisters moved among St. Joseph's, Mount St. Mary's, New York, and Philadelphia as need and their capabilities suggested. Margaret George was in Manhattan, where the orphanage continued to grow, having brought with her mementos and loving encouragement from Elizabeth. Elizabeth Boyle labored there also, her life unimaginably different from what she could have foreseen when as a Protestant teenager she decided to see what the faiths of Baltimore had to offer. The sisterhood continued to attract those who, like Boyle, chose duty over obedience. A German immigrant named Mary Wagner arrived, "a good Dutch girl one eyed, yellow, and all the stiff dignity of what the world calls old maid," as Elizabeth affectionately described her. Her mother had implored her to stay with her family, where there "is plenty of everything and a gig to ride in and a black girl to wait on you." But Mary told her mother, "I would rather work hard at the Sisters and have church every day than walk on gold here."[30]

Cecilia O'Conway had not needed to defy her family to join the sisterhood, but she had struggled ever since against her own contemplative nature. In early 1819, she was deeply unhappy, "very sick of the old sickness she and I so often nursed before," in Elizabeth's sympathetic description. Elizabeth encouraged Cecilia to do as she and Bruté did, finding grace in the bustle of an active life and learning to take "from the hands of all around us every daily cross and trial as if he gave it himself."[31] But so unsettled was Cecilia that council minutes indicate "it was judged proper to put off" her vow renewal; in May, she was brought back to St. Joseph's House.[32] There, with Elizabeth's affectionate guidance, Cecilia regained her composure, resumed her teaching, and renewed her vows. Elizabeth was delighted to have her home, and when Sister Fanny Jordan returned as well, she found their presence "new life to me." As spring turned to summer, Elizabeth was profoundly content. "Keep the straight path to GOD ALONE the little daily lesson to keep soberly and quietly in his presence, trying to turn every little action on his will, and to praise and love through cloud or sun shine, is all my care, and study," she told John Hickey.[33]

"ORDER, PIETY, AND CONTENTMENT REIGN"

In 1819, a severe economic downturn tugged at the Emmitsburg institutions. Everyone from farmers to merchants felt the effects, and as unemployment soared and businesses failed, Elizabeth observed that the nation suffered "trouble of Banks and general distress." Dubois urged care: "No meat at breakfast—nor butter," he instructed Elizabeth Boyle, now at the Philadelphia mission, "shoe-string no other but leather."[34] In his midfifties, Dubois worked as hard and lived as frugally as ever and expected others to do so as well. He, Bruté, and the sisters kept the institutions steady even while tuition monies lagged, and late in the year he received unexpected and valuable help: a young Irish immigrant named John Hughes arrived at St. Joseph's, proposing to do whatever Dubois required in exchange for an education. Dubois employed him as a gardener and laborer, allowing him to board with the students, live in a small wooden cabin, and receive some instruction on the side. Hughes was a brilliant student, and Dubois eventually (and according to undocumented but plausible oral tradition, with some nudging from Elizabeth) admitted him to the Mount. There he proved an able seminarian and a teacher who coolly put an end to any teasing over his Irish accent. Perhaps influenced by his own status as an immigrant and an outsider, Hughes also became the only resident at the Mount to publicly lament the use of slaves, a few years later penning poetry in the voice of an enslaved man who urged his country to "chase foul bondage from its Southern plains . . . to let Afric's sons feel what it is—to be."[35]

Elizabeth's health had never entirely recovered from the days when death grinned in the pot, but she continued to prepare what she called "little talks," in reality ambitious discussions of prayer, charity, and the religious life. They added to an already considerable body of work. By 1820, she had developed and shared her thinking in hundreds of pages of reflections, translations, and meditations, as well as in the words of Bruté's sermons that she'd influenced or simply written. She'd translated a life of Louise de Marillac and all or parts of spiritual books, including works of St. Teresa of Avila and Francis de Sales; she had also produced the first English translation of a *Treatise on Interior Peace,* by the French Capuchin Ambroise de Lombez.[36] She'd even written a variation on the Methodist hymn "Jerusalem, My Happy Home," one that brought listeners to tears and moved John Hickey ("of all people," Elizabeth marveled) to declare, "Ooh it is so delightfully *wild.*"[37] Elizabeth's contemplative nature had caused her to struggle at the demands of leading an active community, and her desire to lead a heroic life for God led her to chafe at the essentially domestic nature of her service. She put those struggles to work creating a distinctive set of teachings about the nature and practice of charity, sacrifice, and love that would animate her spiritual daughters' lives of benevolence for generations to come.

Elizabeth's practical labors continued too, despite her weakening health. She offered discipline and moral guidance to the boarders, and she and the sisterhood's treasurer, Jane Gartland, intercepted accounts before Dubois could charge girls for every pencil and torn stocking. The Harper girls received her special care as they always had. Although less wild than Mary Diana, Emily Harper shared some of her late sister's resistance to Elizabeth's persuasive powers, and one day Elizabeth gave Robert Goodloe Harper an amused account of his little girl's skeptical response to efforts to reason her out of homesickness. "I am sure," Emily declared, "it is very hard to be away from one's parents when they just came from so far off and you was with them such a little while and then separate again." Elizabeth pointed out that Emily suffered much less than an orphaned girl would. It was the kind of instruction that Bec had taken completely to heart, but Emily was unmoved. "Well but," she told Elizabeth, "her Papa and Ma are happy in heaven so you would not pity her."[38] Emily's older sister Elizabeth was far more placid, so there Elizabeth spurred rather than restrained, urging her to use her gift for geography and coaxing her to loosen up her preternaturally neat handwriting. As she grew to love the girls, Elizabeth imagined the possibility of still more ties between the families. "I have two little Harpers with me who are really like a part of ourselves," she wrote to Richard in Italy. "I often look with a loving eye on the eldest and think while her beautiful mind is daily unfolded by me that perhaps I am doing it for you." She and the Harpers even imagined that the virtuous Charles Carroll Harper—who had left for Harvard College—might choose Kit as his wife.[39] Elizabeth still hoped Catherine would one day take religious vows, but marriage to Charles was another welcome possibility.

Amid such pleasant imaginings, grim news arrived about another member of the extended Carroll clan, Louisa Caton. Married to Lord Bathurst just one year earlier, lighthearted Louisa was suddenly a widow. Her husband had survived the loss of an arm during the Napoleonic wars and returned to the battlefield to fight on, but in peacetime an unnamed illness stole his life within a week. Louisa's sister Emily told the sad story. Although she knew he was gravely ill, Louisa had refused to believe that her young, brave husband could die. When he did, "she took him in her arms, began to sing him to sleep as she said, and sung three hours after incessantly." Only "strong opiates" calmed her and she passed "three days out of her senses."[40]

Reading Emily's account, Elizabeth marveled not at the blow struck but at Louisa's capacity to feel it so deeply. "What a hard heart I have ever had," she mused to Julia. She'd felt stupefied by Anna Maria's death and had grieved all of her many losses. But she'd never once doubted death could come or found refuge in delirium when it did. Reading the letter, Julia understood what Elizabeth left unwritten: her "hard heart" came not from insensibility but from faith, and it was the fruit of a lifetime of labor.

Although she did not admit it to Julia, Elizabeth's equanimity still failed in one regard, William. Her son's absence, she told him, "is like a daily Death to me in which every minute carries the pain of that separation."[41] Had Elizabeth known more about the *Macedonian*'s mission, she would not have worried less. Once arrived on the Pacific coast, Captain Downes proved more enterprising than his government intended. American naval regulations permitted captains to hold gold and silver for American merchant ships that might otherwise find their cargoes seized by pirates and to keep for themselves a 2.5 percent fee on the specie. A British commander in the area, Lord Cochrane (the same officer who'd boldly sailed a fleet into the Chesapeake Bay during the War of 1812), had been profiting handsomely from stretching his country's regulations, and Downes quickly went beyond what was permitted as well, accepting specie from a British smuggler happy to pay extra in order to obtain Downes's clandestine services. Before long, he was accepting specie from ships under the Spanish flag. Downes put the *Macedonian*'s crew to work counting the hundreds of thousands of dollars in gold and silver coin he took in.[42]

Having extricated himself from the Filicchis' countinghouse, William now worked aboard a floating private bank. If he had qualms, he kept them out of his letters home. Instead, he wrote of his delight in the voyage, happily anticipating an upcoming sail to the Galapagos, where he hoped to see "wild fowl both of land & seas, species in immense numbers together, the Seal, Sea lions & other amphibious Animals and sea Turtles." He already adored a Galapagos "land tortoise" given the *Macedonian* by a passing whaling captain. "I have frequently seen our little Mid[shipma]n riding him about the gun Deck, without the creature altering its pace in the least," he reported fondly, adding, "Delicious eating."[43]

Amid such adventures, William did not worry much about his soul. During Easter week in Valparaiso, he described a ritual more naval than spiritual: "All the Catholic ships in harbor wore their colours half mast and their yards . . . in a zig zag careless position expressive of mourning—and in the evening a stuffed effigy of Judas with a sword by his side was hung at their jib boom ends." William assured his mother that Easter reminded him of home; "no more two years Cruises for me," he wrote.[44] But while Elizabeth treasured his affectionate words, there was no mistaking one fact: these were letters from a young man happy to be making his way on his own.

Catherine Seton was making her way too, although she preferred to stay close to home, where she could watch her mother's health. Having lost both of her sisters, she found sweet companionship in a boarder named Ellen Wiseman. "They are more united than any sisters I ever saw," Elizabeth happily wrote William."[45] At Elizabeth's urging, Kit resumed visits to friends and family, spending weeks at Carrollton Manor, the huge plantation that lay at the heart of the Carroll wealth. ("I do get so disorderly . . . when I go from St. Josephs I do not know myself," little Emily Harper had declared, "if [Catherine] is with us I shall be very good.")[46] No longer anxiously weighing each gesture and invitation, Kit moved through planter society with a gracious reserve that prompted admiration. Nothing seemed to startle her; when she realized during a visit to Carrollton that the grieving stranger who kept to her room was the widow of Stephen Decatur—just killed in a duel that shocked the nation—she simply noted that the woman "seems truly to feel her loss."[47] Elizabeth trusted her daughter's judgment and piety as she did not trust her sons'. "If she has not what girls at her age call happiness," she wrote Julia, "she has what will ensure her future years that peace and contentment which is as much as any one should expect in this world, that she is doing her duty as it regards her poor Mother, and improving and cultivating her own little endowments."[48] You are, Elizabeth told her daughter, "my only dear companion left of all [God] once gave with bounteous hand—the little relic of all my worldly bliss."[49]

With her father and sisters dead and her brothers off in the world, Catherine likewise saw her mother as the remnant of her familial happiness. Elizabeth's fragile health frightened Catherine for practical reasons as well as emotional. She was more self-sufficient than her brothers: "I beg not to speak of remittance while I am in my present situation," she wrote Julia, "at this time I have no real use for it." [50] But while Richard and William could have careers, Catherine if orphaned must live as a guest until she married. In Livorno, Richard worried over this too, and he offered a home to Catherine as Sam had once offered his rooms to

Harriet. "I hope to have the agreeable burden of so dear a sister, for whose happiness and welfare, I am, and shall daily exert myself to the utmost," Richard wrote. "'Tis not too late to correct my faults," he assured her, "tho' they are numerous."[51]

Richard did not count his love of pleasure among those faults. Along with his pledges of help, he sent Catherine a remarkably direct—and cheerful—rejection of the worldview his mother had so painstakingly instilled. "He who knows how to take care of himself," he wrote, "can find more pleasure and true happiness in a gay and busy world, than he can on the mountainside, listening to the murmuring Brook, and breakfasting, dining, & supping on cabbage leaves and a crust of bread." Richard loved his mother—he'd not known "half her value, nor the 1/3 part how much" until he was far away—but he loved life and himself too. He conceded he might take this latter point a bit far—"I often take care of No. 1 without paying attention to others," he told Catherine—but there was always time for reformation. "You won't mind slight faults, especially when I am fully determined on correcting them."[52] Catherine believed in her mother's teachings; she also adored this brother who so ebulliently cast them aside.

Richard's high spirits held while he believed himself to be advancing at the Filicchi countinghouse. Soon, however, the economic downturn that had begun in the United States spread to Europe. "All business is at a stand," Richard wrote in April, and he no longer had "direct assurance" of his future with the Filicchis. At first he sent brave words about his prospects—"There is such a field in Europe for young men, that if a poor fellow don't succeed in one place, he has but to try another"—and uncharacteristically earnest assurance of his intentions. "My thoughts are concentrated in you," he told Catherine, "and if I can but secure your happiness, I would not pass a second thought on myself."[53] Then Richard's letters, already slowed, stopped. "Not a sentence since last October and this is the last of May," Elizabeth worried to William, "[I don't] understand it."[54] When a letter finally arrived, Richard's European ambitions had been replaced by a new scheme: he would return to the United States and take up residence along the Black River in upstate New York, where his grandfather Seton had long ago bought land and where his bankrupt father had vaguely imagined a new start.[55] Elizabeth and Catherine did not know what the change meant. It was impossible to believe it meant anything good.

By the fall of 1820, more than a year had passed since it seemed that Elizabeth must die. God sometimes seemed as near as her own children had once been. "It will please your so kind heart to know," she wrote Bruté the winter after her illness, that the infant Jesus "has been much more present to me than the beloved Babes of former days when I carried and suckled them." At such times, Elizabeth was not a "broken horse" but still the "delighted, wild one." For all the time she spent translating, reading, and writing, she slipped past the power of words. "I see my God himself in silence and love thro' all," she told Bruté, and broke off her note.[56]

23

ETERNITY

EARLY IN 1820 a young woman wrote to Elizabeth Seton from a plantation on Maryland's Eastern Shore. Ann Tilghman was a Philadelphian who had recently married into an old Maryland family. She and her husband were Protestants, but Ann had sent her unruly young sister Caroline to board at St. Joseph's Academy, hoping the girl would absorb principles of piety and good order along with her geography and arithmetic. Now Caroline wanted to be baptized a Catholic. It was not the first time a Protestant girl had been won over; one boarder had fled the Academy rather than upset her family, exclaiming, "No one can stay in this house without being a Catholic and my sister will die with distress if I am a Catholic!"[1] Caroline, though, wrote to ask her sister for permission to be baptized, and Ann Tilghman was thinking through her response carefully. "I am fully aware my dear Madam," she wrote Elizabeth, "that any objection I may make to Caroline becoming a Catholic, will naturally be imputed to the usual illiberality & prejudice of the Protestants." That, Ann insisted, would be unfair. "Would it not be strange, a person professing & venerating the creed of their own Church, to advise or even permit a child while under their influence to embrace any other?"[2]

Fifteen years earlier, Elizabeth might have responded to such a letter by fervently insisting Caroline become a Catholic. Ten years before that, she might have scoffed at the idea that Caroline's choice of denomination mattered at all. Now she offered an answer that was both nuanced and deeply felt. "Tho I sincerely love and respect . . . other Faith[s]," she wrote, "yet the Faith of the Catholic church is the only one I can teach or advise to any one committed to my charge." Elizabeth honored Ann's searching letter by recounting her own months of deliberation. "The kindest friends among Presbyterians Quakers and Anabaptists invited me to join them," she wrote, "but I could find peace and security only [in] the old church where they all came from." Elizabeth told Ann Tilghman that Catholicism is "so necessary . . . to salvation," then crossed that out in favor of a gentler formulation: Catholicism "is truly the way to Salvation he would have us pursue." Tuning her message to Ann's analytical key, Elizabeth argued that Protestantism abandoned spiritual searchers "in the trackless wilds of self taught creeds and opinions adopted in endless succession."[3] Catholicism might not be the only way to salvation, but it offered the only marked path. She hoped Ann would allow her sister to follow it, but the decision was theirs, and Elizabeth would not press.

GRACE OF THE MOMENT

Serenity thrums through this letter and all of Elizabeth's correspondence from these final years. She marveled at the "good and happy children" whose voices sounded through St. Joseph's House. More than four hundred had so far attended the academy, as well as the unrecorded number who had attended the free school; in 1818, the council approved a plan to hire domestic help so that sisters would have time to pursue their own educations, the better to teach so many students. (The council also deemed that "No Sister shall keep a larger number of children in her class than she thinks she can do justice to.")[4] The sisterhood as well as the school thrived; Elizabeth took great pleasure in the fact that "more postulants have applied than could be received."[5] She had not quite lost her wanderlust—"I think I should have been a traveler . . . If I had had no bairns to nail me," she mused to Eliza Sadler—but when Bruté again spoke of a desire to leave the Mount, this time for a mission to China, she gently warned him against "restless thoughts." "You made the lesson of 'the grace of the moment' so very plain to me," she observed, "I owe you perhaps my very Salvation by the faults and sins it has saved me from."[6]

Finding peace had not required sacrificing her sense of humor. On the contrary, the serene Mother Seton loved moments when a child's rudeness or an adult's unthinking candor sliced through pious convention. Late in her life she wrote up a deathbed scene with mordant delight. "Do you my dear child ask pardon of all your dear Sisters," Dubois had solemnly inquired of a recently arrived sister who'd fallen mortally ill. "I asked their pardon before I came from home," the woman interrupted in a loud voice. "But my dear child,'" Dubois tried again, "if you have given them any bad example, do you ask pardon?" "Oh to be sure," the woman responded, adding dubiously, "if I have." Elizabeth and the black-clad sisters shook with silent laughter. It was funny because beneath the propriety and the striving, everyone was overconfident and absurd; most people just knew enough not to admit it. "I felt my own case so close," Elizabeth explained at the end of the vignette. Her sense of pervasive sin birthed a tragicomic compassion.[7] "The sadness of mine I cherish as a Grace," she told Bruté; it moved her to ask, "Am I indeed in full charity with All."[8]

It was on that very point that Elizabeth felt most unworthy. Her acute powers of observation, her moral urgency, and her passionate love for God had throughout her life led her to find fault with others as well as with herself. The sin she most lamented, harsh judgment, warred with the virtue she most cultivated, charity. "Conscience reproaches aloud," she mourned to Bruté one day, "how little charity and delicacy of love I practice in that Vile habit of speaking of the faults of others, of the short cold repulsive conduct to my betters, as all certainly are." Regretting "words of reproach and disappointment" she'd directed at Bruté himself, she told the priest that she wished that she could extinguish the pain of her criticism "with my blood."[9] When she lost patience with other people, "I find my own [soul] only grows darker and more perplexed."[10]

This unstinting effort to achieve "pure, delicate, sincere charity" led Elizabeth to at last reconsider her memories of New York and to rethink the harsh judgments that had once seemed inseparable from her Catholic self. More than a decade after the angry scenes over Cecilia's furtive conversion, Elizabeth loosened her grip on the story of persecution that she had written. Thanking Julia Scott for sending money, she quietly acknowledged that she had chosen, rather than been forced, to depend on her Philadelphia friend, "not taking what [her family] had voluntarily offered and would no doubt have given if wanted."[11] Elizabeth also acknowledged that her hardest battle had been with her own nature. "I might not have loved my vocation had I tried it," she told Bruté, an admission that would once have devastated but that now amused.[12]

The only thing that could still unsettle Elizabeth's serenity was worry for her three living children. Catherine moved in and out of St. Joseph's House with composure and grace, but Elizabeth sometimes felt a flare of worry even for her: in the summer of 1820, some aspect of Catherine's life in society left her mother feeling "a sort of bitterness I could hardly control."[13] But Catherine proved her circumspect and sensible self and at summer's end returned safely to the Blue Ridge. Richard was a different matter. His letters dreaming about a new life on New York's Black River had been followed by ominous silence. As for William, Elizabeth found it unlikely he would meet his religious obligations on a frigate in the Pacific when he had not done so in Italy. "If you could see from your present scene the agonized heart of your Mother," she wrote in one of many anxious notes she hurled toward the *Macedonian*, "its agony is not for our present separation my beloved one, it is our long eternal years which press on it beyond all expression."[14] The one fear Elizabeth could not transcend was the fear that her beloved boy would not find his way to heaven.

Elizabeth reflected and prayed; Dubois planned. In the summer of 1820, he was absorbed in overseeing the building of the sisterhood's free school. Bruté fretted over the expense, and Elizabeth believed it might be a "bad business," but Dubois's building steadily rose. "Our endless obligations to the Superior the very formation of the House all his—what can we now say," Elizabeth cautioned the fussing Bruté.[15] Not content to have Elizabeth merely tolerate his efforts, Dubois one September day insisted she come with him on a tour of the construction site. She clambered over boards while he pointed to the future. As the two walked the site, a sharp wind started up. After her return to the house, Elizabeth was coughing and feverish.

Everyone, including Elizabeth herself, quietly blamed Dubois, but it was tuberculosis that laid her low, and it would have resumed its assault one way or another.[16] She grew rapidly more frail, and one late September morning as Bruté tended to parishioners in town, Sisters of Charity appeared at the door of the confession room. "Come," they told the priest, "Our Mother is dying!" Frantically commandeering a horse, Bruté rode to St. Joseph's House. There he found Elizabeth, "so calm, so present, so recollected, and wholly trusted to her blessed Lord." He offered her absolution and read the prayers of extreme unction, and when he proposed she renew her vows, she responded, "With all my heart." Sisters of Charity stood near Elizabeth, and so did a desperate Catherine. Tutored all her life to accept the will of God, Catherine was a veteran of deathbeds and a young woman of preternatural composure. Yet she could not stop crying. Bruté gently explained that she must "spare" her mother the sight of her grief. With great difficulty, Catherine gathered herself to pray.[17]

As so often before, consumption declined to deal its fatal blow. "Quiet," Elizabeth answered when asked how she felt, "very quiet." Bruté had never been quiet and was not now. He bustled about trying to ensure his desperately ill friend had all she needed. Elizabeth was grateful for some of his efforts; his offer to "let her former friends know that she was very grateful for their affection and attention" allowed her to seek peace with perhaps her last remaining foe. Ask Father John David "pardon for all pains I have [caused] him," she instructed Bruté. Yet she asked Dubois to restrain the ebullient priest. It was a task, Dubois later explained to Archbishop Maréchal, that Elizabeth entrusted to him alone. "She had expressly asked me before and during her illness," he told the prelate, "not to let her be tormented by the intemperate zeal of [Simon Bruté], whose ill effects she had seen, to remain beside her, if he found himself there to stop him."[18] It is impossible to believe Elizabeth spoke that harshly about her friend and collaborator, but one way or another she'd asked Dubois for help, and he managed to restrain Bruté's unruly love.[19] Whether she realized it or not, Elizabeth's request felt to Dubois like a gift. She needed him.

As Elizabeth's illness dragged on, she repented of any word or gesture that hinted at impatience, once worrying that she'd declined a proffered handkerchief in a peevish way. When pain and failing lungs left her shifting uncomfortably on her bed, she was heartsick at what seemed an involuntary resistance to God's will.[20] Although she had sought comforts for others who lay ill—oysters for one daughter, a feather bed for another—she refused any such ministrations for herself, and when the sisters exchanged Elizabeth's hard mattress for Rebecca's featherbed, she was distraught at the relief it brought. Was she turning away from her cross? Bruté assured her that she must submit to the charity of the women who loved her. "I will," Elizabeth answered, "since you say so."

She now coveted only the sacraments and rituals of the Church. One long night in early October, she refused water despite her fever, determined to fast so that she might receive Communion the next day. The

FIGURE **23.1.** Bruté sketch of "The Contest." APSL 1–3–3–13 158.
Courtesy of the Daughters of Charity Province of St. Louise Archives,
Emmitsburg, Maryland.

next morning, the avidity of Elizabeth's desire surprised even Bruté. "Do
you wish to confess?" he asked her. "No, no!—only give him to me,"
Elizabeth demanded, sobbing with eagerness. "Her whole pale face,"
Bruté marveled, was "inflamed and colored."[21] Struck by Elizabeth's

otherworldliness, he drew a delicate sketch of her suspended between heaven and earth, chains of flowers extending from her shoulders and feet. "My lord thy only Will be done," reads her caption. Above Elizabeth, on a cloud, stands Anna Maria. Clothed as a novice, the girl calmly pulls on a tether to lift her mother toward heaven. Bec, hair flying, stands on another cloud, two chains wrapped around her crutch as she tries with all her might to heave her mother up. Sisters of Charity whom Elizabeth had shepherded in their final hours also pull upward, while from below living Sisters of Charity clad in graceful habits try to keep Mother bound to earth. Alone at the bottom right of the sketch stands Catherine, pulling downward on a tether. "Oh, Bec," reads Catherine's caption, "don't pull so! Have pity."[22]

Bruté was right: Elizabeth was ready to die and Catherine desperate that she live. Dubois saw Catherine's fear no less than Bruté did, and since sensible arrangements rather than sketches were his art form, he made sure the Harpers were prepared to take her in. "St. Joseph's it is true would always be an asylum open to her," Bruté explained, but she "is at an age where such a retreat might appear a kind of Prison, until more experience would point out the blessings of so peaceable an abode."[23] Everyone agreed that Catherine must venture out into the world.

RICHARD

To everyone's surprise, Elizabeth lived through the fall and seemed to grow stronger. Catherine sent word to Julia that her mother was "happily recovering." "This my dear Aunt is a source of heartfelt Joy to me for you know I love her inexpressibly."[24] Then a new crisis arose in the form of a disturbing letter from Richard. Elizabeth's younger son, thought to be in Livorno, was in Alexandria, Virginia, and no one knew why. Witty prose gone, he wrote like a plaintive child. "I hope soon to see you but a bill I brought from Gibraltar is protested and a Mr. Myers on whom I had another, they say is in Emmitsburgh and I send you a duplicate of it," he rambled.[25] Fragile and worried, Elizabeth turned where she so often had before: to Robert Goodloe Harper. "If the Boy is come on business or not is useless to surmise," she confessed, "but knowing how he must wish to be with us it struck me he must be arrested or something wrong in the way." Did Harper have "some friend in Alexandria" who could find Richard? Could he please help? Frightened though she was, she assured Harper that he must set her letter aside if he found her request "unreasonable." She also took the time to tell him that his

"Darlings"—Emily and Elizabeth—"are quite good and lively."[26] Her son might founder, but Elizabeth's composure held.

As the inhabitants of St. Joseph's House tried to imagine what could have brought Richard to ground in Virginia, a letter from Antonio Filicchi made its slow way across the Atlantic, arriving shortly after Richard's cryptic note. "Though of a natural good disposition and right steady principles, I hope," Antonio began—the dubious "I hope" sapping any reassurance the rest of the sentence promised—"Richard's moral conduct of late has not given me that full satisfaction to which I thought perfectly entitled." The merchant informed Elizabeth that Richard "has equally with [William] thoroughly disappointed my expectation in point of abilities & of willingness of rendering himself useful at all in the Counting house." Perhaps Richard might join the navy, Antonio suggested without much conviction, but he did not think he or Elizabeth should help the young man further. "In behalf of your sons, at their age, you cannot do more but advise them well & pray for them, as you surely do," he told her. "Leave the rest to God." His tone thawing, Antonio closed with love. "Consider me, beloved Sister, firm at all times as a Rock in my brotherly sentiments for You," he wrote.[27]

Elizabeth had sent two sons to Antonio; both had failed him. "This then is the earthly fruits of your goodness and patience with us these 20 years," she wrote her old friend, and she agreed that he should help no more. Then she turned his attention away from her children. Antonio's benevolence had not been wasted, she explained, because its truest object, the Sisters of Charity of St. Joseph's, thrived. The "mustard seed you planted by God's hand in America" had grown beyond all expectations. Orphans had been "fed and clothed public and private." Archbishop Marèchal was preparing to bring Sisters of Charity to Baltimore, while from Conewego, Pennsylvania, Jesuits—their order restored by the Holy See just before Carroll's death—asked that a mission be established. Those good works, she reminded Antonio, were the true children of their long friendship. She ended her letter with a startling line: "The Reason of this writing I received the last Sacrament 3 weeks ago."[28] She offered no final farewell beyond that.

Last rites or no, Elizabeth decided she was well enough to work. She donned the black flannel she'd set aside during the worst of her illness and resumed writing—in a newly shaky hand—the letters that had so long formed an important part of her voice as Mother. To Robert

Goodloe Harper she sent a cheerful note about Emily's "singular talent for Geography" and Elizabeth's "regularity of conduct." To Sister Elizabeth Boyle in New York she sent homely encouragement and news. "All you did with regard to the purchase of the goods was exactly right," she wrote warmly, and she relayed cheerful details of the Emmitsburg sisters' work at their looms. The sisters' treasurer, Jane Gartland, had died, and Elizabeth tried to resume their secret task of intercepting the boarders' accounts before they reached Dubois. "You know why," she told Boyle.[29]

Dubois still stood sentry for a world he could not quite enter. He almost certainly knew of Elizabeth's efforts to keep him, as she put it, "in the dark" about accounts, and he had long since accepted the burden of being the uncharitable guardian of the sisterhood's charitable purpose.[30] Without his refusal to give alms, Dubois believed, "St. Joseph's would be daily assaulted by hundreds of those people, who would have reason to complain of a preference given to others much less entitled to relief than themselves." That he accepted his role did not mean he relished it. "One of the most painful circumstances of the vow of poverty," he explained, "is to have nothing to give."[31] All this Dubois would one day tell Rose White, as he chided her and the other sisters for what he deemed ill-considered charity. To Elizabeth, now, he said nothing, love and respect outweighing his desire to be understood.

Dubois prayed that Elizabeth would live to strain the sisterhood's resources for years. He did not think those prayers would be answered, so he did what he always did: he planned. In November of 1820, he and Harper convinced Elizabeth to write a will in which she left neither of her sons a cent. William seemed to be successfully launched, so leaving all her possessions to Catherine solved the problem of Richard without singling him out. "William and Richard can with the assistance of God, provide by their prudence and exertions for their future support," the will reads. "I consider it my duty to provide as far as in my power for my beloved daughter Catherine Josephine Seton." Elizabeth made Catherine her sole executrix as well as heir. Thomas Radford, who had offered a neighborly loan to the Mount, only to angrily leave Mass when Cooper shamed drinkers, stood witness when Elizabeth signed the will.[32]

Days later, Catherine received a letter from Richard. Knowing it would upset her frail mother, she shared it only with Dubois. At a loss, the priest turned to Harper. Richard must have "a mind much disturbed by fever, or agitated by troubles," Dubois told his friend. "Could you not write to find out whether and if any, what relief could be afforded him?" The priest who had more than once told an archbishop what to do confessed that he had no idea how to help this troubled young man. "Little acquainted with the world," Dubois confessed brokenly, "I can only feel for the woes of others, without knowing where to stop." He had money at his disposal, he explained to Harper, and he knew that Elizabeth would wish him to help her son. But was it right to do so, when Richard was so unreliable and the money was—as always—not really Dubois's? "Your prudence, your experience, your judgement, and above all your benevolent heart," he wrote Harper humbly, "will be my compass."[33]

But Richard had himself already written to Harper. "To pretend Sir to give an account of my reasons for leaving Leghorn, to you, would be useless," the young man began, mustering something of his old grace. "Suffice it to say, that religious matters were the principal causes of it. That I have been in the wrong and acted imprudently, I candidly confess—and to pretend glazing my faults with excuses would be but to destroy the merit of confessing them." Insisting that "I have not written to Mama for money, as I know her situation"—a claim both true and misleading—Richard promised that if Harper sent money, he would use it to travel to St. Joseph's House. "I would give half my life to see her," he wrote, "but fear I never shall again."[34] Harper sent him money.

When she learned what he had done, Catherine wrote immediately to her family's stalwart friend. "I cannot express what I feel, my heart is so crowded with feelings truly inexpressible, hearing of your so generous, fatherly conduct towards him," she told Harper, her customary reserve undone. It did not escape Catherine that the brother who had written from Italy promising to support her now presented himself as a boy pleading for help. "Richard has a good heart," she insisted. She told her mother nothing.[35]

Although his family did not know it, William also faced a crisis. While Richard paced in his borrowed lodgings, his brother stood on the deck of the *Macedonian*, shells falling and shouts ringing through the air. The drama had begun with Lord Cochrane. The audacious British commander was blockading Callao's harbor when he managed to "cut out"—to steal—the last remaining royalist ship in the Pacific in order to present her to the rebels. It was an achievement so improbable that naval academies used it as a case study for more than a century, and the royalist Chileans who witnessed it believed the American crew of the *Macedonian* must somehow have taken part.[36] Put at risk first by the battle over the stolen ship—"Being moored close to her we were necessarily exposed to the firing," William wrote—the *Macedonian* the next day faced a murderous royalist assault on a landing party. It was obvious that the frigate must leave the area, but doing so required being let through Cochrane's blockade, and it seemed likely that the British commander would use the opportunity to demand the enormous haul of ill-gotten gold that lay in the *Macedonian*'s hold. William would not have dreamed of explaining the precise nature of the problem to his mother, but he wanted her to know the danger he faced and the determination he felt. He and the rest of the crew would not allow their frigate to be searched, he wrote, if "our guns avail us anything." With that, William announced that he had related all "the news," told his mother to "love and kiss my sweetest Kitt," and signed off.[37]

Had Elizabeth read the letter when it was written, she would have feared not only for William's life but for his soul. His missive was all news and navy, his gauntlets literal, his concern only for the next day. But the letter made its way to the United States slowly, and by the time it arrived at St. Joseph's House, the *Macedonian* had long since sailed unmolested through Cochrane's blockade. Warned by American authorities to cease his freelance banking, Captain Downes docked the frigate at Rio de Janeiro, where he unloaded one million dollars and kept an unknown amount for himself. Then the *Macedonian*, William Seton aboard, began the long voyage back to the United States.

TOWARD ETERNITY

December's shrinking days saw Elizabeth once again too ill to don her habit, her hand stilled from writing, the boarders' accounts set aside. She had stopped trying to discern whether she would live or die. I can't "form the least idea of it," she laughed when Cecilia O'Conway asked what she "thought of her situation."[38] It was as she lay once again bedridden that Richard arrived. He had done as he promised and used Harper's money to travel to St. Joseph's House. There is no record of what he, Catherine, and Elizabeth said to each other, but Cecilia O'Conway wrote that Elizabeth knew it was the last time she would see her son. Richard, who had watched two of his sisters die, knew it too. The love and shame that had brought him home quickly drove him away.

After Richard left, St. Joseph's House centered on the rhythm of the rule and the fragile form of Elizabeth Seton. Lying in bed, a crucifix clasped to her chest, she took pleasure in the sounds of the community she'd created. Children were brought into her room a few at a time so that she might see them. When she overheard sisters chatting about a visit to "several poor around the mountains," she cheerfully asked for details. "O, do tell me!" she exclaimed.[39] Sisters of Charity stayed with her at night when she could not sleep, offering the prayers she seemed most to love—"sometimes of Jesus, sometimes of Mary, sometimes of the Infant Jesus, part of them if all fatigues her," one told Bruté.[40]

Cecilia O'Conway, Elizabeth's companion since the days at Paca Street, spent as much time with her as her duties allowed. One day, the two fell into conversation about a subject Elizabeth had pondered all her life: suffering. Elizabeth started to cry, overcome by thoughts of the agonies endured by those who died without sacraments, by souls in purgatory, and by the friends and relatives whose "bleeding bones" she had tended as they died. Her own pain was nothing compared with theirs, she sobbed. Pressing Elizabeth's frail hand to her lips, Cecilia reassured her that God knew her willingness to suffer and might admit her to heaven without the pains of purgatory. "How far from that thought am I," Elizabeth quickly answered, "of going straight to heaven—such a miserable creature I am!"[41] To Bruté, she'd spoken in even starker terms: she thought she might be destined for hell. "If I am not one of his Elect," she told him, "it is I only to be blamed." Elizabeth's years of prayer had not left her confident of salvation, although that was the purpose she'd had in mind at the start. Yet the thought that no amount of suffering and prayer could be sufficient to gain God's mercy—the possibility that had tormented her after Anna Maria's death—now held no terror. Instead, she felt resigned to God's will even if it brought her damnation. "When *going down*," she had written the spring before, "I must still lift the hands to the very last look in praise and gratitude for what he has done to save me."[42]

When she did allow herself to meditate on the possibility of (an unearned) heaven, Elizabeth no longer summoned the cozy vision of family reunions on which she'd once relied. In her last years, she conceived of an afterlife as unknowable as God. "Time shall be no more," she marveled. "Our imagination places us at the reality of that day half spent, that last day drawing to its usual close; we speak of the ensuing day, but it must not appear—an abyss an immense void is in its place—imagination fails—it has no hold no measure—only a vast, unbounded infinite uncertainty of thought."[43] First drawn to Christianity because she sought certainty and solace, Elizabeth had arrived at a faith that needed no human landmarks. Yet God felt intimately near. "How happy and quiet my day passes," she told Cecilia in December. "It seems as if our Lord stood continually by me in corporeal form, to comfort, cheer and encourage me. I never felt more sensibly the presence of our DEAREST than since I have been sick."[44]

As the last days of 1820 drifted by, Catherine almost never left her mother's side. Elizabeth was reduced "almost to a skeleton in appearance," she wrote Julia. "I am chief nurse and too happy to be so—this employment is dearer to my heart than can ever be imagined or expected."[45] John Dubois and the council faced a different "employment": preparing for life beyond Mother Seton. The council agreed that sisters serving in New York and Philadelphia, as well as those at Emmitsburg, should have a voice in the election of a new Mother, and Dubois worked out the procedures. Each sister would choose two candidates to be presented for election as Mother, he explained to Rose White, and they should write on small scraps of paper and send them all together in order to avoid incurring too much postage.[46]

On New Year's Eve, Elizabeth again refused water, determined to keep the nighttime fast so that she could receive Communion. When Bruté arrived the next morning, she did not speak. On January 2, sisters once again believed Mother was at the point of death. The priest offered urgent prayers "of love, thanksgiving, contrition, acceptation of His will, all his adorable and amiable will in every order of life and death." He urged Elizabeth to recall "the sorrowful soul of our Jesus Christ"; to think of "His blessed bloody sweat of most loving salvation"; to imagine "the nails and spear piercing His divine Heart opened to us, our whole rest in it." Humanity's sin, Jesus's suffering, God's mercy: Bruté was sounding the themes of their long spiritual collaboration. "Don't you thank Him for all, accept all," Bruté asked, "Don't you suffer willingly with our Saviour?" Elizabeth nodded in answer to each question, and Bruté absolved her of her sins.

Early in the afternoon John Dubois came. In his careful, loving way, he had decided that since Elizabeth had seemed truly to recover after receiving last rites in September, she could again be offered the sacrament. Dubois anointed her with oil and prayed for her, the Latin sounding softly through the hushed room. "Oh thankful," Bruté heard Elizabeth say when Dubois began. Dubois told the gathered sisters that Mother wished them to live as "true daughters of charity" and that she had implored him to ask their forgiveness for any "scandal" she caused during her illness. Dubois found it painful to relay Elizabeth's humble plea. "I obey her desire," he told the sisters but explained that she had done nothing but follow the commands of the doctor. Elizabeth herself offered the sisters one instruction. "Be children of the church," she told them, "be children of the church." "Pity me,—pray for me!' she implored, as Dubois and Bruté left the room.

Elizabeth lived through that night. All the next day, Bruté returned to offer prayers and ask her to bless the children. That evening, she asked a sister to find out whether "the children from the new school" had enough for dinner. They should be given her meal, she instructed, if they did not. As the night wore on, Catherine listened as her mother's breath grow more labored, then watched in despair as her stomach distended and she struggled in pain. The young woman began to weep so violently that sisters feared for her life. All the accounts of Elizabeth's final hours mention Catherine's awful grief, and all make clear that Elizabeth did not try to soothe it. While her daughter sobbed convulsively, she lay quietly. "Not the least turn of the head, nor least motion of her could be discovered," Cecilia O'Conway later recalled. Elizabeth knew there could be no consolation, and perhaps after so many years of being both Mother and mother, in her last moments she could be only the first. It was the sisters who tended Catherine, soothing her until she "sunk almost lifeless in [their] arms."[47]

When midnight drew near, Elizabeth again refused the water offered her, hoping for one more Communion. She gasped out a favorite formal prayer. "May the most just, the most high, and the most amiable will of God be accomplished forever," she murmured, the sisters finishing the prayer for her when her voice failed. Sister Mary Xavier whispered in French, "knowing how much she loved" the language. Elizabeth could scarcely draw breath and seemed no longer to know where she was. "I think our Lord is calling you to Himself," a sister told her, but Elizabeth had slipped beyond even pious conversation. "What, dear?" she asked, a straightforward question of the kind that had tickled her at other deathbed scenes. She felt her own pulse, eager to know whether she was truly dying.[48] The night wore on, the sisters praying and Mother Seton repeating phrases as she could. Just after one in the morning, her pains seemed to ease. Her strained and ragged breathing slowed, then stopped. "I don't know if you would call it superstition, what I felt at that moment," Sister Xavier Clark later remembered, "but it seemed the lord was there."

EPILOGUE

Time

THEY BURIED Elizabeth Bayley Seton in the little wood, a cross and rosebush marking her grave.[1] Simon Bruté noted her death in the Emmitsburg parish register. "Let her rest in peace," he wrote, his usual torrent of phrases quieted. "She lived and died in the utmost peace and good will of this congregation—and I thought but proper and according to the feelings of all to enter this memorandum of it here."[2] Baltimore and New York newspapers offered respectful notice of the woman who was the "relict of William Seton" and who had her own accomplishments as well. "To the piety and philanthropy of this excellent lady," read one Baltimore obituary, "the useful institution which is established near Emmitsburg, in Frederick County . . . chiefly owes its foundation."[3] No public notice condemned Elizabeth's faith; she was lauded by a culture that for the moment feared irreligion more than popery.

Clergy, sisters, alumnae, friends, and relatives shared the news in their own way, their admiration for Elizabeth's achievements mingling with a more intimate affection. One of the most expressive remembrances was penned by Charles Carroll Harper. Writing from his room at Harvard, he sketched in a few lines the woman Elizabeth had worked for years to become. "I love to contrast Mother Seton's piety with the austere virtue of some, which becomes a torment to others," the young man wrote. "I love to compare her agreeable conversation with the hypocritical cant of those who can talk of nothing else but Heaven, Penance, and Conversion. Mother Seton did not put on sack-cloth and walk bare-footed in the streets, as if to say, 'see how good I am.' But she accommodated her disposition to that of others. With the ignorant, she was simple, among the learned, she was instructive. She smiled when her friends were gay, and the afflicted were consoled to see her weeping with them."[4] Elizabeth, who to the last lamented what she felt to be her harshness and hypocrisy, would have been grateful to see her burning faith written of as a balm.

The Sisters of Charity elected Rose White their new Mother (Babade, having been sent to France the year before, was not there to see it), and Rose stepped into the role with her usual brusque devotion. The work of the sisters continued. Margaret George, Elizabeth Boyle, and others planted the congregation in cities and countryside, often bringing with them letters and tokens from Elizabeth. The Cincinnati mission began in

FIGURE E.1. St. Joseph's Academy near Emmitsburg, Maryland, lithograph created between 1870 and 1880 from a painting by L. Enke. Courtesy of Library of Congress Prints and Photographs Division.

1829, one in New Orleans in 1839, Richmond the next year, then on to Alabama, Indiana, Massachusetts and, by the 1850s, both San Francisco and Los Angeles. Sisters and Daughters of Charity created the first Catholic hospital in the United States in 1828 and the first Catholic hospital for mentally ill patients in 1840. Daughters tended the wounded during the Civil War, World War I, and World War II and undertook missionary work throughout the globe.

One longtime companion did not participate in the sisterhood's spread; with Elizabeth gone, Cecilia O'Conway was freed to remake her religious life. "My interior attraction for a secluded state was too great to suffer me to live happy in a vocation where intercourse with the world was unavoidable," O'Conway later wrote. Two years after Elizabeth's death, she received permission to leave the Sisters of Charity; not long after, she entered the two hundred-year-old Ursuline convent of Quebec, the institution Elizabeth herself had once hoped to join. Although she sincerely respected the Emmitsburg sisters' Vincentian work, she did not hide her relief at leaving it behind. "Thanks be to God that my bonds are broken *there*, to become a happy captive to rules more congenial to my inclinations," she wrote. O'Conway remained an Ursuline, and content, until her death in 1865, at the age of seventy-six.[5]

Of all those unsettled by Elizabeth's death, none was more staggered than Catherine. The young woman "appeared as if she was struck with a flash of lightning" when her mother died, John Dubois wrote Robert Goodloe Harper. Catherine had no taste for drama, however, even in her own sorrow, and she gathered herself within days. She considered staying in St. Joseph's House and becoming a novice but heeded the counsel of Dubois and Bruté. "A fear of the disappointments of the world," Bruté gently observed, did not a vocation make. Dubois told the young woman that one must "do penance in the world as well as in a religious house. The difference only is that in the world, you must impose it upon yourself, whilst in a religious life, it is imposed on you by your rule." Then he neatly summed up his own and Bruté's thinking: "I am aware of the dangers to which your excursion into the world will expose you—but as it appears to me unavoidable & even commendable, I trust God will protect you."[6] Catherine packed her things. Julia had hoped to take her in, but Catherine did as Dubois advised and went to live with the Harpers. She took with her the red notebook and her mother's wedding ring, artifacts of the two realms through which Elizabeth had moved and into which her daughter might enter.

————

MONTHS LATER, William arrived in Boston aboard the *Macedonian*, eager to see his mother. Catherine sent the news. "I have received the dreadful blow that levels all my hopes," William responded.[7] The grieving young man obtained leave to go to Baltimore, and during the summer of 1821 he stayed with Catherine and the Harper-Carroll clan, unable to bring himself to travel the sixty-odd miles to Emmitsburg. Finally, in late August, he wrote to Dubois. "You who know me so well will not for a moment believe that you have ever been deprived of that place in my esteem and affections which you have so strong a right to command and which truly you will ever possess," William wrote the priest who'd helped raise him. He somberly mused that "Experience is truly a most excellent preceptress, but unfortunately gives her lessons so late that she leaves us no times to practice them."[8] Then William was off again, back to the navy. Despite his respect for the "peaceful abode" Dubois had created, he was determined to make his life outside it.

Then there was Richard. Dubois and Harper ensured that Catherine did not give her brother the $2,500 she inherited from Elizabeth.[9] But no one could control Richard himself. He had yet to find a career, and when news reached Maryland that he intended to marry, Dubois despaired. "Such a match will end in the ruin of both parties," the priest bitterly predicted.[10] Richard made his way to New York, where, turning from his mother's Catholic web of benefactors to her older, familial one, he presented himself at the farm of the Roosevelts, part of the extended Bayley clan. He found no formal job ("that wished thing avoids me," he claimed), but he tended the Roosevelts' farm during their frequent absences and wrote affectionately to his sister. "On the 2 of next February I shall take the fatal oath," he told her of his marriage. "It will I hope render me happy—but may make me eternally miserable." It is an unsettling letter, Richard's lively prose skittering off in odd directions, and he acknowledged his own strangeness near its end. "I'm a lonely miserable being," he told Catherine, "but promise myself much happiness in February, if the lunatic asylum does not bring me up 'twix this and then." Catherine must continue to love him, he added, so "I shan't get crazy."[11]

In the end, it was William, not Catherine, who came to Richard's rescue. February came and went, and Richard did not marry. Instead, William, whom the navy had posted to New York, managed to secure a place for his brother on the ship to which he himself was assigned. Richard was to serve as civilian clerk during the USS *Cyane*'s cruise. Everyone hoped that for three years he would be fed, employed, and under his brother's eye.

The *Cyane* sailed in June of 1822, making its way first through the West Indies and then across the Atlantic to Africa. In April of 1823, as the ship approached the African coast, its captain received a desperate request for help. It came from a tiny settlement planted by the American Colonization Society as part of its efforts to transport manumitted American slaves to Africa. The settlers explained that they'd been attacked by Africans who—unsurprisingly—saw them as hostile invaders. They now faced a shortage of provisions, and their leader, a young minister named Jehudi Ashmun, was severely ill.[12] The *Cyane*'s captain put his crew to work salvaging an abandoned schooner to protect the fragile settlement. Someone else was also willing to help: Richard Seton. He undoubtedly knew of Robert Goodloe Harper's work with the Colonization Society. He may also have been bored by life aboard the *Cyane*. Whatever his mix of altruism and whim, Richard volunteered to go ashore and tend the ailing Reverend Ashmun. "He found me depressed with affliction, burdened with cares, & wasted to the weakness of childhood, by half a year's sickness," the young minister later wrote, and out of "a spontaneous movement of generous feeling, offered to become my companion."[13]

In the weeks that followed, Ashmun saw neither the callowness that had disheartened Richard's family and friends nor the madness Richard himself seemed to fear. Instead, he found a young man of "benevolent and highly accomplished understanding" who prayed daily and—here, the old Richard returned—vowed to give up the "levities" that he'd in the past indulged. It even seemed that Richard's gregarious nature might begin to bridge the grotesque gap between the settlement's intentions and reality. Richard's "open, undisguised character, the simplicity of his manners, and the native kindness of his heart," Reverend Ashmun observed, "won perhaps further on the affections of our black people, than any other agent had ever done in so short a time. I have heard from them no other objection to Mr. Seton, but that he was *a white man*, the only fault which with some of them, unfortunately, is held unpardonable." Richard, who had so loved the company of Italians that he worried he'd forgotten his English, was proving a gifted "agent." Might he have come to understand why "our black people" objected to the settlement and mistrusted the colonizers? Would he instead have failed once again? Before he could do either, Richard fell ill with the fever that had nearly killed Ashmun. The worried minister bundled him onto a ship bound for the United States.[14] A few days out to sea, Richard died. He was twenty-four years old.

Of Elizabeth Seton's five children, only Catherine and William remained. William stayed in the navy, promoted in 1826 to the rank of lieutenant. It was a steady, quiet career, and he retired, still a lieutenant, in 1834, two years after marrying a young woman named Emily Prime. Daughter to an extremely wealthy Episcopalian financier, Emily converted to Catholicism, by all appearances with her family's acquiescence. Although it had been the family's ambition for his sisters, it was William who married well; he and Emily went on to have nine children and to live buoyed by the Primes' wealth. The growing family traveled extensively in Europe, and on her parents' death Emily inherited a home and undeveloped land in the Bronx. William renamed it Cragdon, after the summer house his grandfather had owned long ago, and the family enjoyed it for decades. (In the early twentieth century, the city of New York purchased the land from Seton descendants in order to build a hospital for contagious diseases, writing a poignant if coincidental coda to Richard Bayley's long-ago efforts at the city's quarantine.) William and Emily had their sons educated at the Mount. Two of them joined the military and another, Robert, entered the priesthood, studying at the North American College in Rome and becoming the first American clergyman given the rank of monsignor. One of their daughters, Helen, became a Sister of Mercy.

While William pursued his naval career, Catherine remained with the Harpers. She was self-deprecating about her social graces—"I have . . . endeavored to make myself as agreeable as possible, she once wrote, "though you know I have at best a very slender stock of agreeabilities"— but she captivated most of those whom she met. She was even a favorite of both the Harpers, though the couple agreed on little else. Robert Goodloe Harper was busy with a new dream in these first years after Elizabeth's death: he hoped to found what he called a "seminary farm" in western Maryland, where free black children and enslaved children could be educated to trades, instructed in Christianity (no denomination specified), and then sent to Liberia using the proceeds earned by their labor at the school.[15] Harper's plan mixed the goals of the Washington Society with Samuel Cooper's original dream of a "manufactory," and it placed the seminary farm in the dreamily beautiful landscape of St. Joseph's and the Mount. Sustaining the plan—and gripping it like a vise—was Harper's inability either to accept slavery or to admit the need for its immediate destruction. But in January of 1825, all of Harper's plans came to a sudden halt. Standing in his parlor reading a newspaper, he fell dead of a heart attack, his son Charles Carroll "and a little negro boy" as witnesses. He died still in debt to his father-in-law, and his will freed no one.[16]

In subsequent years, Catherine continued to live as a guest in Carroll and Harper homes, as well as with the Posts in New York; Julia Scott followed her progress affectionately. The young woman received marriage proposals, including one from the British ambassador to the United States—a Protestant—but turned them all down. This left her independent of a husband but lacking a home. William offered to share his, just as Sam had once offered to take in Cecilia and Richard had promised to care for Catherine. This offer, unlike the others, came to fruition, and Catherine joined her brother, his wife, and their children on extended journeys through Europe. She studied Italian and French, learned to play the guitar at a convent in Rome, climbed in the Alps, and, in France after the overthrow of the Bourbons, joined victory celebrations hosted by Lafayette and Talleyrand. Elizabeth Seton had once written that she would have been a traveler if she "had had not bairns to nail me." Catherine did not, and she was.

During one voyage, she toured Rome with an old friend: John Dubois. Dubois had been consecrated bishop of New York in 1826, five years after Elizabeth's death. He was Archbishop Marèchal's third choice, and if he himself had had a say in the matter, he would not have been made bishop at all. But Anthony Kohlmann, the priest who had first led New York's Catholics out of disorder and who had come to admire Cecilia Seton, recommended Dubois to Rome, and his recommendation carried the day. Dubois reluctantly left the Blue Ridge institutions he'd served, loved, and scolded to take charge of a diocese covering all of New York State and much of New Jersey, its Catholic population nearing 150,000. Although Dubois's new position differed from his old in innumerable ways, one thing was familiar: dubious finances. It was while in Europe on a "begging tour" that he and Catherine Seton happily explored Rome.

Catherine enjoyed her years of travel. Yet beneath the glamor it was a transient and dependent life. Nearing forty, she wrote to Julia Scott that "the novelty of Europe" no longer appealed, that she was in fact "weary to death of it."[17] Not long after, she sailed home to New York. There she encountered a Dubois far less happy than the one she'd seen in Rome. New York's ever assertive trustees loathed the bishop's active administration, and he, equally assertive, felt for them none of the affection and respect that had gentled his relations with Elizabeth and the sisters. Dubois had made his way in ancien régime Paris, escaped the Revolution, thoroughly mastered a new language, and created institutions that thrived in rural Maryland. But he could adapt no more. In failing health, unpopular among the city's burgeoning number of Irish Catholics, and stripped of his lifelong confidence, he asked for a coadjutor. In 1838 he was given an able and familiar one: John Hughes, the young man whom Dubois had put to work as a gardener before agreeing to educate him at the Mount. Dubois happily ceded authority to the enterprising—and Irish—young priest. Not long after Hughes's consecration as coadjutor, Dubois suffered a stroke. He survived but led the diocese only in name, instructed by his archbishop to stay out of Hughes's way.

As Catherine spent time with the frail Dubois, they began to discuss both the needs of the city's poor people and the question of Catherine's future. Manhattan offered a wide field for benevolent work, and someone well known to Catherine had already taken it up with surprising dedication: Sam Seton. A lifelong bachelor, Sam had eventually left the Bank of New York and devoted his life to the cause of New York's public schools, working as an assistant superintendent and writing poems and stories for the schoolchildren, pouring into them the humor and charm that had once infused his letters to his sisters. (He also became involved with the American Colonization Society, becoming sufficiently well known that an indigenous Liberian, later to serve as a prominent magistrate, took the name "S. W. Seton" when he converted to Christianity.) When Sam died in 1869, he was buried, as he had requested, in an area of Greenwood cemetery containing the remains of poor children. On his grave appeared a word Elizabeth knew well: "Peace."[18]

As Catherine pondered what next to do with her life, pursuing a path such as Sam's was not an option; both her gender and her faith prevented it. If she wished to be useful, she would need to find a different way, and she knew that life in a Catholic religious community offered it. In 1842 she visited St. Joseph's House, whose superior was now Mother Xavier Clarke, the sister who had prayed with Elizabeth in French as she lay dying. Catherine also visited Baltimore and undertook a spiritual retreat. As she contemplated her future, she endured two losses in quick succession: Julia Scott died that year, and so did John Dubois. "I knelt by his dying bed as his spirit departed," Catherine wrote of Dubois, "and mourned him as my oldest best friend."[19]

CATHERINE HAD TRIED the world and found much to love in it. Now, twenty-five years after departing St. Joseph's House, she was ready to leave the world, or at least to live in it in a changed way. At the age of forty-six, she became a choir postulant in New York's recently established Sisters of Mercy. It's not clear why she chose that community over the Sisters of Charity, but John Hughes, by then bishop, had a sister who was a Mercy, and he asked Catherine to consider them. The founding sisters' last names—O'Connor, Dougherty, Byrne, Breen—make clear their Irish origins, and Hughes and Catherine, whose letters reveal a woman alert to her faith's social and political challenges, may have decided she should cast her lot with this newly ascendant element of the American Church. Catherine may also have wanted to renounce the special status she would have enjoyed as a member of her mother's community, but the superior of the Sisters of Mercy recognized her standing nonetheless: Catherine was, the superior wrote, "a person very influential among Catholics and Protestants of the first distinction."[20]

Thirty-five years had passed between Elizabeth Seton's first vow taking and Catherine's, and the demographic changes that were bringing the Sisters of Mercy and John Hughes into the center of the American Church were also rekindling the smoldering embers of anti-Catholicism. In 1834 rumors flew that a young woman was being held against her will in Boston's Ursuline convent, the kind of rumor everyone at Emmitsburg had feared. A mob of working-class Protestants burned the building. Many Bostonians were embarrassed by the incident, and the convent was rebuilt. But rather than a last gasp of the old, the spasm of hostility proved a harbinger of the new as

Governeur Ogden's prediction of Catholic institutions razed to the ground belatedly came true. In 1844, with Philadelphia's Protestants angered by the growing number of poor Catholic immigrants and by rumors that the King James Bible would be removed from their schools, a mob burned a school run by the Sisters of Charity, then torched St. Michael's Church and Michael Hurley's old parish of St. Augustine's. Philadelphia's mayor tried unsuccessfully to halt the violence. He was John Morin Scott, Julia Scott's son, a man who had grown up with a portrait of Elizabeth Seton in his home. Named for the grandfather who had tried to reduce the privileges of the Anglican Church in colonial New York, Scott watched helplessly as flames from this new combustion of religion, politics, and allegiance lit up his city's sky.

In the late 1840s, as blight struck Ireland's potato crops and poor Irish immigrants jostled for work and space in American cities, economic competition and sectarian mistrust fueled each other. Bishop John Hughes thrived, a new kind of prelate for a changing American Church. Combining a full-throated defense of ecclesiastical authority, an unembarrassed allegiance to Rome, and the cultural and political confidence of St. Peter's old trustees, Hughes commanded the scene, so assertive in manner that the cross he drew near his signature took on a martial air and birthed the nickname "Dagger John."[21] Hughes made clear that violence would be met with violence, and New York saw no riots like those that had occurred in Philadelphia. But in the years to come, the surge of Catholic immigrants continued to elicit the kind of fear and anger that had seemed, by the last decades of Elizabeth Seton's life, to be a relic of the past. Members of the American Party—happy to be called "Know-Nothings"—wanted to limit what they saw as the pernicious effects of immigrants generally and Catholics specifically, and when Jesuits driven from Europe and Latin America arrived in the United States, Americans who feared lurking Catholic influence were further horrified. There continued to be innumerable instances of tolerance and even converts to Catholicism, among them the well-known editor Orestes Brownson and, in 1852, John Henry Hobart's daughter Rebecca. But anti-Catholicism swelled along with the ranks of immigrant Catholics.

The Church's continued involvement with racial slavery heightened some critics' distaste and undermined Catholics' demand for equal treatment. In 1826, when John Dubois left for New York, the Mount still owned sixteen people. Slavery had begun to disappear from the area, undermined by changing laws and proximity to Pennsylvania, and the Mount's bondsmen increasingly resisted and sometimes escaped their captivity. But the Mount was a bit player in the story of the Church and slavery.[22] After leaving Maryland to become bishop of New Orleans, Wiliam Dubourg oversaw a diocese that became, according to one historian, the largest slaveholder in the Louisiana Territory.[23]

Despite its continuing participation in slavery, the Church in the United States was becoming an institution centered less in southern plantations than in the urban Northeast. The Jesuit order divested itself of slaves in 1838, doing so in the most tragic way possible, by selling its remaining bondspeople in order to pay off its debts. As the Church expanded in the nation's cities, the Sisters of Charity were there to meet it, doing work the rest of the Catholic Church—and secular governments— did not. Despite hostile rumors and the threat of violence and in the face of wildly popular novels depicting convents as dens of both forced and consensual sex, that work went on, and the labor and good will of Sisters of Charity, Sisters of Mercy, and other religious communities wove civic ties as well as sectarian. When war with Mexico and the annexation of Texas brought vast new territories into the United States, apostolic women traveled to them, as essential as clergy to the planting of their faith. Sisters of Charity died nursing the sick in the yellow fever epidemics that plagued cities such as New Orleans, Vicksburg, and Galveston in the mid-nineteenth century, and when cholera swept through the country, Sisters of Charity once again nursed, prayed, and died.

As a Sister of Mercy, Catherine Seton focused her efforts on one of the most vulnerable populations of all: New York's prisoners. Spending countless hours at prisons such as Sing Sing in Poughkeepsie and the Tombs in Manhattan, she shared religious materials and counsel, learning new languages in order to communicate with as many men as possible. Understanding that the prisoners' needs were not only spiritual, she collected and distributed writing paper and tobacco; grateful prisoners wrote letters and sent gifts after their release, not least a set of burglary tools that the owner suggested be sold to raise funds for the sisters' work. During her forty-six years in the order, Catherine used the extensive social connections she'd cultivated in the first half of her life to further the sisters' work and wrote meditations and poetry. She died, revered as Mother Catherine, at the age of ninety-one.[24]

————

CATHERINE HAD KEPT the red notebook, filled with her mother's reflections and advice, throughout her long life. After her death, it became part of a growing collection of Seton documents and artifacts. Father Bruté had started this work during Elizabeth's life, and he carried on afterward, urging the preservation of her papers and contributing his own memories and reflections. When Bruté became bishop of Vincennes, he brought with him the Carey Bible he'd given Elizabeth in 1813 (her other Bible was eventually donated to the archives at the University of Notre Dame by Monsignor Robert Seton, who in contrast to Bruté, lamented his grandmother's habit of marking the pages).[25] By his death in 1839, Bruté had ensured the preservation of a large cache of Mother Seton's papers—taking the time to set forth the reasons he believed they belonged to the Sisters of Charity rather than to her family—and had added his own reminiscences, reflections, and notes. In Italy, Antonio Filicchi also worked to preserve his friend's memory and correspondence. Confident that she was a woman of significance within the Church, Antonio found time to bring her life to the attention of Church officials, and he also preserved her memory within his family: his son Patrizio would one day correspond with members of the next Seton generation about Elizabeth and her time in Italy.

Simon Bruté once wrote that under different circumstances Elizabeth might have been a saint, his profound respect for her not quite overcoming his expectation that saints led more dramatic lives than either Elizabeth or Bruté himself had been allowed. Others felt no such hesitation. In 1846 William Seton paid for the construction of a mortuary chapel and instructed that his mother be reinterred there; some took the occasion to see whether Mother Seton's body remained intact, hoping for a sign of her sainthood. When the coffin was opened, Sisters saw, in the words of one there that day, "the black eyeless sockets in the black skull, just for a moment, and then she sank into dust at the bottom of the coffin." "O! those beautiful eyes!" Sister Mary Xavier exclaimed, saddened.[26] But the moment of disappointment passed, and the sisters continued informally to venerate her memory. In 1853, with Catherine Seton's assistance, the Reverend Charles Ignatius White (no relation to Rose or her son Charles) published his admiring *Life of Mrs. Eliza A. Seton*. In 1880, Heléne Bailly de Barberey, working with documents she'd translated into French, portrayed Elizabeth as a saintly figure crucial to the growth of the Church in the United States. Two years after the publication of Bailly de Barberey's work, James Cardinal Gibbons proposed to the community at Emmitsburg that an effort to bring about Mother Seton's canonization—a cause, in the language of the Church—be begun.

Gibbons's proposal was part of a broader effort to convince Rome to canonize an American citizen. As Kathleen Sprows Cummings has argued, prominent members of the faith sought both "to convince Vatican officials of US holiness" and "to display Catholics' Americanness to a skeptical Protestant public." A seventeenth-century Mohawk named Catherine Tekakwitha was also put forth, but it was Mother Frances Cabrini, an Italian who arrived in New York City during a transformational period of immigration, who was honored first. Canonized in 1946, less than thirty years after her death, Mother Cabrini became the first American citizen to be a saint in the Catholic Church.[27]

The cause of Elizabeth Seton, however, had not died. Many admired her holiness; many also believed, in an echo of the long-ago deliberations of Carroll, Cheverus, and Dubourg, that she was uniquely suited to inspire Catholics without alienating Protestants. In 1907 an ecclesiastical court was created to investigate the merits of her cause. The diligent archival work of Sisters and Daughters of Charity, as well as of Antonio Filicchi, Simon Bruté, and others, made it possible for twelve volumes of documents from Elizabeth's life and works to be presented to Rome. World War I interrupted the slow process of review, but the work of documenting her life continued. In 1931, a delegation of American women traveled to the Vatican and petitioned Pope Pius XI on behalf of Elizabeth's canonization. In the same year, the American Catholic hierarchy voted to approve her cause. The Mother Seton Guild formed to advocate for her canonization, and in the 1940s, Sisters and Daughters of Charity authorized a formal biography; the Congregation of Rites in Rome would later laud the usefulness of Annabelle Melville's meticulous and still essential study.[28]

The cause proceeded slowly, though no more slowly than other matters wending their way through the bureaucracy of the Church. American women organized petition drives, signing their name to a polite but assertive request that the pope offer "favorable consideration of the canonization of Mother Elizabeth Seton, pioneer educator and foundress of the American Sisters of Charity, as the first native-born woman of the United States to be raised by Holy Mother Church to the honors of the altar."[29] Elizabeth's nationality had never been of particular interest to her, but the hope of an "American saint"—meaning one born in the United States—inspired many of her followers; by midcentury, as a result of changes in immigration laws and patterns, the American Church was much less significantly peopled by immigrants than it had been fifty years earlier, further enhancing the appeal of a "native-born woman."[30] In 1959, the Congregation of Rites declared that Mother Seton should be honored as "venerable."

Attention turned to authenticating miracles; two were needed for her beatification. In the archive of Elizabeth's cause, science and faith mingle as they did in her life, clerics and physicians pondering whether a recovery was miraculous or simply improbable. In 1961, two miracles were approved, one the healing of a young Baltimore girl afflicted with leukemia and the second the cure of a Daughter of Charity stricken by pancreatic cancer. Elizabeth Seton was beatified on St. Patrick's Day, 1963. Her remains were again exhumed, this time enshrined above the altar in the Sisters' Chapel at what had become St. Joseph College, Emmitsburg. Two more miracles were required for Elizabeth's canonization, and the first was not long in coming: a man named Carl Kalin was cured of a rare illness at St. Joseph's Hospital in New York.[31] In 1974, Pope Paul VI announced that three miracles, rather than the traditional four, would be sufficient. Elizabeth Bayley Seton was to be canonized the next year.

As preparations were made for the canonization, not all Catholics rejoiced: Joel Wells, editor of a Catholic periodical called *The Critic*, was quoted in the *Wall Street Journal* observing that canonization "'belongs to the past, and there's a lot more the Church could do with the money spent on it.'"[32] Yet many Catholics were grateful and moved, including some who recognized that Elizabeth's cause had not proceeded in isolation from the prejudices and competitions of the surrounding society.

The canonization took place in St. Peter's Square, before a crowd of more than 150,000. Among them was a young woman named Ann O'Neill, whose childhood cure from leukemia had been attributed to Mother Seton's intercession. In a departure from tradition, women rather than men approached the pope to ritually petition for the canonization. There were four, and each represented a distinct stage of Elizabeth's life: young girl, wife, widow, founder. The homily placed her in the company of Jane de Chantal and Louise de Marillac, and the ceremony nodded to the fact that the United Nations had declared 1975 International Women's Year. Sisters and Daughters of Charity also remember that when Sister Hildegarde Marie Mahoney, superior general of the Sisters of Charity of St. Elizabeth, served as lector during the canonization Mass, it marked the first time a woman had an official role in a papal liturgy.

———

THE SISTERS AND DAUGHTERS of Charity who rejoiced in Elizabeth's canonization are members of religious communities with complicated histories. As missions spread outward from St. Joseph's House, a shared Vincentian rule and veneration of Mother Seton did not always prevent awkwardness and contention. The most consequential divisions emerged from disagreements over governance, adaptation to American circumstances, and affiliation, much as they had in Elizabeth's own day. In the 1840s, a dispute involving Bishop Hughes and the mother superior at Emmitsburg led to the creation of a diocesan community, the Sisters of Charity of New York. In 1850, Sulpician priests took it upon themselves to unite the Sisters of Charity of Saint Joseph's with the French Filles de la Charité—the union that had been abandoned during Elizabeth Seton's life—and the Cincinnati community declined to go along, instead placing itself under diocesan control. (Margaret George, the Baltimore widow who'd eavesdropped at the bishop's table in an effort to help Elizabeth control her fate, became the community's first Superior.)[33]

For the Emmitsburg community who united to the French Daughters, the simple black flannel of Elizabeth's day was replaced by the Daughters' habit; its cornette, a dramatic white headdress, eventually inspired the 1960s television show *The Flying Nun*. ("They did like their starch," one elderly Daughter, looking at a model of the habit she'd once worn, cheerfully observed to me.) After Vatican II, communities turned to simpler habits or unadorned street clothes, their specific allegiances subtly identified to each other, usually by a unique symbol pinned or worn as a necklace. Through all these changes in dress, affiliation, and governance, and through centuries in which the demography, social standing, and even liturgy of the American Catholic Church were transformed, the work of the religious communities inspired by Elizabeth Seton has gone forward.

Internationally, there are over fifteen thousand Daughters of Charity. Within North America, communities totaling approximately four thousand members form the Sisters of Charity Federation. Sisters work on behalf of vulnerable people including refugees, the poor, and girls at risk of being "left behind," as the federation puts it. Rather than only tend the world's casualties, members of the federation also analyze and seek to undo the structural causes of poverty and forced migration. (They examine their own past as well, their investigations of their community's history marked by both scholarship and a commitment to the Vincentian spirit.) Sisters and Daughters work with lay men and women in organizations including the Vincentian Lay Missionaries, the Vincentian Mission Corps, and the Society of St. Vincent de Paul. Careful attention to the finances of their institutions makes it possible, in the words of Sister Mary Fran Hildenberger, to "do good stewardship" even while the number of women entering the communities has dropped and the average age has risen. (Without financial resources, explained a financial officer who seems a modern-day kinsman to John Dubois, "it's all reduced to good thoughts.")[34]

Members of the religious communities descended from Emmitsburg also continue to collect and interpret documents related to Elizabeth Seton's life and have made this biography possible. Their work is rooted in faith but unconstrained by fear or self-justification; no documents are off-limits and no questions resented. Late in my research, I was fortunate to stay for a brief time at the motherhouse in Cincinnati, where with the help of Sister Judith Metz I worked through meticulously organized letters relating to Mother Seton's life and had the honor of listening to sisters reflect on lives lived in community, prayer, and service.

At lunch one day, two sisters described painstaking efforts to digitize the Cincinnati community's annals and correctly record its past members. One challenge was, as they laughingly told me, "We never know each other's last names." Another was the intricate web of religious names. During much of the nineteenth and twentieth centuries, each entering sister set aside her birth name and was given a new moniker. It was considered a "fault" to use a sister's given name, let alone a nickname, and many of the religious names turned out to be remarkably similar. There were innumerable Mary Josephs and Mary Johns, and although no two sisters were to bear precisely the same name at the same time, when a sister died or left the order, her name was passed on, sometimes very quickly. "One would leave," merrily reminisced the older of the sisters, "and someone might be given her name the next day!" Occasionally things got even more confusing: two Maria Michaels were members of the community at the same time, their names differentiated by the fact that one woman was called "Ma-reeah Michael" and the other "Ma-raye-ah Michael." Seeing my bemused expression—I had, after all, been working in the archive with Sister Judy Metz and had also worked with Sister Betty Ann McNeil—the women explained that since the Second Vatican Council, entering women no longer left behind their birth names. It was one practice among many that Vatican II changed.

Some think those changes began an unwinding of religious life that left communities such as the Cincinnati sisters with echoing hallways and aged members. My lunch companions, though, had embraced it. "Before Vatican II, we served the world but stood apart from it," one said. "So we left our given names and took new ones. Since Vatican II," she continued, smiling, "We keep our given names because we serve the world from within it. We're immersed in it, level with it." The other sister listened and nodded. "It's more like it was in Mother Seton's day."

ACKNOWLEDGMENTS

I CAN'T IMAGINE A BOOK whose worth emerges less from its author than from the people who have guided and sustained her. Sisters and Daughters of Charity have tended Elizabeth Seton's legacy and papers for two centuries; their labor and generosity make scholarly work on Seton not just possible but joyful. Betty Ann McNeil, DC, responded to my early, vague queries with a wealth of information and encouragement and has offered unflagging support since. Regina Bechtle, SC, and Judith Metz, SC, have shared their immense knowledge through publications, correspondence, and conversation; Sister Judy's invitation to use the archive of the Sisters of Charity of Cincinnati, as well as her company and commentary while I was there, proved invaluable at a late stage of my work. I have also benefited from the insights and encouragement Sisters and Daughters of Charity graciously offered as I've visited archives, given presentations, and asked questions. My research into Elizabeth Seton cannot add to the intimate understanding her spiritual daughters possess, but their knowledge has informed my portrait and enriched my life.

My debts to archivists are also unpayable. Denise Gallo, director of the Daughters of Charity Province of St. Louise Archives, has skillfully and patiently aided my work, as has Bonnie Weatherly, who seems to know every scrap of paper in the voluminous Seton collection. Selin James helped me find many of the images that grace this book. Jessica J. Whitmore and Aaron P. Murphy opened the Rhoads Memorial Archive at Mount St. Mary's University to me; William Kevin Cawley led me through the University of Notre Dame's treasure trove; and Tricia Pyne guided me, in person and through her publications, as I used the Archive of the Archdiocese of Baltimore. I am grateful as well to archivists at the Historical Society of Pennsylvania, the Maryland Historical Society, the New York Historical Society, and the New York Public Library.

The Vincentian Studies Institute at DePaul University and the Cushwa Center for the Study of American Catholicism at Notre Dame provided financial support for this work in its early stages and collegial support in every stage since. Kathleen Cummings, the Cushwa Center's director, has quietly assisted me in ways too numerous to list (and too meaningful to forget). The historian Anne M. Boylan has shared research notes and materials with me throughout this project; my gratitude is matched only by my admiration for the model of scholarship she represents. Joseph P. Chinnici, OFM, offered guidance at many moments of my research and writing and also introduced me to Michael J. McGandy, whose criticism and stewardship have been invaluable. At Cornell University Press, Karen Hwa, Jamie Fuller, and Meagan Dermody have brought the manuscript to fruition. I have also benefited from the insights of participants in the UCLA Center for 17th- and 18th-Century Studies' British Atlantic in an Age of Revolution and Reaction conference, the William & Mary Quarterly/Early Modern Studies Institute's Early American Biographies workshop, the Cushwa Center's American Catholicism in a World Made Small seminar, the Jesuit Institute at Boston College's Jesuit Survival and Restoration seminar, and Arizona State University's Provost's Humanities Fellowship. I am grateful to my colleagues in the history, religious studies, and English faculties. Current and former students Chad Deets, James Dupey, Alex Griffin, Jacqueline Willy Romero, Daniel Vigeant, and Jeffrey Wheatley lent research, insight, and inspiration, as did David R. Eaton. As director of the School of Historical, Philosophical, and Religious Studies at Arizona State, Matthew J. Garcia created an environment in which I thrived as a researcher and teacher. I am grateful as well to Kathleen Given, whose competence and generosity have brightened my days and provided me valuable moments to devote to this book.

My children and parents have lived with this project for years, heartening me with their patient faith that I would one day finish; whatever it is I've neglected to do since 2008 please remind me of now. As for my husband, Brian Gratton, who has sometimes reminded me that this book matters and sometimes reminded me that it doesn't, he's been right every time.

NOTES

Documents relating to Elizabeth Seton have been collected, copied, and circulated since her lifetime; as a result, some documents are to be found, with slight or significant variations, in more than one archive and published collection, and others now exist only in reproduction, though the evidence for their authenticity is persuasive. The same is true of documents relating to the broader history of the Catholic Church in Seton's lifetime. I have tried in the notes to direct readers to archives at which they can most readily view the documents that I have used and, using the same logic, have cited the published collection of Seton's writings whenever possible; on occasions when more than one archival version of a source exists, I've noted the version along with the reference to its published form. I recommend that readers who wish to pursue research into Seton consult both the three-volume *Elizabeth Bayley Seton: Collected Writings* and the six-part *Seton Writings Project*, both available digitally through DePaul's Vincentian Studies Institute. I have also cited the published collection of John Carroll's writings when possible, acknowledging in the notes when there are relevant errors or omissions and indicating the archival sources that, in tandem with Thomas W. Spalding's work, remedy them. Finally, although I have preserved much of the distinctive spelling and punctuation in the sources, I have silently intervened at moments where, for example, the use of dashes rather than commas or periods would confound readers; I have used "sic" where an idiosyncratic spelling implies a different word (for example "too" for "two"); and I have filled in obvious abbreviations (e.g., "yours" for "yrs"). In instances in which a torn or illegible manuscript has made more guesswork essential, I have acknowledged speculation with brackets.

ARCHIVAL ABBREVIATIONS

AAB Archives of the Archdiocese of Baltimore, Associated Archives of St. Mary's Seminary and University, Baltimore, MD

AAMP Archbishop Ambrose Maréchal Paper, Archives of the Archdiocese of Baltimore, Associated Archives of St. Mary's Seminary and University, Baltimore, Maryland

AASUS	Archives of the Associated Sulpicians of the United States, Associated Archives of St. Mary's Seminary and University, Baltimore, MD
Act of 1800, NAMP	Act of 1800 Bankruptcy Records of the U.S. District Court for the Southern District of New York, 1800–1809, National Archives Microfilm Publications
AJCP	Archbishop John Carroll Papers, Archive of the Ardiocese of Baltimore, Associated Archives of St. Mary's Seminary and University, Baltimore, MD
AMSJ	Archives of the Sisters of Charity of Cincinnati, Mount St. Joseph, OH
AMSMU	Archives of Mount St. Mary's University, Emmitsburg, MD
AMSV	Archives of the Sisters of Charity of St. Vincent de Paul, Mont St. Vincent, Riverdale, NY
APSL	Daughters of Charity Province of St. Louise Archives, Emmitsburg, MD
ACSCE	Archives of the Sisters of Charity of Saint Elizabeth, Convent Station, NJ
ASCSH	Archives of the Sisters of Charity of St. Vincent de Paul, Halifax, NS, Canada
H-PP, MHS	Harper-Pennington Papers, Maryland Historical Society, Baltimore, MD
L&F R, HSP	Lee and Febiger Records, Historical Society of Pennsylvania, Philadelphia, PA
MPRF	Microfilm of the Congregatio de Propaganda Fide Records, University of Notre Dame, Notre Dame, IN
NYHS	New-York Historical Society, New York, NY
NYPL	New York Public Library
S-J	Seton-Jevons Collection (unless otherwise noted, located at AMSV although copies exist within other archives)
UNDA	University of Notre Dame Archives, Notre Dame, IN

PROLOGUE

1. McNeil, *Vincentian Family Tree,* 28–30.

2. White, *Life of Mrs. Eliza A. Seton*; Bailly de Barberey, *Elizabeth Seton*; McCann, *Mother Seton's Daughters*; Melville, *Seton* (1960) and Melville, *Seton* (rev. ed. by McNeill, 2009); Bechtle and Metz, *Collected Writings.* Other significant studies include Kelly, *Elizabeth Seton's Two Bibles,* and *Numerous Choirs*; Flanagan, "The Influence of John Henry Hobart"; Lee, "Practice of Spiritual Direction"; Bechtle and Metz, *Seton Writings Project: Chronological Lists 1–4*; McNeil, "Historical Perspectives" and "Elizabeth Seton—Mission of Education"; Melville, *Seton,* rev. ed., 314–17; Metz, *Retreat with Elizabeth Seton.*

1. TWO FAMILIES

1. Hancock, "Self-Organized Complexity," 33; Huey, "Old Slip and Cruger's Wharf," 23.

2. Taylor, *Environment and the People,* 116–17.

3. Chopra, *Unnatural Rebellion,* 12; Melville, *Seton,* rev. ed., 1–6.

4. *New-York Gazette, or Weekly Post-Boy,* August 1, 1757.

5. Saint Andrew's Society and Morrison, *History of Saint Andrew's Society,* 184, 284.

6. Thacher et al., *American Medical Biography,* 156–68.

7. Foote, *Black and White Manhattan,* 70–75, 56.

8. Beasley, *Christian Ritual;* Murphy, *Jesuit Slaveholding;* William Bayley will, *Old Wills of New Rochelle,* 70–71; Richard Charlton will, in New York Historical Society, "Abstracts of Wills," 249–51.

9. Scudder, "Biographical Sketch of LeConte," iii; Melville, *Seton,* rev. ed., 2.

10. Mercantile Library Association, *New York City during the American Revolution,* 12–16; Burrows and Wallace, *Gotham,* 175–204.

11. Seton, *Memoir,* 1:31–32.

12. Stevens, *Colonial New York,* 395; Pleasants, *Curzon Family,* 35; *New-York Journal or the General Advertiser,* May 25, 1769.

13. For example, *New-York Gazette and Weekly Mercury,* March 25, 1771; Seton Company trade documents, 100, 101, 4, 2, AMSV, accessed at AMSJ.

14. Henry Pelham to John Singleton Copley, 2 November 1774, in Copley and Pelham, *Letters & Papers,* 268.

15. Chopra, *Unnatural Rebellion,* 22–23.

16. Wilson, *Memorial History,* 4:394

17. Thacher, "Richard Bayley," 159–62.

18. For a contemporary and a nineteenth-century example, see Butler et al., *Religion,* 253, and Seton, *Memoir,* vol. 1.

19. Roberts, *Evangelical Gotham,* 31; Burrows and Wallace, *Gotham* 207–9.

20. J. Duncan, *Citizens or Papists?,* chaps. 1 and 2; Burrows and Wallace, *Gotham,* 135.

21. Quoted in Ketchum, *Divided Loyalties,* 262.

22. *New-York Journal or the General* Advertiser, December 22, 1774.

23. Lamb and Harrison, *City of New York,* 2:22; Jones, *History of New York,* 1:42–43; McConville, *King's Three Faces,* 289–90.

24. Quoted in Papas, "Richmond County," 86.

25. *Rivington's New York Gazetteer,* October 12, 1775.

26. Chopra, *Unnatural Rebellion,* 51.

27. Quoted in Volo, *Blue Water Patriots,* 182.

28. Chopra, *Unnatural Rebellion,* 52.

29. Journal of Lieutenant Isaac Bangs (1890), 75, quoted in Wall, *Equestrian Statue of George III,* 50.

30. Pleasants, *Curzon Family,* 36.

31. Melville, *Seton,* rev. ed., 42; R. Seton, *An Old Family,* 260–61.

32. William Duer to William Alexander, 6 November 1778, in Smith et al., *Letters of Delegates to Congress,* 11:179.

33. Thacher, "Richard Bayley," 63.

34. Charlton will dated 23 June 1777, and proved 10 October 1777, in "Abstracts of Wills," 250.

35. *New-York Gazette and Weekly Mercury,* August 11, 1777.

36. *Royal Gazette,* August 4, 1781.

37. Ryan, *Old St. Peter's,* 33–34.

38. Moffatt, *Barclays of New York,* 112n43; *Royal Gazette,* June 20, 1778.

39. This is a small, partially filled notebook, 1-3-3-26B, APSL; in future references it is cited to its reproduction in Bechtle and Metz, *Collected Writings,* 3a:510–23, quote at 510.

40. Quoted in Stone, *Centennial History*, 224–25.

41. Grabo, "Crèvecoeur's American," 159–61.

42. Acton, "Diary of William Smith," October 1779, 220, 289, 199.

43. William Magee Seton to Elizabeth Seton Seton, 21 December 1782, II–1–a, UNDA.

44. Most modern editions of the Bible, drawing on the Hebrew (Masoretic) text, number this as the Twenty-Third Psalm; those drawing on the Greek version of the Old Testament (Septuagint), number it as the Twenty-Second. Melville, *Seton*, rev. ed., 3.

2. BETSY BAYLEY

1. Quoted in Watson and Watson, *Men and Times of the Revolution*, 275.

2. Barbara Seton to William Seton, n.d., 1–3–3–18, APSL.

3. Elizabeth Bayley Seton to Eliza Sadler, 1 August 1797, Bechtle and Metz, *Collected Writings*, 1:17-18.

4. "Dear Remembrances," *Collected Writings*, 3a:511.

5. ESS to WS, n.d., 1–3–3–18:19, APSL.

6. "Dear Remembrances," Bechtle and Metz, *Collected Writings*, 3a:511.

7. "Dear Remembrances," *Collected Writings*, 3a:511.

8. WS to RC, [August 1784?], 1–3–3–18:20, APSL. See also Melville, *Seton*, rev. ed., 43–45.

9. *Rivington's New York Gazetteer*, December 10, 1783.

10. *Daily Advertiser*, May 23, 1786.

11. WS to RC, [August 1784?], 1–3–3–18:20, APSL; Melville, *Seton*, rev. ed., 46–47.

12. *Independent Gazette*, December 13, 1783.

13. "191 William Seton," in MacBean, Saint Andrew's Society, and Scots Society, *Biographical Register*, 118–19; Rothschild, *New York City Neighborhoods*, 14, 117.

14. January, 1807 bill of sale of "Negro Woman and Child," to William Seton Esq, with appended list of sums received from Cato toward their purchase, S-J 156–57, AMSV, accessed at AMSJ.

15. Burrows and Wallace, *Gotham*, 272; *Pennsylvania Evening Post, and Public Advertiser*, October 3, 1783.

16. "Old New York Hospital," *New York Times*, February 11, 1900.

17. *Daily Advertiser*, September 28, 1786.

18. Bonomi, "John Jay," 9–18; Bulthuis, *Four Steeples*, 33–38.

19. Dix et al., *History of the Parish of Trinity Church*, 2:257–61.

20. Duncan, *Citizens or Papists?*, 39–50; Anti-Federalists quoted in Fea, *Was America Founded as a Christian Nation?*, chap. 10.

21. George Washington to Roman Catholics in America, ca. 15 March 1790, Founders Online, http://founders.archives.gov/documents/Washington/05-05-02-0193; Fea, *Was America Founded as a Christian Nation?*, chap. 11.

22. Duncan, *Citizens or Papists?*, 69–72.

23. Binzley, "Ganganelli's Disaffected Children"; O'Donnell, "John Carroll."

24. New York Common Council and Peterson, *Minutes of the Common Council*, April 1785, 1:137; *Daily Advertiser*, May 26, 1786; *Massachusetts Gazette*, November 17, 1786; Duncan, *Citizens or Papists?*, 63–64.

25. Pleasants, *Curzon Family*, 44–45; Thompson-Stahr, *Burling Books*, 155–58; *Daily Advertiser*, April 25, 1786; WMS to AMS, 28 December 1788, S-J 446–51, APSL; WMS to AMS, 4 March 1789, S-J 317–20, APSL.

26. Codignola, "Gli Imprenditori Livornesi,"43- 66; *Daily Advertiser*, February 23, 1786.

27. *New York Daily Gazette*, January 14, 1790, and June 2, 1790.

28. WMS to AMS, 28 December 1788, S-J 446–51, APSL; WMS to JS, 28 November 1791, A-103.006, ASCSH, accessed at AMSJ; WMS to ESS, 24 December 1791, A-103.006, no. 14, ASCSH, accessed at AMSJ.

29. FF to Cardinal Antonelli, 1794, MPR, reel 1, UNDA; Keneally, *United States Documents*, 7:112; Chinnici, "Organization of the Spiritual Life," 229–30.

30. WMS to JS, 28 November 1791, A-103.006, ASCSH, accessed at AMSJ.

31. WMS to JS, 28 November 1791, A-103.006, ASCSH, accessed at AMSJ; John Thorpe to JC, 3 January 1789, J02; quote in 24 February 1789; 31 January 1789, J03; 6 March 1789, J04; 25 August 1789, J13; 27 December 1790, K14, AJCP, AAB.

32. Petition to the Common Council, 14 February 1788, quoted in de Costa and Miller, "1788 New York Doctors' Riot," 292.

33. *Pennsylvania Packet*, April 28, 1788.

34. *Pennsylvania Packet*, April 28, 1788.

35. Bechtle and Metz, *Collected Writings*, 3a:511. She wrote that she was twelve, rather than eleven, when this occurred, but the reference is clear.

36. Sarah Jay to Susanna French Livingston, 17 April 1788, in Nuxoll, *Selected Papers of John John Jay*.

37. *Daily Advertiser*, April 15, 1788; *New-York Packet*, April 18, 1788.

38. "Old New York Hospital," *New York Times*, February 11, 1900.

39. *Daily Advertiser*, December 5, 1788.

40. Journal to Rebecca Seton, Bechtle and Metz, *Collected Writings*, 1:264.

41. "Dear Remembrances," *Collected Writings*, 3a:511.

42. Quoted in McClymond and McDermott, *Theology of Jonathan Edwards*, 116.

43. Wordsworth, *Excursion*, 14.

44. Sprague, *Annals*, 7:121, 77; Bulthuis, *Four Steeples*, 90–95; Cope, "Salvific Significance," 21–40; Livingston married the Methodist preacher Freeborn Garrettson.

45. Taves, *Fits, Trances, and Visions*, 17; Brekus, *Sarah Osborn's World*, chap. 1.

46. Journal to Rebecca Seton, Bechtle and Metz, *Collected Writings*, 1:264.

47. Quoted in Harmless, *Mystics*, 4–5.

48. Day, *Collection of Psalms and Hymns*, 171.

49. *Daily Advertiser*, February 27, 1786.

50. Burrows and Wallace, *Gotham*,334–35; Desjardins and Pharoux, *Castorland Journal*, 234–42.

51. Erasmus, *Copia*; D. Chytraeus, *De ratione discendi et ordine studiorum in singulis artibus instituendo* (Wittenberg, 1564), quoted in Moss, "Politica," 423; Toner, *Washington's Rules of Civility*; Blecki and Wulf, *Milcah Martha Moore's Book*; Kelley, *Learning to Stand*, 18, 111.

52. New York Society Library, "Circulation Records."

53. EBS to Anna Maria Seton, Bechtle and Metz, *Collected Writings*, 1:219. The commonplace books are RB 30, 31, and 32, APSL, and invaluable extracting and annotation are to be found in *Collected Writings*, 3a:2–17, as well as in Kelly, "Elizabeth Bayley Seton's Commonplace Book."

54. Cayton, *Love in the Time of Revolution*, 46–50; Zagarri, *Revolutionary Backlash*, 40–45.

55. RB 32, APSL. The passage is from Nathanael Lee's *The Rival Queens: or the Death of Alexander the Great* (1677), a work frequently performed and extracted in

eighteenth-century England and America. The three commonplace books (RB 30–32, APSL) are charted in Bechtle and Metz, *Collected Writings*, 3a:2–17.

56. RB 32, APSL, quote from ""Extract of a letter from a gentleman in the English factory at Canton in China, to the Reverend M. in Gloucester," *Gentleman's Magazine*, February 1770.

57. Mary Bayley Post to EBS, 1 August 1808, 1–3–3–11:3, APSL.

58. "Dear Remembrances," Bechtle and Metz, *Collected Writings*, 3a:512.

59. *New-York Daily Gazette*, August 8, 1791, and September 30, 1791.

60. BS to WS, 4 September 1787, 1–3–3–18:21, APSL.

61. RC to WS, 8 June 1791, 1–3–3–18:23, APSL.

62. Uciechowski et al., "Susceptibility to Tuberculosis," 377–88.

63. RC to WS, addendum to 8 June, 1791 letter, 1–3–31–18:23, APSL.

64. Jones, "William Duer," 411–13.

65. WS to AH, 22 January 1792, Founders Online, National Archives, http://founders.archives.gov/documents/Hamilton/01-10-02-0119.

66. *New-York Daily Gazette*, November 7, 1792.

67. *Loudon's Register*, August 24, 1792; *New-York Daily Gazette*, August 25, 1792.

68. Duncan, *New-York Directory*, 200.

69. Post diary, 9 October 1792, NYHS.

70. Post diary, 19 September 1792, NYHS.

71. Post diary, 29 November 1792, NYHS.

72. Post diary, 21 January 1793; 23 October 1792, NYHS.

73. MP to EBS, 1 August 1808, 1–3–3–11:3, APSL.

74. Richard Bayley to EBS, n.d., 1–3–3–9:107, APSL; Booth, *Opium*.

75. EBS to JS, 15 March 1799, Becthle and Metz, *Collected Writings*, 1:65.

76. RB 30, APSL.

77. "Dear Remembrances," Bechtle and Metz, *Collected Writings*, 3a:512.

78. "Dear Remembrances," *Collected Writings*, 3a:512.

79. Bell, "Moral Thermometer" (paper, 2014).

80. MBP to EBS, 5 April [1817], 1–3–3–11:14, APSL.

81. Filippo Filicchi to William Seton, 1793, 1–3–3–18:24, APSL.

82. EBS to WS, n.d, Bechtle and Metz, *Collected Writings*, 1:2–4.

3. A HOME OF ONE'S OWN

1. *New-York Weekly Museum*, February 1, 1794; Melville, *Seton*, 25.

2. EBS to WMS, 23 July 1794, Bechtle and Metz, *Collected Writings*, 1:5–6; WS to EBS, 2 July 1794, A 111 080, AMSJ; 26 July 1794, S-J no. 187–190, ASCSE, accessed at AMSJ; 27 July 1794, A 111 081, AMSJ; Melville, *Seton*, rev. ed., 34.

3. FF to WS, 11 November 1793, 1–3–3–18:24, APSL.

4. From George Washington to the United States Senate, 28 May 1794, Founders Online, National Archives, http://founders.archives.gov/documents/Washington/05-16-02-0124.

5. EBS to WMS, 23 July 1794, Bechtle and Metz, *Collected Writings*, 1:5.

6. EBS to WMS, 23 July 1794, *Collected Writings*, 1:5.

7. Haddock, *Growth of a Century*, 137–38; Desjardins and Pharoux, *Castorland Journal*, xxviii, 75–81.

8. EBS to ES, 11 August 1796, Bechtle and Metz, *Collected Writings*, 1:11.

9. EBS to ES, 1 August 1797, *Collected Writings*, 1:17.

10. "Dear Remembrances," *Collected Writings*, 3a:513.

11. RB to EBS, 23 January 179[7?], 1–3–3–9:93, APSL; EBS to RB, 13 February 179[7?], *Collected Writings*, 1:13.

12. McNeill, "Yellow Jack," 343–64; Estes and Smith, *Melancholy Scene*; Pernick, "Politics, Parties, and Pestilence"; Watts, "Yellow Fever Immunities."

13. Gould, "Literature of Yellow Fever."

14. WMS to EBS, 27 July 1794, A 111 081, S-J 321–324, AMSJ; Parish of Trinity Church, "Baptisms, Marriages, and Burials from 1750."

15. Huler's status has been the subject of speculation, perhaps due to Elizabeth's referring to her as "Mammy." Marilyn Thei has posited that she might have been enslaved. "The Woman Elizabeth Bayley Seton, 1793–1803," 252n94. While this is not impossible, I think it unlikely. The Census of 1800 does not list any slaves in the Seton household, and Seton's language never hints at Huler's enslavement or at any uncertainty caused by New York's gradual emancipation.

16. Duffy, *Public Health in New York City*, 101–23; Cronon, *Diary of Elihu Hubbard Smith*, 16 September 1795, 57.

17. Committee of Health to Gov. John Jay, 4 November 1795, quoted in Davis, *Brief Account*, 54.

18. Bayley, *Account of the Epidemic Fever*, 90–91, 52, 121.

19. EBS to ES, 8 February 1796, Bechtle and Metz, *Collected Writings*, 1:9, 8.

20. EBS to ES, 11 August 1796, *Collected Writings*, 1:12.

21. EBS to JS, 5 July 1798, *Collected Writings*, 1:36.

22. EBS to ES, 8 February 1796, *Collected Writings*, 1:8.

23. EBS to ES, 11 August 1796, *Collected Writings*, 1:10.

24. EBS to ES, 11 August 1796, *Collected Writings*, 1:11.

25. Bayley, 31 July 1796, *Letters from the Health Office*, 7–8; Bayley to Rev. Richard Channing, *Minerva*, August 1, 1796.

26. EBS to RB, 13 February 1797, Bechtle and Metz, *Collected Writings*, 1:14.

27. Bayley, 31 July 1796, *Letters from the Health Office*, 8.

28. Morris, "Letters on the China Trade," 49.

29. WS to WMS, 16 May 1796, A-103.006, ASCSH, accessed at AMSJ.

30. EBS to ES, 15 August 1797, Bechtle and Metz, *Collected Writings*, 1:17.

31. EBS to ES, 15 August, 1797, *Collected Writings*, 1:19.

32. Williams, *French Assault*, 99, 208.

33. *Albany Chronicle*, August 1, 1797; *Loudon's Register*, August 19 and 21, 1797; Wilf, "Anatomy and Punishment."

34. Roberts, *Evangelical Gotham*, 40–41, 53.

35. Boylan, *Origins of Women's Activism*, 96–99, quote at 98. I rely on Boylan throughout my discussion of the society and its connections to Seton.

36. Boylan, *Origins of Women's Activism*, 62, 96–105; Roberts, *Evangelical Gotham*, 53–54.

37. Roberts, *Evangelical Gotham*, 57–59.

38. SB, 19 May 1821, 1–3–3–12:12, APSL.

39. Boylan, *Origins of Women's Activism*, 109.

40. RB to EBS, 4 February 1798, 1–3–3–9:97, 95, APSL.

41. RB to EBS, [June 1793?], 1–3–3–9:105, APSL.

42. MacKenzie to McTavish. Frobisher & Co., 29 January 1798, in Morris, "Letters on the China Trade," 62.

43. EBS to ES, 27 March 1798, Bechtle and Metz, *Collected Writings*, 1:20–21.

44. EBS to ES, 27 March 1798, *Collected Writings*, 1:20–21.

45. EBS to JS, 23 April 1798, *Collected Writings*, 1:24.

46. MacKenzie to Mctavish, Frobisher, 4 March 1798, in Morris, "Letters on the China Trade," 70–71.

47. MacKenzie to McTavish, 30 January 1798, in Morris, "Letters on the China Trade," 64.

48. EBS to JS 9 May 1798, Bechtle and Metz, *Collected Writings*, 1:28.

49. EBS to JS, 16 May 1798, *Collected Writings*, 1:30.

50. EBS to JS, 16 May 1798, *Collected Writings*, 1:32.

51. EBS to JS, 16 May 1798, *Collected Writings*, 1:31.

52. EBS to JS, 3 June 1798, *Collected Writings*, 1:33.

53. *Daily Advertiser,* June 12, 1798.

54. *New-York Gazette and General Advertiser,* June 11, 1798.

4. COURAGE FLIES

1. EBS to Isabella Cayley, fall 1799, Bechtle and Metz, *Collected Writings*, 1:103.

2. EBS to IC, fall 1799, *Collected Writings,* 1:103.

3. EBS to JS, 5 July 1798, *Collected Writings*, 1:36.

4. EBS to IC, 6 July 1798, *Collected Writings,* 1:39.

5. EBS to IC, 6 July 1798, *Collected Writings,* 1:39.

6. Thomas Masters to Miss Rawley, 4 August 1798, Masters Papers, NYHS.

7. EBS to JS, 5 and 9 July 1798, Bechtle and Metz, *Collected Writings*, 1:35–36.

8. EBS to JS, 3 June 1798, *Collected Writings*, 1:34.

9. EBS to JS, 20 August 1798, *Collected Writings*, 1:41.

10. EBS to JS, 8 October 1798, *Collected Writings*, 1:44; EBS to JS, 20 August 1798, *Collected Writings*, 1:42.

11. TM to father, 26 October 1798, Masters Papers, NYHS.

12. TM to mother, 17 November 1798, Masters Papers, NYHS.

13. EBS to Julia Scott, 13 October 1798, Bechtle and Metz, *Collected Writings*, 1:47.

14. EBS to JS, 21 October 1798, *Collected Writings,* 1:48.

15. EBS to JS, 3 November 1798, *Collected Writings*, 1:52.

16. EBS to JS, 28 October, 1798, *Collected Writings*, 1:49.

17. EBS to JS, 25 November 1798, *Collected Writings*, 1:53.

18. EBS to JS, 13 October 1798, *Collected Writings*, 1:47.

19. EBS to JS, 28 October 1798, *Collected Writings*, 1:50.

20. EBS to JS, 25 November 1798, *Collected Writings*, 1:54.

21. RS to EBS, 17 July 1799, 1–3–3–18:49, APSL.

22. EBS to JS, 16 May 1798, Bechtle and Metz, *Collected Writings,* 1:30–31.

23. EBS to Anna Maria Seton, 32 December 1798 (writing on back, with X through it), II–1–a, UNDA.

24. TM to uncle, 26 January 1799, Masters Papers, NYHS; Williams, *Assault on Shipping,* 62.

25. EBS to JS, 15 March 1799, Bechtle and Metz, *Collected Writings,* 1:65.

26. RB to EBS, n.d., 1–3–3–9:100, APSL.

27. EBS to ES, 9 September 1799, Bechtle and Metz, *Collected Writings,* 1:94.

28. EBS to ES, [October 1799], *Collected Writings,* 1:99.

29. EBS to ES [July or August 1799], *Collected Writings,* 1:90.

30. EBS to AMS, 31 December 1798, *Collected Writings,* 1:57.

31. EBS to ES, 1799, *Collected Writings,* 1:95–96.

32. EBS to RB, 24 February 1799, *Collected Writings*, 1:63.
33. EBS to JS, 15 March 1799, *Collected Writings*, 1:64.
34. EBS to RB, 2 February 1799, *Collected Writings*, 1:60.
35. EBS to JS, 2 June 1799, *Collected Writings*, 1:72.
36. Porterfield, *Conceived in Doubt*; Roberts, *Evangelical Gotham*, 40–41.
37. Rousseau, *Emile*, bk. 4.
38. EAS to ES, 1799, Bechtle and Metz, *Collected Writings*, 1:95.
39. EBS to RS, 2 October 1799, *Collected Writings*, 1:100.
40. Williams, *Assault on Shipping*, 306.
41. RS to EBS, 17 July 1799, 1–3–3–18:49, APSL.
42. EBS to RS, 2 October 1799, Bechtle and Metz, *Collected Writings*, 1:100.
43. EBS to JS, 20 December 1799, *Collected Writings*, 1:105.
44. EBS to JS, 20 November 1799, *Collected Writings*, 1:101.
45. TM to WS, 20 October, 1799, Masters Papers, NYHS.
46. TM to uncle, 11 August, 1799, Masters Papers, NYHS; Melville, *Seton*, rev. ed., 46–47.
47. EBS to RS, 23 December 1799, Bechtle and Metz, *Collected Writings*, 1:106.
48. EBS to RS, 3 January 1800, *Collected Writings*, 1:109.
49. EBS to JS, 3 January 1800, *Collected Writings*, 1:108.
50. Act of 1800, roll 8, case 104, NAMP.
51. 31 December 1799, Bechtle and Metz, *Collected Writings*, 3a:18.
52. 31 December 1799, *Collected Writings*, 3a:18.
53. 1–3–3–1:1, APSL.
54. EBS to RS, 3 January 1800, *Collected Writings*, 1:109.
55. EBS to RS, 3 January 1800, *Collected Writings*, 1:109.
56. EBS to RS, 5 February 1800, *Collected Writings*, 1:113.
57. RB to EBS, 8 February 1800, 1–3–3–9:98, APSL.
58. EBS to RB, 17 February 1800, Bechtle and Metz, *Collected Writings*, 1:115.
59. EBS to RB, 12 March 1800, *Collected Writings*, 1:118.
60. EBS to JS, 18 March 1800, *Collected Writings*, 1:120.
61. RB to EBS, [1799], 1–3–3–9:100, APSL.
62. EBS to RS, 5 February 1800, Bechtle and Metz, *Collected Writings*, 1:112.
63. Figure calculated from twenty-four New York City newspapers included in Readex, Early American Newspapers Series I, 1690–1876, during the relevant period. The figure is intended to indicate the decline in Seton's activities rather than to suggest a precise level for that activity.
64. EBS to JS, 18 March 1800, Bechtle and Metz, *Collected Writings*, 1:119.
65. Mann, *Republic of Debtors*, chaps. 1–3.
66. *Daily Advertiser*, May 22, 1800.
67. EBS to RS, [summer 1800], Bechtle and Metz, *Collected Writings*, 1:128.
68. WMS to JS, 7 July 1800, *Collected Writings*, 1:124.
69. EBS to RS, [summer 1800], *Collected Writings*, 1:124; EBS to ES, [July 1800], *Collected Writings*, 1:125; EBS to CD, 14 July 1800, *Collected Writings*, 1:128.
70. EBS to RS, 11 August 1800, *Collected Writings*, 1:134.
71. EBS to RS, 14 August 1800, *Collected Writings*, 1:136.
72. EBS to JS, 19 November 1800, *Collected Writings*, 1:140.
73. EBS to JS, 26 December 1800, *Collected Writings*, 1:143.
74. Act of 1800, roll 8, case 104, Inventory of Goods, NAMP.
75. EBS to JS, 26 December 1800, Bechtle and Metz, *Collected Writings*, 1:143
76. EBS to JS, 7 December 1800, *Collected Writings*, 1:141.

5. KNOT OF OAK

1. *Commercial Advertiser*, March 3, 1801; EBS to RB, 24 March 1801, Bechtle and Metz, *Collected Writings*, 1:154.

2. Act of 1800, roll 8, case 104, NAMP.

3. Act of 1800, roll 8, case 104, NAMP.

4. Coleman, *Debtors and Creditors*, 136.

5. The residences of Fitch and the Setons are recorded in the New York City directories for 1800, 1801, and 1802.

6. EBS to JS, 11 June 1801, Bechtle and Metz, *Collected Writings*, 1:160.

7. *New-York Herald*, November 13, 1802.

8. EBS to JS, 7 January 1802, Bechtle and Metz, *Collected Writings*, 1:196.

9. WM to EBS, 10 June 1801, S-J nos. 438–41, ASCSE, accessed at AMSJ.

10. EBS to JS, 10 March 1801, Bechtle and Metz, *Collected Writings*, 1:150–51; EBS to JS, 16 January 1801, *Collected Writings*, 1:145.

11. EBS to RS, [1801], *Collected Writings*, 1:156.

12. EBS to RS, 20 July 1801, *Collected Writings*, 1:177.

13. EBS to WMS, n.d., *Collected Writings*, 1:231.

14. "James Maitland," in MacBean, Saint Andrew's Society, and Scots Society, *Biographical Register*, 1:339.

15. McKee, *Gentlemanly and Honorable Profession*, 414.

16. EBS to JS, 1 February 1802, Bechtle and Metz, *Collected Writings*, 1:202.

17. EBS to JS, [20 June 1801], *Collected Writings*, 1:170.

18. EBS to ES, 22 June 1801, *Collected Writings*, 1:171.

19. Hobart and Berrian, *Posthumous Works of John Henry Hobart*, quotations at 58, 19, and 71; McVickar and Hook, *Early Life*. The fullest exploration of the collaboration between Hobart and Seton, and a study to which I am indebted, is Flanagan, "Influence of John Henry Hobart."

20. Hobart and Berrian, *Posthumous Works*, 44.

21. McVickar and Hook, *Early Life,* 186.

22. Crumb, "John Henry Hobart and England," 44–49; Mullin, *Episcopal Vision, American Reality,* 10; Doll, "Idea of the Primitive Church," 38; Bulthuis, *Four Steeples,* 88–90.

23. Handschy, "Eucharistic Sacrifice and Apostolic Order," 120–23. Seton appears on Trinity's 1801 list of communicants, but it is not clear whether she became a communicant as a result of Hobart's influence. Flanagan, "Elizabeth Seton's Theological/Spiritual World," 216.

24. EBS to RS, n.d., Bechtle and Metz, *Collected Writings*, 1:144.

25. EBS to JS, 10 March 1801, *Collected Writings*, 1:151.

26. EBS to JS, 16 January 1801, *Collected Writings*, 1:146.

27. EBS to RS, 14 June 1801, *Collected Writings*, 1:162.

28. EBS to RS, n.d., *Collected Writings*, 1:144.

29. EBS to RS 24, July 1801, *Collected Writings*, 1:178.

30. Journal to Rebecca Seton, *Collected Writings*, 1:297.

31. EBS to RS, 27 February 1801, *Collected Writings*, 1:148.

32. EBS to RS, 20 July 1801, *Collected Writings*, 1:176.

33. EBS to JS, 11 June 1801, *Collected Writings*, 1:160.

34. EBS to RS, 14 June 1801, *Collected Writings*, 1:162.

35. EBS to JS, 11 June 1801, *Collected Writings*, 1:160.

36. EBS to RS, Tuesday afternoon, 1801, *Collected Writings*, 1:173.

37. EBS to RS, Tuesday afternoon, 1801, *Collected Writings*, 1:173.

38. EBS to RS, 29 July 1801, *Collected Writings*, 1:180.

39. EBS to RS, 20 July 1801, *Collected Writings*, 1:176. In fact, she was interrupted by a visitor.

40. EBS to RS, n.d., *Collected Writings*, 1:155.

41. EBS to RS, 24 July 1801, *Collected Writings*, 1:178

42. EBS to RS, 24 July 1801, *Collected Writings*, 1:178.

43. Heyrmann, *Southern Cross*, chap. 1.

44. EBS to RS, 1801, Bechtle and Metz, *Collected Writings*, 1:158; EBS to RS, 15 July 1801, *Collected Writings*, 1:174; Lindman, "Spiritual Friendship," 680–700; Lawrence, *One Family under God*.

45. EBS to RS, 11 Oclock Thursday Night, [July 1801], Bechtle and Metz, *Collected Writings*, 1:181.

46. EBS to JS, 5 September 1801, *Collected Writings*, 1:185.

47. EBS to JS, 5 September 1801, *Collected Writings*, 1:185. Bechtle and Metz note that it is possible "Young Bayley" is Joseph Bayley, a nephew of the physician (1:150), but I follow Marilyn Thei's' view that Elizabeth's description of Young Bayley as "one of [my father's] family for fourteen years and to whom he was excessively attached" is, in conjunction with the last name Bayley, likely evidence of the man's enslavement to the physician. Thei, "The Woman Elizabeth Bayley Seton, 1793–1803," 252n94.

48. EBS to JS, 5 September 1801, *Collected Writings*, 1:185–87.

49. EBS to JS, 5 September 1801, *Collected Writings*, 1:186.

50. EBS to JS, 5 September 1801, *Collected Writings*, 1:186.

51. EBS to JS, 7 January 1802, *Collected Writings*, 1:197.

52. *New-York Gazette and General Advertiser*, August 19, 1801.

53. Will of Richard Bayley, New York Wills, no. 490, 43:386–88. Bayley did not free any enslaved people in his will; it is not clear who Young Bayley was or what became of him.

54. Will of William Magee Seton, New York Wills, no. 153, 45:133–34.

55. EBS to JS, 5 September 1801, Bechtle and Metz, *Collected Writings*, 1:186.

56. JS to AG, 10 September 1801, Giles Family Papers, NYHS.

57. EBS to RS, n.d., Bechtle and Metz, *Collected Writings*, 1:198.

58. EBS to RS, Sunday, [1801], *Collected Writings*, 1:204.

59. EBS to JS, 1 February 1802, *Collected Writings*, 1:201.

60. "Adorable redeemer!" passage, *Collected Writings*, 3a:39, near match to "Sunday morning," in Hobart, *Companion for the Altar*, 196.

61. Bechtle and Metz transcribe her annotation, describe its placement, and explain that Bruté brought the book with him when he was made bishop of Vincennes. *Collected Writings*, 3a:38.

62. EBS to JS, 16 November 1802, *Collected Writings*, 1:212.

63. Bulthuis, *Four Steeples*, 78–79.

64. EBS to RS, n.d., *Collected Writings*, 1:203.

65. 20 June 1803, Masters Papers, NYHS.

66. EBS to RS, eleven Oclock Thursday night [1802], *Collected Writings*, 1:182.

67. "Solemnly in the Presence of my Judge," 1 August 1802, Bechtle and Metz, *Collected Writings*, 3a:25.

68. EBS to RS, 5 August 1802, *Collected Writings*, 1:206.

69. EBS to RS, 16 August 1802, *Collected Writings*, 1:208.

70. EBS to RS, 16 August 1802, *Collected Writings*, 1:209.

71. WS to Julia Scott (addendum to EBS letter), 20 August 1802, *Collected Writings*, 1:211.

6. THE OTHER SIDE OF THE FENCE

1. EBS to RS, n.d., Bechtle and Metz, *Collected Writings*, 1:239.
2. EBS to RS, n.d., *Collected Writings*, 1:232.
3. EBS to RS, n.d., *Collected Writings*, 1:239.
4. EBS to CS, 8 April 1803, *Collected Writings*, 1:216.
5. *Morning Chronicle*, May 23, 1803.
6. EBS to AMS, 10 August 1803, Bechtle and Metz, *Collected Writings*, 1:217.
7. EBS to AMS, [1803], *Collected Writings*, 1:219.
8. *Alexandria Advertiser*, March 14, 1803.
9. EBS to ES, 28 September 1803, Bechtle and Metz, *Collected Writings*, 1:220.
10. EBS to ES, 28 September 1803, *Collected Writings*, 1:222.
11. EBS to William and to Richard Seton, *Collected Writings*, 1:223–24.
12. EBS to CS, 1 October 1803, *Collected Writings*, 1:224.
13. EBS to ES, 28 September 1803, *Collected Writings*, 1:221.
14. Rev. JHH to EBS, [1803], 1–3–3–11:B69, APSL.
15. EBS to JS, 1 October 1803, Bechtle and Metz, *Collected Writings*, 1:222.
16. Journal to Rebecca Seton, *Collected Writings*, 1:251–52, drawn from 110:M, II, 12, AMSV.
17. EBS to RS, 2 October 1803, *Collected Writings*, 1:225.
18. EBS to ES, 3 October 1803, *Collected Writings*, 1:245.
19. EBS to RS, 3 October 1803, *Collected Writings*, 1:243; S-J nos. 164–65, ASCSH.
20. EBS to JS 28, October 1803, *Collected Writings*, 1:245.
21. Journal to Rebecca Seton, 8 November 1803, *Collected Writings*, 1:247; 1–3–3:14, APSL; Franchot, *Roads to Rome*, 288.
22. Journal to Rebecca Seton, 11 November 1803, Bechtle and Metz, *Collected Writings*, 1:247; 1–3–3–3:14, APSL.
23. Journal to Rebecca Seton, 19 November 1803, Bechtle and Metz, *Collected Writings*, 1:249; 1–3–3–3:14, APSL.
24. Journal to Rebecca Seton, 19 November 1803, Bechtle and Metz, *Collected Writings*, 1:249; 1–3–3–8:59, APSL.
25. Journal to Rebecca Seton, 19 November 1803, Bechtle and Metz, *Collected Writings*, 1:252; 1–3–3–8:59, APSL.
26. Barnes, "Cargo, Infection," 75–101.
27. Journal to Rebecca Seton, 19 November 1803, Bechtle and Metz, *Collected Writings*, 1:252, drawn from 110:M, II,12, AMSV; all further *Collected Writings* citations in this chapter to the journal to Rebecca Seton are drawn from this source.
28. Journal to Rebecca Seton, 19 November 1803, *Collected Writings*, 1:252.
29. Journal to Rebecca Seton, 19 November 1803, *Collected Writings*, 1:253–54.
30. Journal to Rebecca Seton, 19 November 1803, *Collected Writings*, 1:253.
31. Journal to Rebecca Seton, 20 [November 1803], *Collected Writings,* 1:254.
32. Journal to Rebecca Seton, 20 [November 1803], *Collected Writings*, 1:255.
33. Journal to Rebecca Seton, Thursday [24 November] 1803, *Collected Writings,* 1:258.
34. Journal to Rebecca Seton, Friday [25 November 1803], *Collected Writings,* 1:259.
35. Journal to Rebecca Seton, Tuesday, 13 [December 1803], *Collected Writings,* 1:270.
36. Journal to Rebecca Seton, Tuesday, 29 November [1803], *Collected Writings,* 1:261.

37. Journal to Rebecca Seton, Thursday [24 November 1803], *Collected Writings*, 1:261, 258; Franchot, *Roads to Rome*, 290.

38. Journal to Rebecca Seton, Friday [25 November 1803], Bechtle and Metz, *Collected Writings*, 1:259.

39. Journal to Rebecca Seton, Friday [25 November 1803], *Collected Writings*, 1:258–59.

40. Journal to Rebecca Seton, 1 December 1803, *Collected Writings*, 1:264.

41. Journal to Rebecca Seton, Tuesday, 29 November [1803], *Collected Writings*, 1:261.

42. Journal to Rebecca Seton, 1 December 1803, *Collected Writings*, 1:265.

43. Journal to Rebecca Seton, 30 November 1803, *Collected Writings*, 1:261.

44. Journal to Rebecca Seton, Tuesday, 13 [December 1803], *Collected Writings*, 1:270.

45. Journal to Rebecca Seton, Tuesday, 13 [December 1803], *Collected Writings*, 1:270.

46. Journal to Rebecca Seton, 2 December [1803], *Collected Writings*, 1:266.

47. Journal to Rebecca Seton, 12 December [1803], *Collected Writings*, 1:268.

48. Journal to Rebecca, 14 [December 1803], *Collected Writings*, 1:270.

49. Journal to Rebecca, Tuesday, 13 [December 1803], *Collected Writings*, 1:269.

50. Journal to Rebecca Seton, Saturday and Sunday [18 and 19 December 1803], *Collected Writings*, 1:271.

51. Journal to Rebecca Seton, Tuesday, 20 December [1803], *Collected Writings*, 1:272.

52. Journal to Rebecca Seton, Saturday [24 December 1803], *Collected Writings*, 1:273–24.

53. EBS to RS, 3 January 1804, *Collected Writings*, 1:277.

54. Journal to Rebecca Seton, Monday [27 December 1803], *Collected Writings*, 1:274.

7. THESE DEAR PEOPLE

1. EBS to RS, 3 January 1804, Bechtle and Metz, *Collected Writings*, 1:279.

2. Journal to Rebecca Seton," Monday [27 December 1803], *Collected Writings*, 1:274, drawn from 110:M, II,12, AMSV.

3. Journal to Rebecca Seton, Monday [27 December 1803], Bechtle and Metz, *Collected Writings*, 1:274.

4. EBS to RS, 28 January 1804, *Collected Writings*, 1:289.

5. EBS to RS, 24 [February 1804], *Collected Writings*, 1:292.

6. I draw on Bechtle and Metz's discussion of the shipboard journal as well as on Melville's. *Collected Writings*, 1:304n17, and Melville, *Seton*, 322n59. Robert Seton recalled giving the original journal to Hélène Bailly de Barberey, after having been himself given it by Catherine Seton (his aunt). Bailly de Barberey published a translation, with unknown amounts of editing, in 1868. Code published an English edition as part of *Elizabeth Seton*, in 1927.

7. White, *Life of Mrs. Eliza A. Seton*, 101.

8. EBS to RS, 3 January 1804, Bechtle and Metz, *Collected Writings*, 1:277.

9. Codignola, "Religione e affari tra Italia e Stati Uni,"121–34.

10. Journal to Rebecca Seton, Monday [Tuesday, 27 December], Bechtle and Metz, *Collected Writings*, 1:275.

11. EBS to RS, 6 January 1804, *Collected Writings*, 1:281.

12. Act of 1800, roll 8, case 104, NAMP.

13. EBS to RS, 10 February [1804], Bechtle and Metz, *Collected Writings*, 1:291.

14. EBS to RS, 3 January 1804, *Collected Writings*, 1:277.

15. FF to JC, 2 February 1804 (mislabeled 1807), 3S6 AJCP, AAB.

16. EBS to RS, 3 January 1804, Bechtle and Metz, *Collected Writings*, 1:279.

17. Florence journal, *Collected Writings*, 1:283; this journal is drawn from1–3–3–3:15, APSL.

18. Florence journal, *Collected Writings*, 1:283–84.

19. Florence journal, *Collected Writings*, 1:285.

20. Florence journal, *Collected Writings*, 1:285.

21. Florence journal, *Collected Writings*, 1: 285.

22. Florence journal, *Collected Writings*, 1:286.

23. Florence journal, *Collected Writings*, 1:287.

24. EBS to RS, "St. Francis de Sales Day [29 January, 1804], Bechtle and Metz, *Collected Writings*, 1:289. The dating of this extended letter and the Florence journal is muddled, perhaps arising from a transposition of January and February in her original or a copy.

25. EBS to RS, 2 February 1804, Bechtle and Metz, *Collected Writings*, 1:289.

26. EBS to RS, 10 February [1804], *Collected Writings*, 1:290.

27. EBS to RS, 10 February [1804], *Collected Writings*, 1:290.

28. EBS to RS, 10 February [1804], *Collected Writings*, 1:290.

29. FF to JC, 2 February 1804 (mislabeled 1807), 3S6, AJCP, AAB.

30. EBS to RS, 10 February [1804], Bechtle and Metz, *Collected Writings* 1:291.

31. EBS to RS, 10 February [1804], *Collected Writings*, 1:291

32. EBS to RS, 10 February [1804], *Collected Writings*, 1:291.

33. EBS to RS 18 February [1804], *Collected Writings,* 1:291.

34. EBS to RS, 24 [February, 1804], *Collected Writings*, 1:292.

35. EBS to RS, 18 February [1804], *Collected Writings*, 1:291.

36. EBS to RS, 10 February [1804], *Collected Writings*, 1:292.

37. EBS to RS, 24 [February 1804], *Collected Writings*, 1:293.

38. EBS to RS, 5 March 1804, *Collected Writings*, 1:294.

39. EBS to AF, 6 April 1804, *Collected Writings*, 1:295.

40. Bizzocchi, "Cisibei."

41. Journal to Rebecca Seton, continued, 18 April [1804], Bechtle and Metz, *Collected Writings*, 1:297; this journal is drawn from 1–3–3–8:60, APSL. As Bechtle and Metz explain, this text "contains material not quite identical to the second part of the Italian Journal in the Archives at Mount St. Vincent printed above." *Collected Writings*, 1:296n1.

42. Journal to Rebecca Seton, continued, 18 April [1804], *Collected Writings*, 1:297.

43. Journal to Rebecca Seton, continued, 18 April [1804], *Collected Writings*, 1:297, 296. My thinking is informed by Orsi, *History and Presence*.

44. Journal to Rebecca Seton, continued, 18 April [1804], Bechtle and Metz, *Collected Writings*, 1:297.

45. Journal to Rebecca Seton, continued, 20 April 1804, *Collected Writings*, 1:300.

46. Journal to Rebecca Seton, continued, 21 April 1804, *Collected Writings*, 1:300.

47. Journal to Rebecca Seton, continued, 21 April 1804, *Collected Writings*, 1:301.

48. EBS to JHH, n. d., draft, *Collected Writings*, 1:305.
49. EBS to JHH, n. d., draft, *Collected Writings*, 1:305.

8. THE BATTLE JOINED

1. Journal to Rebecca Seton, continued, 4 June 1804, Bechtle and Metz, *Collected Writings*, 1:308; 110:M II, 12, AMSV.
2. Journal to Rebecca Seton, continued, 4 June 1804, *Collected Writings*, 1:308.
3. Hobart, *Companion for the Altar*, 193; Handschy, "Eucharistic Sacrifice and Apostolic Order," 130–38.
4. EBS to JC, draft, 26 July 1804, Bechtle and Metz, *Collected Writings*, 1:315–16.
5. "Dear Remembrances," *Collected Writings*, 3a:518; the lines are from the Book of Ruth 1:16.
6. Journal to Rebecca Seton, continued, Sunday morning [8 July 1804], *Collected Writings*, 1:310.
7. *New York Evening Post*, July 12, 1804.
8. *New York Evening Post*, July 13, 1804.
9. EBS to JS 15 July 1804, Bechtle and Metz, *Collected Writings*, 1:313.
10. EBS to JS, 15 July 1804, *Collected Writings*, 1:313–14.
11. EBS to AF, n.d., *Collected Writings*, 1:310.
12. Journal to Amabilia, 19 July 1804, *Collected Writings*, 1:368; 1–3–3–10:3a, APSL.
13. John Hobart's response to the Filicchi manuscript, Bechtle and Metz, *Collected Writings*, 3a:616; 1–3–3–20A, APSL.
14. Hobart's response, Bechtle and Metz, *Collected Writings*, 3a:632, 637; 1–3–3–20A, APSL.
15. William O'Brien to JC, 5U1–11, AJCP, AAB; Matthew O'Brien seems to have published *Sermons on Some of the Most Important Subjects of Morality and Religion* (1798) and *Oration on the Death of General George Washington* (1800).
16. JC to JB, 10 January 1805, Hanley, *Carroll Papers*, 2:468–69; this letter references a previous one, not extant. JB to JC, 2E1–5, ACP, AAB. The priest would, Carroll wrote diplomatically to Thomas Betagh, "be still more useful, if he tempered his ardor with more prudence." JC to TB, 14 July 1805, Hanley, *Carroll Papers*, 2:483.
17. AF to JC, 26 July 1804, S2, AJCP, AAB.
18. AF to JC, 26 July 1804, S2, AJCP, AAB.
19. EBS to JC, 26 July 1804, Bechtle and Metz, *Collected Writings*, 1:315–17.
20. AF to JC, 13 August 1804, S3, AJCP, AAB.
21. "Sermon on Occasion of Possessing His Pro-Cathedral," 12 December 1790, Hanley, *Carroll Papers*, 1:477; Dichtl, *Frontiers of Faith*, 8–9.
22. AF to JC, 4 October 1804, S4 AJCP, AAB.
23. AF to JC, 4 October 1804, S4 AJCP, AAB.
24. Journal to Amabilia, August 28 [1804], Bechtle and Metz, *Collected Writings*, 1:369.
25. EBS to AF, 2 September and 12 September 1804, *Collected Writings*, 1:318, 319.
26. AF to EBS, 26 July 1804, 1–3–3–10:4, APSL.
27. EBS to AF, 8 September and 19 September 1804, Bechtle and Metz, *Collected Writings*, 1:319, 320.
28. EBS to AF, 29 September 1804, *Collected Writings*, 1:325.
29. EBS to AF, 27 September 1804, *Collected Writings*, 1:323–24.

30. EBS to AF, 29 September 1804, *Collected Writings*, 1:325.

31. EBS to AF, 29 September 1804, *Collected Writings*, 1:325.

32. EBS to AF, 19 September 1804, *Collected Writings*, 1:321.

33. Seton, *Memoir*, 1:83; Bulthuis, *Four Steeples*, 89.

34. Hobart's response, Bechtle and Metz, *Collected Writings*, 3a: 619; 1–3–3–20a, APSL.

35. AF to EBS, 26 July 1804; 1–3–3–10:4, APSL.

36. Journal to Amabilia, September [1804], Bechtle and Metz, *Collected Writings*, 1:370.

37. Elsner, "Iconoclasm"; Finney, *Invisible God*; King, "Islam, Iconoclasm"; Journal to Amabilia, September [1804], Bechtle and Metz, *Collected Writings*.

38. Journal to Amabilia, September [1804], Bechtle and Metz, *Collected Writings*, 1:369–70.

9. THIS STORM

1. Hamon, *Life of Cheverus*, 70–75; JCh to JC, 10 March 1801, 2N3, AJCP, AAB.

2. AF to EBS, 7 September 1804, 1–3–3–10:7, APSL.

3. AF to EBS, 15 September 1804, 1–3–3–10:8, APSL.

4. EBS to AF, 27 September 1804, Bechtle and Metz, *Collected Writings*, 1:323.

5. AF to JC, 4 October 1804, S4, AJCP, AAB.

6. AF to EBS, 8 October 1804, 1–3–3–10:11, APSL.

7. Journal to Amabilia, Bechtle and Metz, *Collected Writings*, November 1 [1804]; 1:371; 1–3–3–10:31, APSL.

8. EBS to AF, 16 November 1804, Bechtle and Metz, *Collected Writings*, 1:328–29.

9. AF to EBS, [7?] November 1804, 1–3–3–10:15, APSL.

10. FF to EBS, 17 October 1804, 1–3–3–10:13, APSL.

11. FF to EBS, 22 October 1804, 1–3–3–10:14, APSL.

12. AF to EBS, 26 November 1804, 1–3–3–10:16, APSL.

13. EBS to AF, 3 December 1804, Bechtle and Metz, *Collected Writings*, 1:328–30.

14. Journal to Amabilia, November 1 [1804], *Collected Writings*, 1:372.

15. EBS to JS, 13 December 1804, Bechtle and Metz, *Collected Writings*, 1:337; EBS to JS, 28 November 1804, *Collected Writings*, 1:334.

16. EBS to Madame Olive, 20 November 1804, *Collected Writings*, 1:334.

17. Journal to Amabilia, September [1804], *Collected Writings*, 1:370.

18. AF to EBS, 6 December 1804, 1–3–3–10:17, APSL.

19. FF to EBS, 18 December 1804, 1–3–3–10:18, APSL.

20. EBS to AF, 2 January 1805, Bechtle and Metz, *Collected Writings*, 1:340.

21. JC to AF, 12 January 1805, Hanley, *Carroll Papers*, 2:469–70; Gollar, "Father John Thayer"; Jodziewicz, "American Catholic Apologetical Dissonance"; Mullen, *Chance of Salvation*, 226–28.

22. EBS to FF, [after 6 January 1805], Bechtle and Metz, *Collected Writings*, 1:342; Journal to Amabilia, *Collected Writings*, 1:372.

23. Journal to Amabilia, January 1805, *Collected Writings*, 1:373.

24. Seton recalled this years later, EBS to Simon Bruté, [September 1816], Bechtle and Metz, *Collected Writings*, 2:424; Hartfield, "Pluralistic Parish," 30–33; Burrows and Wallace, *Gotham*, 401; Jones, "Pierre Toussaint."

25. Journal to Amabilia, January 1805, Bechtle and Metz, *Collected Writings*, 1:373.
26. EBS to AF, 24 January 1805, *Collected Writings*, 1:342–43.
27. Journal to Amabilia, January 1805, *Collected Writings*, 1:373.
28. Journal to Amabilia, January 1805, *Collected Writings*, 1:374.
29. Journal to Amabilia, January 1805, *Collected Writings*, 1:374.
30. Brownson, "Nature and Office," 247; Brownson, "Review of John Henry Hopkins," 366; Mullen, *Chance of Salvation*, 232–33.
31. Journal to Amabilia, January 1805, Bechtle and Metz, *Collected Writings*, 1:374.
32. EBS to JC, draft, [after March 25, 1805], *Collected Writings*, 1:346.
33. JCh to EBS, 4 March 1805, 100, 115, 1, 12, AMSV, accessed at AMSJ; A.M.M.G., *Life of Mother Elizabeth Boyle*, 26.
34. Journal to Amabilia, [27 February 1805], Bechtle and Metz, *Collected Writings*, 1:375.
35. Journal to Amabilia, [14 March 1805], *Collected Writings*, 1:375. Souvay explains how mistranscriptions of Seton's journal over the years have led to some confusion about the precise dates of the steps of her conversion in "Questions anent Mother Seton's Conversion," 223–38.
36. John Hobart's response to the Filicchi manuscript, Bechtle and Metz, *Collected Writings*, 3a:637.
37. Journal to Amabilia, [20 March 1805], *Collected Writings*, 1:376.
38. Journal to Amabilia, 25 March [1805], *Collected Writings*, 1:376.

10. A CONVERT IN NEW YORK

1. EBS to AF, 22 April 1805, Bechtle and Metz, *Collected Writings*, 1:356.
2. EBS to JS, 5 March 1805, *Collected Writings*, 1:345.
3. EBS to AF, 15 April 1805, *Collected Writings*, 1:352.
4. Duncan, *Citizens or Papists?*, 116.
5. For an admiring account of the Barry family, see Warner, *At Peace with All their Neighbors*, 109–12. Morris is listed as "Assistant Alderman, First Ward, 1802–1806" in New York Common Council and Valentine, *Manual of the Corporation of the City of New York*, 476; on Morris, see also Melville, *Seton*, rev. ed., 145. On St. Peter's trustees in this period, see Wheatley, "Fellow Citizens"; Hartfield, "Pluralistic Parish," 33–34.
6. JB to JC, 25 February 1807, 1K4, AJCP, AAB.
7. EBS to AF, 6 April 1805, Bechtle and Metz, *Collected Writings*, 1:350.
8. EBS to AF 15, April 1805, *Collected Writings*, 1:351.
9. EBS to AF, 6 April 1805, *Collected Writings*, 1:350.
10. EBS to AF, 22 April 1805, *Collected Writings*, 1:356.
11. EBS to AF, 30 April 1805, *Collected Writings*, 1:358.
12. AF to EBS, London, 5 September 1806, 1-3-3–10:31, APSL.
13. EBS to AF, 22 April 1805, Bechtle and Metz, *Collected Writings*, 1:355.
14. EBS to AF, 1 June 1805, *Collected Writings*, 1:365.
15. Sadler to EBS, n.d. but postconversion by internal evidence, 1-3-3–11:B3, APSL.
16. EBS to AF, 30 April 1805, Bechtle and Metz, *Collected Writings*, 1:359–60.
17. EBS to AF, 6 May 1805, *Collected Writings*, 1:362.
18. AF to EBS, 21 May 1805, 1-3-3–10:22, APSL.

19. EBS to AF, 1 June 1805, Bechtle and Metz, *Collected Writings*, 1:365. On Catherine Livingston Garrettson, see Bulthuis, *Four Steeples*, 90–95; Cope, "Salvific Significance."

20. EBS to AF, 1 June 1805, Bechtle and Metz, *Collected Writings,* 1:366.

21. EBS to AF, 6 April 1805, *Collected Writings,* 1:350.

22. EBS to AF, 22 April 1805, *Collected Writings,* 1:357.

23. JC to Joanna Barry, 15 September 1805, Hanley, *Carroll Papers,* 2:487.

24. JCh to EBS, 1 June 1805, 1–3–3–1:2, APSL.

25. EBS to ES, n.d., 1–3–3–11:B3, APSL.

26. EBS to AF, 9 September 1805, Bechtle and Metz, *Collected Writings,* 1:385.

27. EBS to JS, 10 July 1805, *Collected Writings,* 1:380; EBS to JS, 28 August 1805, *Collected Writings,* 1:383.

28. ES to EAS, n.d., 1–3–3–11:B1, APSL.

29. J. Tisserant to EBS, 6 September 1805, 1–3–3–1:20, APSL.

30 J. Tisserant to EBS, 6 September 1805, 1–3–3–1:20, APSL.

31. EBS to Cecilia Seton, 7 October 1805, Bechtle and Metz, *Collected Writings,* 1:389.

32. EBS to JS, 6 May 1805, *Collected Writings,* 1:361.

33. EBS to AF, 6 April 1805, *Collected Writings,* 1:350.

34. Samuel Waddington Seton Diary, New York Public Library.

35. JCP to Charles Plowden, 1 and 13 March 1788, Hanley, *Carroll Papers,* 1:275.

36. Curran, *History of Georgetown University,* 25–35.

37. EBS to AF, 25 October 1805, Bechtle and Metz, *Collected Writings,* 1:394.

38. EBS to JS, 20 November 1805, *Collected Writings,* 1:396.

39 "Memoir of Hurley," 165–80; EBS to FF, 2 November 1807, Bechtle and Metz, *Collected Writings,* 1:481.

40. In a letter explaining his decision to transfer Hurley, Carroll wrote, "There is reason to believe, that besides the reason alledged on account of want of sufficient maintenance, he had assigned other causes, affecting yourself, which perhaps were exaggerated tho' to me he never alluded to those causes. ... If at all founded, you will see at once the most urgent duty of removing a stumbling block, which must be so injurious to religion, and hurtful to the well disposed, as well as to the profligate members of the Church, by furnishing them with a pretence for following their irregular practices." JC to Matthew Carr, 8 July 1805, Hanley, *Carroll Papers,* 2:482.

41. MH to JC, 10 March 1806, 4G9, AJCP, AAB.

42. Matthew O'Brien to John Rossiter, 16 January 1806, 7K2, AJCP, AAB.

43. JB to JC, 25 February 1807, 1K4, AJCP, AAB.

44. EBS to CS, 24 December 1805, Bechtle and Metz, *Collected Writings,* 1:398.

45. MH to JC, 6 January 1806, 4G8, AJCP, AAB. "Since my letter of the second instant [4H1] a general meeting of the Congregation of St. Peters was held in the school room, and took up the consideration of the oath required in this state, with which I have reason to believe Sir, you are acquainted. . . . Already more than two hundred names are affixed to the petition."

46. JT to EBS, 9 March 1806, 1–3–3–1:22, APSL.

47. JCh to EBS, 28 January 1806, 1–3–3–1:4, APSL.

48. Jch to EBS, 3 April 1806, 1–3–3–1:5, APSL.

49. The letter, from a "D. Corvaisier," is cataloged in the archive of the Archdiocese of Baltimore but was removed before 1954, when the collection was microfilmed.

50. JT to EBS, 31 March 1806, 1–3–3–1:24, APSL.

51. EBS to AF, 25 March 1806, Bechtle and Metz, *Collected Writings,* 1:402.

52. JC to JB, 8 April 1806, Hanley, *Carroll Papers,* 2:509–10.

53. Thomas Kelly to EBS, 8 April 1806, 1–3–3–2:54, APSL; Melville, *Seton,* rev. ed., 147.

54. Curran, *History of Georgetown University,* 26.

55. EBS to JS, 20 January 1806, Bechtle and Metz, *Collected Writings,* 1:399–400.

56. MH to JC, 10 March 1806, 4G9, AJCP, AAB.

57. MO to JC, 24 February 1806, 5T5, AJCP, AAB.

58. JC to MO, 4 March 1806, Hanley, *Carroll Papers,* 2:505.

59. This emerges in something labeled "Extract," apparently in Carroll's writing, on the back of a letter from Matthew O'Brien. The final version of the letter is not in the AAB archive, nor is it cataloged there, as some other related missing documents are. The extract is included in the published *John Carroll Papers,* but an editor's footnote incorrectly suggests that Carroll was contemplating the issue of Elizabeth Seton's conversion (rather than Catherine McLennan's accusation, which goes unmentioned). The extract is dated 4 March and is written on M. O'Brien to JC, 24 February 1806, 5T5 AJCP, AAB.

60. Catherine McLennan (cataloged as McLane) to JC, 10 April 1806 (cataloged as 1807), 5D12, AJCP, AAB.

61. JC to Joseph-Octave Plessis, 28 July 1806, Hanley, *Carroll Papers,* 2:524.

62. EBS to JS, 12 May 1806, Bechtle and Metz, *Collected Writings,* 1:407.

63. AF to EBS, 16 June 1806, A 111 118, AMSJ, accessed at UNDA; the sequence of events is also described in Joanna Barry to JC, 17 June 1806, 1M3, AJCP, AAB.

11. DUTY OR OBEDIENCE

1. Friday [1806], EBS to CS, Bechtle and Metz, *Collected Writings,* 1:411.

2. MHS to CS, n.d., 1–3–3–17:14, APSL.

3. CS to MHS, n.d., 1–3–3–4:167, APSL.

4. MHS to CS, n.d., 1–3–3–17:15, APSL.

5. CS to MHS, 1806, 1–3–3–4:168, APSL.

6. EBS to AF, 10 August 1806, Bechtle and Metz, *Collected Writings,* 1:414.

7. EBS to ECF (draft), *Collected Writings,* 1:541.

8. CSO to CS, Thursday [1806], 1–3–3–16:11, APSL.

9. Hatch, *Democratization of American Christianity*; Roberts, *Evangelical Gotham.*

10. MH to EBS, n.d., 1–3–3–1:33, APSL.

11. Joanna Barry to JC, October 1806, 1L2, AJCP, AAB.

12. EBS to AF, 10 August 1806, Bechtle and Metz, *Collected Writings,* 1:414.

13. AF to EBS, 3 November 1806, 1–3–3–10:33, APSL.

14. AF to John Murray and Son, n.d., 1–3–3–10:34, APSL; Melville, *Seton,* rev. ed., 165.

15. Startin eventually removed Seton and her children from her will (Melville, *Seton,* rev. ed. 168 note m) but continued to ask after her well-being and may have thought Seton had found new, permanent benefactors in the Filicchis and the Catholic Church.

16. EBS to AF, 30 March 1807, Bechtle and Metz, *Collected Writings,* 1:431.

17. Neel, "Origins of the Beguines"; Greer, *Mohawk Saint,* 95–125.

18. EF to EBS, undated, 1–3–3–7:100, APSL.

19. EBS to EF, undated, Bechtle and Metz, *Collected Writings,* 1:539.

20. EBS to HS, undated, *Collected Writings*, 1:542.

21. Kaufman, *Tradition and Transformation*; Pasquier, *Fathers on the Frontier*, 28–32; Melville, *Louis William Dubourg*, 1:1–45.

22. Jacques Emery to Louis-Valentin-Guillaume Dubourg, 16 May 1797, quoted in Melville, *Dubourg*, 1:49.

23. Melville, *Dubourg*, 1:46–120.

24. EBS to JS, 10 November 1806, Bechtle and Metz, *Collected Writings*, 1:419.

25. FM to EBS, 25 November 1806, 1-3-3-1:37, APSL.

26. JCh to EBS, 21 January 1807, 1-3-3-1:7, APSL.

27. EBS to AF, 10 April [1807], Bechtle and Metz, *Collected Writings*, 1:432.

28. JC to Joanna Barry, 2 January 1807, Hanley, *Carroll Papers*, 3:4; JC to EBS, 23 May 1807, Hanley, *Carroll Papers*, 3:21–22.

29. JC to EBS, 23 May 1807, Hanley, *Carroll Papers*, 3:21.

30. Burrows and Wallace, *Gotham*, 402.

31. EBS to AF, 14 March 1807, Bechtle and Metz, *Collected Writings*, 1:429.

32. EBS to JS, 20 July 1807, *Collected Writings*, 1:450.

33. CS to EBS, n.d., 1-3-3-4:139, APSL.

34. EBS to ES, 6 October 1807, Bechtle and Metz, *Collected Writings*, 1:469.

35. CS to EBS, 4 July 1807, 1-3-3-4:193, APSL.

36. EAS to CS, 15 August 1807, Bechtle and Metz, *Collected Writings*, 1:460.

37. On the French context, see Ford, *Divided Houses*, who writes of the nineteenth century that women's "religiosity, and the religious vocation more particularly, could and did come to threaten the family, marital relations, and the Catholic hierarchy itself" (14). Schutte argues in *By Force and Fear* that internal Church documents detailing women's petitions to be released from vows in Europe and Latin America render suspect the image made popular by Diderot and Manzoni of helpless women forced into convents.

38. EBS to CS, 15 August 1807, Bechtle and Metz, *Collected Writings*, 1:460; CS to EBS, Wednesday Eve, 11 o'clock, 1-3-3-4 194, APSL.

39. EBS to CS, 1 July 1807, Bechtle and Metz, *Collected Writings*, 1:446.

40. James Barry to JC, 10 June 1807, 1K5, AJCP, AAB.

41. John Rossiter to JC, 27 May 1807, 7K8, AJCP, AAB.

42. JC to Robert Molyneux, 25 February 1807, Hanley, *Carroll Papers*, 3:10–11.

43. Matthias Kelly to JC, 6 November 1806, 4J4, AJCP, AAB.

44. JR to JC, 27 May 1807, 7K8, AJCP, AAB.

45. EBS to CS, [18 July 1807], Bechtle and Metz, *Collected Writings*, 1:449.

46. Michael Hurley to Cecilia Seton, 29 August 1807, 1-3-3-4:197, APSL.

47. EBS to MH (draft), 9 September 1807, Bechtle and Metz, *Collected Writings*, 1:449.

48. EBS to JS, 20 July 1807, *Collected Writings*, 1:451.

49. EBS to ES, 13 November 1807, *Collected Writings*, 1:484; EBS to JS, 29 November 1807, *Collected Writings*, 1:488.

50. JCh to AF, 17 October 1807; 111 112, AMSJ.

51. EBS to JC, 13 November 1807, Bechtle and Metz, *Collected Writings*, 1:483.

52. EBS to AF, 2 November 1807, *Collected Writings*, 1:480.

53. Louis Sibourd to JC, 26 November 1807, 7Q7, AJCP, AAB; LS to JC, 7 December 1807, 7Q8, AJCP, AAB.

54. WD to EBS, 2 May 1808, II-1-a, UNDA; WD to EBS, 27 May 1808, 100, 115, 1, 20, AMSV, accessed at AMSJ.

55. WD to EBS, 2 May 1808, II-1-a, UNDA.

56. JCh to EBS, 12 May 1808, 1–3–3–1:9, APSL.

57. WD to EBS, 27 May 1808, 100, 115, 1, 20, AMSV, accessed at AMSJ.

58. JCh to EBS, 12 May 1808, 1–3–3–1:9, APSL.

59. Quoted in Burrows and Wallace, *Gotham*, 411.

60. JC to Robert Molyneux, 19 June 1808, Hanley, *Carroll Papers*, 3:65.

12. A NEW BEING

1. EBS to ES, 20 January 1809, Bechtle and Metz, *Collected Writings*, 2:48.

2. Rockman, *Scraping By*, chaps. 1–2.

3. Dorsey and Dilts, *Guide to Baltimore Architecture*, 149–50.

4. Quoted in Melville, *Louis William Dubourg*, 1:145.

5. EBS to CS, Thursday evening Corpus Christi, Bechtle and Metz, *Collected Writings*, 2:7.

6. EBS to CS, 20 June 1808, *Collected Writings*, 2:9.

7. EBS to CD, [17 June] and 20 June 1808, *Collected Writings*, 2:7–10.

8. Griffin, "Toothless Priest," 17–21.

9. EBS to JS, 23 March 1809, Bechtle and Metz, *Collected Writings*, 2:60.

10. EBS to CS, 26 August 1808, *Collected Writings*, 2:29.

11. EBS to JS, 4 July 1808, *Collected Writings*, 2:15.

12. Harper's political career is described in Papenfuse, *Evils of Necessity*. He first entered politics in 1790, when he was elected to the South Carolina House of Representatives. After leaving politics in 1801, he resumed his political career, in Maryland in 1810.

13. Alexander, *Notorious Woman*, 118–20.

14. EBS to JS, 8 December 1808, *Collected Writings*, 2:42–43.

15. JC to Francis Neale, 12 November 1805, Hanley, *Carroll Papers*, 2:497.

16. Murphy, *Jesuit Slaveholding*, 73, 54–55, 7, 78; Wilder, "War and Priests," 238–39.

17. Papenfuse, *Evils of Necessity*, 38.

18. JC to Cardinal Leonardo Antonelli, 5 August 1789, Hanley, *Carroll Papers*, 1:375–77 (quotation, 1:376).

19. Quoted in Murphy, *Jesuit Slaveholding*, 55.

20. RGH, "Appius's Letters," quoted in Papenfuse, *Evils of Necessity*, 11.

21. EBS to Catherine Dupleix, 20 June 1808, Bechtle and Metz, *Collected Writings*, 2:12.

22. EBS to CD, 20 June 1808, *Collected Writings*, 2:8; EBS to JS, 6 and 8 December 1808, *Collected Writings*, 2:41 and 2:43.

23. EBS to JS, 8 December 1808, *Collected Writings*, 2:43.

24. EBS to AF, 8 July 1808, *Collected Writings*, 2:17.

25. CS to EBS, 4 August 1808, 1–3–3–4:204, APSL.

26. HS to EBS, 8 November 1808, 1–3–3–8:74, APSL.

27. Catherine Seton (of James), New York, to Annina Seton, 4 August [1808], 1–3–3–4:107, APSL.

28. CS to EBS, 7–23 July 1808, 1–3–3–4:202, APSL.

29. CS to EBS, 7–23 July 1808, 1–3–3–4 202, APSL.

30. Melville, *Dubourg*, 1:20–21, 75–81, 189–92; Bertrand, *Bibliothèque Sulpicien*, 2:172–73.

31. Pierre Babade, 9 August 1808, 1–3–3–1:62, APSL.

32. Rebecca Seton to PB, n.d., 1–3–3–4:46, APSL.

33. EBS to AF, 20 August 1808, Bechtle and Metz, *Collected Writings*, 2:29.

34. Chinnici, *Living Stones*, chaps. 1–3; quotes at 10 and 17; Chinnici, "Organization of the Spiritual Life," 229–30.

35. PB to CS, n.d., 1–3–3–4:34, APSL. The phrase is from the Gospel of Matthew.

36. EBS to CS, 12 August 1808, Bechtle and Metz, *Collected Writings*, 2:26; PB to JC 27, December 1804, 1K1, AJCP, AAB; for Nagot's unease about Babade, see Melville, *Seton*, rev. ed. 190–91, undocumented reference to alcohol use, 472n8; JC to Jacques Garnier, 29 April 1806, Hanley, *Carroll Papers* 2:512–13; Kauffman, *Tradition and Transformation;* Pasquier, *Fathers on the Frontier.*

37. EBS to CS, 8 July 1808, Bechtle and Metz, *Collected Writings*, 2:21

38. EBS to JS, 23 March 1809, *Collected Writings*, 2:63.

39. Cavallo and Warner, *Widowhood;* McIver, *Wives, Widows, Mistresses, and Nuns;* Diefendorf, *From Penitence to Charity;* Dinan, *Women and Poor Relief;* Rapley, *Devotes.*

40. Diefendorf, "Rethinking the Catholic Reformation," 32–34; Lehfeldt, *Religious Women in Golden Age Spain*, 175; Lux-Sterritt, "Mary Ward's English Institute."

41. JC, Report to the Roman Congregation, Hanley, *Carroll Papers*, 2:32; JC to Bernadine Matthews, 1 March 1793, Hanley, *Carroll Papers*, 2:84–85; *Guide to the Catholic Sisterhoods*, 266; Currier, *Carmel in America,*50–59; Binzley, "Ganganelli's Disaffected Children," 278–81.

42. JC to C. and R. Plowden, 3 September 1800, Hanley, *Carroll Papers*, 2:319.

43. Rapley, *Devotes,* 42–43; Clark, *Masterless Mistresses;* Bourguignon, *La Vie du Pere Romillon* (1649), quoted in Bremond, *Histoire littèraire*, 2:29–30, quoted in Rapley, *Devotes,* 51.

44. Rapley, *Devotes,* 55.

45. Evangelisti, *Nuns*, 210.

46. EBS to CS, 6 October 1808, Bechtle and Metz, *Collected Writings*, 2:34.

13. SOME CHARITABLE PERSONS

1. EBS to CS, 6 October 1808, Bechtle and Metz, *Collected Writings*, 2:34.

2. S. Smith, "Philadelphia's First Nun," 417–22; K. Miller, "Margaret Carey Murphy Burke," in Miller et al., *Irish Immigrants*, 349–62.

3. MBP to EBS, 29 October 1808, 1–3–3–11:6, APSL.

4. Act of 1800, roll 8, case 104, NAMP.

5. Joseph Bayley to EBS, Baltimore, 16 January 1809, 1–3–3–2:98, APSL.

6. EBS to FF, 21 January 1809, Bechtle and Metz, *Collected Writings*, 2:52–53, quote at 53; EBS to AF, 16 January 1809, *Collected Writings*, 2:44–47, quote at 45.

7. Matthias O'Conway to Rebecca O'Conway, 9 December 1808, in Smith, "Philadelphia's First Nun," 422.

8. CO'C M & RO'C, 14 May 1809, in Smith, "Philadelphia's First Nun," 429.

9. EBS to MO'C, [Spring 1809], Bechtle and Metz, *Collected Writings*, 2:67–68.

10. SWS and CS to EBS, 22 December 1808, 1–3–3–4:206–207, APSL.

11. CS to EBS, 7–8 January 1809, 1–3–3–4:208, APSL.

12. HS to EBS, November 1808, 1–3–3–8:73, APSL.

13. Shaw, *John Dubois*, 3–5.

14. Shaw, *John Dubois*, 8–9.

15. Champe, *Vincent de Paul;* Purcell, *World of Monsieur Vincent;* Woodgate, *St. Louise de Marillac;* Diefendorf, *From Penitence to Charity;* quote from "Rules

of the Sisters in Parishes," 24 August 1659, in de Paul and Coste, *Correspondences, Conferences, Documents,* 10:530.

16. Dinan, *Women and Poor Relief,* 24–26; 55–57.

17. Shaw, *John Dubois,* 13–15.

18. Shaw, *Dubois,* 20–21, quote at 21.

19. JD to JC, 7 July 1804, 8AG1, AJCP, AAB.

20. JD to JC, 28 November 1805, 8AG2, AJCP, AAB.

21. Daughters of Charity, Bruté de Rémur, and Seton, *Connection with the Community,* 302; Scharf, *History of Western Maryland,* 1:582–83.

22. Quoted in Shaw, *Dubois,* 29; JC to Matthew Ryan, 16 December 1797, Hanley, *Carroll Papers,* 2:226.

23. JD to JC, 14 March 1807, 8AG3, AJCP, AAB; McSweeny, et al., *Story of the Mountain,* 1:14

24. Ruane, *Society of St. Sulpice,* 232–34, Shaw, *Dubois,* 37–42; Melville, *Louis William Dubourg,* 1:171–72, quote at 172.

25. Shaw, *Dubois,* 47.

26. WD to the Rev. Deluol, 15 July 1828, reproduced in Griffin, "Toothless Priest," 18–21.

27. EBS to FF, 8 February 1809, Bechtle and Metz, *Collected Writings,* 2:55.

28. Sulpician Register, 14 March 1809, 39, AASUS; Melville, *Dubourg,* 1:176–77.

29. EBS to FF, 8 February 1809, Bechtle and Metz, *Collected Writings,* 2:55.

30. EBS to AF, 16 January 1809, *Collected Writings,* 2:47.

31. CO'C to R and MO'C, 3 May 1809, in Smith, "Philadelphia's First Nun," 427.

32. MCB to MC, 7 July 1809, 14 July 1809, 19 September 1809, box 65, folder 6, L&FR, HSP; Miller, "Margaret Carey Murphy Burke," 351–55.

33. JC to EBS, 24 March 1810 (but actually 1809), 100, 115, 1, 45 24, AMSV, accessed at AMSJ.

34. EBS to FF, 21 January 1809, Bechtle and Metz, *Collected Writings,* 2:52.

35. EBS to JS, 23 March 1809, *Collected Writings,* 2:62.

36. JCh to EBS, 13 April 1809, 1-3-3-1:10, APSL.

37. EBS to JS, 8 December 1808, Bechtle and Metz, *Collected Writings,* 2:42.

38. JS to EBS, 15 March 1809, 1-3-3-11:B24, APSL.

39. EBS to JS, 2 March 1809, Bechtle and Metz, *Collected Writings,* 2:60.

40. JS to EBS, 15 March 1809, 1-3-3-11:B24, APSL.

41. EBS to JS, 14 June 1814, Bechtle and Metz, *Collected Writings,* 2:273; JS to EBS, 15 March 1809, 1-3-3-11:B24, APSL.

42. EBS to JS, 2 March, 1809, Bechtle and Metz, *Collected Writings,* 2:59.

43. Sulpician Register, 14 March and 16 March 1809, 39RG 1, box 11, AASUS, accessed at AMSJ; Melville observes that the plural of "charitable persons" had been dropped in favor of the singular between the two dates, perhaps reflecting acceptance that the Filicchis might not participate. Melville, *Seton,* 466n41.

44. PB to CS, 26 April 1809, 1-3-3-4:31, APSL.

45. EBS to CS, 3 April [1809], Bechtle and Metz, *Collected Writings,* 2:65.

46. JC to sisters, 20 April 1809, Hanley, *Carroll Papers,* 3:84.

47. EB to CS, 3 April [1809], Bechtle and Metz, *Collected Writings,* 2:66.

48. Papenfuse, *Evils of Necessity,* 24–26.

49. WD to RGH, 8 April 1809, H-PP, MHS.

50. Wake, *Sisters of Fortune,* chap. 7.

51. ET to EBS, 21 March 1809, 1-3-3-2:16, APSL.

52. ET to EBS, 2 May 1809, 1-3-3-2:17, APSL.

53. MBC to MC, 7 February 1810, box 69, folder 4, L&FR, HSP.
54. EBS to MO'C, [May 1809], Bechtle and Metz, *Collected Writings*, 2:71.
55. EBS to CS, 3 April [1809], *Collected Writings*, 2:66.
56. CS to EBS, 20 March 1809, 1-3-3-4:210, APSL.
57. SWS to CS, n.d., 1-3-3-17:11, APSL.
58. CS to EBS, 20 March 1809, 1-3-3-4:210, APSL.
59. Ethelinda Agnes Seton to Anna Seton, 31 May 1809, 1-3-3-4:104, APSL.
60. EBS to CS, [after 25 May 1809], Bechtle and Metz, *Collected Writings*, 2:72.
61. Sister Rose White's Journal, *Collected Writings*, 2:718.

14. HALF IN THE SKY

1. EBS to WD, Winchester Friday afternoon [June 21? 1809], Bechtle and Metz, *Collected Writings*, 2:73.
2. EBS to MO'C, 25 June 1809, *Collected Writings*, 2:75.
3. "Dear Remembrances," *Collected Writings*, 3a:522.
4. MCB to MC, 9 July 1809, box 65, folder 6, L&FR, HSP.
5. PB to HS, 2 July 1809, 1-3-3-1:75, APSL. See also 6, 10, 11, and 20 July, 1-3-3-1:76–79, APSL.
6. PB to HS, 11 July 1809, 1-3-3-1:78, APSL.
7. Red leather notebook, Bechtle and Metz, *Collected Writings*, 3a:480, drawn from AMSV 110: M, III, N1.
8. White, *Life of Mrs. Eliza A. Seton*, 258.
9. Harriet Seton memorandum, n.d., 1-3-3-8:178, APSL.
10. Journal of Cecilia O'Conway, Bechtle and Metz, *Collected Writings*, 2:714, drawn from 1-3-3-4:118,1 APSL; Steele, *Life of Mother Rose White*; McNeil, "Journal of Mother Rose White," 18–22; see also Sister Rose White's Journal, *Collected Writings*, 2:717–37, both drawn from 7-2-1, APSL.
11. MCB to MC, 7 July 1809, box 65, folder 6, L&FR, HSP.
12. JD to Charlotte Melmoth, 28 November 1809, 1-3-3-5:3, APSL; Charlotte Melmoth, in Bordman and Hischak, *Oxford Companion,* 427; Smith, "Lady Macbeth in America," 195nn2, 6, 8.
13. Sister Rose White's journal," Bechtle and Metz, *Collected Writings*, 2:719.
14. 28 July 1809, McNeil, "Memoir of Sister Cecilia O'Conway," 25; Sister Rose White's journal, Bechtle and Metz, *Collected Writings*, 2:720.
15. EBS to JC, [6 August 1809], Bechtle and Metz, *Collected Writings*, 2:76–78.
16. Provisional regulations for St. Joseph's sisters, *Collected Writings*, 2:737; the annotations of the regulations provided by Bechtle and Metz are invaluable.
17. MCB to MC, 7 July 1809, box 65, folder 6, L&FR, HSP.
18. Journal of Rose White, Bechtle and Metz, *Collected Writings*, 2:722–23.
19. EBS to JC, 6 August 1809, *Collected Writings*, 2:77.
20. EBS to JC, 6 August 1809, *Collected Writings*, 2:78.
21. Minutes of first council meeting, Sunday, 20 August 1809, *Collected Writings*, 3b:115. (One page of this book remains, containing three entries.) Sister Rose White's Journal, Bechtle and Metz, *Collected Writings*, 2:721–22.
22. The names are included, without sourcing, in McSweeny et al., *Story of the Mountain,* 1:13. Terms of Nace and "Free Kate" reproduced from a Dubois ledger, entry dated 18 July 1814, in McSweeny et al., *Story of the Mountain,* 1:64. The *Story* documents may have come from the missing "Slavery at the Mount," box 1, AMSMU; all that could be located in 2017 was "Slavery at the Mount," box 2.
23. MBC to MC, 1 February 1810, box 69, folder 4, L&FR, HSP.

24. MBC to MC, 22 May 1810, box 69, folder 4, L&FR, HSP.

25. JD to CM, 28 November 1809, 1–3–3–5:3, APSL.

26. Samuel Waddington Seton to Cecilia Seton, 23 August [1809], 1–3–3–17:23, APSL.

27. EBS to JS, 20 September 1809, Bechtle and Metz, *Collected Writings*, 2:84.

28. BB to HS, 8 August, 1809, 1–3–3–8:81, APSL.

29. Edward Augustus Seton to CS, 6 August 1809, 1–3–3–17:19, APSL.

30. SWS to CS, 11 August 1809, 1–3–3–17:22, APSL.

31. Mary Fitch Bayley to Anna Maria Seton, 6 August 1809, 1–3–3–4:110, APSL.

32. SWS to CS, 27 August [1809], 1–3–3–17:30, APSL.

33. EBS to JS, 20 September 1809, Bechtle and Metz, *Collected Writings*, 2:82–83.

34. MCB to MC, 22 May 1810, box 69, folder 4, L&FR, HSP; Daughters of Charity, Bruté de Rémur, and Seton, *Connection with the Community*, 6n.

35. Melville, *Seton*, rev. ed., 211–12 and 212note g.

36. MCB to MC, 12 September 1809, mislabeled 1810, box 69, folder 4, HSP.

37. PB to HS and EBS, 30 August 1809, 1–3–3–1:64, APSL.

38. EBS to JC, 8 September 1809, Bechtle and Metz, *Collected Writings*, 2:81.

39. WD to EBS, 13 September 1809, 100, 115, 1, 21, AMSV, accessed at AMSJ; Melville, *William Louis Dubourg*, 1:198–200; PB to EBS, 11 October, 1–3–3–1:65, APSL.

40. The letter and Harriet's reaction are revealed in EBS to Andrew Barclay Bayley, [January 1810], Bechtle and Metz, *Collected Writings*, 2:101.

41. EBS to WD (draft), [September 1809], *Collected Writings*, 2:87.

42. EBS to JC, 2 November 1809, *Collected Writings*, 2:87–88.

43. JD to EBS, 6 October 1809, 1–3–3–5:16, APSL.

44. Francis Nagot to EBS, 9 November 1809, 1–3–3–2:7, APSL.

45. EBS to George Weis, n.d., Bechtle and Metz, *Collected Writings*, 2:121.

46. PB to EBS, 20 August 1809, 1–3–3–1:63, APSL.

47. ECF to HS, 28 October 1809, 1–3–3–8:84, APSL.

48. EBS to BB, [draft January 1810], Bechtle and Metz, *Collected Writings*, 2:101.

49. PB to HS, 11 November 1809, 1–3–3–1:89, APSL.

50. SWS to HS, 28 November 1809, 1–3–3–17:5, APSL.

51. GO to HS, 27 November 1809, 1–3–3–8:83, APSL.

52. GO to HS, 27 November 1809, 1–3–3–8:83, APSL.

53. JD to CM, 28 November 1809, 1–3–3–4:3, APSL.

54. CSO to HS, 9 December 1809, 1–3–3–8:85 APSL.

55. Journal of Sister Rose White, Bechtle and Metz, *Collected Writings*, 2:723; PB to HS, 20 November 1809, 1–3–3–1:91, APSL.

56. PB to CS, 4 November 1809, 1–3–3–1:88, APSL.

57. WD to EBS, 15 December 1809, 1–3–3–2:S5, APSL.

58. EBS to GW, 23 December 1809, Bechtle and Metz, *Collected Writings*, 2:93.

15. ENDEAVOR

1. WD to EBS, 28 December 1809, 1–3–3–2:S6, APSL (100, 115, 1, 23 AMSV).

2. Mary Wilkins to CS, 12 February 1810, 1–3–3–16:13, APSL.

3. EBS to GW, 1 January 1810, Bechtle and Metz, *Collected Writings*, 2:96.

4. WD to EBS, 28 December 1809, 100, 115, 1, 23, AMSV; JD to EBS, 28 December 1809, 100, 115, 1, 18, AMSV, both accessed at AMSJ.

5. [Ethelinda] Agnes Seton to AMS, 10 March 1810, 1–3–3–4:111, APSL; Edward A. Seton to CS, 12 March 1810, and 15 March 1810, 1–3–3–16:3, 2, APSL; Mary

Seton Hoffman [mislabeled Charlotte Seton Ogden] to EBS, 13 March [1810], 1–3–3–16:9, APSL.

6. CSO to CS, 12 March 1810, 1–3–3–16:10, APSL.

7. BB to EBS, 22 February [1811?], 1–3–3–7:83, APSL.

8. EBS to JC, 15 June 1810, Bechtle and Metz, *Collected Writings*, 2:142. Melville, *Seton*, rev. ed., 283–85.

9. McSweeny et al., *Story of the Mountain*, 1:23.

10. "Regulations of the School of St. Josephs," 1–3–3–5:9, APSL; when Dubois codified the "School Department at St. Joseph's" as part of the 1812 rule, he began with "This department is under the sole control and inspection of the Mother." Bechtle and Metz, *Collected Writings*, 3b:536; Melville, *Seton*, rev. ed. 287–91.

11. "Rules for the Seminary [1810]," quoted in McSweeny et al., *Story of the Mountain*, 1:43.

12. Several documents set forth the regulations, including "Regulations for the School of St. Joseph's," 1–3–3–5:15, APSL, and Bechtle and Metz, *Collected Writings*, 3b: 124–26; "Employment at St. Joseph's," *Collected Writings*, 3b:127; and "Department at St. Joseph's," *Collected Writings*, 3b:536–40; Melville, *Seton*, rev. ed. 287–91.

13. "Rules for the Seminary [1810]," quoted in McSweeny et al., *Story of the Mountain*, 1:44.

14. XI I, "School Department at St. Joseph's," Bechtle and Metz, *Collected Writings*, 3b:539.

15. MCB to MC, 4 February 1810, box 69, folder 4, L&FR HSP.

16. John Dubois to Sisters of Charity, "Schools at St. Joseph's," 1–3–3–5:9, APSL; "School," 1–3–3–5:13, APSL; "Sundays & Holydays," 1–3–3–5:12, APSL. See also Bechtle and Metz, *Collected Writings*, 3b:534–40.

17. Mattingly, *Secret Habits*, 98–99.

18. MB to MC, 4 Feb 1810, box 69, folder 4, L&FR, HSP.

19. MCB to MC, 25 September 1809, box 65, folder 6, L&FR, HSP.

20. MCB to MC, 18 February 1810, box 69, folder 4, L&FR, HSP.

21. MDH to RGH and CCH, 2 May 1814, H-PP, MHS; CCH to RGH and CCH, 24 November 1814, H-PP, MHS.

22. EBS to Catherine Dupleix, 4 February 1811, Bechtle and Metz, *Collected Writings*, 2:172–73.

23. EBS to ES, 27 May 1810, *Collected Writings*, 2:131.

24. McSweeny et al., *Story of the Mountain*, 1:80.

25. Derks and Smith, *Value of a Dollar*, 231–32; Kelley, *Learning to Stand and Speak*, 98.

26. Mount St. Mary's ledgers, quoted in McSweeny et al., *Story of the Mountain*, 1:40. See also Melville, *Seton*, rev. ed., 285.

27. McSweeny et al., *Story of the Mountain*, 1:46.

28. McNeil, "Historical Perspectives," 285–87.

29. Appendix [to Rule of 1812], "Of the Orphans Educated at St. Joseph's," Bechtle and Metz, *Collected Writings*, 3b:534–35.

30. EBS to JS, 18 October 1819, *Collected Writings*, 2:624.

31. Moran and Vinovskis, "Schools," 292; "Of the Orphans Educated at St. Joseph's," Bechtle and Metz, *Collected Writings*, 3b:534; Kelly, *Numerous Choirs*, 263–64.

32. EBS to JS, 15 June 1812, Bechtle and Metz, *Collected Writings*, 2:219.

33. JD to EBS, 28 December 1809, 1–3–3–3:S1, APSL (100, 115, 1, 18, AMSV).

34. Mattingly, *Secret Habits*, 1–16, quote at 15; see also Stern, *Southern Crucifix, Southern Cross*, 69–108.

35. EBS to RGH, 4 May 1820, Bechtle and Metz, *Collected Writings*, 2:649.

36. EBS to JS, 2 October 1818, *Collected Writings*, 2:581.

37. EBS to ES, 9 January 1810, *Collected Writings*, 2:99.

38. PB to AMS, RS, and EBS, 3 April 1810, 1–3–3–1:67, APSL.

39. JC to Leonard Neale, 24 August 1809, Hanley, *Carroll Papers*, 3:93–94; JC to EBS, 11 March 1810, Hanley, *Carroll Papers*, 3:114.

40. Chinnici, "Organization of Spiritual Life," 236–39.

41. EBS to JC, 25 January 1810, Bechtle and Metz, *Collected Writings*, 2:107.

42. St. Teresa of Avila, "The Book of Her Life," *Collected Works of St. Teresa of Avila*, vol. 1, chap. 13, pts. 14 and 19.

43. JD to EBS, 23 February 1811, AMSV 100, 115, 1, 19, accessed at AMSJ.

44. JC to EBS, 11 March 1810, Hanley, *Carroll Papers*, 3:114.

45. A.M.M.G. and Dougherty, *Life of Mother Elizabeth Boyle*, iv, 7–15.

46. CS to PB [likely], in Bailly de Barberey, *Elizabeth Seton*, trans. Code, 286. No original. Code gives date as 1 February 1810.

47. CS to PB [likely], in Bailly de Barberey, *Elizabeth Seton*, trans. Code, 287. No original. Code gives date as 1 March 1810.

48. AMS to EBS, 7 May 1810, 1–3–3–9:30, APSL.

49. EBS to ES, 8 March 1810, Bechtle and Metz, *Collected Writings*, 2:110.

50. EBS to Julia Scott, 30 May 1810, *Collected Writings*, 2:133–34.

51. Melville, *Seton* rev. ed., 235–36.

52. EBS to JC, 13 May 1811, Bechtle and Metz, *Collected Writings*, 2:184 (Seton is describing her 1810 request in this 1811 letter).

53. EBS to ES, 6 May 1810, *Collected Writings*, 2:123.

54. EBS to ? [Identified as John David, but the tone of the letter makes that improbable], n.d., *Collected Writings*, 2:120–21.

16. TRIALS OF THE PASSAGE

1. Journal of Sister Rose White, Bechtle and Metz, *Collected Writings*, 2:727.

2. EBS to CD, 4 June 1810, *Collected Writings*, 2:137.

3. Draft of EBS to Mr. Smith, n.d., *Collected Writings*, 2:695.

4. EBS to ES, 27 May 1810, *Collected Writings*, 2:132.

5. EBS to ES, 8 March 1810, *Collected Writings*, 2:110-11; EBS to ES, 27 May 1810, *Collected Writings*, 2:132.

6. AMS to EBS, 7 May 1810, 1–3–3–9:30, APSL.

7. Description of labor (1823), "Slavery at Mt. St. Mary's," box 2, AMSMU; Melissa DiVincenzo, "Slavery at Mt. St. Mary's," honors thesis, ca. 1998, Mt. St. Mary's, AMSMU.

8. Dubois ledger, page from 1813, "Slavery at Mt. St. Mary's," box 2, AMSMU; McSweeny et al., *Story of the Mountain*, 1:55.

9. Joseph Shorter purchase of John Butler from the Revd. John Dubois, January 1814, "Slavery at Mt. St. Mary's," box 2, AMSMU; July 1814, "ledger," quoted in McSweeny et al., *Story of the Mountain*, 1:64.

10. Daughters of Charity, Bruté de Rémur, and Seton, *Connection with Community*, 187; "Bruté's Thoughts on the eve of Corpus Christi, and on the Solemnity Itself," 1814, in Seton, *Memoir*, 2:165.

11. McSweeny et al., *Story of the Mountain*, 1:34.

12. Still, *Underground Rail Road*, 461, 465, 71, 392, 524, 226; Byron, "'Catechism for their Special Use,'" 184–205; Miller, "Failed Mission"; Miller, "Black Catholics in the Slave South"; Raboteau, *Slave Religion*, 112–16.

13. Sulpician Register, 51, 16 July 1811, AASUS, RG 1, box 11, accessed at AMSJ. See also Melville, *Seton* rev. ed., 235, 266–67.

14. JC to EBS, 18 July 1810, Hanley, *Carroll Papers*, 3:120.

15. EC to GW, 9 August [1810?], *Collected Writings* 2:155.

16. JC to EBS, 18 July 1810, Hanley, *Carroll Papers*, 3:120.

17. John of the Cross, *Dark Night of the Soul*, bk. 2, chap. 5, 78.

18. AMS to EBS, 7 May 1810, 1–3–3–9:30, APSL.

19. AMS to EBS, 8 May 1810, 1–3–3–9:31, APSL.

20. AMS to EBS, 4 June 1810, 1–3–3–9:34, APSL.

21. AMS to EBS, 23 May 1810, 1–3–3–9:32, APSL; 30 May 1810, 1–3–3–9:33, APSL.

22. EBS to JS, 23 October 1810, Bechtle and Metz, *Collected Writings*, 2:162.

23. EBS to JS, 10 July 1811, *Collected Writings*, 2:191.

24. EBS to JS, 10 July 1811, *Collected Writings*, 2:191.

25. EBS to ES, 22 July 1811, *Collected Writings*, 2:192–93.

26. JC to EBS, 11 September 1810, 100, 115, 1, 3, AMSV, accessed at AMSJ (absent from Hanley, *Carroll Papers*).

27. JC to EBS, 11 September 1810, 100, 115, 1, 3, AMSV, accessed at AMSJ (absent from Hanley, *Carroll Papers*).

28. EBS to JC, "9" (apparently for September) [1810], Bechtle and Metz, *Collected Writings* 2:157–58.

29. EBS draft to John David, n.d., *Collected Writings*, 2:159.

30. MG to EBS, 25 December 1810, 1–3–3–2:19, APSL.

31. JC to EBS, date uncertain; improbably dated as 10 March 1810 in Hanley, *Carroll Papers*, 3:112–13; 1–3–3–143, APSL.

32. EBS to JC, 16 March 1811, Bechtle and Metz, *Collected Writings*, 2:179.

33. EBS to JC, 13 May 1811, *Collected Writings*, 2:184.

34. EBS to JC, 13 May 1811, *Collected Writings*, 2:185.

35. JCh to EBS, Boston, 4 January 1811, 100, 115, 1, 13, AMSV, accessed at AMSJ; Benedict Flaget to SB, 17 October 1811, II–3–n, UNDA; Melville, *Seton* rev. ed., 223.

36. JC to JD [1814], Hanley, *Carroll Papers*, 3:251, and "Comment on James [sic] David Letter," 17 September 1814, Hanley, *Carroll Papers*, 3:295. As many as eighteen sisters were at one point designated for America. The plans and their collapse can be glimpsed in documents collected in 1–3–1–6:2 (no. 3), APSL, which meticulously explores this incident. See also Marie Bizeray et al. (French Daughters) to Emmitsburg community, 12 July 1810, in White, *Life of Mrs. Eliza A. Seton*, 282–83.

37. EBS to GW, 24 June 1811, Bechtle and Metz, *Collected Writings*, 2:186–87.

38. EBS to AF, 24 June 1811, *Collected Writings*, 2:187–89.

39. Pasquier, *Fathers on the Frontier*, 24.

40. MCB to MC, 3 September 1814, box 88, folder 4, L&FR, HSP.

41. MCB to MC, 4 February, 18 February, and 22 May 1810, L&FR, box 69, folder 4, HSP.

42. EBS to MCB, 21 March 1810, Bechtle and Metz, *Collected Writings*, 2:115.

43. Melville, *Seton*, rev. ed., 215–17.

44. Quoted in McCann, *Mother Seton's Daughters*, 1:29.

45. Berner, "Epicurus' Role,"43–59; Newman, "Disciplining the Body," 90–115.

46. Olivera and Roberts, *Sun at Midnight*, 62. One can love oneself for God's sake, the only legitimate form of self-love, in Bernard's thinking.

47. Kauffman, *Tradition and Transformation*, 17.

48. JD to EBS, 23 February 1811, 100, 115, 1, 19, AMSV, accessed at AMSJ.

49. CO'C to M and RO'C, 8 November 1809, reproduced in S. Smith, "Philadelphia's First Nun," 439; MCB to MC, 18 February 1810, box 69, folder 4, L&FR, HSP.

50. Bynum, *Fragmentation and Redemption*; Bynum, *Holy Feast and Holy Fast*.

51. Passages are from a section labeled "Sickness by our own fault," in the Notebook of St. Matthew, A 111 074, AMSJ (the notebook appears to have originally been a business ledger, perhaps from Seton & Maitland); Bechtle and Metz, *Collected Writings*, 3a:559–72; I am indebted to Bechtle and Metz's annotations.

52. Charlotte [Nelson] Smith to EBS, 23 March 1812, 1-3-3-3:73, APSL.

53. A clear and extensive comparison, as well as a discussion of the fragmentary American documents through which the regulations can be traced, is to be found in 1-3-16:2 (no. 3), APSL, a document prepared by Sisters of Charity at Emmitsburg in the twentieth century in response to questions put during the investigation of the cause (consideration for sainthood) of Elizabeth Seton.

54. Rule of 1812, RB no. 29b, APSL and Bechtle and Metz, *Collected Writings*, 3b:500–501.

55. JC to JD, 22 December 1811, Hanley, *Carroll Papers*, 3:165.

56. JC to EBS, 11 September 1811, Hanley, *Carroll Papers*, 3:155–57; Melville, Seton rev. ed., Tessier also approved the constitution: "After having read the constitutions of the Sisters of Charity with great attention and approved of everything contained therein I have presented them to the most Reverend Archbishop Carroll for obtaining his approbation, and at the same time I have confirmed and hereby again confirm the nomination of the Reverend Mr. Dubois for Superior-general." Quoted in McCann, *History of Mother Seton's Daughters*, 1:60. The official confirmation is also reported in Bailly de Barberey, *Elizabeth Seton*, trans. Code, 328–29, but archivists have found no original.

57. JC to EBS, 11 September 1811, Hanley, *Carroll Papers*, 3:155–56.

58. EBS to JS, 2 December 1811, Bechtle and Metz, *Collected Writings*, 2:201.

59. MBP to EBS, 7 February 1812, 1-3-3-11:9, APSL.

60. EBS to RGH, 28 December 1811, Bechtle and Metz, *Collected Writings*, 2:207.

61. Elizabeth Seton's journal of [Anna Maria] Seton's last illness and death,1-3-3-3:18, APSL; this journal, recounting Anna Maria Seton's illness and death, is not in Seton's handwriting; Bechtle and Metz posit that it is a copy made by Ellen Wiseman, a student at St. Joseph's who remained a correspondent of Seton. *Collected Writings*, 2:747–48.

62. EBS to GW, 13 December 1811 and [December 1811], *Collected Writings*, 2:202–3; EBS to PB, [December 1811], *Collected Writings*, 2:204–5.

63. JC to EBS, 20 January 1812, 100, 115, 1, 6, AMSV, accessed at AMSJ; omitted from Hanley, *Carroll Papers*; no. 158 in Spalding, *John Carroll Recovered*.

64. WS to EBS, 22 December 1811–6 January 1812, 1-3-3-16:2, APSL.

65. Elizabeth Seton's journal of [Anna Maria] Seton's last Illness and death, 1-3-3-3:18, APSL; see also Bechtle and Metz, *Collected Writings*, 2:749.

66. Annina's Decury Rules, n.d., APSL,1-3-3-3 66, APSL.

67. Elizabeth Seton's journal of Anna Maria Seton's last illness and death, 19 March [1812], 1-3-3-18, APSL; see also Bechtle and Metz, *Collected Writings*, 2:755.

68. Journal of Anna Maria's last illness and death, 12 March [1812], *Collected Writings* 2:755; EBS to JS, 29 April 1812, *Collected Writings*, 2:215–16. Bechtle and Metz, *Collected Writings*, 2:213n2, report that the hymn is identified "on a blue slip of paper in *Hymns for the Use of the Catholic Church in the United States of America* (John West Butler, Baltimore, 1807); APSL Rare Book 6."

69. EBS to ES, 19 March 1812, Bechtle and Metz, *Collected Writings*, 2:213.

17. DEATH, JUDGMENT, HELL, HEAVEN

1. EBS to ES, 14 September 1812, Bechtle and Metz, *Collected Writings*, 2:227.
2. EBS to GW, 30 July 1812, *Collected Writings*, 2:224–25.
3. MBP to EBS, 24 May 1812, 1–3–3–11:16, APSL.
4. In J. Bayley, *Memoirs*, 49, no original found.
5. JD to SB, 7 May 1812, AMSMU.
6. JC to JT, 13 September 1812, Hanley, *Carroll Papers*, 3:199–200.
7. EBS to ES, 3 May [1812], Bechtle and Metz, *Collected Writings*, 2:216–18.
8. EBS to RS, n.d., and 5 July 1812, *Collected Writings*, 2:221, 222.
9. Rowland, *Charles Carroll of Carrollton*, 2:292.
10. MCB to MC, 16 February 1814, box 88, folder 4, L&F R, HSP.
11. Ruane, *Beginnings*, 25.
12. "Well now our Dearest," Thursday, [1812], Bechtle and Metz, *Collected Writings*, 3b:7.
13. "Well now our Dearest," Thursday, [1812], *Collected Writings*, 3b:7.
14. EBS to SB, 22 September 1812, *Collected Writings*, 2:228–29.
15. Kelly, *Elizabeth Seton's Two Bibles*, 23–24.
16. See, for example, SB to EBS, n.d., 1–3–3–13:11; n.d., 1–7–3–1–2; n.d., 1–7–3–1–2:B52; 1–7–3–1–2:B61, all in APSL; Lee, "Practice of Spiritual Direction," 263–313; Melville, *Seton*, rev. ed., 311–20 and passim.
17. Daughters of Charity, Bruté de Rémur, and Seton, *Connection with the Community*, 21, 31.
18. EBS to SB, n.d., Bechtle and Metz, *Collected Writings*, 2:591.
19. Daughters of Charity, Bruté de Rémur, and Seton, *Connection with the Community*, 61.
20. Lee, "Practice of Spiritual Direction," 275–77. I am indebted to Lee for highlighting this figure and for her illuminating discussion of the Bruté-Seton spiritual collaboration.
21. Daughters of Charity, Bruté de Rémur, and Seton, *Connection with the Community*, 25–26; Bechtle and Metz, *Collected Writings*, 2:296 and n3.
22. Daughters of Charity, Bruté de Rémur, and Seton *Connection with the Community*, 9.
23. CCH to CCH, 29 December 1813, H-PP, MHS.
24. EBS to Margaret Stinson, 16 April 1813, Bechtle and Metz, *Collected Writings*, 2:244.
25. EBS to JS, 14 September 1812, *Collected Writings*, 2:228.
26. EBS to ES, [17 September 1813], *Collected Writings*, 2:252.
27. St. Teresa of Avila, "The Constitutions: On the Order to be Observed in Spiritual Matters," "On the Sick," in *Collected Works*, vol. 3, pt. 28.
28. Katz, "Mysticism and Ethics; Thurman, "Mysticism and Ethics."
29. "Pyamingo Reflections" (series of reflections that Seton seems to have written across a number of years, often drawing on other spiritual writers), Bechtle and Metz, *Collected Writings*, 3a:195.
30. "Gospel of Matthew Notebook," A 111 074, AMSJ; *Collected Writings*, 3a:525.
31. EBS to SB, 6 August 1814, *Collected Writings*, 2:280.
32. EBS to JC, 10 September 1813, *Collected Writings*, 2:251.
33. EBS to JS, 25 January 1813, *Collected Writings*, 2:239.

18. WAR AND BUSTLE

1. Beitzell, *Jesuit Missions*, 104–20.

2. MCB to MC, 3 September 1814, box 88, folder 4, L&FR, HSP.

3. McCann, *Mother Seton's Daughters*, 1:68–69.

4. EBS to JS, 1 June 1814, Bechtle and Metz, *Collected Writings*, 2:272.

5. MP to EBS, 16 July [1813?], 1–3–3–11:18, APSL.

6. EBS to ES, 29 October 1812, Bechtle and Metz, *Collected Writings*, 2:231–32.

7. EBS to JS, 11 August 1813, *Collected Writings*, 2:247.

8. CS to RS, 11 July [no year], 1–3–3–9:51b, APSL.

9. CS to RS, 1812, 1–3–3–11:B43, APSL.

10. Daughters of Charity, Bruté de Rémur, and Seton, *Connection with the Community*, 187.

11. EBS to ES, 3 May 1812, Bechtle and Metz, *Collected Writings*, 2:217–18.

12. Bruté's eulogy on Maria Burke, 7–3–1–3:193, APSL.

13. Rebecca Mary Seton notebook, 1–3–3–9:42h, APSL.

14. EBS to JS, 25 January 1813, Bechtle and Metz, *Collected Writings*, 2:238.

15. "Retreat Meditations," 1–3–3–20, APSL; see also "Retreat Meditations," Bechtle and Metz, *Collected Writings*, 3a:316.

16. Mannard, "Widows in Convents," 111–32; McNeil, "Demographics," 77–80.

17. EBS to JS, 1 December 1814, Bechtle and Metz, *Collected Writings*, 2:286.

18. EBS to SB, n.d., *Collected Writings*, 2:259.

19. HD to EBS, September 1813, 1–3–3–4:75, APSL.

20. Register of women who entered the Sisters of Charity during Elizabeth Seton's lifetime, Bechtle and Metz, *Collected Writings*, 2:784–85.

21. John Grassi to SB, II-3-n, UNDA.

22. EBS to RGH, 15 October 1814, Bechtle and Metz, *Collected Writings*, 2:282; EBS to RGH, 6 December 1814, *Collected Writings*, 2:288; CCH to parents, 29 December 1813, H-PP, MHS. He added a plea that his parents send him a New Year's present large enough to share, "as you know I would have no pleasure in enjoying it alone."

23. JD to RGH, 2 February 1813, H-PP, MHS.

24. Papenfuse, *Evils of Necessity*, 7–8, 42; quote from "A Discourse on Learning," 15 March 1788, at 7.

25. Quoted in Wake, *Sisters of Fortune*, chap. 9.

26. PB to EBS, 28 March 1814, 1–3–3–1:69, APSL; Melville, *Seton*, rev. ed., 269.

27. Wharton, *Social Life in the Early Republic*, 96–97; Wake, *Sisters of Fortune*, chap. 9.

28. JC to CP, 5 January 1815, Hanley, *Carroll Papers*, 3:318.

29. Quoted in Porterfield, *Conceived in Doubt*, 86–90, at 88.

30. Boylan, *Origins*, 26–27.

31. Walsh and Earley, *Sisters of Charity of New York*, 1:26; McCann, *Mother Seton's Daughters*, 1:74; Hacsi, *Second Home*, 13–17; journal of Sister Rose White, Bechtle and Metz, *Collected Writings*, 2:732–35.

32. Journal of Sister Rose White, Bechtle and Metz, *Collected Writings*, 2:733.

33. Journal of Sister Rose White, *Collected Writings*, 2:733–34.

34. White, *Life of Mrs. Eliza A. Seton*, 352–53; no original found.

35. Walsh and Earley, *Sisters of Charity of New York*, 1:20–72.

36. JD to SB, 10 March 1812; BF to Leonard Neale, 26 June 1816, both quoted in Pasquier, *Fathers on the Frontier*, 43–44.

37. JD to SB, 12 July 1813, II-3-n, UNDA; BF to SB, 13 July 1813, II-3-n, UNDA; JD to SB, 7 September 1813, II-3-n, UNDA; BF to SB, 21 September 1813, II-3-n, UNDA; Melville, *Seton*, rev. ed., 257–60.

38. Council minutes, 18 August 1814, council book, 1:2, APSL; PB to EBS, 19 October 1814, 1–3–3–1:70, APSL; JD to JC, 27 October 1814, 8H2, AJCP, AAB; JD to JC, 10 October 1814, 8H1, AJCP, AAB; JD to JC, 27 October 1814, 8AF1, AJCP, AAB; JD to JC, 10 October 1814, 3F14 AJCP, AAB; JD to JC, 5 December 1814, 3F16, AAB; JD to JC, 27 December 1814, 3F17, AJCP, AAB; Melville, *Seton*, rev. ed., 258–62.

39. HB to EBS, 4 February 1814, 1–3–3–1:B38, APSL.

40. Maynard, *Reed and the Rock*, 106, suggests Bruté went in order to explain the purposes and conduct of Mount St. Mary's to the Sulpicians, but Bruté later wrote that he went "for" St. Mary's College of Baltimore; accordingly, Melville suggests he may have gone "to persuade them to reconsider their decision about withdrawal of Sulpician sponsorship" of Mount St. Mary's. Melville, *Seton*, 319nI and 339n48.

41. EBS to JC, 28 December, 1814, Bechtle and Metz, *Collected Writings*, 2:291.

42. EBS to AF, 20 December 1814, *Collected Writings*, 2:291.

19. OUR MEANING

1. Kelly, *Elizabeth Seton's Two Bibles*, 23–24. EBS to WS, [January 1815], Bechtle and Metz, *Collected Writings*, 2:298.

2. ES to EBS, 16 April 1815, 1–3–3–11:B16, APSL.

3. WS to EBS, 5 April 1815, S-J 339–341, 1–3–2–2, APSL.

4. WS to EBS, 26 October 1816, A 111 085, AMSJ (also S-J 227–230).

5. RS to WS, 18 May 1815, Seton, *Memoir*, 2:191–92.

6. Pasquier, *Fathers on the Frontier*, 36. Note of Father Bruté's: "13 May, 1813: Mr. Monroe of the post office of Washington, recommended by Mr. R. Brent, came with his two sons, but Mr. Dubois has returned his expenses and refused to admit them, being Protestants. (Atlee, our last, discharged shortly before)." Quoted in McSweeny et al., *Story of the Mountain*, 1:62.

7. Journal [to SB], 1815, Bechtle and Metz, *Collected Writings*, 2:315, 318, 320.

8. Journal [to SB], 1815, *Collected Writings*, 2:324, 326.

9. Journal [to SB], 1815, *Collected Writings*, 2:323.

10. Journal [to SB], 1815, *Collected Writings*, 2:323, 324, 330.

11. Journal [to SB], *Collected Writings*, 2:331. As a rule, women did not preach in Protestant denominations of the era either, although occasionally Free Will Baptist or Christian Connection congregations permitted it; Southern evangelicals encouraged women to pray and even exhort but not to preach. Brekus, *Strangers and Pilgrims*, 125–39.

12. L. Preudhomme de Borré to SB, 16 June 1815, II-1-a, UNDA.

13. WS to SB, 2 September 1815, S-J 542–544, APSL.

14. EBS to JS, 30 March 1815, Bechtle and Metz, *Collected Writings*, 2:308.

15. Shaw, *John Dubois*, 78, quoting John Tessier to John Hickey, September, 1815.

16. JD to Antoine de Puget Duclaux, n.d. quoted in Melville, *Seton*, rev. ed., 344.

17. RW to Rev. Mr. De Barth, 8 October 1815, 7-2-1-1, APSL.

18. McCann, *Mother Seton's Daughters*, 1:77. Joanna Smith was chosen procuratrix.

19. JD to EBS, [1815], 1–3–3–5 18, APSL; McNeil, Bechtle, and Metz identify Martha as Martha Hartwell.

20. "Notebook of Sister Margaret George," 44, APSL, quoted in McNeil, "Demographics," 77.

21. Journal [to SB], Bechtle and Metz, *Collected Writings*, 2:325, 330.

22. EBS to WS, 4 August 1815, *Collected Writings*, 2:337.

23. MSH to CS, 21 August 1815, 1–3–3–11 B49, APSL.

24. EBS to JS, 15 December 1813, Bechtle and Metz, *Collected Writings*, 2:255–56.

25. RS to EBS, [October 1815], 1–3–3–9:46, APSL.

26. F and AF to SB, 24 May 1815, Seton, *Memoir*, 2:188–89.

27. EBS to WS, 21 April 1816, Bechtle and Metz, *Collected Writings*, 2:389.

28. R and CS to WS, n.d., 1–3–3–18:9, APSL.

29. EBS to WS, 21 April 1816, Bechtle and Metz, *Collected Writings*, 2:389.

30. The Sulpicians' objections emerge in correspondence between Dubois and Tessier and later Dubois and Bruté. JD to JT, 18 January 1816, RG 1, box 17, AASUS, accessed at AMSJ; JD to SB, 5 February 1816, AASUS, accessed at AMSJ.

31. JD to JT, 18 January 1816, RG 1, box 17, AASUS, accessed at AMSJ.

32. JC to JT, 13 September 1812, Hanley, *Carroll Papers*, 3:199; JD to AG, 18 April 1816, RG 24, box 7, AASUS, AAB, accessed at AMSJ.

33. SB to EBS, 7 November 1816, 7–3–1–3:B276, APSL.

34. ES to SB, 30 November 1816, 1–3–3–11:B19, APSL.

35. EBS to ES, [September 1816], Bechtle and Metz, *Collected Writings*, 2:423–24.

20. SWIFT ROLLING EARTH

1. WS to CS, 29 December 1815, 1–3–3–18:26, APSL.

2. RS to WS, 30 March 1816, 1–3–3–18:27, APSL; 1 April 1816, A-103.006, ASCSH, accessed at AMSJ; 3 April 1816, 1–3–3–18:28, APSL; 9 April 1816, S-J 290–93, ASCSE, accessed at AMSJ; 19 April 1816, A-103.006, ASCSH, accessed at AMSJ; 9 May 1816, II-1-a, UNDA.

3. EBS to WS, 18 May 1816, Bechtle and Metz, *Collected Writings*, 2:397.

4. EBS to RBS, 25 April 1816, *Collected Writings*, 2:392; EBS to WS, 3 April 1816, *Collected Writings*, 2:382.

5. SWS to RBS, 1816, 1–3–3–18:33, APSL.

6. RBS to RS, 21 June 1816 1–3–3–18:29, APSL.

7. EBS to WS, 20 May 1816, Bechtle and Metz, *Collected Writings*, 2:398; Wake, *Sisters of Fortune*, 73–76.

8. MDH to RGH and CCH, 11 July 1816, H-PP, MHS.

9. Jerome Bonaparte to EBS, 21 June 1816, 1–3–3–4:100, APSL.

10. CS to EBS, [summer 1816], 1–3–3–9:52a, APSL.

11. CS to EBS, 16 July 1816, 1–3–3–9:50, APSL.

12. EBS to Catherine Dupleix, [January 1816], Bechtle and Metz, *Collected Writings*, 2:366; EBS to WS, 4 February 1816, *Collected Writings*, 2:371.

13. RS to WS, 2 July 1816, S-J 74–77, APSL.

14. RS to WS, 2 July 1816, S-J 74–77, APSL.

15. EBS to SB, [5 May 1816], Bechtle and Metz, *Collected Writings*, 2:393.

16. EBS to SB, 20 May 1816, *Collected Writings*, 2:433.

17. Journal of Rebecca's illness, 17 May [1816], 1–3–3–12:B20, APSL; see also Bechtle and Metz, *Collected Writings*, 2:433, and for document description, 432.

18. EBS to RS, [May 1816], Bechtle and Metz, *Collected Writings*, 2:399.

19. JD to WS, n.d. [1816], 48 S-J 531–534, APSL.

20. Daughters of Charity, Bruté de Rémur, and Seton, *Connection with the Community*, 105.

21. MBP to EBS, 12 February [1816], 1–3–3–11:13, APSL.

22. Journal of Rebecca's illness, 20 [July 1816], 1–3–3–12:18, APSL; see also Bechtle and Metz, *Collected Writings*, 2:441–42.

23. RS to PB, June 1816, Seton, *Memoir*, 2:215–16, no original found.

24. PB to RS, 26 September 1816, Seton, *Memoir*, 2:224, no original found.

25. SB to RS, 9 June 1816, Seton, *Memoir*, 2: 216–17, no original found.

26. JD to WS, n.d., [1816], S-J 531–34, APSL.

27. WS to EBS, 28 July 1816, S-J 223–26, APSL.

28. EBS to WS, 15 August 1816, Bechtle and Metz, *Collected Writings*, 2:418; EBS to CS, [July 1816], *Collected Writings*, 2:418.

29. CS to JS, 14 September 1816, 1–3–3–11:B51, APSL.

30. JS to EBS, 20 September 1816, 1–3–3–11:B30, APSL.

31. RBS to EBS, 3 September 1816, 100, 115, 1, 35, AMSV, accessed at AMSJ.

32. Journal of Rebecca's illness, [15 October, 20 July, 14 October 1816], Bechtle and Metz, *Collected Writings*, 2:444, 442, 435, 436.

33. Journal of Rebecca's illness, [October 31, November 1 1816], 1–3–3–12:B20, APSL; see also Bechtle and Metz, *Collected Writings*, 2:438–40.

34. Journal of Rebecca's illness, [October 31, November 1 1816] 1–3–3–12:B20, APSL; see also Bechtle and Metz, *Collected Writings*, 2:440; EBS to WS, 11 November 1816, *Collected Writings*, 2:447.

35. JD to SB, [4] November 1816, 1–3–3–5:25, APSL.

36. JCh to EBS, 28 November 1816, 1–3–3–1:16, APSL.

37. "Pen and ink sketch by Bp. S. Bruté of EA Seton & Josephine Seton at communion; Annina & Rebecca departed—rising from altar," 1–3–3–13:150, APSL.

38. MBP to EBS, 7 December 1816, 1–3–3–11:23, APSL.

39. EBS to SB, [2 September] 1816, Bechtle and Metz, *Collected Writings*, 2:420.

40. JD to SB, December 1816, quoted in McCann, *Mother Seton's Daughters*, 1:86.

41. RBS to WS, 8 November 1816, A 103.006, ASCSH, accessed at APSL, 1–3–3, box 18, photostats.

42. RBS to EBS, 13 December 1816, SJ 503–506, APSL.

21. WRITTEN BY HERSELF

1. JCh to EBS, 30 December 1816, 100, 115, 1, 16, AMSV, accessed at AMSJ.

2. JC to SB, 5 January 1820, II-1-a, UNDA, quoted in Melville, *Seton* rev. ed., 341n121.

3. Walsh, *Sisters of Charity in New York*, 1:32–34, quote at 33; McNeil, "Demographics," 80.

4. Burrows and Wallace, *Gotham*, 456–57, 494, Trollope quoted at 457.

5. Boylan, *Origins*, 110–11; Burrows and Wallace, *Gotham*, 493–95, SPP quoted at 494 and 495.

6. Walsh, *Sisters of Charity in New York*, 1:41.

7. Walsh, *Sisters of Charity in New York*, 1:42.

8. JD to Bishop John Connolly, 24 July 1817, 7–10–2:6, APSL; Curtis, *Educating the Faithful*, 64.

9. Walsh, *Sisters of Charity in New York*, 1:65–69.

10. EBS to CO'C, [before August 13, 1817], Bechtle and Metz, *Collected Writings*, 2:499.

11. EBS to CO'C, [November 1817], *Collected Writings*, 2:516.

12. JD to JC, 24 July 1817, 7–10–2:6, APSL.

13. *Columbian*, March 11, 1817; *New York Evening Post*, April 18, 1817.

14. Quoted in Walsh, *Sisters of Charity in New York*, 1:50.

15. EBS to EG, 23 August 1817, Bechtle and Metz, *Collected Writings*, 2:502.

16. 17 January 1817, Laws of Maryland, vol. 6, chap. 95. The law limited the sisters to eight hundred acres of land and a personal estate of $50,000.

17. WS to EBS, 18 May 1817, S-J 335–58, APSL.

18. EBS to AF, 1 April 1817, Bechtle and Metz, *Collected Writings*, 2:471.

19. EBS to WS, 25 April 1817, *Collected Writings*, 2:477.

20. EBS to WS, [1817], *Collected Writings*, 2:459.

21. RBS to EBS, 12 October 1816, SJ 395–398, APSL; RBS to EBS, 18 March 1817, 1–3–3–18:10, APSL.

22. EBS to WS, [1817], Bechtle and Metz, *Collected Writings*, 2:459.

23. RBS to JD, 20 June 1817, AMSMU.

24. EBS to JS, October 1817, Bechtle and Metz, *Collected Writings*, 2:510.

25. CS to JS, 18 October 1816, 1–3–3–11:B52, APSL.

26. EBS to WS, [1817], Bechtle and Metz, *Collected Writings*, 2:458.

27. EBS to AF, 24 February 1817, *Collected Writings*, 2:468.

28. RBS to Rev. John Hickey, 11 June 1817, AMSMU.

29. RBS to EBS, 19 June 1817, SJ 402–405, APSL; RBS to JD, 20 June 1817, AMSMU.

30. AF to EBS, 4, June 1817, 1–3–3–10:46, APSL.

31. EBS to SB, [January 1816], Bechtle and Metz, *Collected Writings*, 2:366.

32. EBS to ES, 24 August 1817, *Collected Writings*, 2:503.

33. AF to EBS, 4 June 1817, 1–3–3–10:46, APSL.

34. Robert Fox to EBS, 8 September 1817, 1–3–3–4:72, APSL.

35. D. W. Know, Captain, USN (Ret.), to Sister Aurea, Secretary to the Vice Postulator, Mother Seton Guild, 7 February 1940, Seton Writings Project, AMSJ.

36. EBS to AF, 16 September 1816, Bechtle and Metz, *Collected Writings*, 2:507.

37. RBS to EBS, 19 September 1817, 1–3–3–18:52, APSL.

38. "Biddy" to CS, 17 May 1817, 1–3–3–18:15, APSL.

39. 1–3–3–30, APSL 81–89. Rollin was also in the library of the Sisters of Loretto, in Kentucky, and was used in Jesuit men's colleges as well. Mattingly, *Secret Habits*, 104.

40. Daughters of Charity, Bruté de Rémur, and Seton, *Connection with the Community*, 89.

41. CS to EBS, 24 February 1818, 1–3–3–9:53, APSL.

42. CS to EBS, 24 February 1818, 1–3–3–9:53, APSL; CS to EBS, 6 March 1818, 1–3–3–9:54, APSL.

43. *Memoirs of Mrs. S*, 10–11.

44. CS to EBS, 26 May 1817, 1–3–3–9:52, APSL.

45. PB to EBS, 12 July 1818, 1–3–3–1 71, APSL.

46. Bruté memo, "This Collection of Papers," 1834, 1–3–16:2, APSL; Porterfield, *Conceived in Doubt*.

47. Bruté memo, "This Collection," 1–3–16:2, APSL; Bruté, addendum to document, 1–3–3–12:8, APSL.

48. Catherine Seton's little red book, Bechtle and Metz, *Collected Writings*, 3a:489–90, drawn from 1-3-3-25B, APSL.

49. CS's red book, *Collected Writings*, 3b:505, 506, 502.

50. CS's red book, *Collected Writings*, 3b:495, 508.

51. ? Byrne to JD, 20 September 1817, AMSMU.

52. Edmond Pratt to EBS, 2 November 1819, 1–3–3–2:94, APSL.

53. N.d., quoted in White, *Life of Mrs. Eliza A. Seton*, 342–43.

54. EBS to JH, [before 19 March 1818], Bechtle and Metz, *Collected Writings*, 2:536.

55. EBS to WS, 6 April 1818, *Collected Writings*, 2:544.

56. RGH to EBS, n.d., 1–3–3–2:42, APSL.

57. EBS to RGH, 5 April 1818, Bechtle and Metz, *Collected Writings*, 2:543.

58. Report card quoted in McSweeny et al., *Story of the Mountain*, 1:86. Francis William Elder reminiscence (he entered the school in 1818), quoted in *Story of the Mountain*, 1:78–81.

59. ? Byrne to JD, 20 September 1817, AMSMU.

60. McSweeny et al., *Story of the Mountain*, 1:71–72; Melville, *Seton*, rev. ed., 381; Shaw, *John Dubois*, 80–81, quotes at 81.

61. JT to JH, 27 May 1818, quoted in Melville, *Seton*, rev. ed., 382.

62. McSweeny et al., *Story of the Mountain*, 1:76.

63. EBS to WS, 1 July 1818, Bechtle and Metz, *Collected Writings*, 2:566.

64. Melville, *Seton*, rev. ed., 301–4.

65. JD to Garnier, 17 February 1819, AMSMU.

66. RS to WS, 29 April 1818 101, 1, 6D, AMSV, accessed at AMSJ.

67. RBS to CS, 30 April 1818, S-J 511–514, APSL.

68. RS to CS, 11 June 1818, ASCSH, accessed at APSL, 1–3–3, box 18, photostats.

69. RBS to EBS, 1 July 1818, A.103.006, ASCSH, accessed at AMSJ.

70. RBS to EBS, 27 January 1818, SJ 406–409, APSL.

71. AF to EBS, 5 January 1818, A 111 05 (no original located), AMSJ.

72. EBS to JS, 5 October 1817, Bechtle and Metz, *Collected Writings*, 2:510.

73. Burin, *Slavery and the Peculiar Solution*; Clegg, *Price of Liberty*.

74. Joseph Shorter purchase of John Butler from the Revd. John Dubois, January 1814, Slavery at the Mount, box 2, AMSMU.

75. RGH, *Letter to Elias Caldwell*, 7, quoted in Papenfuse, *Evils of Necessity*, 57; RGH to JD, 15 November 1819, Slavery at the Mount, box 2, AMSMU.

76. Mary Egan to RS [1816], 1–3–3–3:92a.1, APSL.

77. "Regulations for the Colored Servants at the Washhouse, to be enforced by the Sister who has Charge of Them," n.d., Slavery at the Mount, box 2, AMSMU.

78. JD to AM, 9 February 1818, 15T17, AASUS.

79. JD to JT, 4 November 1817, quoted in Melville, *Seton*, rev. ed., 335; JD to AM, 9 February 1818, 15T17, AJCP, AAB.

80. Tessier, "Epoques," 3 June 1818, quoted in Melville, *Seton*, rev. ed., 335–36.

81. McSweeny et al., *Story of the Mountain*, 1:98–99.

82. EBS to SB, [November 1818], Bechtle and Metz, *Collected Writings*, 2:591.

83. Bruté, *Mother Seton*, 86–87.

84. Bechtle and Metz, *Collected Writings*, 3b:79.

85. EBS to SB, [November 1818], *Collected Writings*, 2:593.

86. EBS to WS, 6 April 1818, *Collected Writings*, 2:546.

87. EBS to SB, [November 1818], *Collected Writings*, 2:594.

88. EBS to SB, [November 1818], *Collected Writings*, 2:594.

89. EBS to JH, [before 19 March 1818], *Collected Writings*, 2:536.

22. I SEE MY GOD

1. EBS to ES, [December 1819], Bechtle and Metz, *Collected Writings*, 2:632–33.

2. EBS to ES, 5 May 1818, *Collected Writings*, 2:550; EBS to WS, 9 May 1818, *Collected Writings*, 2:554; EBS to CS, 5 May 1818, *Collected Writings*, 2:553.

3. EBS to WS, 27 May 1818, *Collected Writings*, 2:558.

4. Daughters of Charity, Bruté de Rémur, and Seton, *Connection with the Community*, 193.

5. EBS to SB, 21 April 1818, Bechtle and Metz, *Collected Writings*, 2:549.

6. JCh to EBS, 11 August 1818, 100, 115, 1, 17, AMSV, accessed at AMSJ.

7. PB to EBS, 12 July 1818, 1-3-3-1:71, APSL.

8. EBS to SB, 2 July 1818, Bechtle and Metz, *Collected Writings*, 2:566.

9. EBS to CO'C, 20 July 1818, *Collected Writings*, 2:568.

10. EBS to CO'C, 20 July 1818, *Collected Writings*, 2:658–59.

11. EBS to ES, August 1818, *Collected Writings*, 2:575.

12. De Kay, *Chronicles of the Frigate,* 129–31.

13. JCh to EBS, 11 August 1818, 100, 115, 1, 17, AMSV, accessed at AMSJ; Melville, *Seton*, rev. ed., 361–62.

14. EBS to WS, 8 September 1818, Bechtle and Metz, *Collected Writings*, 2:761.

15. WS to EBS, 29 August [1818], 1-3-3-18 59, APSL.

16. EBS to Ellen Wiseman, [October 1818], Bechtle and Metz, *Collected Writings*, 2:587.

17. De Kay, *Chronicles of the Frigate,* 130–39.

18. EBS to MFC, 1 November [1818?], Bechtle and Metz, *Collected Writings*, 2:629.

19. Helen Bayley Craig to EBS, 17 November 1818, 1-3-3-11:B41, APSL.

20. MFBB to EBS, 25 October 1819, 1-3-3-11:B40, APSL.

21. Marèchal, 21 and 23 September 1818, "Diary of Archbishop Marèchal," 432, quoted in McCann, *Mother Seton's Daughters* 1:101, 432.

22. Report to Sacred Congregation de Propaganda Fide, Marèchal to Cardinal Litta, 16 October 1818, quoted in Melville, *Seton*, rev. ed., 348.

23. AM to EBS, 18 December 1818, 115, 1, 29, AMSV, accessed at AMSJ.

24. "Interview with Sister Martha Daddisman, recorded July 1, 1877, St. Joseph's, Emmitsburg," APSL, in Shaw, *John Dubois*, 87, 80.

25. Melville, *Seton*, rev. ed., 387.

26. Bruté, Description of Emmitsburg in 1823, 7-3-1-1:14, APSL.

27. SC to AM, 15 March 1819, 15D7, AAMP, AAB; Marèchal to JD, 22 March 1819, quoted in Melville, *Seton*, rev. ed., 389; JD to AM, 23 April 1819, 15U13, AAB; Melville, *Seton*, rev. ed., 388–91.

28. SC to AM, 13 April 1819, 15D8, AAMP, AAB.

29. Register of women who entered the Sisters of Charity during Elizabeth Seton's lifetime (1809–1820), Bechtle and Metz, *Collected Writings*, 2:783–84; EBS to AM, [June 1817], *Collected Writings*, 2:481; EBS to AM, September 1817, *Collected Writings*, 2:506.

30. EBS to SB, [August 1817], *Collected Writings*, 2:497–98.

31. EBS to CO'C, January 24, 1819, *Collected Writings*, 2:600.

32. Council minutes, 1819, 3-3-5:1, APSL.

33. EBS to JH, 14 June 1819, Bechtle and Metz, *Collected Writings*, 2:614.

34. JD to EB, 27 August 1820, 1-3-3-5:19, APSL.

35. Loughery, *John Hughes*, quote at 31.

36. For a definitive accounting of Seton's translations, with reference also to Bechtle and Metz's *Collected Works*, see Lee, "Practice of Spiritual Direction," 296–98, esp. n313.

37. EBS to SB, n.d., Bechtle and Metz, *Collected Writings*, 2:690.

38. EBS to RGH, 25 October 1819, *Collected Writings*, 2:625.

39. EBS to RS, 8 May 1820, *Collected Writings*, 2:651.

40. EBS to JS, 18 April 1820, *Collected Writings*, 2:645.

41. EBS to WS, 7 November 1819, *Collected Writings*, 2:627.

42. De Kay, *Chronicles of the Frigate*, 140–60.

43. WS to EBS, 13 March 1819, 1-3-2-2, APSL.

44. WS to EBS, Seton, *Memoir*, 2:282–83, no original found.

45. EBS to WS, 7 November 1819, Bechtle and Metz, *Collected Writings*, 2:627.

46. EBS to RGH, 21 May 1820, Bechtle and Metz, *Collected Writings*, 2:652.

47. CS to ES, 10 July 1820, 1-3-3-9:61, APSL.

48. CS and EBS to JS, 19 August 1819, 1-3-3-1:B55, APSL.

49. EBS to CS, [28 June 1819], Bechtle and Metz, *Collected Writings*, 2:619.

50. CS to JS, 19 August 1818, 1-3-3-11:B4a, APSL.

51. RBS to CS, 29 December 1818, 1-3-3-18:11, APSL.

52. RBS to CS, 29 December 1818, 1-3-3-18:11, APSL.

53. RBS to CS, 10 April 1819, 101, 1, 65, AMSV, accessed at AMSJ.

54. EBS to WS, 27 May 1820, Bechtle and Metz, *Collected Writings*, 2:653.

55. EBS to Ellen Wiseman, [29 June 1820], *Collected Writings*, 2:656.

56. EBS to SB, [Christmas season, 1818], *Collected Writings*, 2:597.

23. ETERNITY

1. EBS to SB, [April or May 1817], Bechtle and Metz, *Collected Writings*, 2:479.

2. Ann C. Tilghman to EBS, 1 January 1820, 1-3-3-7:84, APSL.

3. EBS to ACT, [after 1 January 1820], Bechtle and Metz, *Collected Writings*, 2:638–39.

4. Mattingly, *Secret Habits*, 90; McNeil, "Elizabeth Seton," 196–97.

5. St. Joseph's Academy and Free School roster, 1809–1821, Bechtle and Metz, *Collected Writings*, 3b:565–79; EBS to MFC, 31 December 1819, *Collected Writings*, 2:634; EBS to JH, January 1820, *Collected Writings*, 2:637; EBS to JH, 28 February 1820, *Collected Writings*, 2:640.

6. EBS to ES, December 1819, *Collected Writings*, 2:632; EBS to SB [spring 1819], *Collected Writings*, 2:606.

7. EBS to CO'C, 9 November 1818, *Collected Writings*, 2:589.

8. EBS to SB, November 1818, *Collected Writings*, 2:588.

9. EBS to SB, August 1820, *Collected Writings*, 2:664.

10. EBS to JH, June 1819, *Collected Writings*, 2:615.

11. EBS to JS, 19 February 1819, *Collected Writings*, 2:601.

12. EBS to SB, November 1818, *Collected Writings*, 2:588.

13. EBS to MFC, 24 August 1820, *Collected Writings*, 2:665.

14. EBS to WS, 23 July 1820, *Collected Writings*, 2:662.

15. EBS to SB, September 1820, *Collected Writings*, 2:668.

16. EBS to EB, 25 October 1820, *Collected Writings*, 2:671.

17. 24 September–6 October, Bruté, "Notes on Elizabeth Seton's 'last illness,'" in *Mother Seton*, 3–20. Except when other sources are given, the following description is drawn from "Account by Rev. Simon Bruté, S.S. of Elizabeth Seton's Last Days," Bechtle and Metz, *Collected Writings*, 2:765–70.

18. JD to AM, February 1821, 15V25, AAMP, AAB.

19. SB to EBS, 1–3–3–12:2, APSL.

20. Bruté, "Notes," 25.

21. White, *Life of Mrs. Eliza A. Seton*, 440; McNeil explains that no original can be found, although one seems to have existed into the twentieth century. Melville, *Seton*, rev. ed., 409n102.

22. Bruté sketch, September 1820, 1–3–3–13:158, APSL.

23. JD to RGH, 5 October 1820, 11L13, AASMSU, AAB.

24. CS to JS, 4 October 1820, 1–3–3–11 B56, APSL.

25. Quoted in EBS to RGH, 15 October 1820, Bechtle and Metz, *Collected Writings*, 2:668.

26. EBS to RGH, 15 October 1820, *Collected Writings*, 2:668–69.

27. AF to EBS, 8 August 1820, A 111 106, AMSJ.

28. EBS to AF, 19 October 1820, Bechtle and Metz, *Collected Writings*, 2:669–79.

29. EBS to Elizabeth Boyle, 25 October 1820, *Collected Writings*, 2:671–72.

30. EBS to EB, 25 October 1820, *Collected Writings*, 2:671.

31. JD to RW, [after January 1821] 1–3–3–5:40, APSL.

32. Will of Elizabeth Ann Seton, 1–3–1–6:2, no. 6, APSL, reproduced from Register of Wills for Frederick County, Liber H.S., no. 2, fols. 475–76.

33. JD to RGH, 21 November 1820, 11L14, AASMSU, AAB.

34. RBS to RGH, 23 November 1820, 20N20, AASMSU, AAB.

35. CS to RGH, 1 December 1820, 1–3–3–18:14, APSL.

36. De Kay, *Chronicles of the Frigate*, 166–71.

37. WS to EBS, 20 November 1820, 1–3–3–18:60, APSL.

38. CO'C to SB, 28 February 1821, 1–3–3–12:6, APSL.

39. CO'C to SB, 28 February 1821, 1–3–3–12:6, APSL.

40. Bruté, "Notes," 23.

41. CO'C to SB, n.d., 1–3–3–12:6, APSL.

42. EBS to SB, [spring 1819], Bechtle and Metz, *Collected Writings*, 2:606.

43. Red notebook, *Collected Writings*, 3a:508.

44. CO'C to SB, 28 February 1821, 1–3–3–12:6, APSL.

45. CS to JS, 26 December 1820, 1–3–3–3:11B58, APSL.

46. He explained the procedures in a letter that also tersely reported the death of "our beloved Mother." JD to RS, 6 January 1821, 1–3–3–5:37, APSL.

47. CO'C to SB, 28 February 1821 1–3–3–12:6, APSL.

48. Mary Xavier Clark to SB, n.d., 1–3–3–12:5, APSL.

EPILOGUE

1. White, *Life of Mrs. Eliza A. Seton*, 426.

2. Melville, *Seton*, rev. ed., 403n v.

3. *American and Commercial Daily Advertiser*, February 7, 1821.

4. CCH to RGH, 31 January 1821, H-PP, MHS.

5. CO'C to MO'C, 18 July 1823, and 9 July 1823, in Smith, *Philadelphia's First Nun*, 454.

6. SB to CS, 15 February 1821, II–1–a, UNDA; JD to CS, n.d., 1–3–3–5:32, APSL.

7. WS to EBS, 21 June 1821, S-J 545–65, APSL.

8. WS to JD, 22 August 1821, AMSMU.

9. RGH to JD, 14 January 1821, Gallagher Collection, APSL.

10. JD to RGH, 7 January 1821, AMSMU.

11. RS to CS, [1821], 110, 11, 1, AMSV, accessed at AMSJ.

12. D. W. Know, Captain, USN (Ret.), to Sister Aurea, Secretary to the Vice Postulator, Mother Seton Guild, 7 February 1940, AMSJ.

13. JA to CS, 28 December 28, 1823, 1–3–3–18:18, APSL.

14. JA to CS, 28 December 28, 1823, 1–3–3–18:18, APSL.

15. Papenfuse, *Evils of Necessity*, 70.

16. Papenfuse, *Evils of Necessity*, 71–72.

17. CS to JS, 28 November 1838, quoted in Gallagher, "Catherine Seton," 102.

18. Kiddle and Schem, *Cyclopaedia of Education*, 789; Bourne, *History of the Public School Society*; "Annual Message to the Legislature, December 15, 1908," in Dunn, *Annual Messages of Presidents of Liberia*, 471.

19. CS to James Roosevelt Bayley, 1843, quoted in Gallagher, "Catherine Seton," 104.

20. Gallagher, "Catherine Seton," 104–7; Mother Agnes O'Connor to Mother Cecilia Marmion, 15 October 1846, quoted in Gallagher, "Catherine Seton," 107.

21. Loughery, *Dagger John*.

22. Deed between John McGerry, president of Mt. St. Mary's, and Francis B. Jaison and John B. Purcell, 9 December 1829, containing evidence of a prior transfer of property from John Dubois to McGerry and Michael D. Egan on 4 October 1826, Slavery at the Mount, box 2, AMSMU; JB Purcell to unknown, 10 September 1830, Slavery at the Mount, box 2, AMSMU; Edward Lynch, Esq. to Rev. Thos. R. Butler, Principal, Mt. S. Mary's College, 28 August 1835, Slavery at the Mount, box 2, AMSMU.

23. Ochs, *Black Patriot*, 22; Pasquier, *Fathers on the Frontier*, 166–99.

24. Gallagher, "Catherine Seton," 106–10.

25. Kelly, *Elizabeth Seton's Two Bibles*, 17, 23.

26. "First Exhumation of Mother Seton's remains in 1845," 1–3–3–9 B:19, APSL.

27. Cummings, "American Saints," 220–24; Cummings, "Native Daughters"; Greer, *Mohawk Saint*.

28. Melville, *Seton*, rev. ed., xxi.

29. "Petition," 1–3–1–63:1, APSL.

30. Cummings, "American Saints," 223.

31. Thomas C. Guthrie, MD, to Reverend Sylvester A. Taggart, 29 May 1973, 1–3–1–63:5, APSL.

32. *Wall Street Journal*, 25 June 1975.

33. Metz, "Sisters of Charity of Cincinnati," 232–40.

34. Quotations from Elizabeth Williamson, "Emmitsburg Nuns Keep Legacy of Charity Alive," *Washington Post*, 5 June 2003.

BIBLIOGRAPHY

PRIMARY AND SECONDARY SOURCES

A.M.M.G. *Life of Mother Elizabeth Boyle: One of Mother Seton's First Companions, the Assistant Mother under Her for Eight Years, and First Superioress of "The Sisters of Charity of St. Vincent De Paul," in New York City.* Edited by James J. Dougherty. New York: Mission of the Immaculate Virgin, 1893.

Acton, James A. "The Diary of William Smith, August 26, 1778 to December 31, 1779." PhD diss., University of Michigan, 1970.

Alexander, Elizabeth Urban. *Notorious Woman: The Celebrated Case of Myra Clark Gaines.* Southern Biography Series. Baton Rouge: Louisiana State University Press, 2001.

Bailly de Barberey, Hélène Roederer. *Elizabeth Seton.* Translated and adapted by Joseph B. Code. New York: Macmillan, 1927.

———. *Elizabeth Seton Et Les Commencements De l'église Catholique Aux États-Unis.* 2nd ed. Paris: Poussielgue Frères, 1869.

Barnes, D. S. "Cargo, 'Infection,' and the Logic of Quarantine in the Nineteenth Century." *Bulletin of the History of Medicine* 88, no. 1 (Spring 2014): 75–101.

Bayley, James Roosevelt. *Memoirs of Simon Wm. Gabriel Bruté, D.D.* 1911. Reprint, Victoria, Aus.: Leopold Classic Library, 2017.

Bayley, Richard. *An Account of the Epidemic Fever: Which Prevailed in the City of New-York, during Part of the Summer and Fall of 1795.* New York: Printed and sold by T. and J. Swords, 1796.

———. *Letters from the Health-Office, Submitted to the Common Council, of the City of New-York.* New York: John Furman, 1799.

Beasley, Nicholas M. *Christian Ritual and the Creation of British Slave Societies, 1650–1780.* Race in the Atlantic World, 1700–1900. Athens: University of Georgia Press, 2009.

Bechtle, Regina M., and Judith Metz, eds. *Elizabeth Bayley Seton: Collected Writings.* 3 vols. in 4 pts. Hyde Park, NY: New City Press, 2000.

——. *Seton Writings Project: Chronological List 1a (1767–June 1804)*. DePaul University Library, Via Sapientiae, 2015. http//:via.library.depaul.edu/seton_stud/3.

——. *Seton Writings Project: Chronological List 1b (June 1804–June 1808)*. DePaul University Library, Via Sapientiae, 2015. http//:via.library.depaul.edu/seton_stud/2.

——. *Seton Writings Project: Chronological List 2a (June 1808–December 1809)*. DePaul University Library, Via Sapientiae, 2015. http//:via.library.depaul.edu/seton_stud/1.

——. *Seton Writings Project: Chronological List 2b (January 1810–December 1813)*. DePaul University Library, Via Sapientiae, 2016. http//:via.library.depaul.edu/seton_stud/5.

——. *Seton Writings Project: Chronological List 3 (January 1814–December 1816)*. DePaul University Library, Via Sapientiae, 2016. http//:via.library.depaul.edu/seton_stud/6.

——. *Seton Writings Project: Chronological List 4 (January 1817–December 1820*. DePaul University Library, Via Sapientiae, 2017. http//:via.library.depaul.edu/seton_stud/7.

Beitzell, Edwin Warfield. *The Jesuit Missions of St. Mary's County, Maryland*. Abell, MD, 1959, 1960.

Bell, Richard. "The Moral Thermometer: Rush, Republicanism, and Suicide." *Early American Studies: An Interdisciplinary Journal* 15, no. 2 (2017): 308–31.

——. "The Moral Thermometer: Republicanism and Suicide." Paper presented at the Republics of Benjamin Rush Conference, Dickinson, PA, March 2014.

Berner, Ulrich. "Epicurus' Role in Controversies on Asceticism in European Religious History." In *Asceticism and Its Critics: Historical Accounts and Comparative Perspectives*, edited by Oliver Freiberger, 43–60. New York: Oxford University Press, 2006.

Bertrand, L. *Bibliothèque Sulpicien, Ou La Littèraire De La Compagnie De Saint-Sulpice*. 2 vols. Paris: Alphonse Picard, 1900.

Binzley, Ronald A. "Ganganelli's Disaffected Children: The Ex-Jesuits and the Shaping of Early American Catholicism, 1773–1790." *U.S. Catholic Historian* 26, no. 2 (2008): 47–77.

Bizzocchi, Roberto. "Cisisbei: Italian Morality and European Values in the Eighteenth Century." In *Italy's Eighteenth Century: Gender and Culture in the Age of the Grand Tour*, edited by Paula Findlen, Wendy Wassyng Roworth, and Catherine M. Sama, 35–58. Stanford, CA: Stanford University Press, 2009.

Blecki, Catherine L., and Karin A. Wulf, eds. *Milcah Martha Moore's Book: A Commonplace Book from Revolutionary America*. University Park: Pennsylvania State University Press, 1997.

Bonomi, Patricia U. "John Jay, Religion, and the State." *New York History* 81, no. 1 (2000): 8–18.

Booth, Martin. *Opium: A History*. New York: Simon & Schuster, 1996.

Bordman, Gerald Martin, and Thomas S. Hischak. *The Oxford Companion to American Theatre*. New York: Oxford University Press, 2004.

Bourne, William Oland, and Making of America Project. *History of the Public School Society of the City of New York*. New York: W. Wood, 1870.

Boylan, Anne M. *The Origins of Women's Activism: New York and Boston, 1797–1840*. Greensboro: University of North Carolina Press, 2002.

Brekus, Catherine A. *Sarah Osborn's World: The Rise of Evangelical Christianity in Early America*. New Directions in Narrative History. New Haven: Yale University Press, 2013. E-book.

——. *Strangers and Pilgrims: Female Preaching in America, 1740–1845*. Gender and American Culture. Chapel Hill: University of North Carolina Press, 1998.

Bremond, Henri. *Histoire littèraire du sentiment religieux en France*. 6 vols. Paris: Edition Jérôme Millon, 2006.

Brownson, Orestes. "Nature and Office of the Church." *Brownson's Quarterly Review*, April 1844, 243–56.

———. "Review of John Henry Hopkins, *The Novelties Which Disturb Our Peace*." *Brownson's Quarterly Review*, July 1844, 349–67.

Bruté de Rémur, Simon Guillaume Gabriel. *Mother Seton. Notes by Rev. Simon Gabriel Bruté (Bishop of Vincennes.) from Original Papers in the Possession of the Community*. Emmitsburg, MD: Privately published, 1884.

Bulthuis, Kyle T. *Four Steeples over the City Streets: Religion and Society in New York's Early Republic Congregations*. Early American Places. New York: New York University Press, 2014.

Burin, Eric. *Slavery and the Peculiar Solution: A History of the American Colonization Society*. Southern Dissent. Gainesville: University Press of Florida, 2005.

Burrows, Edwin G., and Mike Wallace. *Gotham: A History of New York City to 1898*. New York: Oxford University Press, 1999.

Butler, Jon, Grant Wacker, and Randall Balmer. *Religion in American Life: A Short History*. 2nd ed. New York: Oxford University Press, 2011.

Bynum, Caroline Walker. *Fragmentation and Redemption: Essays on Gender and the Human Body in Medieval Religion*. New York: Zone Books, 1991.

———. *Holy Feast and Holy Fast*. New Historicism. Berkeley: University of California Press, 1987. E-book.

Byrd, William. *The Commonplace Book of William Byrd II of Westover*. Edited by Kevin Berland, Jan Kirsten Gilliam, and Kenneth A. Lockridge. Chapel Hill: University of North Carolina Press, 2001.

Byron, Tammy K. "'A Catechism for Their Special Use': Slave Catechisms in the Antebellum South." PhD diss., University of Arkansas, 2008.

Carter, Michael S. "'What Shall We Say to This Liberal Age?' Catholic-Protestant Controversy in the Early National Capital." *U.S.Catholic Historian* 26, no. 2 (2008): 79–95.

Cavallo, Sandra, and Lyndan Warner. *Widowhood in Medieval and Early Modern Europe*. Women and Men in History. New York: Pearson Education, 1999.

Cayton, Andrew R. L. *Love in the Time of Revolution: Transatlantic Literary Radicalism and Historical Change, 1793–1818*. Chapel Hill: University of North Carolina Press, 2014.

Chinnici, Joseph P. *Living Stones: The History and Structure of Catholic Spiritual Life in the United States*. Makers of the Catholic Community. New York: Macmillan, 1989.

———. "Organization of the Spiritual Life: American Catholic Devotional Works, 1791–1866." *Theological Studies* 40, no. 2 (1979): 229–55.

Clark, Emily. *Masterless Mistresses: The New Orleans Ursulines and the Development of a New World Society, 1727–1834*. Chapel Hill: University of North Carolina Press for the Omohundro Institute of Early American History and Culture, 2012.

Chopra, Ruma. *Choosing Sides: Loyalists in Revolutionary America*. American Controversies Series. Lanham, MD: Rowman & Littlefield, 2013.

Clegg, Claude Andrew. *The Price of Liberty: African Americans and the Making of Liberia*. Chapel Hill: University of North Carolina Press, 2004.

Coakley, John Wayland. *Women, Men, and Spiritual Power: Female Saints and Their Male Collaborators*. New York: Columbia University Press, 2006.

Codignola, Luca. "Gli imprenditori Livornesi Filippo & Antonio Filicchi e il Nord America (1785–1806)." In *Storia e Attualità Della Presenza Degli Stati Uniti a Livorno e in Toscana*, edited by Paolo Castignoli, et al., 43–66. Pisa: Università di Pisa, 2003.

———. "Religione e affari tra Italia e Stati Uni, 1785–1847: Alla ricerca Dei Filicchi." *Rivista Della Civiltà Italiana* 36, no. 1–2 (1992): 121–34.

Coleman, Peter J. *Debtors and Creditors in America: Insolvency, Imprisonment for Debt, and Bankruptcy, 1607–1900.* Madison: State Historical Society of Wisconsin, 1974.

Cope, Rachel. "Salvific Significance in Personal Life Stories." *Magistra* 20, no. 1 (2014): 21–59.

Copley, John Singleton, and Henry Pelham. *Letters & Papers of John Singleton Copley and Henry Pelham, 1739–1776.* Boston: Massachusetts Historical Society, 1914.

Crumb, Lawrence N. "John Henry Hobart and England: Two Unpublished Letters." *Anglican and Episcopal History* 65, no. 1 (1996): 44–49.

Cummings, Kathleen Sprows. "American Saints: Gender and the Re-Imaging of U.S. Catholicism in the Early Twentieth Century." *Religion and American Culture: A Journal of Interpretation* 22, no. 2 (2012): 203–31.

——. "Native Daughters: Making Saints in a Divided Church." *Commonweal,* June 1, 2013.

Curran, Robert Emmett. "Ambrose Marèchal, the Jesuits, and the Demise of Ecclesial Republicanism in Maryland, 1818–1838." *U.S. Catholic Historian* 26, no. 2 (2008): 97–110.

——. *The Bicentennial History of Georgetown University.* Washington, DC: Georgetown University Press, 1993.

Currier, Charles Warren. *Carmel in America: A Centennial History of the Discalced Carmelites in the United States.* Philadelphia: J. Murphy, 1890.

Daughters of Charity of St. Vincent de Paul, Emmitsburg Province, Simon William Gabriel de Bruté de Rémur, and Elizabeth Ann Seton. *Rev. Simon Gabriel Bruté (Bishop of Vincennes.) in His Connection with the Community: 1812–1839.* Emmitsburg, MD: Daughters of Charity, 1886.

Davis, Matthew L. *A Brief Account of the Epidemical Fever Which Lately Prevailed in the City of New York; with the Different Proclamations, Reports and Letters of Gov. Jay, Gov. Mifflin, the Health Committee of New York, &c. upon the Subject. to which is Added, an Accurate List of the Names of Those Who Have Died of the Disease, from July 29, to Nov. 1.* New York: Matthew L. Davis, 1795.

Day, William. *A Collection of Psalms and Hymns, for Public Worship.* Evesham, Eng.: Printed and sold by John Agg, 1795.

de Costa, C., and F. Miller. "American Resurrection and the 1788 New York Doctors' Riot." *Lancet* (London), January 22, 2011, 292–93.

De Kay, James Tertius. *Chronicles of the Frigate Macedonian, 1809–1922.* New York: Norton, 1995.

De Paul, Vincent, and Coste, Pierre, "Correspondences, Conferences, Documents, Volume X. Conferences to the Daughters of Charity vol. 2" (2006). *Vincentian Digital Books,* Book 35. http://via.library.depaul.edu/vincentian_ebooks/35.

Derks, Scott, and Tony Smith. *The Value of a Dollar: Colonial Era to the Civil War, 1600–1865.* Millerton, NY: Grey House, 2005.

Desjardins, Simon, and Pierre Pharoux. *Castorland Journal: An Account of the Exploration and Settlement of Northern New York State by French Émigrés in the Years 1793 to 1797.* Edited and translated by John A. Gallucci. Ithaca, NY: Cornell University Press, 2010.

"Diary of Archbishop Maréchal." *Records of the American Catholic Historical Society of Philadelphia* 11 (1900): 417–54.

Dichtl, John R. *Frontiers of Faith: Bringing Catholicism to the West in the Early Republic.* Lexington: University Press of Kentucky, 2008.

Diefendorf, Barbara B. *From Penitence to Charity: Pious Women and the Catholic Reformation in Paris.* New York: Oxford University Press, 2004.

——. "Rethinking the Catholic Reformation." In *Women, Religion, and the Atlantic World, 1600-1800*, edited by Daniella Kostroun and Lisa Vollendorf, 39–51. Toronto: University of Toronto Press, 2009.

"The Diocese of Baltimore in 1818. Archbishop Maréchal's Account to Propaganda, October 16, 1818." *Catholic Historical Review* 1, no. 4 (1916): 439–53.

Dinan, Susan E. *Women and Poor Relief in Seventeenth-Century France: The Early History of the Daughters of Charity*. Women and Gender in the Early Modern World. Burlington, VT: Ashgate, 2006.

Dix, Morgan, John Adams Dix, Leicester Crosby Lewis, Charles Thorley Bridgeman, and Clifford Phelps Morehouse. *A History of the Parish of Trinity Church in the City of New York*. 7 vols. New York: Putnam, 1898.

Doll, Peter. "The Idea of the Primitive Church in High Church Ecclesiology from Samuel Johnson to J. H. Hobart." *Anglican and Episcopal History* 65, no. 1 (1996): 6–43.

Dorsey, John R., and James D. Dilts. *A Guide to Baltimore Architecture*. 2nd ed. Centreville, MD: Tidewater, 1981.

Duffy, John. *History of Public Health in New York City*. New York: Russell Sage Foundation, 1974.

Duncan, Jason K. *Citizens or Papists? The Politics of Anti-Catholicism in New York, 1685–1821*. Hudson Valley Heritage Series, vol. 3. New York: Fordham University Press, 2005.

Duncan, William, ed. *The New-York Directory, and Register, for the Year 1792*. New York: Printed by T. and J. Swords, 1793.

Dunn, D. Elwood, ed. *Annual Messages of the Presidents of Liberia, 1848–2010*. New York: De Gruyter, 2011.

Elsner, Jaś. "Iconoclasm as Discourse: From Antiquity to Byzantium." *Art Bulletin* 94, no. 3 (2012): 368–94.

Erasmus. *On Copia of Words and Ideas (De Utraque Verborem [sic] Ac Rerum Copia)*. Mediaeval Philosophical Texts in translation, no. 12. Milwaukee: Marquette University Press, 1963.

Estes, J. Worth, and Billy G. Smith. *A Melancholy Scene of Devastation: The Public Response to the 1793 Philadelphia Yellow Fever Epidemic*. Canton, MA: Science History Publications/USA, 1997.

Evangelisti, Sylvia. *Nuns, a History of Convent Life, 1450–1700*. New York: Oxford University Press, 2007.

Fea, John. *Was America Founded as a Christian Nation? A Historical Introduction*. Louisville, KY: Westminster John Knox Press, 2011. E-book.

Fernow, Berthold, comp. and ed. *Calendar of Wills*. Ancestry.com, 2002. First published in 1896 by Colonial Dames of New York (New York).

Fingerhut, Eugene R., and Joseph S. Tiedemann. *The Other New York: The American Revolution beyond New York City, 1763–1787*. An American Region. Albany: State University of New York Press, 2005.

Finney, Paul Corby. *The Invisible God: The Earliest Christians on Art*. New York: Oxford University Press, 1994.

Flanagan, Kathleen. "The Influence of John Henry Hobart on the Life of Elizabeth Ann Seton." PhD diss., Union Theological Seminary, 1978.

——. "Some Aspects of Elizabeth Seton's Theological/Spiritual World." *Vincentian Heritage Journal* 14, no. 2 (1993): 215–26.

Fogarty, Gerald P. *Patterns of Episcopal Leadership*. Bicentennial History of the Catholic Church in America. New York: Collier Macmillan, 1989.

Foote, Thelma Wills. *Black and White Manhattan: The History of Racial Formation in Colonial New York City.* Oxford: Oxford University Press, 2004.

Ford, Caroline C. *Divided Houses: Religion and Gender in Modern France.* Ithaca, NY: Cornell University Press, 2005.

Franchot, Jenny. *Roads to Rome: The Antebellum Protestant Encounter with Catholicism.* Oakland: University of California Press, 1994.

Freiberger, Oliver. *Asceticism and Its Critics: Historical Accounts and Comparative Perspectives.* American Academy of Religion Cultural Criticism Series. New York: Oxford University Press, 2006.

Gallagher, Ann M. "Catherine Seton and the New York Mercy Experience." *American and Commercial Daily Advertiser* (Baltimore) 27, no. 1 (2007): 97–112.

Gollar, C. W. "Father John Thayer: Catholic Antislavery Voice in the Kentucky Wilderness." *Register of the Kentucky Historical Society* 101, no. 3 (2003): 275–96.

Gould, Philip. "Race, Commerce, and the Literature of Yellow Fever in Early National Philadelphia." *Early American Literature* 35, no. 2 (2000): 157–86.

Grabo, Norman S. "Crèvecoeur's American: Beginning the World Anew." *William and Mary Quarterly* 48, no. 2 (1991): 159–72.

Greer, Allan. *Mohawk Saint: Catherine Tekakwitha and the Jesuits.* New York: Oxford University Press, 2005.

Griffin, Martin I. J. "Toothless Priest, Reverend Samuel Sutherland Cooper: The Founder of Mother Seton's Institution." *American Catholic Researches* 15 (1898): 17–32.

Guide to the Catholic Sisterhoods in the United States. Compiled by Thomas P. McCarthy. Washington, DC: Catholic University of America Press, 1955.

Hacsi, Timothy A. *Second Home: Orphan Asylums and Poor Families in America.* Cambridge, MA: Harvard University Press, 1997.

Haddock, John A. *The Growth of a Century: As Illustrated in the History of Jefferson County, New York, from 1793–1894.* Albany, NY: Weed-Parsons printing company, 1895.

Hamon, André Jean-Marie. *The Life of Cardinal Cheverus: Archbishop of Bordeaux, and Formerly Bishop of Boston.* Boston: J. Munroe, 1839.

Hancock, David. "Self-Organized Complexity and the Emergence of an Atlantic Market Economy, 1651–1815: The Case of Madeira." In *The Atlantic Economy during the Seventeenth and Eighteenth Centuries: Organization, Operation, Practice, and Personnel,* edited by Peter A. Conclanis, 30–71. Columbia: University of South Carolina Press, 2005.

Handschy, Daniel J. "Eucharistic Sacrifice and Apostolic Order: American Contributions to the Ecclesiology of the Oxford Movement." PhD diss., Saint Louis University, 2012.

Hanley, Thomas O'Brien, ed. *The John Carroll Papers.* 3 vols. Notre Dame: University of Notre Dame Press, 1976.

Harmless, William. *Mystics.* New York: Oxford University Press, 2008.

Hartfield, Anne. "Profile of a Pluralistic Parish: Saint Peter's Roman Catholic Church, New York City, 1785–1815." *Journal of American Ethnic History* 12, no. 3 (1993): 30–59.

Hartnoll, Phyllis, and Peter Found, eds. *The Concise Oxford Companion to the Theatre.* 2nd ed. Oxford: Oxford University Press, 1996.

Hatch, Nathan O. *The Democratization of American Christianity.* New Haven: Yale University Press, 1989.

Heyrman, Christine Leigh. *Southern Cross: The Beginnings of the Bible Belt.* Chapel Hill: University of North Carolina Press, 1998. E-book.

Hickey, Donald R. *The War of 1812: A Short History*. Urbana: University of Illinois Press, 1995.

Hobart, John Henry. *A Companion for the Altar . . . According to the Form Prescribed by the Protestant Episcopal Church in the United States*. New York: Peter A. Mesier, 1804.

Hobart, John Henry, and William Berrian. *The Posthumous Works of the Late Right Reverend John Henry Hobart . . . : With a Memoir of His Life*. New York: Swords, Stanford, 1832.

Hoffman, Ronald, and Sally D. Mason. *Princes of Ireland, Planters of Maryland: A Carroll Saga, 1500–1782*. Chapel Hill: University of North Carolina Press, 2000.

Huey, Paul R. "Old Slip and Cruger's Wharf at New York: An Archaeological Perspective of the Colonial American Waterfront." *Historical Archaeology* 18, no. 1 (1984): 15–37.

Jodziewicz, Thomas W. "American Catholic Apologetical Dissonance in the Early Republic? Father John Thayer and Bishop John Carroll." *Catholic Historical Review* 84, no. 3 (1998): 455–76.

John of the Cross. *The Dark Night of the Soul; and the Living Flame of Love*. Translated by David Lewis and with corrections and introduction by Benedict Zimmerman. London: Thomas Baker, 1908.

Jones, Arthur. "A Slave, Society Hairdresser, Philanthropist, Pierre Toussaint May Become Nation's First Black Saint." *National Catholic Reporter* 36, no. 37 (2000): 12.

Jones, Robert F. "William Duer and the Business of Government in the Era of the American Revolution." *William and Mary Quarterly* 32, no. 3 (1975): 393–416.

Jones, Thomas. *History of New York during the Revolutionary War*. Edited by Edward Floyd de Lancey. 2 vols. New York: New York Historical Society, 1879.

Katz, Steven T. "Mysticism and Ethics in Western Mystical Traditions." *Religious Studies* 28, no. 3 (1992): 407–23.

Kauffman, Christopher J. *Tradition and Transformation in Catholic Culture: The Priests of Saint Sulpice in the United States from 1791 to the Present*. New York: Collier Macmillan, 1988.

Kelley, Mary. *Learning to Stand & Speak: Women, Education, and Public Life in America's Republic*. Chapel Hill: University of North Carolina Press, 2006.

Kelley, Mary, and Robert A. Gross. *An Extensive Republic*. A History of the Book in America, vol. 2. Chapel Hill: University of North Carolina Press, 2010.

Kelly, Ellin M. "Elizabeth Bayley Seton's Commonplace Book of Poetry: Archives, St. Joseph Provincial House, Rare Book 31." *Vincentian Heritage Journal* 29, no. 1 (2009): 35–132.

——. "Elizabeth Seton: Key Relationships in Her Life, 1774–1809." *Vincentian Heritage Journal* 14, no. 2 (1993): 305–27.

——, ed. *Elizabeth Seton's Two Bibles, Her Notes and Markings*. Huntington, IN: Our Sunday Visitor, 1977.

——. *Numerous Choirs: A Chronicle of Elizabeth Bayley Seton and Her Spiritual Daughters*. 2 vols. Evansville, IN: Mater Dei Provincialate, 1981.

Kenneally, Finbar. *United States Documents in the Propaganda Fide Archives. Index to Calendar, Vols. I–VII*. Publications of the Academy of American Franciscan History. Washington, DC: Academy of American Franciscan History, 1981.

Ketchum, Richard M. *Divided Loyalties: How the American Revolution Came to New York*. New York: Henry Holt, 2002.

Kiddle, Henry, and A. J. Schem. *Cyclopaedia of Education; A Dictionary of Information for the Use of Teachers, School Officers, Parents and Others*. New York: Steiger, 1877.

King, G. R. D. "Islam, Iconoclasm, and the Declaration of Doctrine." *Bulletin of the School of Oriental and African Studies, University of London* 48, no. 2 (1985): 267–77.

Lamb, Martha J., and Burton Harrison. *History of the City of New York: Its Origin, Rise, and Progress*. 3 vols. New York: A.S. Barnes, 1877.

Lawrence, Anna M. *One Family under God*. Early American Studies. Philadelphia: University of Pennsylvania Press, 2011. E-book.

Lehfeldt, Elizabeth A. *Religious Women in Golden Age Spain: The Permeable Cloister*. Aldershot, UK: Ashgate, 2005.

Lee, Shin Ja. "The Practice of Spiritual Direction in the Life and Writings of St. Elizabeth Ann Seton." PhD diss., Catholic University of America, 2010.

Lindman, Janet Moore. "'This Union of the Soul': Spiritual Friendship among Early American Protestants." *Journal of Social History* 50, no. 4 (2017): 680–700.

Longworth, David. *Longworth's American Almanac, New York Register, and City Directory, for the Twenty-Eighth Year of American Independence*. New York: D. Longworth, 1803.

——. *Longworth's American Almanac, New York Register, and City Directory, for the Twenty-Sixth Year of American Independence*. New York: D. Longworth, 1801.

Longworth, David, and Abraham Shoemaker, eds. *Longworth's American Almanac, New York Register, and City Directory*. New York: D. Longworth, 1800.

——. *Longworth's American Almanac, New York Register, and City Directory, for the Twenty-Seventh Year of American Independence*. New York: D. Longworth, 1802.

Loughery, John. *Dagger John: Archbishop John Hughes and the Making of Irish America*. Ithaca: Cornell University Press, 2018.

Lux-Sterrit, Laurence. "An Analysis of the Controversy Caused by Mary Ward's Institute in the 1620's." *British Catholic History* 25, no. 4 (2001): 636–47.

MacBean, William Munro, Saint Andrew's Society of the State of New York, and Scots Society in New York. *Biographical Register of Saint Andrew's Society of the State of New York*. New York: Printed for the society, 1925.

Mann, Bruce H. *Republic of Debtors: Bankruptcy in the Age of American Independence*. Cambridge, MA: Harvard University Press, 2002.

Mannard, Joseph. "Widows in Convents of the Early Republic: The Archdiocese of Baltimore, 1790–1860." *U.S. Catholic Historian* 26, no. 2 (2008): 111–32.

Mattingly, Carol. *Secret Habits*. Carbondale: Southern Illinois University Press, 2016.

Maynard, Theodore. *The Reed and the Rock, Portrait of Simon Bruté*. New York: Longmans, Green, 1942.

McCann, Mary Agnes. *The History of Mother Seton's Daughters, the Sisters of Charity of Cincinnati, Ohio*. 2 vols. New York: Longmans, Green, 1916–17.

McClymond, Michael J., and Gerald R. McDermott. *The Theology of Jonathan Edwards*. New York: Oxford University Press, 2011.

McConville, Brendan. *The King's Three Faces: The Rise & Fall of Royal America, 1688–1776*. Chapel Hill: University of North Carolina Press, 2006.

McIver, Katherine A. *Wives, Widows, Mistresses, and Nuns in Early Modern Italy: Making the Invisible Visible through Art and Patronage*. Women and Gender in the Early Modern World. Burlington, VT: Ashgate, 2012.

McKee, Christopher. *A Gentlemanly and Honorable Profession: The Creation of the U.S. Naval Officer Corps, 1794–1815*. Annapolis, MD: Naval Institute Press, 1991.

McNeil, Betty Ann. "Demographics of Entrants: Sisters of Charity of St. Joseph's, 1809–1849 and Daughters of Charity, Province of the United States, 1850–1909." *Vincentian Heritage Journal* 31, no. 1 (2012): 71–92.

——. "Elizabeth Seton—Mission of Education, Faith and Willingness to Risk." *Vincentian Heritage Journal* 17, no. 3 (1996): 185–200.

——. "Historical Perspectives on Elizabeth Seton and Education: School Is My Chief Business." *Catholic Education: A Journal of Inquiry and Practice* 9, no. 3 (2006): 284–306.

——. "The Journal of Mother Rose White: The Earliest History of the Sisters of Charity of Saint Joseph's, Emittsburg, Maryland." *Vincentian Heritage Journal* 18, no. 1 (1997): 18–56.

——. "Memoir of Sister Cecilia O'Conway: Sisters of Charity of St. Joseph's." *Vincentian Heritage Journal* 29, no. 2 (2009): 20–49.

——. *Vincentian Family Tree.* Chicago: Vincentian Studies Institute, 1996.

McNeill, J. R. "Yellow Jack and Geopolitics: Environment, Epidemics, and the Struggles for Empire in the American Tropics, 1640–1830." *Review of the Fernand Braudel Center* 27, no. 4 (2004): 343–64.

McSweeny, Edward Francis Xavier, Mary M. Meline, John J. Tierney, and Peter A. Coad. *The Story of the Mountain; Mount St. Mary's College and Seminary, Emmitsburg, Maryland, Begun by Mary M. Meline . . . and Continued by Rev. Edw. F. X. McSweeny.* 2 vols. Emmitsburg, MD: Weekly Chronicle, 1911.

McVickar, John, and Walter Farquhar Hook. *The Early Life and Professional Years of Bishop Hobart.* Oxford: D. A. Talboys, 1838.

Melville, Annabelle M. *Elizabeth Bayley Seton, 1774–1821.* New York: Scribner, 1951.

——. *Elizabeth Bayley Seton, 1774–1821.* Rev. ed. Edited by Betty Ann McNeil. Hanover, PA: Sheridan Press, 2009.

——. *Louis William DuBourg: Bishop of Louisiana and the Floridas, Bishop of Montauban, and Archbishop of Besancon, 1766–1833.* Chicago: Loyola University Press, 1986.

"A Memoir of the Very Rev. Michael Hurley, D.D O.S.A." *Records of the American Catholic Historical Society of Philadelphia* 1 (1887): 165–212.

Memoirs of Mrs. S.; A Fragment of Real History. Elizabethtown, NJ: Isaac A. Kollock, 1817.

Mercantile Library Association of the City of New-York. *New York City during the American Revolution.* New York: Privately printed for the association, 1861.

Metz, Judith. *A Retreat with Elizabeth Seton: Meeting Our Grace.* Cincinnati: St. Anthony Messenger Press, 1999.

——. "The Sisters of Charity of Cincinnati, 1829–1852." *Vincentian Heritage Journal* 17, no. 3 (1996): 201–44.

Miller, Kerby A., Arnold Schrier, Bruce D. Boling, and David N. Doyle, eds. *Irish Immigrants in the Land of Canaan: Letters and Memoirs from Colonial and Revolutionary America, 1675–1815.* New York: Oxford University Press, 2003.

Miller, Randall. "Black Catholics in the Slave South: Some Needs and Opportunities for Study." *Records of the American Catholic Historical Society of Philadelphia* 86 (1975): 93–106.

——. "The Failed Mission: The Catholic Church and Black Catholics in the Old South." In *The Southern Common People: Studies in Nineteenth Century Social History,* edited by Edward Magdol and Jon Wakelyn, 37–54. Westport, CT: Greenwood Press, 1980.

Moffat, R. Burnham. *The Barclays of New York: Who They Are and Who They Are Not, and Some Other Barclays.* New York: Robert Grier Cooke, 1904.

Mooney, Catherine M. *Gendered Voices: Medieval Saints and Their Interpreters.* Middle Ages Series. Philadelphia: University of Pennsylvania Press, 1999.

Moran, Gerald F., and Maris A. Vinovskis. "Schools." In *A History of the Book in America*. Vol. 2, *An Extensive Republic: Print, Culture, and Society in the New Nation, 1790–1840*, edited by Robert A. Gross and Mary Kelley, 286–303. Chapel Hill: University of North Carolina Press in Association with the American Antiquarian Society, 2010.

Morris, Grace Parker. "Some Letters from 1792–1800 on the China Trade." *Oregon Historical Quarterly* 42, no. 1 (1941): 48–87.

Moss, Ann. "The Politica of Justus Lipsius and the Commonplace-Book." *Journal of the History of Ideas* 59, no. 3 (1998): 421–36.

Mullen, Lincoln. *The Chance of Salvation: A History of Conversion in America*. Cambridge, MA: Harvard University Press, 2017.

Mullin, Robert Bruce. *Episcopal Vision, American Reality: High Church Theology and Social Thought in Evangelical America*. New Haven: Yale University Press, 1986.

Murphy, Thomas. *Jesuit Slaveholding in Maryland, 1717–1838*. Studies in African American History and Culture. New York: Routledge, 2001.

National Archives. "The Papers of Alexander Hamilton." Founders Online. htttp://founders.archives.gov/Hamilton.

———. "The Papers of George Washington, Presidential Series." Founders Online. htttp://founders.archives.gov/about/Washington.

Neel, Carol. "The Origins of the Beguines." *Signs* 14, no. 2 (1989): 321–41.

Newman, Martha G. "*Disciplining the Body*, Disciplining the Will: Hypocrisy and Asceticism in Cistercian Monasticism." In *Asceticism and Its Critics: Historical Accounts and Comparative Perspectives*, ed. Oliver Freiberger, 91–115. New York: Oxford University Press, 2006.

New York Common Council and Arthur Everett Peterson. *Minutes of the Common Council of the City of New York, 1784–1831*. Vols. 1–19. New York: M. B. Brown Printing & Binding Co., 1917.

New York Common Council and D. T. Valentine. *Manual of the Corporation of the City of New York, 1861*. New York: New York Common Council, 1861.

New York Historical Society. "Abstracts of Wills." In *Collections of the New York Historical Society for the Year 1904*. Vol. 37, 1–381. New York: Printed for the society, 1905.

New York Society Library. "Circulation Records, 1789–1792." http://cityreaders.nysoclib.org/.

New York Wills, 1626–1836. Ancestry.com.

Nuxoll, Elizabeth M., ed. *The Selected Papers of John Jay Digital Edition*. http://rotunda.upress.virginia.edu/founders/JNJY-01-04-02-0326.

O'Brien, Matthew. *Sermons on Some of the Most Important Subjects of Morality and Religion*. Cork, Ire.: James Haley, 1798.

Ochs, Stephen J. *A Black Patriot and a White Priest: André Cailloux and Claude Paschal Maistre in Civil War New Orleans*. Conflicting Worlds. Baton Rouge: Louisiana State University Press, 2000.

O'Donnell, Catherine. "John Carroll and the Origins of an American Catholic Church, 1783–1815." *William and Mary Quarterly* 68, no. 1 (2011): 101–26.

Old Wills of New Rochelle: Copies of Wills by Citizens of New Rochelle, N.Y., 1784–1830. New Rochelle: New Rochelle Chapters, Daughters of the American Revolution, 1991.

Olivera, Bernardo, and Augustine Roberts. *The Sun at Midnight: Monastic Experience of the Christian Mystery*. Monastic Wisdom Series, vol. 29. Collegeville, MN: Liturgical Press, 2012.

Orsi, Robert. *History and Presence*. Cambridge, MA: Belknap Press of Harvard University Press, 2016.

Papas, Philip. "Richmond County, Staten Island." In *The Other New York: The American Revolution beyond New York City, 1763-1787*, edited by Joseph Tiedemann and Eugene R. Fingerhut, 83–106. Albany: State University of New York Press, 2005.

Papenfuse, Eric Robert. *The Evils of Necessity: Robert Goodloe Harper and the Moral Dilemma of Slavery*. Transactions of the American Philosophical Society, vol. 87, pt. 1. Philadelphia: American Philosophical Society, 1997.

Parish of Trinity Church. "Baptisms, Marriages, and Burials from 1750." https://registers.trinitywallstreet.org/files/history/registers/registry.php.

Pasquier, Michael. *Fathers on the Frontier: French Missionaries and the Roman Catholic Priesthood in the United States, 1789–1870*. Religion in America Series. New York: Oxford University Press, 2010.

Pernick, Martin S. "Politics, Parties, and Pestilence: Epidemic Yellow Fever in Philadelphia and the Rise of the First Party System." *William and Mary Quarterly* 29, no. 4 (1972): 559–86.

Pleasants, J. H. *The Curzon Family of New York and Baltimore, and Their English Descent*. Baltimore: Privately printed, 1919.

Porterfield, Amanda. *Conceived in Doubt: Religion and Politics in the New American Nation*. American Beginnings, 1500–1900. Chicago: University of Chicago Press, 2012.

Pujo, Bernard. *Vincent De Paul, the Trailblazer*. Notre Dame, IN: University of Notre Dame Press, 2003.

Purcell, Mary. *The World of Monsieur Vincent*. New York: Scribner, 1963.

Raboteau, Albert J. *Slave Religion: The "Invisible Institution" in the Antebellum South*. New York: Oxford University Press, 2004.

Rapley, Elizabeth. *The Devotes: Women and Church in Seventeenth-Century France*. McGill-Queen's Studies in the History of Religion. Buffalo: McGill-Queen's University Press, 1990.

Rappaport, Roy A. *Ritual and Religion in the Making of Humanity*. Cambridge Studies in Social and Cultural Anthropology. New York: Cambridge University Press, 1999.

Roberts, Kyle B. *Evangelical Gotham: Religion and the Making of New York City, 1783–1860*. Historical Studies of Urban America. Chicago: University of Chicago Press, 2016.

Rockman, Seth. *Scraping By: Wage Labor, Slavery, and Survival in Early Baltimore*. Studies in Early American Economy and Society from the Library Company of Philadelphia. Baltimore: Johns Hopkins University Press, 2009. E-book.

Rothschild, Nan A. *New York City Neighborhoods: The 18th Century*. San Diego: Academic Press, 1990.

Rousseau, Jean-Jacques. *Emile: Or On Education*. Introduction, translation, and notes by Allan Bloom. New York: Basic Books, 1979.

Rowland, Kate Mason. *The Life of Charles Carroll of Carrollton, 1737–1832, with His Correspondence and Public Papers*. New York: G.P. Putnam's Sons, 1898.

Ruane, Joseph William. *The Beginnings of the Society of St. Sulpice in the United States, 1791–1829*. Washington, DC: Catholic University of America, 1935.

Ryan, Leo Raymond. *Old St. Peter's, the Mother Church of Catholic New York (1785–1935)*. United States Catholic Historical Society. New York: United States Catholic Historical Society, 1935.

Saint Andrew's Society of the State of New York and George Austin Morrison. *History of Saint Andrew's Society of the State of New York, 1756–1906*. New York: Printed by the order of the society at Press of the Evening Poet, 1906.

Scharf, J. Thomas. *History of Western Maryland. being a History of Frederick, Montgomery, Carroll, Washington, Allegany, and Garrett Counties from the Earliest Period* to the Present Day; Including Biographical Sketches of their Representative Men. Philadelphia: L. H. Everts, 1882.

Schutte, Anne Jacobson. *By Force and Fear: Taking and Breaking Monastic Vows in Early Modern Europe.* Ithaca, NY: Cornell University Press, 2011.

Scudder, Samuel H. "A Biographical Sketch of Dr. John Lawrence LeConte." *Transactions of the American Entomological Society and Proceedings of the Entomological Section of the Academy of Natural Sciences* 11, no. 3 (1884): i–xxviii.

Seton, Elizabeth Ann. *Memoir, Letters and Journal of Elizabeth Seton: Convert to the Catholic Faith, and Sister of Charity.* Edited by Robert Seton. 2 vols. New York: P. O'Shea, 1869.

Seton, Robert. *An Old Family; Or, the Setons of Scotland and America.* New York: Brentano's, 1899.

Shaw, Richard. *John Dubois, Founding Father: The Life and Times of the Founder of Mount St. Mary's College, Emmitsburg, Superior of the Sisters of Charity, and Third Bishop of the Diocese of New York.* Yonkers, NY: United States Catholic Historical Society, 1983.

Smith, Gay. *Lady Macbeth in America.* Palgrave Studies in Theatre and Performance History. New York: Palgrave Macmillan, 2010.

Smith, Paul Hubert, Gerard W. Gawalt, Rosemary Fry Plakas, Eugene R. Sheridan, Ronald M. Gephart, and Library of Congress. *Letters of Delegates to Congress, 1774–1789.* Vol. 11. Washington, DC: Library of Congress, 1976–2000.

Smith, Sara Trainer. "Philadelphia's First Nun." *Records of the American Catholic Historical Society of Philadelphia* 5, no. 5 (1894): 417–522.

Souvay, Charles L. "Questions Anent Mother Seton's Conversion." *Catholic Historical Review* 5, no. 2 (1919): 223–38.

Spalding, Thomas W., ed. *John Carroll Recovered: Abstracts of Letters and Other Documents Not Found in the John Carroll Papers.* Baltimore: Cathedral Foundation Press, 2000.

Sprague, William B. *Annals of the American Pulpit; or, Commemorative Notices of Distinguished American Clergymen of Various Denominations.* 9 vols. New York: R. Carter and Brothers, 1859–69.

Steele, Delphine, ed. *Life of Mother Rose White.* Emmitsburg, MD: Saint Joseph's Central House, 1936.

Stern, Andrew H. M. *Southern Crucifix, Southern Cross: Catholic-Protestant Relations in the Old South.* Tuscaloosa: University of Alabama Press, 2012.

Stevens, John Austin. *Colonial New York. Sketches, Biographical and Historical, 1768–1784.* New York: J.F. Trow, 1867.

Still, William. *The Underground Rail Road: A Record of Facts, Authentic Narratives, Letters, &c., Narrating the Hardships, Hair-Breadth Escapes, and Death Struggles of the Slaves in Their Efforts for Freedom, as Related by Themselves and Others or Witnessed by the Author: Together with Sketches of Some of the Largest Stockholders and Most Liberal Aiders and Advisers of the Road.* Philadelphia: Porter & Coates, 1872.

Stone, William Leete. *The Centennial History of New York City, from the Discovery to the Present Day.* New York: R.D. Cooke, 1876.

St. Teresa of Avila. *The Collected Works of St. Teresa of Avila.* 2nd ed. Translated by Kieran Kavanaugh and Otilio Rodríguez. 3 vols. Washington, DC: Washington Province of Discalced Carmelites, 1987.

——. *The Interior Castle.* The Classics of Western Spirituality. New York: Paulist Press, 1979.

Taves, Ann. *Fits, Trances, and Visions: Experiencing Religion and Explaining Experience from Wesley to James.* Princeton, NJ: Princeton University Press, 1999.

Taylor, Dorceta E. *The Environment and the People in American Cities, 1600–1900s.* Durham, NC: Duke University Press, 2009.

Thacher, James. "Richard Bayley." In *American Medical Biography, Or, Memoirs of Eminent Physicians Who Have Flourished in America.* Boston: Richardson & Lord and Cottons & Barnard, 1828.

Thei, Marilyn. "The Woman Elizabeth Bayley Seton, 1791–1803. *Vincentian Heritage Journal* 14, no. 2 (1993): 227–66.

Thompson-Stahr, Jane. *The Burling Books: Ancestors and Descendants of Edward and Grace Burling, Quakers (1600–2000).* Baltimore: Gateway Press, 2001.

Thurman, Howard. "Mysticism and Ethics." *Journal of Religious Thought* 27, no. 2 (1970): 23.

Toner, Joseph M., ed. *George Washington's Rules of Civility and Decent Behavior in Company and Conversation.* Washington, DC: W.H. Morrison, 1986.

Uciechowski, P., H. Imhoff, C. Lange, C. G. Meyer, E. N. Browne, D. K. Kirsten, A. K. Schroder et al. "Susceptibility to Tuberculosis Is Associated with TLR1 Polymorphisms Resulting in a Lack of TLR1 Cell Surface Expression." *Journal of Leukocyte Biology* 90, no. 2 (2011): 377–88.

Volo, James M. *Blue Water Patriots: The American Revolution Afloat.* Westport, CT: Praeger, 2007.

Wake, Jehanne. *Sisters of Fortune: America's Caton Sisters at Home and Abroad.* New York: Touchstone Books, 2011.

Wall, Alexander J. *The Equestrian Statue of George III, and the Pedestrian Statue of William Pitt: Erected in the City of New York, 1770.* New York, 1920.

Walsh, Marie de Lourdes, and Mary Elizabeth Earley. *The Sisters of Charity of New York, 1809–1959.* New York: Fordham University Press, 1960.

Warner, William W. *At Peace with All Their Neighbors: Catholics and Catholicism in the National Capital, 1787–1860.* Washington, DC: Georgetown University Press, 1994.

Watson, Elkanah, and Winslow C. Watson. *Men and Times of the Revolution, or, Memoirs of Elkanah Watson.* 2nd ed. New York: Dana and Co., 1857.

Watts, Sheldon. "Yellow Fever Immunities in West Africa and the Americas in the Age of Slavery and Beyond: A Reappraisal." *Journal of Social History* 34, no. 4 (2001): 955–67.

Wharton, Anne Hollingsworth. *Social Life in the Early Republic with Numerous Reproductions of Portraits, Miniatures, and Residences.* Philadelphia: Lippincott, 1902.

Whatley, Harlan Douglas, Duncan A. Bruce, and Randall Lenox Taylor, eds. *Two Hundred Fifty Years, 1756–2006: The History of Saint Andrew's Society of the State of New York.* NY: St. Andrew's Society of the State of New York, 2008.

Wheatley, Jeffrey. "Fellow Citizens: Catholic Lay Trustees in New York City, 1785–1815." Honors thesis, Arizona State University, 2012.

White, Charles I. *Life of Mrs. Eliza A. Seton, Foundress and First Superior of the Sisters or Daughters of Charity in the United States of America.* 4th rev. ed. Baltimore: J. Murphy & Co., 1862.

Wilder, Craig S. "War and Priests: Catholic Colleges and Slavery in the Era of Revolution." In *Slavery's Capitalism: A New History of American Economic Development,* edited by Sven Beckert and Seth Rockman, 227–42. Philadelphia: University of Pennsylvania Press, 2016.

Wilf, Steven Robert. "Anatomy and Punishment in Late Eighteenth-Century New York." *Journal of Social History* 22, no. 3 (1989): 507–30.

Williams, Greg H. *The French Assault on American Shipping, 1793–1813: A History and Comprehensive Record of Merchant Marine Losses.* Jefferson, NC: McFarland, 2009.

Wilson, James Grant. *The Memorial History of the City of New York: From Its First Settlement to the Year 1892.* New York: New-York History Co., 1892, 1894.

Woodgate, Mildred Violet. *St Louise De Marillac, Foundress of the Sisters of Charity.* St. Louis, Mo., London: B. Herder Book Co., 1946.

Wordsworth, William. *The Excursion, Being a Portion of the Recluse, a Poem.* London: Printed for Longman, Hurst, Rees, Orme, and Brown, 1814.

Zagarri, Rosemarie. *Revolutionary Backlash: Women and Politics in the Early American Republic.* Early American Studies. Philadelphia: University of Pennsylvania Press, 2007.

NEWSPAPERS

The Albany Chronicle
Alexandria (Virginia) Advertiser
American and Commercial Daily Advertiser (Baltimore)
Columbian (New York)
Commercial Advertiser (New York)
Daily Advertiser (New York)
Independent Gazette (New York)
Loudon's Register (New York)
The Massachusetts Gazette (Boston)
The Minerva (New York)
Morning Chronicle (New York)
New-York Daily Gazette
New York Evening Post
New-York Gazette and General Advertiser
New York Gazette and Weekly Mercury
New-York Gazette, or Weekly Post-Boy
New-York Herald
New-York Journal or the General Advertiser
New-York Packet
The New York Times
New-York Weekly Museum
The Pennsylvania Evening Post, and Public Advertiser (Philadelphia)
Pennsylvania Packet (Philadelphia)
Rivington's New York Gazetteer
Royal Gazette (New York)
The Wall Street Journal
The Washington Post

INDEX

Page numbers for illustrations are in italics.